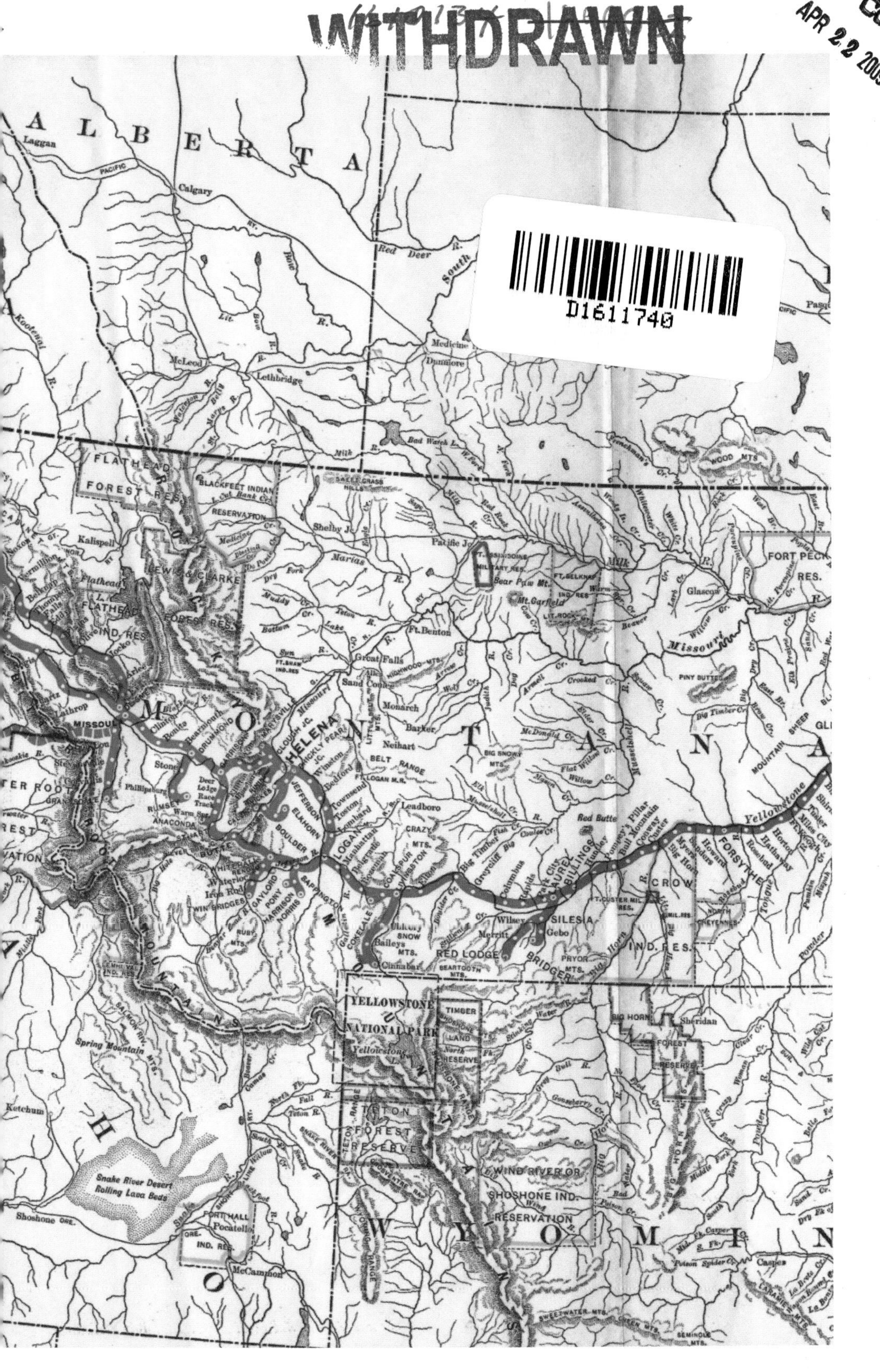
ALBERTA
Laggan
PACIFIC
Calgary
Red Deer R.
Kootenai R.
McLeod
Lethbridge
Medicine
Dunmore
Milk R.
FLATHEAD FOREST RES.
BLACKFEET INDIAN RESERVATION
SWEET GRASS HILLS
Shelby J.
Marias R.
Kalispell
Flathead L.
FLATHEAD IND. RES.
LEWIS & CLARKE FOREST RES.
Pacific Jc.
FT. ASSINIBOINE MILITARY RES.
Bear Paw Mt.
Mt. Garfield
FT. BELKNAP IND. RES.
Glasgow
FORT PECK RES.
Missouri
WOOD MTS.
Ft. Benton
Great Falls
HIGHWOOD MTS.
Sand Coulee
Monarch
Barker
Neihart
BELT RANGE
MISSOULA
HELENA
BIG SNOWY MTS.
PINY BUTTES
MONTANA
Yellowstone
Townsend
Toston
Lombard
Leadboro
CRAZY MTS.
Phillipsburg
ANACONDA
BUTTE
BOULDER
ELKHORN
JEFFERSON
LOGAN
Manhattan
Red Butte
Pompey's Pillar
Bull Mountain
Conway
Custer
BILLINGS
LAUREL
FORSYTHE
Big Timber
Columbus
Whitehall
Waterloo
Iron Rod
GAYLORD
PONY
HARRISON
NORRIS
TWIN BRIDGES
SAPPINGTON
COKEDALE
Baileys
SNOW MTS.
RED LODGE
Cinnabar
BEARTOOTH MTS.
SILESIA
Gebo
BRIDGER
PRYOR MTS.
CROW IND. RES.
YELLOWSTONE NATIONAL PARK
Yellowstone L.
TIMBER LAND North RESERVE
BIG HORN FOREST RESERVE
Sheridan
Spring Mountain MTS.
SALMON RIV. MTS.
Ketchum
TETON FOREST RESERVE
Snake River Desert
Rolling Lava Beds
WIND RIVER OR SHOSHONE IND. RESERVATION
Shoshone
FORT HALL IND. RES.
Pocatello
McCammon
WYOMING
Casper
SWEETWATER MTS.
SEMINOLE MTS.

Banking on Global Markets

Banking on Global Markets uses the story of the U.S. business and political dealings of Germany's largest bank to illuminate important developments in the ongoing globalization of major financial institutions. Throughout its nearly 140-year-long history, Deutsche Bank served as one of Germany's principal vehicles for forging economic and other links with the rest of the world. Despite some early successes in the face of severe obstacles for Deutsche Bank, the U.S. market probably remained its highest foreign priority and its most frustrating challenge. As with many foreign investors, Deutsche Bank found its hopes of harnessing America's enticing opportunities often dashed by many regulatory and political barriers. Relying on primary-source material, *Banking on Global Markets* traces Deutsche Bank's involvement with the United States in the context of a changing national and international regulatory and economic environment that set the stage for its strategies and activities in the United States, and, at times, even in its home country. It is the story of how international cooperation furthered and conflict hindered those endeavors, and how international banking evolved from a very personalized business between nations to one dominated by enormous transnational markets. It is a work designed for anyone interested in how cross-border flows of information and capital have affected history and how our modern form of globalization distinguishes itself from that of earlier periods. A professor of finance and writer of history, Christopher Kobrak weaves together the story of how these financial, political, and institutional developments have helped shape the emerging new international order.

Christopher Kobrak holds a BA degree in philosophy from Rutgers University and MA, MBA, and PhD degrees from Columbia University in history, finance/accounting, and business history. He is a CPA and has spent ten years working in numerous business positions for Sterling Drug, Inc. He teaches corporate finance and business history at ESCP-EAP, European School of Management, concentrating on international finance, history of capital markets, and financial theory. His publications include: *National Cultures and International Competition: The Experience of Schering AG, 1851–1950* (Cambridge University Press, 2002), *European Business, Dictatorship and Political Risk, 1920–1945*, edited with Per Hansen (2004), and articles and reviews in many business history journals. He has taught at Columbia University, Warsaw University, and Toulouse University, from which he received his Habilitation in Management. He is currently working on the economic contribution of family businesses, corporate governance, and foreign direct investment in the service sector.

Cambridge Studies in the Emergence of Global Enterprise

Editors

Louis Galambos, *The Johns Hopkins University*
Geoffrey Jones, *Harvard Business School*

Other books in the series:

National Cultures and International Competition: The Experience of Schering AG, 1851–1950, by Christopher Kobrak, ESCP-EAP, European School of Management

Knowledge and Competitive Advantage: The Coevolution of Firms, Technology, and National Institutions, by Johann Peter Murmann, Australian Graduate School of Management

The World's Newest Profession: Management Consulting in the Twentieth Century, by Christopher D. McKenna, Saïd Business School, University of Oxford

Global Brands: The Evolution of Multinationals in Alcoholic Beverages, by Teresa da Silva Lopes, Queen Mary, University of London

Banking on Global Markets

Deutsche Bank and the United States, 1870 to the Present

CHRISTOPHER KOBRAK

ESCP-EAP, European School of Management

CAMBRIDGE UNIVERSITY PRESS
Cambridge, New York, Melbourne, Madrid, Cape Town, Singapore, São Paulo, Delhi

Cambridge University Press
32 Avenue of the Americas, New York, NY 10013-2473, USA

www.cambridge.org
Information on this title: www.cambridge.org/9780521863254

First published 2008

Printed in the United States of America

A catalog record for this publication is available from the British Library.

Library of Congress Cataloging in Publication Data

Kobrak, Christopher.
Banking on global markets : Deutsche Bank and the United States, 1870 to the present / Christopher Kobrak.
p. cm. – (Cambridge studies in the emergence of global enterprise)
Includes bibliographical references and index.
ISBN 978-0-521-86325-4 (hardback)
1. Deutsche Bank – History. 2. Banks and banking – Germany – History.
3. Banks and banking, Foreign – United States – History. I. Title. II. Series.
HG3058.D4K63 2008
332.1′540943 – dc22 2007016836

ISBN 978-0-521-86325-4 hardback

To the many young people in my life who contribute to my sense of purpose and energy – Pierre, Stéphane, and François Chapelle; Mark and Caitlin Farewell; Owen and Milena Hanenberg; Max, Rowena, Ben, Jake, and Kai Kobrak; Julius and Moritz von Rohrscheidt; Nora and Sina Schecker; Sammy Schoenberg; and all the many cousins in Ireland and England – in hopes that they will strengthen the ties between Europe and America.

Contents

Series Editors' Preface

Two of the world's most successful economies during the Second Industrial Revolution were Germany and the United States. Both made excellent use of their resources, capital, people, and business and political institutions to push ahead of their competitors among the developed economies. There were marked similarities in their large businesses, in their approach to protectionism, and in their patterns of investment in some of the leading industries – especially the electrical, chemical, electro-chemical, and steel industries – of the late nineteenth and twentieth centuries. There were also many differences grounded in their resource endowments, their political systems, and their cultures, differences that were and still are highlighted by the experiences of two world wars and the brutal Holocaust. The United States and Germany have through these long years been competitors, enemies in war, and more recently allies.

Christopher Kobrak's *Banking on Global Markets: Deutsche Bank and the United States, 1870 to the Present* opens a large window on that remarkable history. He takes us inside of the Deutsche Bank, Germany's leading financial institution, and helps us understand why and how the bank's officers chose to invest in the rapidly expanding American business system. It was not easy to acquire the information they needed to make prudent investments. It was not easy to establish working relationships with Americans and their enterprises in transportation and other leading industries. Nor was it a simple matter after World War I to monitor the flow of capital from the United States to Germany. But, as Kobrak explains, the Deutsche Bank persisted and restored investments after the wartime ruptures and the troubled postwar recovery in Europe. Readers should find the personal as well as the institutional links between the two countries of great interest. The contrasting styles of the American investor Henry Villard and the bank's Georg von Siemens provide an intriguing story within a story, as do the institution's troubled experiences between 1914 and 1948.

Geoffrey Jones
Harvard Business School
Louis Galambos
The Johns Hopkins University

Preface and Acknowledgements

> Why, the chances are a thousand to one against there being any connection between your so-called evidence – a pitiful heap of books and letters and music and furniture – and the vast reality you pretend to reconstruct. What culture leaves to the historian is but vestiges of the doings of a very few. The more articulate your sources, the less likely they are representative. You fill in and sketch out with your imagination and in the light of your present-day concerns.
>
> Jacques Barzun, "Cultural History: A Synthesis."

> The German element in the United States had its first permanent settlement at Germantown, Pennsylvania, in 1683, since which time its political, moral, social and educational influence has been recognized and appreciated.
>
> Edward Adams, Deutsche Bank representative in the United States, November 10, 1913.

The more I pursue business and financial history, the more I become persuaded of serendipity's role not only in one's personal and professional life but also in what one learns about the past. This project with Deutsche Bank fell in my lap, as it were, at an ideal personal and professional time. Professionally, I had wanted to tackle a range of themes in more detail for which a study of Deutsche Bank was ideal. These included: how and why German and American business cultures and corporate governance were distinct; what we could learn from the past about the evolution of economies from so-called emerging status to developed; how the so-called globalization of markets in our era differs from or resembles such processes in the past; and, lastly, how the apparent need for increased foreign direct investment was influenced by the change in macro economics and political conditions after World War I. To investigate these questions, I was very lucky to have access to Deutsche Bank archives and the bank's assistance. As one of Germany's most important economic institutions, Deutsche Bank served as a rich source of material for better understanding the multifaceted history of Germany's relationship with the United States as well as the role of financial institutions in the modern world.

This access has allowed me to pursue the long-term goal of writing a multi-dimensional business and financial history that relies on primary sources while putting business into its broader political and economic context. In this book, as with other studies, I have tried to integrate cultural, professional, and personal influences on management's assessment of its complex reality and its attempts to shape effective strategies and tactics to reap economic value out of an unknown, evolving future. In short, I have sought to combine what is sometimes called the *institutional* and *social* approaches to business history. I have tried here, too, to write a history that shows business's effect on society with sufficient background and detail so as to be useful to historians, economists, and business practitioners. Given the breadth of audiences I want to address, as well as the cross-cultural dimension of this story, providing the appropriate contexts is more demanding than usual.

In this daunting task I hope that I have been faithful to Marc Bloch's challenge to historians to question sources and reflect on the issue, "How can I know what I am about to say?"[1] This involves perhaps more footnoting and more discussion of the reliability of evidence than some readers would like. For this, I apologize in advance. Thanks to Deutsche Bank, I had ample "raw material." Unlike many business historians, I not only had access to public primary sources but also to unpublished documents. Each of the sources poses separate difficulties and opportunities, which must be addressed. Moreover, I sought to give the reader not just a factual account of what happened but also a sense of how businesspeople thought and talked about a broad range of issues. In a sense, I have tried to convey how those economic actors perceived their activities and social-political environment. I can only hope that my commitment to Bloch's challenge is matched by a set of imaginative questions emanating from my knowledge of business history and business. Even for a writer trained in business – indeed, with ten years of business experience and who earns his living teaching management – finding the right balance of the general and particular, one that uses business contexts to enrich commercial detail, while building from detail to reformulate generalizations and create a coherent whole, is an intimidating endeavor.

The more I study history, the more too I realize it is about sources as much as about subjects. Fortuna influences Clio – if I may mix a Roman god with the Greek muse of history – that is, what we know about the past, in countless ways. A word, then, is called for about my sources. Given their importance, this book might be viewed as two, not one. The vast majority of the source material for this book came from Deutsche Bank's American Collection, 1,400 folders with documents about the bank's business in North America from 1870 to 1941. Using a subject matter index, I selected nearly one-third of those folders, and, much to the chagrin of Deutsche Bank, copied a large number of documents – by last count around 19,000.[2] I cannot be sure that I have seen everything relevant to the period and my subject that currently exists at Deutsche Bank, but there were no restrictions put on me. I was denied nothing I asked for and have no reason to believe anything was hidden from me, quite the contrary. The documents, though at times self-serving, were unlikely to have been written with the intention of influencing an historian in the twenty-first century. Collectively, they provide an unusual glimpse of the men and attitudes that shaped international business before the telephone, e-mail, and mergers destroyed much of our ability to recapture business's past.

For many reasons, it was necessary to approach the post–World War II period differently from the earlier years. First, the archive does not have all the documents. Some have stayed with various Deutsche Bank departments. Second, the volume is too great. I could never scan all the documents for the 1980s and 1990s the way I did those from the 1880s and 1890s. There are just too many. Third, many of the transactions involve subjects that might give rise to legal issues for Deutsche Bank, though I stumbled on nothing of that nature.

I adopted a different approach for this period. I relied to a large extent on the files of Hermann Josef Abs, a key figure in German and Deutsche Bank's financial history. I have examined these files in his substantial *Nachlass* pertaining to the United States with the view that nothing of importance in Deutsche Bank's history in the United States would have escaped his attention. In addition, for the later years of this narrative, I have relied on oral history and, to a greater extent than for the pre-1945 period, on newspaper accounts to bolster what I had from other public primary sources such as annual reports. Although some scholars have focused on the benefits or liabilities of one or another of these, none of the three sources is without some advantage and risk.[3] The challenge for the historian with these or any other sources is to compare and contrast the information they provide, try to assess bias, and determine their plausibility in light of reasoned judgment. The alternative is to give up our profession and write fiction.[4] Even the most casual of readers will observe that no effort has been made to avoid describing transactions and incidents that might be embarrassing for Deutsche Bank.

For the entire narrative, I am indebted to several other archival sources: the New York Federal Reserve Bank; the National Archives in Washington; the Bundesarchiv in Berlin; the Historisches Archiv der Deutschen Bundesbank, Frankfurt; the Deutsches Technikmuseum, Berlin; the Morgan Library, New York; Harvard University, Baker Library, Cambridge, Massachusetts (Henry Villard Collection); and the Edison Papers at Rutgers University.

This book owes a great deal to several institutions and individuals. First and foremost among these is Deutsche Bank itself. Those who are in the field generally recognize that Deutsche Bank has led efforts to devote more resources to furthering our knowledge of the evolution of economic institutions. This work is merely the latest in a long line of books and articles that the bank has helped bring into print. These include many important additions to general business study, such as *The Deutsche Bank*, written by Lothar Gall and colleagues, and specific contributions to the study of National Socialism. Through my research, I learned that this tradition of supporting scholarship at Deutsche Bank goes back to 1913, when Deutsche Bank helped arrange for the publication of the English edition of Karl Helfferich's *Deutschlands Volkswohlstand* in the United States.[5]

For the support it gave me, the bank made only two demands on the content of the final work. The first was that the book deal mainly with Deutsche Bank's activities in the United States, leaving out an elaborate history of any of the companies it acquired over the years. Second, that I include some discussion of its activities in the United States over the past twenty years without the benefit of primary-source material at the bank. For those years, as discussed, I relied on secondary sources and interviews with senior executives. For all other periods, I was given wide access to its archival materials and even encouraged to supplement those documents with research in other archives. The more I plunged into the work, the more I was convinced that these conditions were reasonable, because the history of Deutsche Bank in the United States itself was extensive enough to pique any historian's interest, and that for the most recent period too little time had elapsed, in any case, for normal historical judgment.

The reasons why Deutsche Bank made this commitment involve important aspects of German history and the history of the bank. Deutsche Bank, for good or ill, has always been identified with the modern history of its country. For at least 200 years, Germans have cultivated a special relationship with history. In Germany, more than in any country I know, historical reflection serves as a first step to self-consciousness and activity, despite that country's painful past. German firms, more than their counterparts in most countries, feel a special responsibility for cultivating consciousness about business's social role. The financial theorist Michael Jensen once argued that industry must be able to clear dead plants from a garden for new ones to grow.[6] For this, American industry has been rightly praised, but tending the garden as an ecosystem is important, too, and here German firms excel. As a leader of German business, it is only natural that Deutsche Bank takes its role as gardener very seriously.

A commitment of this sort requires not only an extraordinary amount of courage but also consistent organizational implementation on various levels, beginning with senior management. Deutsche Bank at no time attempted to exercise control over what I wrote. Indeed, I maintained legal control of the copyright and responsibility for errors. In its willingness to take these risks, Deutsche Bank is fortunate to have had and still has executives for whom a commitment to the past is as natural as the profit motive. Current managers are only the latest in a long line of Deutsche Bank executives who refuse to allow Deutsche Bank employees to forget their history and culture. One mark of that strong corporate culture is the attachment of retired managers to their companies' histories. Among those who at one time worked for Deutsche Bank or Bankers Trust (most retired but not all) and who have made important contributions to this book are Michael Rassmann, Detlev Staecker, John Ross, Charles Sanford, Klaus Jacobs, Mark Yallop, Rolf-E. Breuer, Hilmar Kopper, and Otto Steinmetz. Several managers who are still with the bank – Seth Waugh, Donna Milrod, Frank Fehrendorf, Gary Hattem, and Gene Guill – have also graciously contributed their time and documents.

Another mark is Deutsche Bank's outstanding archive, an intellectual nerve center and memory bank for Deutsche Bank's historical consciousness. Without the help of Angelika Raab-Rebentisch, Martin Müller, Reinhard Frost, and especially Bernd Kulla, whose knowledge, meticulous eye, and general insights about the American and Abs files saved me countless hours, this work could neither have been contemplated nor completed. They all contributed many useful comments to this work and are all first-rate historians in their own right.

It has been my privilege to belong to several groups of scholars who have nourished my intellectual life and contributed to this book in more ways than I can count. Among the historians who are involved in the principal European historical associations of which I am a part, there are (as one of them affectionately refers to the grouping) the "usual suspects" of colleagues/friends: Gerald Feldman, Harold James, Alice Teichovà and Mikulàš Teich, Hubert Bonin, Margarita Dritsas, Jeff Fear, Youssef Cassis, Duncan Ross, Per Hansen, Peter Hayes, Andrea Schneider, Peter Hertner, John Wilson, Gabriele Teichmann, Phil Scranton, and Christopher McKenna, to whom I am particularly indebted for improving the English title of this book. This group has reinforced my conviction that economic institutions cannot be properly understood separately from their political contexts. Some members of the group even did me the honor of reading significant portions of the manuscript. Special thanks in this regard must go to Mira Wilkins, the little lady who is for most of us in the field the "grande dame" of the history of multinationals and international investment. For at least two decades, her work has been the starting point for the historical and theoretical study of cross-border investment, especially in and out of the United States. This book is no exception. To these names, I must add several economists and historians, who have given me useful suggestions or influenced this work in other ways. They include: Geoffrey Jones and Lou Galambos, editors of this series; Jean-François Hennart; John Dunning; Michèle Saboly; Catherine Schenk; Ray Stokes; Jana Wüstenhagen; Krys Obloj; Carl-Ludwig Holtfrerich; and Don Brean. Several nonhistorian friends had to put up with my endless stories about the project, from which they tried to divert me, and consoled me with ample quantities of good food and wine. Some, especially Bonnie Hoffman, were even kind enough to help with editing. These friends include: Johannas and Karin Costa (whose mother was née Gwinner, a name that will figure large in this story); Robert and Bonnie Hoffman; Christian and Petra von Rohrscheidt; Udo and Beate Schecker; Kevin and Gale Farewell; and Barbara Lindheim and Michael Capek. I would like especially to thank Jeanne Weckler and Marie-Claude Howard, without whose typing and proofreading help this book simply could not have been written.

The Center for the Study of Europe gave me a home during the early stages of this work. Its director, Volker Berghahn, who has since I met him a decade ago been a true and valued counselor and friend, shared his well-studied views on American-German relations. This book is peppered – in a manner hard to footnote – with his insights about writing history and about those relations, drawn from his many written contributions and from morning walks in Riverside Park. As always, Fritz Stern was there, too, in spirit, the embodiment of the historian's conscience and imagination. At virtually all stages, Frank Smith and his co-workers at Cambridge provided intelligent guidance.

I am indebted to ESCP-EAP, European School of Management, for according me two sabbatical semesters and the International Club for some additional funding. ESCP-EAP also contributed to this book by funding a host of international students who made various contributions to this book and made the whole exercise a more pleasant undertaking for me. They include: Sushmita

Banerjee (Indian); Rajiv Gupta (Indian); Chandi Neubauer (American); Christian zu Sayn-Wittgenstein (German); Valerie Spiegelfeld (Austrian); Patricia Szerszenowicz (Polish); Erin Patten (American); Greylen Erlachen (American); Unsang Jo (South Korean); and David Tabet (Lebanese and French). Finally, I would like to express my appreciation to several of my colleagues in ESCP-EAP's finance department – Cécile Kharoubi, Alain Chevalier, Franck Bancel, Christophe Moussu, Michael Troege, Bruno Thiry, and Jyoti Gupta – who took the time to give me valuable suggestions during an internal seminar in May 2006.

Christopher Kobrak
Paris, May 2007

Abbreviations

ABH	Association of Business Historians
AEG	Allgemeine Elektricitäts-Gesellschaft
AG	Aktiengesellschaft (Joint Stock Company)
AMRO	Amsterdam-Rotterdam Bank
APC	Alien Property Custodian
B&O	Baltimore and Ohio Railroad
BCCI	Bank of Credit and Commerce International
BEC	Banque Européenne de Credit
BIS	Bank for International Settlements
CEO	Chief Executive Officer
CMI	Capital Management International GmbH
CSAT	Central and South American Telegraph Co.
DB	Deutsche Bank
DM	Deutsche Mark
EAB	European American Bank
EABC	European American Bank Corporation
EABTC	European American Bank & Trust Corporation
EBIC	European Banks' International Company SA
EC	European Community
EEC	European Economic Community
EGE	Edison General Electric
EMS	European Monetary System
EPS	Earnings Per Share
ERISA	Employee Retirement Income Securities Act
FBI	Federal Bureau of Investigation
FDI	Foreign Direct Investment
FDIC	Federal Deposit Insurance Corporation
FED	Federal Reserve Board
GAAP	Generally Accepted Accounting Principles
GDP	Gross Domestic Product
GE	General Electric
GNP	Gross National Product
HABBk	Historisches Archiv der Deutschen Bundesbank (Historical Archive of the German Bundesbank)
HADB	Historisches Archiv der Deutschen Bank (Historical Archive of Deutsche Bank)

HSBC	Hongkong and Shanghai Banking Corporation
IAB	International Acceptance Bank
ICC	Interstate Commerce Commission
K&L	Knoblauch & Lichtenstein
LTCM	Long-Term Capital Management
M&A	Mergers and Acquisitions
MBA	Master of Business Administration
NAC	North American Company
NAFTA	North American Free Trade Agreement
NATO	North Atlantic Treaty Organization
OEEC	Organization for European Economic Cooperation
OM	Organization and Management
OMGUS	Office of Military Government of the United States
OPEC	Organization of the Petroleum Exporting Countries
OR&N	Oregon Railway & Navigation Company
OTC	Over-the-Counter
P&G	Procter and Gamble
RAROC	Risk-Adjusted Return on Capital
S&H	Siemens & Halske
SEC	Securities and Exchange Commission
SWIFT	Society for Worldwide Interbank Financial Telecommunication
WMR	Western Maryland Railroad Company

1

Overview of the Title and Terrain

Deutsche Bank Representative: "Do you know where I am from? I know that there is gambling going on in there."

Rick (Humphrey Bogart): "Yes, I do. You're lucky that your money is good at the bar."

Casablanca, 1942.

I believe that we in Berlin must also take an interest in American affairs. America is closer to us than Italy after all, the Gotthard notwithstanding.

Georg von Siemens, first spokesman of Deutsche Bank management board, 1870–1900.

Cooperation and Conflict, Men and Markets

In our internet age, globalization sometimes appears like a linear, inevitable process. In reality, over the past 150 years, the integration of world markets and homogenization of world culture have progressed fitfully. In the face of technical and political obstacles, moving from international connections to multinational integration required enormous individual and institutional commitments to the value of cross-cultural interchanges. This is in part the story of how German and American capital markets became more integrated with one another, particularly of the role played in that process by one major institution, Deutsche Bank. It is the history of Deutsche Bank's nearly 140-year-long relationship with the United States. Whether one bemoans or rejoices in these transformations, there is little doubt that Deutsche Bank was one of the key bridges over which finance and ideas traveled between the United States and Germany. From its inception, the bank was conceived as a project to deepen German economic links to the rest of the world.

The story is set in very contrasting economic and political environments. First and foremost is the contrast between periods during which Deutsche Bank pursued profit in the context of relatively peaceful corporate and national competition and those periods characterized by much more violent national conflict that filtered into business relationships – the former dominated by cooperation and the Gold Standard and the latter by unbridled competition and aggressive conflict among nations. To be sure, political risk, especially America's uncertain support of the value of its own currency, and national ambitions were never far from the minds of German managers at nearly every stage of the years covered by this narrative, but the contrast between the pre-World War I period and the decades that followed is very striking. The relative stability of long-term interest rates in most countries and complete convertibility of many currencies were replaced in a few short months in 1914, for example, by previously unimagined volatility and blocked funds.[1] Moreover, much of business's macroeconomic and political environment even during the second half of the twentieth century was set in motion by the events connected with World War I. For much of Deutsche Bank's history, national conflicts and macroeconomic instability have been more the norm than the exception. Though many of us hoped that the world had turned a new corner in the 1990s, more recent events have cast a shadow on that optimism.

Paralleling these developments has been another transformation involving the contrast between financial transactions dominated by personal contacts and those done in huge, impersonal capital markets.[2] Although the term "market" is hard to define, it suggests the institutionalization of transactions with relatively open access governed by rules, not by individuals. Capital markets are today not only vastly larger than they were in the nineteenth century, they are also more standardized and directed by much more regulation designed to reduce the influence of private information in determining price movements. In most of Europe and North America, the issuance and distribution of government debt, an enormous part of debt markets, have become routine, nearly automated affairs by comparison to the nineteenth century. Technology and developments in financial theory have helped make financial markets and pricing of instruments more transparent and, for many practitioners and theorists, an exercise in stochastic modeling. Indeed, most of the financial tools applied today to market analysis are based on random price movements around patterns predicted by economic theory, which reflects a high degree of information dissemination and an extremely rapid transmission of new data. From the 1930s on, at least – if not sooner – American regulators tended to emphasize transparency, arm's-length transactions, and diversification for market regulation and the governance of corporations rather than keeping key stakeholders, such as bankers, close to firms.

The public today is understandably shocked by the degree to which "movers and shakers" can still manipulate prices and the distribution of assets, but the story of Deutsche Bank in the United States is a useful reminder of how much financial regulators have taken bankers out of the management and the corporate governance loop. This regulatory decision has had costs and benefits. Although venture-capitalist and some boutique-financing firms still maintain close contact with the users of their capital, the vast majority of bankers are no longer at the hub of creating new companies and financing old ones in the way they were 100 years ago. For regulatory and other reasons, they keep their distance. Moreover, new players have challenged their place as providers of capital. These intermediaries, such as pension and mutual funds – with different interests in companies and different limits on their involvement in corporate management – channel institutional funds into companies. More often than not, the access that governments, companies themselves, and investors have to one another is now so easy that the efforts of bankers are not needed to acquire or loan funds – certainly there is enough access in most cases to avoid paying large fees for many services that were commonplace and the "bread and butter of banking" 100 years ago. All this is not meant to imply that modern bankers do not earn huge commissions from individually driven deals, such as those portrayed in the book and film *Barbarians at the Gate*. Rather, the overall weight in the gamut of bank affairs has shifted to many more "standardized" (commodity-like) transactions, capable of mathematical description, such as currency trading (by itself a nearly unimaginable $2.2 *trillion a day*), asset management, and bond trading, with high volumes but low margins, which lend themselves to stochastic modeling. As Ron Chernow pointed out in an excellent book about precisely this theme: "At bottom, the real power of old-line bankers lay in their monopoly over information, a commodity even rarer than capital in those days."[3] The creation of modern capital markets has narrowed the range of transactions about which "monopoly" information can be acquired and used by men and institutions. Only the very quick and innovative can earn above-average rents.

In the early stages of this story, both the United States and German financial scenes were dominated by closed-door negotiations about prices and costs among participants, sometimes elites of different nationalities that shared a common culture. By the end of the twentieth century, America's decision to force finance into public markets with relatively transparent standardized transactions, came, by dint in part of its huge volumes and easy access, to dominate the world of finance, a transformation with which Deutsche Bank has had difficulties coping. It is the story of how international capital markets and their regulation grew from this infancy to a troubled adolescence. It is also the story of how banking evolved from a quite broadly defined activity, which included active management of companies, in the nineteenth century to a much narrower, technical one in the late twentieth century.

Through all of these structural changes, Deutsche Bank's management may have altered its strategies and tactics for doing business with the rest of the world but it rarely wavered in its faith that international business made social and economic sense. In the face of dire challenges, the bank's leaders held steadfast to the conviction that more cross-cultural interaction ultimately profited all those who engaged in it.

This book takes a somewhat novel approach to business and financial history. It proposes to make a contribution to our understanding of these great transformations in financial institutions and capital markets by focusing on one bank and its relationship to one country. For some readers, putting a firm and a nation – especially the largest economic and military power in the world – on an "equal footing" in the title, connected by the word "and," might appear as just another example of corporate arrogance, which for many critics taints modern globalization.

I have two reasons for treating this country and this company together. First, the size of U.S.-styled capital markets and the weight of their regulation have been of paramount importance to understanding Deutsche Bank's entire history. Second, during many of the years of this narrative, Deutsche Bank was not *in* the United States in any meaningful sense. For the first fifty years, Deutsche

Bank sold an enormous amount of American securities in Europe and did considerable amounts of other types of business with American institutions and individuals without operating a subsidiary or branch – not even a joint venture. During the interwar and post-World War II period, Deutsche Bank and Germany in general were highly dependent on American capital and regulation, again without operating a legal entity in the United States.[4] Through most of this narrative, too, Deutsche Bank served as, and may still be, the most important German institutional financial connection to the United States. For these reasons, I hope the reader will be patient with my coupling of the United States with Deutsche Bank and with my use of the broader "and" both in the title and the approach to the book.[5]

Linking the country and the bank, moreover, emphasizes the role of national and international politics and regulation in business, and therefore business history. For virtually all of the period covered by this book, the size and regulation of American markets made that country a special case for most businesses. Political conflict quickly helped transform America's great need for capital into an overabundance of funds. Not until the New Deal did the United States succeed in creating extensive regulation of its capital markets, and then did so in a new, particularly American form. Although hardly adapted to the rest of the world, that system, in part because of political events, has had an extraordinary influence over international capital markets. The American combination of abrupt changes in capital flows and regulation has proven both extremely enticing and challenging even for U.S. companies, let alone their foreign rivals.[6] Despite a high degree of internationalization of business and many new limits on national governments' abilities to assert their sovereignty over business, political contexts are still important for determining the strategy, structure, and timing of foreign investments. Even though business is global or regional, politics is still largely national. Relations between the United States and Germany have been one of the most decisive factors in Deutsche Bank's overall success or failure in any period. Although business was never easy, at times antagonisms were so great that Deutsche Bank's very existence was threatened.

If these reasons are not sufficient for focusing on how one business dealt with one country, I ask the reader to imagine how different the story would be if I were writing about a British bank investing in the United States, or conversely about Deutsche Bank investing in Russia.

In the recent past, historians and economists have become more attuned to the value of comparative history and the limits of narrowly defined national histories, which neglect the international dimension of many events and movements. Yet even some excellent new studies ignore the business element of those connections. Although it is unquestionably true, as one author put it, that countries are "enmeshed in each other's histories," how business has helped cross the semipermeable lines that divide nations is less well understood.[7] Writing a cross-cultural history is commendable but difficult. It requires mastering the political, economic, and social stories of multiple countries, and it risks losing focus. It is my hope that the story of Deutsche Bank in the United States will provide that institutional focus which can help clarify the complex modes of economic interaction between nations, and international business's role in bringing together diverse cultures.

A Broad Outline of Deutsche Bank and German-American Relations

Probably no institution or trade name is more closely identified in public, professional, or academic minds with the accomplishments and failures of German commerce than Deutsche Bank. Though ranked by some measures among the top ten banks in the new century, Deutsche Bank has lost some of the clout in world, European, and even German financial markets that it once had.[8] However Deutsche Bank's significance goes well beyond financial yardsticks. For much of the past 140 years, Deutsche Bank has symbolized Germany's special blend of financial capitalism – with its close, long-term relationships of investors to commercial companies, consensus building, innovation, resilience against catastrophe, and drive to establish international markets – which, by most accounts, helped make the German economy revered by imitators and feared by competitors. Deutsche Bank has been thought of, until very recently, as the quintessential universal bank with a wide range of financial services – taking deposits from individuals as well as institutions and using these relationships to bring to market securities and to hold long-term positions in client companies, in whose governance the bank often takes an active role. Sadly, too, Deutsche Bank has also been implicated, as the above quote from an American movie suggests, in German business's complicity with some of history's most notorious crimes.[9] Recently, along with other icons of German capitalism such as Daimler-Benz and Hoechst, the bank has even been criticized, paradoxically on both sides of the Atlantic, for promoting German resistance to change and, alternatively, for efforts to emulate slavishly America's "cowboy" capitalism.[10] For better or worse, Deutsche Bank's history, in short, has been tied to that of the country in which it was founded, and its activities in the United States to the relations between those countries.

With the cautious support of the Prussian government, Deutsche Bank was founded in 1870 by a group of small banks and investors for the purpose of representing German financial interests on international markets. As one of the first banks organized as a joint stock company and with excellent political connections, Deutsche Bank was well positioned to survive and even expand during the financial crisis of the 1870s through acquisitions and diversification of its banking services. Soon, those activities included not only international trade financing but also cross-border commercial and investment banking under the same roof. Led by Georg Siemens, a second cousin of the founder of the electrical giant Siemens & Halske, Deutsche Bank was one of the first banks to pursue a strategy of universal banking, a model that the bank has kept and that remains one of the hallmarks of the German financial system.[11]

Although Deutsche Bank came into existence a few months before the Reich whose name it bore, its creation was a truly national project. Its primary purpose was to pool the efforts of its participating banks to circumvent the dominance of British banks in international trade financing. However, Deutsche Bank soon exceeded its original charter. It played an intimate role not only in the unprecedented increase of German business activity, new commercial forms, and technologies, but also with public and private attempts to grapple with vast economic and social upheavals. Its investors and regulators consciously saw it as combining the "national idea with one of the key ideas underlying the founding of the German Customs Union in 1834 ... to give Germany as much autonomy as possible in commerce and industrial production."[12] The German financial community understood its mission. As Otto Jeidels, the distinguished banker from the Berliner Handels-Gesellschaft, wrote early in his career, a country that wanted to be a dynamic exporter had to have an international banking network to clear transactions, absorb foreign debt, and take positions in foreign firms.[13]

Even though Deutsche Bank was founded to further international development, its greatest successes and failures occurred in Germany – many of them due to the bank's close relationship to the German government. Ironically, and probably unintentionally, the banks that had contributed to its founding also contributed to the creation of a powerful new domestic competitor. Deutsche Bank's willingness to support many projects, from the acceptance of the Mark to the furtherance of German trade, gave it a privileged position in its home market. Its consolidation with troubled institutions after the Crisis of 1873 made Deutsche Bank a major player in Germany, giving it access to much greater amounts of domestic capital. From 1876 to 1899, Deutsche Bank transformed itself from a bank with a small share in the consortium that handled government issues of securities to one that handled some issues all alone. It expanded domestic lending and other services to industrial firms, and vastly enlarged its branch office network in Germany.[14] Its size and excellent political connections made Deutsche Bank both the object of political attacks within Germany and one of the most favored banks for governmental control of capital markets. Wherever the government used private institutions to "guide markets," from the Baghdad Railroad before World War I to control of foreign exchange transactions, Deutsche Bank played a pivotal role. By 1913, Deutsche Bank had become not the oldest, but Germany's leading representative of the so-called banking revolution, combining the advantages of its corporate statute as a joint-stock company with a branch network for collecting deposits and investment banking. In that year, Deutsche Bank was roughly twice the size of the largest American joint-stock bank and more than 50 percent bigger as measured by assets than its closest German rival.[15]

Despite these wide-ranging international activities, probably no other country in the world, apart from its home country, played a greater role in Deutsche Bank's history than the United States. Unlike some other major financial institutions of the nineteenth century, Deutsche Bank quickly perceived America's potential and pivotal role.[16] The above quote by Siemens, which introduces nearly every work about Deutsche Bank's relationship to the United States, accurately captures management's strongly held feelings about and strategic commitment to that part of the world.

America's startling economic growth as the country emerged from the effects of its civil war reinforced its dominant economic and political position in the region and, by the end of the century, transformed it into the largest economy in the world.[17] America and Germany came to industrial maturity at the same time, just as Deutsche Bank came into existence. Indeed, in a sense, both countries became "unified" nations by dint of "blood and iron" during the decade following the shots fired on Fort Sumter. As Fritz Stern wrote in a different context:

> In the three decades before the Great War, Germany was the country in ascendancy, and its physical power, with its strident militaristic ethos, seemed to be balanced by cultural, especially scientific achievement.... The only other country at the time growing with similar energy was the United States, it too marked by immense material power, embarked on an imperial course, and exemplary in the promotion of scientific-technical innovation.[18]

Quoting the German theologian and academic statesman Adolf von Harnack, Stern added that it seemed America was the nation most "intellectually and spiritually" akin to Germany.[19] How these two countries, seemingly moving along similar trajectories at the end of the nineteenth century, should have such different experiences in the twentieth, unavoidably serves as the backdrop for this narrative.

Although differing labor costs and views about stability contributed to contrasting control institutions and attitudes toward production, marketing, and competition, it is not sufficiently recognized in economic history literature that the two economic systems shared many common characteristics before World War I. These commonalities included: reliance on banks for corporate control; a federal political system that made regulation more complicated; and an uncomfortable reliance on foreign models and markets. Despite a capitalism with very different roots and orientations, the intellectual, cultural, and business ties between the two countries ran deep. Many German refugees from the Revolution of 1848 ended up in the United States and played important roles in America's intellectual and commercial development, including in the affairs of Deutsche Bank. In the last quarter of the nineteenth century, German immigration to the United States was running nine times higher than the combined flows from the Netherlands, Belgium, Luxembourg, Switzerland, and France.[20] Many of those immigrants returned home to encourage others to come or at least to invest in the "New World." Generations of American professors in numerous disciplines trooped off to "validate" their studies at German universities, whose organization and research orientation became models for some of America's most important institutions of higher learning. German Jewish bankers and merchants played an integral role in American capital markets. Investment from Germany to the United States grew rapidly and came in many forms. Long-term investment in securities went from $0.2 billion in 1899 to $1 billion in 1914, 15–16 percent of all German foreign investment.[21] American patents issued to German nationals went from 218 in 1885 to 1,475 in 1914, surpassing those granted to English citizens in that year.[22] As early as 1900,

U.S. insurance companies, savings banks, and trust companies held nearly $34 million in foreign securities – approximately $10 million of which were those of the Austrian and German governments.[23]

But Germany's and America's financial capitals – Berlin and New York – were relative newcomers to the world of international finance, still dominated by London. The battles of both cities to solidify their new roles also form an important backdrop to this story.[24]

Ironically, given its initial purpose, the bank seemed to make little direct profit from its early international activities. Although Deutsche Bank's foreign activities in and of themselves often brought the bank little joy and were hard to manage, those activities, nevertheless, helped distinguish Deutsche Bank from other German banks, with few or no financial links to the rest of the world. The bank's first international efforts were focused on supporting the commercial activities of German firms abroad, for which it needed to build up a network of affiliates to handle international transactions. However, as Germany's supply of loanable funds increased with the maturity of some industries and the nationalization of German railroads, German investors and regulators wanted to broaden the range of German investment. Deutsche Bank expanded into underwriting international loan and equity issues that could add to its portfolio of alternatives for domestic clients. In the mid-1880s, it began to invest in foreign loans, first in South American and then in U.S. companies. Only a few years later, it started to take the lead in financing projects in the Balkans and Middle East. Most of its initial investments had little or nothing to do with Germany's colonial enthusiasm and policy; yet by the mid-1890s, Germany's "web of influences from ... diplomacy, military aid, and private business" became more of a factor in investment decisions, especially in Turkey, China, and Morocco.[25]

Despite many obstacles, business structures in the nineteenth century reflected macroeconomic and political circumstances that were very favorable to the free flow of goods, services, and funds. Though far from easy, the bank required far less direct investment then to engage in international finance. During this period, the many modern financial routines were not yet commonplace, so even greater potential rewards accrued to those institutions that could access new opportunities and profit from managing uncertainty. To be sure, many investments were backed by mortgages on land or pledges of securities, for example, but legal recourse was often cumbersome at best. With varying degrees of success, for much of its history in the United States, Deutsche Bank was obliged to rely on personal relationships and mutual trust as a basis for managing investments.

Even where politics played little or no role in business decisions, assessing risks and evaluating returns was hard for Deutsche Bank's executives, leading to abrupt changes in structure. Soon after joining the bank, Hermann Wallich (member of the management board from 1870–94) emphasized in a memo to the board the necessity of establishing as fast as possible a network of branches in Germany's principal trading centers. Wholly owned offices in London, Bremen, and Hamburg were quickly followed by holdings in foreign banks in New York and Paris, as well as two branch offices in Asia. The Asian market was particularly interesting to German merchants, in part because the area had been recently opened to westerners. Germany's conversion to the Gold Standard in 1873 freed its own silver reserves for sale to China, which remained on the silver standard. Deutsche Bank was active in the transaction. On the heels of the financial crisis in 1873, however, some of these investments were terminated. By 1875, the decision was made to close the Shanghai and Yokohama branches. For a time, ironically, English banks represented Deutsche Bank's interests in Asia. By the late 1880s, Deutsche Bank, following the lead of the German government and of commerce, became much more interested in South America. Most of its Latin American investments would be carried out, however, through a new German subsidiary, the Deutsche Ueberseeische Bank.[26] Investments in other regions were often conducted in joint ventures with other German firms, and even English banks.

Although German politics played little role in the bank's decisions, America was one of many countries where Deutsche Bank's early investments were plagued by great difficulties. For Deutsche Bank, the absence of adequate financial regulation was its greatest challenge in tapping into early opportunities in the United States – but it also increased the rewards for clever perseverance. Extraordinary capital flows passed between the two countries without computers, instantaneous price information, and, for the most part, this was accomplished without audited financial statements and other currently commonplace forms of capital market regulation. Investments could earn higher nominal rates than in Germany or England, but, as Deutsche Bank discovered to its chagrin, with many sharp ups and downs of fortunes, in both senses of the word. In general, investors enjoyed more governmental assurances about foreign exchange rate movements before World War I than they do today. Without a central bank, however, the United States was one of the weakest links in that era's foreign exchange regime and the American banking system was more subject to panic. Moreover, America's multi-layered banking regulation hindered Deutsche Bank from opening its own wholly owned operation in the United States to service the bank's main business interests there. In the pre-1914 environment, Deutsche Bank's strategy of relying on independent agents and correspondent banks – though not without significant drawbacks – did not prevent the bank from handling a large part of German-American capital movements.

Before World War I, Deutsche Bank's failure to sell German securities in the United States was frustrating. Despite many obstacles, the bank's entry strategy served it better in finding and marketing American securities in Europe than marketing European ones in the United States. Deutsche Bank managers had expected that cash flows would flow back and forth between Europe and the United States – it did, but in unwelcome ways. Deutsche Bank complained bitterly about the lack of advertising for German securities offered in the United States by the bank and its friends. State and city bonds from Frankfurt and Saxony were poorly marketed. And even the selling of Imperial Bonds was botched. Many of the loans were resold in Germany through arbitrage firms, leaving German firms with the greatest possible expense and smallest possible benefit.[27]

There were serious weaknesses in German and American economic and political relations that would affect Deutsche Bank. Despite American-German economic and cultural ties, much of the business activity between the United States and other parts of the world, even before the war, was filtered through Germany's European economic rival, England. This riled many Germans, who felt that German culture deserved greater weight in diplomatic, colonial, and business matters.[28] Around the turn of the century, as the world passed from a period during which the sentiments of nationalism and internationalism could easily coexist and even complement one another to a period of passionate antagonism, England's role as conduit produced multifaceted strategic disadvantages for Germany.[29]

Moreover, some of the economic policies of the two countries – Germany and the United States – jeopardized closer relations. America's protective tariffs, designed to shield "infant industries," closed it off to many German manufactured goods. Germany, for its part, began raising tariffs on agricultural and other products of particular interest to American exporters in the late nineteenth century. America's cavalier macroeconomic and regulatory environment increasingly shocked Germans. During that same period, Germany's approach to regulating competition also increasingly distressed Americans. In short, America and Germany were two of the most important emerging markets of the late nineteenth century, with all the opportunities and threats for doing business that developing markets entail today, including potential for mutual national antagonisms.

For the first forty years covered by this book, both America's economic growth and need of foreign capital brought the two nations into closer association. From 1870 to 1914 the American economy grew by 4.3 percent a year, well over 1 percent faster than even Germany's dynamic rate of growth. Much of the growth in both countries was built on exports to the rest of the world and to each other. By 1914, total foreign investment in the United States came to $7 billion, approximately 20 percent of America's GNP. German investors went to pains to understand and live with the chaotic and impersonal patterns of American investment behavior. Yet, some reacted with awe and amazement.

The topsy-turvy pattern of German and American relations in the twentieth century greatly affected the nature and success of Deutsche Bank's business. During the interwar years, financial markets appeared to those trained in the pre-1914 era to have an "Alice in Wonderland" character. Among other changes, Germany went, in the eyes of many Americans, from a disciplined lender to an undisciplined, unscrupulous debtor. Americans, once justly infamous for their shoddy regulatory and financial practices, preached to Germans about sound money practice, clear accounting, and fair banking.

However, not even world wars, economic collapse, and this bizarre reversal of roles significantly altered Deutsche Bank's interest in American business. In a sense, they intensified it. Yet whereas Deutsche Bank's principal preoccupation with North America before World War I was to find and monitor suitable investments for its German clients, after 1918 it was to encourage and monitor investment into Germany. The economic and political chaos following

World War I transformed Germany into a country desperate for capital. In the space of a decade, German businessmen were transformed from welcome foreign investors to holders of enemy assets, targets for "abnormal" gains by American companies. America seized more foreign assets than any country in history, and Deutsche Bank's affairs in the United States were dominated by activities aiming to get those assets back. During the Weimar Republic, for several years, German companies became the darlings of American speculators and of serious companies looking for significant foreign investment. By the 1930s, however, German borrowers were considered unreliable defaulters and, soon after, for many Americans, even considered to be vile anti-Semites and wartime enemies, capable of contributing to the gassing of harmless civilians. For the first seventy years of this story, Deutsche Bank's connection to America evolved from trusting German-born Americans, to working with Americans with little prior contact to Germany, to relying on its own employees, to finally watching, helplessly, the virtually complete breakdown of its American business relations, which paralleled the changes in the world economic and political environment. Remarkably, despite the loss of much its property and, to some extent, its prestige in the world and in the United States (from 1914 to 1957), by the end of this narrative, Deutsche Bank is not only still Germany's largest bank, it has also become a major force in American and world financial markets.

The Personal, Institutional, and Technological Dimensions

The story of Deutsche Bank in the United States is also the story of people and other institutions. Although human capital makes up the value to a large extent of financial service firms, we know less than we should about those who manage banks.[30] Over the years, Deutsche Bank was blessed with a number of entrepreneurial senior executives who were politically active German nationals, yet had a strong set of liberal convictions and were very comfortable in the world outside of Germany. Before the creation of Deutsche Bank, Georg Siemens, spokesman of the management board for the first thirty years of the bank's life and liberal member of the Reichstag, had worked in London and Tehran for Siemens & Halske, the electrical company founded by his father's cousin. According to many accounts, Siemens was a visionary, whose eyes were always focused on the big picture and the long run. Siemens was in many ways the guiding spirit whose faith in international and American business was so great that it sometimes clouded his judgment.

In addition to Siemens, men like Arthur Gwinner, who shared responsibility for American business, were trained outside of Germany and spoke several languages. Born in Frankfurt am Main in 1856 to a family of lawyers, Gwinner had ten years of bank training in England and Spain.[31] He joined Deutsche Bank's management board in 1894 – serving as its spokesman from 1910 until 1919 – just at a time when the bank's activities in the United States began a crucial period. His relationship with several important investors and bankers in other countries and his excellent working relationship with Deutsche Bank's representative in New York were key elements in the bank's success before political conflicts made internationalism seem like an atavistic element of the past. Although Gwinner, too, was an ardent internationalist and very ambitious for Deutsche Bank in the United States, he seems to have been more of realist and more cautious than Siemens.

This is, then, the story of how a wide range of human emotions and attributes – including ambition, professionalism, creativity, betrayal, and loyalty – affected high finance in the context of new technologies and colossal social transformations. Here Deutsche Bank's two American representatives during the thirty years preceding World War I – Henry Villard and Edward Adams – offer a sharp contrast. Both brought an enormous amount of business to Deutsche Bank by dint of their contacts and business sense, but then the comparison ends. In some sense, their roles in the United States for Deutsche Bank paralleled those of Siemens and Gwinner in Germany.

Villard (1835–1900) always thought big, making and losing several fortunes in the process. A roguish visionary, he could charm sober businessmen and frustrate even the most adventuresome entrepreneurs. He rarely lost his optimism, a proclivity to think in large terms, and his gift for self-promotion. Villard often felt confused by Deutsche Bank's unwillingness to invest more in his grandiose projects and by the bank's indignation over his, to say the least, "sloppy" management of some of its investments.

Adams, by contrast, came from old, conservative New England stock. Distantly related to heroes of the American Revolution, there was little he had to prove to himself or the world. Although he started several businesses, Adams was always cautious and methodical. Despite his inability to speak German fluently, Adams instilled confidence in his Berlin colleagues, who, at a critical junction in Deutsche Bank's history in the United States – a point at which indeed the bank might even have stopped investing in that country – gave him more leeway than they did their compatriot Villard. For two decades prior to World War I, Adams invested the bank's and other German funds, managed their holdings, and served as one of the principal links between the United States and German capital markets. Similar to those dealing through Morgan and other banks, these links were based on personal relationships among individuals.

Adams performed many functions for Deutsche Bank. Like Villard before him, he sought out new investments, helped control the ones that the bank had, and kept Berlin managers informed about American political and economic events.[32] His correspondence with Deutsche Bank managers often revolved around the character and judgment of executives in prospective investments.[33] Obviously, the workings of American banks and their managers were of special interest.[34] Adams' relationship with Deutsche Bank was curious: he was neither an employee nor a fully independent agent. Adams was not averse to pursuing his own personal agenda alongside Deutsche Bank's.[35] His efforts were key to finding a workable solution to Deutsche Bank's gravest economic problem in the United States; his talents and Yankee character helped him resolve some conflicts, but created some others arising out of his lucrative and unusual position.

In addition to Deutsche Bank employees and agents, some of the leading figures of the past two hundred years played supporting roles – Edison, the Rockefellers, Westinghouse, J. P. Morgan, and Benjamin Strong, for instance.

This book is also the story of many ancillary institutions and markets. It would be unintelligible without a great deal of background about other banks – the houses of Morgan, Speyer, and Warburg, for example – with which Deutsche Bank worked, and an explanation of changes in banking regulation and financial products. Over the course of this story, German and American attitudes about economics and institutions influenced one another greatly, sometimes subtly – sometimes aggressively.

This story is even relevant to the development of accounting in both countries. The private ownership of American railroads, a stimulus to German investors whose share in German railroads had been bought up by the German state, attempts at regulation, and financial distress all combined to further the development of the American accounting profession and accounting standards. Although German economists influenced the American accounting profession, the presence of railroad shares and bonds on U.S. capital markets furthered the use of accounting as a control mechanism in the United States. The same issues contributed to a very different response in Germany.[36] The general instability of American capital markets and the specific troubles of many American firms, especially railroads, led to the transformation of the Deutsch-Amerikanische Treuhand-Gesellschaft AG (Treuhand), a company dedicated to the protection and development of German assets in the United States. In the 1890s, it moved into auditing American and German firms. With its strong relationship to Deutsche Bank, the Treuhand became a model for German auditing and corporate governance that has had a great influence on German accounting to the present day.[37]

Deutsche Bank's U.S. affairs were conducted in radically different technological environments. When this story begins, there were no direct telex lines between Germany and the United States, certainly no telephones. Crossing the Atlantic took approximately two weeks in each direction. Business letters were handwritten and clerks checked figures by hand. News of an American bankruptcy, for example, could take weeks to reach Germany. By the time the story ends, communication and money transfers have become almost instantaneous, and getting extensive business news is a question of turning on a computer or television. These changes have played an important role in this story, and did not occur overnight.

The Layout of the Book

The bulk of this book is divided into three Sections (Founding of Deutsche Bank in 1870 to 1914, 1914 to 1957, and 1957 to the Present Day), broken roughly by two great political events that radically changed Deutsche Bank's business environment. I will begin each Section with a short introduction designed to place Deutsche Bank's activities in the United States in their larger political and economic environment.

The first is the outbreak of World War I, an event that, as most readers recognize, shattered the international consensus of the first era of industrial globalization. Whereas the bank's national and international activities comfortably coexisted before World War I, the economic and political "disorder" unleashed in August 1914 made integrating those two poles of Deutsche Bank's activity significantly more difficult. In the wake of the Great War, Deutsche Bank became more dependent on German government business, chaotic regulation, and its ability to fend off hostile criticism of the role played by banks during the Weimar Republic. With many depositors wiped out by inflation and with many corporations relatively cash rich and able to access international capital markets directly, Deutsche Bank lost much of its power over commercial clients and grew more dependent on attracting deposits from foreigners – especially Americans – whose expectations were harder to manage than those of its traditional investors. The whole banking system, moreover, lost much of its public credibility during the interwar years. Because Deutsche Bank executives were involved in repatriation negotiations, in the economically questionable financing activities of German government and private concerns during the 1920s and in the financial "coordination" of the Third Reich, the bank paid a high price for its visibility as an icon of German finance capital. As a target of Allied occupiers who were convinced that concentration of banking had contributed to Hitler's coming to power, Deutsche Bank was initially split into many entities after World War II. Nevertheless, even before its reunification in the 1950s, Deutsche Bank began to play a pivotal role in steering American funds into West Germany's "economic miracle."

The second transition, in 1957, although less dramatic, involved the nearly simultaneous reunification of Deutsche Bank and the signing of the Treaty of Rome. Occurring as they did in the same month, they roughly coincided with German reestablishment of currency convertibility and the first appearance of sizeable cracks in the Bretton Woods economic system. Both developments contributed greatly to our current financial system. Although once again one of the largest banks in the world, in the new economic world order Deutsche Bank has found that breaking into certain segments and regions of the world is difficult. Through most of its history, Deutsche Bank relied on third-party representatives or partially owned banks to handle its affairs in the United States, but by 1979, it had several equity interests in American banks and a New York State branch office. Twenty years later, its purchase of a 100-year-old U.S. bank, Bankers Trust, became a *cause célèbre* in many quarters, igniting discussions about the loss of domestic control of assets, the power of global capitalism, and crimes against humanity committed five decades before the purchase. Although Deutsche Bank has lost market share and profits in some segments over the past twenty years, at the millennium it still controlled nearly 1 trillion Euro in assets and employed over 65,000 full-time workers (nearly 40,000 outside of Germany). By 2002, approximately a quarter of its assets and total revenues came from North America.[38]

I conclude with a Chapter on the future of multinational banking and explain how Deutsche Bank's history might add to our understanding of the salient features of financial institutions in the twenty-first century.

Because the book is specifically designed for businesspeople, economists, and historians from at least two cultures, I have made an effort to provide more contextualization than might ordinarily seem appropriate, and that at times may seem tedious for those already familiar with one or more of the dimensions of the story. For this, I apologize in advance. I have also intentionally provided more detail about some events than is commonplace, to give the reader a better sense of the people in the narrative and how they communicated with one another. Wherever possible, I describe the financial impact of Deutsche Bank's strategies and transactions and the terms of its business, along with some benchmarks to indicate the order of magnitude they represented. In addition to material in the text, I provide several appendices with comparative financial data.

Those readers who are looking for more details about Deutsche Bank's involvement with National Socialism will be disappointed. This terrain has been ably covered by Harold James, among others. Only as the Nazi seizure of power affected Deutsche Bank's business in the United States, debt negotiations, and ability to reestablish its business after World War II will it be dealt with here. The reader should remember that one of the consequences of that regime's autarchy policy was to make normal international banking virtually impossible. Between the crises in financial markets and the efforts of the Nazis to control German external capital flows, little was left of Deutsche Bank's business with the United States by 1938.

Although this book is not intended to be a business manual, I hope that it will make a contribution to bridging a long-standing and unfortunate gap between historical and economic studies, and at the same time, deepen our appreciation of commercial phenomena in general. This is not an easy task for many reasons. For the most part, those interested in business and those interested in history have conflicting orientations and different vocabularies. Even among academics the challenge is great. What Gertrude Himmelfarb wrote over fifteen years ago is probably truer today than in the late 1980s: "For all the brave talk about interdisciplinary studies, scholarship has never been as factional and parochial as it is today."[39] Much of Deutsche Bank's business involves transactions that are complicated even for those trained in accounting and finance, and in the broad historical framework of two or more countries. Finding the right balance of financial and historical context has been, to say the least, a daunting enterprise. I can only hope that I have risen to the challenge.

Section I

On Golden Chariots – Deutsche Bank's U.S. Business, 1870 to 1914

Each morning, Helios rose into the heavens in a gold chariot driven by four snow-white horses.

Using wings that Daedelus had fashioned from feathers and wax, he and his son Icarus escaped from Minos (king of Crete), who had imprisoned them; but Icarus, exulting in his power, flew too close to the sun, which melted the wax and he fell into the sea.

Robinson and Wilson, *Myths and Legends of All Nations*, pp. 66 and 186.

This town, one third of whose inhabitants were German, lay in a culturally rich area, which had increased its number with waves of immigrants. It contained in those days, I believe, five churches, among them two German ones. The Germans found themselves in the best circumstances and had several associations, even a hunting club.

Karl May, "*Weihnacht!*," 1897.*

* Karl May was a prolific German writer, whose works of fiction were for many Germans their first introduction to the United States. His popularity and this description of a town in the "Wild West" are testimony to the importance of German-American connections.

Introduction

> The fact is, there are in the world only two great progressing countries: the United States and Germany.
>
> Arthur Gwinner to James Hill, June 15, 1909, HADB, A1365.

When my story opens, the United Kingdom was the premier economic and political power in the world, a preeminence that exceeded the relative size of its national product.[1] In 1873, its stock exchange already had a total value of £2.3 billion ($10 billion, nearly as large as Germany's in 1913), of which more than 60 percent were private issues.[2] In addition to having the most vibrant capital market in the world, most relevant to this story, Britain in 1870 was the world's largest capital exporter, with an aggregate total of £770 million ($3.8 billion), of which 25 percent went to the United States, an amount that had increased by a factor of eight from 1830 to 1870.[3] By 1910, investment in other countries accounted for 7 percent of its gross national product.[4] Its banks led the way in the globalization of financial services.[5] The bulk of world trade was transacted with bills of exchange drawn for the most part on London banks.[6] Comparatively low transaction costs and a robust money market drew German and other foreign banks to create agencies in London.[7]

Britain was at the hub of a nearly worldwide economic global order of free trade and capital flows only surpassed in the last few decades, if at all.[8] Adherence to the Gold Standard served as the financial "Good Housekeeping" seal, largely awarded and then maintained by the Bank of England. Although the system was neither as automatic or simple as some believed – and was subject to periodic panics and depressions – fiscal discipline of national governments permitted an era of extraordinary and stable low inflation, low interest rates, and high real economic growth, especially compared with what preceded it and what would follow.[9] Wholesale prices even fell between 1872 and 1913, in Germany, the United States, and the United Kingdom.[10] Although several countries fell off the Gold Standard – or nearly did, like the United States – for much of this period the western world enjoyed unprecedented exchange rate stability.[11] The world order also included an extensive albeit incomplete commitment to free trade, for which the United Kingdom fought by words and example. From 1850 to 1913, world trade by some estimates increased tenfold.[12] Even in 1913, when protectionist passions began once again to run high, England's general tariffs level on industrial products was zero, Germany's only 13 percent.[13] With its large fleet and colonial empire, Britain policed a European "global dominance," a shield against "political risk" as defined by the great powers.[14] Under British leadership, the "European world" enjoyed its second – even its third by some measure – era of globalization with a good deal more consensus than earlier and even later periods.

By the time the era ended, however, much had changed. While the British economy was still growing strongly, the empire still covered the face of the earth, and London remained the center of the financial world, by 1913, it had lost a great deal to the United States and Germany in relative terms. Spurred by huge population increases, resolution of many internal political difficulties, industrial investment, and a managerial revolution, as well as the opening of its western regions, the U.S. economy stood at the economic pinnacle of the western world. Its index of output per capita was more than 10 percent higher than Britain's and approximately 50 percent higher than Germany's.[15] While the U.K. enjoyed real GDP and GDP per-capita growth of 1.9 and 1.0 percent respectively from 1870 to 1913, its continental and New World rivals' growth rates outstripped it by 50 percent and 100 percent respectively during the same period.[16] In 1913, the economies of Germany and England were roughly the same size; the U.S. economy was 30 percent larger than each of the others.[17] Moreover, unbeknownst to nearly everyone, European dominance as expressed in economic power and breadth of colonial domination stood at a precarious peak.

Deutsche Bank thrived in this political-economic environment. For the first forty-five years of its existence, Deutsche Bank's business grew at an astonishing pace. Although there is no one comprehensive public financial statement – or internal analysis – of how much impact business with North America had on that development, there is a great deal of circumstantial evidence that the U.S. business played a significant role in that growth, albeit to some extent indirectly. During the first forty years of its existence, Deutsche Bank's assets climbed from zero to 2.2 billion Mark, profits to 68.3 million Mark, and paid-in capital to 200 million Mark, an amount equal to 1 percent of the par value of all the equity traded on exchanges in Germany. In 1913, its stock was selling at two and a half times book value, a whopping 500 million Mark of market value, a sum that represented approximately 1 percent of Germany's 1913 gross domestic product.[18] From 1870 to 1913, business volume grew from 239.3 million Mark to 129.2 billion Mark.[19]

During those years, the United States went from an insignificant part of Deutsche Bank's business to one of its main foci. As late as 1880, even though foreign revenues realized in Berlin – not the bank's main center for international business – had grown in that city alone by 6 million Mark, Deutsche Bank managers wrote nothing about the United States in that year's annual report.[20] During the next twenty years, however, that was to change greatly.

Although there is no single document or series of memos laying out strategic decisions, soon after the bank's founding, Deutsche Bank's managers, convinced of America's economic potential, turned their attention to finding some way to participate in and manage the risks of that country's vibrant growth.[21] Although we know the United States was important to the bank's business, it is hard to determine both how and how much money Deutsche Bank made (or lost) in the United States. Financial reporting in Germany in this period did not require disclosing regional and business segment analyses. Nevertheless, not only did its 1900 annual report devote an entire sentence to the effects of the American presidential elections and economic conditions on the bank's prospects, the report prophesized that the American rail industry would create great rewards for Germany. By 1914, there was a whole paragraph devoted to U.S. business conditions, although nothing about precisely what Deutsche Bank was doing there. By that time, too, the bank had invested in and, in many cases, played an important role in the development of General Electric (Edison General Electric); the Northern Pacific, Baltimore & Ohio, Atchison, Topeka and Santa Fe, Missouri Pacific, and Chicago Rock Island Pacific railroads; Allis-Chalmers; Anaconda Copper; Lehigh Coke; and Niagara Power; as well as various government and other utility, construction, and commercial ventures. These investments came in many forms: bonds, term loans, preferred shares, and common shares. Some were short-term investments, often only distributed among European clients. On occasion, some short-term investments, regrettably, became long-term ones. With some, Deutsche Bank asserted or tried to assert management control, others were merely passive portfolio investments. It performed other banking services, such as trade financing, but these tended to be handled by correspondent banks in the United States and through its London office. Its primary activity during this period was underwriting and trading American securities in Europe, from which Deutsche Bank ultimately derived much prestige and profit, but even today's financial disclosures would not have been able to reveal all their indirect costs and benefits.

The first phase of the story in the United States, from 1870 to 1914, involves some drama and turbulence, but on a scale that is hardly comparable with the second. It is set against the background of inconsistent efforts by the United States to move away from an unregulated emerging market with enormous economic potential but without a central bank. Punctuated by severe economic crisis and aggressive nationalism, Deutsche Bank's activities in the United States played an integral but insufficiently recognized part of the first forty-five years of the bank's history.

International banking during this period differed from modern multinational banking[22] in some respects and resembled it in others. Few banks had a strong network of subsidiaries or branches in more than one country. Some foreign banks, such as Berliner Handels-Gesellschaft, purchased and for many years kept an equity interest in a U.S. bank, but this was rare. Other banks were tied to a foreign bank by family relationships. No matter what their entry strategy, the banks were hungry for deals and knowledge, and eager to avoid opportunity costs associated with not having the right partner at any one moment. Therefore, domestic and foreign banks continually restructured informal alliances. In any case, before 1914, at least, international banking, though highly competitive, was probably by necessity also a very cooperative, almost "collectivist" undertaking.[23]

The form of investment in the United States depended greatly on what kind of business a foreign bank wanted to pursue. For some aspects of banking, local regulation posed a problem, for others not at all. Well before the turn of the century, banks performed a wide range of tasks. They took deposits (mostly from wealthy individuals and firms), cleared and guaranteed bills of exchange, wrote letters of credit (a bank's promise to pay on behalf of a buyer), financed companies with direct loans, traded securities for customers, and underwrote debt and equity issues for corporate clients. Some even had the right, as very few banks do today, to issue their own currency.

For most banks, even those which, like Deutsche Bank, aspired to service the international needs of their clients, a strong network of correspondent bank relationships served as the principal means of extending their international reach. Before World War I, much of what banks now do through their own subsidiaries – clearing transactions, gathering information, and buying and selling securities – was done through correspondent bank accounts and by offsetting entries in each country's home office. Not only European banks in the United States operated this way, but also American ones in Europe.[24]

Local public banks had only a few competitive – or regulatory – advantages, as even they had to work with very strict limits in the United States and many of its states. Until 1914, U.S. banks with national (federal) charters, for example, could not accept bills of exchange. The creation and processing of letters of credit – then an important part of international banking and an activity that Deutsche Bank was supposed to take away from British banks – remained a largely London-based affair generally handled on the U.S. side through private banks in New York. Even most German trade transactions were processed through London. Under a letter of credit drawn on a London correspondent bank, a U.S. bank would collect from an importer, convert the funds to Sterling, and make the transfer to Britain, where a bank would make the payment to the exporter. Domestic banks still serviced travelers, a growing segment, whose main means of paying in a foreign country were with letters of credit drawn on their home bank, a correspondent of the U.S. banks.[25]

Moreover, even in the first decade of the twentieth century international investment banking was terribly one-sided. U.S. investment in Germany was only one-quarter of the total German investment in American capital markets. Although well-regulated in comparison to U.S. markets, and hungry for foreign investment, German capital markets shunned some kinds of trading, as evidenced by a ban on forward sales. Some Germans feared the influence of foreign capital in their markets, an ambivalence that was only reinforced by repeated American financial crises.[26]

To varying degrees, all of Deutsche Bank's business – even in the United States – reflected a sense of national mission. Deutsche Bank's earliest forays, including those in the United States and South America, were designed to give German traders a German financial contact in those regions. Like American banks, German banks served as a kind of national ambassador,[27] subject to the ups and downs in relations between the respective home countries.[28]

America was one of many countries where Deutsche Bank's early foreign investments were plagued by difficulties. In the later third of the nineteenth century, like many foreign banks, Deutsche Bank had already purchased an interest in a U.S. private bank.[29] The failure of that bank, and a reassessment of its needs in the United States led to a strategic combination of correspondent relationships, third-party representatives, and a changing constellation of relationships with strong American investment banks for underwriting business, based on personal contacts and market conditions.

This approach was not the only option and by no means a guarantee of success. Disconto-Gesellschaft, the bank with which Deutsche Bank was merged in 1929, worked almost exclusively through the Warburgs and Kuhn Loeb. Some banks interested in routine trade or transfer business opened up subsidiaries or branches. Crédit Lyonnais, for example, the largest bank in the world in 1913 as measured by assets, had opened a branch in New York in 1879, only to close it two years later. For much of the next fifty years, the French bank's business was handled by a representative, but despite its size the bank was less successful than some other European banks. As Crédit Lyonnais felt legally or perhaps just morally bound not to hold shares as a bank whose liabilities contained considerable deposits from individual investors, its underwriting activities were less effective than those of Deutsche Bank in investment banking.[30]

U.S. banking regulation was complicated but not horribly restrictive, making it rather unique among "developed" countries. But for virtually all of its history, the U.S. banking system significantly hindered Deutsche Bank's ability to operate and control an entity there as a universal bank that could offer the same wide range of services as it did in Germany and many other countries.

Many different kinds of banks existed in the United States, some with strong international connections. Banking activities were regulated both by individual states with different requirements, and the federal government. Foreign agencies were licensed in most states by state banking departments, including New York's, but until 1911 foreign agencies could not accept deposits and perform other banking activities.[31] By 1914, only twenty foreign banks operated agencies licensed for business in New York, by far America's most important financial center. Deutsche Bank was not among them.[32]

Before 1914, three kinds of banks tended to be owned by the public and were regulated by some layer of government. National banks received a charter from the federal government, had capital requirements and, for much of the pre-World War I period, were subject to deposit, acceptance, and loan limits.[33] State banks – and here New York law was the most important as it was where foreign banks wanted to do business – could take deposits and have multiple sites within a state, but were limited to business in one state. Several of these public banks relied on close ties with private banks and rich individuals to overcome these statutory limitations. As will be discussed later, around the turn of the century, a third type of bank, trust companies, developed rapidly to fill the void in universal banking. The great competitive strength of all these public institutions – the ability to acquire cheap retail deposits – took on much greater importance as the number of individuals with savings increased significantly and banking regulation loosened. If Deutsche Bank wanted to apply for a charter to operate as a bank, it too, would have to live with these constraints, as well as others.

U.S. banking law imposed two other impediments specifically to foreign-owned subsidiaries. None of the directors could be foreign nationals, which hampered foreign control. The federal government also limited the geographic operations of foreign-owned subsidiaries.[34]

Despite the rough setting, Deutsche Bank found a great array of potential bank partners to choose from, each with different strengths and weaknesses, perhaps because of the nature of the New York/U.S. banking system. Some kinds of banks and banking activities, even international ones, were relatively easy to set up in the United States. Unlike in Continental Europe, private banks needed no special licensing.[35] As discussed, some foreign banks elected to take equity positions in U.S. private banks, as Deutsche Bank did for a few years. Although some private banks served rural interests, the most important ones were money-center institutions that competed against state and national banks with many financial services. They filled a gap in the banking sector, especially between 1870 and 1914.[36] They dominated international banking in the United States and other markets. Their strength was the trust that wealthy clients from all over the world put in them and the ease of internal communication, which allowed them to become the focal point for international investing as well as many other aspects of cross-border banking for individuals and institutions. Some based in New York had a quasi-multinational status. As American institutions, they avoided some restrictions on foreign entities and concentrated on activities for which they had an immense competitive advantage over local banks. Many of the larger and most interesting ones, such as Drexel, Morgan (J. P. Morgan, after 1893), and Kuhn, Loeb and Co., had long-standing family or other ties to European institutions and families, such as August Belmont's to the Rothschilds.[37] They used their own capital and that of wealthy corporate or individual clients as brokers, investment bankers, venture capitalists, hedge funds, and security analysts, all rolled up into one institution.

In short, like many of its international rivals, Deutsche Bank did business with the United States but was insufficiently interested in local banking and internalization of clearing trade documents in New York to wrestle with national or state banking law, which would have at the very least confined the German bank's local operations or, worse still, risked loss of control of transactions generated by a local affiliate. Of the ten largest banks in the world measured by deposits in 1913 – of which Deutsche Bank was ranked sixth with £79 million – most were active on U.S. markets but only a few had salaried representatives, branches, or subsidiaries.[38] Although Deutsche Bank, which often suffered from a lack of information, considered sending a German representative to the United States, it discovered that during this period underwriting American securities and placing them in Europe could be achieved without its own U.S. subsidiary or agency. Only after the turn of the century, when Deutsche Bank became more interested in marketing American securities in Germany, and licensed agency constraints were loosened by New York State, did a greater presence become really feasible.[39] As this Section shows, moreover, there are many ways "to enter" a financial market.

2

First Steps

Trade Financing and Henry Villard

The trip was extraordinarily interesting. The land comes out of the desert and is transformed into the highest culture.... Amidst dirty and exhausted Indians in miserable conditions, ladies in the best silk fashions go for walks, and well educated men, who could fit in with the best salons in Europe, are next to revolver-toting cowboys.

Georg Siemens to his wife; Portland, September 12, 1883 (Helfferich, Vol. 3, pp. 310–311).

Georg Siemens circa 1890. Spokesman of Deutsche Bank's management board from the bank's inception to 1900, Siemens shared Villard's passion for America's potential, political outlook, and activism, as well as his innovative spirit. He is credited not only with spearheading Deutsche Bank's American investments, but also with the vision to create a universal bank with a wide range of services to companies, individuals, and governments, including taking deposits, making loans, and underwriting securities. Although a better administrator than Villard, Siemens' years at Deutsche Bank's helm were not without controversy over his decisions and conflict with the bank's founders over management's prerogatives and the scope of Deutsche Bank's activities.

The Carrot

Gaining a foothold in the U.S. market was for Georg Siemens – the Deutsche Bank leader probably most fascinated by the United States – an essential part of the bank's international strategy. Not only was America's size and growth potential in the 1870s an irresistible business pull for Deutsche Bank, New York was also seen as a jumping-off point for the lucrative South American market.[1] However, the reasons for this strategic commitment went beyond purely economic interest, according to Siemens' biographer (and son-in-law Karl Helfferich); it was a political, intellectual passion. The allure of America – with its population growth drawing European masses, its almost unimaginable stretches of land and "virgin fecundity" – was almost impossible to resist.[2] As his biographer put it, "The development of the United States in the nineteenth century was the wonder of human history."[3] According to Helfferich, Siemens' desire for closer transatlantic relations emanated not only out of his perception of America's economic potential, but also out of its potentially positive influence on "old Europe" with its "constantly threatening political contradictions and tensions."[4] For Siemens, it was not merely a question of obtaining the future profits to be gained from the connection between American and German capital, but rather "furthering, through active financial activity between the countries, to build and preserve closer economic relations between Germany and the United States."[5] Although America's businesses and economic structure were very different than Germany's, all the prosperous and difficult periods showed how interconnected the two countries were.

Yet not all Germans were as convinced as Siemens of America's positive influence. Even before World War I, some powerful German interests railed against the export of German capital and the listing of foreign securities on the German stock exchange – particularly in reference to the American *Gefahr* (danger) seen in the poor regulation of American markets and the protectionist disposition of its populace.[6] Selling the idea of cross-border investment, especially in the United States, required a strong intermediary such as Deutsche Bank.

From Trade Financing to Securities Trading

Despite natural and man-made obstacles, between 1870 and 1914, economic contact between the United States and Germany developed briskly. During that period, both German imports and exports in general increased by a factor of five. By 1913, Germany was the second and the United States the third largest exporter of manufactured goods, but with advances in transportation, agricultural commodities were traded over wider areas, too.[7] Despite high U.S. tariffs after the Civil War and the long distance between them, the two countries became major trading partners,[8] which reinforced German interest in American capital markets. Although trade between Germany and the United States grew by 5 percent per annum[9] between 1896 and 1913, the distance and restrictive trade policies held by both countries against goods for which the other had competitive strengths retarded commerce between the two nations. During this

Deutsche Bank.

Eingezahltes Capital: 15 Millionen Thaler.

FILIALEN:

Bremen, Hamburg, London, Shanghai, Yokohama

Commandite: **NEW-YORK.**

Deutsche Bank letterhead circa 1873. Bremen, Hamburg, London, Shanghai, and Yokohama listed as branches, with a limited partnership in New York.

period, the exchange of people and capital remained the principal economic contact, and even that was terribly one-sided.

Soon after Deutsche Bank's founding, bank officials decided to establish an American presence with an ownership interest in a private bank. The German bank organized, guided, and financed the creation of a new American private bank, Knoblauch & Lichtenstein (K&L).[10] Several of Deutsche Bank's most important investors and managers spearheaded K&L's creation and nurtured its development.

Similar to many German companies and many private banks, Deutsche Bank's first connections to the United States were reinforced by intimate personal ties. Paul Lichtenstein, for example, one of the two managing partners of the new firm in New York, was the nephew of Herman Marcuse, Deutsche Bank's third largest investor in 1870, and the son-in-law of Friedrich Kapp, a close friend of many of Deutsche Bank's investors and of leading managers, as well as a member of the Deutsche Bank's administrative board (*Verwaltungsrat*, an earlier form of supervisory board) from 1871–84. Kapp probably contributed much to Deutsche Bank's knowledge of the American market and the formulation of the bank's strategy. As a left-leaning intellectual, Kapp had fled there after the failed revolutions in 1848. He worked in the United States as a lawyer, journalist, and author until his return to Germany in 1870.[11] As was common among Deutsche Bank's early leaders, he was active in liberal politics and particularly interested in Deutsche Bank's involvement in the United States.

The origin of the partnership idea is unknown, but Lichtenstein was in the United States in summer 1872, with final arrangements awaiting his return to Germany in July.[12] In October 1872, shortly after his marriage to Kapp's daughter, Lichtenstein left for the United States again and K&L opened for operations. Although less is known about his partner, Charles Knoblauch, he seems to have been already established in New York as a currency broker.[13] Deutsche Bank provided the lion's share of the capital ($500,000 of the total $600,000). The American bank's purpose was to further the interest of its main investor in all forms of banking, and especially to further trade transactions with North America, Europe, and East Asia – however its ownership interest and control was left somewhat unclear.[14] Although Deutsche Bank wanted to have its ownership interest fully acknowledged and to take an active role in management, American law at the time stipulated that only owners whose liability was unlimited could exercise control.[15] Marcuse played a role in these discussions, but it is not clear from the files what exact compromise was worked out to take account of Deutsche Bank's desire to manage actively and American restrictions on "silent partners."

The investment was part of a long and frustrating process of trial and error that tested the patience of German investors and managers searching for a way to profit from contact with the American market. Located at 37 Broad Street and later at 29 William Street, K&L was organized as a limited partnership in New York. It seemed to be a relatively safe way to enter the market.[16] Despite the personal ties, Deutsche Bank managers tried to exercise control from Berlin with questionable success. They stipulated to K&L that total transactions were to be limited to $500,000 and facilities were only to be arranged with reputable banks, within bounds for each bank agreed with Berlin managers, and preferably secured by goods. The term of advances were not to exceed six months. Some other forms of guarantees were permitted: Fully paid-up securities, for example, were acceptable but not land, houses, ships, or easily spoiled goods. The partnership agreement also stipulated that Berlin was to be informed regularly about all business that was done in New York. This included providing a list of transactions and financial statements.[17] With this seemingly conservative approach, K&L survived the crisis of 1873, which had hit German and American markets particularly hard. Nevertheless, despite its limited original scope, by 1877, the New York bank had expanded into non-trade credits.[18] It was this activity that got the bank into trouble.

Initially, the U.S. firm was part of a larger global vision of how Deutsche Bank would become involved in German trade financing.[19] Siemens had in mind creating a bank in the United States that could also contribute to the exchange of German-manufactured items against imported goods from North and South America. Although branches seemed to be the most reasonable course in other parts of the world, Siemens believed that Deutsche Bank should ultimately create a German subsidiary (originally Germanische Transatlantische Bank) with branches all over North and South America to handle trade transactions in cooperation with other German banks. The realization of the plan, however, was delayed and transformed. In its final form and with its new name, the Deutsche Ueberseeische Bank serviced mainly South America. Although Deutsche Bank continued in many ways to cultivate business in Latin America and Spain from New York, U.S. restrictions on foreign banks taking deposits and on issuing and discounting bank acceptances made using a United States-based subsidiary as the focal point of operations in the Western Hemisphere impractical.[20]

Through its contact with K&L, however, Deutsche Bank started trading in converted U.S. Civil War debt and investing in railroad securities.[21] These activities and the investment in K&L did not work out well. In the late 1870s, the New York bank started to roll up large losses on some bank acceptances and loans in the petroleum sector.[22] By 1882, K&L's speculative investment losses led to Deutsche Bank writing down its own shareholding, and, finally, to the New York bank's liquidation.

As the American firm's problems mounted, the personal ties probably lost some of their luster for the German managers. By 1885, Lichtenstein had a new partner (Baltzer). Siemens had to confirm to Marcuse that the new New York partnership was once again asking for loans, which the German bank was not disposed to extend, despite the likely negative impact on the American bank's reputation. Siemens could see no reason why anyone in Germany, including Marcuse, a major shareholder in Deutsche Bank, should take further losses due to the mistakes of the American partners.[23] The losses suffered by the partnership in that year, connected with a small American rail line, even touched other German banks. Although Marcuse felt that Deutsche Bank and other related parties could avoid serious losses, he conceded that the German bank should proceed with the liquidation of the American private bank.[24]

Like some other German banks such as Darmstädter Bank, Deutsche Bank began to rely more heavily on closer ties with stronger U.S. banks without making an equity investment.[25] Perhaps the volume of U.S. trade business was not sufficient to justify the investment. Perhaps, too, Deutsche Bank chose not to have its own affiliate in New York because London continued to dominate trade business and it already had a branch there. Undaunted by K&L's failures, Deutsche Bank's management plunged into investing in the securities of American commercial companies. Deutsche Bank shifted its main interest in the United States from trade financing, for which it would use correspondent banks, to underwriting securities.

With the growing importance of the U.S. economy and the capital needs of U.S. firms, long-term investment in American firms became more interesting business than short-term transactions like trade financing, but it required communication and knowledge to manage the considerable risk – capacities that were not easily acquired. Exchanges of views were slow and cumbersome by twenty-first-century standards. Not until 1882 did the United States and Germany have a cable link, and that was through an English company.[26]

Railroad Securities

For German investors, like the English before them, American railroads seemed, understandably, to be an ideal object for cross-border financing. Helfferich recognized, long before business historians did, that the railroad played a special role in America's development. Not only did this sector have the same spin-off effects that it had everywhere else – iron production, the telegraph, construction of terminals and railroad cars, for example – in the United States it opened whole new markets hitherto isolated from trade. In 1840, the United States already had over three times the rail network of Great Britain and seven times the area that would become the German Reich. The growth in tracks was staggering. By 1890, there were nearly 163,000 miles of track, more than all of Europe's and nearly seven times that of Germany.[27] American creativity contributed to new service industries designed to exploit the faster and more reliable transportation method. American firms led the way in developing new management and accounting techniques to cope with the large companies that were growing rapidly.[28]

The market for railroad securities was large and international. Even conservative, distant investors understood what railroads did and what security they

Henry Villard circa 1890.

could offer. They flocked especially to the secured bonds and preferred stock of these firms.[29] By the early 1890s, the controlling interest in many U.S. railroads was held outside of the United States. In total, 33 percent of the nominal value of all U.S. railroad securities was owned by non-Americans.[30]

But like many sectors in the United States in the last quarter of the nineteenth century, transportation was still highly splintered. (In 1880, there were 43 companies each with over 500 miles of track.)[31] Railroad firms suffered from duplication of services, a lack of interconnection and compatibility between lines, over-construction, price competition, heavy fixed costs, and client pressures – all of which contributed to boom and bust cycles and to a desperate need for consolidation that provided a great deal of opportunity for clever bankers.

Moreover, by the 1880s, Germany was nationalizing its own rail system, putting a great deal of cash into the hands of companies and individuals who had once held railroad securities. By 1899, German investment alone in this U.S. sector amounted to $103 million. Fifteen years later, it had tripled.[32] As early as 1881, Deutsche Bank had purchased bonds in three American railroads from "friendly banks" in London and was trading convertible U.S. Civil War debt in London.[33] With the demise of K&L, moreover, Deutsche Bank took over its first Northern Pacific Securities, a 6 percent First Mortgage Bond issued while the line was still under the control of its founder, the notorious Jay Cooke. The acquisition of this investment coincided with the raising of a new question for Siemens and his colleagues: Who should replace K&L as Deutsche Bank's representative in the United States?[34] At this time, serendipity – or a Cheshire Cat – smiled on Deutsche Bank in the person of a German-American immigrant, one of the most extraordinary financial characters, some might say rogues, of the nineteenth century.

Henry Villard

For approximately a decade, Deutsche Bank's affairs in the United States were handled by one of the most remarkable figures of American finance, Henry Villard. Born Heinrich Hilgard, a German refugee, his anti-Prussian, antimilitaristic, and strong liberal sympathies – together with some adolescent career aspirations – brought him into conflict with his conservative, upper-middle-class family, and led to his flight to the United States at age eighteen.[35] His German roots and tireless self-promotion would serve him well throughout most of his life. A friend of many diverse and important figures, such as Carl Schurz, the German-born American leader, his life illustrates the opportunities and risks for entrepreneurial, energetic, international visionaries in growth economies with a shortage of business talent. He is not only a key figure in this narrative, but is also the source of material about the financial and railroad doings of the whole period.

Villard came to his relationship with Deutsche Bank through a convoluted route. After entering the United States in 1853, he first became a successful journalist. Deeply devoted to Lincoln's vision for America, Villard made some good political connections, by all accounts and in all respects married well, and entered the world of finance. Adaptable and with a taste for the good life, he used his close connections in the 1860s with liberal reform groups in the United States as a springboard to a lucrative career. Villard came onto the American financial scene right after the Civil War, when America's relations with the rest of the world were at a low ebb. America needed to build up its hinterland, which required a lot of new labor and capital, a fact that contributed a great deal to German influence on American affairs. For nearly twenty years, in a variety of roles – counselor, bondholder representative, entrepreneur, manager, and financier, roles taxing even for his considerable versatility and energy – Villard served as one of the main conduits of German-American business exchanges.[36]

His first experience in this newfound career came in the late 1860s, when he traveled to Germany to broker U.S. securities. In 1873, when the financial crisis hit the United States – and Germany – a group of Frankfurt bondholders led by Jacob S. H. Stern, a leading German private bank, sought out Villard, who was convalescing in Heidelberg, to represent them in the default proceedings of the Wisconsin Central railroad, a line that they had bought a year earlier. Privately, he also agreed with Stern to look for possibly undervalued investments among the many shaken properties. Enchanted by the Northwest and confident of future tourism and immigration, which were sure to bring high profits, Villard convinced Stern to lead a group to buy out the Oregon and California line.[37] From this chance opportunity with the bankers sprung a whole new professional life. As early as the mid-1870s, he confided to his beloved wife, Fanny, his thrill at personally earning vast sums, while building up the Northwest.[38]

Fascinated by railroads, Villard put together America's first hostile takeover and one of the largest mergers of the Gilded Age. In Oregon, he uncovered a great deal of fraud and mismanagement, but his confidence in the potential viability of the region and the company never wavered. The German group agreed to his reorganization plans and forced the agreement of the other investors. Villard was able to create a new company, the Oregon Railway & Navigation Co., which effectively controlled all of the transportation infrastructure between Oregon and San Francisco. As president of the new company, his reputation in the industry and among German investors grew, but his dream of controlling the transportation of the whole Northwest brought him into conflict with other railroads – notably the Union Pacific, the Northern Pacific, and the Great Northern – all of which would play a significant role in Deutsche Bank's activities in the United States.[39]

Villard's vision of how to make the railroads of the region profitable did not change substantially over the next decades. Like many of his competitors, such as Jay Gould, he dreamt of controlling the transportation for the whole region, a monopoly of service that would go well beyond the pooling arrangements or other loose consolidations of separate companies that were often attempted to stave off ruinous competition.[40] It was probably the only sensible way of dealing with structural problems in the sector. Regulatory constraints and his own management deficiencies, however, hindered realization of his dream.

The first step in his strategic plan entailed getting out from under the control of his largely foreign investors. Using the railroad's own assets as collateral, Villard engineered one of history's first management (leveraged) buyouts. He cajoled the Frankfurt group into selling its holdings to him at a loss. By 1881, the demoralized Frankfurt committee turned over to Villard what they had sent him to America to protect. He was now owner and manager of a large, highly leveraged transportation business, yet he was to a large extent free, at least temporarily, of the sorts of controls that always seemed to irk him.[41]

Completing his dream of a line that stretched across the west was costly – requiring, for example, a conversion to standardized rails, aquisition of more debt, and gaining control of other rail lines. To this latter end, Villard began negotiations with the Northern Pacific, which he feared would soon have its own line to the Pacific, undermining the monopoly position he so badly wanted.[42]

The Northern Pacific Line

Founded in 1864, the Northern Pacific possessed construction and use rights for rail and telegraph lines from Lake Superior (Minnesota) to Puget Sound (Oregon), as well as other rights in the region and ample land-grant rights for property around the lines (forty-seven million acres in all). In the year that Deutsche Bank was founded, the Northern Pacific began construction of America's second cross-continental line, but progress was impaired by the financial crisis of 1873. Because of the reorganization that followed its first bankruptcy, the Northern Pacific had the wherewithal to work on the completion of the cross-continental line and even to expand its activities into areas that brought the company into direct competition with the Villard-run company.

Short of funds, Villard first came to an agreement with Northern Pacific management for use of his Oregon company's lines. But the Northern Pacific's

Celebration of the Northern Pacific's completion of its cross-continental rail connection September 8, 1883. Villard is in the middle on the engine.

ability to secure long-term financing (a $40 million mortgage bond) through Drexel Morgan and Belmont & Co. (Rothschild's representative in New York) rekindled the company's ambition to finish its own line all the way to the west coast, which would link up to its lines to the east, creating intolerable competition for the Oregon Railway & Navigation Co.

Showing his daring, in 1883 Villard determined that the only way of saving his line would be to acquire the majority of the Northern Pacific shares, put those shares into a holding company with the shares of the Oregon company, and eventually to merge the rail lines.[43] With the Northern Pacific not generating enough cash to add to its debt, his earlier financial ploy of borrowing against the company's assets would not work. Despite his double-dealing with German investors, his reputation on Wall Street was sufficiently good that he was able to convince, within twenty-four hours of his private announcement, fifty-three investors to join a blind pool – that is, they did not know what the precise object or terms of the investment were – to put up a total of $8 million against a vague promise to share in the profits of the consolidated lines under Villard's control. Villard was reported to have invested $900,000 of his own money. Even Jacob S. H. Stern – who had made good money on Villard's earlier handling of defaulted debt in Kansas and who was not part of the Frankfurt group that Villard had just bamboozled – participated.[44]

In short order, Villard controlled the stock of the two companies and put the shares into the newly formed holding company, Oregon & Transcontinental Co., creating a somewhat unified firm with 2,700 miles of track. There was little that could stand in the way of connecting the companies' western and mid-western lines. Laying track at a rate of three miles a day required 25,000 men (15,000 of those from China) and monthly expenditures of $4 million – a huge expenditure overrun – but it allowed Villard to meet his opening deadline of September 1883. As the work proceeded, it passed close to where another overreacher had been massacred together with much of the 7th cavalry seven years earlier.[45]

As a darling of the stock exchange in the early 1880s, his creation now could do business from the Mississippi to the Pacific, operating the second cross-continental line – a railroad line the distance of Paris to Moscow. Its construction required a great deal of new financing. Relying on his charm and charisma, Villard saw to it that the consolidated companies took on another $10 million in watered-down stock (exaggerated asset values used to inflate par values) and borrowed another $40 million. In the space of a year, Villard had created a giant new line, completed a cross-continental rail connection, made himself a short-lived fortune, and witnessed it all – or nearly all – disappear, as the company's stock price collapsed and the firm found itself in financial distress by late 1883.[46]

As with almost all his undertakings, Villard's faith in his dreams had blinded him to the value of cost-benefit analysis. Even at this early stage in his career, Villard's lack of management discipline was apparent to some. His unwillingness to get involved in details, and contempt for accounting and operational policies, made him overly dependent on subordinates, and even more vulnerable to his own excessive enthusiasm.[47] His contagious enthusiasm and his life-long distaste of budgetary constraints were evident in the celebration of the completion of the cross-continental line in September 1883. Georg Siemens and distinguished businessmen and scientists, along with U.S. federal officials, representatives from seven other governments, an ex-President of the United States, and various other notables, were invited to the ceremony.[48] There were three hundred guests, including twenty-five Germans, and all paid for by the company. It was a veritable parade from *Who's Who* in America and Europe. Wine flowed freely.[49] But as his biographer put it, the trip to Montana turned out to be a "prelude to failure."[50]

For Siemens the invitation was the fulfillment of a burning desire to personally get to know the United States and its leading business figures. He arrived in New York in August 1883. Before heading to the West, he spent two weeks as an honored guest getting to know the leading banking people in New York – Morgan, Belmont, Lanier, Drexel – as well as leading industrialists especially in the railroad and electrical sectors. In two special trains, the Northern Pacific executives and guests wound their way to the site, in what Helfferich called a "veritable triumphal march." Helfferich also reported that Siemens was overwhelmed by the vistas, the wealth, and, most importantly, the possibilities for future development he saw. In all the major cities, there were demonstrations honoring Villard and his guests. Six days after their departure from

New York, the group reached the mountain site of the linkage and the ceremony. Siemens used the opportunity of his stay in the United States to visit the west coast as far south as Los Angeles. The trip, which lasted until October, bolstered Siemens' passion for the United States and his conviction that Deutsche Bank must become a significant player in this vibrant market.[51] His letters home to his wife during his stay are full of the details of whom he had met and what he had seen, capturing his first impressions and enthusiasm for the United States. For him, it was a land of unbelievable growth, promise, and contradiction.

But the inevitable hangover hit the participants shortly after the party. Before the end of September, *The New York Times* reported that the firm's financial condition was shaky.[52] Northern Pacific bond prices tumbled. Despite the evident lack of confidence, the company issued another $18 million in debt, half of which was sold in Germany by Stern and Deutsche Bank. The expansion of the Northern Pacific's main line required at least another $14 million of new financing. Further needs of the Oregon & Transcontinental Co. exceeded the $40 million prior lien financing, forcing the company to draw on short-term credit lines. Although some of the German press seemed very cautious about new investment in the United States, Deutsche Bank bought up most of a Second Mortgage Bond ($20 million) at a price of 82½ (prices expressed as percentages of face value of debt and nominal or par value of stock), despite protests from other debt holders. In October, the German press reported that the market for Northern Pacific preferred shares was weak. By October 25, 1883, the price of common and preferred stock had fallen from 51 and 88 in 1881, to 27 and 62, respectively.[53]

With the stock price falling, Villard got board permission to buy shares as a defense against a hostile takeover, which further increased the company's debt to equity ratio. The hope that equity markets could bail out the beleaguered company was dashed by the general stock market crisis during the fall of 1883. The price of Villard's holding company, Oregon & Transcontinental, fell from 83 percent of its nominal value to 34 percent by October. Despite the crisis, Siemens did not lose confidence: Deutsche Bank took up a large number of the second lien bonds issued by the railroad at the end of 1883 for distribution in Germany, which helped bail out the Northern Pacific, at least for the time being. However, the spending by the companies seemed out of control, and Villard's personal situation critical. The drop in the companies' stock prices led investors to lose confidence in him, and his own personal losses from railroad and other investments weighed heavily on him. In December 1883, his situation became so desperate that he finally confessed his predicament to a close circle of friends. Audits led to his personal bankruptcy, and pointed to further dangers for the Oregon & Transcontinental Co.[54]

Wrapped in self-pity and blaming bad luck, Villard refused to see his own lack of management skills as a contributing cause for the poor 1883 operating results. Though some agreed with his view, he resigned as president and was succeeded by a veteran railroad man, Robert Harris, in whom Wall Street had more trust. In any case, bankers would take more active management in the

Villard's short-lived home on Madison Avenue circa late 1880s. Villard only spent a few weeks in this vast mansion he had constructed before the Northern Pacific's financial crisis hit in 1883.

running of the line.[55] Led by Morgan, who had joined the Northern Pacific board in September, a bank syndicate was formed to handle Villard's personal as well as the companies' financial problems on the condition that he resign his posts with the railroads.[56] Morgan's reorganization saved the Northern Pacific from its second bankruptcy in ten years.[57] The rescue worked well without Villard in the short run, unfortunately only postponing a future day of reckoning, as will be discussed. By 1885, Northern Pacific mortgage debt instruments were selling at a premium (above their face value).[58]

Nevertheless, the financial help and Villard's resignation provided little in the way of long-term respite for the companies. Under the new president, construction work proceeded, but serious tensions remained between management and its financial backers, among whom Deutsche Bank was now included. Deutsche Bank stepped up its lending and other sorts of business with the company. In 1886, along with Belmont, Deutsche Bank managed issuance of another *tranche* of First Mortgage Bonds on European markets.

Villard as Conduit of German Capital

In 1884, Villard returned, ostensibly, to live in Germany. Ironically, once again, his German roots saved his financial fortunes.[59] Two men had not lost faith in him: his friends Thomas Alva Edison, and Georg Siemens. Edison commissioned him to find German investors for his new company aiming to launch electrical power in the United States, as well as to find a partner in Germany (see next Chapter). While in Germany, Villard met with Siemens, who contracted him to represent Deutsche Bank's interests in the United States.

Villard's more intense relationship with Deutsche Bank coincided roughly with the liquidation of K&L's successor firm and with Siemens' successful attempts to win more independence for Deutsche Bank managers from their investors. Germany as a whole changed its German company law, creating a clearer separation between the responsibilities of managing and supervisory boards. While in Berlin during 1884, Villard reestablished contact with a fellow German-American whom he had known in the United States, Friedrich Kapp.[60] Kapp, a member of Deutsche Bank's administrative board, and a good friend of Siemens', had returned fourteen years earlier to Germany from the United States, where he had gotten to know Villard. After Villard's embarrassing financial predicaments, Kapp seems to have contributed greatly to rekindling Siemens' willingness to do business with Villard. The three shared similar politics and a passion for America's potential. Perhaps, too, Kapp's death shortly after Villard's arrival in Berlin somehow cemented the connection between his two surviving friends. Beyond finance, one could imagine a mixture of many emotions drawing the two men together: Siemens' memories of his American adventure; his envy of Villard – a compatriot living a life that he might have wanted for himself; or Villard's innate charm. We will probably never know. In any case, Siemens put his faith in Villard. In 1886, Villard left for New York, a nearly rehabilitated man.[61] At this time, the Siemens-Villard relationship seems to have been very close.[62]

Despite the first collapse of Villard's empire, Deutsche Bank was still ready to jump into the American waters with both feet. For good or ill, Villard presented himself as the bank's "swimming instructor." Understandably, Deutsche Bank liked getting information about its investments in the United States and general economic-political circumstances from sources that it knew and could understand.[63] In 1885, the bank had already grown impatient with Northern Pacific's management for its reluctance to provide information about the American market in general and the railroad line in particular.[64] Inspired by his own trip to the United States and undaunted by Villard's sudden financial difficulties, Siemens resolved to convince his colleagues to take on more significant investments in the United States. Some said of Siemens that he shared Villard's unchecked passion for big ideas and impatience with detail.[65]

Deutsche Bank's activities with U.S. securities had hitherto consisted mainly of American debt instruments purchased and held for a short time for sale on the German market. It had taken a long time, but the bank was now ready to make a greater commitment. If Villard were willing to get involved again in the Northern Pacific, this railroad enterprise might be an ideal object with which to start making significant equity investments in the United States. With a strong equity position, Siemens argued, the bank would be in a better position to protect the bondholders from "unfortunate occurrences."[66]

In September 1886, Deutsche Bank and Villard signed a formal contract for Villard's services. Considering his activities, his employment conditions seem very liberal. He represented both Deutsche Bank and Jacob S. H. Stern. The two German banks gave Villard a choice between 25 percent of any investment he brought them or 10 percent of the profits they made. Under special circumstances, he could even accept remuneration from the companies in which the banks were investing. Most, if not all, of his expenses were paid by the banks, and he received fees for serving on the boards of companies in which Deutsche Bank held an interest.[67] Villard kept large accounts in his and his wife Fanny's names with Deutsche Bank in Berlin.[68] Little remains to tell us about how large his staff was – only the work of one of his assistants, Arnold Marcus, found its way into the Deutsche Bank files.[69] Villard delegated some responsibility and nearly all writing chores to Marcus, who served as secretary in many Villard companies and corresponded, almost always in German, with Deutsche Bank and Stern.[70]

Villard's new activities quickly provided the bank with ample American opportunities. Villard seemed ideally suited to convince German investors to invest funds in the United States. As Deutsche Bank's investment advisor, he reportedly sold $64.3 million in U.S. securities, mostly issued by American railroad companies, to German investors. Some were reorganizations, others were attempts to acquire control. During the late 1880s, Deutsche Bank participated in the creation of the Rocky-Fork Railroad, the reorganization of the Southern Pacific, the Denver and Rio Grande Railroad Co., and the reorganization of the Chesapeake and Ohio Railroad, which would later involve Deutsche Bank in extensive negotiations with the American government for a $28 million bailout of the line.[71]

Within a few weeks of receiving his appointment, Villard responded with a tempting offer. The Oregon & Transcontinental was once again in difficulty. Management offered Villard both the chairmanship of the Oregon and Northern Pacific boards and the deciding vote on the Northern board in exchange for an equity investment of $5 million. Thirty-six hours after Villard sent the telegram to Berlin, he had the cash from Germany, causing a sensation on Wall Street, where such speed in transatlantic decision-making was hitherto unknown.[72]

Like the region that it served, the railroad was enjoying tremendous but highly variable growth, purchased at a steep price. To keep up with the 100,000 new arrivals to Washington and Oregon in that year, by 1887 the Northern Pacific network had already expanded enormously. It consisted of 2,800 miles of lines, of which 2,300 were owned and the others leased. Capital investment was also growing. This included purchasing some of the lines that had been leased, and leasing of new branch lines. Its expansion also brought the Northern Pacific into further conflicts with competitors, notably the Union Pacific. Its borrowing needs, understandably, also increased substantially, leading to a Third Mortgage Bond ($12 million) in 1887, of which Deutsche Bank, Jacob S. H. Stern, and Belmont took a large portion to list on the Berlin and Frankfurt exchanges in 1888. The financial difficulties of the railroad and the new bond elicited a great deal of criticism, even at Deutsche Bank, but Siemens' confidence prevailed. Nevertheless, the bank felt compelled to warn investors of the new issue's reduced security. The first two mortgage bonds had been launched at premiums; the third, in contrast, reached the market with an over 10 percent discount, yielding a 7 percent rate of return. Two smaller issues were brought to market but, according to Helfferich, the bank told its customers that only those who were willing to accept the higher risk should expect this higher return.[73]

The bonds of the late 1880s brought only short-term relief for the railroad. Further investments in new lines, rolling stock, and other improvements quickly used up the $12 million. Siemens argued that the expansion period should finally come to an end. By this time, it seemed clear that the Northern Pacific needed to restructure its debt. A $160 million bond, envisioned to consolidate all the mortgage bonds and reduce the company's financial charges, could not be brought to market. A general economic downturn quelled the market's appetite for debt, but sadly, not the Northern Pacific's ambitious expansion plans in the early 1890s.[74]

The North American Company

It is a little hard to understand why Deutsche Bank gave Villard such a wide berth. Although there were often rumors in the market that the bank had abandoned Villard,[75] the bank's new concerns with Villard should have begun in the late 1880s, when even he recognized many of the problems. But as was often the case, Villard had his eye on a grandiose solution to them: He became convinced that the railroads in the west had to be brought under the control of one group in order to maintain their profitability. Considering the developments in the story of the Northern Pacific and many other railroads, this may not have been such a crazy idea – in theory. However, as he and others found out, the scheme had many obstacles in practice.

Villard wanted to form a holding company that would include the shares of the Northern Pacific, Wisconsin Central, St. Paul, Minneapolis & Manitoba, as well as other lines, at a total cost of $24 million. Considering its own resources, this was an intimidating sum even for Deutsche Bank, which had roughly $20 million in capital in 1890, $50 million in total deposits, and $14 million in total loans outstanding.[76]

While in Berlin in 1889, Villard probably pleaded his case. In an undated, unsigned, extensive memo entitled "Projekt," it was argued that tensions persisting between the companies' managements could only be resolved through common ownership. For his project, Villard required $12 million for the Oregon Railway & Navigation, $10 million for the St. Paul, Minneapolis & Manitoba shares, and $2 million for the St. Paul & Northern Pacific shares, as well as an unnamed sum for the Chicago Terminal Project already known to the directors of Deutsche Bank. All of this investment would be built around the cornerstone of his holding in the Oregon & Transcontinental Company. Clearly, the acquisitions also entailed taking on responsibility for the outstanding debt of those companies. He optimistically stressed that "never has a better American business opportunity come to Europe."[77]

Judging from the plan, this was the birth of the North American Company, which never got Deutsche Bank's full backing nor achieved its intended purposes, and which was expanded to include other securities including those connected with Edison General Electric (see next Chapter). But Deutsche Bank, as well as many other prestigious institutions and individuals, did invest in Villard's plan. Although little is known of the North American Company and how much and in what form investors contributed, a rough outline of its purpose and activities can be gleaned from existing documents.

Much of Deutsche Bank's hesitation about the project was due to the amount of capital, which would exceed internally set limits on American investments, not to the idea itself. Villard had asked for an amount equal to Deutsche Bank's entire paid-in capital. With this and other investments, Deutsche Bank representatives had to remind Villard that they had limits to their American exposure. Many of the deals arranged by Villard called for long holding periods for the securities Deutsche Bank and other German firms had bought.[78] In spring 1890, Deutsche Bank was already holding close to its internal limit on U.S. securities: $2.4 million of Northern Pacific securities; $0.8 million of Edison Electric; $0.6 million in Oregon & Transcontinental shares; and another $0.5 million from other railroads, which came to approximately $4.3 million (18 million Mark). Villard's method of building syndicates effectively blocked Deutsche Bank from selling these investments and replacing them with new ones. Villard was, therefore, not free to commit the bank to anything new. His proposal arrived at a moment when the bank was so burdened with U.S. investments that it could no longer react positively to initiatives, no matter how much its officers wanted to participate. These orders would hold until Deutsche Bank's commitments in the United States had been reduced. Siemens added in a postscript to his letter to Marcus that the bank would have had no problem getting out of all of its Northern Pacific holdings, for example, if it were not prevented by commitments Villard himself had made.[79]

Villard was more than disappointed by Deutsche Bank's reluctance to invest more. He was bitter. He felt that Deutsche Bank questioned his ability to represent them in the future and that he had wasted two years of his time and effort in trying to put together a deal that was in Deutsche Bank's interest. He could not allow its rejection of his plans to make those efforts useless.[80] Even though he achieved much of what he wanted through lease agreements, Villard pushed ahead with other aspects of his plan in the face of deteriorating business and financial conditions. The worst days lay ahead.

Villard would eventually get limited backing from Deutsche Bank, although not nearly the initial amount he proposed to the German bank. The rest came from others who helped form the North American Company (NAC). The problem, obviously, was not just Deutsche Bank's internal policy about American exposure. There were also limits to how much American paper the bank could place while maintaining a reasonably liquid and stable price on German and other European exchanges.[81]

Marcus defended Villard by saying that his boss always wanted to do the "right thing," which led him to jump over obstacles that stood in his way. Marcus felt confident that Siemens and Villard would resolve their differences, but intimated that Villard was looking to bring money from London to the United States to replace the German sources that had dried up, a thinly disguised threat that probably did not go down well in Berlin.[82] In the summer, Villard was using Morgan's banking house in London as his European address, emphasizing, perhaps, that there were other "paths" to European investors interested in the American market.[83] Marcus cautioned that Villard's ideas had become quite gigantic of late, but hoped that with time things would improve. A stay away from New York would do him and his nerves, which appeared to be overwrought, much good.[84]

Finally founded in June 1890, the North American Company's only assets were the securities of other companies, mostly equity and debt of the Northern Pacific, but also of several adjacent lines and Edison General Electric. The purpose of this holding company seems to have been to unite some ownership interests as well as to provide a market for the securities of the related companies, especially those in the rail and electrification sectors. Organized under the laws of New Jersey, $40 million of the company's $50 million in new capital came from a simple swap of old Oregon & Transcontinental equity for shares in NAC. With Villard as its president, the new holding company had many powerful backers, including a syndicate in which Deutsche Bank, Morgan, Kuhn Loeb, and Speyer were represented.[85] Some of its financing seems to have come from direct loans from important individuals and institutions, such as both John D. and William Rockefeller, Deutsche Bank, Speyer & Co., and Drexel, Morgan & Co., backed up by securities of other companies. Deutsche Bank and Stern also had options on some of the securities held by North American. Even in September 1890, when markets were still fairly strong, over half of North American Company's book value was financed in the form of short-term loans. The company in effect collected securities of competing companies. By bringing in new equity capital and borrowing against its assets, it could make a market for the securities in its portfolio and diversify risk. Relatively early on, despite new loans supplied by Deutsche Bank and others, the North America Company's stock began a long slide. In part this was a result of Villard's apparent intent to keep its affairs as murky as possible, even from some of his chief investors.[86]

The inherent weakness of NAC was made clear in fall 1890 soon after its creation, but it is hard to know the degree to which the parties understood the risks. NAC's financial structure and general business purpose required regular new injections of capital. Soon after its founding, they ground to a halt. The U.S. Congress, under pressure from populist agricultural groups, passed the Sherman Silver Purchase Act, which required the U.S. Treasury to buy up 4.5 million ounces of silver per month. The act called into question the United States commitment to the Gold Standard and panicked foreign investors, who held an amount of U.S. securities roughly equal to ten times the federal government annual budget. The near collapse of Baring Brothers in November further spooked capital markets.[87]

The crisis tested Villard's magic. In mid-November 1890, NAC shares fell precipitously. Deutsche Bank sold some of its NAC holding to buy Northern Pacific shares.[88] Nearly all NAC's short-term facilities were collateralized by its securities holdings and its own stock. Villard counted on continued European interest in the securities held by NAC to insure its financial health, and he himself was reluctant to take responsibility for them.[89] NAC could not meet $2 million in obligations. During this period, Villard was obliged to travel twice to Frankfurt to negotiate (beg) for more financing. The original $2 million quickly ran out. Another $3 million was pried loose. His success probably came at a great cost. Even Villard had to recognize that he had lost a good deal of credibility with the Germans and that many of the underlying financial issues had not been resolved.[90] Even though some of the U.S. securities were perceived in Germany as cheap, Deutsche Bank reduced its lending to NAC, which obviously hurt the already shaky company. In part, Deutsche Bank was pulling back its commitment because it seemed to have lost confidence in Villard's ability to manage numerous financial issues in the United States.[91]

A year later, Villard still blamed American monetary policy for the troubles that beset "his" companies. The low prices of NAC holdings ruled out their sale as a viable means of raising cash to pay its debts. He recommended staying the course with a more limited range of investments. Although the Northern Pacific was still highly dependent on good harvests, cost cutting, and effective integration of new branch lines, other forms of traffic left the line in solid financial shape.[92] Although the situation had calmed, in December 1891 the value of NAC's securities was still only under $8 million. Its short-term debt was one-third of its total obligations.[93]

By 1892, with capital markets still edgy about America's commitment to the Gold Standard but near their highs, NAC's share price had reached $7.50. Many shareholders still complained about the absence of adequate financial statements and a board comprised of a cabal of insiders. Some accused them of engaging in speculative trading. Villard defended his actions and offered more detailed financial information. Despite his protestations of ill health caused by his efforts on behalf of the North American Company and promises of better results in the future, the minority shareholders seemed unimpressed.[94] Not only did Villard have to wrestle with the management of several diverse businesses at this time, he had to deal with illness and personal tragedy.[95]

During the early 1890s, with Siemens' support, Villard was still given a relatively free hand as Deutsche Bank's representative, especially to sort out the internal difficulties of the Northern Pacific. Deutsche Bank seemed increasingly aware of some of the risks but also seemed to see little alternative to sticking with its man at the scene. Its patience would be costly. In 1890, Villard seemed unwilling to bring himself to give up further expansion projects for the line, for which he sought and received intermittent Deutsche Bank support. Despite the shaky markets, Northern Pacific management went ahead with some of its projects, many of which involved investments in new lines and terminals to keep up with its main competitive threat, the Union Pacific's own overexpansion. Instead of just consolidating lines as had been agreed, the Northern Pacific used the added funding to increase its capacity. Later, Villard claimed that he could not control Northern Pacific executives as he was one voice among thirteen on the board. At the very least, revenues and operating profits through 1892 were still growing.[96]

Although they had several serious spats, by summer 1891 Villard and Siemens seemed to have temporarily smoothed over some of their differences. It is hard to assess the overall state of the relationship, which had many ups and downs, and moved along many axes. Their correspondence dealt with the importance of the silver question to America's overall economic health, Villard's assurances of the soundness of Northern Pacific's financial situation, how well the Edison company (next Chapter) was doing, and how Villard would throw himself into new railroad ventures.[97] That winter Villard had bought a considerable amount of U.S. securities for Deutsche Bank.[98] Nevertheless, by spring 1891, there were persistent rumors in the market that Deutsche Bank was withdrawing its support of Villard.[99] Clearly, in 1892 Deutsche Bank and its partners became alarmed by Villard's unwillingness to commit his own resources to projects he recommended to them, and by his inability to deal with the continuing problem of the Northern Pacific,[100] whose securities were once again suffering. Villard seemed to recognize how essential Deutsche Bank's support of Northern Pacific stock was for the overall financial health of the company and for the realization of what he called the company's "beneficial consequences."[101]

Just as the situation seemed to become more difficult, in March 1893 Villard wanted to "jump ship" – or "train," as it were.[102] In response to pleas to postpone his retirement as president of the Northern Pacific board until after the current financial problems had passed,[103] Villard agreed to do all he could to help with a refinancing but, knowing Deutsche Bank's reluctance, he had become pessimistic about restructuring the rail line with new funds.[104] A few months later, Villard made his departure a *fait accompli*; this time he made his announcement publicly, as if to make it irreversible. In a published report, he justified his decision by arguing that it had never been his intention to enter the "management" of Northern Pacific. His election to the board was virtually an accident at the 1887 shareholders' meeting, a consequence of his ambition to use the support of German friends to build up a "large and profitable finance business."[105] He knew from the beginning that misunderstandings and faulty expectations would cause him problems, so as if he were preparing his later defense he had practiced "a hands-off policy" as chairman of the board. Insofar as he was involved in decisions, Villard claimed that he made sure that the other members of the board were aware of his involvement in other companies and the nature of those undertakings. Despite his protestations of cultivated distance from management and of his "innocence" of any blame for the railroad's problems, Villard was already viewed by much of the press and others as responsible for the railroad's financial difficulties. Despite what he believed to be selfless efforts, he felt he had been made into a scapegoat by the press and by speculators. Without trust, he contended, he could achieve nothing. Resignation was the only sensible course.[106] A few days later, capital markets sealed the Northern Pacific's fate.

In many respects, even during this period, the business provided by Villard was very lucrative for Deutsche Bank. The bank alone or in consortia provided many credit facilities at high effective rates and with the line's own shares as security.[107] New agreements ostensibly even gave the banks more collateral by substituting securities with a higher nominal value, but also exposed them more to the vagaries of the market and Northern Pacific's ability to manage its business.[108] The willingness of Deutsche Bank to enable Northern Pacific to struggle along belies some of the bank's later righteous indignation. As some were to charge, the line seemed to be run simply to provide a seemingly endless supply of new securities for bankers to market. Most of the concerns expressed seemed much more about the general financial market conditions, not the operating and investment decisions of the line.

Despite Villard's resignation, the sharp drop in equity markets, and other warning signs, in June Siemens seems to have naively entertained some hope that the new financing and investors could stabilize the situation. Even though Villard had not received permission to resign this key post as Deutsche Bank's representative, Siemens congratulated Villard for bringing Rockefeller to the Northern Pacific board (spelled Roccefeller and Ronnefeller in the letter). He pointed out, though, that Rockefeller was no replacement for Villard, should Villard fulfill his dream of retiring to Germany. More importantly, Siemens chastised Villard for publishing his explanation for leaving the board. To resign was one thing; to do it so publicly was another, especially with subjective expressions of pessimism which the public was ill-adapted to appreciate. It showed a "willingness to pursue money ruthlessly."[109] It is clear that for some time Siemens and Deutsche Bank knew of the Northern Pacific's problems, but perhaps not how grave they had become in the midst of the financial panic passing through the United States in spring 1893. The collapse of capital markets and Villard's public comments effectively ruled out an infusion from capital markets. Siemens, for one, also believed Villard had contributed to the problems, and perhaps even exploited them for his own personal gain.

Neither the involvement of important new investors nor new complicated financial structures had salvaged the situation. In the face of further expansion in railroad and related properties, concerted action by all the investors, threats of legal action, and fancy new financial vehicles all proved inadequate for solving the Northern Pacific's financial problems. If Deutsche Bank did not see through much of this, it was not alone. Many sophisticated investors had bought up Northern Pacific shares. Most regulators did not see through it, either. For many, decoding control and evaluating railroad assets presented an extraordinary conundrum.[110] To some, it appeared a shell game. Even Villard admitted that when he originally took control of the Northern Pacific in 1882, he voted 365,799 shares of a total 754,193 outstanding, without personally owning one himself. Much of the extensive debt he raised in one company was used to fund other companies that he controlled, always, it seemed, with his first transportation love, the Oregon property, standing above the fray, providing management to other companies and controlling key rights of passage, so no matter which other line won other battles for business, Villard's personal holdings would prosper.[111]

What is more, these railroad holdings were not the only major financial interests requiring active management by Villard and Deutsche Bank, and transportation was not the only "high-tech" growth sector the bank was following. In addition to handling Deutsche Bank's affairs and his own personal interests, Villard ostensibly attempted to manage one of the most important companies of the Second Industrial Revolution. The range of his activities was only matched by the breadth and depth of his ambition.

3

Deutsche Bank and American Electrification

As I told you, the consolidation of the two companies will create a great firm, out of which the greatest enterprise in the world will emerge.

Villard to Deutsche Bank, March 7, 1890, about the prospects of a merger between the Edison company and Thomson-Houston, which eventually formed GE, HADB, A404.

Introduction

The electrification of the developed world stands as one of the great technological and economic revolutions of modern times, ranking in importance with the introduction of the railroad and the telegraph. The huge investment in power generation and distribution during the last two decades of the nineteenth century and the first three decades of the twentieth century set the stage for the invention and marketing of a series of products without which – it is no exaggeration to say – the events and lifestyles of our era would be impossible to imagine. From the lightbulb to the television, ours has been an electrical age.

But before the new gadgets could be marketed in sufficient quantity to cover their initial development costs and to reduce their unit production costs, enormous power generation and distribution capacity had to be installed. Small inner-city lighting projects of the 1880s evolved into huge regional grids in the 1920s. The process had a momentum of its own. As the uses grew, decisions had to be made about local generation versus greater centralization, for example. Once concentration was chosen, more investment in moving electricity over greater distances had to be made.[1] From 1882 to 1920 in the United States, for example, electrical power generation went from one kilowatt hour (kWh) to 44 billion kWh.[2] As one of the most important chroniclers of the century wrote, "Of the great construction projects of the last century [nineteenth, my note], none has been more influential in its social effects, and none has engaged more thoroughly our constructive instincts and capacities than the electric power system."[3]

It was an international phenomenon of extraordinary proportions not just because of the patterns of development but also because of the international flows of equipment, know-how, and capital. Although many of the new uses, as well as the social and architectural impact of electrification, have been chronicled, considerably less attention has been given to financing.[4]

Deutsche Bank came to its special interest in electrical engineering by many paths. Not only was Georg Siemens related to one of Germany's great family businesses in the field, Villard had brought the bank into contact with the "Wizard of Menlo Park." Villard and Edison had a symbiotic but conflictual relationship, which bore much fruit for them and their bankers. Edison's single-mindedness, which may have served him well as an inventor, sometimes got him into trouble as a businessman. Villard was pivotal to Edison's ability to clean up many of the inventor's difficulties in the United States and Europe. In 1886, Villard convinced Edison that he had just the right contacts and expertise in Europe to raise money, resolve disputes that already existed among the European partners, improve the already existing contracts between Edison and Siemens & Halske and, in general, improve the earnings of Edison's ventures in Europe. A year after Villard's return to the United States, the German Edison company was reorganized into Allgemeine Elektricitäts-Gesellschaft (AEG). By 1887, too, Villard had wrung out a substantial payment from Edison's Paris partners for the abrogation of their contract with Edison, revised the Siemens contract, and increased AEG's capital from 5 to 12 million Marks to finance power-station development. Despite losing much control, Edison was reported to have been pleased. Villard had gotten Deutsche Bank involved, returned to the United States with the power to negotiate with Morgan for German investment into U.S. electrical power generation, and to reorganize the Edison companies with substantial financial backing from German companies and bankers.[5]

Many undertakings followed, entailing investment into and from the United States. By 1914, Deutsche Bank could look back with pride on assisting Siemens & Halske's entry into the United States, bringing many U.S. patents to Germany, helping to create the largest power-generation facility in the world, Niagara Power Co., and contributing to the growth of several other companies connected with the revolution in electrical power generation. This effort included what came to be one of the largest companies in the world, GE.

Although Deutsche Bank was not involved in the creation of Deutsche Edison Gesellschaft, the company Edison founded with Emil Rathenau in 1883 to bring Edison's inventions to Germany, by 1887 Georg Siemens sat on its board. Siemens served as chairman until 1896, when he decided that the conflicts of interest between AEG and Siemens & Halske were too great for him to continue in that capacity.[6] Siemens and Deutsche Bank played a central role for many years in coordinating the interaction of German and American firms' pursuit of cross-border exchanges of capital and know-how. Deutsche Bank, for many years, was at the hub of a network of organizations that were collectively bringing electricity to much of the world.[7]

The broad outlines of Deutsche Bank's involvement in what led to the creation of GE are well known. The details, however, provide many insights into the risks of foreign direct investment, especially in novel sectors and with untested management, involving big up-front investments with little in the way of modern accounting information.

Edison is seen here at roughly the age when he first met Villard, circa 1880. Despite conflicting views about finance, Edison and Villard shared an almost single-minded ambition and a common vision of how electrification could change the world. They remained attached to one another over the years. Edison was one of the mourners at Villard's funeral.

The Founding of Edison General Electric (EGE)

Villard enjoyed a long and intense involvement in Edison's projects.[8] He arranged the first demonstration of Edison's dynamo and lamps for trains while still head of Oregon Railway & Navigation Company. As an early shareholder in Edison's electric light venture, Villard asked Edison to install lights on his company's steamships. Villard gave Edison extensive financial assistance. As early as 1880 Villard had tried to get German investors interested in Edison's U.S. company and to bring his patents to Germany, as well as the rest of Europe.[9] Despite the usual setbacks, Villard maintained his optimism.[10] It was on an 1884 trip to market Edison's generating plants in Germany that Villard renewed his earlier acquaintance with Georg Siemens.

Yet there was always an element of tension between Edison and Villard, due to their different interests and management philosophies. Edison hated dependence on capital houses, preferring to rely on personal supervision by owners, partnerships, or closely held companies, which maintained the personal representation and relationship of owners. Villard thought big by nature, which required banks and capital markets.[11] Ironically, Edison's own vision of how electricity should be provided helped to tie the two men together, creating a mutual dependence. Better known as an inventor, Edison also believed that his inventions could only be utilized in a world in which giant electrical systems generated and distributed electricity efficiently. Individual generators would never do. Light without a lighting system, which required vast expenditures, a giant technical, legal, financial, and even legislative undertaking, was unthinkable to Edison. In 1878, once technological innovation made spreading electricity through large cities possible, he set his sights on creating the necessary techno-infrastructure.[12]

Creating that infrastructure required Edison to contain his mistrust of bankers. As early as 1882, the opening of the Pearl St. station, the first central station for the supply of electricity – a mere one-square mile area in lower Manhattan – told the story. It was no accident that the first lights were switched on at Morgan's office. Despite financial difficulties throughout the mid-80s, by 1888, Edison had established large facilities in Detroit, Philadelphia, Chicago, Brooklyn (then a separate city), New Orleans, St. Paul – with 1,698 customers and 64,174 lamps in the United States alone – and internationally in Berlin and Milan.[13]

Villard and Deutsche Bank's involvement in Edison projects coincided with a relative decline in Morgan's interest. Although Edison remained close to the Morgan Bank, the firm – not the partners – declined his 1886 offer of 1,000 shares of electrical stock to relieve the inventor of a cash-flow problem. Morgan still managed much of Edison's finances and participated in both his international and domestic relationships, but the firm seemed reluctant in the late 1880s to invest more than it already had in technology that still had some rough spots and whose economic viability was still unproven.[14]

With his close ties to both Edison and Deutsche Bank, Villard, once again, was in the "catbird seat."[15] He was the prime mover for Edison's entry into Europe, drawing finance from Europe to the American Edison companies, and in the reorganization of the Edison companies in the United States.[16] Although Edison had already started up operations in France in 1880 with George Barker, as Edison moved into other countries Villard became more involved, both in the creation and management of new European companies.[17] Villard assisted with the negotiations that led to the transformation of Deutsche Edison into AEG, while representing in the United States both Deutsche Bank and Siemens & Halske, which wanted to get more value for its patents in America.[18]

In addition to his duties with Deutsche Bank, Villard had the authority to handle the production rights for the Siemens' armored cables and couplings. He always had a broad range of activities. Indeed, the period of his most intense preoccupation with Edison coincided with the deterioration of Northern Pacific's business and his campaigning for the election of President Cleveland. To circumvent high U.S. tariffs, Villard suggested that Siemens & Halske manufacture in the United States. He tried in vain to get an Edison company to do the manufacturing under a licensing agreement. Failing in this endeavor – and never one to think small – in 1888 he tried to get the Siemens company to buy all of Edison's business in the United States. Supposedly, in a meeting with Deutsche Bank, Siemens, and AEG, he got the support of all the Germans, even though the two electrical companies had some competing product lines. Edison, who was laboring under severe working capital difficulties, also responded favorably.

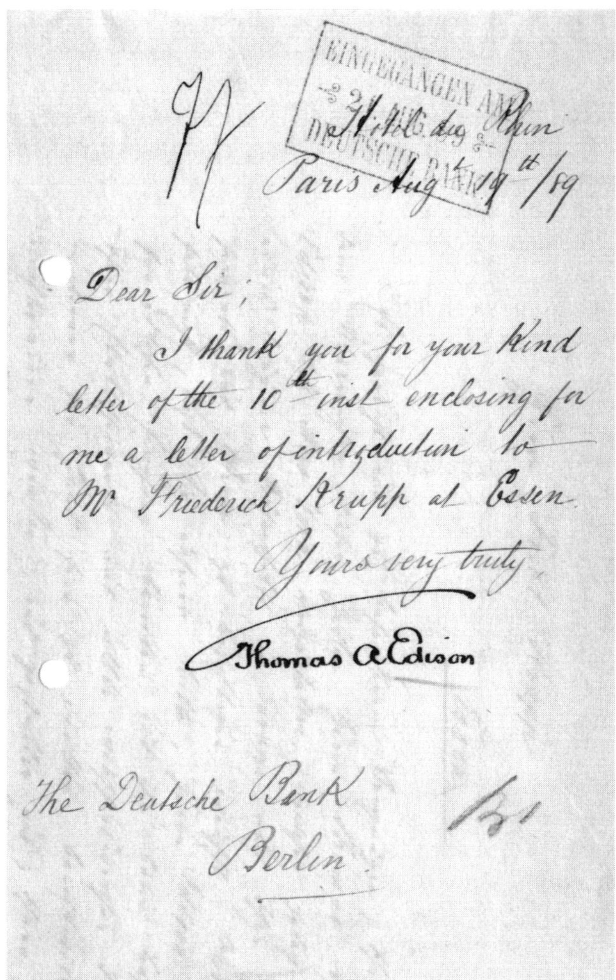

Hôtel du Rhin
Paris Aug 19th/89

Dear Sir;

I thank you for your kind letter of the 10th inst enclosing for me a letter of introduction to Mr Frederick Krupp at Essen.

Yours very truly

Thomas A Edison

The Deutsche Bank
Berlin

Edison thank-you letter to Deutsche Bank for arranging an introduction to the Krupps, August 19, 1889.

Edison General Electric Company was formed in April 1889 with sizeable amounts of German capital, though the timing and exact amounts are somewhat unclear. Although several sources indicate that the creation of Edison General Electric was a Morgan deal, it was actually organized by Villard and Deutsche Bank, with Morgan only taking \$312,000 in stock (at nominal value) at a price of \$215,000, corresponding to only 3,125 of the 30,000 shares issued.[19] Accounts of the positions of the German shares differ greatly, although all agree that Deutsche Bank, Stern, Siemens & Halske, and AEG were heavily involved, varying in total from \$3 to \$8.3 million. There are many reasons for the discrepancies. Some of the sources are not dated. We know that the amounts of share capital changed over time, as Edison General Electric's financing needs increased. Some of the investors lent money, which included an option on common shares. Some of the confusion, too, may come from the difference between nominal value and price or market value, which was often impossible to determine.[20] It is beyond doubt that for the period these were immense sums of foreign direct investment and that the Germans were heavily involved, not only with cash but also with valuable licenses from Siemens in Germany to Edison General Electric.[21]

The German capital achieved many things. It allowed the Edison companies to consolidate and expand. By providing him with a fresh pot of cash from distant investors, Edison felt relieved of financial pressures that allegedly distracted him from his technical work. Moreover, it avoided ceding control to Drexel Morgan, which Edison felt would squeeze him more than distant investors. However, not only had Edison lost much control of his foreign business, his American one was now in the hands of German interests, with whom Edison shared technical orientations and foibles, but with whom at times he disputed concerning organization.[22]

Villard, as representative of the Germans, became the company's first and only president. In contrast to many accounts, there is ample evidence that Villard pursued a combination with one U.S. competitor, Thomson-Houston, soon after Edison General Electric was formed. (See quote that opens this Chapter.) As usual, in his position as president, Villard focused on big deals rather than operational efficiency. The merger to create General Electric led to his own, the Germans', and Edison's departures from the company that had, until that time, born Edison's name.

The Business Model

The beginning of the Edison side of GE was rocky, to say the least. It was still a very speculative business. The story of Deutsche Bank's involvement in Edison illustrates how important financial planning and adequate financing were – and are – to the success of start-up operations.

The management team and business premises of the new company made a good deal of sense. The first Annual Report of the Edison General Electric Co. contained many names important to this narrative. In addition to Villard as president, Marcus served as its first secretary. Edison himself and a representative of Morgan – Charles Coster, very important to the Northern Pacific story – also sat on the board (see next Chapter). Edward D. Adams served on the board of one of the subsidiaries. The stated purpose of the company was to combine the Edison Electric Light Company with three other Edison manufacturing companies: Edison Machine Works, Edison Electric Illuminating Company, and Bergmann & Company. The new consolidated company was intended to profit from gradual integration and closer cooperation among the various "divisional activities." The production of cable was only one of those activities. As Villard wrote to the shareholders, "The formation of your Company was mainly due to the belief of the principal shareholders of the different companies that the protection and development of their respective interests would be better assured by a practical consolidation of the patent-owning and the manufacturing interests." Moreover, the new structure would allow the companies better access to

TWENTY-SIXTH STREET STATION.

Edison Electric Illuminating Co. Twenty-Sixth Street Station, New York, circa 1880s.

capital, vitally needed for the expansion of electric light and power production. Power stations for major metropoles such as New York, Boston, Chicago, and Milwaukee had yet to be built.[23]

The Edison General Electric Company (EGE) business model was ambitious, to say the least. Recognizing that electrification required an enormous investment to create the power and lines to conduct electricity, the firm assisted in the creation of local power companies. It sold them power-generating machinery and cable. In return for technical assistance and equipment, EGE took some cash and shares in the local generating company.

The Edison Electric Illuminating Company diverged from this model somewhat. It purchased the plants of local electrical companies with its own shares, then installed an incandescent light plant, at a fixed cost and for a fixed period of time, and paid the local company a royalty (in the case of the San Francisco company 30 percent or 1,500 shares). Its parent, the Edison General Electric Company, then agreed to purchase stock in the new company. The proceeds of the shares were used for the construction costs of the company. Other shares would be issued to various promoters of the project, with some also sold off to local potential partner companies.[24]

Through its fee income, moreover, Edison General Electric intended to double its holdings of securities in local companies, which helped insure orders for its manufacturing establishments. A further promising note came from the expected growth in the electric railway business.

At its conception, the new company had $11.1 million in assets (its subsidiaries were listed and carried at cost) and virtually no debt. Its leverage would soon change. To implement the business plan, the company required large inputs of equity and debt over the next few years, of which, until 1892, Deutsche Bank was one of the principal suppliers.[25] The EGE's head office permitted the subsidiaries to create and own their own subsidiary companies.[26] But everyone seemed to recognize that further growth and efficiency required a consolidation of the operating units and more support staff. At times, the development of Edison General Electric even had to rely on infrastructure from other companies controlled by Villard.[27]

Financial and Other Difficulties

As usual, Villard was optimistic about the results. He predicted that the consolidated company would earn $1 million in 1889.[28] But even before the contracts were signed, the partners evidenced very different interests and an unwillingness to leave a lot of cash in the firm. Siemens & Halske's participation was contingent on a contract for the consolidated company to build cable, though oddly there was no commitment to purchase the cable for the U.S. company's own needs. Siemens & Halske wanted 20 percent of the profits on the U.S. company's sales to outsiders off the top. The new company was also to represent the Siemens products (patents) in the United States against a percentage of the profits derived from their introduction. According to Deutsche Bank, Emil Rathenau of AEG was ready to accept this,[29] although one could imagine that a special relationship between Siemens and Edison in the United States would rile him. A special 8 percent dividend on preferred shares was to be declared from the beginning, but not paid until there were more profits, so as to leave cash in the firm but commit the company to paying it out to shareholders relatively early on.[30] Technical issues also came to the fore. Some of the participants began to question the safety of direct versus alternating current,[31] a technical problem that would plague the Edison company for many years.

The conflicts broke wide open in February 1889. Villard wrote Marcus from Germany that there were so many objections to the agreement that he could not list them all in a cable. The main one involved the inclusion of electrified railway patents in the new company, even though the original proposal called for organizing other companies later for their commercialization. The resolution of all these issues required extensive negotiation, which endangered the whole deal. Villard suspected that the American partners would grow impatient and withdraw. Siemens & Halske seems to have been one of the objecting parties, but Villard believed another potential German partner, of which he claimed there were several – presumably AEG and others – could be substituted.[32] Although these initial problems were worked out,[33] before the ink dried on the corporate certificates of Edison General Electric, Villard had constructed new and typically ambitious plans. He recommended that the new company purchase two motor companies.[34] As ever, Villard was the "happy warrior," reporting to Georg Siemens, still his honored friend, in spring 1889, about his success with a battle concerning the Northern Pacific and the great prospects for the official launch of Edison shares in July. He quite rightly predicted that the electrical business was going to be a big success, but as usual his confidence and especially his underestimation of the cost and difficulties would get him in trouble with his investors.[35]

Within a few months, to his great regret, Villard was obliged to report bad news. The stock had not yet been listed on the New York Stock Exchange. There were not even private quotes, which would give Deutsche Bank an idea of the price it could get should the bank want to sell some of its holding. Deutsche Bank pressed him for more information, but Villard claimed there was none to report, a fact which was also bound to undermine confidence. A few transactions were done at 95 percent of the par value, but only in small amounts. Villard could only promise the bank a price of 92, and that price could not be had for the bank's entire holding. Actually, only sales of these shares among members of the syndicate were allowed. Villard tried to assure his German colleagues that the quoted prices had nothing to do with the real worth of the stocks, which would, in his opinion, be much higher with time. After all, the company's operating results progressed according to plan.[36]

The business expanded in many directions – among other things these were new German products to be produced in the United States – but conflicts flared up even among the Americans. Villard and Edison were friends, but their friendship was volatile. They did not share the same attitude about money. Villard had lent money personally to Edison over the years, and named one of the Northern Pacific's stations after him, but the inventor felt that Villard's financial dealings were complicating his life and creating unneeded pressure by making Edison accountable to banks.[37] It is not clear whether at this time "his German friends" lost faith in Villard, but in September 1889, Jacob S. H. Stern wrote Deutsche Bank suggesting they remove their American stock certificates from Villard's care and put them with Speyer Brothers in London.[38]

By the fall, with vigorous company revenues, Villard was hopeful that the Edison shares could be listed on the New York Stock Exchange.[39] He forecasted a 2 percent dividend on preferred shares, based on expected earnings of nearly $1 million in subsidiary profits and nearly the same for the parent company. According to Villard, the board believed that an 8 percent dividend on common shares was likely and should be considered "permanent" for investors, even with liberal depreciation. "The whole business is as mentioned earlier in glowing shape and seems to want to continue on this path."[40] But even this expansion was not rapid enough. He also mentioned that Edison General Electric was ready to acquire Sprague Company for $520,000 of its own preferred and common shares.

There were, however, some "operational clouds on the horizon." Early in December, Villard warned that Edison's two major competitors (Westinghouse and Thomson-Houston) were creating companies to raise capital. Their success might cause price competition.[41] Further bad news came in mid-December, when Villard announced to Deutsche Bank that the Edison General Electric syndicate had ordered its members to hold on to the stock until April 1, 1890, instead of the original date of January 1.[42] A few weeks later, Deutsche Bank received word that the Edison company had invested $0.7 million in New York Illuminating Company stock, whose central station had just burned down. Ostensibly, the station was insured and would shortly return to service.[43] Four days later, Deutsche Bank learned that the $0.7 million had grown to $1.4 million, though much of the additional amounts would be sold off, in order to help with the restructuring of this related company. According to Villard, the lighting company would provide Edison General Electric with approximately $2 million in orders. EGE had also committed itself to taking 20 percent of the new capital ($120,000) of Boston Illuminating Company, but this capital contribution came merely in the form of a license agreement for its products, which was to generate another $0.5 million in sales. In Philadelphia, EGE was working out the same sort of arrangement. These and other new contracts led to an additional $3.5 million in new sales. Sprague motor sales were also developing faster than expected. Just after the year's end, Villard forecasted that the final sales number would be 40-50 percent higher than the previous year.[44] As Mira Wilkins wrote of EGE, the start-up, like many fast growing companies, was plagued by working capital problems. In this case, however, the problem was compounded by the unfortunate fact that the receivables were from related companies.

With these expenditures came more requests for capital. Villard proposed that the syndicate exercise its option to purchase another $2 million and to take another $2 million at the same price. Even before all the details for the financing were worked out, Villard, consummate salesman that he was, wrote that because demand was so high for the new shares he could only promise to try to reserve $1 million for Deutsche Bank – one-third of the entire new offering. However, if the bank committed immediately to $0.5 million – a step that he heartily recommended – he could guarantee at least that much. In his view, in a short time the stock would be listed in the United States and then Deutsche Bank would have little difficulty, once the market was more liquid, to offload at a price above its purchase cost whatever shares the bank did not want to hold. He assured the bank that Edison General Electric's credit was still good, which would make further development of the business a lot easier.[45] It is not clear how Villard convinced Deutsche Bank, but after a long, difficult meeting with Stern, Deutsche Bank reported that the two banks were inclined to participate in the new offering of the syndicate for at least $1 million, even though a listing of $3 million was improbable in Berlin before some months because of the many formalities there.[46]

The problems persisted throughout the winter and spring. In February 1890, Villard announced the company's working capital needs were growing so quickly that he and Drexel Morgan had upped the amount of new capital expected from the syndicate from $3 to $4 million in a combination of new equity and debt, 10 percent of which Deutsche Bank and its group would have to ante up under the terms of the agreement.[47] If participants wanted stock in this fast growing firm, they would have to underwrite a portion of the loan, too, a fact at which they balked even if the stock was priced at a 10 percent discount from its par value and the loan carried an 8 percent interest rate.[48] The rate of growth of sales and profits was phenomenal – fivefold for sales and over eightfold for profits from the 1887 actuals of the formally independent companies to 1890 estimates of the merged firm. From 1887 to 1889, the number of local companies grew from 303 to 587 and orders of lamps during the same period from 84,500 to 318,000. But with the increase in investment and funding requirements, actual net earnings per share (EPS) dropped from $25 in 1887 to an estimated $23 in 1890.[49] Nevertheless, in early March, Rathenau was thinking about investing more,[50] and according to Villard, Morgan was buying up shares for important clients like Vanderbilt.[51]

Part of Deutsche Bank's hesitancy was caused by internal factors at the bank. As discussed earlier, management had set a 20 million Mark ($4.8 million) cap on U.S. investments for its own account. With its various railroad interests having a value of approximately $3.4 million and the Edison holding already at $0.8 million, the bank's total investment in the United States came to 18 million Mark, just under the limit, or over 25 percent of the bank's paid-in capital in 1890. In addition, as with the Edison commitment, Deutsche Bank found that it was obliged to hold on to many of these investments for extended periods, which Villard kept extending.[52] Deutsche Bank also seemed concerned by the fact that stock in the United States was not in the form of bearer certificates but rather registered in the name of the company or person that owned it,[53] a legal technicality that would come back to bite the Germans thirty years later.

Villard looked to mergers to solve some of the company's problems. In an apologetic letter, Villard, nevertheless, pressed for the acquisition of other companies, namely Thomson-Houston. He claimed to have a preliminary agreement to acquire all its shares as of a certain market price on a given date, for an amount that came to roughly $24 million, a figure a reader in Berlin at Deutsche Bank underlined and put a question mark next to. On the positive side, only half the sum needed to be paid immediately. The two companies together would form a "giant" – the largest company in the field – with its main strength in electrified trains and train station lighting. What is clear from the letter is that Villard had not yet sent the details about the company to Berlin, even though he had already negotiated a price.[54] Ostensibly, too, the merger was designed to avoid competition in the construction of electrified trains,[55] but one might wonder how Siemens and AEG greeted the emergence of a new giant in the field.

Less than two weeks after divulging his intentions, Villard once again optimistically reported that sales were surprisingly brisk but that the working capital requirements had once again outgrown the company's borrowing lines. The board recommended issuing nearly $2 million more in stock, from the unauthorized $12 million that remained, and borrowing another $2 million. A further bonus of $363,000 in shares would be given to the syndicate for underwriting the stock and providing the loan.[56] Deutsche Bank seems, once again, to have been a little recalcitrant, as it delayed supplying its part of the loan.[57]

By May 1890, according to Villard, the company was doing even better and would pay an 8 percent dividend on the $9.3 million of outstanding common shares.[58] Despite investor frustrations, Villard demanded more capital. Enamored of his company's profitability to date and future prospects, Villard seemed willing to circumvent Deutsche Bank to fulfill his dreams by going directly to London and other capital markets.[59] His threats seemed to pay off. By June, he got a fresh capital infusion. The stock was still illiquid and some of the investors wanted to reduce their exposure. Morgan even threatened to quit the syndicate, which by this time included Kuhn Loeb and five other New York private bankers, but even he finally agreed to contribute to additional capital of $3.6 million.[60]

The situation became even tenser in July. It was determined that "under current conditions" Edison General Electric stock could not be introduced in Germany. This news came nearly a year before Georg Siemens learnt that Villard tried to circumvent Deutsche Bank's affiliate for the listing. After the announcement, Drexel, Morgan & Co., and other U.S. parties to the syndicate decided that the syndicate itself should be shut down immediately. The stock closed in New York at 111.5. Fearing that individual shareholders would get the information about the delay in the German listing, which would probably temporarily drive down the price,[61] they dissolved the syndicate, releasing Deutsche Bank and its fellow German investors, such as Jacob S. H. Stern and Siemens & Halske, from their commitment to hold on to the stock – in other words, to allow the syndicate members to get out before the news of the German problems hit the press. The stock did drop over the next few weeks, but according to Marcus, none of the large American shareholders tried to dump their holdings, just smaller participants.[62]

In contrast to the American syndicate members, Deutsche Bank by this time was more interested in selling its shares than in acquiring new ones. Perhaps the Germans felt the Americans were double-dealing. Over the next few days Deutsche Bank tried to unload its shares, but with little success. According to Marcus, the market was just too thin – had too few transactions – to absorb a block sale. He described the share price as "purely nominal."[63] In September, Villard himself bought a thousand shares from Deutsche Bank at 105. The overall market for the shares was still "listless." Marcus apologized for not being able to sell at 107. "There was no reason, though; the company's business was doing well."[64] A few weeks later he unloaded small lots at 100. This sort of "investment stock," according to Marcus, had a very limited public. Dropping the price had little effect.[65]

By fall 1890, the long-awaited reorganization of the "sub-companies" (subsidiaries) was virtually complete. Even though they had been folded into the parent in 1889, and Edison General Electric was planning to issue one consolidated balance sheet for the prior year (a full consolidation would have presumably eliminated intercompany earnings), the separate companies had not merged many of their operating activities. Even though realization of the operating efficiencies was behind schedule, the parent company prepared for a remarkable 8 percent dividend on its $12 million in common share capital, paid for largely by new capital. Nevertheless, despite additional capital construction needs, Marcus maintained that the company's cash flow was quite good. Some of the subsidiaries were already collecting licensing fees.[66] However, the stock price had fallen to 88, if there were any public sales at all.[67] Some investors seemed to see through the charade of EGE's "extraordinary" accounting earnings for the year ending October 31: $2 million in net income, of which $.8 million was paid out as a dividend. This profit figure supposedly did not include another $1.5 million of undividended Edison Light Co. profits.[68]

The company's cash needs were acute. With all this accounting prosperity came news that the planned new equity capital of $2 million – the third increase in 12 months – would probably be insufficient. An additional million would be better. The parent company had established companies and operations in Brooklyn, Boston, Philadelphia, Washington, and Chicago. Supposedly, the new companies were consolidated – with the exception of the Edison Light Company – with the results of the parent, which made the whole operation easier to understand.[69] Nevertheless, Deutsche Bank appeared to have many questions about the accounts. Understandably, there was much confusion especially about the handling of intercompany payables and receivables, and the nature of customer receivables. Villard felt obliged to personally respond. No record of his comments survives.[70]

The company's capital increase was approved by the shareholders and by February the stock had climbed a little – to the low 90s. The company was attracting interest among powerful investors. The Vanderbilts wanted to acquire a large position in Edison General Electric. Drexel, Morgan & Co., Villard, and Edison himself had offered them 1,000, 2,000, and 1,000 shares respectively from their own holdings. Marcus hoped news of the purchase would jolt the stock from its doldrums, which indeed occurred. Within a few days the price jumped to 102.[71]

By the spring, listing the shares on the German stock exchange was once again a hot topic. For Siemens, the only obstacles were technical and easily overcome. He proposed having an official of the Treuhand, a Deutsche Bank subsidiary formed specifically to administer foreign listings in Germany, serve as special transfer agent.[72] Although the Treuhand had been Villard's idea, Villard now balked at its involvement. Villard's reluctance to allow Deutsche Bank to handle the German listing violated all their previous strategic joint intentions and shook Siemens' trust in Villard's integrity. Siemens saw no reason to abandon these plans. If one listing worked, the stocks of Northern Pacific and other companies could be sold in Germany. These problems had come up before with other companies without any serious consequences for Deutsche Bank. Now Villard's reaction threatened Deutsche Bank's connection to New York capital markets, the very bond he had been employed to build.[73] Siemens revealed that he feared Villard had gone from being Deutsche Bank's representative to its enemy.[74]

Other legal disputes also haunted the Edison company. Even favorable verdicts by judges failed to give the stock a big boost. The expansion brought Edison into conflict with other companies over patents and many local interests. Successful decisions also raised complicated issues for the company as to how it should react; whether it, for example, could go into immediate manufacture of products with questionable patents and immediately go after other infringers, or wait until appeal processes had been worked out. According to Marcus, even the favorable rulings provided further evidence that trading in the stock was really dead. The public just did not understand the significance of the company or the decisions.[75] Deutsche Bank continued to sell shares slowly, as much as 2,200 at approximately 99 in late October 1891, even though during the previous week only a total of 1,100 shares had been traded on the market.[76]

In October, other investors started getting nervous. Rathenau wrote directly to Villard, who in turn gave Marcus a piece of the correspondence requesting more information about the progress of the Edison companies. Unfortunately, Marcus, though claiming to be ready to provide any help he could, seemed unclear about what the questions were. Marcus did write that the dividends and profits would be at least as good in 1891 as in the previous year, even though the company, like all companies, had suffered from a general business decline. He sent a long a list of licensing fees collected, which showed an improvement over the previous year of 22 percent and included income from nine U.S. cities outside of New York.[77] Nevertheless, with the company results sufficient but not extraordinary in 1891, the price for Edison stock languished for the rest of the year and the market remained thin and volatile.

Despite some apparent progress, the company's cash situation deteriorated. In September, a $1 million convertible loan (due in March 1892) was issued. Drexel, Morgan & Co. took up half the loan, with J. P. Morgan and Villard each taking $100,000 personally.[78] Two months later the company sold another $1 million of common stock raising its outstanding to $15 million.[79] As a sign of his greater interest and involvement in EGE's finances as 1891 closed, Morgan underwrote the new issue for $90,000. This 9 percent commission was just a prelude, however, to Morgan's reasserting financial control in electrical and other sectors.

The Merger

As with rails, Villard's office in New York continued pushing for further consolidation of the electrical sector as a remedy for the company's problems. In winter 1892, Marcus wrote Deutsche Bank that the merger of Edison General Electric Co. with Thomson-Houston Electric Co., which Villard had been trying to arrange for at least two years, was finally imminent.[80] As usual, if further examination confirmed, the "combination promises colossal profits."[81]

Founded in part by the third most prolific inventor in American history, Elihu Thomson, who remained close to the research of all the companies he helped create, Thomson-Houston Electric Company was simply better run than the Edison Company. It combined scientific and craft knowledge with good business sense. The successor company of several early ventures since its relocation and restructuring in 1883, Thomson enjoyed solid financial backing. It broadened its product line including both direct (DC) and alternating (AC) current, incandescent lighting systems, electric motors, street railways, and electric meters. Unlike the Edison company, it recruited many skilled managers, including Charles Coffin, a former shoe company manager, who seemed particularly gifted at linking strategy, marketing, business organization, and technological innovation. Under his leadership, Thomson developed a functional structure around designing, manufacturing, marketing, and financing functions. Without accepting equity in new utilities as the Edison Company did, Thomson only took bonds; by 1891 Thomson had become the leading supplier of electric-lighting stations.[82]

The merger represented an important step for Edison General Electric. Except for Westinghouse, the new company would have no serious competitors. Marcus, however, personally saw "a little fly in the ointment."[83] In the past, careful examination of company balance sheets had revealed interesting information. This step had evidently been skipped. The new company would have another $17 million reserve of unissued common shares for future acquisitions, which represented a risk of loss of further control and dilution of earnings per share. The combined companies' high debt levels also added risk.[84] A large group of Edison company personnel would have to leave the consolidated company. As Deutsche Bank's holding had become far smaller over the years, these changes were of less importance for the bank. According to Marcus, though, even Thomas Alva Edison's relationship to the new firm would surely change. There was no telling how much. Despite his technical stubbornness over such issues as direct current, the connection to Edison seemed to be important to Deutsche Bank.[85] His reduced role along with other factors may have diminished the German bank's enthusiasm. This reorganization, unlike the others, was a Morgan operation. He controlled the financing and management decisions.[86]

Villard, as usual, was euphoric, at least at first.[87] Taking credit for both the founding of the Edison General Electric Co. and the new merger, Villard characterized the new company as an opportunity to combine the technical skill and experience of two of the most important firms in the field, a project which held much promise for the public.[88] The sector was growing at an outstanding pace. Between 1887 and 1889, Thomson's sales and profits, for example, had nearly quadrupled.[89] Nevertheless, the industry needed to attract more capital, reduce competition, and enhance organizational compatibilities.[90] Soon after the approval of the merger, Villard reminded the participants of his early support of the combination and announced his intention to resign as president. Although all the board members had tendered their resignations, Villard's seems to have been in earnest. Morgan wanted him out. The fact was, Thomson was twice as profitable as Edison General Electric, and Villard's personal responsibility for EGE's deficiencies seemed lost on no one.[91]

The Drexel Morgan people inquired through Marcus whether Deutsche Bank and their friends would like to become more closely involved with the merged company, but there seems to have been little interest. The terms of the merger gave the U.S. bank a free hand with the new company, a fact which seemed to lessen the appeal of participation.[92] Marcus could not shake his conviction, moreover, that the insiders had paid too high a price for Thomson, reducing the value of the Edison shares, but there was little Deutsche Bank could do to oppose the merger – even if it wanted to. Given the price, perceived as high, this might have been an ideal time to get out. Drexel Morgan could keep the new shares selling at their high nominal price for a while, but without real economic sense behind the valuation even they could not keep it there for long.[93]

There were probably other reasons for the Germans' change in heart. Villard needed more capital and his German "friends" were growing weary of his control – or lack thereof – of their railroad and other interests. The German electrical companies seemed to get few operating advantages from the final GE entity. Only AEG's cable factory, which became part of GE, retained its close relationship to the German interests. The only recourse left to Siemens & Halske, in contrast, involved sending family members to the United States to search for new American uses for its patents.[94]

It is not clear whether Germans made a substantial profit. EGE shareholders got only $15 million of the new company's $50 million in common stock. The German investors left the field to Morgan, who wanted complete control or nothing.[95] Although some sources indicate that they earned 200 percent on their shares, the nominal value of all Edison General Electric shares was already $15 million. Perhaps, too, seeing an overvalued stock and the growing signs of macroeconomic weakness in the United States, the Germans were anxious to get out.[96]

Edison withdrew from active involvement in the new company, General Electric. Moreover, passage of the Sherman Anti-Trust Act dimmed prospects of forming an international electrification cartel, if that had been the German hope. Perhaps, too, the bank grew tired of tying up so much of its capital and committing management time to controlling the "animal spirit" of its representative.

For the better part of the next twelve months, Villard directed those spirits at American politics, namely the effort to elect his friend Grover Cleveland to the presidency, and at salvaging the holding company for his other interests. But in a little over a year, Deutsche Bank's worst fears about Villard and the American economy were confirmed.

Electricity and rails had a common need for a great deal of start-up capital and top-flight management, both of which were in short supply in the United States. With financial markets periodically booming, managers had to tread a delicate path between investing in a prosperous future and preparing for the worst. Even General Electric narrowly escaped bankruptcy in the Depression of 1893. By that time, Deutsche Bank was probably glad for any transaction that pared down its U.S. exposure. The Edison General Electric story illustrates, like those to follow, that doing business in the United States required more than just good business ideas. It might be argued that until the early 1890s Deutsche Bank approached its investments in the United States quite naively. Even though German bankers complained about missing information about cash flows and future prospects, they seemed to assume that they enjoyed the same regulatory protection in the United States that they could count on in Europe. Not only did Deutsche Bank and many of its banking associates not understand Villard's failings, but they also underestimated the fragility of American markets and some of its institutions. As will be discussed in subsequent Chapters, these experiences changed the form, but not the depth, of Deutsche Bank's expressions of enthusiasm for American electrification.

4

The Northern Pacific Bankruptcy Saga

> Remember the Frenchman who wanted his dog to jump a ditch with water in it. The ditch was too wide, so the Frenchman told the dog to take two jumps.
>
> A joke that James Hill told to Arthur Gwinner to highlight his determination and impatience, Gwinner to Adams, April 25, 1898, HADB, A685.

Introduction

The Northern Pacific Railroad enjoyed one of the most turbulent histories in a sector full of such stories. It is a story that has been told many times in the biographies of key players, including Siemens and Morgan, and in the histories of warring companies. This is the first time that it will be told by a non-Deutsche Bank employee using extensive materials from the bank's archive. The cast of characters includes many of the most important figures of nineteenth-century international banking and rail management. During the first thirty years of its existence, the line went bankrupt twice, changed the seat of its headquarters among three different cities, and saw much of its debt converted into equity instruments. Backed by Deutsche and other banks, it emerged from its *third* bout of financial distress with lower fixed financial and other charges, but no real solution to its fundamental problems. The story illustrates the degree to which banks in the late nineteenth century managed the details of some struggling corporations' activities. It also shows the degree to which investment bankers took responsibility for what they had sold to their clients.

Deutsche Bank's nearly two-decades-long experience with Northern Pacific was not one of the prettiest pages in its relationship with the United States, but the bank learned many lessons that would prove useful in the United States and elsewhere. It disabused bank managers of the notion that only German-speaking confidants could be trusted and that railroads were virtually riskless investments.[1] Its problems and final success reinforced a capacity to take on long-term projects. Most importantly, it culled the bank's ability to deal with troubled companies, whose difficulties it learned could sometimes produce abnormal profits. The reorganization produced conflicts, not just between equity and debt holders – even though many investors held both forms of securities – but also among various other stakeholders in the firm: Northern Pacific's community; state and local governments; suppliers; management; old and new investors; and, if I might stretch the notion of stakeholders, competitors. Although the Northern Pacific's financial distress was an embarrassment for Deutsche Bank with its clients, its handling of the crisis may have ultimately enhanced its reputation both in and outside Germany.

Northern Pacific Railroad Company was an impressive institution by many standards. In 1883, even before its perhaps too-rapid expansion, the Northern Pacific controlled nearly 1,500 miles of track, making it, as measured by the length of its lines, the tenth largest railroad in the United States.[2] By 1896, despite two bankruptcies, it controlled 4,706 miles of track (approximately 3 percent of the total U.S. track),[3] forty-three million acres of land (an area roughly the size of 50 percent of modern-day Germany), and various terminal, logistic, coal, and navigation companies. It also held bonds, stocks, and receivables from several companies. The land, which had been granted by the United States as part of the Public Lands Acts, was being sold off and formed a significant part of the company's revenues. The firm's operations actually consisted of forty-four separate companies, with $380 million in bonds of various sorts and maturities outstanding.[4]

Here lay many of the problems. In 1893, the parent company alone had $10.9 million in annual interest and sinking fund payments to make. With total annual revenues averaging around $24.5 million for the preceding three years and operating income averaging approximately $9.8 million, there should have been some concerns much earlier. Although its operating margins were obviously very rich, even in its best years, operating return on assets was less than 2 percent, a figure that implies that volumes were not high enough to justify its huge investments and their related costs. Although the company went into receivership in 1893, the real crunch came in 1894 and 1895, when revenues and operating profit fell to $16.5 million and $4.7 million, and $17.4 million and $6.1 million, respectively.[5] Not only were its general operating revenues down, but Northern Pacific's land sales had also fallen, putting pressure on sinking fund payments. Like many western railroads, the Northern Pacific's revenue was highly dependent on cyclical commodities prices and markets. These operating problems were compounded by periodic capital market shortages of liquidity and confidence.

In early spring 1893, Deutsche Bank managers seemed more worried about the fall in preferred shares prices than bankruptcy.[6] By May 11, 1893, much had changed. The Northern Pacific had to give investors public assurance that the company's obligations would be met. By that time, too, Deutsche Bank was privately looking for ways to reduce its exposure, but it was already too late.[7]

In early May 1893, panic hit U.S. capital markets. A slip in stocks in May led to lenders calling in short-term loans, and a series of bank failures. Panic spread across the country.[8] The turndown in the economy was one of the worst in American history, lasting two years. By July, the Dow had lost a third of its value. Many banks, manufacturing companies, and, of course, railroads went bankrupt. Thousands were out of work and farm prices, already in decline, fell even further. According to many, the panic was a delayed reaction to the Sherman Silver Act, which precipitated a loss of faith in the Dollar and a general loss of confidence.[9] Despite the election of the pro-Gold Standard Cleveland, on whose campaign Villard had so effectively worked, the Democrats, with many Populist silverites, swept both houses of Congress.

By early June 1893, too, in some private correspondence, the question was being discussed as to whether the Northern Pacific could survive any further fall in revenues. Much of the discussion about Deutsche Bank's position revolved around its loans to NAC. Villard, too, seemed more focused on the difficulties NAC suffered. As capital market conditions worsened, Deutsche Bank's American representative put his faith in his "off balance sheet" financing scheme, even though NAC might suffer too. Its real risk was the deteriorating foreign exchange situation, which was drying up money markets. If the NAC suddenly stopped financing itself with debt, it could not provide roll-over loans and make a market for its securities, for which there was no market price.[10] By late June, though, Deutsche Bank's dissatisfaction with the quantity and quality of information it received from New York had grown to the extent that it refused further financing to NAC.[11] Any number of contingencies threatened to drive the Northern Pacific into bankruptcy – for example, the failure to reach an agreement with competing lines about pricing or the inability to get fresh financing.[12] By this time, many of the threats seemed beyond management's control. Reaching an agreement with competitors was a crucial aim, as this was probably the factor over which management had the most influence.

Price competition with other lines continued unabated. Northern Pacific common shares were selling at 7.5, less than 8 percent of their par value, reflecting Northern Pacific's financial distress. At this price, Deutsche Bank did not want to sell. Undaunted by the general crisis, in mid-summer, the bank was even considering new investments in the United States in both General Electric bonds and stock.[13] However, rumors of an imminent receivership for the Northern Pacific hit the market in mid-July.[14] For both the Northern Pacific and NAC it was not just a question of higher interest rates that they would have gladly paid. No one was willing to lend at any price.[15]

Marcus, perhaps still under Villard's spell, saw reasons for some optimism among the gloomy details. According to him, even if the poor economic conditions continued for a while unabated, the land and notes the Northern Pacific held, which were pledged to the preferred shareholders, guaranteed at least their par value. Although there was no absolute certainty, he added, this seemed like a good time to buy into the market.[16] Less than a month later, the shock came.

The Initial News

Deutsche Bank first received official word of the bankruptcy on August 13, 1893. Oddly, Deutsche Bank cabled Marcus that Villard had written Farmer's Loan & Trust, as trustee of all mortgages and collateral, that he (Villard) insisted that a receiver be appointed. Naturally, Deutsche Bank management was miffed about the apparent absence of prior consultation about the precise terms of the receivership with those debt holders whom Villard ostensibly represented. Deutsche Bank and Stern reported that they had no objections to the receivers already proposed, but because they were so bound up in the present management, Deutsche Bank wanted to add some new and independent ones.[17] Though Marcus committed himself to protect the bank's interest, changing the receivers was impossible until the bondholders took collective action, a task Marcus suggested Deutsche Bank should initiate across Europe.[18]

In contrast to Deutsche Bank's assertion, there had been some prior consultation. On August 3, 1893, Villard cabled that he had reluctantly come to the conclusion that a reorganization of the company was inevitable and advised that Siemens come immediately.[19] By August 5, Villard started to make suggestions about how to reorganize the troubled line.[20] At best, it seems that Deutsche Bank never gave its formal permission to call on the courts.

On August 15, 1893, Villard himself finally wrote to Siemens, addressing the letter, "to my honorable friend." The "long-feared" catastrophe had occurred: Northern Pacific came under a court-appointed receiver. Although claiming the letter was difficult for him to write because he felt so responsible, Villard then defended his actions and asserted that the bankruptcy hurt him more than others. According to him, his personal investment in the company was greater now than at any other time. (Given that he had bragged about his original purchase of the company without a single share, this is not terribly surprising.) The letter dripped with emotion and self-pity, detailing how much he personally sacrificed to achieve the company's many ambitious goals. Villard set out his view of what caused the failure. There were few surprises in his explanation: excess competition; weak commodities prices; and high investment in new lines. To him, all hope was not lost, because the potential for recovery was great. After all, many other lines had come back.[21] In some respects, his forecast for the future was accurate.[22] Investors had ignored many operational and governance warning signs[23] and the risks inherent in volatile capital markets. According to his great-granddaughter, and in contrast to his own declaration, however, Villard, to whom some of the Northern Pacific debt was owed, was well prepared for the crisis and lost little of his personal fortune.[24]

Deutsche Bank was certainly not alone in underestimating the problems and complexity of railroad investment. Bankruptcy law, even for Americans, was a quagmire, largely determined by states and by trial and error. Ideology, rather than economics, moved the structure of receiverships and the choice of individuals to run them. The rights of junior claimants often were not protected. Not unlike today, the transportation sector was hit particularly hard. Perhaps, too, Deutsche Bank did not realize how much American monetary and anti-trust policies would affect the feasibility of Villard's plans.

The receivership of the Northern Pacific in 1893 was part of the third great spike in American railroad bankruptcies of the nineteenth century – the first two came in 1873 and 1884, falling at ten-year intervals but with different durations. In 1893 alone, an astounding 74 rail companies with $1.8 billion in capital and 30,000 miles of track went into receivership, nearly one-sixth of America's 1890 rail capacity and nearly as many miles of track in one year as during the prior nine years combined.[25] The Northern Pacific, even with the addition of its sister company, the Oregon Railway & Navigation Co., which followed it into bankruptcy in the fall, together accounted for 5,500 miles of track, but were not the largest companies to go bankrupt. Like many American railroads, they too suffered from the poorly controlled practice of allowing equity shareholders to own shares of stock without paying the full par value of the stock up front. Because of this faulty financial practice and poor accounting, companies were under-capitalized and overly dependent on debt financing, which also shifted more risk to the bondholders.[26] By 1896, 20 percent of all U.S. rail track was controlled by receivers. Not until 1900 did the percentage fall below 10 percent. The whole process left its mark on financing by shifting financing from fixed to contingent sources.[27]

According to Siemens' biographer and son-in-law, the news of the reorganization hit Berlin management like a "thunderbolt." But given the early August telegram discussions, Deutsche Bank knew of the line's dire straits. Deutsche Bank's anger about not having been informed was a little disingenuous. The public, on the other hand, was no doubt less well informed. For Siemens, however, the bankruptcy of the Northern Pacific was probably his most discouraging business experience. Not only did it shake his hopes about the future of American railroads, his personal trust in Villard was also crushed. Not surprisingly, he felt responsible for the losses of German capital invested in American railroads with his encouragement.

The public reaction in Germany to Deutsche Bank's and Siemens' role in the Northern Pacific debacle was quick and hostile. Deutsche Bank was hammered with criticisms. Old friends wrote Siemens insulting letters, which upset him so much he devoted much of his fortune to covering their losses. But according to his biographer, Siemens never lost his nerve and set out immediately to develop a plan for salvaging as much as could be saved.[28]

The first step in the plan was to organize the bondholders in Germany, a step that Deutsche Bank, by virtually all accounts, led quite efficiently, though with several bumps along the way. Within twenty-four hours of the announcement, Deutsche Bank put out a public circular calling for all investors to deposit their bonds with the bank's offices in Berlin and Frankfurt. The bank called a meeting of the investors for September 8, at which time the groundwork was laid for an agreement about how to proceed. Siemens wrote a history of the line and an explanation of what the receivership meant for the investors.[29]

In the early stages, the receivership in particular gave the Germans much cause for concern. Siemens explained to the investors that it was a structure very foreign for Germans. It was a temporary administration designed to keep as much of the property together as possible so as to fulfill the obligations of the firm. The court appointed managers and overseers whose responsibility was to verify that the Northern Pacific managers respected their duties and to prepare the firm for foreclosure, that is, the sale of property so as to pay off as many creditors as possible in order of their legal priorities. These court-appointed officials had a primary responsibility to follow the law, not economics. This made them reluctant to shed branch lines that were uneconomical, and led them on occasion to propose acquisitions of new assets.[30]

Although it was not clear that the company was actually in default and who had initiated the proceedings, receivers were nominated by the company and approved by the court. Villard, who had earlier in the month advised Deutsche Bank that the receivership was the only sensible course, now claimed that he only learned at the last moment of the move. The bank was not overly enthusiastic about the choice of receivers. All three nominees, however, would contribute something to the process. Thomas Oakes, for example, a former president of the line and longtime Villard associate, had experience running the railroad. He knew the key relationships, but there was no one to represent the interests of the German bondholders. The others, Henry Payne and Henry Rouse, were considered independent of the previous management, but also very much under the influence of the Rockefeller family, which had a significant interest in the company.[31]

While Siemens and others tried to organize skeptical bondholders in Germany, Ludwig Roland-Lücke, later a member of Deutsche Bank's management board, arrived in New York two days after the Northern Pacific passed into receivership. He had been sent from Germany as the crisis mounted in early August, a sign that the bank had some prior indication – probably with Villard's August 3 cable requesting Siemens' presence – that matters were about to come to a head. Roland-Lücke was the first Deutsche Bank manager on the scene and key to the bank's early assessment of the crisis. He received his instructions directly from Siemens. His primary objective was protecting Deutsche Bank's clients' financial interests. From the very beginning, Siemens recognized that the Northern Pacific represented a great threat to the bank's future credibility. The bank considered protecting the value of its own holdings of securities connected with the Northern Pacific – a not insignificant sum of approximately 10 million Mark ($2.4 million) – to be a secondary consideration. Roland-Lücke's briefing for the task ahead stressed that whenever there was a conflict between reputation and money, reputation should have unquestioned priority.[32]

Before Roland-Lücke's departure, Siemens felt that Villard's expansion of the railroad had gone well until the company had signed contracts that brought the line to Chicago via the Wisconsin Central, a company in which Villard had a large interest. For Siemens, the solution to the current difficulties lay in getting rid of this connection. The company had simply paid too much, and thereby incurred too much debt. No foreseeable increment to revenues could cover these fixed charges, even if the general economic circumstances improved enormously. Villard had pushed these new investments not only because of his arrogance, but also to protect other personal investments that were connected with the purchase, a clear conflict of interest. Deutsche Bank's reputation for launching securities depended on a successful completion of the Northern Pacific restructuring, which in turn depended on temporarily not pursuing the issue with Villard, who still had influence, especially with the choice of receivers.[33] Although Siemens came to believe that the market had overreacted to the bad news, he knew Deutsche Bank's position was delicate.[34]

The immediate task was to assemble information about financial issues, agreements, and the relevant law. That news did not cheer the Germans.[35] Through most of the rest of August, Marcus and Roland-Lücke's attention was turned to preventing the receivers from handling the railroad's cash flows in a manner that would hurt the bondholders. The receivers had gotten permission from the court to issue $5 million receiver certificates (originally thought to be only $4 million), a sort of promise to pay suppliers, other contractors, and salaries, all of which would have first priority over the company's other debts. The certificates would allow the railroad to function, but without quick action from the bondholders a significant reduction in the net value of pledged assets would result.[36]

With Villard virtually in hiding at his country home, Roland-Lücke spent his first days getting briefed by Marcus. At this point, it was not clear just how many of the Northern Pacific's obligations had not yet been paid.[37] A month later, Villard announced plans to leave the country. His initial itinerary avoided Germany. After a stop in Munich, he was advised not to visit Berlin.[38]

Siemens' Arrival in New York

Convinced of the overwhelming importance of turning the Northern Pacific around, Siemens took charge of the early stages of the investigation and negotiations. In late September he left for New York, accompanied by a team of distinguished German businessmen. As soon as he arrived, he confronted Villard. Although he defended Villard in public, according to Helfferich, in private, Siemens did not hold back his anger. He accused Villard of seeing the problems and violating his duty to Deutsche Bank by not spelling out clearly exactly how vulnerable the railroad had been. Villard's feeble defense – namely, that he had done all he could for the bondholders and that he had offered his resignation – did not quell Siemens' anger. He reminded Villard that the resignation letter emphasized that he (Villard) was tired and wanted to return to Europe, not a warning that the company was going "to hell in a handbasket."

Although Siemens was optimistic that investors would eventually recoup everything but the unpaid interest, the crisis shook him badly. Letters written by and about him to family members indicate how troubled he was before and during his second stay in the United States. He was overwhelmed by a sense of responsibility to those he had advised, and committed to do all in his power to recover their investments;[39] over $15 million of the consolidated mortgage bonds alone were said to be in Germany.[40] With revenues falling quickly, the situation demanded prompt action. It was not clear, however, whether Siemens was more enraged by Villard's perceived incompetence and dishonesty or by Villard's failure to inform Deutsche Bank soon enough of the Northern Pacific's predicament.[41]

German bondholders were in no mood to follow Deutsche Bank blindly. Many feared becoming too dependent on Deutsche Bank for information. Complaints arose over Deutsche Bank's compensation for its out-of-pocket costs and fees. One can imagine that under the circumstance the "professional fees" particularly grated. Given the recent past, questions came up about Deutsche Bank's ability to protect German investors from Americans and whether there were just too many conflicts of interest between the German bondholders and Deutsche Bank. Reducing or eliminating these tensions would be one of Siemens' and Deutsche Bank's chief challenges through the whole process.[42]

There were two important immediate decisions the bondholder committee needed to make: determine a common strategy and select a point man. Next on the agenda was deciding what to do with Villard and his pals, and financing the short-term cash needs of the line. Once these decisions were made, work could proceed on the real reorganization. All these considerations were set against a further August shortfall of $800,000, which gave everything a sense of urgency.[43] Moreover, as late as September 13, 1893, $1.5 million in subscriptions to Northern Pacific securities were still unpaid by investors. Oakes promised to get an agreement from the other receivers to keep Deutsche Bank informed of the details, even before they were presented to the court. By then, too, Roland-Lücke had confirmed that the Northern Pacific's recent leasing deals put an undue hardship on the rail line. The total amount of payments from the Northern Pacific to the lessors was equal to the railroad's gross profit. The bankruptcy offered an opportunity to renegotiate the agreements.[44]

Early on, it was clear that uniting investors with different interests would not be easy. For the Germans who were dealing with very "foreign" circumstances, there were complicated conflicts of interest. Deutsche Bank recognized that the shareholders' immediate interest was to block a rapid sale of assets and force the assessment of common shareholders for damage, still unlimited in some states, whereas the short-term interest of the bondholders was to liquidate some assets to get cash for interest and principal payments. Even at this early stage, however, Deutsche Bank seems to have come to the conclusion that its own long-term interests and those of the other bondholders would best be served by controlling the receivership process sufficiently to avoid a rash disposal of assets, while preventing the shareholders from using them in their own interest. With patience, perhaps, a reorganization could be worked out that would provide bondholders with a far greater return than they would receive by an immediate sale of mortgaged property. All this required building a consensus among the powerful groups represented.[45]

There was much suspicion about who was saying what to whom, and about whether everyone was getting the same information. Roland-Lücke was also concerned, for example, about the role August Belmont, who represented the Rothschilds, would play with management – that is, whether he would work with Deutsche Bank or make a deal directly with Brayton Ives and his group of shareholders. Ives was already trying to put a committee of shareholders together with the United States Trust: John D. Probst; a partner at Stern, representing the German interests; a representative of John D. Rockefeller; the president of Mercantile Trust; and a representative of the Cromwell Committee, a group that, according to several letters, was closely allied with Villard and Oakes. Marcus, for example, was appointed its secretary, raising a question about his loyalty to Deutsche Bank. According to many of

Roland-Lücke's letters, communication among the parties was less than perfect. In an atmosphere of public rebuke, falling revenues, uncertainty, claims and counter-claims in the press, and further railroad failures – including that of the Chicago & Northern Pacific, which Speyer, Probst, and Deutsche Bank encouraged to go into receivership – the investors naturally remained highly suspicious of one another, management, and the receivers through the end of September and early October. These groups vied to control the votes of the most investors. It was a race in which Deutsche Bank fared very well.[46]

In October, the shareholders installed a new board, some of whose members had already been approved in September or were part of the old board. It included Belmont, Brayton Ives, Robert Harris, the former president of the line, and Wilbur S. Sanders, a large shareholder from the west, and at Siemens' personal recommendation, August Ruetten. Ives was made president, Harris vice president, and several other employees remained at their functions including the company secretary, auditor, and treasurer. But the day-to-day running of the company was left to the receivers, who controlled even disbursements to the board.[47]

Given the untested nature of the board and the difficult, uncertain economic and financial circumstances, Roland-Lücke recommended that a competent representative of the German bondholders be appointed as quickly as possible. On the same day that Marcus reported that the new board had been selected, Roland-Lücke wrote the directors back in Berlin that Edward D. Adams had already been named representative of the 5 percent bondholders. With his experience, energy, contacts, and knowledge of finance, Adams seemed ideal for the job. In October 1893, Deutsche Bank formally offered Adams a contract to replace Villard. Understandably, one of Deutsche Bank's chief concerns was Adams' financial interest – of which he assured the bank there was none – in the Northern Pacific or related companies.[48]

An experienced banker and industrialist, Adams served as Deutsche Bank's representative in the United States for the next two decades. Born in Boston, Adams had worked for several banks and brokerage houses. As a partner of Winslow, Lanier & Company, he had achieved significant national financial recognition that had come to the attention of J. Pierpont Morgan, who believed, at least after their initial dealings, that Adams had an extraordinary genius for organization. Villard must have known Adams for several years. They even served together on the board of one company before the Northern Pacific bankruptcy, but there is no record of what kind of relationship they had, although Villard took credit for finding Adams for the reorganization. Adams was probably already known to the bank through projects in which Deutsche Bank had a long-term interest. A great believer in electrification, he was involved in Edison's project to bring electric light to the streets of New York, holding positions with Edison's corporations and working on the financing of the Northern Pacific Terminal Company in Portland, Oregon, as well as the financing of other railroads.[49] His activities during the period of his collaboration with Deutsche Bank were not limited to handling the bank's affairs, and even after their formal relationship ended, he continued to serve as a confidant and agent of

Edward D. Adams circa 1895.

senior management in Germany.[50] At the early stage, he seemed to enjoy the support of both the German and American bondholders.[51]

Adams was a deal maker who also worked on a commission basis, with only his office space and a fixed sum of $12,000 paid annually (nearly $300,000 in today's Dollars) by Deutsche Bank. But unlike his German predecessor he had a fine sense of administration and of the need for consistent follow-up. Adams' role in the Northern Pacific reorganization and with Deutsche Bank quickly expanded.

Despite all of Deutsche Bank's many preparations, the task of working out a reorganization plan was indeed gargantuan. It lasted nearly three years. Although the $49 million in common equity holders (at par) and $36 million of preferred (at par) were not as well organized as the debt holders, neither the equity nor the debt holder group was homogeneous. There were many small shareholders among the common and preferred owners (only 60 held more than 1,000 shares, the largest shareholders had 13,000 shares).[52] Some of the debt holders had assets pledged to their securities; others had relatively few securities and ranked low in priority. Some investors came in after the collapse, others had been along for the whole ride. As the line's results deteriorated between 1893 and 1895, alliances shifted. According to some, the protracted negotiations served Deutsche Bank's interests. Many of the participants had their own credibility to defend.[53] Behind the ongoing agonizing efforts to unite

James J. Hill after his many battles to control the Northern Pacific.

the investors stood a man who was the source of many of the Northern Pacific problems and perhaps ultimately its best hope of their resolution.

The Great Northern and James J. Hill

The solution for Northern Pacific involved a consolidation of all the companies in the region, but this proved to be difficult to achieve, to say the least. The owners of the other lines wanted to use their financial muscle to force the breakup of the Northern Pacific so that they could buy up those assets themselves. In order to understand how the Northern Pacific's fate was dependent on the resolution of conflicts between old and new investors and on its competitors, at this junction it is necessary to introduce the Great Northern Railroad, James J. Hill, its owner-manager, and his group of investors. The relationship between Hill and Deutsche Bank changed a great deal during the course of the bankruptcy. At times, his desire to grab or destroy the Northern Pacific's assets put him into conflict with Deutsche Bank and its representatives. After time, though, Deutsche Bank came to the position that the financial interests of their holdings would best be served under Hill's leadership, although perhaps not under his terms.

Born in Canada in 1838, Hill came to the United States (New York) in 1856 and then moved to St. Paul, Minnesota. He began running a steamboat company in 1871 out of St. Paul, where he had learned the transportation business.[54] In old age, at least, he was dark and bearded, resembling Karl Marx, a similarity at which both men would have chafed. For much of his 78 years (he died in 1916), transportation was his passion. In 1877, with the help of Donald Smith and George Stephen, he raised $5.5 million of "other people's money" to buy the bonds of a bankrupt rail company, whose worth Hill estimated at $20 million. If this master of transportation strategy, especially of rate cutting, was correct, the group stood to make a fortune. As it turned out Hill had underestimated the value of the property. With Stephen as president, the Canadian Pacific Railroad was born and soon made the group a small fortune.[55] Although Hill withdrew from the Canadian Pacific Railroad in 1883 to form a new venture, an American transcontinental railroad that linked Manitoba to St. Paul, he stayed close to his Canadian associates and the Canadian Pacific Railroad. They maintained a sort of "community of interest" with Hill's new enterprise, the Great Northern, which was finally founded in 1889.[56]

From the beginning, Hill's ambition and the Great Northern's business brought it into conflict with the Northern Pacific railroad, as well as other lines in the region. The Great Northern, for example, was totally dependent on Oregon Railway & Navigation for access to the Pacific.[57] As early as 1889, Hill resolved that the best strategy for the Great Northern was to take control of the Northern Pacific. He had little respect for Deutsche Bank's absentee management, especially with Villard in New York working on Edison affairs. Hill suspected early on that Villard's ego would lead to clashes and later that Adams, whose financial ability he respected, was merely a front for "those whose interest were served by a protracted receivership." Hill's biographer contends that, in short order, Hill placed a spy in Northern Pacific's office to learn more about its rate cutting.[58] The bankruptcy of Northern Pacific and its related companies, though a competitive threat, was also a welcome opportunity for Hill to achieve his goal of controlling transportation in the Northwest. For Hill, neither voluntarily ending rebates and rate discrimination – as had often been tried – nor even government action, nor the dictates of J. P. Morgan in New York could hope to stop ruinous competition. Only consolidation of lines would solve the fundamental dilemmas of rail service. It was Hill who would profit most if the assets of the Northern Pacific were auctioned off quickly.

Hill recognized that many of the problems with the Northern Pacific had little to do with the line itself. Rather, they were brought on by Villard's strange ability to persuade investors to throw good money after bad, coupled with, at the very least, Villard's proclivity to close his eyes to conflicts of interest between the railroad and its managers. For years the line had been borrowing to pay interest and dividends, ignoring much-needed improvements.[59]

But like Villard, Hill was driven by a dream of realizing a giant rail network in the west. Unlike Villard, though, he was relentless, focused, and, in many ways, close to the project. He was an inveterate, skilled cost-cutter. Moreover, Hill was not above using politics and politicians to get his way.[60]

In his conflicts with many investors and competitors, Hill maintained the faith of an impressive, knowledgeable group of investors. The most formidable of these in the United States was Jacob H. Schiff of Kuhn, Loeb & Co., who took his job as a director of the Great Northern very seriously. Through Schiff, Hill gained access to many continental European financial sources.[61]

Hill assembled a group of distinguished investors, principally from his native Canada. Chief among his investors and advisors was his friend and confidant, George Stephen.[62] An immigrant from Scotland, Stephen was one of Canada's most successful businessmen, first in dry goods, in which he made a fortune, then in banking and railroads. As with many of the leaders of Deutsche Bank in Germany (Siemens and Gwinner), in the United Kingdom Stephens was elevated by Queen Victoria to the peerage as Lord Mount Stephen in 1890. He settled in England after his retirement from Canadian business and political affairs. Along with his longtime associate, Donald Smith (also elevated to the peerage as Lord Strathcona), he bounced back and forth between country and city homes, enjoying the role of one of England's most financially savvy members of the House of Lords.[63] Although he spent his last 30 years mostly in England, he never lost his attachment to Canada and Canadian Pacific Railroad, whose president he was for approximately ten years, or to Canadian politics.[64]

As the Northern Pacific's troubles mounted in 1892, both Mount Stephen and Schiff advised Hill to consider taking a role in the eventual reorganization of the line. Hill felt that some of the management's decisions were so poor and self-serving – especially Oakes' insistence on purchasing the Wisconsin Central Railroad – that they bordered on criminality. Hill agreed with nearly all the reports about the condition of the Northern Pacific commissioned by Siemens, discussed earlier, copies of which had been given to him surreptitiously by Schiff – all except their assessment of the weakness of the Great Northern, of course. In truth, the bankruptcy of the Northern Pacific was both an opportunity and a threat for Hill. If Hill could gain control over all or some of the Northern Pacific's assets, he could reduce his own costs and eliminate competition. On the other hand, freed from its interest burden during the period of a receivership, the Northern Pacific could drop its rates.[65] In any case, Hill had to act.

Following the company's progress or lack thereof in spring 1893, Hill wrote Mount Stephen prophetically in May that the Northern Pacific was on the verge of bankruptcy – three months before the company filed – and had to be completely reorganized, which would wipe out the present common and preferred shareholders. He predicted that, even without investing, his group would have to be consulted in all transportation matters to avoid conflict. Handled the way Hill handled his own properties, the Northern Pacific could be a great line, but it was being run to make new financial instruments, not money. He also correctly foresaw that the Great Northern could survive the competitive pressures produced by the Northern Pacific's and, later, the Union Pacific's financial distress.[66]

From 1893 to 1896, the reorganization moved slowly, at least too slowly for Hill, who came to see Adams along with the group around Ives as the major obstacle to his plans. Gleaned largely from the frontiersman's perspective, Hill's biographer's assessment of Adams is damning: overly proud of his distant connection to famous revolutionary Adamses; cultivated to the point of bordering on prissy; thin-skinned; arrogant; with only a good sense of finance and some experience with railroad organization to recommend him.[67] Not everyone in the Hill group, however, shared Hill's opinion of Adams. At least Jacob Schiff of Kuhn Loeb, who very much supported the idea of merging the activities of the two railroads, wrote in 1894 that Adams "is very capable as you know, but he has a Herculean task before him. In my opinion, your friends of the Deutsche Bank could do nothing better than to induce Mr. James J. Hill to interest himself in the affairs of the Northern Pacific Company."[68]

Schiff was pushing with other bankers for a virtual consolidation of the two lines with fresh capital. The plan involved leasing a reorganized Northern Pacific to the Great Northern and a shared division of joint earnings.[69] According to Stephen's biographer, at this juncture Hill, although he could think of nothing but the Northern Pacific, had not developed concrete plans of his own and was reluctant to accept responsibility for the bankers' ambitious consolidation plan, which he considered operationally and financially flawed.[70] Too many anxious bondholders were waiting for any improvement in the market to dump what they held, which would then depress the market and put additional pressures on the finances of both railroads.[71]

In spring 1895, to Hill's dismay, Adams presented an alternative plan. All the parties seemed to recognize that some sort of merger was needed, but Adams submitted to Deutsche Bank a plan for reorganization in which the Great Northern would guarantee Northern Pacific debt. The reaction of the Hill group was predictable and vociferous.

That spring an up-tick in Great Northern revenues and bond prices increased Hill's confidence that only in his capable hands could the two railroads be profitably run, a view shared by his band of financial supporters. Although Deutsche Bank and Hill shared many common interests and views, combining the lines was a long-term project, to say the least. By 1895, Hill had set out to convince Adams and his German backers that unifying the two corporations under his control was the only sensible solution to the Northern Pacific's problems.

The London Agreements

London became the center for a series of talks designed to break the logjam. Hosted initially by Mount Stephen and later by Morgan, two meetings were held in London to achieve this unification. They led to two separate plans (The First and Second London Agreements): The first and most straightforward, calling for the Great Northern to absorb the Northern Pacific, was thwarted by public reaction and regulators; the second, more complicated and probably also illegal, was held together under great turmoil for nearly five years.

Getting to the point required a great deal of agonizing negotiation. In April 1895, Hill and Adams sailed together for Europe, where they met with Siemens to work out a reorganization that would put the Northern Pacific into Hill's hands; a solution both companies favored, according to some, but to which Hill seemed, at this stage, lukewarm.[72] In London they met with Mount Stephen and J. Pierpont Morgan, who uncharacteristically seemed willing to leave the reorganization to others. Improvements in the market for Northern Pacific securities probably made the negotiations more difficult, and Hill was frustrated by the rejection of his straightforward plans. Reportedly Hill offered the First Mortgage Holders to take their bonds at par and with interest. If he owned the bonds, Hill could simply foreclose on the mortgaged assets, take possession, and thereby avoid a merging of the companies, a neat solution for him and certainly one that would have shortened the reorganization at the expense of some investors.[73] The offer certainly had less appeal for the holders of other debt and equity instruments and may have been thwarted by the fact that many individuals and institutions held several different classes of securities.

Following the rejection of his offer, intense negotiations led to a much more complicated agreement about how the strengths of each line could best be used to work toward a common good, and how their financial interests could be tied together.[74] Tantamount to an acquisition, the First London Agreement entailed many steps that were difficult to arrange. In order to insure that the financial reorganization would be a success, the participants agreed to pool their efforts to buy as many of the new bonds as required and up to 25 percent of the new stock. The bankers would receive a $1 million fee to compensate them for the reorganization, and the syndicate would receive $3 million for underwriting the new paper. According to Siemens, the greatest danger to keeping the railroad together was still the immediate demands being made on the company. He proposed creating a syndicate, which would include the largest American and German interests, to buy up the so-called Receiver Certificates.[75]

Opposition to the "merger" came from many sources. Some investors feared that the Germans were favoring the interests of the bonds held in Germany, mostly Second Mortgage Holders. Even some of Hill's own shareholders in the Great Northern protested against some parts of the agreement. Stephen feared that litigation would undermine the Great Northern's ability to obtain credit.[76] Despite Hill's assertions about the value of the combination for the community, many of the residents in the area opposed the Great Northern's takeover, because it would give the line a near monopoly over rail service in the area, transferring power from the users to the providers of transportation services. Some of the old shareholders and different classes of bondholders sensed that they would lose value to those who bought up securities at depressed values, and that they would commit themselves to taking further risk without sufficient compensation.[77] The large number of bondholders in Germany and at its branch in London gave Deutsche Bank a great deal of power in the process, but some of those they represented feared being sold out by powerful interests.[78] Minnesota corporate law prevented one railroad from holding the securities of another that it paralleled in the state.[79] Even the U.S. Congress got into the act by forbidding the acquisition of the Northern Pacific's assets by a parallel line as a condition of its approval of the reorganization agreement.[80] Improving Northern Pacific profits and increasing local agitation against the merger, which stimulated a series of court cases, finally convinced Morgan and

Deutsche Bank that Hill's scheme was tainted as a "monopoly" and perhaps unnecessary.[81] The first agreement was effectively dead, but a solution had to be found.

By January 1896, pressures from bankers and investors mounted. Hill began to fear that Deutsche Bank, via Adams, was trying to assert more control than he (Hill) had, an affront that Hill found intolerable. To reassert his influence, Hill put forth a new plan for the Northern Pacific restructuring.[82] Even before the awaited Supreme Court decision – which indeed held in late March that the original plan was illegal – in February 1896 Hill wrote Mount Stephen about a restructuring that would circumvent the legal obstacles and perhaps some of the criticism. It was based largely on the first agreement, but instead of corporations, individuals or syndicates would hold the shares. This time Morgan would be more strongly involved. Financing would come from a Morgan–Deutsche Bank syndicate furnishing $45 million to underwrite the restructuring of securities and $5 million for improvement of the property. Hill was not a member of the syndicate, but he agreed with Morgan and the other members of the syndicate to take those securities that the old investors had declined. The plan also called for all classes of equity to be held in trust for five years by the members of the syndicate.[83]

In February, Morgan lined up behind changes to the First London Agreement and consented to taking on a direct role in the reorganization, which chagrined Hill, who was still disappointed that the Great Northern had not simply absorbed at least the assets of the bankrupt line, a failure for which he in part blamed Morgan,[84] who wanted to model the reorganization on those he had arranged for the Erie and Reading lines.[85] Arriving in Europe in March with a draft agreement, Morgan intended to finalize plans with the other participants.[86] By this time, too, some investors saw Northern Pacific securities as a buying opportunity.[87]

Characteristically, the Hill group, though participants in the first agreement, refused at first to participate in the new syndicate, at least for the time being, despite Morgan's offer to sell the group a substantial number of shares. Although they kept an option to buy shares later, their initial reluctance to take responsibility for the new financing did not bode well for the future.[88]

By this time, too, it may have seemed to the Hill group that it could take substantial control of the Northern Pacific through operational agreements without any out-of-pocket expense at all. Deutsche Bank evidently was also not enthralled by the terms of the agreement. It called for the bank to continue to hold equity in Northern Pacific, a commitment for which, by this time, it understandably had little enthusiasm.[89] Nevertheless, Deutsche Bank agreed to take a one-third interest and lead the syndicate with Morgan.

The potential profits were substantial. The syndicate members committed themselves to purchasing nearly $8.9 million in old bonds, $18.7 million in preferred stock, and $77.5 million in common stock for a price of $19.9 million plus any accrued interest on the bonds. They were also requested to purchase $3.6 million in new 4 percent prior lien mortgage bonds and $9.7 million of 3 percent general bonds when issued for a price of $8.9 million. The members also committed themselves to advancing further funds if needed, up to $15 million, carrying an interest rate of 6 percent for new company purchases. The total obligations of the syndicate were capped, however, at $45 million. For their services, the syndicate managers claimed a commission of 6.66 percent of the total subscription.[90] On the nominal value of debt and equity, this probably came to around $18 million (well over $400 million in today's Dollars) split three ways. As of January 1, 1896, $169 million of various Northern Pacific bonds alone were still held by the public.[91]

But the final plan preserved several key objectives of the participants in the London meetings. The first was to keep as much value for the bondholders as possible, which meant staving off efforts to sell off assets quickly and piecemeal, and to wrest control of the company from the old shareholders. The second was to attract new capital, which required creating a structure that had a reasonable chance of avoiding friction with competing lines in the region. In addition to the financial and other arrangements, the company changed its name from the Northern Pacific Railroad to Northern Pacific Railway.

By March, all the stakeholders, including management and receivers, seemed reconciled to the plan – everyone except Hill, of course, for whom this was only meant to be a quick palliative on the way to complete control of the line. The plan proposed a four-pronged approach to improve the line's financial and operational prospects. The first two involved business and corporate restructuring. The last two were financial in nature. First, the railroad would abandon Chicago as its eastern terminus, limiting its eastern access to the Mississippi and Great Lakes. This entailed disposing of its assets connected therewith. Second, all of the main line, branches, and terminal properties would be brought, as far as possible, under the ownership of a single company and covered by its new mortgages.[92] Costs would be cut and greater attention paid to servicing its financial obligations.

The syndicate had put together a series of proposals for debt restructuring. These included various ways of swapping old debt for new interest-bearing instruments and equity, and the promise of new capital. All this was aimed at bringing down the companies' annually fixed financial expenditures and securing future borrowing power in times of distress, or for future improvements, which were expected to be $9 million over the next five years. With "net income applicable to fixed charges" – roughly equivalent to our operating profit before depreciation – fluctuating between $10.1 million and $4.4 million during the prior five years, averaging $7.8 million, the committee believed that a fixed financial expenditure (charge in their terms) would be prudent.[93]

The agreement held many advantages not only for investors but for the company, too. The company was able to reduce significantly its interest expense, received approximately $2 million in new paid-in capital, and the promise of credit lines to tide it over if there were additional cash flow problems. The bondholders who decided to stay with the company's securities received new bonds carrying a lower coupon rate, but they received higher face values for the debt: in most cases, also preferred shares, and in some cases equity shares for their trouble. Those equity holders who were willing to pay in additional funds saw some dilution of their holdings by the issuance of new equity, but they could presumably hope that the turnaround would work and that their shares would be worth at least their par values in the near future. In some sense, none of the investor groups had much choice.

The terms of the financial reorganization of Northern Pacific were complicated and more favorable to the bondholders. Surprisingly, however, the shareholders took less of an economic hit than would be expected. All the debt was to be consolidated into prior and general lien bonds, $105 million and $56 million respectively.[94] The bondholders were to receive a mix of cash and securities, new debt carrying 3 percent and 4 percent as well as preferred stock. General Second Mortgage Bondholders received, for example, 4 percent in cash, 118.5 percent of prior lien new bonds, and 50 percent of preferred stock for the face value of the bonds turned in. Those who opted not to take the new securities would be compulsorily retired under the terms of the old bond, presumably at the market, not face value.[95] The new bonds would be secured by all the assets of the company – main line, land, rolling stock, etc. – with the prior lien creditors maintaining their priority. The new bonds also had the advantage of being 100-year, noncallable instruments.

In short, the purely financial part of the restructuring involved a debt for debt, debt for equity, and equity for new equity swap. Old equity holders would have to put in new cash if they wanted to exchange their shares for those in the new company, while their percentage ownership was halved. It doubled the company's paid-in capital and reduced its debt burden substantially, as well as adding over $11 million in new cash from the old shareholders.

Morgan and Deutsche Bank agreed to underwrite Northern Pacific securities for ten years (that is, to make a market) in return for a fee and full information about the companies' activities and a privileged position with any new securities issued by the conversion.[96] There were significant costs and risks for Deutsche Bank in the reorganization plan. Senior Deutsche Bank executives got involved in relatively trivial decisions of the new company.[97] Ultimately, the bank had to offload most of the securities it had bought. This was not always easy. If the bank wanted to avoid having a large inventory of bonds on hand by the end of the year, it would have to stop buying them in November 1896.[98]

Understandably, the authors of the plan focused on the interest expense and the expected preferred dividend – $6.1 million and $2.9 million respectively – as a measure of the fixed financial cost the reorganized firm would have to cover. They also used an interesting measure for valuing the reasonableness and risk of the plan. All the debt, equity capital, interest expense, and preferred dividends were converted to their per-mile-of-railroad-track values. Total gross cost was divided by 4,706 miles. In other words, each mile of railroad track was to provide an operating profit available to cover financial costs of $1,286 in interest payments and $616 in preferred dividends, leaving $1,902 for the common shareholder.[99] The participants took comfort that the plan would in effect reduce the company's fixed annual financial charges by nearly 35 percent.

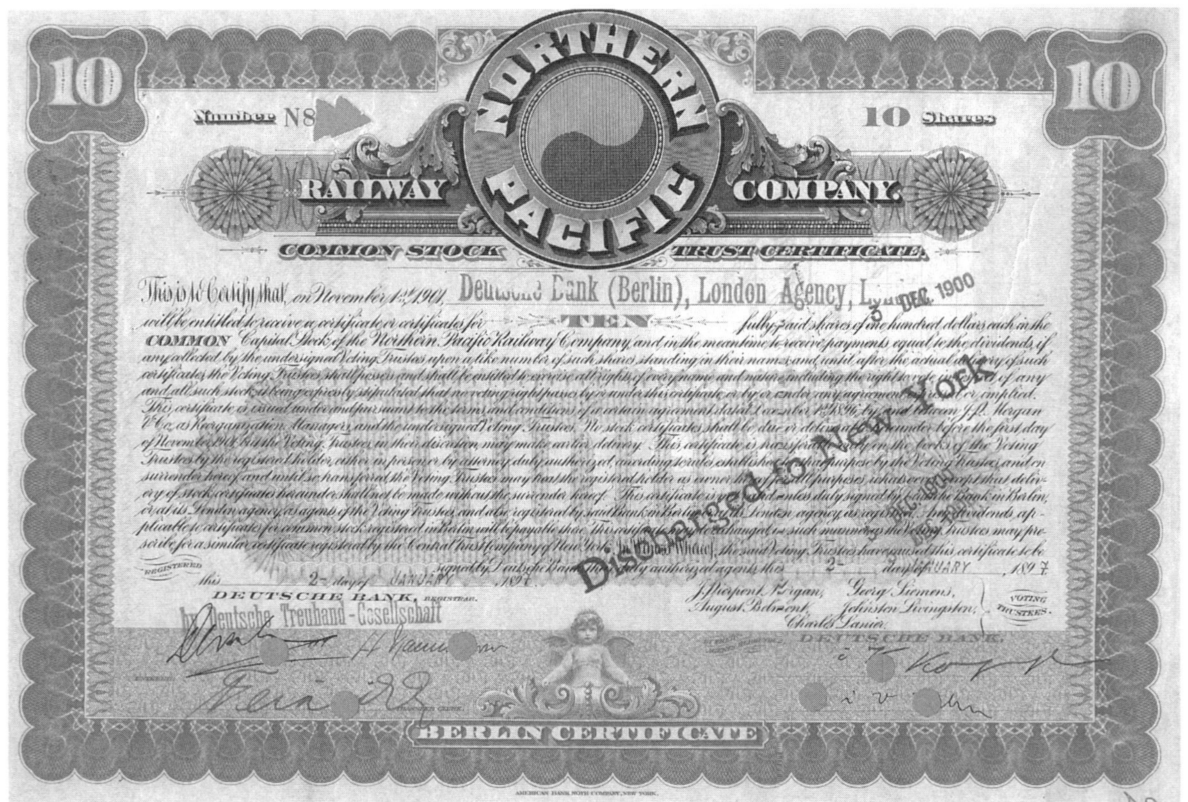

Northern Pacific Common Share Trust Certificate dated November 1901. This security points to many interesting aspects of the reorganization. Not only was it held by Deutsche Bank's London Branch, Deutsche Bank's Treuhand-Gesellschaft processed (certified) the transfer of shares, which then had to be sent to New York. It was actually a Trust Certificate that gave the holder rights to dividends and eventually normal common shares, under the terms of the agreements made in 1896, especially the Voting Trust agreement. The certificate bears the names of the Trustees: J. Pierpont Morgan, Georg Siemens, August Belmont, Johnston Livingston, and Charles Lanier.

Voting Trust

The bankers took many precautions to avoid conflicts that might disturb the rebirth of the Northern Pacific. Along with the Reorganization Plan, they created a Voting Trust, in which all preferred and common shares (except those in the hands of directors) were deposited. Voting Trusts were a popular device during the period, often used by Morgan to steer companies out of bankruptcy. Shareholders were willing to yield their voting rights to directors in exchange for trust certificates, to avoid penalties that bondholders and other creditors might be able to win from shareholders when a company went bankrupt. Unlike today's limited liability companies, there was a real risk of shareholders being assessed for damages. This "Morganization" of companies was viewed benignly by many shareholders who wished a bankrupt company to be guided by competent bankers and a strong board, which under banking house guidance exercised much more control over managers than is commonplace today.[100] For the next five years, the affairs of the Northern Pacific passed from one crisis to another, punctuated by periods of prosperity, tranquility, and hopes that a long-lasting solution could be found.

Morgan, Siemens, Belmont, Johnston Livingston, and Charles Lanier were named the five voting trustees. To further the independent reorganization and administration of property, they would hold and vote the shares for a maximum of five years. The stock could be returned to the shareholders at an earlier date if the trustees felt, at their discretion, that the return was called for. Shareholders would receive Stock Trust Certificates, transferable in New York and Berlin, until such time as the prescribed number of shares in the company was distributed by the trustees.[101]

The bankers had taken another step to ensure the success of the reorganized company, one that was kept secret and would not have held up in U.S. courts. Signed that April by the parties in London, the agreement to avoid competition became a major object of dispute for the next five years, perhaps illustrating some of the dangers of cartelization versus merger. After the breakdown of the first agreement with the Great Northern because of public and legal pressure, the participants searched for another means of ending the harmful effects of cutthroat competition and overcapacity. In the end, Hill and Lord Stephen agreed to do all in their power not to hinder the independent reorganization (i.e., without the Great Northern) of the Northern Pacific, even to discourage the bondholders of Northern Pacific branch lines from pushing for better terms. For this, the two "competing" lines would form a permanent defensive alliance (cartel) in order to avoid "competition" and "aggressive policies" that might work against the "common interests of both companies." All competitive business would be divided on equitable terms between the two companies. Tariff wars and rate cutting were absolutely forbidden. Both companies agreed not to pursue business in each others' territory. They also agreed to work together to prevent anyone else from taking control of the Oregon Railway & Navigation Co. and to block any other line such as the Union Pacific from using the line. The agreement included some equity ownership by the Great Northern group in the Northern Pacific. It was to be, in short, a merger not in the technical, operational sense, but in effect, because some of the key shareholders would be the same in both companies. The bankers offered Hill and Stephen shares in the new Northern Pacific at a price that matched the best received by any of their customers. All the parties agreed to use their voting shares and proxies only after consultation with the other parties and in concert.[102]

> The four parties hereto subscribing promise to use their best endeavors towards loyal fulfillment of this purpose of friendly and harmonious working of the two systems, with insistence of good faith on the part of the operating officials in *maintaining rules and rates fixed by the respective superior officials and Boards of Directors.*[103] [My italics]

The agreement concluded with a pledge not to make the contents of the document known to other parties without the consent of the other signatories.[104]

Although reasonably happy with the reorganization in general, Deutsche Bank seemed to prefer Hill's original approach and his later efforts to consolidate the two lines. However, the bank had to respect Morgan's fears of regulatory interference and became annoyed by their representative's precarious position among the parties. Over the next few years, the Germans cautiously unloaded some of their securities, just as Hill and Morgan were building up their own positions.[105]

By November 1896, Deutsche Bank was understandably satisfied by the performance of its remaining Northern Pacific holdings. The price of preferreds was between 33–34 and 54, and that of prior lien bonds between 83 and 85, although European markets were showing some resistance to the American price climb. The bank itself was still holding on to or responsible for 400,000 prior liens ($40 million at face), 250,000 general liens ($25 million at face), and 72,000 preferred shares ($7.2 million at face), against which there was Hill's option on 6,250.[106] But the problems were not over.

Oddly, as the plan was put into place, the approaches of some of the banking "partners" did not reflect the stereotypes of their national business cultures. The Germans seemed more willing to accept a real integrated merger; Morgan, who was now much more involved, insisted on keeping the cartelized, Voting Trust approach with the lines remaining independent. Within less than a year of agreeing to the reorganization terms and the secret London protocol, Hill started to augment his direct control of the Northern Pacific and frictions increased. Perhaps due to its distance from American regulators, Deutsche Bank encouraged attempts at merging the two lines, as long as certain principles from prior agreements were respected.

A few days after the first annual meeting of the reconstituted line, Stephen approached Gwinner about whether Deutsche Bank still favored ultimately merging the two properties. Gwinner replied that Deutsche Bank had nothing against Hill taking a larger chunk of Northern Pacific stock to gain more influence, but he confronted Stephen with evidence that Hill was undermining the profits of the Northern Pacific in violation of their agreement. Respectful of Hill's knowledge of the business, Gwinner especially looked to Hill's increased ownership interest in the Northern Pacific as the best way to reduce conflict and Deutsche Bank's own exposure.[107]

Arthur Gwinner circa 1896. Gwinner brought to Deutsche Bank in the mid-1890s banking experience and family connections, which were particularly useful in overcoming the stigma of the Northern Pacific collapse and restoring the bank's credibility as a representative of German capital in the United States. His relationship with Adams, too, helped create a steady flow of business between Germany and the United States, for the most part, with less "Sturm und Drang" than experienced during the Villard years. Like Adams, Gwinner enjoyed a broad range of scientific interests.

But Deutsche Bank's management was understandably afraid of two circumstances: Hill's cheating on his pledge to curb competition, and a making public of the terms of the London agreements, which were in large part initiated to circumvent public and legal obstacles to the merger. Gwinner implored Mount Stephen to use his influence to stop Hill from "bragging" about the agreement and to stop new Great Northern expansion projects without consulting Adams. Mount Stephen seems to have been in agreement with his German colleague, even with the latter's request to have all stock transactions processed in Europe, far away from curious journalists who might report that the Great Northern group was buying up shares of the Northern Pacific from the syndicate.[108] Giving Hill control of the two lines would, however, relieve the bank of both its financial risk and the risk of embarrassment and an antitrust case should the details of the two lines' cooperation become public.

Hill's excitement about finally getting control of the Northern Pacific grew in the new year. For at least two years, this had been one of his primary business objectives. Even the London market, which had been lukewarm to Great

Northern, was showing signs of interest in combining the ownership of the two railroads. Seemingly unconvinced about the advisability of Hill gaining more control, Adams, in contrast to Gwinner, recommended offering some Deutsche Bank holdings in Northern Pacific shares to Morgan, James Stillman of National City Bank of New York, or William Rockefeller, younger brother of John D., as a counterweight to Hill. Nevertheless, in late January, the Hill group acquired 26 percent of the par value of the company's equity capital for a total price of $7.5 million. Hill's group now had in its hands, with the addition of this one transaction, 41.3 percent of Northern Pacific's common shares.[109]

Meanwhile, back in London, Mount Stephen, who professed ignorance of his friend's precise plans but faith in his overall abilities, was understandably getting nervous. He wrote that he was in basic agreement with Gwinner and Siemens that merging the activities of the two companies was the best hope for making the two lines economically viable. Hill had promised that he could wring an extra $2 million in operating profit out of the Northern Pacific and $1 million from the Great Northern.[110]

But the selection of management soon brought the investors into open conflict. Edwin Winter, the first president of the reorganized line, quit, apparently over Hill's interference. With the backing of the European investors, Hill wanted to give Winter orders.[111] For months the participants battled over who would succeed Winter. Hill pushed for Daniel Lamont, then secretary of war; Morgan for Charles Mellen, an experienced rail man, but one without his own property and not universally liked.[112] Morgan eventually got his way and Lamont took the post of vice president. Morgan was furious with Hill for driving out Winter, for whom Morgan had a lot of respect. He also never forgave Adams, who had supposedly divulged something to Winter that ostensibly had been the last straw for the proud, experienced rail man. Although the letters do not indicate what Adams said, his indiscretion contributed to Morgan's decision to remove Adams as chairman of the board in the fall, as will be discussed later.[113] Adams himself blamed Ives for poisoning his relationship to Morgan.[114] In May 1897, Ives was giving interviews to local newspapers, pushing his view of the Northern Pacific situation. The atmosphere of charge and counter-charge must have taxed everyone's nerves.[115]

Because of Hill's objection, Mellen was not installed in his new position until the end of the summer, a delay that must have created management havoc.[116] Born in 1851 in Lowell, Massachusetts, Mellen came to the Northern Pacific with twenty-eight years of experience in a variety of companies and functions, the most recent one being vice president of the New York–New Haven line. He had never worked in the West.[117] Judging from a letter to Adams, Mellen recognized that he had fallen into a snake pit without any rope to pull himself out. He turned to Adams for advice, a practice which he would continue for many years, even though his closest confidant remained Morgan's right-hand man, Charles Coster, until the latter's death.[118]

In summer 1897, Gwinner's concern about Northern Pacific's insufficient profitability made him and his colleagues in Berlin even more anxious to have the railroad interests in the West work closer together. Despite greater population density and a better class of freight trade, Northern Pacific's profitability was less than that of Great Northern, although it was acknowledged that some of this may have been due to a different accounting system. Gwinner had high hopes that this could be rectified. The line was in great shape. The receivers had made massive investments in improving the physical conditions of the track. Gwinner advised that uniform standards of equipment, tools, and methods could do much to further improve efficiency and that the company should move toward adopting the same procedures as the Great Northern, an acknowledged sector leader.[119]

Even within the structure of the Voting Trust, many new and old personal conflicts could not be resolved. Gwinner felt that Ives was trying to work mischief, but Morgan did not share his concern. In order to gain cooperation with Northern Pacific's prior board and owners, Morgan had granted them many concessions prior to their agreeing to the restructuring, including the promise to keep the railroad independent of Hill's interests, a promise of which some of Morgan's partners seem to have been unaware. The departure of some of Northern Pacific's management, ostensibly because of conflicts with the Hill group, also displeased the Morgan group.[120]

In June 1897, with a strong sense of urgency, Hill approached Mount Stephen with the charge that Morgan's intransigence was trying his patience and costing the property $2.5 million a year in violation of promises.[121] Stephen and Gwinner interceded to convince Hill to keep calm and give some consideration to Morgan's position – otherwise there would be a risk of furthering tensions, which would do neither side any good.[122] To Hill, Morgan's people were acting strangely. They were allowing sentiment and promises to Ives and the old stockholders to overshadow good business, that is, the structuring of the Northern Pacific to unite the financial interests of investors in both railroads by a share swap or dividend agreement.[123] According to Hill, Morgan, despite his faith in Hill's competence, had "sentimental notions in regard to what he calls 'an independent reorganization,' even though it was a great weight for the property to carry."[124]

Much came down to individuals and geographic distance. With most of the combatants very far away from the property – Hill was the only shareholder actually based in the Midwest – the selection of the railroad's president and board was obviously an issue of paramount importance. Despite their long association and earlier confidence, Morgan and his people came to detest Adams, a problem that concerned many of the parties. Morgan could not abide divided loyalties. He also disliked the idea of a strong presence on the board of directors that could interfere with his own control. Deutsche Bank wanted Hill to take over; Morgan, on the other hand, had control of the Voting Trust and wanted to keep it that way. Adams was left in the middle, between his employer and the most powerful banker in America, who insisted on having his own way, independent of any outside influence. According to Adams, Morgan was upset with Hill, Deutsche Bank, and Adams because they were all trying to undermine his control and reputation. Although Adams continued to maintain a close relationship with his German employers, his effectiveness for handling the problems of the line was diminished.[125] Denying that he ever promised Hill or anyone else control, Morgan recommitted himself to keeping the Trust going and dealing with the overall situation.[126]

How much of a role Hill played in undermining Adams is unclear. Although Hill claimed that he appreciated Adams as a "hard-working, clear-headed businessman," his conflicts with the Morgan people seemed to create too many frictions for the company to realize investor hopes. Hill predicted correctly that Morgan would try to get Adams off the board as quickly as possible, perhaps at the next annual meeting, despite the success of the restructuring and Adams' support in Berlin.[127] To Mount Stephen, Hill confided that replacing Adams would be a mistake and an injustice, but by August 1897, at least, Hill felt strongly that Adams' relationship with Morgan had become a significant liability to the Northern Pacific and to his own plans. Even though Hill personally had seen nothing of the lack of business integrity of which Morgan and his associates now charged Adams, the want of harmony between Adams and the Morgan group could do much harm.[128] Though all of this may have been a convenient ruse for Hill to get rid of someone who had opposed his plans, Mount Stephen, at least in his communication with Deutsche Bank, pledged to take no part in ousting Adams so long as Adams remained Deutsche Bank's representative. He would support Adams even if Hill recommended a change.[129]

For Deutsche Bank, these controversies posed special problems. Although most of the participants were far away, the German managers were the furthest. At the end of the nineteenth century the bank was going through its own expansion of its capital base and absorbing provincial banks with many branches, which required committing a substantial amount of its reserves.[130] The pressure to remove Adams mounted in spring and summer of 1897. Finally, Deutsche Bank caved in. In light of the completion of the reorganization and the recovery of much of the German investors' funds, in October 1897 the bank agreed that Adams would be re-elected chairman (as a face-saving gesture) and would then turn the appointment down.[131]

Although preserving the independence of the company was necessary for legal and other reasons, avoiding friction was also a high priority, and Adams was only part of the problem. Judging from Gwinner's comments, Morgan, though in principle in agreement with the merger as a long-term aim, was reticent to topple the "apple cart," that is, to allow much more integration between the two companies.

By 1897, German shareholders, in contrast, were also growing impatient. Though cautious about the regulatory obstacle, Deutsche Bank shared Hill's view that current management seemed to be an ongoing obstacle, because it refused to do all it could to work more closely with Hill, a view Mount Stephen also shared. The desire of all parties to achieve greater operating efficiency and avoid price wars required greater cooperation. Controlling the assets of both companies, although clearly in restraint of trade, might not run afoul of the Sherman Anti-Trust Act and might achieve nearly the same result. Increasingly, Hill saw the Voting Trust and the existing management as the root of the problem.[132] But even within the framework of the Voting Trust, management ran regulatory risks.[133]

Battle of the Titans

Despite a large block of stock and the tacit support of Deutsche Bank, Hill was unable to break Morgan's will for several years. Hill alternatively used the tactics of threatening to acquire more Northern Pacific shares or conversely to unload his block – and then acting on his threats. Conflicts with other lines and prosperous economic circumstances distracted the participants and relieved the sense of urgency. Although the Voting Trust was obviously no panacea for dissipating conflicts – and may have even caused a few – until the turn of the century Morgan categorically refused to find a legal means of casting it aside. The Voting Trust did lead to the realization of some coordination of business and operational improvements. In spite of the seemingly unending international battles over staffing, procedures, pricing, and financing, by 1899 both lines and their shareholders were doing much better.

In contrast to many accounts that present Hill and Morgan as working together, through much of the life of the Voting Trust the relationship was extremely tense. Taking instructions from Morgan's partner Charles Coster, the great turnaround specialist, seemed particularly irksome for Hill. He still resented Northern Pacific's intention to build lines that would compete with his own, in manifest contradiction to the intention of the London agreement and the interests of all parties. Hill was tired of waiting. In September 1898, he began to issue threats. If the situation were not rectified, he would unload his shares at the current inflated share price.[134]

Morgan provided him with a lengthy response (thirty pages, perhaps written by Coster) a week later. In this management tome, Morgan seemed like a cross between the "terror of Wall Street" and a scolding second-grade teacher. He dressed down Hill for a plethora of sins ranging from sloppy accounting to a faulty memory. Although recognizing that some major change was necessary, Morgan neither found Hill's ideas sufficient nor had he a plan of his own. He reminded Hill that even though the idea of Great Northern acquiring a controlling interest in Northern Pacific common stock was indeed the basis of the original London Agreement in June 1895, it had been found to be unworkable, leading to the independent reorganization in 1896. The reorganization called for the creation of a Voting Trust, into which both classes of shares would be put, so as to ensure that the Northern Pacific would remain independent of Great Northern influence. The second London Agreement (April 1896), signed by all the parties, began with a passage acknowledging that the first agreement was abrogated and that the reorganization would be accomplished with Northern Pacific remaining independent of Great Northern or any other interest.[135]

Morgan emphasized that on numerous occasions Hill had been told that he could not be allowed to control Northern Pacific during the period of the Voting Trust. Nevertheless, all parties had expressed the strongest desire that Northern

The Northern Pacific's competitive position vis-à-vis its competitors relied greatly on its access to the Pacific Ocean and the Great Lakes. The rival companies fought over building or leasing branch lines and the shortest routes to the sea. Both Villard and Hill dreamt of building a transportation empire that would include rails and shipping. This 1885 photo taken at the Willamette River near Portland, Oregon, shows elements of that potential network.

Pacific and Great Northern should "work in harmony." But "harmony" did not include Hill choosing the railroad's senior management. The company had been paying a dividend on preferred stock and would shortly begin paying a small dividend on common shares. Morgan flatly denied Hill's charge that the Northern Pacific was building lines that would injure his interests.[136] Although everyone agreed in principle that cooperation was essential, the squabbling over which lines should be built, who was trying to undermine whom, and how long the Voting Trust should remain in force continued for well over a year.

Unable to attain the control he wanted, Hill's relations with the Northern Pacific managers and others deteriorated in the late fall of 1898. It was an open secret that there was "great bitterness" between Morgan's group, in particular Coster, and Hill. Although Adams hoped to avoid being drawn into the controversy and to be able to complete the tasks Deutsche Bank had set out for him, he also believed that a contest between the House of Morgan and Hill, the two interests most deeply concerned, was inevitable. Coster charged that the Great Northern people were using newspapers to further their attacks. Adams received information from sources he considered reliable that Hill was even less "controllable" than ever, even enlisting politicians to support his ideas about the so-called overcapitalization of and reduction of dividends at the Northern Pacific. Adams concluded that "Mr. Hill will not rest quietly, attending to his own business, but will pursue his attacks until he obtains control of the Northern Pacific, or as some express it, 'goes to the Insane Asylum.'"[137] At the very least, the atmosphere of jealousy and suspicion that prevailed between the two railroads' managements, if left unchecked, would breed disaster for both.[138] Though Mount Stephen continued to defend Hill, many of the main parties, including Deutsche Bank, must have been very frustrated by trying to understand and manage the situation from such long distances.[139]

In defense of the Voting Trust, Adams, who still represented Deutsche Bank's interests even after his "retirement" as chairman of the Northern Pacific board, argued that American public opinion desired it as a means of maintaining the independence of rail lines, in compliance with the Supreme Court decision, an odd point of view considering how the two lines were "restraining trade." Its abolition would be a breach of faith, especially toward Northern Pacific securities holders, who counted on it lasting for the prescribed five years (until December 1, 1901) as a buffer against competitive rail lines having influence on the profitability of the Northern Pacific through aggressive pricing. Adams reported, probably quite correctly, that Hill had never accepted this and had admitted as much to Adams. Hill was relentless and willing to litigate or push for legislative changes to alter the arrangement; Adams believed, however, that this would not only be fruitless, but it also would poison any chances of the lines working together in an amiable fashion. According to Adams, Hill had even resorted to a new, unscrupulous tactic: adverse press and Northern Pacific stock manipulation to pressure Morgan in hopes of getting his way. All of this had resulted in a greater intensity of feeling among all the parties, which the London investors, who were friends of Hill, advised could only be resolved by the parties committing themselves to surrendering control to Hill, a solution that Adams still believed impractical. By this time, the two seemed to have had a very tense personal relationship. Hill had stopped calling on Adams. Moreover, the two great magnates, Hill and Morgan, had drawn a line in the sand. The issue had become personal, not business.[140]

Adams tried to maintain a balanced take on the personnel situation. He found Mellen at times overly ambitious and a little headstrong, but quite capable. Mellen's unrest, about which Adams often reported, came from his desire to expand the Northern Pacific. As someone who had studied railroads for a long time, Mellen, like Hill, felt strongly that in the next few years larger rail systems had to be developed. Companies with fifteen thousand miles or less could not continue to exist, because there were too many fixed costs that could not be absorbed. The Northern Pacific not only had to shorten its lines and get a western outlet, it also had to combine with lines east of it, such as the St. Paul company, which was controlled by William Rockefeller and his family associates. Mellen was in a rough position. Appointed by Morgan and approved by Hill, Adams reported that within two weeks Hill's brother publicly expressed his contempt for Mellen, shortly after assuring the Morgan group that the Hill group trusted him.[141] Mellen had left his family in New Haven, Connecticut, to take the position based in St. Paul, where he lived in a hotel, without many social connections. The support from his directors, reflecting Hill's influence, was not unanimous. In particular the support of Morgan, upon whom Mellen was also dependent for future assignments, was crucial. On many matters Mellen's hands were tied. Nothing was brought to the board without Coster's prior approval and many of the normal administrative functions, such as finance, were taken out of Mellen's control by him.[142]

But in winter 1898–99, some of the pressure was taken off. Convinced that the unification of the Northern Pacific and Great Northern had ceased to be a practical alternative, Hill's friends sold their Northern Pacific common stocks, while conserving their holdings in preferred. Adams' relations with Morgan improved, but Gwinner decided that for important matters he would address the Morgan people directly, in hopes of "sparing their jealousy," which might have been the root cause of the Morgan hostility to Adams.[143] Adams ostensibly approved this decision on condition that in affairs of mutual interest, including problems with Hill, Coster should submit matters to him for revision and advice.[144]

For the moment, Hill bowed to the bankers' preferences. But pursuing the strategy laid out in the London Agreement was even more critical to him now than before. The two companies effectively controlled all the rail lines in seven large and rapidly developing northwestern American states. "There is no such opportunity elsewhere to secure the permanent protection, security, and advantages which are offered here."[145]

By 1899, the Northern Pacific was doing very well in some regions in its competition with the Great Northern.[146] However, a month after Adams reported the good news about volumes, a new rate war broke out, once again putting at risk the progress and profits of the Great Northern and Northern Pacific.[147] According to Mellen, since January 1, Hill had cut his rates to try to divert mail business from Northern Pacific to the Great Northern. Though unnecessary, Mellen found that the rate reductions had actually increased passenger travel and more general rail usage, off-setting the price reduction.[148]

Hill's own enthusiasm for the unification of the companies was also temporarily dampened by other factors. Favorable state rate decisions, higher profits, and the rise in company share prices also contributed to delaying the decision about the merger until after the turn of the century. Despite higher capital expenditures, Northern Pacific paid higher dividends. Nevertheless, Gwinner feared that the Hill group would always try to underprice their Northern Pacific shares in whatever new equity conversion structure was suggested.[149] New disputes lay beneath the surface.

The story of the attempts to unite the western lines and Deutsche Bank's involvement was not finished. Although both railroads were doing better, nearly everyone hoped that they would do better still. Mount Stephen reported to Gwinner that, during a twelve-hour walk with Hill, the railroad magnate could talk of nothing else. He was "full to the brim" with hope. To accurately evaluate his plans required a great deal of knowledge of the terrain, which many of the investors did not have. According to Mount Stephen, "permanent peace and harmony will never be attained until the two properties are practically owned by one and the same proprietary, in short unification," as Siemens had been the first to point out five years earlier. Mount Stephen felt strongly that Hill's reputation as a railway administrator was well earned and that he would put the line into permanent prosperity.[150] In December 1900, Mount Stephen, whose faith in Hill as the premier railway administrator of his generation was undiminished, personally held 6,000 shares of Northern Pacific common and 1,000 preferred, and intended to add to his holdings when he knew more about the personnel changes at the House of Morgan and about Morgan's new willingness to see the dissolution of the Voting Trust.[151]

Somewhere around this time Deutsche Bank seems to have lost a good deal of patience with the personalities in the Northwest and with some aspects of America's distinctive form of regulation. At the very least, the bank was drawn to other interests. In 1901, the Northern Pacific was once again the object of an acquisition battle, this time between the Union Pacific and, amazingly, a Hill-Morgan group. At the very least, the bank was happy to take on the role of spectator as some of the giants of American finance battled American regulators to solve the Northern Pacific dilemma.

5

The Fallout

> We do not have the time in Germany to repeat all the developmental steps of the U.S. and England. We can spare ourselves many difficulties by carefully following the development in the United States. . . .
>
> Fritz Mezger, in *Der Wirtschaftsprüfer*, May 31, 1932.

Introduction

The persistence of management and governance disputes and the inability of the parties to find a long-term solution that they perceived to be both financially in their interests and acceptable to regulators took a heavy toll on many of the participants. Many investors had become frustrated with the line's inability to deal with its core problems. By 1901, the bank and its customers had significantly reduced their exposure.[1] At times, only Deutsche Bank's loyalty to Morgan based on his commitment to his partners kept the Germans involved at all.[2]

The experience with the Northern Pacific was critical to Deutsche Bank's relationship to American markets. Although Deutsche Bank did not lose its interest in U.S. investment, it and Germans in general approached new deals with more caution. Moreover, by the end of Deutsche Bank's intense involvement with the line, the actions of the participants dealing with the effects of the bankruptcy had a profound impact on both American and German financial regulations and business practice.

The Human Toll

The reorganization made enormous demands on those involved. In March 1900, Charles Coster, Morgan's loyal lieutenant and able railroad expert who had taken over as chairman of the board of the Northern Pacific, died at age forty-seven. Some said he had worked himself to death. Although the Northern Pacific was probably one of the more complicated dossiers he handled for the House of Morgan, thanks to Morgan's system of Voting Trusts he sat on forty-eight other corporate boards.[3] According to Adams, whose office was a few doors down from the House of Morgan and who had frequent, albeit not always pleasant visits there, Coster's presence would be sorely missed. Morgan had grown quite dependent on Coster's tireless efforts, and studious and intuitive judgment. Morgan could not conceal his grief at losing his most trusted colleague.[4]

Wall Street circa 1895. On the left is Morgan's headquarters. On the right (far corner) is the site of Bankers Trust's first building. The structure on the corner was demolished to put up Bankers Trust's first headquarters.

Coster's successor, Robert Bacon, fared little better. Soon after taking over Coster's duties, his nerves became too shot to continue working. On doctor's orders he retired from banking, and later picked up a less pressured career in government that included roles as secretary of state and ambassador to France.[5] Apparently, working for the president of the United States was less taxing than a position with Morgan. The great toll it took was perhaps, too, an indication of the short supply of top management.

Villard followed Coster seven months later, dying in bed of an apoplectic stroke after a long series of illnesses.[6] Deutsche Bank's relationship with Villard had been effectively at an end for many years, although he still had a few occasional business contacts with the bank.[7] Ever modest, in his autobiography, he claimed to have saved all the money of all the investors who had hung on until 1900 through his cool handling of the bankruptcy and by recommending Adams.[8] It is clear that he protected himself against the bankruptcy and profited from the reorganization. Much of the debt owed by the Northern Pacific was owed to him or his companies. According to his great-granddaughter, fearing a collapse after the Silver Act he had taken steps to protect his own finances, a fact that had outraged Siemens.[9] First tried for fraud and then sued for malfeasance, after a few years he escaped all legal punishment.[10]

Much of his remaining life was devoted to writing his memoirs, a two-volume work that he never completed, 90 percent of which is devoted to his prebusiness early life as a journalist. His Horatio Alger life left legacies in many arenas. For a while, he had been a trusted member of two societies, one of the main links between German and American finance, and an icon of the hopes and aspirations shared by the two countries. He died a symbol of America's poor financial regulation and governance, and Germany's difficulty in assessing economic opportunities from afar.

His public persona was full of contradictions. Many contemporaries appreciated his contribution to the development of the Northwest and institutions such as Harvard. He also made large donations to other universities such as Washington, Oregon, and Columbia, as well as to German charities. He shared with his friend Edison both deafness to certain kinds of criticism and the standard sort, as well as a stubborn faith in progress. His ideas lived on in the *Evening Post*, which he had bought and was run by his surviving son. Shocked by the "war-racket" that got the United States into the Spanish-American War, he and his wife preferred to stay in Europe until the peace treaty was signed.[11] Siemens felt personally betrayed by what he characterized as Villard's regular disregard of commitments he had made to his "friend." Villard's passion for private and public self-promotion seemed to have a much higher priority than his duty to his clients.

Siemens died a year later, a few days after his sixty-second birthday. Some said that neither he nor Villard had ever fully recovered from Northern Pacific's collapse and the blow that it was to their reputations. Long before he had realized that much of his whole legacy was bound up with the Northern Pacific, other U.S. investments, and, above all, with his inability to control Villard. But his faith in the potential of America and the money that could be made there was undiminished. As the Northern Pacific crisis unfolded he wrote, "One does not need to lose money here, and in the next three years, it will be lying on the streets for the taking. One just needs the right people."[12] He urged his colleagues not to fear the future but rather recognize how the bank had erred in the past. Although the lost funds would be made up, Villard was "an awful person."[13] Perhaps Siemens' best consolation for the mistakes he and Deutsche Bank had made during Villard's tenure was the recognition that Villard had taken in many who were better able to judge affairs in the United States than Siemens.[14] In any case, at Deutsche Bank, too, some shift in personnel was called for. In 1894, Arthur Gwinner joined Deutsche Bank and took much responsibility for U.S. business, traveling there in 1896. For some at the bank, his attention to detail was as necessary a change as the one from Villard to Adams.

New Ownership Structures and Alliances

At times, when the conflicts between Hill and the Northern Pacific management were particularly intense, the investors turned to more radical – that is, desperate – ownership structures. Some had even suggested forming a British holding company for the two lines, effectively transferring ownership out of the country to avoid regulation against combining the two lines. Adams and Gwinner seemed to think that the many great legal and other obstacles to the move would be insurmountable.[15] By the end of April 1900, perhaps because of Coster's death, Morgan at last resolved to disband the Voting Trust. Gwinner, for his part, could not conceal his frustration at having no workable solution to the Northern Pacific's conflicts.[16] Mellen and the other managers feared that the dissolution of the Voting Trust would remove the last buffer against Hill.[17]

But in a series of meetings during January 1900, the partners hatched a new scheme with a new structure, Northern Securities. The new plan did not resolve all the regulatory and personal issues – indeed it created some new ones. But it did attempt to eliminate the incentives for overbuilding and underpricing, while giving the lines better access to the Pacific. They used Villard's old company, the Oregon Railway & Navigation Company, whose complex ownership structure and conflicting agreements complicated transport matters in the whole region, to achieve that end. Unfortunately, the agreement required close continued cooperation with Hill's longtime rival, E. H. Harriman, and the agreement of U.S. regulators.[18]

Even when the main characters reached agreement, there were still many other powerful actors who needed convincing. William Rockefeller and the Vanderbilt family, for example, held big blocks of shares in the lines. Only a consolidation of the properties through individual holdings, as opposed to corporate consolidation – as Morgan had done with the Pennsylvania line – would work. Any attempt by the Great Northern to acquire the Northern Pacific, for example, would result in the legislature taking away any profit that could be realized. Morgan felt strongly that settlement of the Oregon line problem was key to an overall settlement and stressed that Hill would have to find a way to give the other participants Great Northern stock.[19]

The "unification" occurred in December 1901 in a way that was not contemplated when Siemens had first floated the idea in 1894. The Northern Securities Company was a holding company for the shares of the four major western rail lines. Its intention was not only to resolve the conflicts between the Great Northern and Northern Pacific and link all the transcontinental railroads but also to build a worldwide transportation network. Its investors included bankers and some of the most important rail men of the era, such as Hill and Harriman who had dominated the restructuring of Western railroading around the turn of the century.[20] Created two months after McKinley's death, Northern Securities quickly ran afoul of state and federal regulators.

Deutsche Bank kept its distance. Although Deutsche Bank had little direct interest, both Gwinner and Adams made use of insider information – information Gwinner had promised not to share with anyone – to buy shares.[21] Deutsche Bank rejected, however, a $10 million investment in the new company and was particularly adamant about not tying up any amount for a long period.[22] The German group had many concerns. Adams was still worried about the treatment of minority shareholders, and he feared that he was not getting full information. Hopefully Morgan would keep Gwinner better informed.[23] Gwinner wrote to Adams, clairvoyantly and somewhat tongue in cheek: "The Northern Pacific Board seems to be arranged on the happy family principle. Wonder whether they will eat each other."[24] After years of rancor with Hill, many of the Northern Pacific managers began to jump ship during the summer of 1901.[25]

But in a climate of stupendous combinations, even Adams started to become somewhat more optimistic about combining the interests of the three main disputing lines and proposed his own ideas about how it might be accomplished using purchases of noncompeting, but related, lines.[26] All this was set against the background of "phenomenal" Northern Pacific earnings in the summer of 1901 and confirmation of Hill's control of the line. Harriman, Morgan, and Hill seemed to have agreed to terms that allowed Morgan to name the present board and redeem the preferred stock with common.[27] According to Gwinner, by this time Deutsche Bank's relations with the Hill faction had ceased.[28] He added a favorable assessment of Hill balanced by an equally condemning one of Morgan:

> I ought to say that we can hardly complain of Mr. Hill's dealings towards us. In fact, if we had accepted the many overtures for an alliance which he made us in the course of the last few years, we would have fared better than by keeping faith unto Mr. Morgan, who ignored us upon all occasions. You will have heard possibly of the latest German philosopher Friedrich Nietzsche, who died in a lunatic asylum last year and in my judgment was crazy all his life. In one of his much-read and much-quoted books he puts forward, as a consummation to be wished, the development of man into the "Uebermensch," ignoring good and bad. Mr. Morgan seems to be well on his way towards Nietzsche's ideal.[29]

Although by this time Deutsche Bank's financial interests in Northern Pacific had diminished greatly, as late as October 1901, Deutsche Bank still held 45,501 preferred and 20 Northern Pacific common shares in its own name.[30] Mistrust among the banks was evident. Reports surfaced that Deutsche Bank had accused Morgan of treachery in its sale of shares to the Union Pacific interests (Harriman).[31] Adams no longer could count on his good relationship with Mellen, or Mellen's with Coster, to ensure that Deutsche Bank was always well informed.

The magnitude of the deal that took shape in the fall of 1901 captured a lot of public interest and illustrated Morgan's duplicity. Sales were being negotiated at above market prices by Morgan, who had used Adams and Deutsche Bank to fight battles with Hill, and other banking houses to aid Hill's creation of Northern Securities. Even Harriman stood to gain personal profits of around $20 million – once the Northern Securities had a market, a development that did not come easily – for his concession securing the rights to the international boundary. Hill became so rich and so confident, he even moved to New York. With Morgan's financial interest reduced, he positioned himself as arbiter for the competing interests to keep harmony on the boards he created. Adams believed that the deal would prompt important litigation, a prophecy that would come true. Adams was still of the conviction that Hill had already caused and would cause even more damage to the Northern Pacific property. Many of those who had defended its independence would be most hurt.[32] Certainly, Morgan and Hill were not hurt. Morgan's profits, helped by Northern Pacific, were $22 million, $12 million more than the year before. Hill's son stated that his father had just distributed $25 million among his four children.[33]

Fears of Morgan, even among shareholders, persisted well into the new century. In 1903, Adams reported that many investors in New York believed, with much reason, that the venerable banker deliberately attempted to unload comparatively worthless shares at high prices upon the unsuspecting public, bringing the so-called Morgan securities into further disfavor. "Many of those who have entertained great admiration for the energy, courage, ability and the breadth-of-view of Morgan, view this development with sincere regret, as likely to affect the influence that has so often been exerted for the highest national good in so many ways."[34]

The Regulatory Reactions

The Northern Securities party did not last long. President Theodore Roosevelt decided to make an example of the new holding company and pushed for fast-tracking the case right to the Supreme Court, which decided in March 1904 by a slim margin of five to four that the company had violated the law and should be divided.[35] The manner of dissolution was complicated and required extensive negotiation, the details of which are beyond the scope of this book.[36]

Gwinner understood why the Supreme Court had rejected the Northern Securities Company. Although the decision had strange aspects, according to Gwinner, America "will not stand the concentration of what the people consider an exaggerated power in the hands of a few, and a nation may violate and act its own laws, particularly in a republic [sic]."[37] Nevertheless, the case of Northern Securities was one of the first in which the Supreme Court battled over what kinds of business consolidations, which industrial development seemed to demand, best combined economic efficiency with social good. America was just beginning to tackle a problem that went to the heart of two American core values: relatively unconstrained competition and industrial efficiency. Whereas the coordination needs of large commercial and transportation undertakings seemed to require greater internalization of activities, the legislature and courts still had not determined acceptable principles for judging them. Neither cartels, nor trusts, nor even enormous consolidated companies fit into America's picture of socially useful competition. The ambivalence of American regulators and their constituencies augmented Deutsche Bank's perception of political risk in the United States. In contrast, the organizers of Northern Securities were unmindful of public concern. They understood business better than politics. Unlike their German colleagues, they seemed to have little respect for the social role of business.

The failure of the reorganization, moreover, to address many ongoing operational and regulatory issues reinforced fears in Europe that America's control of its economic system was not sufficiently mature. Not only were many Americans unable to understand the benefits of disciplined government planning in the growth of rail service, as argued by Colleen Dunlavy about an earlier era,[38] they were ambivalent about which level of government should make determinations concerning bankruptcy, accounting, and consolidation rules. The ambivalence added to the political risk of the world's largest economy. For many decades, Americans would not only argue about what controls were necessary, but who should be empowered to make them. As great as growth was, for most observers this regulatory paralysis retarded the creation of a truly national market and led to higher risk premiums for investors.[39] However, the experiences of the 1890s spurred reforms to make some effort to tighten U.S. regulation. Although the first permanent independent federal agency, the Interstate Commerce Commission, was established in 1887, a series of court cases further clarified its role and gave the commission more teeth. It benefited users but contributed to a decline in the quality of railroad equipment. Its activities had been supported even by owners of lines anxious to prevent ruinous competition. The benefits of sensible regulation were becoming clearer in many areas.[40] The Republican victory in 1896 led directly to legislation that effectively ended the debate about silver and gold. Many Republicans and Democrats, moreover, saw the utility of a central bank.

The crisis with the Northern Pacific had forced Deutsche Bank to step up its involvement with U.S. investments and also to augment its efforts to reduce risk. With Northern Pacific's reorganization and the U.S. government's financial crisis in the mid-1890s, the United States's regulatory environment must have been "dead center on the radar screens" of Deutsche Bank executives. The reader must remember that part of the quick decline of the Northern Pacific was caused by the illiquidity of American capital markets. Some of the decisions made by the line were predicated on the confidence of managers in their ability to tap into strong capital markets to get the line through hard times. The abrupt changes – from highly liquid to highly illiquid – hurt the railroad by creating an economical environment at times too anxious to lend and at times too stingy. The issue of American monetary discipline was so important for German investment into the United States that Villard threw himself into Grover Cleveland's 1892 presidential campaign, raising millions of Dollars and attempting to influence much of the twelve-and-a-half-million-strong German-American community to vote for Cleveland, a Democrat who strongly supported the Gold Standard.

The mid-1890s seemed to be a regulatory turning point for the United States. The series of crises awoke many to the contradiction between America's economic maturity and regulatory adolescence. Momentum gathered among reformers to find some reconciliation between American fears of concentrating power and public control of private abuses, a contradiction Germans such as Siemens found baffling.

In the mid-1890s Deutsche Bank turned its attention to marketing U.S. government gold bonds in Europe, which had the advantage of both shoring up the American financial system and being easier to sell to suddenly more cautious European investors.[41] A syndicate led by Morgan in 1896 attempted to transact a private placement of $100 million in U.S. government debt to bolster America's sagging gold reserves, as Morgan had done a year before with the Rothschilds. Although the 1896 bond issue turned out to be smaller than planned and was sold at a public auction, Deutsche Bank took a large portion of the securities, effectively replacing the Rothschilds as the distributor in Europe. The mid-1890s also marked the end of what some, especially contemporaries, have described as the Great Depression, a twenty-year period that stands out principally for falling commodity prices, corporate restructuring, and general instability. Resolution of some monetary and regulatory problems, as well as tariffs, unfortunately, helped pave the way for growth and price increases in many vibrant, young business sectors.[42]

Deutsche Bank's effort to improve transparency and its own control of American financial information had profound effects on the development of German accountancy. Paradoxically, the Treuhand, a Deutsche Bank subsidiary that after 1893, ran audits and helped reorganize companies in financial distress, was also one of the first beneficiaries, and then casualties of the railroad crisis. Formed in 1890 to help introduce American shares in Europe by overcoming regulatory impediments in Germany (minimal nominal value of shares, for example) and alleviate worries about U.S. capital market weaknesses,[43] the Treuhand was originally conceived as a kind of trust company, which would sell its own debt and invest the proceeds in American securities. Management quickly determined that the risks of future investment in this kind of mutual fund were too high. The Treuhand's first name reflected the original mission, Deutsch-Amerikanische Treuhand-Gesellschaft (German-American Trust Company). Based on information provided in part by Villard, it took its original model from the London & New York Investment Corporation, which helped bring companies to capital market by guaranteeing a price for their securities on exchanges, in much the same way as underwriters do today for an all-in launch of securities. The British investment company earned healthy commissions and reimbursement for expenses, allowing for very high dividends at times.[44] One of Treuhand's first projects – and controversies – also came from Villard: the purchase of $5 million in Edison General Electric stock and bonds, funded by a Treuhand bond.[45]

The Treuhand's relationship to Deutsche Bank was obviously very close. In fact, it was at times hard to separate the two, a fact that would play an important role in the development of the German accounting profession.[46] As the Northern Pacific unraveled, Deutsche Bank turned the Treuhand into a company for reviewing financial statements, especially troubled foreign firms. By the turn of the century, the Treuhand played a central role in Germany's nascent audit sector. In contrast to the United States, where banks were forbidden to offer this service, banks in Germany were encouraged to take on this function as an almost natural add-on to their supervisory board responsibilities. The special role of banks in a broad range of corporate governance functions became one of the hallmarks of the German economic system for the next hundred years. In contrast to the United States, Germany increasingly looked to bankers to oversee companies and, perhaps more importantly, capital markets.[47]

Investor Impact

It is not clear how much money Deutsche Bank made or lost with its Northern Pacific experience, but an undated memo gives us some indication. According to the calculations, its share of the holding of various Northern Pacific securities had a market value of $10.3 million, for which it paid $7.2 million, leaving a book profit of $3.1 million. The worksheet indicates that if Hill and others exercised their options, most of the book profit would be transformed into cash, implying that there were some concerns about the marketability of the securities held.[48] Clearly, the profit for the syndicate lay in part in buying up the outstanding old securities (up to $45 million worth) and trading them for new securities with a higher value. Adams felt very confident that the new securities would trade well.

In 1901, with Adams gone from the Northern Pacific board, the bank no longer had a strong link through which it would receive direct information about profits and other matters.[49] But by then the bank's direct financial interest had become much smaller. As early as spring 1897, Deutsche Bank had sold some of its own holding of Northern Pacific preferred stock to facilitate Hill's control at a price that Siemens still felt was below its intrinsic value.[50] Those investors who stayed with the company until 1901 made large gains. According to Deutsche Bank's annual report for that year, German investors had made $15 million from their investment in the Northern Pacific, but little indication is given about how and from what starting point this calculation was made.[51] Nevertheless, the Northern Pacific continued to create problems and opportunities for Deutsche Bank even well into the interwar period. (See Section II.)

Despite all the conflicts, the reorganization itself appeared to be a resounding success for the company. From 1896 to 1900, the rail company had increased its mileage by approximately 33 percent and its equipment by over 38 percent. It had sold nearly 12 million acres of land during the same period. Profits had increased by 50 percent, working capital had quadrupled, and cash assets were just under $35 million. By every operating measurement – for example, freight carried by mile and earnings per mile – there was vast improvement.[52] With a good deal of pride, the trustees recounted the progress made by the rail line. The company had already declared thirteen dividends on preferred shares. Even a 4 percent dividend on par value common was expected. Significant improvements had been made to the quality of the line. Utilization of capacity had dramatically improved. Land sales and prices increased, which was particularly important to bondholders whose payments were guaranteed by the land and who had been particularly threatened by the soft land market in the mid-1890s.[53]

More importantly for my story, the experience with Northern Pacific was a turning point for Deutsche Bank in its investment strategies in the United States. By 1901, Deutsche Bank had few American securities left on its own books, but it seemed to have had a positive enough reaction to the final outcome of the reorganization process that it and Germany had an appetite for more. Gwinner reported that, during the past few years, the bank itself had earned 12 million Marks from its American activities, but here, too, he provided no breakdown of how this was calculated and whether it included business passed on to related companies or how much of its own capital had been tied up.[54] Two things were clear, though: The results would have been very different if calculated in 1894, and Deutsche Bank had no intention of tying up such sums itself in the United States for the foreseeable future.[55]

By and large – with the possible exception of Morgan and Deutsche Bank – the parties remained on good terms. Hill wrote Gwinner in 1908, praising the German economy and its regulation and expressing his hope to visit him in Berlin during an upcoming trip to Europe.[56] Gwinner was still in many respects equally enthusiastic about America and Hill. Returning the compliment in 1910, as a member of the Prussian House of Lords, and in a manner that would surprise many observers, then and now, including Hill, he argued that American rail management should be the model for Germany.[57]

By 1905 those investors who had been patient received a handsome gain. Northern Pacific's common was selling at twice its par value and the company's bonds were doing well. Gwinner regretted that he personally had not held on to Northern Pacific shares. But the saga was not over.[58] Deutsche Bank continued to follow the internal and external conflicts through the end of the decade.[59]

In 1906, Hill had a new plan for resolving the problems on the plains. The Great Northern would pay from $40 to 50 million for the Northern Pacific's interest in the Chicago Burlington line. That holding would be consolidated into the Great Northern. Hill promised gains of approximately 400 percent for Great Northern and Northern Pacific shareholders if Great Northern could capitalize on an agreement with United States Steel for the shipment of Minnesota ore.[60]

In reality, however, the Northern Pacific's fundamental problems had changed little. In 1912, Moody's concluded that Northern Pacific had once again over-invested and was poorly positioned to weather the region's downturn in economic activity. Moreover, according to Moody's, most observers believed that Hill still shifted business between the Great Northern and Northern Pacific as he liked. As he made his reputation with the former, it was with the former that he was most personally attached. The Great Northern was still likely to get the better choice of business.[61]

Deutsche Bank's Investment Strategies

Northern Pacific was a seminal experience for Deutsche Bank. Perhaps the saddest aspect of the whole story is what it said about the characters of many of the people involved. To be sure, there were some examples of gentlemanly behavior – for example, when Adams' tenure as chairman became untenable, Siemens insisted that he be re-elected and allowed to resign[62] – but bitter disputes among many of the participants before and after the final reorganization agreement were more the rule and revealed high levels of animosity and unbridled ambition.[63] After the Northern Pacific saga, the reliability and good character of those with whom they worked played an even greater role in the investment analyses of Deutsche Bank managers. Adams' letter accepting his appointment with Deutsche Bank is revealing. Although he had many independent financial interests, Adams pledged above all to keep Deutsche Bank informed about any of his business that might conflict with theirs.[64]

The story also gives a sad indication of how bad the control system in America was at the turn of the last century. Much has been said in favor of the close working relationships that existed between banks and their clients. Nevertheless, if half of the accusations leveled after the company's collapse were true, many banks viewed "their special relationship" as a grab bag of commission income. It seems that all concerned, including Ives -- who himself profited from land sales – bemoaned the absence of control over the company's properties. Villard's "confession" of his own case provides examples of how bank representatives almost seemed to be competing with each other in their generosity at distributing business and commissions. According to Villard, on some new issues the banks were earning profits of 10 percent of the value of the bonds.[65] If Deutsche Bank ever had this disposition toward one of its clients, the bankruptcy disabused the Germans of anything so foolhardy for a long time.

What remains a mystery is the role of Villard in North American Company, a holding entity he created and which Deutsche Bank helped finance. Villard remained as president for a time. As discussed, shares of Oregon & Transcontinental had been exchanged for those of North American Company, which borrowed to invest in other companies. It used the assets of companies that it controlled to borrow further. On two occasions, it could not make payments and turned to Deutsche Bank for further financing. Among its holdings was a large packet of Northern Pacific common shares.[66] It is unclear what happened to that ownership interest – though it was probably restructured in the 1896 reorganization – but soon after Villard's death, several of the parties seemed to expand their holdings. This holding had been the centerpiece of Villard's personal investments and railroad consolidation strategy, but it was threatened by the Sherman Anti-Trust Act.[67] The holding must also have been involved in the 1901 restructuring.[68] According to one source in 1901, it still held one-third of Northern Pacific stock and over half of the Navigation Company.[69]

The experience with the Northern Pacific reshaped Deutsche Bank's attitude about risks and rewards in the United States, and fundamentally about structuring its activities. Henceforth, it would avoid tying up large amounts of capital there, as was the case with Villard, and large U.S. holding companies like North American Company, which ostensibly diversified their investments while making a market for securities through leverage. The bank worked with numerous companies, concentrating less on just one or a few interconnected firms, while at the same time diversifying its client services.

Deutsche Bank had learned, too, that these structures ran the risk that no one was "watching the store," as Villard so amply proved. Control required a controller. Henceforth, Deutsche Bank would focus on assembling a group of investors to make substantial, but often not controlling, investments in companies or sectors (pools and syndicates). Although it – and also its managers – would hold some of these securities, its primary business would be marketing them in Europe, especially Germany, and giving advice much like a modern investment bank. Its success in helping work out the Northern Pacific's problems combined with the upturn in the United States and world economies reinforced its faith in the value of cross-border business. As illustrated in the next Chapter, despite the difficulties, its enthusiasm for American securities remained strong.

The bank found some aspects of the experience and its aftermath reassuring. In spite of America's inconsistent and different views about corporate consolidation, there were many signs that a worldwide consensus around regulatory reforms was developing. Starting in the 1890s, the opinions of American progressives and businesspeople alike, along with their conservative and liberal counterparts in Germany, seemed to be coalescing around policies designed to find a more workable, happy medium between *laissez-faire* capitalism and antimodern populism. In part because of the nagging economic crises, resistance to government serving as a counterweight to markets and large business interests gathered momentum.[70] Ironically, in contrast to the quote that introduces this Chapter, before World War I, for many in the United States and Germany, Rhine capitalism was viewed as a paragon of regulatory virtue and American a wastrel cousin. For the time being, like capital, the flow of reform ideas moved much more from East to West.

6

Other Transportation and Commercial Investments

> My thoughts have been frequently following you across your continent on the track I so well remember.
>
> Gwinner to Adams, July 1, 1898, HADB, A45.

Introduction

Although Deutsche Bank changed for the most part its strategy for buying, selling, and controlling U.S. investments, it continued to focus on transportation and electrification. The opportunities were too enticing. Between 1900 and 1913, U.S. per capita income grew in real terms by just under 30 percent, nearly 50 percent faster than Germany's. Railroad construction and productivity slowed but was still substantial. Other sectors such as machinery and chemicals picked up the slack.[1] Although Adams and Deutsche Bank sometimes took an active role in the management of these companies, none of these investments entailed anywhere near a commitment of time and capital comparable with the Northern Pacific.

The ups and downs of the Northern Pacific only temporarily quelled Deutsche Bank's and Germany's enthusiasm for American railroads. Their long-term interest in railroad investment seemed insatiable. Deprived of virtually all opportunity to invest in private German railroad securities by the turn of the century, German investors turned to foreign "iron horse" projects. Between 1876 and 1890, Bismarck's nationalization policy had put 2.8 billion Mark of cash in the hands of former owners of German railroad common stock,[2] an amount equal to over 20 percent of the nominal value of shares traded in Germany in 1902. Although Deutsche Bank's reach in railroad investment stretched both considerably east and west of its base in Berlin, America's needs for capital in this sector were vast compared with the rest of the world's.[3] With America's vast spaces, agricultural and mining potential, and the great influx of immigrants anxious to spread out from eastern cities, railroads had a greater social, economic, and political impact there than in any other country in the world.[4]

Deutsche Bank's interest in railroad securities shifted from investing itself to passing on securities, advice, or making secured loans. After the problems with the Northern Pacific, the bank seemed, at least with the vast majority of its American railroad and energy securities, more of an investment bank in the modern, Anglophone sense. Deutsche Bank more often than not would underwrite securities, that is, buy them up for a short period for the purpose of selling them to other investors. It would only rarely try to exercise management control.

Fortunately, most of these railroad stories were far less complicated and far less dramatic than that of Northern Pacific, at least those that involved Deutsche Bank. During the twenty years following the reorganization of Northern Pacific, Deutsche Bank bought for its own or customer accounts securities of many famous American lines, concentrating on those railroads with low fixed costs and whose shareholder configuration would not lead to conflicts, especially conflicts of interest.[5] It is clear that financing rail lines was a lucrative business full of pitfalls, but Deutsche Bank's files about these investments, in some sense, may present a distorted picture of the risks and rewards. Companies in financial distress require more time and effort.

In the end, Deutsche Bank's difficulties in these investments were not so much a result of poor management or competition, but politics. Poor regulation inhibited consolidation and hindered effective control, while decreasing operation cash flows and maintenance. The railroad magnates – the Harrimans, Vanderbilts, Goulds, and Hills – seemed all too willing to oblige the bankers' desire to lend by building more, leading to more and more restructurings. The flows in American railroad regulation added to the lines' capital dependencies. As the sector and the country's economy passed from one "hurricane" to another, there was "considerable wreckage to be cleared away."[6] The only way to secure foundations was to pull down (liquidate and consolidate) endangered structures,[7] a step for which Americans were ill-prepared. Despite its continued willingness to invest, Deutsche Bank's management was painfully aware of the magnitude of problems in the rail sector. The combination of increasing financial, management, and restructuring needs that they found in the rail sector was a booby-trapped gold mine for bankers.

However, Deutsche Bank had learned many valuable lessons from its Northern Pacific experience. As a report about the New York Central makes clear, for Deutsche Bank, company management was everything:

> This company continues to give evidence of a lack of direction by its directors and of an accumulation of problems that are best fitted in their complex character and magnitude to the solutions of a Harriman or a Hill than to those of a Vanderbilt. The company requires money, a large amount, and soon....
>
> By the unwillingness of the Vanderbilt interest to recognize the condition of the company, its requirements and the condition of the market, and by their lack of attention to the details of the situation, which would have enabled them to grasp these conditions two or three years ago, the company has gone drifting along with injury to its credit, depreciation of its securities and now the necessity of paying a higher rate of interest and of pledging its assets for new loans.[8]

Deutsche Bank concluded that staying away from the New York Central was a good idea.

These stories illustrate the variety of Deutsche Bank's activities in the United States, and how the bank had learned to eat the American pie in smaller, more easily digested morsels. Even before the collapse of the Northern Pacific, from time to time Germany's ability to absorb huge chunks of American issues became limited, forcing Deutsche Bank and Stern to look to other European markets to distribute American securities to avoid holding them for their own account.[9] Deutsche Bank did not want to repeat its experience with Northern Pacific, but despite its best efforts in this volatile sector, some repetition was probably inevitable.

The Baltimore and Ohio

In the case of the Baltimore and Ohio Railroad (B&O), Deutsche Bank's significant involvement seems to date from the railroad's emergence from bankruptcy instead of from the time preceding it. In comparison with the Northern Pacific, it was a minor undertaking. As was the case for many American railroads, bank syndicates and default were very much a part of the B&O's history.[10] But with demand for its securities high, the line launched many new issues toward the end of the nineteenth century and through the first four decades of the twentieth, making it a good and consistent customer for banking services.

Deutsche Bank played only a minor role in the Speyer-led syndicate, which led the B&O's 1898 restructuring.[11] Despite its financial difficulties and trouble with the Interstate Commerce Commission, by 1910 the B&O had more than doubled its rail mileage and revenues.[12] As early as 1903, B&O was once again seeking new financing.

Many German investors were safely out of their Northern Pacific holdings, and they seemed willing to take on more risk. One of the many important aspects of the 1903 launch was that it consisted of common shares, not the less risky preferred shares or debt.[13] Deutsche Bank, however, committed itself to only 10,000 common shares, less than 1 percent of the whole issue.[14] The shares were to be listed on the Berlin Stock Exchange. In fall 1903, Deutsche Bank sent one of its bright, young managers to work out the details of the listing.[15] With the German stock market seemingly ready to take on even speculative risks that fall, the bank was very hopeful for a successful launch.[16]

The B&O was the first of many other companies the bank intended to bring to European markets with the help of Speyer in New York.[17] Although the actual amount of Deutsche Bank's involvement was small, the issue had enormous symbolic importance. The B&O became the first American railroad since the Northern Pacific problems to be listed on the Berlin Stock Exchange. The railroad seemed to be an excellent candidate for this step. Coming to market at a fortunate time, it had the wind at its back.[18]

The issue was important to German capital markets and German-American relations. German capital markets had lost some of their international stature compared with other markets. Several German newspaper articles reported that the launch filled a vacuum for American rail stocks on the Berlin exchange. The

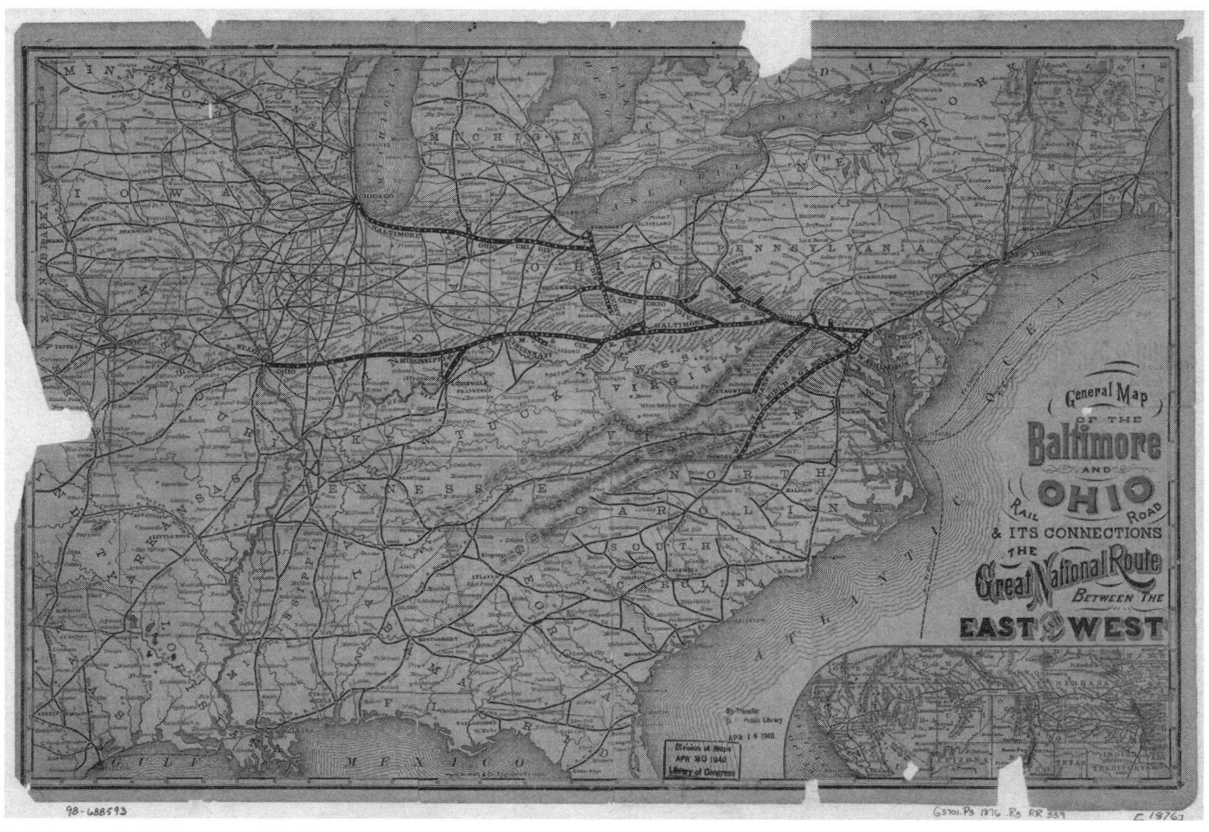

Baltimore & Ohio map. No date.

absence of American rail stock led to a loss of business with other European exchanges, especially London's.[19] Profitable arbitrage transactions necessary to maintaining prices were shifted away from Berlin, putting that market in an unfavorable position vis-à-vis competitors, primarily those in London. The listing served as an excellent indication of how important financial intermediaries like Deutsche Bank were to turn-of-the-century capital markets. Since the retirement of Northern Pacific preferred shares in 1902, only one North American railroad, the Canadian Pacific Railroad, was listed in Berlin. The new listing would give German investors more of an opportunity to participate in the upturn in American economic activity which followed the Spanish-American War. The fall of railroad stock prices in the 1890s afforded a buying opportunity. The listing would even help stimulate trade with the United States by showing German interest and commitment to that country, expressing trust and "a friendly disposition."[20] Moreover, American banks used the rigor of European capital market controls and the success of the issue in Europe to subsequently market the B&O in the United States.[21]

Speyer seemed especially pleased with its German collaborator's participation in the introduction of B&O shares on the Berlin exchange. Deutsche Bank had sold more shares than its original allotment. The B&O share price remained relatively strong, despite the announcement of generally weak rail earnings and the overall weakness of rail stocks. But some of the buying of B&O shares amounted to arbitrage transactions or covering short positions.[22] Deutsche Bank, for its part, was a little less enthusiastic than Speyer. Paul Mankiewitz, a board member and later spokesman of Deutsche Bank's management board from 1919 to 1923, wrote from London that he was concerned that the initial price increase was a product of demand from Deutsche Bank competitors, who bought the security up to have a "piece of the action." Even Deutsche Bank's purchases were in part intended to provide a floor for the market, an operation Mankiewitz feared Speyer would harm by its lack of discretion. Buying the securities at virtually any price, Speyer seemed to ignore many unresolved business issues at the B&O.[23]

But Deutsche Bank continued for several years to recommend B&O securities to its customers, emphasizing the line's tight cost controls and good margins, which left plenty of cover for the preferred dividends and other financial payments.[24] By some measures, the bank's efforts met with success. By 1910, approximately 6,500 common shareholders of B&O stock – with an average holding of thirty-six shares – lived in Germany. Making a market for the B&O carried a price, however. Deutsche Bank's own holding of B&O common shares had climbed from 38,000 in March 1904 to 234,000 in September 1910.[25] By then, the German market seemed saturated with B&O securities.[26] Despite several exotic features and favorable terms for underwriters, later B&O attempts to raise money in Europe held little interest for Deutsche Bank and European investors.[27] Both the B&O's active use of capital markets and its financial troubles continued into the post-World War I period. By 1932, at the height of the depression, its president was pleading with investors and regulators for help.[28]

Western Maryland Railroad

Deutsche Bank's involvement with Western Maryland Railroad Company (WMR) began very differently, with a short-term loan of $3 million (notes due April 1, 1907, shared with some other European banks) and collateralized by $4 million of the company's First Mortgage 4 percent bonds, due in 1952. Though different in form, the WMR experience once again illustrated the holes in America's regulatory safety net. Deutsche Bank held the option to purchase the bonds at 85 (85 percent of their face value) less commissions to Deutsche Bank and Adams of 1.5 and 0.5 respectively. In winter 1907, WMR requested an extension and increase of the loan, which Deutsche Bank granted, subject to some additional conditions being met.[29] The loan seemed to have everything: a high real interest rate, collateral, and the upside of a profit with the option. Once again, appearances were deceptive.

Controlled by the son of another of the era's roguish railroad magnates, the WMR had been operated until 1906 as a series of disconnected properties. George Jay Gould seemed to lack the discipline of his father, robber baron Jay Gould, the "most hated man in America," who made a fortune buying up and reorganizing railroads.[30] After several years of handling some difficult projects for his father, who believed his spoiled and pampered first-born son had a good head for business, George took over the reigns of the family's interest. Too susceptible to flattery and lacking his father's genius and appetite for work, George soon proved incapable as heir to the family fortune. Unlike his father, too, he was careless with details and came into conflict with other important financial and railroad interests, such as Harriman.[31]

WMR had some powerful shareholders. Ignoring Adams' advice and its own bad experience with powerful investors, Deutsche Bank seemed to think that the loan was without significant risk. In addition to the Gould family itself, the Rockefellers owned a substantial chunk of WMR shares. Those who supported Gould controlled 178,000 of the 313,708 shares outstanding.[32] Reported to have invested heavily in good properties and equipment, the WMR was small by comparison to Deutsche Bank's other rail investments. In other regards, however, it was similar. The company needed further funding to improve some of its properties and acquire more freight cars. What seems to have made this company attractive for investment was its ownership not only of rail lines and equipment, but also of coal properties. Even this somewhat dubious competitive advantage, according to one source, seems to have relied on weak accounting practice to improve the railroad's earnings. During times of industrial downturns, WMR could increase the output of its mines and, thereby, manufacture freight business for itself. Moreover, much of its $8 million debt was in the form of short-term funds, a risk not lost on the company's management.[33]

The company's most serious weakness, however, came from the ambition of its principal owner. George Gould fell under the spell of many a rail man's dream. In the first decade of the twentieth century, no one had managed to create a single coast-to-coast system. Harriman and Gould's father had come close, but both failed. George Gould tried to outdo his father. He already owned

Missouri Pacific from St. Louis to Pueblo in New Mexico, just short of the west coast. From Missouri, he reached Toledo and Detroit with another line. In 1900, he bought Wheeling & Lake Erie, which connected Toledo to Wheeling, West Virginia. If he could acquire an East Coast line, he would certainly have a powerful grouping of railroads. In 1902, he got control of the Western Maryland to outflank a stunned Pennsylvania Railroad, which tried many tactics, including court injunctions, to stop Gould.[34]

In addition to the Pennsylvania line, WMR's business antagonized other larger companies such as the B&O. For a long time these conflicts led to negotiations between Gould's interest and those of "other great powers" in the sector, such as New York Central. The management of WMR seemed conscious of its isolation and the rise of new competitors. Despite its small investment in WMR credit, the possibility of successful negotiations with a larger line, as well as other underdeveloped assets of the company, provided Deutsche Bank with an interesting upside for its position in WMR's debt.[35]

But by June 1907, there were many worrisome signs at WMR. Even before the financial crisis hit in 1907, earnings for 1906–07 were worse than expected. For the following year, fixed charges exceeded net earnings. Adams and others were looking into ways to improve the situation for shareholders.[36] Unable to withstand the downturn, WMR found itself in the hands of a receiver. The ultimate financial health of WMR was very much linked, however, to the coal demand in the United States, which at the time, fortunately for the railroad, was high in relation to supplies, a fact not lost on Deutsche Bank.

It tried to buy WMR's 25,000 acres of coal land, but curiously, and presumably illegally, ownership was passed instead from the company into the hands of some of the Goulds, the owners of most of WMR's equity. The sale should have been advantageous for WMR, but the price to its principal shareholder was not at arm's length.[37] In short, the company had owned an asset the long-term value of which was seemingly assured by the long-term demand for coal, now lost to the company and other investors.

Deutsche Bank had been enticed to extend the loan by an offer of participation in a complex restructuring of WMR's debt, and sale of assets, a kind of off–balance-sheet transaction, which the Enron scandal of our day has made infamous. Gould offered to sell a portion of his now personal interest in the land in return for the bank's extending its loan to WMR. Based on this deal, Adams recommended renewing the loan.[38] Gwinner himself had invested in the original syndicate, and even he asked Adams to let him know when it would be a good time for him and some friends/partners to add to their portfolio at a lower price.[39] With the company in receivership and general prices down, the loss of the sale to a third party hurt WMR's other shareholders. In the difficult market, however, even Gould may have regretted the deal. He was having difficulty selling the coal acres at cost ($3.2 million). Offers had dried up.[40]

Now Deutsche Bank's original mortgaged debt had lost value, and it had put new funds into an asset that no one seemed able to unload – others, too, had been fooled. For some, the general economic downturn and the railroads' particular problems had been perceived as a buying opportunity. In summer 1907, James Speyer had been very interested in funding George Gould's expansion. This included a rapprochement with the Chicago Rock Island & Pacific Rail Line. Six months later, Speyer offered his services to handle the receivership of WMR and Western Pacific, which seemed to require some permanent financial assistance and guidance.[41] Deutsche Bank's ambitions were limited. Unfortunately for the bank, neither the sale of the collateral nor the issuance of new collateral was possible at that time. Adams hoped, however, that the negotiations with Gould and John D. Rockefeller, who was a large investor in WMR debt, might lead to a financial organization. With Blair & Co. and Speyer participating, this might produce new securities in a company combining many lines in a larger, integrated rail system.[42] A familiar dilemma, and one with no easy solution.

Once burned, Deutsche Bank seemed in this case completely focused on getting its money back immediately rather than taking any new position in the troubled, albeit soon-to-be-reorganized, company. Over a few days' negotiations among Gould, Rockefeller, and Adams, the group tried to hammer out an agreement. Deutsche Bank would only agree to further investment in the railroad if Gould personally guaranteed the money owed to Deutsche Bank under the original loan.[43] Not unsurprisingly, he refused.[44] The bank was furious at the company for taking the receivership route.[45] Deutsche Bank was particularly outraged by Gould's double-dealing, what it perceived as his treachery. At the time of the original loan, Gould had pledged that he would keep Deutsche Bank informed about the financial affairs of the railroad well in advance of any dramatic downturn in the company's fortunes. In addition to this violation of trust, Adams discovered that a company controlled by the Goulds had foreclosed (attached property) on other mortgaged property of the railroad, which would in effect give the family prior claim to the assets that should have served as securities for the bondholders.[46] Given this extraordinary lapse in due diligence, Deutsche Bank and Adams agreed that the only recourse open was to file suit against the railroad for the remainder of the interest and principal owed after the bank sold the bonds.

In any case, in April 1908, Adams reported that J. D. Rockefeller held 51 percent of WMR's shares, including Gould's holding, which had been deposited with the oil baron, who was empowered to sell them to the B&O.[47] By 1909, Deutsche Bank reportedly had sold its First Mortgage Bond to Blair & Co., which it had held as security against its $3 million loan to WMR. The amount it received was sufficient to help the bond prices, convince the bank to drop its lawsuit against WMR, and help the prospects of a reorganization of the line.[48]

Nevertheless, the restructuring was filled with many clashes. Gould seemed ready to put his property in better order, so long as that did not wound his vital financial interests or his ego, his "*amour propre.*"[49] Restructuring, like always, led to animosity among different classes of investors and stakeholders.[50] Further problems with the line caused significant tension between Adams and Deutsche Bank management. WMR was also plagued by personnel problems well into 1912.

Although Deutsche Bank flirted with forming other syndicates to market other transportation securities, especially New York subway and New Jersey and New York tunnel bonds in Europe, in the end, investing and selling securities of an incomplete and untried value hurt the bank.

By 1912, too, Deutsche Bank had more systematic concerns about the whole transportation sector. Adams believed, for many reasons, that industrial securities were a better bet. Gross railroad revenues had been increasing, but net earnings were decreasing. Tighter regulatory supervision as well as higher labor and other costs led to lower dividends and share prices. Industrial organizations, in contrast, had enjoyed very favorable publicity due to their existing operations and potential for diversification into fields of activity less subject to public regulation. Adams understandably looked to water power projects as one of those areas winning public confidence and likely to profit from America's increasing population and foreign trade. Dividends, both for preferred and common shares, were growing in this sector. Most serious for the rail sector, in contrast, was the number of short-term obligations coming due in the near future.[51] For many years, Deutsche Bank had actively marketed and traded American railroad securities, but the WMR loan and syndicate seemed to mark the end of Deutsche Bank's strategic interest in American rail investments.[52]

Nevertheless, Deutsche Bank was still anxious to list American rail shares in Germany.[53] Even in the midst of the WMR crisis, Deutsche Bank continued to look for buying opportunities in the American transportation sector.[54] Although in 1903 it organized a pool of investors to put money into a variety of mining companies in North America,[55] its principal interest outside of transportation was in another of the great growth sectors of the Second Industrial Revolution: electrification.

Siemens & Halske's American Operations

Despite the formation of GE and Deutsche Bank's sale of its interest in the merged firm, Deutsche Bank continued to provide services and financing to American and European companies involved in American electrification. After the crisis of the mid-1890s had passed, GE's financial strength and European ambitions worried the bank and its German clients. Its interest in GE became more defensive than anything else. For this reason, Adams continued to report on General Electric's plans in Europe well into the new century.[56] The growth and associations of this new American giant in the sector complicated the plans of German companies to develop the U.S. market.

For many reasons, Deutsche Bank used its connections to further the interests of Siemens & Halske (S&H). In addition to the family connection, in 1897 Deutsche Bank helped S&H transform itself from a partnership to a joint stock company. Although the majority of shares were held by family members, in 1899 the shares were, nevertheless, traded at double their par value.[57] When the company contemplated the unusual step of launching some of the shares of its English subsidiary on the London stock exchange – a large chunk of the shares were to be held by Morgan and Deutsche Bank – Deutsche Bank turned to its longtime associate, Lord Mount Stephen, for advice about whom to add to the board.[58]

Deutsche Bank's efforts to help German companies in the United States sometimes led to conflicts of interests and loyalties, and they pointed to some weaknesses in the structure of its business. S&H's attempts to sort out its U.S. operation for the production of steam turbines with the help of its long-term banking ally's representative in the United States provide an excellent example. The story shows that maintaining property rights and managing subsidiaries, alliances, and agents in the United States at the beginning of the twentieth century was fraught with difficulties, not unlike those in emerging markets at the end of the twentieth century. Unfortunately for all concerned, not the least the reader of this book, the story was long and complicated.

Having established an American subsidiary, S&H relied on American management and soon lost control over the company. It struggled to free itself from its commitments to its subsidiary. For a time, it even lost the rights to its patents in the United States and to manufacture under its own name or any other name there. By 1904, it had finally won back the right to manufacture under another name in the United States and to import from Germany under its own name.[59] The ensuing story is not one of the prettiest pages in the annals of Siemens' management history.

In July 1903, S&H asked Deutsche Bank to determine whether Edward Adams would be willing to handle its negotiations in the United States to solve a series of problems with its American subsidiaries and General Electric in consideration for some of S&H's shares in Allis-Chalmers (338 to be exact, with a total value of $28,413, more than $650,000 in today's Dollars), a sum for his expenses, and an option on the future purchase of S&H's entire Allis-Chalmers holding (nearly 7,000 shares at $200 per share).[60] Allis-Chalmers, an electrical engineering company, and competitor of General Electric and Westinghouse, was a major client of Deutsche Bank, which probably had placed the shares with S&H. Adams and Deutsche Bank agreed to his being lent out for the purpose of the negotiations.[61]

The origin of the difficulties seems to have lain in steps taken by S&H after the merger of EGE and Thomson to find a substitute way of making and marketing its products in the United States. In March 1892, S&H had entered into an agreement with its American company, in which it assigned its rights, title, and interest in virtually all its inventions and patents relating to electricity. By virtue of that agreement, the German company kept all its rights to European markets. Pursuant to this agreement, as in other sectors, the companies had exchanged their inventions and patents over several years. According to S&H, the American company had violated the agreements by allowing employees to obtain their own patents, which were then submitted for patent protection in Europe on behalf of the American company. Moreover, by 1903, it claimed that the American company had stopped production in the United States and that it had had no functioning board of directors since the last general meeting.

Moreover, since 1900 GE had been acquiring a considerable amount of the U.S. company's shares not controlled by S&H. Holding a large portion of the shares of the seemingly bankrupt company, GE began disposing of some of its assets. GE labored under the misapprehension that it was now the successor of the American Siemens and demanded that S&H fulfill its obligations under the 1892 contract, effectively putting S&H's most cherished assets in the United States in the hands of a U.S. competitor with a close relationship with its primary German rival, AEG. S&H felt strongly that, under these circumstances, it was unreasonable for GE, even as majority shareholder of the American Siemens, to hold the German firm to its agreements.[62]

The American subsidiary seemed beset by problems from inception, at least from the perspective of the German parent. In July 1894, its Chicago factory burnt down. Despite additional share capital from Germany, the Siemens family seemed to lose interest in the American subsidiary, allowing the Americans to take effective control. The subsidiary just seemed to slip out of the German firm's hands. When in 1897, the American firm's capital was once again raised, this time to buy Pennsylvania Iron Works, a project that was completely alien to the subsidiary's original purpose, S&H began to withdraw completely.[63]

The president of GE, Charles Coffin, visited Germany and discussed the matter with Wilhelm Siemens in Berlin. Both sides expressed their desire to find some understanding between the two companies. Coffin initially proposed that S&H should pledge not to establish or allow anyone else to establish a new American firm under its name, but Wilhelm Siemens refused to bind the company to an agreement of this sort for an unlimited period. He agreed to consider an obligation with a fixed duration such as five years, to which Coffin countered with an offer of ten. Both seemed ready, once a period of noncompetition had been accepted, to release S&H from its obligation under the 1892 agreement and to dissolve the American company.[64]

By fall 1903, Adams had sketched out the terms of an agreement between GE and S&H along the lines of the Berlin discussions the previous spring. Under the terms of the agreement, all the property of the American Siemens acquired before March 30, 1900 under the terms of the original agreement of 1892 would be ceded to GE. If GE submitted these assets into any pooling of patents with AEG, S&H in Germany would receive the benefit. All European patents, however, were ceded back to S&H. In return, the German company accepted the ten-year limit as opposed to the five-year limit on its entry into the United States. This turned out to be a small sacrifice, since World War I effectively made entry into the United States virtually impossible for decades. Adams suggested deferring to a later date any issues about electrical generation for railroads and new standards for generators arising out of work in Niagara Falls – a project with which he was intimately connected, as will be discussed shortly. Solving these issues would delay signing an agreement about the original, more urgent issues.[65] Unfortunately, although both sides were content with the draft agreement, many new issues quickly arose for the participants.

Coffin signed the agreement but was obliged to bring the agreement to the attention of the board of control – as the executive controlling patents belonged to General Electric and Westinghouse Electric – on which both patent experts from GE and Westinghouse sat to rule on matters that affected the patent rights of either company. George Westinghouse declined to give his permission for the deal based on the general principle: "surrender nothing."[66] Coffin pledged to press the matter. Adams was convinced that this had essentially become a dispute between GE and Westinghouse. With the strain in their relationship, Westinghouse was probably piqued that he had not been consulted in advance by GE. Adams felt confident that Westinghouse's desire to maintain friendly relations with S&H – particularly important in Germany and England, where he was isolated due to GE's strong alliances – would eventually assure his permission for the agreement.[67]

Within a fortnight, Adams recognized that the matter was not so simple. As the American Siemens was still a corporation, albeit inactive, any agreement had to be made with it. For this and other reasons, changing the terms of the agreement in any significant way would risk losing the consent of the other parties and probably lead to litigation. The problem with Westinghouse's approval was more complex. GE had bought the shares of the American Siemens with permission of the patent pool, asking Westinghouse to assist with the purchase of the American company. To the horror of regulators (had they known), Westinghouse declined, but he granted GE a larger percentage of the patent pool as compensation for "extinguishment of a competitive organization."[68] In short, while the two companies labored to keep the terms of their agreements secret, Adams had discovered that the original intent had been to eliminate competition from Siemens' products. Westinghouse pressed for compensation for relinquishing the benefits of controlling a portion of the assets of the American company, which GE ostensibly could now enjoy for ten years. Coffin disputed this claim as the employees of the American company had misused their responsibility. S&H believed, moreover, that the inventions of the Americans had little value.[69] Despite Adams' pleas and offers to mediate between the two competing electrical giants, Westinghouse was unmovable. Adams began to fear that litigation could not be avoided, but he still hoped that Siemens and Gwinner might move Westinghouse when the latter visited Europe in January in search of alliances.[70]

The issue dragged on well into 1904. With Westinghouse blocking the transfer, GE and S&H had two other options: complete liquidation of the American Siemens or removal of the Siemens name from the company, with a promise by S&H not to allow anyone else to use the Siemens name in the United States for ten years. S&H would relieve its former American holding of any liability to the German company.[71] The only saving grace of the managers of the American Siemens seems to have been their incompetence. The patents that they tried to establish in their own names lacked essential follow-up.[72] S&H regretted Westinghouse's intransigence, but it believed there was little to be done by the German company, because the matter was purely between GE and that company.[73]

Finding an amiable compromise was made even more complicated by the relations of another company, Allis-Chalmers (see following extensive discussion of this company and Adams' connection), to several of the parties. Allis-Chalmers, on whose board Adams sat, had just hired away one of Westinghouse's top managers – who had been head of production there for approximately two years – to become president of the Chicago-based company. That manager, in turn, was recruiting his former colleagues at Westinghouse to join him at Allis-Chalmers. Adams feared that the recruiting would alienate Westinghouse before his planned visit to Berlin in March. With a little luck, Westinghouse would not get the news about the recruiting and Adams' connection to Allis-Chalmers until after his return to the United States.[74]

For whatever reason, the first discussion in Germany among Westinghouse, Wilhelm Siemens, and Gwinner in March did not go well. Despite repeated pleas by Siemens and Gwinner to permit the signing of the agreement between GE and S&H, Westinghouse felt that the agreement violated basic parts of the agreement between GE and Westinghouse for dividing the American electrical field. He had no problem with S&H in Germany, but many with Coffin and GE.[75]

Fortunately, at a second luncheon with Siemens, followed by a tour of the Berlin elevated and underground metro, Westinghouse and Siemens seemed to have developed a "friendly feeling." Westinghouse gave the impression that he would not make too many difficulties for the contract between GE and S&H upon his return. Deutsche Bank cautioned Adams about contact with Westinghouse, because the latter might feel less friendly toward Adams after he found out about Allis-Chalmers' personnel poaching, even though Westinghouse was rather dismissive of Allis-Chalmers as a competitor.[76] Even with the many new hires, according to Westinghouse, it would never become an effective player in the energy sector, a damning but, as it turned out, insightful criticism of a company in which Deutsche Bank invested a lot.[77]

It seems, however, that Siemens and Gwinner both underestimated their charm, and, unfortunately, how easily Westinghouse could get his "Irish up." In his thank-you note for the hospitality in Berlin, Westinghouse indicated he would give his consent to the GE–S&H deal even before his departure for the United States, a decision he postponed after getting the news about the lost personnel. As Adams feared, Westinghouse had put off the decision. Despite his contemptuous comments about Allis-Chalmers, Westinghouse wrote Gwinner that the whole situation had become more complicated due to Adams, whom he personally blamed for the delay in any resolution until he (Westinghouse) returned to the States.[78]

In his response, Gwinner chose to emphasize the positive. Ignoring Westinghouse's change of mind, he congratulated him for his quick and sensible decision to terminate his opposition. Around Adams' Allis-Chalmers connection, he had "to do a little dance." While acknowledging Adams' relationship to Allis-Chalmers, Gwinner wrote that Adams had "no interest at all in the S&H concern." Gwinner compounded "the dishonesty" by stressing that Adams had handled the negotiations as a favor for Deutsche Bank "without retribution or personal interest." If his involvement with the negotiations and Allis-Chalmers posed a problem, the parties would be happy to put the finalization of the agreement in the hands of a lawyer. Gwinner did not believe that Adams' presence should be a hindrance, because all the American parties, including Westinghouse (once again ignoring Westinghouse's seeming change of heart) were now in agreement.[79]

Despite the legitimate worry that Adams' involvement in both Allis-Chalmers and the negotiations had caused severe damage, Gwinner's tactic worked. Westinghouse wrote from America that he had not meant to imply that Adams' connection to Allis-Chalmers really posed a problem. His staff had recommended waiting until Westinghouse's return owing to Adams relationship to Allis-Chalmers.[80] In the end, Westinghouse did not seem to want this affair to affect future business opportunities with S&H. Deutsche Bank was inclined to let Adams decide whether his conflict of interest required bowing out of future discussions with Coffin and Westinghouse. The bank seems to have gotten its way. Adams cabled in June that the contract (virtually the same as the November 1903 draft) had been signed, despite further strains in the GE–Westinghouse relationship. Although there were many administrative details to work out, all the parties in Germany seemed very happy with the "clever way" Adams had brought the matter to a successful conclusion. Adams received his compensation.[81]

Niagara Power

Some of Deutsche Bank's investments in electricity came directly from Adams' own activities. This was the case, for example, with Niagara Power. He had a long and abiding interest in electrification. Despite his extensive duties for Deutsche Bank, Adams' most important business interest was, remarkably, Niagara Power and its related companies, for which he served as president for twenty years, and about which he wrote a two-volume book in the 1920s. Niagara Power grew out of a New Jersey company, Cataract Construction Company, which was founded in 1889 and got a charter from New York state to develop water power for the region. Its lack of success in getting financial backing led to its acquisition by Lynde Stetson, a New York lawyer, who put together a group of associates that sold its rights to Niagara Power for $2.4 million in cash and stock.

With these funds, Cataract was in the position to serve as construction contractor for the power facility. The agreements called for the Cataract Company to design, finance, and construct the plant. For these services it would receive fees. Ultimately it would be folded into the power company. Niagara Power was formed to own and run the actual facility. From the very first attempts to use the Falls for electrical power in the early part of the nineteenth century, the project of harnessing Niagara Falls' power was seen as a key step to industrializing the region and a project of international scope, which included financial backing from Adams' old firm, Winslow, Lanier & Co. and Drexel Morgan, Brown Brothers, and Deutsche Bank. Oddly, in his history of the company, Adams makes no mention of Deutsche Bank, his friend Gwinner, or Siemens. By 1927, Niagara had become the largest hydroelectric plant in the world.[82]

Georg Zwilgmeyer, head of Deutsche Bank's London Branch (left), and Baron Seidlitz, on a business trip to the United States. Photo ostensibly taken at Niagara Falls in 1903.

During the entire time he worked for Deutsche Bank, Adams was associated with the development of hydroelectric power in the Niagara area. It predated his relationship with Deutsche Bank. Certainly, Adams' involvement reflected his and Deutsche Bank's long-term strategic interest in the sector. As discussed,

Adams had been a director of Edison Electric Illuminating Company of New York (1884–89), a position he held until resigning to become president of the Cataract Construction Company,[83] which had already begun developing electrical power at Niagara Falls. As president of Cataract Construction Company in 1890, he spearheaded the initial project at a cost of $1.2 million. It was a venturous scheme with a great deal of risk, as evidenced by the Subscription Agreement of January 17, 1890.

> While the Directors are of the opinion that in a work of this novel character, frequently calling for a change of plan, it is not desirable to forecast with too great particularity the details of the proposed expenditure, they are prepared to make use of this sum in the extension of the tunnel beyond the first section, the completion of the wheel-pits, additional development of hydraulic and electrical power, the construction of a power house, with its appurtenances, and the construction of a line of transmission for manufactures on the company's property, as well as some eighteen miles to Buffalo, where abundant opportunity and demand for Niagara power has already developed.[84]

By 1897, the subscribers' list was made up of prestigious international investors including Lord Rothschild of London, August Belmont, John Jacob Astor, J. Pierpont Morgan, Kuhn Loeb, James Speyer, and William K. Vanderbilt. Neither Deutsche Bank nor any of its key executives are mentioned by name,[85] but Adams had already bought a sizeable lot on Deutsche Bank's behalf ($400,000).[86] In June 1898, however, Adams seems to have purchased another $25,000 in Niagara Power for the Deutsche Bank "pool" bonds, for a price of $23,415.[87] After the turn of the century, when Niagara was up and running with healthy operating profits, Deutsche Bank, the Treuhand, and several Deutsche Bank executives shared $300,000 of Niagara debentures. They had really wanted to purchase $500,000, but even Adams could not allocate that much to his German friends.[88] Despite the solid footing of the project and Adams' already close contact with the company, Niagara Falls Power remained a mostly personal interest of Adams, of which Deutsche Bank liked to be kept informed. Perhaps Adams wanted to avoid any appearance of a conflict of interest here. Although Deutsche Bank had an appetite for securities in the sector, Adams evidently was cautious about hawking his own company.[89] He was not, however, averse to using his experience with the project to gather information about other companies.[90]

Allis-Chalmers

Although Deutsche Bank invested in other electrical, transportation, and food companies, one of Adams' and Deutsche Bank's main interests during the twenty years that preceded World War I was an engineering company mentioned in the previous section, Allis-Chalmers, which grew out of short-lived, atypical British direct investment in the United States.

Allis-Chalmers was a product of foreign investment and the merger of two companies. One strand came from the Reliance Works of Edward P. Allis & Co., a Wisconsin company that had been in operation, albeit under different management, since the Civil War, and whose main activity was the production of flour and iron mill equipment. After running into financial troubles in 1873, it was taken over in 1876 by Allis, a local entrepreneur.[91] The other half of the business came from England.

In January 1890, Fraser & Chalmers, Ltd. was registered in London to purchase an American company of the same name and to build a factory in England. The Chicago firm was founded by two Scottish émigrés forty years earlier to make mining machinery. The company supplied U.S. mining firms and exported its machinery. In order to supply diamond mines in South Africa, the British Rothschilds and Wernher, Beit & Co. decided to bring the manufacturing of mining equipment to the United Kingdom. Their intention resulted in the formation of Fraser & Chalmers, with a distinguished list of British investors, the founders of the American firm, and Chalmers' son, William J., on its board. The British firm acted as a sales agent for the Chicago factory while a new English facility was being built. Once up and running, the British works shared the international business with the Chicago plant.[92]

In 1901, the American Fraser & Chalmers was merged with the Edward P. Allis Company of Milwaukee and two other smaller firms. The merger was designed to offset the poor business prospects of the Chicago firm, which had shaky finances. With the merger the British parent received a sizeable holding in the new firm, but not a controlling interest. Consisting, actually, of four separate companies and maintaining ambitious expansion goals to exploit the turn-of-the-century optimism and prosperity, Allis-Chalmers always seemed to be strapped for cash.[93] Alas, the investment required more management time than Deutsche Bank probably wanted to give.

Adams' first involvement with Allis-Chalmers dated from 1901. He served on its board, probably because Deutsche Bank had underwritten much of the financing for the reorganization of the company in that year. At the same time, Adams tried "to find a safe harbor for the Pennsylvania Iron Works," in which either he or Deutsche Bank had ostensibly already invested through the U.S. Siemens subsidiary discussed earlier.[94] To force the Pennsylvania company to accept a purchase offer from the Allis-Chalmers Company, he himself took a large interest in the former, investing $1 million in the syndicate personally, and $0.5 million for Deutsche Bank, as well as money from other sources, all to turn the Pennsylvania into a cash asset. The later S&H problem (see above) was not the first conflict of interest involving Adams and Allis-Chalmers. Adams had handled the negotiations for the iron works while he served on Allis-Chalmers Co.'s finance and executive committee.[95]

Although Deutsche Bank participated heavily in the financing of the Allis-Chalmers reorganization, for a long time it was not anxious to hold a large position in that company. As the company was merged in 1901 with $25 million in new common and preferred stock, the bank created a syndicate for investing in Allis-Chalmers, which held $13 million of the common and $8.4 million of the preferred.[96] The bank itself, the Treuhand, and managers took positions. But as early as the end of 1902 Gwinner was becoming apprehensive about the bank's investment. The bank was never really happy with Allis-Chalmers' management and its returns from this company, but Deutsche Bank seemed to make some money from the company's financial and other weaknesses. Gwinner hoped that a market for Allis-Chalmers stock could be made, as he thought that America would experience a financial crash no later than the fall of 1903. Unless the bank got out of its interest before that time, it would be stuck with the investment until the next boom, which might be years in the future.[97] Gwinner expected that Adams, who agreed about the risks, would find some way to avoid losses.[98]

Adams' idea seems to have been to take a more active role in Allis-Chalmers' management. Although he criticized the company's technical developments, Deutsche Bank soon became even more involved in financing and managing the company.[99] By 1904, Adams had become chairman of the board. He reputedly helped push Allis-Chalmers' move into electric generators to complement its steam turbine business.[100] Along with its U.S. expansion, Allis-Chalmers joined the English steam turbine syndicate and aggressively pursued the development of its other patents in Europe.[101]

Competitive pressure from other companies led Allis-Chalmers Co. to consider taking up steam engineering. There had been a tacit agreement between the Westinghouse and General Electric companies to avoid direct competition with each other's lines. Adams was quite convinced that steam turbines were no longer experimental. They had reached a commercial stage and, in his view, represented a revolution in steam engineering and electrical manufacturing. He tried to get Rathenau, who was touring the United States, interested in manufacturing the Stumpf turbine in the United States with Allis-Chalmers, but Rathenau indicated that his company, AEG, was not ready to build the turbine in the United States.[102]

Adams and Deutsche Bank served as a conduit for closer relation between Allis-Chalmers and European business partners. With other companies, such as General Electric, coming out with new turbines, Adams reminded Deutsche Bank of Allis-Chalmers' efforts in this area. He pushed for a joint venture between Allis-Chalmers and S&H to manufacture turbines. If S&H were to show little interest, Adams proposed another European firm as an eventual partner. Westinghouse had not shown much interest in improving its already functioning turbine, but Westinghouse was having too many problems in Europe to invest heavily in this area.[103] Illustrating the delicate balance that Deutsche Bank had to forge among its competing clients, Gwinner replied that all of this information was of special interest and that he had passed it on to Siemens, "as could be done without prejudice to the AEG."[104]

In April 1904, Adams announced to Gwinner that he had finally gotten the preliminary agreement for Allis-Chalmers to manufacture the Zoelly Steam Turbine, one of the best of the new steam turbines in the United States. Adams wanted the chief engineer of Allis-Chalmers, who was visiting Germany to make the final tests on the turbine, to meet Siemens' engineers, who Adams claimed were interested in the subject. Perhaps the Zoelly turbine syndicate could be brought into "a sphere of mutual business interest." Adams suggested that these meetings along with a visit to Borsig and a discussion about Westinghouse business should be on the engineer's agenda when he was Berlin.[105]

The Allis-Chalmers' steam engines built for the New York City transit companies around the turn of the century. The seventeen "Manhattan Engines" were among the most powerful ever built. The largest produced 12,000 horsepower.

For six months, Adams had been very preoccupied by Allis-Chalmers matters – sorting out its management and governance difficulties. After the general economic downturn in 1903, Allis-Chalmers had been viewed by Adams as an interesting turnaround situation. He expected that Allis-Chalmers would "resume its former position of business success and high reputation for engineering ability for the class of work that it turns out," allowing him to turn his attention to other matters of interest to the bank.[106] Gwinner seemed relieved, but the pace of improvement was disappointing for both Adams and Gwinner.[107] At this time, Adams was very optimistic about the technical and marketing results, which he contended would give the company the inside track over competitors like GE and Westinghouse. Good government relations were crucial. "I continue to congratulate myself upon securing the services of Mr. Mattice for the Allis-Chalmers Co." One of Mattice's attributes was a close connection to America's Navy Department, via a classmate at

Annapolis who was one of the principal naval advisors for steam engineering. If the final tests of the turbine were successful, Adams wanted to move immediately toward establishing an Anglo-American Turbine Company aimed at acquiring the Zoelly steam turbine for Britain. They could work with the English turbine advisory syndicate (Fullagar), and divide the share capital and licenses, as had been done in Germany. This might be followed by a close affiliation between the new organization and its German counterpart, with exchange of experience and representatives.[108]

Unfortunately, Allis-Chalmers' goals were probably too ambitious for the company. Gearing up for turbine production, for example, required serious capital expenditures. The expansion of Allis-Chalmers' facilities was costly and required a lot of Adams' time.[109] The problems of the Allis-Chalmers company were still sufficiently important that Adams considered postponing his departure to Europe in the spring of 1906. Like other companies in the sector, that company's growing machinery business and use of installment-sale financing were causing it to have grave working capital difficulties. Some of its competitors were even borrowing abroad to fund their working capital.[110] Allis-Chalmers urgently needed a financial plan to complement its marketing scheme, a situation that made many financial people nervous. Although according to Adams other investors viewed his role with Allis-Chalmers as crucial,[111] Deutsche Bank was becoming reluctant to invest more.[112] Even Adams was getting more anxious. Company managers continually assured Adams that the "light was just around the corner," but each time they disappointed Adams and Deutsche Bank. Now Adams was loath to believe anything that they said, no matter how reasonable: for example, the forecast for improved earnings. For Adams, even increased sales and operating profit were just another indication that short-term borrowing would have to go up to fund inventory and receivables. Borrowing to fund working capital, coupled with a downturn in the economy, which loomed on the horizon in spring 1907, seemed like a near lethal combination for Allis-Chambers, as it was for many other companies.[113]

As capital markets tumbled in the United States in 1907, rumors of Allis-Chalmers' possible bankruptcy circulated. The market for its securities was thin. Deutsche Bank finally bought more preferred shares at depressed prices. The board planned to concentrate more authority in a new chairman, elected to replace Adams, who had wanted to reduce his involvement and who felt that he could do little to stem the crisis.[114] With the new management, Allis-Chalmers' preferred shares seemed to Adams to be a reasonable deal. In the new year, those holding abundant amounts of cash would find many irresistible bargains. By December, Gwinner, too, was more optimistic. Although attention had been given to Allis-Chalmers' floating debt, he felt confident that Adams, with Deutsche Bank's help, would overcome the difficulties. New financing would tide the company over this rough spot and new management would insure that it would reap the benefits of the recovery which was sure to come.[115] In January, the volume of Allis-Chalmers' business picked up, which in turn helped it improve its credit.[116] Even though Adams was a little hesitant, Gwinner was ready to commit more of his own funds to the market.[117]

But by 1911, Allis-Chalmers was in trouble again. A downturn in business put pressure on the company's cash flow. The company had not solved many core problems, but it had a certain staying power, although not necessarily in the segments that Adams and Deutsche Bank had envisioned. As head of the executive committee and in the face of heavy opposition, Adams pushed for large bonuses for company officers to encourage greater efforts. Even with these measures, Allis-Chalmers still had only 2 percent of the $130 million U.S. electrical machinery business, a pitiful third behind GE and Westinghouse with 54 percent and 44 percent, respectively.[118] Western banks, however, wanted to help, as they considered the company important for western industry. They had been lending liberally and were expected to consider a reorganization, after which time Speyer and Deutsche Bank could advantageously enter a syndicate.[119] In March 1912, the company was reorganized, despite the active opposition of its British shareholders, who sold the rest of their interest in 1911. Even then there were still many management problems and margins were slim.[120] In 1913, Deutsche Bank organized a new financing that brought the troubled company another $5.2 million in cash from both old common and preferred shareholders.[121] Like many businesses, Allis-Chalmers has not remained intact to the present day. Various divisions were sold off to other American and European companies in the 1980s and '90s. Although the company no longer is in business, its trade name in some sectors, such as tractors, persists.[122]

With no detailed records of purchases and sales of Allis-Chalmers securities, it is impossible to reconstruct how much Deutsche Bank made or lost on its investment. The stock was turbulent enough that the bank may have made money on short-term movements, even though the company's strategic goals through 1914 were not met. It continued to hold Allis-Chalmers shares into the 1920s, a fact that would play a role in the bank's struggle to recover from the effects of World War I.

Above all, the Allis-Chambers' and other stories here show the great breadth of Deutsche Bank's participation in the U.S. market around the turn of the century. It served as a provider of straight loans, an underwriter of international loans, a broker of companies and processes, and a management consultant. Its principal role of conduit of European money to American enterprise had expanded, but in smaller increments and with better information flows and follow-through. In the decade following the Northern Pacific shock, Deutsche Bank had made a significant contribution toward calming German fears of new American investment and helping avoid further panic, on both sides of the Atlantic. Like many of its American and German competitors (collaborators), Deutsche Bank played an integral role in filling regulatory gaps and reducing information asymmetries. Without these efforts – then and perhaps even now – cross-border investment would seem unimaginable.

Although Deutsche Bank, through Adams, did exercise a good deal of control over Allis-Chalmers for many years, that manufacturing firm never required the management time nor other resources that had plagued Deutsche Bank's connection with the United States during the Villard–Northern Pacific era. Only one other investment in the United States before 1914 approached that level of Deutsche Bank involvement. It took nearly two decades after the Northern Pacific went into receivership, and the creation of GE, for Deutsche Bank to once again take significant management responsibility for an American company. In this case America's high tariffs, and not its chaotic regulation, in all likelihood provided the challenge and the incentive.

7

A Taste for Start-Ups

Deutsche Bank as Venture Capitalist in the United States

Happy families are all alike; every unhappy family is unhappy in its own way.

Leo Tolstoy, *Anna Karenina*.

The biological analogy, so prevalent in an age in which biology and biotechnologies are enjoying impressive triumphs, would lead us to consider failed cases and defunct firms as trivial.

Patrick Fridenson, "Business Failure and the Agenda of Business History," *Enterprise & Society*, Vol. 5 (2004), no. 4, p. 562.

In contrast to Deutsche Bank's overall strategy for U.S. investments during the twenty years preceding World War I, one example stands out. Although the creation of Lehigh Coke, a Greenfield investment, was a novel undertaking for the bank in the United States, it was hardly unique in the annals of bank-led foreign direct investment. Although not a vast "industry" as it is today, venture capital is as old as risky investment with significant upfront assets and several periods of negative earnings. As evidenced by the GE story in the nineteenth century and the early days of the last century, banks played an important role in selecting projects, gathering capital, and monitoring start-ups.[1] Unlike virtually all other Deutsche Bank investments after 1896, Lehigh Coke involved very active and intense direct management. It coincided with Deutsche Bank's interest in other new energy sources outside of Germany.[2] This investment, in contrast to the European ones, did not rely purely on German capital organization. Nor was it predicated on Germany's desire to block American dominance of new, chaotic energy markets, such as Deutsche Bank's Russian oil venture with the Rothschild and Nobel families. It was, rather, an attempt to exploit German technical expertise in coking and the production of coke ovens. It was, in short, designed to diversify already existing German businesses and technology by expanding their markets internationally. Despite these technological advantages and a partnership with one of its main suppliers and customers, the project was plagued by technical difficulties, personal clashes, and political conflicts.

Using German ovens and coking technology, Deutsche Bank led a syndicate for the construction of a coke and coke by-product facility in eastern Pennsylvania. Coke is produced by heating and pressurizing raw coal in blast furnaces so that it melts and fuses. The result is a substance that burns more homogenously, longer, and more evenly than coal and is therefore very useful for steel plants.

A number of by-products such as sulfuric acid, ammonia, and benzene are produced, from which coking companies get much of their profit.

Pivotal to the investment were two German firms, Berlin-Anhaltische Maschinenbau-Aktiengesellschaft (Bamag) based in Berlin, and Stettiner Chamotte-Fabrik Aktiengesellschaft vorm. Didier (Didier). These two companies were members of the syndicate and contracted to build the plant: an entire facility – including roads, buildings, shipping docks, coal elevators, storage areas, electrical equipment, and the coking ovens and condensation facilities for gases, capable of coking 4,300 long tons per day and of recovering their by-products – for a price of no more than $3,250,000 and a share in the new company's equity. The construction time was not to exceed two years commencing from May 1, 1910. Moreover, the two companies were responsible for the factory's maintenance until it was turned over to its eventual owner, Bethlehem Steel Company.[3]

In principle, the investment had all the success factors one could imagine: partnership with an important supplier-customer, German technical skill, experienced local businessmen on the ground, and long-standing relationships among most of the key parties. American press reports were favorable. *The New York Times* reported in early 1910 that the project seemed to offer enormous benefits. It was bringing coke and gas by-product production to Pennsylvania, allowing the state to rival Indiana as a center for coking. In addition to supplying coke and its gas by-products to companies in the region, the project would bring sophisticated state-of-the-art German technology to America as well as a 1,000 new jobs.[4] In the end, it was a nightmare.

The Concept

The origins of the project remain a bit murky, but fundamentally the idea was that Bethlehem Steel wanted these two German firms to build a coking factory for them, for which the American company would provide the land and guaranteed purchases of coke. The intent was for the coking company to be sold eventually to Bethlehem, although the steel company had a twenty-year right, not an obligation, to purchase at 10 percent over construction costs (excluding patent rights) after ten years or at 50 percent over construction cost after twenty years. As with most coking facilities, the cost of the coal was to be covered by coke sales. Covering other costs and profits relied on the sale of by-products, mainly gases. The plan called for the formation of a new company to run the facility. The German companies were responsible for the technical know-how to build and help operate the plant at the early stages for a percentage of the new company's shares.[5] Deutsche Bank was to provide financing and management – in the form of Adams – in the United States, for which the bank and is representative would receive shares.[6]

At first, Deutsche Bank was relatively optimistic. The managers in Berlin seemed a little swept up by the faith that the leaders of the German companies had in the ultimate profitability of the project. The high demand in the United States for coke and its by-products made the project sound. The bank's principal concern was the project's long-term dependence on an industrial corporation like Bethlehem.[7]

Nevertheless, Deutsche Bank's original conditions to the German companies evidenced a good deal of caution. The bank made its participation contingent on the partners convincing Adams of the project's viability and giving him "unrestricted influence in drawing up the contracts – particularly those relating to patents – and also in all steps and actions to be taken for establishing the new company to be formed. His circumspection and wide experience will be of the greatest advantage."[8] But even at the early stages, Deutsche Bank's attempts to assert control provoked its German partners to rebel. They claimed that Adams had no right to involve himself in any technical matters.[9] One of the engineering managers working in New York threatened to use other Berlin banks for financing, an assertion that Deutsche Bank dismissed as a bluff and one that was quickly retracted.[10] As early as winter 1910, Adams cautioned Deutsche Bank about the unwillingness of the German engineers to consult with Americans who might be able to inform them about relevant local conditions that would affect the project.[11]

Before the new company had a name, it had a financial plan with a healthy projected return. Equity capital was divided into equal parts of preferred (16.8 million Mark) and common (16.8 million Mark), each of which was expected to earn 12 percent, although in an earlier letter Deutsche Bank talked about only 6 percent. (The higher projected return might have been a result of an increased sense of risk.)[12] With a gas price of eight cents, the planners projected 16,870 Mark of profit per day, for a total annual income of 6.2 million Mark, or what they called a 14.6 percent return on the preferred and common capital invested, which they calculated after reducing income by a reserve of 1.3 million Mark and correctly adding that amount to the equity denominator.[13]

The deal included an unusual supply, delivery, and purchase contract with Bethlehem Steel, a company run by Charles M. Schwab, whom Adams described as antagonistic and whose management style was untrustworthy.[14] From the very beginning, this agreement, which effectively made Bethlehem a partner in the new facility, was integral to the deal. In effect, the syndicate was constructing and running a coking facility for Bethlehem until Bethlehem felt that it could do it for itself. There were still many unresolved issues related to the amount of land to be used, water rights, and the quality and quantity of coke and by-products to be sold.[15] The parties tried to avoid legal costs by submitting disputes to arbitration and even sharing any political risk by splitting the effects of any laws of the state of Pennsylvania or the United States that would adversely affect one of the parties.[16] Despite Adams' misgivings about Schwab, both sides seemed pleased by the last stages of negotiation.

Additional German Support

Enthusiastic about the agreement, the Germans, nevertheless, had been advised to try to get the American subsidiary of a German firm, Oberschlesische Kokswerke & Chemische Fabriken (Kokswerke), involved in the project, although the exact nature of the cooperation was never made clear. At the time, Kokswerke was largely a distribution company, therefore in all likelihood its help was probably sought for selling coke and by-products in the United States. With what appeared to be state-of-the-art production, adding reliable selling competence to free the new company from too much dependence on one customer seemed to make sense. No one seems to have taken note of the possibility that the new plant's existence might run contrary to the interests of Kokswerke, which supplied coke and by-products from Germany and was building its own plant. As with so many other aspects of the project, the participants misjudged the breadth and depth of the problem.[17] The issue of whether or how the completed facility would work with Kokswerke was left for later consideration by the new company's (Lehigh Coke) executive committee.[18] Confident that some sort of arrangement could be worked out, they discussed adding Kokswerke to the group and changing the original split of 50/50 between Deutsche Bank (together with the syndicate, which included American banks) and Bamag-Didier to a revised one-third share for each participant.[19]

Founded in 1890 by Jewish entrepreneurs with the help of banking interests, Kokswerke had built up an extensive business based in Silesia to mine coal, and to produce and distribute coke and coke by-products.[20] Because of intense competition in Europe, Kokswerke established a sales group in the United States. Paul Mankiewitz, who took the lead for Deutsche Bank in the Lehigh project, contacted one of the bank's principal connections in Silesia, Emil Berve of Schlesischer Bankverein, who in turn promised to pass the information from the group on to Kokswerke's management.[21] Berve reported a few months later that Kokswerke was, in principle, interested, but that he doubted it would take part in the contract with Bethlehem Steel. His reasons were not spelled out, but Kokswerke already had developed a good relationship with United States Steel. Berve suggested some sort of community of interest to avoid excessive competition.[22]

Kokswerke feared that the project would clash with its own plans in the United States. It owned 60 percent of the German American Coke and Gas Company, which was based in New York and which was involved in building coking ovens in the United States. Founded in 1909, the company had two construction projects and had also acquired interests in companies that sold coke by-products such as coal tar and ammonia.[23] One of these firms, American Coal Products Company, was incorporated with $15 million in New Jersey and controlled nearly all the coal tar and by-products in the United States. It used Otto-Hoffmann ovens, which relied on a different process than that used by Bamag and Didier.[24] With this in mind, Berve wisely thought that having the choice between two different technologies would lessen the considerable risks of entering the U.S. market.[25]

Confident in their own process, though, the two German construction companies were lukewarm to the idea of working closer with Kokswerke's American interests on the construction. In contrast, Deutsche Bank became increasingly concerned. Relatively early on, the bank grew impatient with its partners' inability to nail down certain important administrative details. The bank was quite willing to leave the choice of U.S. contractor to Bamag, but wanted to know what its charter would be.[26] How would payments be made, and who would have the final authority to release funds? Deutsche Bank was happy to have the "thorough" Adams on the ground, but the German negotiators had not kept Adams well informed, even when he became chairman of the board and president of the new company. Bamag and Didier suffered from a "lack of transparency." Even if all the outstanding questions were answered, the project was still fraught with a lot of business risk, which they were reluctant to address seriously. Deutsche Bank could forgive the disregard of some of the original planning decisions that had been laid out that September, but within a few months the situation had devolved to a point that the bank wished that it had never approved the project. Increasingly skeptical about the projected profits, the bank came to quickly regret Bamag-Didier's choice of representatives sent to the United States for the negotiations.[27] Even at this early stage, they seemed ill adapted to the task.

"Uncommon Interests"

What became increasingly clear, despite the equity interests of Bamag and Didier in Lehigh Coke, was that there were significant conflicts of interest. By the summer of 1910, Deutsche Bank resolved to hire an independent coke engineer to coordinate with the chief operating manager, someone who was "fully competent to exactly examine the estimates and to supervise and superintend the construction work as confidential man of Lehigh Coke Company." Adams reported back a month later that he had hired Thomas Clarke for that purpose.[28]

The technical difficulties led to conflicting analyses early on. Correctly assessing the sort of coal to be used for coking was essential. Nikodem Caro, a technical chemist from the Deutsches Laboratorium sent to the United States in the fall of 1909, essentially found that the American coal Bamag-Didier intended to use lacked certain characteristics needed for the processing – for example, it was too damp – which would delay the coking and might even damage the ovens. Bamag-Didier's position was always clear and optimistic: either Caro's calculations were wrong, the right coal could be easily found, or the ovens could be easily adjusted. Not one of these assumptions turned out to be true.[29]

But some of the participants maintained that the dispute had little to do with the extent of Caro's or his critics' knowledge, but rather with personal animosity and differences in their economic interests in the matter. Other, nontechnical matters were important, moreover. In America, many of the by-products from coking played less of an economic role in coke profitability than in Germany. Benzene and ammonia, for example, were much harder to sell in the United States.[30]

In June 1910, the Bamag people painted a rosy picture. Bamag asserted that the latest coking test with the Didier oven under adverse conditions had shown that the system – and the gentlemen involved – were completely up to the task. Any possible difficulties would be limited to the initial stages of construction and operation. Settling amounts of moisture in the coal could be worked out

Paul Mankiewitz circa 1920. Mankiewitz sponsored one of Deutsche Bank's most unusual undertakings in the United States. Despite Lehigh Coke's disappointing and time-consuming launch, Mankiewitz became Deutsche Bank's first Jewish spokesman of the management board when he succeeded Arthur Gwinner in that post in 1919.

easily with Bethlehem. Representatives of Bamag and Didier wanted to go to the United States in the fall to sound out potential customers for the by-products, thus circumventing the need to involve Kokswerke.[31]

Mankiewitz was in the United States at the early stage of the project. He was the point person for Deutsche Bank in this investment; Gwinner's name, for example, is hardly mentioned. Many of the issues involved personnel and other matters, such as the compensation of participants, and were handled in Germany rather than in the United States. As with many deals, Adams and others were rewarded in large part with stock or percentages of the profits. In 1910, Mankiewitz took the position that the construction company should receive no cash until the facility was up and running, categorically refusing to allow Deutsche Bank to take any responsibility for payments and advice before the system had proved successful.[32]

The Guarantee

Even before the coal problem arose, as Deutsche Bank's frustration and doubts grew, Bamag-Didier gave the other parties a formal guarantee. It stipulated financial penalties if a working plant was not delivered at the agreed price and by the stipulated date to Lehigh. In exchange, the other parties agreed not to interfere with the construction.[33] It seems that neither party completely respected the terms of this agreement. Adhering to its conditions taxed Deutsche Bank's resolve.

Confident of its ability to fulfill the terms of the guarantee, Bamag-Didier provided Deutsche Bank with an even rosier picture of profits based on a capacity of 4,300 tons of dry coal. After salaries, coal purchases, repairs, supplies, and taxes, the plant would provide a 16 percent return before depreciation, with nearly 20 percent of the revenues derived from by-products.[34]

Not surprisingly, technical issues plagued the project for years. The process of testing various kinds of coal and finding a reliable supplier continued into 1914. Many of the substitute sources of coal found created new problems. Caro seems to have been completely vindicated, much to the chagrin of Bamag-Didier. The only workable solution seemed to be mixing coals, but one of the engineers believed that even this solution would cause many other technical and logistical problems, reducing the profits of the firm.[35] The conflicts cost one member of the group his job. Through the next four years, confusion and mistrust existed about who would perform the tests and verify their validity. Moreover, although for a time Deutsche Bank relied on the guarantee for completion, Adams and others worried that not enough attention had been paid in the agreement to the quality of the facility that would be delivered. His deep-seated concerns, reinforced by the comments of some New York associates who shared his reaction to the behavior of the German businessmen, and stories about the failure of many similar coke facility construction agreements, were so strong that he refused to sign the guarantee on behalf of Lehigh.[36]

Sadly, the guarantee was no panacea for resolving conflicts. As mentioned earlier, to allay Adams' fears, Lehigh resolved to hire an experienced American construction expert to advise it and Deutsche Bank, a precaution that seemed to irritate the construction company and others. Even August Putsch, who had moved from England to become the superintendent of production for the new facility once it was up and running, protested the interference. During the construction, Putsch was supposed to work for Lehigh to inspect the company's chief engineer's work and to advise the engineer about the coke ovens. He had an odd dual-reporting relationship, both to the chief engineer and the board of Lehigh Coke.[37] Appointing another engineer would cause even more conflicts with the construction people, undermining Putsch's authority and ability to fulfill his contractual responsibilities. Only if the new engineer reported to him with the understanding that they were both working in the interest of Lehigh Coke could these potential conflicts hope to be avoided.[38] The representatives of Bamag and Didier disagreed. In their view, the new engineer should work only on inspections, and should not, nor should anyone else, work under Putsch. After the plant went into operation, Putsch would serve as its manager, as long as Bamag-Didier was happy with his services. At that time, the American engineer could become his assistant, but not before.[39] In order to preserve the peace, Deutsche Bank agreed to give Bamag-Didier veto power over the selection of technical support.[40]

Just setting up the U.S. company caused conflicts. The "coal tar hit the fan," as it were, in the fall of 1910 when Bamag and Didier's representatives returned to the United States. Their arrival led to a rash of angry meetings and letters. It took months to restore calm. At the first meeting, Adams expressed the hope that the Octava, as he referred to the group, made up of himself, Bruno Axhausen – a Deutsche Bank employee who had been sent to New York on temporary assignment to help Adams – Edmund Hohmann and Fritz Grumbacher (members of the Didier and Bamag management boards, respectively), two representatives from the construction company, the company lawyer, and Lehigh's secretary, could iron out the details of the new company's by-laws around principles that had already been worked out in Berlin.

Hohmann and Grumbacher believed, however, that their companies' covenant gave them the right to make further demands in the United States. They infuriated Adams by ignoring him, his instructions, and other members of the Octava and by insisting that their lawyers be present for all the negotiations. For Adams, the Octava's charter was quite simple: to implement what had been agreed at Berlin meetings on June 8 and 9, 1910, at which he had not been present, but about which he had clear instructions from Deutsche Bank. Hohmann and Grumbacher, in contrast, believed that their companies had done everything possible with the guarantee and other statements to protect Deutsche Bank's interest. Their mission in New York was to see to establishing a company in the United States that protected the long-term interests of Bamag-Didier, which included their reputation in the United States and Europe. The meddling of Americans, especially those such as Adams with little or no technical training, was most unwelcome. The Germans seemed to have little appreciation of American customs and laws[41] and refused to be guided by interpretations of the minutes of the Berlin meetings, because they themselves had no copy.

Understandably, part of the problem lay in the conflicting interests of the parties. Deutsche Bank endeavored to organize and manage the company in such a way that it could be listed and sold on the New York Stock Exchange as soon as possible.[42] The interest of Hohmann and Grumbacher was protecting the rights of their companies, not just through the construction phase, but thereafter, from any change in management or a new American owner. They sought legal advice. Although their companies' voting rights on the board exceeded their shareholding by a factor of twelve, they insisted on further protection of their voting power in the new company, as well as other changes to the by-laws. Mankiewitz took the reasonable position that it was unnecessary at this early stage to make provisions in the by-laws covering subjects such as how much cash to hold or what accounting reserves to make.[43]

By the beginning of November, Hohmann and Grumbacher seemed to have given up their initial attempts to change the by-laws, at least as those changes concerned the calculation and distribution of profits. Many points were just tabled, however, for the time being; as Grumbacher put it, "the entire matter of the By-laws is still open for discussion," but even his own lawyer seemed to lose patience with him.[44] Hohmann sailed back to Germany to explain the situation to his colleagues.[45] In his summary to Deutsche Bank, Adams repeated that taking away the directors' responsibility for distribution of earnings was an unwise and embarrassing provision with which he preferred not to be involved.

Although it was the legal responsibility of the board to make provisions for profits, working capital, repair, and other needs of the company and to protect Bamag-Didier's interest from future actions of the American board of directors, some sort of compromise had to be found. Adams seemed to soften on these points. For example, if the stockholders agreed, some provision, which capped preferred share payments until common stock received a dividend and which set other limits on directors' bonuses until sinking fund and dividend payments were made, might be incorporated into the by-laws.[46] These were unusual provisions but doable, if all the parties stated their desires clearly.[47] In the end, conflicts between American and German stakeholders were destined to take a completely different form.

Despite these compromises, the animosity seemed to deepen. Adams, according to Mankiewitz, warned that accepting Hohmann's and Grumbacher's demands and behavior would make his own participation on the board impossible. Standing behind his man in New York, Mankiewitz threatened Bamag-Didier that Adams' departure would make Deutsche Bank's financial involvement untenable.[48] Mankiewitz reminded Bamag-Didier that their demands went against the previous agreements and that Hohmann's and Grumbacher's visit had just exacerbated tensions. In mid-November, he took the German managers to task for the manner in which both Adams and Axhausen had been treated by Bamag-Didier representatives, who continued to maintain they were acting on instructions from headquarters. With or without the March guarantee, Adams and the board had to have full information in accordance with all the agreements as well as with Adams' position as chairman of Lehigh Coke and as Deutsche Bank's representative in the United States.[49] He repeated his threat to withdraw Deutsche Bank as head of the syndicate. Although Bamag-Didier denied the accusations and pursued counter-charges – such as that all of this had arisen because Deutsche Bank was having "cold feet anyway" about the project – Axhausen's support of Adams helped convince Deutsche Bank that its German partners were making life very difficult for their American representatives. For many reasons, Bamag-Didier had lost credibility.

But as a result of a meeting held at Mankiewitz's request in mid-November, a temporary cease-fire came into effect. Grumbacher, despite his close relationship with Schwab, was called home. Hohmann was instructed to keep Adams better informed. All technical plans and contracts, especially personnel contracts, had to be presented to Adams.[50]

Nevertheless, a month later, Adams complained that the construction company was keeping important information from him. In a personal letter to Mankiewitz, he also charged Bamag-Didier with conducting secret negotiations with Hallgarten & Company, an associated company of Kokswerke, which represented many of the Silesian firm's interests in the United States, ironically in hopes of having the firm, whose participation they had once opposed, replace Deutsche Bank in the U.S. venture. He speculated that these negotiations might be behind their recent threats. This attempt at finding a new partner was consistent with Grumbacher's original intent to form a larger syndicate. The various Kokswerke associates in the United States seemed anxious to have a closer relationship to Bethlehem Steel, and this project might have provided the vehicle. They even considered taking over Bethlehem's coking business themselves.[51]

Though many issues had been swept under the carpet, a fragile peace held sufficiently well to proceed with work on the ill-fated facility. As evidence of how topsy-turvy the situation was, four days after charging Bamag-Didier with trying to circumvent the syndicate, Adams found some consolation in the guarantee agreement, which he conceded relieved the syndicate of worrying about some technical details and concerns about releasing cash.[52]

Still unresolved, however, was another issue that troubled the careful Adams: patents. According to some of his advisors, patents being used by Bamag-Didier were insufficiently protected. Moreover, according to the agreements with the construction company and the employment contract with Putsch, all the engineers kept the patent rights to devices that they had created while working on the project and later for Lehigh.[53] For Adams, there was one loose end after another.[54] As late as February 1913 they were still arguing about whose responsibility it was to acquire the rights for several essential processes.[55]

Information Flows and Personnel

Choosing personnel for the new firm was not an easy matter. It was not only a question of finding employees with the technical competence, a great deal of patience and people skills were required to survive in the highly charged internal political environment and to avoid alienating one or more of the combating stakeholders. The distance, both cultural and geographic, hampered resolution of many problems.

Back in Berlin, the parties held meetings at the end of December and beginning of January to discuss various matters, including Caro's last analysis, which provided some good news about the question of the firebrick used in the plant. An American engineer, Thomas Clarke, was formally accepted by Bamag-Didier as Adams' technical assistant. Despite the bankruptcy of some local coal mining companies, supply of coal seemed to have been assured, even if Bethlehem itself was not to up to furnishing the facility's demands. Despite nagging doubts about the coal quality – at least about the cost of substitution or other adjustments – the participants agreed to stay with the project for a period of twenty years. They also agreed to use their voting stock and influence on the board to ensure that, out of the twelve board members, eight were appointed by Deutsche Bank and four by Bamag-Didier.[56] Contacts continued with Kokswerke's associate companies, which, according to Adams, were still interested in contracting Lehigh for its potential by-products.

That contact had two unforeseen consequences. United States Steel had worked with American Coal Products, one of Kokswerke's affiliate companies. Although Adams cautioned against "ruinous competition," he did see an opportunity to win over a new customer. There was no long-term contract between the two companies, which left an opportunity for Lehigh to win the business away from the Kokswerke affiliate.[57] Moreover, thanks to the discussions with the Kokswerke affiliate, Adams soon felt that he had found a viable candidate for president of the new Lehigh Coke; Edward McIlvain, assistant to W. H. Childs of American Coal Products, had handled the negotiations for American Coal Products and impressed Adams.

In spite of all the difficulties, through much of 1910 and 1911 Deutsche Bank engaged in an aggressive campaign to market the shares of the new coke company to clients and other banks.[58] One letter maintained that the preferred stock would sell at 140 percent of its par value on the U.S. market. The stock was being marketed with relatively precise financial targets and planning assumptions.[59] According to another undated memo, probably written in late winter 1910, Deutsche Bank would control $2,334,000 in shares, Bamag-Didier, $1,116,000, of which Kuhn, Loeb & Co. would receive $500,000. Deutsche Bank had already sold $1,110,000 of its holding. Dresdner Bank, Schlesischer Bankverein, and Credit Suisse were among the foreign institutional holders of the equity. Gwinner and Mankiewitz personally held substantial amounts. In addition to Adams, Blair & Co. and Winslow Pierce, the chairman of the board of Western Maryland Railroad, were among the shareholders.[60]

The project enjoyed numerous other forms of support. Along with the company guarantee, Hohmann claimed to take his personal responsibility very seriously. It was his duty to his firm to finish the project on time and at the stipulated cost. He even pledged to complete the project below the agreed $3,250,000. Unfortunately for the project and the individuals, several of those who had personally guaranteed its successful completion were outside of their previous experiences and competencies.[61]

Agreeing on a qualified president for the new company with whom all parties were happy and who in turn wanted the challenge was not easy. Many of the participants felt that it had to be someone with close ties to Schwab. Some candidates made too many demands; others put off one or several of the partners. Consensus was required by the parties.[62] As Adams expected, his first candidate rejected the job.[63] In 1911, the parties finally settled on Edward McIlvain, a manager who had worked for Schwab and for the Kokswerke affiliate, agreeing a salary of $18,000 and a guaranteed bonus of $7,000 (approximately, 400,000 and 150,000 in today's Dollars).[64] Given the technical and other challenges, McIlvain's salary did not come easily.

The team at Lehigh had divided into two enemy camps, the pro- and the anti–Bamag-Didier groups. Some of the issues were questions of style, others of substance. Almost all the experts on the ground began to realize that completion would be delayed at least by a few months. Charges that the Bamag-Didier group would not listen to criticism and refused to communicate reemerged.

Although Deutsche Bank had Bamag's guarantee, Axhausen felt that Mankiewitz had to know about these difficulties, considering how much capital the bank had put in and the possibility of lost interest due to delays or other problems. Axhausen feared that the reports to Bamag-Didier, as usual, would be full of optimism and certainty.[65] Mankiewitz seemed resigned to the problems and hesitated to inform Bamag-Didier that Deutsche Bank knew of the potential delay for fear of only "throwing oil on the fire." It was bad enough for them all that Caro had been right all along: only certain kinds of coal would work – for all intents and purposes, only that from western Maryland.[66]

Other Stakeholders

Another additional cost of the project, which had not been originally envisioned, was housing for workers. Estimates for the purchase of land and the construction of workingmen's houses for 50–75 workers, were for approximately $100,000. The issue naturally arose: Were these "necessary buildings" under the terms of the contract? If in the judgment of the "gentlemen associated with the construction work" they were necessary, then it was their responsibility to pay for them.[67] If not, why were they building them?

Adams labored to line up another success factor, the cooperation of powerful, local citizens. To this end, he recommended W. A. Wilbur for the Lehigh board. Wilbur, a local banker who was interested in the syndicate as an investor, was also a member of the executive committee of the Western Maryland Railway Company. He and his family, who had been established business people in the area for generations and were active in community affairs, such as Lehigh University, also owned a large holding of anthracite coal property of the highest grade, around 100,000 acres in West Virginia. Wilbur was very interested in coking and might even have been interested in installing a facility for his coal holdings. Especially as Lehigh Coke was obliged to have one-third of its Board of Directors reside in the state of Pennsylvania, Adams felt strongly that the group could not select a better local director. He felt confident that Axhausen, who respected Wilbur's "intelligent and gentle manner," would agree.[68]

A new issue cropped up, this time with Lehigh's principal U.S. stakeholder. Bethlehem refused to assume the cost of freight charges for the delivery of coal and coke. This added cost seemed high enough to threaten the economic viability of the whole project. When the coking concern suggested sharing the profits from Bethlehem's rail line, it was told, in no uncertain terms, that this would violate American law, which prohibited related parties from profiting from freight and rail charges under those offered to the general public. Unlike German *Interessengemeinschaften* (Communities of Interest) agreements, not a penny could be paid back by the rail company to its customers, especially if they were related in any way.[69]

The "bloom had been off the Bethlehem rose" for a while. In December 1910, Schwab confided to Adams that he had hidden his own difficulties with Bamag-Didier in deference to Adams' own concerns. Schwab complained that the Bamag-Didier team and their experts had tried to sell him a defective idea to assure the regularity and evenness of the coal mixture, allegedly allowing hearth furnaces to use gas. Based on Grumbacher's "brag" that he had invented and patented the device, Schwab had reluctantly agreed to spend $1 million to adjust his equipment, but the process did not work. "In other words, he made his contract for the purchase of gas at 8 cents per 1,000 feet upon the faith of the statement made by Bamag-Didier's representatives, which, he feels, cannot be substantiated."[70] Despite his disappointing experience, however, Schwab maintained his intention to exercise his right to buy Lehigh before the expiration of his twenty-year option, provided satisfactory terms could be found.[71]

Deutsche Bank's problems with the project were as much in Germany as in the United States. In the fall of 1911, Deutsche Bank's frustration built, in part because of its conflicting loyalties. Unable to suppress its fears that Bamag-Didier would fail to deliver the plant at the agreed price and date, the bank was obliged to show its willingness to use the guarantee to protect the American and German syndicate. However, Bamag-Didier were "valued clients of long standing, for whom we feel under a certain obligation to do something when necessary and practicable." Mankiewitz was a member of Bamag's board. He was particularly inclined to "take this side of the question into account." Gwinner and Axhausen lobbied Adams to find a way of helping Lehigh Coke while "at the same time help[ing] Bamag-Didier out of the hot water they have got into." Paying the contractually promised penalty of $400,000 would be very burdensome for the companies. If Lehigh rigidly enforced its rights, the potential operating period of thirty years would be full of "unpleasant strife, accusations, recriminations, and litigations," which would only end up hurting the operating company. Convincing the German participants of this wisdom would not be difficult. The bank relied on Adams to do the same with the Americans.[72]

Adams seems to have come up with a solution: convince everyone that the extra costs were due to improvements on the original plans. Adams employed Price Waterhouse and an engineering company, and defended their conclusions that the extra costs helped to avoid problems with future expansions of the plant. Getting the desired agreement to this analysis was not simple, because of the ownership and employment situation at Lehigh. There were local directors responsible to the company to consider. Although Adams was chairman of the board and executive committee until 1914, only five of the board members represented the interests of Bamag-Didier, seven the interests of investors.[73] In the end, Lehigh contracted with Bamag-Didier to improve on the already existing plant, for which the coke company would pay substantial funds as long as the four coking batteries were delivered and tested by January 1, 1913.[74] Adjusting the contractual cost of the plant was only one of many unresolved problems.

In winter 1912, Adams once again felt compelled, despite all the promises during the previous year to avoid criticizing the participants, to alert his colleagues at Deutsche Bank about the problems at Lehigh. As he wrote:

> For a long time past I hesitated to have a *little chat* with you about our mutual interests in the Lehigh Coke affair. There are a number of details that I prefer not to include in my regular correspondence, as they may seem trivial, and are inherently criticisms and necessary reflections upon the mismanagement of others.[75]

His "little chat" was twenty-three pages long. It was so long that a two-page German summary, which did not capture his obvious frustration and many key points, was attached. Adams cautioned that the plant would not be fully ready until July 1913, over a year later and should be run only experimentally for some period to verify Bamag-Didier's claim that its capacity would be greater and costs lower than in the original plan. A test period of several months was necessary and even this test would be inconclusive, if all the batteries were not complete. According to some sources, the construction company was cutting corners because it already had exceeded its budget. Inferior design, workmanship, and defective material would exacerbate the already severe frictions in management and unsatisfactory results. The construction manager had interfered with coal tests designed to determine what sort of coal could be used in the ovens, leading to open quarreling between him and the Lehigh engineers. Despite Adams' efforts to establish clearly differentiated responsibilities, overlapping responsibilities remained a sore point. McIlvain, by then installed as president of Lehigh, reported to Adams that despite Putsch's great dignity – and unexpected "backbone" given his generally mild manner – the relatively inexperienced construction manager refused to heed his advice. McIlvain exhibited "a painstaking care to consider all questions" and remained on very good terms with the key executives at Bethlehem Steel. Nevertheless, important issues such as the water supply and land purchase went unresolved. Unless Bamag-Didier negotiated water supply and sewage facilities, the plant could not be operated. Both McIlvain and Clarke believed that the machinery, acquired in Germany, could have been purchased more cheaply in the United States, even considering the high duties and transportation costs. These machines might even require more manpower than originally forecasted. The bricks and cement used for construction had led to persistent failures, and many cracks had been found in the buildings. Although it had been agreed in December 1911 that all gas would be sold to Bethlehem, Bamag-Didier had done nothing to acquire the contracts. Only after Adams' insistence and with great difficulty did McIlvain get Bamag-Didier to approach Bethlehem, whose goodwill the Germans seemed to be taxing. Seven months later the contracts were still not negotiated.[76] The list seemed to go on and on, but the commentary was prescient. In September 1912, months after the due date, the facility was still not ready to perform in accordance with the plan. The batteries were not functioning and the promised cost savings were only a dream, leaving the Lehigh company in a dangerous financial position.

Even Adams' position was somewhat precarious. He confided to Deutsche Bank management that he felt constrained in criticizing the project managers. His negative comments always seemed to reach Bamag-Didier, inflaming a relationship that had been poor since the first visit of their representatives to the United States. Despite Deutsche Bank managers' sharing confidential communications with Bamag-Didier, Adams pledged to continue to communicate fully, frankly, and fearlessly, trusting Deutsche Bank's judgment about whom they would share his letters with. Based on his communication with Lehigh managers, Adams was convinced that the bank was being misled by the Bamag-Didier managers.[77]

Adams seems to have won his fight, at least for the moment, but it may have been a Pyrrhic victory. According to Deutsche Bank, even the boards of Bamag and Didier were shocked and disappointed by their technical experts. They finally acknowledged that the board of Lehigh had responsibilities to the

American company. Nevertheless, the bank could not make up its mind whether to take action against Bamag-Didier under the terms of the guarantee, even though the delivery of the plant was already at least two months overdue – a failure that caused grave financial hardship for Lehigh, especially vis-à-vis Bethlehem Steel. Once again the bank implored Adams to be patient, as the German companies had an unimpeachable technical record and were close friends of the bank. The companies had already acknowledged their fault, paid out $100,000, and were preparing to raise another $600,000. They were even considering a Deutsche Bank proposal to return the plant to Bamag-Didier, thus annulling the contracts. The German companies were prepared to use their combined 50 million Mark in capital and 4 million Mark in earning power to fulfill their obligations. Deutsche Bank still felt that their managers, despite everything that had happened, were men of good faith.[78] The bank concluded:

> We wish to express to you our regret at the inordinate amount of labor and unpleasantness that this business has put you to. As we have unfortunately missed our chance of getting out of this business in December 1910, we must see it through now, and we sincerely wish that your energy may not be overtaxed.[79]

Deutsche Bank also began to inform investors that things were not going well. Referring to reports from that May, the bank confessed to clients that even the delayed targets for opening the coke batteries would not be met. Pledging to get more information, Deutsche Bank tried to reassure investors that Bamag-Didier understood its duties.[80]

Relieved by Deutsche Bank's response, Adams, however, still feared that the situation was growing worse faster than the German side seemed to realize. Begging that his new letter be held in strictest confidence, Adams warned that Deutsche Bank's reputation in the United States was at risk due to Lehigh's financial distress. He confided that the operations of the coking batteries were even worse than he had described in his last letter and, more seriously, that Bamag-Didier representatives in the United States were deliberately trying "to mislead the officers and the Board of Directors of the Lehigh Coke company."[81]

Hohmann's return only made the situation more grave. Coal shortages had been used as an excuse for the lack of coking, when the real reason was construction flaws in at least one of the batteries. Replacement of the flawed brick would entail an investment of around $700,000. According to Adams this implied that the Didier coking system, which had been installed and which was more expensive than similar systems in the United States, was a complete failure. Adams wanted to press Lehigh claims without any further delay, a view which he believed Kuhn, Loeb & Company would probably share. The coke company was hemorrhaging cash. Lehigh's liabilities for undelivered coke already amounted to between $270,000 and $345,000 per month, with no foreseeable end in sight. Clients, especially Bethlehem, would undoubtedly attempt to establish a personal liability of the stockholders because payment of the par value of stock was not made at the time of issuance.[82] The unprecedented scarcity of coal and coal rail cars made delivery of coal even harder, compounding Lehigh's woes.

Despite the unproductive year, costly delays, and misinformation, as late as November 1912, Mankiewitz respected the old agreement. As long as Bamag-Didier took full responsibility for the construction, with all the consequences and costs, it could control personnel decisions. Mankiewitz reluctantly agreed to fire August Putsch, the technical advisor loyal to Lehigh. Putsch's dismissal aroused Adams' suspicion. It coincided with Caro's return to investigate the plant's condition. Losing his expertise seemed like a high price to pay for placating Bamag-Didier. This concession came when the plant was already nearly four months behind schedule. In other words, to avoid further tensions with its unreliable "stakeholder," Lehigh would lose its best source of information about what was going on. The decision embittered those like Adams who had relied on Putsch and tried to protect him. Mankiewitz repeated the complaints about Bamag-Didier representatives, who seemed to have done everything in their power to alienate Adams and McIlvain, to Bamag-Didier's management in Germany.[83] Although he had not lost faith in the leadership of Bamag-Didier and knew that it, too, had suffered, Mankiewitz felt that his efforts had been betrayed by the conduct of the German firm.[84]

The frustrations of those connected with Lehigh Coke continued well into spring 1913. Lehigh's management was completely convinced that the Bamag-Didier staff either did not appreciate the gravity of the situation or suffered from the delusion that Deutsche Bank's close relationship with the German company would spare them from the financial consequences of their blunders. In any case, the day of reckoning was at hand.

The Coup de Grâce

Caro's trip report in 1913 provided "the straw that broke the camel's back." It made grim reading. The installation had to be completely rebuilt. Bamag-Didier needed to hire and pay for a new superintendent. A new schedule of deliveries would have to be negotiated with Bethlehem Steel. One estimate indicated that the needed coking batteries' cost would be enormous: 75 ovens, capacity 1,375 tons, $707,000; two batteries with 150 ovens, capacity 2,750 tons, $1,234,000; and finally four with 300 ovens, capacity 5,500 tons, for a total cost of $2,450,000. Two new batteries would take eleven months to build; no estimate was offered for all four. According to Caro, Lehigh could not even fulfill its obligations under the Bethlehem agreement, although he did find Bethlehem's claims for damages somewhat excessive.[85]

Some of the venture's problems were derived from what had been good news. Pursuant to the agreement, in late 1913, Bethlehem decided to raise the quantities of coke it required from Lehigh. Because of construction delays and inappropriate mixtures of delivered coal, the coking company had insufficient supply of the proper coal. The construction company, Didier-March, was panicked.[86] Bethlehem was furious, too. It claimed that the failure to deliver coke had led to great damage in its operations, for which it would hold Didier-March directly responsible. Any additional costs born by Bethlehem due to Didier-March's failure to deliver the required coke would be passed on to that company.[87]

Deutsche Bank seemed desperate to extricate itself from the situation which seemed to be moving inexorably from bad to worse. It even tried to get Bamag-Didier to purchase its holdings. By the end of 1913, the construction company finally admitted all its follies. In late winter 1914, the various parties – Lehigh Coke Syndicate, Bethlehem Steel, and Bamag-Didier – finally resolved their disputes, as Mankiewitz himself wrote, "after prolonged and excruciating negotiations."[88] Although exceedingly onerous to Bamag-Didier, the failure of the construction company to fulfill its agreements meant that the German company was liable under the terms of its guarantee, but on a more favorable basis than Mankiewitz anticipated at the start of the negotiations. After all the rancor, Bamag-Didier acknowledged its errors and agreed to pay the added cost but with loans provided by Deutsche Bank.[89]

Yet the intense discussion and delay were not completely in vain. Amazingly, the syndicate's technical advisors were unanimous in their view that the profits for the syndicate would be higher than originally hoped, despite the problems. Happy to have the facility reconstructed using better ovens, Bethlehem had largely reduced its demands for damages and extended its original contract with Lehigh Coke for another three years. The German syndicate partners agreed to return one-half of their original stock bonus in the venture. Deutsche Bank itself consented to give up a large percentage of its commission for managing the syndicate and agreed to finance Lehigh Coke's cash needs up to $1 million. Unlike the Germans, the American partners, who accounted for one-fifth of the whole syndicate, would not have to give up any part of their bonus shares.[90]

Mankiewitz's letter is somewhat ironic considering his official report to the syndicate in 1912, in which he had stated optimistically that all the technical problems had been solved, and that profits would be at least as high as in the original (March 1, 1910) estimate. Although its premise – namely, that the technical problems had been resolved – was faulty, its conclusion had merit. Bamag-Didier's guarantee protected the shareholders, Bethlehem had increased its orders, and the facility would use ovens better adapted to the project. Even though the revised start date (August 1, 1912) had not been achieved, perseverance seems to have borne fruit.[91] On March 10, 1914, a new agreement was drawn up to cover the $3.3 million cost to Lehigh of rebuilding the facility, the damages to Bethlehem Steel, and other expenditures related to the German firms' failures. Two and a half million Dollars of these funds were provided by the construction firms, the rest by the syndicate or the bank directly. In return, the construction companies were issued $2.6 million in new common and preferred shares. In addition to normal interest, Deutsche Bank received an option for new shares for the loan given to Lehigh. By early 1915, two of the batteries were fully operational; the remaining two were being tested.[92] Persistence and restructuring the financial rewards and responsibilities seemed to have paid off.[93] By that time, however, Lehigh and Deutsche Bank were confronted by a new set of challenges in the United States.

Unfortunately Lehigh's travails were not at an end. By this time, too, Deutsche Bank had resolved to change its representation in the United States. That decision was as much a part of its specific investments in the United States as the transformation in the American economy, regulation, and political role in the world. However the Lehigh Coke story pointed to some weaknesses in Deutsche Bank's U.S. strategy. Building a stronger link with American markets might require more investment in personnel and reducing some of its ties and loyalties in Germany. In any case, the bank was reflecting on how best to adapt to changes in the U.S. financial environment.

8

Transitions

American Banking, Deutsche Bank, and German-American Politics on the Eve of World War I

> [B]ut the officers of the Deutsche Bank, of whom I met a good many, including Herr von Gwinner, the head of the establishment, impressed me as being the best informed and the most alive of them all [*German bankers, my note*]. In fact, there is no reason for us to change our opinion that our banking connections abroad are the best that possibly could be made.
>
> Benjamin Strong to Dan Pomeroy, a Bankers Trust Director, June 9, 1914, Strong's Trip to Europe May–June 1914, Federal Reserve Bank of New York, Strong Papers, 1000.1.

> It is noteworthy that during the past few years, never more so than at present, financial interests in this country watch very carefully the financial conditions in European financial centers in the order of London, Berlin and Paris. The position regarding Berlin is comparatively new, as five years ago Paris would have been considered the second in importance.
>
> Adams to Deutsche Bank, November 1898.

> "When will this damned prosperity cease?"
>
> Adams reported a merchant asked in connection with his difficulty about finding financing, because everyone was expanding. Adams to Gwinner, November 21, 1906, HADB, A47.

Introduction

As illustrated by many stories in this Section, the American financial system at the turn of the twentieth century was fragile. Corporate law was fragmented, and accounting standards and reporting inconsistent at best.[1] Moreover, the hodge-podge construction and inadequacy of federal and state regulation over banking contributed to a special system of international banking dominated by private banks.[2] Not only were international private transactions handled to a large extent by family banks, they served the public function of keeping the U.S. monetary system tied in a reasonably orderly fashion to the rest of the world.

The volatility and lack of regulation of the U.S. capital markets played a paradoxical role in Deutsche Bank's history. These twin financial hazards, the Charybdis and Scylla, as it were, of investing in the United States, blocked a good deal of cross-border flows but offered the promise of magnificent rewards to the heroes brave enough to navigate them. Although Germany was not immune to financial crisis, since 1873 at least that country enjoyed many institutional safeguards against outright panic. Were it not for the risk and, they hoped, correspondingly high payouts, however, intermediaries such as Deutsche Bank would have little in the way of international *raison d'être* and little to justify their high fees for guiding investors through the straits. Even before World War I, the U.S. economy and political environment created a dilemma for much of the world. By 1900, it was already the largest economy in the world and held twenty-two percent of the world's gold stock, more than any other nation. But many key activities of developed economies were uncontrolled or poorly regulated by comparison to world economic powers such as Germany. Unlike England (since 1694), France (1800), and Germany (1876), in 1900 the United States had no central bank. Political opposition prevented forming a central bank to regulate the banking system and the currency until 1913. As this was the first time such an institution had existed in over seventy years, and most of its leading members had much more domestic rather than international experience, much of its early work was concentrated on national concerns.[3] Above all, banking and business were highly personal, often familial.

Deutsche Bank and New York Banking Circa 1900

As illustrated by many transactions, maintaining solid contacts with U.S. banks was crucial to Deutsche Bank's strategy in New York. Pursuing this strategy was not always easy. It required having special relationships with some, but avoiding exclusivity, which might be abused and lead to a loss of business from other institutions. Personal and institutional rivalries came to the fore. Deutsche Bank had to stay abreast of the politics and rumors in New York banking circles. It was part of Adams' job to keep his German colleagues informed about the shifting strengths and allegiances of financial institutions in America's financial capital before most foreign banks operated branches or subsidiaries there.[4]

Despite antagonism and conflicts, international banking in the first decade of the twentieth century was conducted in a relatively tight-knit community of men with similar values and educations. Many such as Jacob Schiff and James Speyer traveled together regularly. The success of German-Jewish investment houses relied on their cosmopolitan outlook and international relationships. Despite lingering anti-Semitism, this world view characterized national and joint-stock banks, too. Although their approaches to problems and interests reflected national cultures and priorities, the bankers shared a tendency to look beyond national boundaries for opportunities and solutions.[5] Many shared a common education through international internships within one bank or experiences with related banks.[6]

For much of the period covered in this Section, international banking relations in the United States stood in the shadow of Drexel, Morgan & Co. It was a partnership designed to exploit the U.S. knowledge and contacts of Anthony Drexel in Philadelphia and the U.K. contacts of J. P. Morgan's father, Junius Morgan. It fulfilled its purpose with astonishing success. In 1894, Drexel retired. J. P. continued to dominate American public and private financing with the renamed firm, J. P. Morgan & Co.[7]

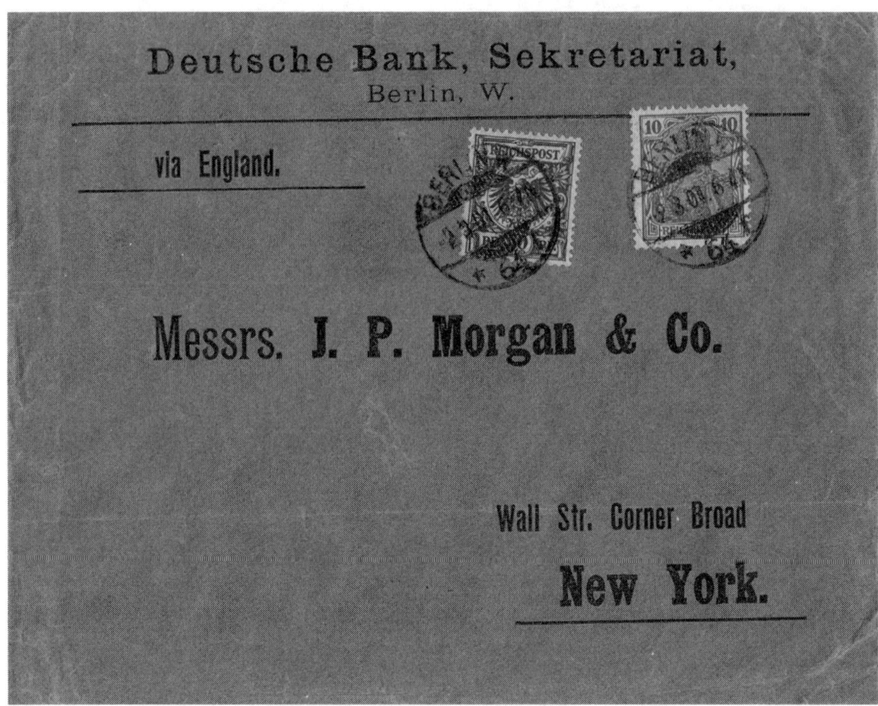

Deutsche Bank preprinted envelope to Morgan, via England, evidencing the amount of business between the two banks (1901).

But Speyer & Co. was the U.S. bank to which Deutsche Bank was closest, particularly between 1896 and 1910. His wife Anna (née Speyer) brought Gwinner into contact with many important private bankers, especially those from her family. Gwinner and Edgar Speyer, head of Speyer's English office (Speyer Brothers), for example, were cousins by marriage. The two communicated regularly over day-to-day banking matters as well as American and European political concerns – one of the few sets of correspondence using the informal form of address 'Du' – but the relationship was not without difficulties. The Speyer group's position with Deutsche Bank started to weaken shortly before World War I. Although James Speyer, who took over as head of the New York office, was raised in Frankfurt, the group seemed to have lost a natural leader and familial contact with Deutsche Bank after the death of Edgar Speyer.[8]

Speyer was one of the oldest banks in Europe. The House of Speyer could trace its roots back to the fourteenth century to the town near Frankfurt (100 kilometers) whose name it bore. At the end of the eighteenth century, the Speyers were reported to have been richer than the Rothschilds.[9] In 1837, showing a great deal of foresight, Philip Speyer created an operation in New York to deal in foreign exchange and trade European merchandise. The House of Speyer or Speyer group operated in London as Speyer Brothers, in New York as Speyer & Co., and in Frankfurt as Speyer-Ellissen. (I will refer to them as Speyer, unless the distinction is important.) As one of the first European houses to be represented in New York, Speyer played a leading role in the financing of the American Civil War and turning New York into one of the leading banking centers in the world. Other family members followed Philip, and in 1878, Speyer & Co. joined the New York Stock Exchange. Though it performed many banking functions until the 1930s,[10] including retail operations, Speyer became particularly well known for its financing of Latin American and Philippine projects.[11]

For nearly fifty years, Speyer and Deutsche Bank were connected in many activities in the United States. They cooperated in underwriting many U.S., European, and Latin American securities, a relationship that was substantial but not without conflict.[12] The question seems to have arisen in early 1905 as to whether Deutsche Bank would do business exclusively with Speyer in the United States. Speyer also desired a seat on the Deutsche Bank supervisory board. James Speyer seemed to have pushed the hardest to do more business, on occasion even used Deutsche Bank's name for transactions before discussing them with his larger "partner." Deutsche Bank, for its part, liked Speyer's good connections in Mexico and Cuba, which Speyer dangled as incentive for a closer relationship.[13]

For many reasons, though, Deutsche Bank wanted to remain flexible in its dealings with U.S. financial institutions. Gwinner naturally felt strongly that the relationship with Speyer had helped Deutsche Bank fare better than its German competitors in America. But by avoiding a more exclusive arrangement, Deutsche Bank combined James Speyer's stirring and energetic presence with its own excellent representation and information sources in the person of Adams. With this freedom came the option to do some business with other banks, such as Kuhn Loeb, which belonged to the Warburg network. At least for business that might come to Germany in the foreseeable future, the Loeb-Warburg group needed Deutsche Bank, because alone the group just was not strong enough.[14]

With Disconto-Gesellschaft in Germany, in contrast, the bank with which Deutsche Bank merged in 1929, there was no hope of regular peace and an honest meeting of the minds. Disconto-Gesellschaft was nearly twenty years older than Deutsche Bank and had been doing business longer in the United States. It had particularly tight relations with Belmont and, thereby, with the Rothschilds and Bleichröder.[15] Yet despite the earlier start in the United States and good connections, according to Gwinner, Disconto-Gesellschaft seemed less successful than Deutsche Bank. Its partner in the States was too deceptive and completely unreliable. In hopes of opening better cooperation with Disconto-Gesellschaft, Adams naively suggested that he perform for Disconto-Gesellschaft the same services he did for Deutsche Bank, an arrangement that Gwinner, understandably, categorically rejected.[16]

Cooperation with other German-connected banks had limited benefits. Gwinner considered few of them upright and competent. Some lacked the proper quality and stature as representatives. Most of them were not decision makers or were busy with other matters.[17]

Nonetheless, Deutsche Bank was sizing up its overall strategic alternatives in the United States and with Speyer. It was not just Gwinner's personal tie to

Speyer that kept Deutsche Bank from establishing its own subsidiary or working more closely with another U.S. bank. The two banks seemed to complement one another. Even though it occasionally used other New York banks, Deutsche Bank preferred Speyer for routine transactions. However, James Speyer was very sensitive. The Speyer group seemed to want Deutsche Bank to go through it for all its U.S. transactions.[18] During the 1896 gold bond negotiations, with Deutsche Bank trying to build its own weight in American finance, Speyer was deliberately held at a distance.[19] Competition even within the German part of Deutsche Bank's network could not be completely contained.[20] Speyer's contacts with some German financial institutions aroused Deutsche Bank's jealousy. In 1905, Deutsche Bank found Speyer's flirtations with other German money-center banks, like Dresdner Bank, a reason for concern.[21] The relationship, in short, illustrated the advantages and disadvantages of networking as opposed to internalizing functions. Neither the relationship with Speyer nor with its other connections, moreover, could solve one long-standing Deutsche Bank problem in the United States: marketing European securities in New York.

Deutsche Bank's position in the United States became more complicated as New York banks became larger and more interested in international expansion. Despite its relative decline, the House of Morgan in the decade before World War I was still the center of New York financial activity. Morgan's sales and purchases of securities were tracked by Deutsche Bank through Adams. His United States Steel holdings were of particular interest because Morgan had tried to introduce them onto the French market. Adams saw all the interest in France as a prelude to American banks opening up offices there, a natural reaction to French interest in the United States.[22]

Pressure from Americans to tap European markets came from various sources, which increased the interest of American banks in better European connections. The Empire Engineering Corporation, for example, where Adams was a board member and shareholder, received the suggestion to promote the construction and development of hydraulic industrial works in the United States but to raise the capital in Europe. The company had some heavyweight backing in the United States, including Kuhn Loeb, Speyer, and National City Bank, and, in Germany, friends of Deutsche Bank in Berlin and others in Frankfurt. According to Adams, the company was well equipped for its undertaking, but which bank would take the lead for "bridging transatlantic finance" was still unclear.[23]

Paul Mankiewitz, who joined Deutsche Bank in 1879 and served on Deutsche Bank's management board from 1898 to 1923, visited the United States in 1910 and gave a revealing picture of American banking and its relationship to Deutsche Bank from the eyes of an informed German. Tied to the private bank Ladenburg, Thalmann & Co. by family relationships, he came under considerable pressure to do more business with that bank. When he visited Speyer, James Speyer came out to the sidewalk to greet him. Suffering from lower foreign exchange volumes and pricing pressure from Morgan, many other bankers were eager to do business, whereas some banks, such as George Baker's First National Bank, were firmly in the hands of wealthy families like the Rockefellers. Morgan appeared to be delegating more and more to subordinates, who were reinforcing ties to Dresdner Bank and pushing Morgan's own Paris branch.[24] As early as 1904, Morgan, the great financial bridge across the Atlantic, was showing signs of losing interest in the markets. His many activities, especially the time-consuming reorganization of American companies, of which the Northern Pacific was only one of many, had evidently taken a toll on him, too. Disappointed by a decline in public faith in his judgment, he was considering retiring from business affairs and putting his holdings into a trust company.[25]

As early as 1898, the rising star in New York seemed to be National City Bank of New York (now Citibank). Deutsche Bank had many ups and downs with National City Bank. Ostensibly, it had a good relationship with the future Citibank, but the New York bank had ambitions to develop more international financial muscle. James Stillman, its president, claimed that he would invariably give preference to Deutsche Bank in international transactions, but Gwinner believed that Stillman's subordinates, at the very least, did not faithfully carry out his instructions.[26] Stillman was eager to expand what was already America's largest national bank. In 1899, Stillman worked very hard to get Jacob H. Schiff, a partner at Kuhn Loeb, as a director for his bank, with particular responsibilities for encouraging foreign exchange transactions.

Most of the investment banks tried to develop closer ties to National City. Morgan and National City at times had very intimate relations. Bacon, from Morgan, sat on National City's board. Kuhn Loeb was looking to develop a similar relationship with National City. Sometimes, conflicts between the corporations were fought out at the banks. For example, Morgan was a large shareholder in National City Bank, Hill in Chase National Bank.[27] But National City Bank's assets in 1901 were still only $67.4 million, making it roughly one-third the size of Deutsche Bank's.[28]

The other "comer" among New York banks was Kuhn Loeb. According to Adams, by 1898, it had increased its prestige and power enormously in New York, even more so than Speyer, which had also enlarged its influence. Morgan's relative decline had helped make Kuhn Loeb, in Adams' view, the most influential of the private bankers in New York, causing much friction between that bank and Morgan.[29] Schiff played an important role in Kuhn Loeb's ascendancy. He was popular and close with both Hill and his adversary Harriman, but Gwinner, for one, found him difficult to negotiate with and wanted to keep his distance.[30]

The affairs of the great private banks were run a little like those of the ruling dynasties of Europe. Adams reported to Gwinner that Kuhn Loeb's relationship with Heidelbach, Ickelheimer & Co. and Probst, Wetzlar & Co. "are so intimately associated by marriage and social ties that they may be considered practically as one as far as information is concerned that is not of vital importance at the moment to the particular firm interested."[31] Abraham Wolff of Kuhn Loeb, for example, had one daughter married to a Wetzlar and another to one of his own partners, Otto H. Kahn, who was both a director of Kuhn Loeb and the Union Pacific Railroad, with which there had been so many conflicts.

The partners of these firms lunched almost daily with one another.[32] The banking community was a relatively close-knit, cosmopolitan group. The highly cultivated Kahn, son of well-to-do, liberal Jewish parents, had done his training with Deutsche Bank's London office. After his experience in the money center, he was promoted to vice-manager of Deutsche Bank's London office and sequestered for a period to Speyer & Co. in New York, where he married into the "Kuhn Loeb family."[33]

Some of the New York banks tried to circumvent Deutsche Bank in Germany by creating alliances with other European banks. Morgan and Dresdner Bank had struck up an association as a counterweight to the Speyer/Deutsche Bank relationship and the ties among Kuhn Loeb, Disconto-Gesellschaft, Warburg, Barings, and others. The initiative for the Morgan tie seemed to come from Dresdner Bank, led by Johann Jacob Schuster, the son-in-law of Eugen Gutmann, the leading director of Dresdner Bank. With his good manners and excellent command of French and English, Schuster spearheaded a strong drive to compete with Deutsche Bank's international expansion. Speyer's success with the Cuban and Mexican loans troubled Morgan and, no doubt, contributed to his interest in other European connections. As for Deutsche Bank, unfortunately, James Speyer's conflicts with Schiff of Kuhn Loeb impeded closer relationships between the two banks.[34]

The conflicts among the banks sometimes had trivial causes, but their rewards were not. This was truly a "Gilded Age." According to Adams, Stillman and Speyer both claimed to have a special privilege in transacting Deutsche Bank business in the United States. The dispute about who was "more privileged" set off a war of words between the two banks. James Speyer grated on many people, but he also had a loyal following. Although he served on many boards, Adams doubted that Speyer had much influence. Schiff, in contrast, was very popular, because of his many charitable works. The politics and personalities coupled with the risks and rewards of doing good business between the United States and Europe forced Deutsche Bank to reconsider its New York banking relationships regularly. Fortunes were there to make and lose, and personal relations counted. In the spring of 1904, William K. Vanderbilt left for Europe, inviting Stillman and Edward Harriman and Harriman's family to join him. The group hired a "fleet" of cars, some of which they brought with them from the United States, to transport the entourage with servants. The European tour included a stop in Berlin to see Deutsche Bank executives.[35]

The meeting between Stillman and Gwinner in Berlin that summer seems to have passed amiably. Stillman tried to impress on Deutsche Bank management that he sought to establish full confidence between the two banks in order to prepare the way for larger mutual transactions. His confidence about American markets did not include, however, a bullish short-term forecast for some sectors, such as rails. They did not discuss National City's plans to open a London office, but Stillman offered his opinion that banking in New York would become more and more concentrated in larger organizations and that George Gould was not a reliable businessman. (See earlier Chapter.) Stillman appeared afraid that Gwinner would share too much with Adams. *En garde* but duplicitous, Gwinner cautioned Adams not to betray his "indiscretion" of describing the whole conversation by using with Stillman any turn of phrase that might be attributed to their private meeting.[36] Despite Deutsche Bank's growing dependence on ever-stronger American banks, Adams was still the lynchpin of its U.S. business.

These developments point to an overall weakness in its American business. Without a bank of its own in the United States, Deutsche remained dependent on American institutions for carrying out transactions, accessing American capital, holding its own investments kept in the United States, and even servicing German clients traveling to the United States. Its only competitive advantage rested in its ability to bring German capital to the United States. As long as America needed capital and Germany was willing to provide it in large quantities, Deutsche Bank's strategy and structure were tenable. By 1900, Deutsche Bank had, however, two new sorts of competition in connection with its American affairs. The first was symbolized by Stillman's visit to Europe. American bankers became more aggressive about cultivating their own business in Europe, circumventing, as it were, their European colleagues. In addition, a completely new competitor arose in both the United States and Europe.

As discussed earlier, trust companies emerged in the late nineteenth century to perform services for clients that had been commonplace in much of Europe. As more American individuals and institutions accumulated wealth, they needed secure companies that would not only hold on to their securities, but would also insure that dividends, interest, and other administrative services were handled properly. National banks were forbidden to take on these services. Although the original purpose of trusts was to hold on to deposits that secured transactions, they could take normal deposits, give credit, and discount notes, which allowed them to become formidable competitors to the national banks. The only function denied to trusts was issuing notes. Starting with little capital, they began to grow like mushrooms in the main American financial centers, New York and Chicago. Between 1894 and 1904, their number in New York doubled. By 1914, there were 1,564 in the United States, one-fifth the number of national banks.

Although many trusts remained just trust companies, Bankers Trust, founded in 1903 by a group of New York commercial and private bankers, was specifically designed to exploit the trust companies' advantages, while avoiding cannibalizing business away from commercial banks. As a trust bank for banks, it was to serve as a kind of "banker of last resort." Within a few years, it was also aggressively marketing a new retail instrument in Europe, travelers' checks. It survived the 1907 Panic (see following) with greater prestige than many other financial institutions. By 1914, it had grown considerably by merging with other banks and acquiring new deposits. Without the national banks' reserve requirements, the trust movement was leading competitors and regulators alike to talk about a "trust crisis." Some, such as Guaranty Trust, developed strong foreign-exchange departments. Moreover, unlike national banks, which had been offering traditional banking services outside of the United States through established banking relationships, during the first decade of the twentieth century, the trusts had few limits on how to develop their international business.[37]

Some Americans were considering creating an international bank, much like Deutsche Bank had been for Germany, to penetrate international markets. In short, before World War I American bankers began to see themselves as competitors in European capital markets, selling themselves to European clients, and helping Europeans access American capital. They had learned from the methods used by Germans to handle financial transactions, especially from their ability to handle cross-border finance.[38]

The Panic of 1907

The year 1907 was pivotal for the institutionalization of many aspects of America's financial system. In the overheated economic atmosphere of the time, gold, the fulcrum of the system, was once again leaving the United States. The economic crisis of that year set off a decade of reforms that would not be matched in intensity until the 1930s. Tired of both business scandal and simplistic populism, the country seemed ready to tackle reform in a more systematic, less politicized manner than under the administration of Teddy Roosevelt, whose brand of Republicanism was scorned by many business people. After 1907, both "staunchly conservative and unbridled" business people finally gave grudging recognition to the need for many reforms and could make common cause with "firebrand" progressives about many aspects of the regulatory environment.[39] Though very much an international movement, the changes were probably most profound in the United States. A country of the size and economic importance of the United States, for example, could no longer rely on a few private bankers to salvage its currency.

These problems were neither new nor confined to the period. Americans have always had a somewhat spotty loyalty to financial discipline, both before and after 1907. With 21,000 state and federal banks with no coordinated regulation and little federal oversight of the amount of money available for investment, it was no wonder that the system often imploded. Deutsche Bank executives often complained about how the chaos in America's financial system made marketing securities in Germany difficult. Although the crisis that had begun in the fall was relatively brief, it once more underlined, to the chagrin of much of the nation, how dependent the country was on private bankers like Morgan.[40] The Age of Reform did not begin then, but it reached a certain maturity after the crisis.[41] Within six years of the 1907 panic, America finally restored its central bank, the Dollar was put on a firm gold footing, accountants made great strides in codifying professional standards, and, through a series of court cases, the United States determined the legal framework for putting new limits on monopolistic activity.

As early as spring 1906, Adams began to have severe concerns about the American economy. Although industrial and agricultural sectors were both vibrant, according to Adams, the investigations of Standard Oil and popular sentiment in favor of the likely Democratic candidate for the president, William

Jennings Bryan, hurt market confidence.[42] Indeed, Adams also reported that the progressive Republican Teddy Roosevelt was helping the Democrat's cause. The President was making more enemies than friends. His popularity was sure to decline. In Adams' view, many of the maverick Republican's views undermined stability.[43]

Of particular concern were the Interstate Commerce Commission's investigations of the financial transactions of Union Pacific, an investigation ostensibly initiated by Hill to get at his rival. The whole sector came under a microscope. The conflicts seemed to pit those who genuinely wanted to control railroad lines against those who wanted to make a quick buck. Harriman's interest in the rival line was merely an attempt to control its pricing policy. Bankers were nervous. Stillman departed town suddenly for Europe, possibly to avoid embarrassing questions. The drive to consolidate and regulate the sector involved many imponderable outcomes affecting Deutsche Bank's investment. According to Adams, the disclosures verified Harriman's suspected ambition to get an Atlantic seaboard connection linking his Baltimore & Ohio interests to west coast lines, eventually taking in the Western Maryland line.[44]

Although he was optimistic about some additional railroad investments in January, by February, Adams feared that many railroads and industrial companies were once again in need of financial assistance, specifically those firms to which bankers were least likely to give credit.[45] Precisely a month before the panic, Adams signaled that the major obstacle to the country pulling out of its slowdown was the President's proclivity to undermine markets by stimulating class war as embodied in the Standard Oil and other investigations.[46]

Three months after the panic hit, Gwinner, although agreeing with Adams' overall assessment, emphasized other things – for example, the need for a governmental bank, which would allow the country to enjoy many of the benefits of the Gold Standard without the need of importing more gold. He sent a long cable to Adams, which Adams then forwarded in a letter to the president of the American Chamber of Commerce. According to Gwinner, a large part of the problem was America's juvenile attitudes about financial matters, particularly a central bank. America needed $100 million more in circulation, which could not be furnished from outside of the country, even if "gold-loving France" were involved. Efforts to draw more gold into the United States would worsen the crisis. Currency, not gold, was necessary. America could help itself, a recognition that would find general approval all over the world and relieve those who feared that at present the "United States financial markets wreck all others."[47]

Nevertheless, Deutsche Bank's long-term confidence in the United States was such that, by summer 1907, in the midst of the crisis, it started looking for new investment opportunities. Deutsche Bank was not averse to doing a little "bottom fishing." Adams thought that the period between October 1907 and the end of March 1908 would see the steepest depression and would therefore be the ideal time to acquire cheap securities. The market would be ahead of the real economy. People were moving from extravagant living to savings, which would later turn into investment. The greatest strain for companies looking for money would come during the fall.[48] After that period the idea of

This cartoon from a U.S. newspaper (circa 1907) illustrates the perception of Morgan's power and control over the American economy.

an investment trust under French auspices, as some investors had wanted to create, could be revived once confidence had been restored to the market.[49]

Adams believed that, as in 1893, the savings of American companies and individuals during the crisis, coupled with the nation's innate optimism, would get the country through the crisis without material assistance from Europe. He foresaw a rapid recovery. The banking system was basically solid. New York banks, in contrast to others, had shown especially great strength. He blamed the increase of telephone and national newspaper coverage for the speed with which the crisis spread. By the same token, prosperity would also spread rapidly. With this crisis, Americans had been made more aware of the international nature of finance and commerce, which helped to lay the political groundwork for the creation of a national clearing house or better still a Federal Reserve.[50]

There was no doubt in Adams' mind where to lay the blame for the crisis and whom to praise for the recovery.

> The last six months will unquestionably prove to have been pregnant with incidents from which new history will be made and of all the incidents of importance, I deem none more significant in their bearing upon the future than the part that was carried out so boldly and skillfully by J. P. Morgan in the Roosevelt panic of 1907.[51]

Through the winter, Gwinner became guardedly optimistic and a little philosophical:

> We are in the state of a man that [sic] has drunken too much champagne and is suffering the next day from seasickness. First he puts himself or is put by his doctor to a severe régime, next he begins to take food of easy digestion until again he will return to beef and burgundy and ultimately again commit excesses. Our market is just beginning to work itself out from the first stage into the second which financially you style the taste for time securities returning a fixed return.[52]

The 1907 crisis initiated a period of extensive reflection and proposals for new banking legislation, in which German bankers in general, and Deutsche Bank in particular, took part. Not only did much of the gold used to support the currency in 1907 come from German vaults, many of the American regulators looked to Germany for inspiration. Germans took a great interest in the American regulatory problems because American markets were now so large that their destabilizations would send tremors around the world. Like the American legislature, the Reichstag initiated a discussion of banking reform. The ensuing legislation produced fewer dramatic changes in Germany, but German and American representatives discussed various aspects of their respective reforms.[53]

In a speech at the American Association of Commerce and Trade in 1911, Arthur Gwinner, identified as "the Fatherland's leading banker," weighed in. He emphatically declared that America would continue to have profound economic crises without a central bank, and that it should adopt Germany's model. As the latest and best central bank, its regulations provided for a self-correcting currency system, which proved to be an effective check on unsound financial and industrial expansion. Any central bank needed a strong constitution to avoid control and manipulation by political or special financial interests. "If the bank became the plaything of special interests it would prove more fatal than the disease which it was created to destroy."[54] Within four years, America had a strong Federal Reserve System modeled on Germany's. Not all the economic interaction between the countries passed so well.

In the first decade of the new century, some political problems between the United States and Germany threatened Deutsche Bank's business. America and Germany showed signs of regulatory and other conflicts. The U.S. government began to complain about German control of oil fields in central Europe and

Russia. Press reports indicated that the American government was prepared to "lock horns" over Germany's granting of monopolies to German banks for the purchase and distribution of oil. Deutsche Bank was mentioned by name, and its investments in Russian oil fields and those of Disconto-Gesellschaft in Romania highlighted.[55]

Sometimes American and foreign investors differed in how they wanted to resist or cooperate with government regulation. As the government prepared in 1911 to mount its attacks on U.S. Steel under the terms of the Sherman Anti-Trust Act, Adams reported that some shareholders preferred that the company find some sort of arrangement with the government to dissolve the company in order to avoid criminal procedures against the directors and managers. Others, including foreign shareholders, preferred a vigorous resistance to the government, even if this meant prolonged litigation and entailed financial and other risks.[56] Rumors were rife in Germany that a dissolution would mean that U.S. Steel shares would become worthless.[57]

Although America still had much to do to prove itself as a financial center, its companies were beginning to develop international clout. In 1912, much to Deutsche Bank's chagrin, Standard Oil was able to organize an effective political campaign in Germany against legislation that it deemed unfavorable to its interest. Gwinner, who had helped restructure German entry into the petroleum sector, was livid with indignation and shocked by the extent of Rockefeller's political power, even in the Fatherland. Content with his victory, Standard's representative returned home in December from Liverpool on the *Lusitania*,[58] a sad symbol of future, more severe conflicts.

Personal and Structural Changes

The correspondence between Adams and Deutsche Bank during the twenty years preceding World War I was friendly and covered a wide range of subjects: personalities of business associates; relationships with other institutions, especially financial ones; companies in which they had invested; the prospects of the American and German markets; politics; and, of course, new ventures. After the turn of the century, their letters dealt more and more with two important transitions, which were key to Deutsche Bank's American business: the United States's coming of age as a world power and finding a successor for Adams.[59]

The letters varied from short notes to thirty-page tomes, sometimes handwritten, almost always affectionate and respectful, sharing confidences about business associates and views about the world of politics and economics. As Georg Siemens moved away from day-to-day involvement in the business during the waning years of the nineteenth century, Gwinner took charge of managing the American business. Gwinner enjoyed an especially good rapport with Adams. The two discussed Adams' passionate hobby, to which Gwinner contributed by helping to find rare coins in Europe.[60]

Their correspondence included discussions of meetings between the families, their health, and outside interests, which for Adams, especially, entailed many charitable and scientific interests. Adams' daughter Ruth, referred to in letters by Adams as "your little friend," was obviously particularly fond of Gwinner. The Adams-Gwinner relationship was complicated, however, because of the distance between them, their own loyalties and commitments, their business cultures, and other business interests. Adams' and Deutsche Bank's affairs were so complex and intertwined, it was hard sometimes to know where one started and the other stopped. Occasionally, the "friends," as they would refer to one another, would get miffed about something, especially payments from other companies.[61]

But they shared both triumphs and tragedies, the greatest of which was the untimely death of Adams' son Ernest in summer 1904 at age thirty of nephritis. A graduate of Yale and Columbia, he was considered a gifted electrical engineer. Because of his father's work with Niagara Power, Ernest had contact with some of the most important electrical engineers and projects in the United States. Adams' son was one of the main foci of his life. He even used his many contacts in electrical engineering to find and buy a company for his son to manage. In Berlin, Ernest had married Margarethe Seefeld, whose father was the military commander of the Grand Duchy of Baden. Together the couple had a child, reinforcing the family's German ties.[62] Adams seemed genuinely touched by his German colleague's expressions of grief over his son's death. Nevertheless, he was soon back to work.[63]

Despite their personal-business relationship, Gwinner had a balanced view of Adams' strengths and weaknesses. As Gwinner wrote in a file note, Adams had a clear head and was a precise worker. Though Adams could be touchy, Gwinner felt that he was someone Deutsche Bank people could work well with and should be open towards. Adams' loyalty to Deutsche Bank and Gwinner personally was beyond question.[64] In spite of frequent rifts between Adams and Speyer – Deutsche Bank's most important banking relationship in New York – all the parties seemed to prosper and, until shortly before World War I, Deutsche Bank and Adams were reluctant to run the risk of changing their *modus operandi*.[65] Nevertheless, Deutsche Bank was always on the lookout for ways of expanding and improving its American business.

As Deutsche Bank's frustration about marketing European paper in the United States and competition for selling U.S. securities in Europe grew, it turned to new ideas. During the latter stages of the 1907 Panic, Gwinner and Adams gave cautious support to the idea of an international consortium of banks, which would bring financial stability to capital markets and engage in cross-selling of international securities. Although the idea had a great deal of support from major financial institutions, especially Crédit Lyonnais, a formal structure was never established. The idea was brought to Deutsche Bank by Albert Kahn, a French financier with excellent connections, broad interests, and an uncertain future.[66] Kahn seems to have received strong support from the French bank, but the Germans and some Americans felt the time was not ripe.[67] However, Deutsche Bank increasingly structured its U.S. investments in pools and syndicates with private investors. Perhaps influenced by Gwinner, Adams took a lively interest in Kahn and in the project.[68] The idea of working in conjunction with other European financial institutions in the United States was an idea, moreover, that would be floated again and tried in the 1960s. For the time being, despite great losses in 1907, and the insecurity and costs of investment banking in and from the United States, large financial institutions balked at banding together for anything more than ad hoc transactions and particular investment groupings.[69]

Much of Adams' and Gwinner's discussions revolved around expanding their U.S. activities as a base of operations in other geographic areas. Gwinner considered working more closely with the International Banking Corporation, a Connecticut-based bank, which did business in South America. A possible purchase of that bank's shares in exchange for shares of the Deutsche Ueberseeische Bank,[70] Deutsche Bank's subsidiary for Latin American business, was considered.

Especially after the Spanish-American War in 1898, Gwinner and Adams shared an enthusiasm for American imperialism and what it would mean for conquered regions, the American psyche, and New York as a financial center. Both saw American influence in what had once been Spanish controlled areas as an opportunity to run more business through New York. Along with the opportunity for German and American banks came the challenge of adapting the American political and economic system to its new role of world financial and political power. New York was now on equal terms with the other great money-centers – London, Berlin, and Paris – but without many of the necessary safeguards.[71] As discussed earlier, their concerns continued well into the new century.

The complexity and politics of some of Deutsche Bank's new undertakings produced problems for managing its U.S. business. As Deutsche Bank's worldwide interests grew, Adams feared that it would be harder and harder for him to represent them. Even though Deutsche Bank left him wide discretion for handling its affairs in the United States, Adams felt out of the loop of Deutsche Bank's strategic decisions.[72] By the turn of the century, Deutsche Bank had become very aggressively involved in other parts of the world – for example, in the Middle East and Russia. Adams felt that he did not have sufficient knowledge of these other commitments to adequately speak for Deutsche Bank in the United States. He assured Gwinner that his reaction to the bank's investments was not a criticism, merely an expression of frustration that he was unable to explain them to American clients. "You undoubtedly recognize that I am jealous of the reputation of your Bank in this country and am constantly watchful for everything that will protect it and augment it, feeling a personal interest in its personnel, quite apart and beyond the interest that I have directly in the results of management."[73]

In the face of these complications, Adams and Deutsche Bank managers began thinking about altering the structure of the bank's representation in America. The discussions about various options lasted nearly two decades. Deutsche Bank sometimes regretted not having more of an administrative presence in the United States, though none of the possible structures was ideal.[74] The issue was only resolved by a near-complete reversal in Deutsche Bank's business fortunes in the United States. Adams seems to have launched the first salvo, an idea to create a small private bank with him as head. Although the German bank wanted to strengthen its bonds with Adams by establishing some sort of organization, creating that structure would add expense and perhaps damage existing relationships. Creating a subsidiary had severe regulatory drawbacks and foreign agencies were not yet allowed in New York. Likewise, taking a sleeping interest in a partnership with a private firm would be against Deutsche Bank's policies, probably because it did not want to repeat its K&L experience.[75] Adams understood the logic of Gwinner's assessment, but regretted not having more information.[76] Gwinner felt compelled to restate the bank's policy of not going beyond Germany's frontiers with branch offices and subsidiaries, despite some temptations, particularly in Italy. The only exception was the London agency, which was necessary for its transoceanic business. The bank sought to avoid anything but pure commission banking business,[77] a policy which Adams found "conservative and conducive of the highest credit for international business and the greatest strength for domestic affairs."[78] However, some changes had to be made.

In the new century, Adams' age and health became more of a factor. Adams turned 60 in 1906, an age comparable to 80 today. Preoccupied also by the health of his wife,[79] Adams felt that he should have help in the New York office, both secretarial and other kinds. He wanted Deutsche Bank to send a representative to New York to whom he, Adams, could gradually transfer responsibility. Adams preferred Carl Bergmann, who had worked on studies of several American railroads and was willing to transfer to New York from Berlin. Concerned by the growing competition of Disconto-Gesellschaft and its New York bank connection Kuhn Loeb – whose business was mostly European but for whom Gwinner had little patience – Adams openly wondered whether Deutsche Bank could maintain its predominant position among German banks in the United States.[80] Preferring to send someone Adams had selected, Gwinner was ready to send Bergmann to New York as Adams' eventual replacement, but he feared that Adams would not share enough of the work with the young German he had selected.[81] For a while, the issue was once again tabled, but in January 1909, Deutsche Bank wrote to a pleased Adams that it was contemplating sending Bergmann to the United States.[82] Around this time, too, Axhausen went over to the United States and got involved in Lehigh Coke and other matters.

Delaying a succession plan for Adams was in part a sign of the bank's great confidence in him, but also reflected the bank's fear of the administrative consequences of replacing him with employees. The trust that Deutsche Bank exhibited in Adams was quite extraordinary. According to Gwinner, no individual in the world enjoyed more authority to commit the bank than Adams did. As a matter of fact, no Deutsche Bank executive in Berlin could exercise as much power as he could. Under the bank's articles of association, the signature of two bank executives was necessary to engage the bank. No director could buy or sell securities alone. Gwinner reminded Adams of the telegram drafted in the mid-1890s (probably around the time of the Gold Bond) between three and four in the morning by Siemens, his wife, and Gwinner authorizing Adams to lend $25 million of the bank's money whenever he thought fit. Gwinner had personally carried the message to the telegraph office.[83]

Not all the comments from Deutsche Bank about Adams, however, were positive. Some of the younger managers in Berlin complained that he sent too many undigested articles to the Berlin office. It seemed that he himself had not looked through them enough to know whether they were really important and, if there was some essential information, to make sure that it was appropriately highlighted. Complaints were voiced about unnumbered telegrams and expensive methods of sending messages.[84] Axhausen expressed concerns after his 1911 trip to the United States that he could not judge Adams' health, but that Deutsche Bank's American representative had clearly drawn himself away from the details of running the office and from pushing the publication of Deutsche Bank's financial results in American newspapers.[85]

But Adams' desire to reduce his office visits by building up his support staff to handle transactions always brought the bank back to the problem of authority.[86] Deutsche Bank would not extend its confidence to his whole office, not even to Bergmann, who was a Deutsche Bank employee. Even though Gwinner had confidence in Adams' staff of two or three, some of whom he had never met, he could not possibly authorize the individuals to sign for the bank. "That must be done by you and under your responsibility."[87]

As late as 1913, Deutsche Bank senior management seemed reluctant to let Adams retire. In response to a letter in which Adams talked about the difficulties with the coke company and other pressures, Gwinner asked him to consider ways to obtain relief from the workload short of retirement.[88] Even the older idea of a partnership was still on the table. A purely local group was unfeasible, though, for several reasons, not the least of which was that some of the members might have conflicting interests to those of the German bank. Gwinner wrote, "What the Bank wants in New York is that we should have hitherto a confidential advisor, a friend conversant with the Bank's principles, on whom we can call when his advice and counsel is needed."[89] Adams' desire to get away from the day-to-day business was not completely at odds with this mission. If he could retain his former role, the bank could strive to spare him from the time-absorbing execution and administration of transactions. Slowly, he could disengage from many troubled companies and some of his directorships.

Several possibilities were considered. To reduce the necessity of Adams coming into the office every day, the executives from Berlin might cable in instructions every day to correspondent banks. Adams could name brokers, with whom Deutsche Bank could settle up periodically. Some of the transactions required special secrecy, though, for which another alternative might be arranged.[90] Shortly before World War I, Deutsche Bank could have created a licensed agency in New York to conduct a great deal of banking business for which it relied on correspondent banks. Although an agent needed an official license, it resembled a branch but could not accept deposits apart from credit balances derived from trade transactions. By 1913, however, New York state had amended its banking law to permit agents to perform many more banking services, especially international ones.[91] Deutsche Bank seriously considered opening a branch for some of its business. No document lays out how the bank intended to configure its business, but some of Deutsche Bank's activities were to have been conducted by an agency (or branch as they are called in Deutsche Bank documents), but with the coming of World War I the plans were postponed "temporarily" – unforeseeably for those involved the postponement was to last seven decades.

Unfortunately, Deutsche Bank's general needs in the United States, and for Adams' services in particular, increased. Though the bank tried to avoid leaning on Adams too much, none of the "junior partners" envisioned by 1914 – Alfred Blinzig, Bergmann, or Axhausen – were ideal. Gwinner ruled out Blinzig, who could not be spared in Berlin. Bergmann had become too involved in South American affairs to add U.S. business to his workload, and Axhausen had just left New York to live with his aged mother, a decision the bank respected. Gwinner suggested that Bergmann continue some of his South American activities from New York and that he work closely with John McClement, an American banker who was already handling some of Deutsche Bank's affairs in New York. Bergmann and McClement were very friendly. Gwinner felt that they could work well together, take many of the burdens off Adams, and handle the South American affairs, so that Adams could focus on just those issues that required his judgment and experience.[92] Although the decision to have Bergmann take up an assignment in New York in September seemed final, unforeseen circumstances relieved the bank from having to address just how Bergmann would work with Adams and McClement.

There were many other transitions, too, in American banking. Ironically, Adams wrote Gwinner with fascination about the construction plans for the great new Bankers Trust building on the corner of Wall and Cedar Streets. The plan called for an elevation of five hundred feet above the street and several stories below the sidewalk to house the expanding new bank.[93] In 1910, Edgar L. Marston, the president of Blair & Co., which was closely tied to the Rockefellers, informed Adams that the partnership had decided to disband. The closing of Blair held special significance for Deutsche Bank and its fortunes with the Western Maryland Railroad. For several years, Blair and Deutsche Bank maintained a tight relationship. Blinzig and Marston in particular seemed to work very closely together. Deutsche Bank relied on Blair to control WMR. In return, Deutsche Bank put Blair on its list of "most intimate friends."[94]

Even without a branch or subsidiary in one of the most important capital markets, by virtually any financial measure, on the eve of World War I, Deutsche Bank was still a worldwide player in financial markets. Exceptionally, Deutsche Bank's files contain a 1913 report listing all its securities, including its American holdings. The American paper amounted to 9 million Mark ($2.2 million), less than in 1890, but roughly 20 percent of all the securities the bank held for its own account, even though much of its Lehigh Coke, Kerbaugh Empire Company, and Allis-Chalmers holdings were carried at a nominal value of 1 Mark. It was a diverse package including: rail debt; U.S. coal equity; and notably two

American trust ventures (pools), Société Financière de Valeurs Américaines and Zurich American Trust.[95]

As early as 1899, Deutsche Bank and Adams had begun looking into the possibility of selling European securities in the United States. According to Adams, more and more public attention was turning to foreign loans. The prospect first of Russian bonds and then German bonds coming onto U.S. capital markets had excited much interest. He was confident that German bonds, owing to the greater interest in and knowledge of Germany, would be better received. A campaign of education was required that would be a sensible investment only if the institution providing the business was assured of regular business.[96] There were some regulatory obstacles.[97] Before World War I, to Deutsche Bank's continued frustration, this business never got off the ground.

America's lack of regulatory discipline continued to disturb German executives. Although prosperity was restored in 1908, the ups and downs of the U.S. capital markets reduced business and personal enthusiasm for further U.S. investment. In winter 1910, the U.S. market was once again under pressure. The death of the older Harriman, whose estate was much more indebted than anyone in the market had thought, led to large sales of Central Pacific, Union Pacific, and other shares. Among the shares were some that Adams had advised the Metropolitan Museum of Art, on whose board he sat, to buy. Morgan, he claimed, had been manipulating the market with regard to some shares.[98]

More seriously, disputes between European countries sometimes undermined German relations with the United States. The American press often showed a hostile reaction to Germany.[99] Relations with Britain, too, had clearly deteriorated since the Boer War. As early as 1903, Gwinner was concerned about British agitation for tariffs. His comments to Mount Stephen about British policies show how nineteenth-century liberal principles and tolerance were beginning to fray.

> Although I am a free-trader myself I do not see why Great Britain should not make a trial with Protection. British Industries, I take it, are not suffering the effects of insular free trade which has brought about such a wonderful development in your country during the past 50 years, but rather of Trade Unionists of which you are sorely afflicted. We are having some experiences of that ourselves in your country. Then again, some of your countrymen have become lazy, precisely as a result of their great prosperity.[100]

In spring 1914, Deutsche Bank in Berlin finally resolved to replace Adams, but Adams, as late as mid-June, still seems not to have been informed of the decision. In the end, his handling of some aspects of the Western Maryland investment, and the perception in Berlin by some that he was not sufficiently popular with New York bankers to make and keep friends for Deutsche Bank, a quality essential for representing the bank's interests there, prompted the final decision. The transition was one of the main subjects of a series of meetings in Berlin between representatives of the bank and Benjamin Strong, then president of Bankers Trust, but who would soon become governor of the New York Federal Reserve in mid-June 1914.[101] Obviously, none of the participants could have known how much the subjects of the talks would be affected by the assassination of the Archduke at Sarajevo on June 28, 1914. Hugo Schmidt, the Berlin manager at Deutsche Bank responsible for North American affairs, took the lead from Deutsche Bank's side.[102] He feared that Adams would be annoyed and hurt by the change. Perhaps this was inevitable, but the change was necessary due to the continuing problems with Western Maryland Securities that had been widely purchased in Germany, especially in Berlin, based on Deutsche Bank's advice. According to Schmidt, many German investors had bought the stock, now selling at 15 or 16, for 65, hurting the reputation of American investments in general.

Strong, in contrast, defended Adams' representation of Deutsche Bank's interests. All WMR's directors had been deceived. Bankers Trust, however, was the only exception, declining a loan, which annoyed both Adams and Rockefeller. Strong confidently predicted that the stock would turn around, because the company was fundamentally sound and had good relationships with other important lines.[103]

Their conversations give an excellent glimpse of what business people were discussing just weeks before World War I broke out. Schmidt insisted that Strong spend enough time at the bank to meet with all of Deutsche Bank's leading managers. Strong did see Blinzig and Gwinner, but he left no specific record of their conversation. In general, Strong reported that Deutsche Bank management displayed a wide range of knowledge about U.S. affairs but still distrusted American political conditions. In a private meeting with Strong, Bergmann expressed a great deal of interest in cultivating a closer relationship with Bankers Trust once he got to New York. As there were no outstanding business issues between the banks, Schmidt and Strong spent most of their time talking about general business conditions in the United States, France, Germany, and Cuba. Although confident that the German banking system was in excellent shape, Schmidt expressed his concern about the French "extravagant sale of foreign securities of doubtful value," especially Russian bonds. Despite some criticism by Schmidt of American pricing for some transactions, Strong hoped that the American and German banks could work closer together in the future.[104] Strong even pushed for Deutsche Bank to set up a new office in the Bankers Trust building in New York. He wrote to Schmidt from Amsterdam just after his visit to Berlin: "The location is so central, and his [a Deutsche Bank representative, author's note] facility on that account for making use of our office would enable us to be of more value to him than if he were situated further away."[105] Strong felt confident, too, that Bankers Trust would develop an even closer relationship to Deutsche Bank.[106] His confidence in that relationship and Schmidt's fears about Russian bonds turned out to be more well-founded than either could have dreamt.

As Europe was "turning off the lamps," Adams, apparently now informed of Bergmann's planned arrival, wrote that he agreed completely with the transition plan and pledged to "take Mr. Bergmann at once into my full confidence and try to convince him of its sincerity and completeness."[107] The intended mixture of personnel to replace Adams in June became even more complicated than anyone could have imagined, and would continue to cause problems for the next few years. Deutsche Bank was about to have employee representation in the United

States but was still very far from internalizing its U.S. banking business. For many decades, it remained dependent on a series of personal relationships with "outsiders" rather than on an operation of its own. Sadly, just as the regulatory doors to cross-border banking operations in the United States were opening, the international political ones were shutting. Not a word was written in Strong's notes about the possibility of a coming war. Less than two months after Schmidt and Strong's conversation, Deutsche Bank had a completely new set of worries in the United States. Within five months Schmidt arrived in New York instead of Bergmann, who had been recruited into government service.[108]

Section II

Deutsche Bank and the United States During the "Great Disorder,"[1] 1914 to 1957

Since beginning to work in banking, I have endeavoured to avoid consistently public affairs. Public matters produce conflict with business or conviction, and I do not wish to come in conflict with either of these fundamental aspects of human life.

Otto Jeidels of Berliner Handels-Gesellschaft to Emil Georg Stauss of Deutsche Bank, March 21, 1922.

I almost wish to say that I have come to just the opposite conclusion, because I fear that business people in the future will not be able to avoid political issues, as was the case in the past. I believe the British system is better and that we would not have come to war, if businessmen here in Germany had had more influence over politics.

Stauss to Jeidels, March 23, 1922, both HADB, S3626.

Introduction

> ...[T]he state has everywhere played a greater role in economic life. The preparation and conduct of major wars have served as the catalyst of this process, but it is obvious that the growth of private economic power, the recognition that the state could itself take action to relieve and mitigate the effect of economic crisis, and the intensified demand by large segments of the population for an increasing measure of social security in the broadest sense, have all served to increase the functions of the state.
>
> Gerald Feldman, *Iron and Steel in the German Inflation*, p. 9.

The years covered by this Section, 1914 to 1957, invite comparison with some of history's most dismal periods. The decades following the French Revolution or those of the Thirty Years' War come to mind. Like these earlier periods, few firm markers clearly designate their beginnings and ends, only somewhat arbitrary signposts. One could reasonably ask whether this period opened with the assassination of the Archduke or with the recognition that the interminable trench war required total mobilization, denying both sides a glorious, quick victory. For Deutsche Bank, as for other firms, some of the effects of the war took hold gradually. Although the forty years before World War I knew panics, depressions, and war, as Mira Wilkins wrote of a period covering roughly the same time frame, the decades following the outbreak of the Great War lacked the consistency of the pre-World War I period.[2] Another economic historian provided a vivid image of the transition when he wrote that in a few weeks of 1914 the economic world went from a calm stream to "white water."[3] During the fifty some years following the opening salvos in August 1914, the world witnessed two world wars taking tens of millions of military and civilian lives, several "smaller conflicts," hyperinflation, deep depression, the rise of the modern totalitarian state, and, above all, genocide on a scale of probably unprecedented proportions. This Section covers, like these earlier periods, too, a time of seemingly relentless struggle, cruelty, and suffering, but it also heralded the foundations of a new, more constructive political and economic environment.

As the historian Harold James wrote of the mid-twentieth century, after World War II Europe witnessed a rebirth. The geographic – and gender – spreading of democracy; mass access to new goods and services – and some goods and services once reserved only for economic elites; shorter working hours with better working conditions; greater social and economic entry possibilities for minority races and women in the developed world; and, above all, more leisure, more mobility, and better health care for those living in Western Europe and the United States all seemed not only to form a convincing break with the past but also greater hope for the future.[4]

As James notes elsewhere, the first half of the twentieth century witnessed a huge shift in international political economy and regulation of capital markets. Gone were government restrictions on themselves and the semi-automatic mechanisms for regulating macroeconomic imbalances. For much of the period that followed the outbreak of hostilities in 1914, many governments tried in vain to replace the prewar system with supranational organizations designed to replace their nationally based disciplined regulation of the world economy, while simultaneously dooming those efforts with trade and capital movement restrictions, wasteful spending and, finally, to some, bellicose nationalism and autarky.[5]

Above all for business, the period is associated with two enormous "sea changes." The first is the economic and political entrance of the United States on to the world stage. To be sure, many changes did not occur overnight, and American financial and other business institutions were not the only ones to profit, but the relative shift in the positions of American vis-à-vis British and German capital markets was staggering.[6] As this Section opens, the United States was by far the largest economy in the world and its citizens felt reasonably secure within its borders behind vast oceans and a large navy. It was a net borrower nation; its capital markets were still overshadowed by Britain's. Although America maintained a few colonies, in 1914, its army was relatively small and stationed mainly in the United States. Few American businesses had operations or investments beyond U.S. borders or those of nearby dependent countries.

By the end of this time period, however, fear of fascism and then communism helped transform a tradition of American self-confidence and self-reliance to anxiety and a web of international interdependencies. America's reluctant and inconsistent internationalism spanned economic, political, and military spheres. From Seoul to Berlin, by 1957, the United States had large numbers of troops stationed outside its borders. By 1957, it spearheaded the creation and deployment of two large military alliances and fought two major wars and one "police action." Moreover, by 1957, American money, movies, management, and modes of thought seemed to many European business and intellectual leaders as a stronger invading force than its divisions.[7] For Deutsche Bank, America's new – albeit inconsistent – international economic and political hegemony transformed its regulatory and strategic horizons.

The second is epitomized by the preceding quotes by Otto Jeidels of Berliner Handels-Gesellschaft, Emil Georg Stauss of Deutsche Bank, and that by Gerald Feldman. Suddenly, politics took on a paramount importance for business. This is not to say that politics had no significance for business people before 1914. Some businessmen, such as Siemens, were active in political parties and ran for office. However, whereas before 1914 governments used their sovereign powers sparingly, after 1914, driven first by military conflicts and then the misery that followed them, governments and politics played a far greater role in economic life. Politics became so important and so strident that indeed many seemed to forget that economics counted at all. Not until John Maynard Keynes wrote his *General Theory* in the 1930s did both economics and politics receive theoretical justification for how much the two were inextricably intertwined. Like economic theory, much of the business community tried for a long time to live as if the two were independent, as in the nineteenth century. As in other eras with different passions – religion, freedom, and nationalism, for example – now politics was on the ascent. The war not only increased the scope of government activities, it changed their spending habits. From 1913, tax revenues climbed from less than 5 percent of Germany's GDP to approximately 20 percent of the Federal Republic's GDP in 1960.[8] Most countries in the developed world lost much of their fiscal discipline and increased their borrowing.[9] From 1914 to 1940, German treasury bills went from less than 20 percent of Deutsche Bank's assets to approximately 70 percent.[10]

The added power government assumed, even in liberal democracies, created a new dimension – or at the very least, one that had been dormant for 100 years – for businesses in North America and Europe: systematic political risk. In the hundred years before World War I, bankers always had to worry about how national tensions might reduce the value of some new securities issues, or how a country's commitment to the Gold Standard might suddenly be called into question – notably the United States and Argentina. But after 1914, not only did governments substantially shift responsibility to firms for managing foreign exchange exposures, they tried to manage flows of capital, goods, and services, pushed their own national economic projects, entered labor relations, increased taxes, and expropriated property on a scale unimagined before.[11] For most of the next three decades, economic imbalances, such as excess capacity and divisions between capital-rich and poor nations, were encouraged by, or at least insufficiently addressed by, governments and other financial regulators, making military conflict for many an acceptable remedy.

9

Personal, Communication, and Financial Breakdowns

From Banking to Blockade Running

It would be useless for me to deny that the prolonged duration of the war and the ensuing and continuing weakness of the Mark exchange has been a severe disappointment, my expectation having been that our enemies would be reasonable enough, in view of the marked success of our arms, to put an end to the slaughter by coming to terms. As they insist upon receiving still severer punishment before acknowledging the truth and bowing to the hard logic of facts, and as present indications therefore are that the exchange situation will not be relieved for some time to come, I have been giving constant thought to the financial problems created by the exchange situation, and which are now threatening to perpetuate themselves unless some remedy is soon devised.

Mankiewitz to Adams, November 20, 1915, HADB, A528.

You will share our pleasure about the splendid success of our troops. Sadly, we have already lost a young friend, married for only four months, at Donon. Another lies with a bad lung wound close to death.

Blinzig to Axhausen, September 1, 1914, HADB, A461.

Personal and Personnel Matters

The outbreak of World War I created many strains for Deutsche Bank and its managers. By early August 1914, drafts went unpaid, stock markets closed, and German banks experienced a significant drop in deposits.[1] The war and its aftermath not only buffeted the world financial system, it also called into question personal relations, such as those between Gwinner and Adams and Blinzig and Marston. It tore the New York banking community into pro-German and pro-English factions.

Although Blinzig and Marston, for example, continued to discuss business matters, especially WMR issues, the war and each nation's perceptions of the other played an increasing role in their correspondence. An atmosphere of blame and counter-charge replaced the older amiable business ties. For example:

You mention in your letter that you had been unable to communicate with your friends by cable due to the action of the German Government [sic]. Now I may assure you that it is certainly not the German Government [sic] that puts itself in the way of a free intercourse between your country and ours: you may put that blame solely upon the English who have cut the German cable immediately after declaration of war and not let pass since any cables with addresses in Germany.

The English have always been clever enough to work the opinion in the various countries of the world according to their desires. The cable monopoly they have now is used by them to an astounding degree. The newspapers that come now from your side show the result thereof, and all the opinions and reports therein about Germany's doings and intentions and the state of our country are really most surprising news for us. It would be inconceivable that so much falsehood could be believed by anybody who knows our people if it were not exactly for the fact that our adversaries have made the fullest use of their power to prevent us from stating our case as it really is.[2]

Blinzig wrote pages about how Germany really wanted to avoid a war that was forced on her by the Allies, particularly Russia. Despite Allied press claims to the contrary, he wrote, now that it had been declared all Germans were behind the war effort to an astonishing degree. Through the winter of 1915, Blinzig worried that Americans in general and Marston in particular "might be influenced by the distorted opinions now prevailing in your country about everything German."[3]

Clearly, America's relationship with Germany took a turn for the worse with the sinking of the *Lusitania*. Schmidt wrote Blinzig of the "colossal agitation" ignited by this event and how much it reinforced America's strong "love of England" and "hatred of Germany." "The newspapers ritualistically scream with anger."[4] Marston wrote that he only forgave his old friend and colleague Blinzig because Germany had finally changed its policy and because he was convinced that his friend could never have supported the unrestrained submarine warfare. "I have been unable to date to bring myself to the belief that my own personal friends have approved of the Lusitania disaster and some other actions reported in the press."[5]

Nevertheless, many of these relationships survived the war. Blinzig and Marston exchanged personal letters after the end of hostilities.[6] Blinzig, though, seemed very bitter:

These years have been terrible ones for us, and one of the sadest [sic] experiences for me was to see, [sic] how the campaign of the press and the calumniations of everything German, that may or may not be considered as a weapon of war as well as justified by others, have borne fruit. I am confident however that in time our German people may still expect a more just appreciation. I always felt sure that you, knowing more of our people, than most of your countrymen, would not allow to have your view and judgement obscured. I was glad to receive your card. . . . There is already a good deal of improvement. Our people are willing to work, but in order to be able to work they want coal and food. The peace makes it well nigh impossible to provide both and therefore it is a bad treaty. It does not deserve its name.[7]

The war threw Deutsche Bank's personnel plans for the United States up in the air. As discussed in the last Chapter, the plan to send Carl Bergmann, who would take responsibility for many Latin American transactions and much of Adams' activities, had to be scrapped. He was to work closely with John McClement, an American who would take over from Adams as the bank's American spokesman with local banks and corporations. McClement had worked with several railroad and electrical companies, including the Western Maryland Railroad. Since

Lusitania Sinking, the Greatest of Ocean Tragedies

THE LUSITANIA, WHICH SAILED FROM NEW YORK FOR LIVERPOOL MAY 1, 1915, WITH 1,959 SOULS ON BOARD, WAS SUNK BY A GERMAN SUBMARINE MAY 7, WITH A LOSS, INCLUDING WOMEN AND CHILDREN, OF 1,195.

THE SINKING OF THE LUSITANIA, THAT GREATEST OF OCEAN TRAGEDIES, IS HERE PORTRAYED BY A BRITISH ARTIST FROM DESCRIPTION AND WITH THE AID OF SURVIVORS. THE MARKINGS ON THE PICTURE GIVE THE MOST IMPORTANT DETAILS. THE MOMENT CHOSEN IS WHEN BOATS ARE PULLING AWAY WITH SURVIVORS

SERVICES AT THE GRAVESIDE OF THE LUSITANIA VICTIMS IN THE CEMETERY AT QUEENSTOWN, IRELAND, WHILE ON THE OTHER SIDE OF THE OCEAN ALL AMERICA MOURNED IN SYMPATHY.

(© International News Service.)

358

The sinking of the British passenger liner, RMS *Lusitania*, on May 7, 1915, which resulted in the deaths of over a thousand crew and passengers, including women and children, aroused enormous anger in the United States and contributed greatly to American willingness to enter World War I, albeit two years later. American troops going into battle in France were said to have shouted, "Remember the *Lusitania*." Considered by some in Germany a strategic necessity brought on by British use of passenger ships to convey war materials shielded by civilians, as the *Lusitania* was actually doing, the sinking was a moral burden for many Germans and certainly a propaganda catastrophe that ultimately undermined the German war effort.

1905, he had represented the interests of German banks and served as president of Empire Engineering. This contact with Deutsche Bank was particularly close in 1914–15, when Deutsche Bank was selling a lot of Empire's securities in Europe.[8] However, as the threat of hostilities grew in Europe, Adams' willingness to devote time to help the bank increased. At the end of July 1914, he even offered to house Bergmann in his own offices, a working arrangement Deutsche Bank seemed eager to avoid.[9] The war delayed Bergmann's departure and finally led to the decision that he would not return to the United States. The uncertainty caused by the war also seemed to make the bank reluctant to "change horses." For the foreseeable future, it would rely on Adams, at least for some business. The trick was determining how to avoid offending everyone. Although the exact timing and explanation is not clear, within a few months of European nations declaring war, Hugo Schmidt was on his way to the United States with a somewhat different mandate than his junior, Bergmann, had had.

Many important issues – even the date of Schmidt's arrival – were unclear. His departure from Germany coincided with growing anti-German sentiment. English agents were promoting hostility toward Germany, including German business interests. Even private banking houses with German connections were suffering.[10] During the first month of Schmidt's stay, Adams and Schmidt saw each other daily to compare notes on their perceptions of conditions and to help Schmidt make more contacts. Plans for creating a formal branch agency had to be dropped. The time was not right. Adams preferred to let Schmidt do more of the communications with Berlin, though he personally pledged to continue to write about things he considered particularly important.[11] According to Adams, Schmidt gave the impression that Deutsche Bank's affairs in the United States were their joint responsibility, even though friction still persisted over the WMR refinancing.[12]

This lack of clarity contributed to tension and provoked awkward situations. After his arrival, Schmidt had to contend with all the different personalities and the indecisive, unclear assignments. "My situation with Adams and McClement is not pleasant, as I have to go back and forth between the two without the other noticing, or feeling preferred or ignored," Schmidt reported in December.[13] Even though he felt his relationship with Adams was excellent, Schmidt feared that he had made no progress on the issues that concerned the bank most and that he would soon have to turn to McClement. Giving Adams no new assignments would be helpful, because they kept Adams' hopes up that he would continue to represent the bank. Schmidt intended to use Adams' six-week stay in California that winter to take over many of the affairs, especially those concerning Lehigh Coke, as will be discussed later. In the context of a cold New York winter and anti-German press, Schmidt, left largely alone, doubted whether Adams realized he would be replaced and whether he would be really happy with the idea.[14]

Schmidt and his superiors disagreed on how to handle the situation, perhaps because of the communication difficulties or perhaps because of their varying proximities to the players and problems. It took three weeks for Schmidt's views to reach Berlin, where Deutsche Bank's management had already come to the conclusion that the war necessitated postponing the plans for Bergmann and McClement to work together. Adams still was chairman of the board of Lehigh and held a share of the profits, but it was not just money or the bank's long-term relationship to Adams that counted. Since the war broke out, the bank had been forced to make greater demands on Adams because many clients knew only him and they could not make direct contact with Deutsche Bank in Berlin, a fact that the bank had taken pains to explain to McClement. What made the situation even more delicate was Adams' own ambivalence. On the one hand, he wanted to be relieved of work; on the other, he displayed an unwillingness to break the old ties. In the judgment of the Berlin managers, Adams was struggling to balance his own personal wishes to tend to his health with his commitment to his Deutsche Bank's affairs.[15] But all of the bank's main contacts in New York – Marston, Otto Kahn (Kuhn Loeb), James Speyer, for example – were asking: Who represents Deutsche Bank in New York? Answering the question with Adams or McClement around was not simple for Schmidt and led to some embarrassment.[16] Moreover, Adams was beginning to convince Schmidt that he had been right all along about some issues.[17] New to the city, the personalities, and some of the problems – and with delayed communications with his head office – Schmidt wrestled with assessing complicated questions and situations.

With communication difficulties and anti-German sentiment mounting, Schmidt must have felt more and more isolated in the United States. One year into the war, the parties were beginning to feel its consequences. Letters between New York and the head office contained a good deal of personal news. Blinzig shared news of his father's death, his children's illness, and his fears about the future, especially in light of what then seemed to be a long, drawn-out war.[18] Schmidt also shared his concerns about the consequences of a long war. Each year seemed to bring new and severe challenges.

Although many of Deutsche Bank's American investments were doing well, such as Western Maryland (WMR) and Allis-Chalmers, more conflicts among banks and their surrogates as well as other stakeholders arose.[19] In early 1916, with greater risks for the bank and favorable exchange rate and stock prices, Deutsche Bank began to speed up the liquidation of somc of its investments.[20] However, getting additional dividends out of companies sometimes brought Deutsche Bank into conflict with other investors, who did not share the bank's need for transferable cash.[21] As early as fall 1914, German businessmen and those associated with them were watched by both British and American agents. Adams himself was probably on British lists of German sympathizers. By January 1915, U.S. firms with which Deutsche Bank did business had been interviewed by the State Department about associations with and associates of Deutsche Bank. Deutsche Bank representatives believed that British agents were actively spreading rumors about the bank to undermine its business and that of other German firms. Britain had taken the position that companies in neutral countries with majority ownership from enemy lands were considered hostile companies.[22]

There was some reason for British concern. Deutsche Bank participated in cloaking some companies from hostile nations through neutral countries.

The steamship *Steaua Romana*, for example, originally owned by Romanian investors, found its way into the hands of Americans with the help of Deutsche Bank.[23]

The personal relationships between Schmidt and several Americans seemed to deteriorate during the war, sometimes for political reasons, sometimes for other reasons. In one letter he expressed very critical views of Speyer & Co. and called one of the board members of a company in which Deutsche Bank had a large investment a pighead. Many sorts of issues remained between Adams and Schmidt. Although Adams always tried to be nice and helpful, Schmidt condescendingly remarked that Adams' age made any kind of serious discussion complicated and took up a great deal of his (Schmidt's) ever more precious time.[24]

In contrast to its New York German representative, Deutsche Bank in Berlin had nothing against Adams' involvement in complex issues, but did in day-to-day matters and sensitive cross-border transactions, which included several deals with Speyer.[25] In early January 1916, Adams finally handed over to Schmidt the keys and responsibility for a safe deposit box containing loan agreements and insurance policies carried on key executives of companies in which the bank invested.[26] But Adams remained the primary contact person for WMR – whose shares Deutsche Bank tried to unload in spring 1916 just a few days before an erroneous earnings report knocked the bottom out of its share prices – and for Lehigh Coke, which was still causing all concerned enormous headaches, as will be discussed further in the next Chapter.[27]

Communication and Transfers

Stopping normal messages between Germany and the rest of the world was one of Britain's early war aims. Five hours after war was declared on August 5, the British cable ship *Teleconia* dragged her grappling irons along the North Sea cutting five of Germany's main cable links with the world. On the same day, a British cruiser cut two cables near the Azores, effectively cutting communication for Germany beyond Europe – all part of the effort to disrupt the German economy.[28] The outbreak of hostilities necessitated a change in how Deutsche Bank communicated and did business with the United States. The basic plan was put into place in September 1914. It was agreed that Credit Suisse would establish a "special account" with National City Bank in its name but for Deutsche Bank and its customers. For this service the Swiss would charge a 1 percent commission on all transactions from both the seller and buyer. Deutsche Bank had to bear all the risk. The plan would eventually involve other New York banks such as Guaranty Trust but not Speyer, for obvious reasons. In effect, Deutsche Bank as far as New York transactions were concerned became, like many others, a client of Credit Suisse, except that settlement would be in Dollars instead of Swiss Francs.[29] Communication would flow from Berlin, to Munich, to Zurich, and then to New York. Nearly all this was clearly stated to National City Bank by the end of September,[30] but the system did not function perfectly.[31]

Private dealings became more dependent on national governments. German banks began to rely on diplomatic services to deliver their mail. Telegraph service between Germany and Russia was lost on August 1, and between Germany and France on August 3. Only coded cables through the Azores passed from the United States to Germany, beginning on August 3. A few days later, all direct cable lines between the United States and Germany were broken. Senders of cables that passed through the complicated routing system were uncertain about when and if they would reach their destination. Some were censured and most delayed with far-reaching effects for transactions. Access to diplomatic cable services through Denmark offered German banks one of the few reasonably reliable alternatives but made them dependent on government priorities and whims. Even mail connections required intermediaries. The American government discouraged use of radio communications.[32]

Simple financial transactions became cumbersome. With the exchanges closed, efforts of many Europeans to liquidate their U.S. holdings during the early days of the war were virtually paralyzed. Payments of checks and bills of exchange, many through London, were blocked after Britain declared war. Approximately 150,000 Americans were traveling in Europe when the war broke out. For a few weeks, continental banks refused to change money or take tourist travelers checks until leading institutions such as Bankers Trust and Deutsche Bank devised together with government representatives a means of sorting out the mess.[33]

The situation for German banks in London was particularly important, yet confusing. On August 6, Deutsche Bank received permission to continue its London operations, but a day later the government closed it. On August 10, the British government decided to limit the branch's activities – but gave the bank no explicit written explanation of how and in what way. Later Deutsche Bank learned that the London branch had to fulfill all its prewar commitments, but was not allowed to enter new ones.[34] With the restrictions inconsistently applied, amazingly, some German banks' branches were permitted to conduct business in London through much of early August 1914.[35] All communication, bookings, and so on had to be postponed until permission was received to restart them.[36] The authorities appointed a commissioner to oversee the German banks' London branches.[37]

All governments stiffened controls on gold and foreign exchange movements, but in different manners reflecting their different economic systems and immediate needs. A patriotic appeal for gold by the Reichsbank actually increased the central bank's reserves during the first few years of war, postponing the almost inevitable – a plunge in the value of the Mark and future gold purchases at a high premium. By 1916, the Reichsbank, however, had to control the public price of foreign exchange transactions. In the United States, the war coincided with some of the first activities of the Federal Reserve System. Few members of the new Federal Reserve Board had foreign experience. It was preoccupied by internal matters and slow to relieve the problems caused by the war for international transactions. In the end, the claims on U.S. gold were stemmed, not by the Fed, but by America's status as the only major country to avoid the worst effects of the war and maintain gold convertibility. For Germany, sale of American securities and repatriation of the proceeds became a high priority.[38]

German institutions were obliged to work through neutral countries. Almost immediately after war was declared, Deutsche Bank sent Bruno Axhausen to Switzerland to coordinate communication between the United States and Germany. Although very useful, Axhausen's mission was not completely successful. His position at the Swiss bank was delicate. Only some senior managers knew what he was doing. The Swiss bankers were understandably anxious that no one in Britain or France learn of Axhausen's office and activities. He was warned by the Swiss many times to avoid any communication of a military nature. The German bankers had to change their Swiss mailing address several times. Even letters from Americans to Americans were delayed. Letters tended to mix several languages or were written in code. All the participants were confused about when and if their letters were received. Axhausen worried that the Allies falsified cables to confuse them. For some of his communications, Axhausen was obliged to cross the border into Germany, a long and tiring trip under war conditions. News about his own family and his draft status was much too infrequent.[39] During the first few weeks of the war, there seems to have been delays in receiving letters in Germany even from neighboring Switzerland.

Adams was a key figure in keeping some of the correspondence flowing between the Berlin and New York offices of Deutsche Bank.[40] His letters flowed through neutral countries with greater ease.[41] He was still entrusted with holding many of Deutsche Bank's American securities,[42] but as early as August 1914, even Adams and Deutsche Bank experienced communication problems. Deutsche Bank received word through Axhausen that Adams had not heard from Deutsche Bank since the beginning of August, and that Adams wanted to update Berlin about many matters, such as about how and when emergency payments were being made by New York banks, when the stock exchange would reopen, and what other measures were being studied in the United States to handle the crisis.[43] Cables through Switzerland were being held up at the French border and censors in Germany and Switzerland added to the delays.

Communication often ran through Denmark and the Netherlands, despite both countries' desire to preserve strict neutrality. The work was dangerous – two couriers were arrested.[44] Adams would receive batches of letters, sometimes through the German Embassy. No cables were accepted for Germany, but by using disguised German names (Smith for Schmidt), first names, using the names of officers for institutions, using street names (preferably Anglicized) instead of the person's name, and avoiding use of currency names, the messages could get through.[45] During the first six months of the war, Deutsche Bank received correspondence in huge batches (one day 50 items, letters, and articles from Copenhagen; another time 20 from Rotterdam). Some arrived three weeks after the date sent; others seven weeks.[46]

Despite the use of intermediaries, by early September Deutsche Bank was concerned that its payment instructions were not being processed in New York.

The success of British censors had added a great deal of uncertainty about transactions, which became even more serious once the stock exchange was reopened. The bank considered giving up direct control over future orders from Berlin. New York transactions were cloaked, appearing to be one of many others processed by Credit Suisse for customers.[47]

Finance

It is hard to imagine a more profound break in the financial affairs of any institution than that which was felt by Deutsche Bank during World War I and its aftermath. In sharp contrast to the prewar years, during and after the war salvaging as much of its own and its customers' assets in the United States and raising funds on U.S. markets became the German bank's principal U.S. activity. In July 1914, no one seemed to have foreseen these consequences of the war. World stock markets hardly took notice during the week that followed the assassination of the Archduke Francis Ferdinand on June 28, 1914. Prices slumped, but not until mid-July did "unusually" large sales indicate that investors had begun to take a European war seriously. Large drops in European stock prices were followed by sales of American securities.[48] European sales of American stocks first hit American markets heavily during the last week of July, but even then few observers imagined the extent to which the coming war would overturn existing economic relationships.

The financial implications for Deutsche Bank were mixed well into the war. *The New York Times* reported correctly in May 1916 that Deutsche Bank paid a 12.5 percent dividend on the nominal value of its shares, with substantial increases in reserves and assets. But the Deutsche Bank annual report, released nearly five months after the financial year end, also suggested the gravity of the true situation in terms of long-term costs: 226 Deutsche Bank employees had died in the line of service, 49 more than the year before – over 2 percent of the bank's entire staff. The bank also noted that the British estimated that their own equity values had dropped by $2 billion. Some analysts believed that New York had already surpassed London as a financial center.[49]

It is an exaggeration, but only a small one, to say that Germany and her allies were undone by their inferior position in financial and trade relations. Even before America's entry into the war, Germany lost the battle to harness American resources that could potentially have been utilized for the war effort. This fact did not go unnoticed in Germany and at Deutsche Bank. The Allies were far more successful at raising capital in the United States to pay for purchases there. Indeed, the use of the money for American purchases played an important part in marketing the loans to professional investors and the public at large. Although some banks, especially those with German connections, were reluctant to contribute to the Allied war efforts – especially Russia's – and powerful Americans like John D. Rockefeller were reluctant to get involved at all, the loans were, by and large, fully subscribed.[50] By July 1915, the Allies had borrowed nearly $10.3 billion; Germany, Austria-Hungary, and Turkey only $5.3 billion.[51] Despite Deutsche Bank's efforts to market and safeguard German government securities offered to the market during the war, German debt had an enormous disadvantage: it appeared riskier and German purchases in the United States were made more difficult by the Allied embargo.

Those sympathetic with Germany mounted a campaign to stop America's financial support of the Allies. The secretary of the German-American Chamber of Commerce, Heinrich Charles, wrote to bankers, investors, and to the U.S. government complaining about America's "unneutral" financial behavior. He pleaded that new loans should be tied to embargo concessions allowing supplies for Germany via neutral ports to proceed.[52] According to Charles, the U.S. Treasury had taken steps to bolster Sterling but did nothing to help the value of the Mark.[53]

Charles' missives brought him into a war of words with Deutsche Bank's old "friend" James J. Hill. Charles reminded Hill of German-Americans' great respect for him as a financial magnate, and took him to task for encouraging Americans to do business only with Britain and France. He reminded Hill that the Allies might lose the war, making the amounts owed to Americans virtually worthless. Would not Americans be wiser to cultivate business in other parts of the world, and Hill personally better off not to risk his "reputation in a lost cause?"[54] In another letter, a day later, he encouraged Hill to use his energies and influence for finding ways to allow the American farmers' wheat, corn, and cotton to reach the civilian populations of Germany, Austria-Hungary, and Turkey, countries that were solvent and would pay cash.[55] Charles even wrote to the New York superintendent of insurance, charging that any insurance company investment in Allied debt was illegal and immoral.[56]

Despite the misgivings of some, without a doubt, the hostilities contributed to a huge shift in the world's financial balance of power and the configuration of international investment. When most of Europe plunged itself into war, America was the largest debtor nation in the world. Foreigners held nearly $7.1 billion in U.S. assets, mostly in the form of bonds. Over $5 billion was portfolio investment; in principle it could be easily liquidated. By the end of the war, foreign investment as a percentage of America's GDP had not only dropped dramatically, its composition and purpose had also changed dramatically. Most importantly, in the space of four years, America became the largest creditor nation in the world.[57]

The liquidation and repatriation of those securities posed many economic and administrative problems. The New York Stock Exchange was closed until November 28, 1914. Fortunately for many foreigners, there were sufficient domestic buyers for the orderly absorption of foreign securities sales. German investors, however, faced special obstacles. In addition to the closing of exchanges, many of their securities were held physically in London and the shipment of the proceeds of security sales in gold from New York was dangerous. Here Deutsche Bank's correspondent relationships with major U.S. banks, most importantly National City Bank, came in handy.[58] Moreover, Deutsche Bank representatives used the bank's offices to facilitate commodities transactions that were more difficult to handle from Germany,[59] a particularly important function beginning with the onset of hostilities because Germany's ability to feed itself was of great concern.[60]

The German government tried to use the funds obtained from the sale of securities by its nationals in the United States to support its war efforts. According to journalists in the United States, Deutsche Bank records revealed that many of the 32,000 subscribers to German and Austrian war loans were German nationals living in the United States, who had sold other securities to buy German bonds. Some of the funds were even used to support German "plots."[61]

The war shifted long-established risk and reward tradeoffs, and tore asunder financial relations. It split the U.S. banking community. The House of Morgan and National City, so important to Deutsche Bank's transactions in New York, tended to favor the Allies, but, for example, Speyer & Co. and Goldman Sachs had very pro-German partners.[62] For Deutsche Bank, even before the outbreak of war between the United States and Germany in 1917 – which effectively severed the bank from its American holdings – managing some of its already hard-pressed investments became much more difficult. Oddly, as business opportunities in the United States became less lucrative and more risky, America became more important for Deutsche Bank's business in Germany. By 1916, Deutsche Bank had misgivings even about dealing with some American banks with which it had enjoyed long-standing business relations.[63] National City Bank had become an "Allied bank par excellence." Many New York banks were tripping over themselves to give the Allies credit.[64]

American banks seized the opportunity presented by the war to expand their international business. By 1916, National City Bank had opened up branches in London, Barcelona, and Madrid, and was considering establishing an operation in Paris. More tied to British banking interests, it also grew closer to Dutch banks. Likewise, Guaranty Trust Company of New York hired a Frenchman, who would likely become its representative in Paris. That bank was also in negotiations with a Dutch bank to develop a more intimate relationship.[65] With the war, National City Bank and other American institutions also started to expand into South America.[66] Shortly after the war began, Adams contended that the increase of American international financial muscle coupled with the likely increase in American exports, especially to Latin America, pointed even more convincingly to establishing a Deutsche Bank branch (licensed agency) in New York for foreign exchange and trade transactions with a strong, new correspondent bank such as Guaranty Trust.[67] As the war dragged on, his idea became less and less feasible.

Germans realized that they were in an economic, in addition to a military, war, which included mobilizing neutral nations. Schmidt reported that American journals published unfavorable articles about the condition of German banks and requested material with which to refute the "lies." Some American banks refused to hire Germans, "even German Jews."[68] For a few years, the American government pressed all banks to avoid lending to one side or the other. Although American trust companies guaranteed (confirmed) letters of credit drawn on German banks such as Deutsche Bank, the Allies had an easier time raising trade credits. Sterling bills, even for large amounts, were particularly easy to discount on the U.S. market, and some U.S. banks geared up to finance exports to the Allies.[69]

By fall 1916, some German journals expressed worry about what Germany would lose not to Britain, but rather to the American juggernaut. The *Frankfurter Zeitung* implied that Germany had already lost an economic war to the United States.[70] Although America went through a difficult financial period just after war was declared in Europe, by 1916[71] America had already transformed itself from a raw material supplier to an industrial producer, and from a debtor to creditor nation – largely through the war. Adams expressed his concern that America was ill prepared for this change in fortune with all the demands that would be made on it as by far the largest neutral power.[72] After early financial losses and blocked shipments in the United States, by 1916 Europe was enriching America and thereby strengthening it as a competitor.[73] Despite its "small weakness of always wanting to set records" – everything had to be the highest, the best – America, according to one German journal, had already become the largest producer of many critical goods. Even before the war, German exports to the United States had been dropping, and since the war began Britain's and France's economic relationship with the United States was growing. A country that a few years before did not even have a central bank and that stumbled from one economic crisis to another was now witnessing an upsurge in banking investment, even international outward investment and transactions.[74] Its agricultural sector was flowering, with one record harvest after another since the beginning of the war.

By then, too, American capital markets were soaring. Some stocks held by Deutsche Bank, such as Allis-Chalmers, Bethlehem Steel, and General Electric, for example, witnessed their share prices grow enormously (500 percent, 1500 percent, and 25 percent respectively).[75] As the Mark fell, German investors' nominal paper profits became even larger, but they had to balance the risk of remitting gold proceeds against the possibility that the oft-turbulent American equity markets would once again tumble.

Blockade Running

The war clearly pushed Deutsche Bank interests into new directions. Of these, the Deutsche Ozean-Reederei was probably the strangest. As communication became more complicated, the German government and German business looked for new ways of transporting letters, important documents, and some raw materials. On November 8, 1915, just six months after the sinking of the *Lusitania* threatened American–German relations and put a temporary halt to unlimited submarine warfare,[76] a syndicate took over two submarines built by Krupp. They were delivered to Deutsche Ozean-Reederei on May 5, 1916 (the *Deutschland*) and on July 20, 1916 (the *Bremen*).[77] With its capital of 2 million Mark divided between Deutsche Bank and Norddeutscher Lloyd (1.5 million Mark), and Kaufmann Alfred Lohmann (0.5 million Mark), the company appeared to be a completely private concern. The Deutsche Versicherungsbank

The war naturally drove up the cost of communication. These stamps were used for transport on the submarines financed by Deutsche Bank. The rate for a normal postcard had been 7½ Pfennig. These stamps came in denominations of 5 to 50 Marks.

stood as a silent partner. It had contributed the first boat, which ostensibly had a value of 2.7 million Mark. It also insured the new enterprise.[78]

But the new enterprise had a rather odd relationship to the government. All the documents list Deutsche Bank as the primary owner of the new company, but a good deal of the financing and guarantees for the firm came from the Reich. The Reichsbank served as the clearinghouse for all the documents and goods transported, and one report indicates that the Reich was to receive 80 percent of the company's profits. Moreover, the original agreement among the participants entailed a commitment of the Reichsschatzamt (Treasury) to guarantee the participants a 5 percent annual return and repayment of their capital, while taking responsibility for any losses incurred.[79] To pay for future purchases of boats, the government guaranteed Deutsche Bank's credit line to the new company up to 18 million Mark.[80] Although the origin of the idea for the company is unclear, the parties seemed to recognize the danger that sooner or later the real ownership or impetus for the Deutsche Ozean-Reederei would be discovered and some excuse would be found to intern the ships in the United States.[81]

Deutsche Ozean-Reederei activities were both lucrative and beset by many dangers. The *Deutschland* made its maiden voyage on June 14, 1916, returning to Bremen on August 25, netting a 4.2 million Mark profit.[82] The *Bremen*'s first voyage, which began on the day the *Deutschland* returned, ended in disaster with the loss of its entire crew and goods. The company took full responsibility for the support of the crew's families and received insurance payments, which covered a substantial portion of its future risks. By October 1916, its profits amounted to nearly 1 million Mark. A month later, it contracted with the

German navy for the purchase of six more trade submarines and two surface ships, though the Reich reserved the right to recover the submarines for military or other purposes, which it did with the *Deutschland* as soon as relations with the United States broke off in February 1917.[83]

Oddly, the activities of the company seemed to be no secret. The *Frankfurter Zeitung* published an article in July 1916 that described in great detail the company's commercial undertakings. It reported the kinds of goods and documents transported and even the departure point, Bremen. It proudly recounted the miles covered by the company's boats and the technical achievements required for success.[84] In addition to letters and valuable documents, the *Deutschland* carried rubber and chemicals. The company received praise from many quarters, and its services seemed to be in high demand.

It stayed in business at least until 1925. Some of its property, not ships, ended up in U.S. government hands. The Reich took over the liability to the families of the seamen lost on the *Bremen*. Its retained earnings of nearly 6.4 million Mark were distributed 80 percent to the Reich and 20 percent to the owners, in accordance with the original agreements.[85]

Given the desperation that drove the submarine and other ventures, it is no wonder that supply independence weighed heavily on Germans in the 1920s and '30s facing the possibility of another war. Deutsche Bank's ill-fated involvement with Lehigh Coke Company served as another illustration of the risks of overseas supply dependencies.

Although the increase in uncertainty led some, understandably, to want to keep their assets close to home, this was not easy for Deutsche Bank, which had made its reputation in large part by managing international investment – and some of the bank's assets were not completely liquid. Not only were fundamental pillars of its prewar business collapsing, governments, including Deutsche Bank's own, limited the free deployment of its assets and personnel.

10

War Supplies, Espionage, and Expropriation

I fervently hope that the clouds which are now collecting... between your and our country... will soon be dispersed and that we will thus be saved from further complications in connection with the Coke business just when we are all beginning to look hopefully into the future.

Mankiewitz to Adams, September 3, 1915, HADB, A528.

"All the News that's Fit to Print."

Motto of *The New York Times*.

Introduction

In some areas, Germans actually expanded their investment in the United States. In order to avoid shipping goods into the United States, many companies increased their production there to service American and other markets. But given communication difficulties and anti-German attitudes, these increased commitments entailed new and acute management challenges. Lehigh Coke was the only American company over which Deutsche Bank attempted to exercise management control after war was declared in Europe.

Its Lehigh Coke failures continued to weigh on Bamag-Didier. Bamag replaced one member of its board because of the problems in the United States. Despite vigorous war business and solid reserves,[1] Bamag-Didier had difficulty meeting its commitments under the terms of the March 1914 settlement (see previous Section). Acquiring the foreign exchange necessary to fulfill its pledge was difficult. At the very least, management felt that the current strength of the Dollar against the Mark led to unwarranted short-term financial losses, because the rate was sure to reverse itself eventually. Bamag-Didier had to borrow $500,000 in the United States to pay its commitments to Lehigh Coke; unfortunately it had already mortgaged all of its current and future holdings of Lehigh Coke securities as collateral for previously issued credits. The syndicate was not prepared to advance any more money.[2] Lehigh Coke itself ended up advancing the funds to Bamag-Didier to pay for the new construction firm, raising the money with a guarantee from Adams, agreed upon with Deutsche Bank, despite delayed communication with Germany, but this initial loan was not sufficient. In late 1914, with winter coming on, Lehigh needed to invest in coal inventories.[3] Deutsche Bank was still torn between its loyalty to Bamag-Didier, which the bank did not want to burden with further borrowing and foreign exchange transactions at unfavorable rates, and its loyalty to and interest in Lehigh Coke. It advised McIlvain, Lehigh's president, to hold off further construction until the foreign exchange situation improved. The bank felt sure that Bethlehem could not, under existing contracts, demand the completion of the last two batteries, as long as Lehigh could maintain supplies with the two up-and-running batteries. Despite extraordinary communication difficulties, German management, for many reasons as will be made clear in the following, felt obliged to micromanage the U.S. coking company, even in details such as the coal mixture that should be used for optimal ash content and in the minutae of acquiring needed financing.[4]

Deutsche Bank's involvement in Lehigh Coke during the war has been misconstrued in many accounts. According to some sources, Deutsche Bank's involvement with Lehigh Coke was sponsored by the German government in order to have a U.S. plant for the production of Benzol and Toluol intended for the German war ministry. Once the project came to light, Deutsche Bank was forced to sell Lehigh Coke to Bethlehem Steel before America's entry into the war.[5]

Political Football

The evidence suggests that, in reality, the story was much more complex. The original prospectus called for a Benzol processing facility. The first interest in the military significance of the plant came from the Allied side, not the Germans. According to Adams, the English showed interest in Lehigh's capacity to provide Benzol before German officials did. He reported to Deutsche Bank on December 31, 1914 (the letter did not arrive in Berlin until January 20, 1915, just prior to Deutsche Bank's meeting with German government officials) that "an English officer here" was "manifesting much interest in the subject."[6] But there was more than just military interest. Demand for Benzol and its products was very high at the time. Thomas A. Edison, for example, was so anxious to obtain Benzol for the manufacture of phonographic record plates that he twice called on Adams to seek a contract.[7]

The British interest and German concerns created a dilemma for the bank. From the very beginning of the controversy, Deutsche Bank recognized that the bank had a financial interest in an immediate and complete sale of Lehigh, while keeping the parties from knowing all the facts.[8] Unfortunately, the first goal could not be accomplished in the short run because it ran counter to German national interest and the second could not be achieved in the long run.

Coking was only economical if all of the spin-off chemicals could be captured and sold efficiently. The question was when, not whether, a Benzol plant should be built. According to a somewhat strange February 1915 letter, the idea to build a plant for the production of Benzol and Toluol somewhat ahead of schedule was brought to Deutsche Bank by Wilbur, an American member of Lehigh's board. Indeed, a few months earlier, in November 1914, the president of Lehigh himself wrote to Deutsche Bank that in the near future a Benzol plant could be made profitable and that the matter had already been broached with Wilbur during the previous summer so that Wilbur could discuss it with Deutsche Bank when he visited Germany. McIlvain was only awaiting the right moment to sketch specific plans for board approval. He knew that Deutsche Bank was reluctant to finance the plant with its own funds.[9] Although he never explained how, Wilbur even offered to arrange the financing.[10] Lehigh's president was enthusiastic about the idea, but it put Deutsche Bank and its German partners in an awkward position.

The bank suspected that the idea for the facility was to supply not only American but British and French customers with the chemicals, the price of which had been driven up by war demand. The project included, in addition to the above-mentioned products, Xylol, the solvent Naphtha, and other products used in making explosives. Therefore, the decision was crucially important to the war efforts of the two sides. Loyal to their country, the German parties wanted to prevent their property from being employed for the Allied war effort. Patriotism, however, was mixed with good business sense.

Under pressure from its own government not to allow the strategic chemicals to fall into enemy hands, Deutsche Bank believed that it had only four options. Two options involved complicated and economically uninteresting changes in how and what was produced and delivered. In short, some of the most essential raw materials for the war effort would not be produced at all or would be stored instead of sold. The third alternative was to finance the construction with "other peoples' money." The fourth was to sell the whole company.[11] Solutions three and four made some financial sense, but could hardly assuage the bank's patriotic conscience, which, given the dilemma as outlined, could only be achieved by scuttling Lehigh and its capacity to aid the enemy. The fourth option seemed to include Bethlehem because it had several years left to exercise its option. Deutsche Bank gave Smith (Schmidt) some indication of reasonable pricing – around $9–10 million – and asked him to use "Edward Dean's absence" (presumably Adams) to begin negotiations with Bethlehem. All this had to be kept quite secret. "In any case neither Edward [presumably Adams, my note] nor the gentleman at the coke company can learn that we as a matter of principle will withhold our permission for the Benzol project, as long as the war lasts."[12]

Until early 1917, Deutsche Bank bounced back and forth among the options listed above. For resolution of this dilemma, at first, Deutsche Bank turned to its own government. If the German government were willing to finance the plant and purchase of the raw materials, both the bank's financial and patriotic interests could be satisfied simultaneously. As long as the syndicate had sufficient external financing to purchase and store the chemicals in question, politics and private finance would not come into conflict.[13] The critical products would be controlled by Germany, the syndicate's ultimate goal of selling Lehigh would not be impaired, and the patriotic and private interest of protecting the ultimate Dollar foreign exchange rate would be preserved. No further investment would have to be made by the syndicate, and the bank would be spared further discussions with officials. By May, Deutsche Bank seems to have lined up the German government's financial support ($150,000 at first, later $300,000) and the U.S. Lehigh board approval for the plan.[14] Obviously, the Reich wanted to control how the much-sought-after raw materials would be used. This would not be easy.

The situation was made more complicated by Bethlehem Steel's sales to the Allies, its interest in the project, and by financial problems at Lehigh. Bethlehem wanted to ensure supplies of coke by-products, and through much of 1915 still preferred to outsource that production, as had been provided for in the original plan. Its business was booming, much of which was connected with Allied arms sales.[15] Relations between the two Pennsylvania companies had improved considerably. Deutsche Bank management cautiously hoped that the worst was over.

Once again, the bank would be disappointed. By December, even though much of the facility was up and running, this was by far not the end of the matter. Lehigh Coke continued to have quality and timing problems, even with the new construction company, Koppers. Worse still, by summer 1915, with the steel company deluged with Allied munitions contracts, Bethlehem wanted to buy the plant immediately and take control of not only coking, but also the by-products. Struggling against communications obstacles, Adams requested considerable freedom to move ahead without specific instructions from Berlin. He also assured his Berlin colleagues he would keep Schmidt informed and seek out his advice.[16]

It became increasingly clear that Bethlehem wanted to purchase Lehigh precisely for the gases that Deutsche Bank wanted to keep out of the steel company's hands. As Schmidt and others cautioned, any expectation that Bethlehem would buy the plant without the ability to make Toluol and Xylol, for example, was unrealistic. Knowing what leverage it had, Bethlehem could only be delayed temporarily. Only if the German war ministry were ready to buy and hold the products for an extended period, at the very high American price, could Bethlehem be prevented from getting the products. The Americans had considerable control of the company and were still committed to the sale of Lehigh, which would be problematic for the German war effort.[17]

Any delay seemed favorable. Mankiewitz counted on the end of the war solving the problem.[18] As in so many areas, Deutsche Bank and Germany pinned their hopes on an early peace. Many tactics were explored to put off the sale. These included delayed payments of funds needed to complete the other batteries. In winter 1915, the company's financial situation was still complex and unfavorable. It had a total of $9.1 million in equity capital ($5.1 common, $4 million in preferred, but $650,000 issued to Bamag-Didier had not been paid in), $10.2 million in assets, of which nearly $8 million was the net amount invested (after depreciation) in the plant and equipment, a $1.5 million receivable for stock issued but not yet paid in, and little in retained earnings. Gross margin on its $1.6 million in sales was less than 10 percent. With selling and general administration costs of $50,000, net profits provided a less than

1 percent return on gross assets. As it stood, the project was less than a roaring success. Clearly, invested assets were still underutilized.[19] Moreover, the sale was made more complicated by the inability of Bamag-Didier to determine the full cost of construction, which in the original contract was to be the basis of the purchase price.

In the end, these economic factors were not crucial. Patriotic sentiment and government pressure were too great to allow the sale. German officials in Washington kept in close touch with Adams about the Benzol factory. The bank, along with German public officials, had to go to considerable effort to quash German public criticism of the bank's involvement with the supply of Allied munitions in the United States. Based on these pressures, a sale of the company in the summer of 1915 was "out of the question," even if it appeared that "this country's interests would be just as well protected as heretofore." As the purchaser, wrote Mankiewitz presumably, "continues to be the chief exponent of factual and material support to the Allies in the line of arms and munitions, and as long as a large majority of the Coke Company's stock is held by interests in this country, a sale would raise such a violent outburst of public clamor and misrepresentation that I cannot for a minute continue to consider any further negotiations."[20] In addition, Deutsche Bank expressed confidence that this decision was in the financial interests of the German members of the syndicate, as the improving economic value of the plant and the favorable foreign exchange rates would more than make up for what was lost by postponing the sale. "All we can do therefore is to continue our attitude of patient expectation until such time when the clouds have disappeared from the political skies and when the earning power of the plant will induce prospective purchasers to bid such price for the Syndicate's holdings as will fully compensate it for the prolonged risk it has been carrying."[21]

The bank's primary focus continued to be keeping Benzol and other by-products out of Bethlehem's hands, if not for patriotic reasons, at least for fear of government or public rebuke. In September, Deutsche Bank addressed its concern directly to McIlvain. Deutsche Bank thanked him for his loyalty and reminded him of how Benzol by-products could be used for war-related production. It implored Lehigh's president to "preclude any such use of the Benzol to be produced by you."[22] A little over a week later, the bank reiterated its hope that the Lehigh company would only sell "commercially pure" Benzol, without the other by-products. "We must rely upon you to most consciously protect the Bank in that respect, because we are sure that the production of any crude Benzol at your plant would be considered a breach of contract by our friends here, which would necessarily *lead to most fatal consequences for all of us* [my emphasis]."[23]

The bank and the company were still between a "rock and a hard place." On one hand, there was the German government and public pressure. On the other, Bethlehem threatened to build a Benzol plant for itself. Deutsche Bank could only plead that the American Lehigh board should try to protect the syndicate's interests as well as Germany's national interest.[24] As Bethlehem persisted, Deutsche Bank hoped to find a better buyer, one that would use the chemicals for peaceful purposes.[25]

Inadequate information frustrated Deutsche Bank. Revealing the weakness of financial information in the first decades of the twentieth century, the bank complained, for example, in 1916 that it got accounting reports with little commentary from management, which left the bank in the dark as to what was really going on.[26] By early 1916, communication had become so cumbersome that Deutsche Bank gave Adams full authority to act for the Germans. The bank added the cautionary note that his action should be consistent with the bank's views as expressed in previous correspondence with the necessary formalities.[27]

Delegating the decision cautiously to Adams, as it did, might eventually give the bank an ideal way out of its predicament. Adams could sell, which was in the syndicate's financial interest, but Deutsche Bank could argue with the German authorities that the sale was out of its hands and that it had advised Adams to respect the bank's wishes. In any case, exercising control was getting more and more difficult.

Adams was clearly aware of how political the issue had become. Debates about the sale of Lehigh ran parallel with negotiations with German government representatives in the United States, whose intentions seemed to change with German military fortunes. As early as summer 1915, he had met with representatives of the German government for the building of the Benzol processing facility. In April 1915, Adams had been in contact with Count von Bernstorff, the German ambassador, who had asked Adams' assistance with various matters and who introduced him to Captain Franz von Papen, future chancellor of Germany in 1932 and vice chancellor for a short time under Hitler. Adams had many dealings with the captain about war materials and explosives. He duly informed Papen about the interest in and the action taken by the board to utilize the Benzol obtained for peaceful purposes. The subject was understandably of great interest to Papen. Ostensibly, Papen told the Americans that he was satisfied with the idea of storing the materials and would communicate this to his government.[28] In reality, the wily Papen had an idea of selling the chemicals to the Norwegian government, which might have used them to supply Germany. Unfortunately – Papen's luck with schemes was rarely very good – his communications fell into British hands.[29] In September 1915, the contract was signed with Carl Still, a German-owned company founded by Papen for the construction of the chemical processing facility. Deutsche Bank would buy the Toluol for example (an exclusive right for six months after construction of the facility), pay for its storage, and advance $300,000 to Lehigh Coke for the construction.[30] In fact, the German government supplied the cash. In January 1916, Mankiewitz suggested that the war ministry take one-third of Deutsche Bank's profits on the sales. In spite of Deutsche Bank's offer, the war ministry expected to be protected against foreign exchange risk as well as the storage and handling risk of Toluol by the bank.[31] (What had been a government responsibility just two years earlier, foreign exchange management, had already been delegated to private hands.) At the same time, despite growing recognition in Germany of chemical shortages, the German authorities approved the sale of Lehigh by-products on the U.S. market to a nondefense buyer, a decision Papen ostensibly approved.[32]

In a somewhat confusing letter, Deutsche Bank reminded the ministry of the difficult position it was in. The original contracts required Lehigh to sell by-products from its second Benzol extraction facility to Bethlehem. In order to keep the Toluol out of Bethlehem's hands in accordance with the bank's perception of its duties Deutsche Bank took control over the inventory of the first by-product facility, which had been financed by the ministry and could produce Toluol. The second facility still had to be built, however, in a manner designed to ensure the removal of the objectionable chemicals. Deutsche Bank had not discussed all the details with the ministry in Berlin because Papen in the United States had approved them.[33] Deutsche Bank was growing impatient and nervous about how precarious its position was between its own financial interests and patriotic duties.

The public pressures on Deutsche Bank's sense of patriotism mounted during 1916 as the harsh effects and long duration of the war became more clear. Those pressures were multifaceted. The *Frankfurter Zeitung* reported that the war business in the United States was creating millionaires and multi-millionaires. Bethlehem Steel was singled out as one of the most aggressive suppliers of Allied armaments. It also conceded that some Toluol was finding its way from New York through Sweden to Germany.[34] Although since early 1915, even before the German authorities raised the issue of strategic chemicals, Deutsche Bank had looked for ways of exporting from the United States to Germany, its efforts received little recognition.[35]

Not until February 1916 during a visit by Papen at Deutsche Bank's office in Berlin, did the new position of the war ministry become clear. It demanded control of all the Toluol – even that to be produced by the new facility. A way had to be found to remove Benzol (and related gases) from the gas by-products delivered to Bethlehem Steel. In retrospect, the war ministry regretted approving and funding the first part of the construction, now that the demands on Lehigh were so great that it needed a second facility. Despite his own direct involvement with the earlier decision, Papen was now convinced – and would get his way eventually – that a new solution for the Toluol problem had to be found. When they concocted the original plan, bank and government officials had assumed that the war would not last beyond spring 1916. Even though everyone had been informed, no one had envisioned a longer war and the construction of a second facility.[36] Deutsche Bank representatives reminded Papen of the great danger for all German interests should the American participants, whose agreement was necessary and who had not seen much profit from Toluol production in the first facility, withhold their consent for eliminating Toluol from the second. All these new provisions might cause enormous losses for Deutsche Bank. Papen, whom Axhausen described as usually polite and accessible, retorted brusquely that his only interests were protecting the investment of the war ministry and preventing the loss of Toluol.[37] While the Americans continued to try to sell the company, Deutsche Bank and the German government got their way about the new plant. By July 1916, the Lehigh Board had accepted the limits on production at the extension plant.[38]

Opportunities and Divisions in the United States

Summing up the situation and the personalities involved in January 1916, however, Axhausen reported that Adams was still embittered by the whole coke business because he had not been fully compensated for his efforts and because the Lehigh developments had hurt his relationship with Deutsche Bank. According to Axhausen, McIlvain, who maintained strong contacts with Bethlehem, his former employer and main client, was nevertheless intellectually inferior and obedient to Adams. Though unsure of the reliability of his sources, Axhausen perceived a lot of tension between the American and German representatives. Deutsche Bank had to live with an imperfect situation. Axhausen reminded his colleagues, for example, that they took McIlvain precisely because of his good relationship with Bethlehem. With the Benzol plant on the property, on which Bethlehem had an option, McIlvain's relationship with Bethlehem was quickly changing from an asset into a liability. The bank might have to prepare itself for a significant change in its American personnel, including replacing the chairman and president. Schmidt, at the very least, had to be on guard for a major change in staffing and alert for new information.[39]

While the political conflicts mounted, the commercial difficulties disappeared. By the end of 1916, both coke and by-product processing were in full swing. Even earlier, McIlvain reported that the company could sell all the coke and by-products it processed. Sales figures reinforced the impression that the market was almost limitless. Even in late 1915, although Lehigh still needed to borrow and was still awaiting some share payments from stockholders, the company's cash problems had dissipated and the board approved a large wage increase.[40] Ostensibly the participants were now secure with each other's role. McIlvain wrote in response to Deutsche Bank's expressions of confidence that the bank's sentiments "inspire us to bend our very best efforts towards making this Company a grand success."[41] Deutsche Bank also urged Adams to forget past difficulties with Bamag-Didier, defending the bank's view, ironically, by arguing that the factions "can afford to let the past be buried now when the presence [sic] has done up [sic] to our previous expectations and when the future looks even more promising than expected."[42]

Despite the acute political problems, Deutsche Bank's regular reports to syndicate members in 1916 grew more and more optimistic at least about the business. Although the bank and Lehigh managers continued to look for a "white knight" who would free the investors from their impossible political pressures with an economic gain commensurate with the frustration and risk endured by all, Lehigh was about to pay its first dividend. Its profits had climbed over tenfold in two years, reaching $1 million for the first eleven months of 1916.

But in late 1916, Deutsche Bank's relationship with the American Lehigh Coke participants was in fact unraveling. With communications' blockages becoming more severe, the delicate balance of German control versus American independence swung toward the Americans.[43] Because Deutsche Bank felt that it was losing control, in August 1916, it asked Martin Nordegg (né Cohn and born in Germany), a well-known Canadian pioneer in the coal sector who was visiting New York, to join the board, report on the coke company's activities, and to take a hand in solving Lehigh's political problems. He confirmed the bank's worst fears. Not only were many normal business problems not adequately reported, such as coal shortages, accounting problems, and production problems, management was acting in the interests of only the American and not all the shareholders. It would be impossible to prevent the use of Toluol for Allied military production. He recommended a sale or a change in management, because the current situation was untenable. Adams, he believed, felt that Deutsche Bank's expectations had become unrealistic.[44] Mankiewitz shared Schmidt's and Nordegg's views, but was saddened that Lehigh Coke would be sold at that time, after all their efforts, just as the facility was beginning to show its promise.[45]

Deutsche Bank, understandably fearful of German governmental retribution for selling the factory without restrictions, asked for legal advice, which it received from Axhausen's brother Paul. In his opinion, if there was no alternative and the Reich received benefit from the sale, there would be no risk of legal retaliation.[46] Presumably the remittance of a large amount of money from the United States counted as a benefit for the Reich.

After receiving Nordegg's unfavorable reports about McIlvain, the bank demanded that McIlvain come to Germany to report on the situation.[47] In December, Mankiewitz wrote Adams that McIlvain had lost the confidence of the German investors and had to be removed in favor of Nordegg.[48] The order seems to have been ignored. At any rate, probably before the order reached Adams, plans for the sale by the American interests were well under way.

The End Game

By January 1917, armed with legal advice, Deutsche Bank came to the recognition that local management had to be given a free hand to sell the company to an American purchaser for the best possible price with little expectation that any political influence could be exercised over the transaction, a fact that indeed helped its position with its own government.[49] As German relations with the United States deteriorated in winter 1917 – in February the United States cut off diplomatic relations with Germany – Deutsche Bank removed any remaining obstacles to dispose of its interests in Lehigh Coke. By mid-January 1917, negotiations with Bethlehem Steel were in full swing. Although Schmidt and some of the American representatives of Lehigh were involved in the negotiations and Schmidt held the power to act on behalf of Deutsche Bank, Kuhn Loeb, with its Warburg and Bamag-Didier connections, handled the actual transfer of money against shares. The precise terms of the sale had been hammered out by early February, but the anxious Berlin managers did not receive the letter with details until April 18, nearly two weeks after America declared war on Germany.[50]

At the time of the sale, Lehigh Coke had approximately sixty shareholders divided into the German Bamag-Didier syndicate, the German Deutsche Bank syndicate – several major German banks and Deutsche Bank executives were among the shareholders – an American syndicate, of which Deutsche Bank managers, Deutsche Treuhand-Gesellschaft, Bamag, Didier and other bankers also participated – and a separate group of common shareholders (including the companies Bamag-Didier) who had received shares as a commission. Deutsche Bank's own holding consisted of $420,000 common and $500,000 preferred at par value. Adams' holdings amounted to $150,000 preferred and $153,000 common. In total, Lehigh had issued over $4.2 million of preferred and $5.1 million of common, both at par value.[51] The price seems to have been $105 for the preferred and $50 for the common, for a grand total of approximately $7 million, less commissions (5 percent for Deutsche Bank) and payments of outstanding loans owed by the parties.[52] It was an amount nearly one-third less than what the bank expected a year earlier.[53] Most of the shares held by Bamag-Didier were in the form of common shares. As soon as payment was received in Dollars, the German participants could receive Marks at a rate of 5.8 to the Dollar.[54] The funds were sent to Switzerland as Marks, where presumably, at least, some of the investors kept accounts, at least for a while.[55] Bamag-Didier for one was furious with Deutsche Bank's commission, a reaction some might view as ungrateful considering the degree to which for so many years Deutsche Bank managers had fought with other participants to protect the engineering and construction companies.[56]

Whether the other participants came away from the Lehigh Coke experience happy with the result is difficult to determine. Despite the war-related sales, Bamag-Didier were nearly bankrupt by the investment, their reputations severely tainted. Its error of judgment contributed to the early deaths of two of the key managers involved in the project – Grumbacher and Hohmann.[57] Many of the German syndicate members had paid full nominal value for their subscriptions. Even though the depressed exchange rate gave them more Marks than they had invested, investors were probably disappointed – but by spring 1917, also relieved to get anything out.

Deutsche Bank seemed to make a good return for its enormous effort. It had not paid anything for the stock it held – this was for service – and its loans were repaid. The bank realized about $700,000 for the stock and the commission (about $11 million in today's Dollars). With some justification, Deutsche Bank felt that it had earned this reward. As Mankiewitz stressed to Adams much earlier in December 1915, the bank had taken many risks and worked out many compromises among the participants, contributing to the successes the coke company had already achieved. Reviewing the whole history of Deutsche Bank's efforts, he hoped, might mollify the American investors. Perhaps self-servingly, Mankiewitz wrote that remembering the reasons why Deutsche Bank had only pushed Bamag-Didier gingerly might help give the American investors some perspective. In any case, he concluded with the obvious: The fighting had put them all under great strain.[58]

The New York Times *Declares War*

For nearly two years Deutsche Bank's name made the U.S. press, but for reasons the bank would have preferred to avoid. Even before America's entry into

World War I, many German nationals came under intense scrutiny. As early as November 1915, *The New York Times* had highlighted Hugo Schmidt's and Deutsche Bank's involvement with a "pro-Teuton Bridgeport Company."[59] In July 1917, one German banker, Richard Adam Timmerscheidt, opened his veins and threw himself out of a ten-story window, ostensibly because he was being investigated for aiding German agents to report on troop movements.[60]

After war was declared by the United States, some German businessmen, suspected of working as foreign agents, were detained, including Deutsche Bank's representative, 54-year-old Hugo Schmidt. The news of his first incarceration came to Deutsche Bank via a *Times* article. As the bank claimed to believe that the charges were absurd, it asked the Swiss authorities in Washington to intercede on his behalf to gain his release, to gather more information about why Schmidt was in custody, and to determine whether he could be freed by posting bail.[61] Released for a time, like other Germans in the United States, Schmidt was closely monitored. Deutsche Bank officials in Berlin were able to receive some news from him through Rotterdam. Only personal correspondence was allowed. Schmidt pleaded that he had not heard from his family since December 22, 1916, and at that time only from his future son-in-law. Through Deutsche Bank's efforts, Schmidt finally got some news of his family. In June, the Deutsche Bank's Dutch representative finally reported that Schmidt had been released and seemed better than he had feared, but further business discussions would probably be even more dangerous.[62]

In July 1917, Schmidt was questioned as part of a U.S. government investigation of Guaranty Trust transfers in connection with the steamships *Barbarossa* and *Friedrich der Grosse* – prepayments of $.6 million from the North Lloyd Line orchestrated by Schmidt, allegedly under suspicious circumstances. According to Schmidt, before coming to the United States, his work in Berlin provided no contact with the North Lloyd account, and therefore, he had little idea whether that company owed Deutsche Bank money or the contrary. Although this may have been true, Schmidt also falsely maintained that he had had no communication with Deutsche Bank Berlin since arriving in the United States and that he had probably exceeded his authority by arranging for the payment. Under the circumstances, this was a stupid lie. The U.S. officials argued that the suspicious transfer was in reality a means by which North Lloyd paid a debt to Deutsche Bank, an explanation that Schmidt vehemently denied. If the line had owed money to Deutsche Bank, a receivable for the bank, it could have in principle settled the amount by paying a debt for the bank. By arranging for payment, Deutsche Bank, according to the U.S. government, was transferring one of its assets to avoid its seizure. In the end, the government seized the funds for "safekeeping."[63]

But Schmidt's real problems began in the fall. American agents raided Deutsche Bank's office, taking thousands of files that not only supposedly documented Deutsche Bank's normal business dealings but also indicated that it had $100 million in cash and negotiable securities in the United States – an amazing amount, considering Deutsche Bank's share capital in 1913 was roughly $48 million and total assets $500 million. Soon after the raid, Schmidt was taken into custody again. In reporting the public accounts of Hugo Schmidt's questioning, *The New York Times*, in a sensationalist fashion, not only listed the amounts Deutsche Bank reportedly had in the United States, but also, on flimsy evidence, that Schmidt controlled their use for espionage.

The scandal involved Bolo Pacha, a French citizen, and Count von Bernstorff, the former German ambassador to the United States. These two had allegedly conspired specifically to corner the wool market, in general to hurt French interests in the United States, and plot, of all things, to "engineer a peace." A communiqué from Bernstorff to the German foreign secretary asked for $1.7 million in funding for a sinister activity – a "peace action." Deutsche Bank and Schmidt's crime was to have transferred money to Bolo.[64]

In a front page article, *The New York Times* presented evidence of Bernstorff's attempts "to influence Congress for peace," of his engineering both a Bolo Pacha plot to buy up French newspapers "for pacifist purposes," and a "Big Deutsche Bank Fund." For the second accusation about the Deutsche Bank "slush fund," the paper's only evidence was Bernstorff's request to his government that it instruct "Deutsche Bank to hold nine million Marks ($2 million) at the disposal of Hugo Schmidt, who acted as American agent for Bolo."[65] According to *The New York Times*, Schmidt's admission that he had paid the money out on Bernstorff's instructions nailed the case for the government against the former ambassador for the payments to Bolo as well as other espionage activities, but there was no evidence presented in the articles that Schmidt knew to what purpose the money was being used.[66] Most importantly, it should be noted that most of the telexes produced as evidence of Bernstorff's activities dated from a period before America's entry into the war.

According to Schmidt, he was not responsible for all of Deutsche Bank's business in the United States, "only some special business of the bank." He had no general power of attorney, only one covering matters with Guaranty Trust Company. His power of attorney did not cover, for example, transactions at National City Bank. In November 1917, while in custody, Schmidt volunteered that sometime in 1916, on orders of Bernstorff, he had also paid $6,000 to a man in Paterson, New Jersey.[67]

Schmidt was not officially arrested until January 1918. Before his arrest he was obliged to report once a week to federal agents. On January 20, 1918, he and 35 other Germans, labeled by *The New York Times* as "spies, agents, propagandists, and other enemy trouble makers" were shipped from Ellis Island to a prison camp near Fort Oglethorpe, Georgia. The paper singled out Schmidt, whom it described as "the paymaster of the Bolo Pacha-Bernstorff plot" and went on to report:

> The Teutons embarked on the Ellis Island ferryboat for the Battery shortly after 3 o'clock. They sang "Die Wacht am Rhein," "Deutschland über Alles," and other German patriotic songs and made contemptuous remarks as their craft steamed past the Statue of Liberty.[68]

Among the passengers bound for this early-twentieth-century Guantánamo Bay instillation was an editor of a newspaper whose only crime was to be pro-German, and Baron Seebeck, described as "one of Deutsche Bank's agents" in London. The article did not spell out what kind of agent was meant, but the term seemed to carry a sinister quality in the context.[69] In its lead paragraph on the front page the next day, *The New York Times* cited reassuringly Hugo Schmidt's internment as evidence of the government's more rigid policy against enemy alien spies and agents.[70]

Unfortunately, it seems that we will never know what was actually in the letters and other documents seized by the American authorities from Deutsche Bank's office, but *The New York Times* claimed to have them and to have found in them proof that Schmidt had come to the United States to "further the war purposes of his Fatherland."[71] Papers locked in Schmidt's safe, the paper reported – once again on the front page – recorded his seeking to buy wool and other commodities in neutral and even Allied countries for German companies, financing those transactions, and arranging for payments. All the transactions discussed were well before the United States entered World War I, when plenty of American companies were selling to the Allies and Germans.[72] We can never know whether Schmidt's application for citizenship a few months after arriving in the States was sincere, which *The New York Times* ridiculed as evidence of his malicious intent to further the German war effort. He later became a citizen, despite his treatment, and as the reader knows from Section I, no less than the head of the New York Federal Reserve attested to Deutsche Bank's plans to send a representative to the United States at least six weeks before war was declared in Europe. Moreover, Deutsche Bank had been thinking about replacing Adams with someone from Berlin for years.

The story attracted much attention up to and just after the armistice. Even *The New York Times* recognized that there was something odd about Schmidt's failure to hide or destroy so many "incriminating documents." Undaunted, it printed more stories with "revelations" about their content. According to the paper, the documents provided "conclusive evidence" that Germans owned a lot of property in the United States. Without the documents, "ferreting out the trade footholds of the Hun in America" would be an almost impossible job. With the information, this property, once thought to be owned by neutrals such as the Hamburg-America Line could be seized and auctioned off to "bona fide Americans." In addition to some information already mentioned, the paper reported that a list of 32,000 subscribers in America to war loans for the Central Powers had been found. It failed to point out that the loans were made when it was perfectly legal to do so. Payments made by Deutsche Bank on behalf of the foreign office and plans for expanding business in South America and continuing business in neutral countries were also normal under the circumstances.[73]

Even after the armistice, the harangues continued. In subsequent Congressional hearings, Kuhn Loeb and other institutions with strong German connections were besmirched. Otto Kahn felt that he had to defend publicly his loyalty to the United States. Alfred Becker, the deputy attorney general handling the cases against the Germans, charged Schmidt during the hearings with hoodwinking the British by creating a dummy organization, Standard Mercantile Agency, for dealing in bills of exchange with South America that were really from Deutsche Ueberseeische Bank. Schmidt even succeeded in discounting some of the bills on the London market. Neither the deputy attorney general, nor the Congress, nor the press paid much heed to the fact that all this occurred before America entered the war while the business was permitted in a neutral country. By this time, even John McClement got into the news, as someone who also represented Deutsche Bank in the United States.[74] Schmidt was not released from detention until summer 1919, nearly a year after the Armistice.[75] Bolo was tried for treason in France during the last winter of the war and executed.

Hostility extended beyond individuals. Once war had been declared by the United States, Americans became even more nationalistic in their approach to economics. Many acts passed by Congress during and after the war were specifically designed to free America from dependence on foreign investors. Higher tariffs, shipping controls, investigations of the radio industry, and many new aspects of tax legislation during the war foreshadowed interwar attempts to make the American economy more "American." Perhaps most importantly, more often than not the United States "failed to rise to the challenges of world economic leadership." The nation seemed to want to separate itself from dependence on any part of the world where "un-American values held sway."[76] Fortunately or unfortunately for Deutsche Bank, like other banks, they still held securities and cash in New York and London.

Expropriating German Assets

In October 1917, the Trading with the Enemy Act became law, setting up the Alien Property Custodian (APC), which was authorized to sequester the properties of German and other enemy investors. By January 1, 1918, that office had launched extensive investigations and gathered 11,170 reports on enemy property. According to Mira Wilkins, the data found in Deutsche Bank records and the extent of foreign investments in the United States "astonished the APC."[77] Some saw the APC's mission as an opportunity to separate Germans from their American property forever and to give Americans access to German technology. Early on, a great deal of seized property was sold, in seeming contradiction to the intent of the law.[78]

German fears of losing property made the APC's initial work, in some sense, easier. Many German holdings had already been sold and transferred long before war was declared. To get at what was left, the American authorities launched themselves into their task with a great deal of zeal. On July 1, 1914, Germans held $1.1 billion of long-term U.S. investments. By December 1918, thanks to sales and expropriation, German holdings amounted to nothing.[79] Several agencies of the U.S. government moved quickly to coordinate their varied activities to determine the extent of enemy holdings in the United States. Officers of the Department of Justice interviewed executives of companies thought to be controlled by enemy companies.[80] The impounding of enemy assets had long-term effects on capital flows. By war's end, U.S. earnings on foreign-held investment had already surpassed that of foreign holdings in the United States, in part because of increases in U.S. foreign investment but also because of reductions in the amounts held in the United States by all foreigners.

Outward investment flows took on greater significance for international U.S. banks during the war and interwar period. German investment in the United States during the interwar period, moreover, never exceeded more than 40 percent of its prewar level and for the most part stayed under 20 percent.[81] Foreign borrowers had to pay substantial premiums on their debt, ranging from 144 basis points to 181 between 1920 and 1924.[82] The nature of investment changed, too. Tax and political considerations played a much greater role, making the structures employed more complicated and the collection of data on investments more difficult.

Deutsche Bank had already taken steps to take funds out of the United States before war between the United States and Germany was declared. National City Bank reported to the authorities that Deutsche Bank held only $28,291 in cash with it but had borrowed $172,448, due April 2, 1918, collateralized by 5,000 shares of Western Maryland Railway common, 4,319 in Seaboard Air Line Railway preferred, and 5,469 in Temporary Voting Stock Certificates of the same company. The borrowed funds seemed to have been transferred out of the country.[83] Acquiring an overview of Deutsche Bank's U.S. holdings was not easy. The justice department had some difficulty breaking Deutsche Bank's code and determining the method by which Deutsche Bank correspondence flowed, which involved using various neutral countries and couriers who would mysteriously drop off correspondence at designated mail boxes. On at least one occasion, the courier was arrested, the letters opened, and resealed in a manner so as to avoid any suspicion that they had been opened.[84]

In November 1917, the APC began extensive interviews with Adams, Schmidt, and McClement. These earliest conversations centered around the Kerbaugh Empire Company, which was a holding company for several engineering firms suffering financial difficulties. Deutsche Bank had put equity capital into these companies and lent them money. Schmidt denied that Deutsche Bank still had an interest in Allis-Chalmers Company and in Niagara Power Company.[85] The government persisted, claiming that it had received reliable information refuting Schmidt's contention. Even Adams came under suspicion because of his German connections.[86] On many occasions, Schmidt repeated his claim that the bank had already liquidated its holdings of securities in the two electrical power companies, a contention that McClement supported.[87] Indeed, some of these transactions may have been cloaked or handled by Adams.

In addition to the shares and loans with National City Bank, discussed earlier, in December 1917 Deutsche Bank had its main accounts with Guaranty Trust Company, Equitable Trust Company, Bankers Trust Company, Chase National Bank, Speyer & Company, Shearson, Hammel & Company, and smaller amounts with twelve other institutions.[88] The bank's holdings included a piece of land in Pennsylvania.[89] Even some Deutsche Bank subsidiaries had deposits in New York, but Deutsche Bank's net deposits had understandably decreased from their prewar levels.[90]

For several years the assets of the bank and its clients were in a state of limbo. Deutsche Bank seemed to recognize that only after passage of the German-American Peace Treaty in 1921 could the bank even attempt the difficult work of getting back its property and the property of its clients. Bergmann realized that the staff working on recovering property would have to commit to a long process with a great deal of cost, hopefully followed by a "nice profit."[91] Nevertheless, Berlin management was probably not prepared for the grueling eight-year ordeal that would follow. There was an enormous number of individuals, institutions, and securities involved. In one message to the New York office, Berlin sent sixteen separate documents, mostly lists of clients from various branches ordered by customer and security.[92] The process involved Deutsche Bank's close banking contacts, such as Speyer, which had held certificates for the bank or which were involved in transactions with the bank. Starting from the onset of the war in Europe and continuing for at least a decade if not longer, Deutsche Bank's activities in the United States shifted largely from doing new business to preserving as much as it could of the old. It is a story that highlights business's vulnerability in the face of dramatic, unforeseen political events, even in countries reputed to hold private property sacrosanct. When nationalist passions run high, economic and other principles suffer.

11

Salvaging Assets and Business Prospects in the War's Immediate Aftermath

> I thank you for your thoughts and the charitable gift. I personally am not suffering, but every German has in his circle of friends many once well off friends who through the terrible inflation are driven into poverty and who feel hunger knocking at the door. These include women alone and old people for whom the foreign generosity is a real blessing. I will use your gift for this purpose.
>
> Gwinner to von Bargen & Ebeling, March 11, 1921, HADB, A1031.

> Alexander Hamilton said that he could find no words to express the abhorrence that he felt for the proposal that private property should be seized and confiscated because of war between nation and nation.
>
> It will soon be four years since the Armistice was signed, yet no policy has been adopted by the American government with reference to the seized property in question.
>
> A. W. Lafferty, attorney of several property holders such as Stollwerck to APC, March 17, 1922, HADB, A1035.

Introduction

Deutsche Bank's business relationship with the United States after World War I must be seen against the background of a loss of trust among key financial players and tumultuous financial upheavals punctuated by brief spells of quiet and growth. The armistice hardly brought relief to Germany. Though Allied troops had not reached German soil, Germany was starving and chaotic. Regular assaults from both the right and left undermined the fragile Social-Democratic government. The decade following the armistice bears the name of Weimar, because the constitutional convention had to flee Berlin to Goethe's old home to draft the document. In addition to the direct war casualties it suffered – three million dead – under the humiliating terms of the treaty the Germans were forced to sign, Germany lost 13 percent of its European territory and population, 15 percent of its prewar assets, and all of its colonies. Under the terms of the May 1921 reparation assessment, too, Germany was obliged to pay in installments a nominal amount totaling $31.5 billion, two-and-a-half times its 1913 gross national product. This bill would have been difficult to pay in the halcyon prewar world, but with the devastation and disequilibrium in 1921, it was and would remain a political and economic millstone around

Germany's and the world's neck for the next fifteen years. Gone were virtually all of Germany's foreign investments: $7 billion, or 10 percent of its total national wealth. Even with this, it did not have peace with the world's largest economy, the United States, whose rejection of the Versailles Treaty meant the two countries remained, technically, in a state of war until 1921.[1]

Much of the sense of crisis and catastrophe that existed during the war remained during the interwar years. Political tension, disputes over reparations, and chaos in prices, money supply, foreign exchange rates, capital movements, trade, and banking were prominent features of the economic history of the whole interwar period. A short-lived postwar boom was followed by a slump and a serious banking crisis in many countries in 1920–21. Although confidence and production revived in the mid-twenties, both were short-lived. Well before the Great Depression, international monetary cooperation on a scale approaching the prewar level was hardly to be found, which itself contributed to a high degree of disequilibrium in capital and other markets and greater investment risks. Certainly after 1931, the world seemed divided into hostile economic blocks each pursuing some version of autarky. By effectively destroying the Gold Standard and factor mobility and removing the Bank of England as the banker of last resort, World War I "brought down" the "pillars of the nineteenth-century international economic order."[2] The German banking system was particularly hard hit by these developments. With much of its international business destroyed, its home capital base sharply reduced, and internal demands for financial assistance increased, Germany came under considerable domestic and foreign political and economic pressure.[3]

In addition to the economic and material consequences of the war, national attitudes impaired the healing process. Whereas the Allies enshrined German guilt in the Versailles Treaty, most Germans held the Allies responsible. Nearly a decade after the armistice, Gwinner felt so strongly about the matter that he published an article accusing France and Russia of fomenting the war. Under the title "Who were the war criminals of 1914?" he presented considerable evidence that France and Russia not only conspired to start the war, but they also left Germany no choice but to fight.[4]

Even Adams, for a while, distanced himself from his German "friends." In the 1920s, letters between Adams and Deutsche Bank became rarer. In 1925, the Engineering Society organized a dinner at the Waldorf Astoria to honor Adams on the occasion of his seventy-ninth birthday. The dinner committee itself was impressive. It included Thomas Edison, Will Durant, Nicholas Murray Butler, Philip Dodge, Vernon Kellogg, Charles M. Schwab, and H. H. Westinghouse.[5] No one from Deutsche Bank attended, but the entire Deutsche Bank management board sent a telegram, one of hundreds of congratulatory messages sent to the hotel, crediting Adams with the successful completion of the Northern Pacific reorganization and the bank's participation in the 1896 U.S. Gold Bond.[6] A year later, Adams was awarded the John Fritz medal, previous winners of which included Edison, Thomson, and Marconi. All the others had won the award for their inventions; Adams for his achievement as an engineer, financier, and scientist, "whose vision and courage and industry made the birth at Niagara

The board of the Germanistic Society in New York early in 1929: Ferdinand W. Lafrentz (president of the Germanistic Society), Gaffron Prittwitz (German ambassador), Nicholas M. Butler (president of Columbia University), Edward D. Adams, Frederick W. J. Heuser (in charge of Deutsches Haus).

Falls of hydro-electric power" an effective source of energy.[7] Yet Adams made no mention of Deutsche Bank in his history of Niagara.

Every once in a while he was asked to comment on old banking matters, especially on problems dealing with railroads, which never seemed to go away. He also took a lively interest in German-American relations, helping to dedicate the new Germanistic Society House at Columbia University in 1929, for example, which replaced the original one that he had donated years before.[8] In his last correspondence to Gwinner, long after he left any official role with Deutsche Bank, and shortly before both passed away, Adams resumed his earlier habit of cutting out articles of interest to Gwinner, commenting on American–German politics and the goings on of companies in which the bank had invested.[9] Adams died in 1931, living just long enough to witness another panic and shock to the world financial system, a crash that might best be understood as a delayed reaction to events and circumstances set in motion by World War I. Gwinner followed him in December.

Above all, the first few years after the Armistice will always be associated with hyperinflation and the rollercoaster ride of the German currency, the effects of which dominated international economics for much of the interwar period leaving economic and cultural scars on the German psyche to this very day. With inflation came the uneven collapse of the Mark, the destruction of savings, and destabilization of the middle class. From 1914 to November 1923, the value of one Dollar went from 4.21 Mark to 4.2 trillion Mark, only to miraculously return after the stabilization and introduction of a new currency, to 4.2 again.[10] Shaken to its core, the German economy, even in the best years of the Weimar Republic, never recovered its prewar vitality, nor business its prewar

As this cartoon from the period shows, American funds were greatly appreciated at first. Loans poured into all sorts of public and private projects, including some of dubious value, and in amounts that made repayment in foreign currency at the appointed maturities virtually impossible. Within a short period, they became just another hated symbol of foreign dependencies.

compass.[11] The eventual and necessary stabilization of the currency with the introduction of the Rentenmark in November 1923 (transformed into the Reichsmark in August 1924) brought on a steep recession and was fraught with political pitfalls. The stability it achieved was short-lived and extremely fragile. By 1928, Germany was once again showing signs of recession and in the following year "saw the beginning of a series of damaging banking panics and failures in Europe, culminating in 1931 in the collapse of the largest Austrian bank, and serious bank crises in Germany and the USA."[12]

During the 1920s, North America presented unusual opportunities and challenges for all German business. Although American authorities administered expropriated German assets in the United States, some private Americans looked at Germany as a veritable "candy store" of cheap goods and companies with which to satisfy a hunger to invest newly won profits. The American markets, both financial and consumer, grew rapidly in the 1920s. It was by far the richest country in the world. Between 1926 and 1929, the nation manufactured 42 percent of total world output. U.S. foreign portfolio and direct investment flowed in large quantities out into the world, but inward investment slowed. By 1929, U.S. outward investment amounted to $27.1 billion, whereas inward investment was down to $5.8 billion, considerably less than the amount in 1914. Foreign governments alone owed the U.S. government $11.7 billion.[13]

Deutsche Bank profited in many ways from the flow of funds from the United States, but these transactions included many new risks. The bank helped arrange several loans for German companies on American capital markets and used its reputation in the United States to raise funds for middle-sized (*Mittelstand*) German firms who would otherwise have little access to Dollar financing. The bank itself was the beneficiary of American interest in its shares and considered listing directly on the New York Stock Exchange.[14] Moreover, Deutsche Bank helped negotiate several loans for public German institutions, including the $50 million loan in 1929 to the German Reich.[15]

Deutsche Bank and the New York Banking Scene

Despite the new challenges, Deutsche Bank made little change in how it structured its U.S. business. Without control of the securities it still owned or held for clients, however, Deutsche Bank had little need for an American to represent its interests with U.S. companies. Schmidt, as an employee of Deutsche Bank, ran a representative office with no legal status and no special rights or responsibilities as a bank. Deutsche Bank still relied on correspondent banks and personal relationships with other banks, but the strong ties with Speyer were unraveling and other New York banks were changing their international orientations. Competition, distracting administrative tasks, and trouble at home limited Deutsche Bank's ability to profit from the wave of international banking expansion and cross-border investment that characterized the 1920s.[16] Nationalist and populist feeling was sufficiently high that several acts during the mid-1920s limited the ownership of foreigners in companies in several U.S. sectors, but much of the sentiment was directed more toward British, not German, companies.[17]

American banks quickly used the opportunity of European weakness to move into markets where the Germans had been strong. Equitable Trust Co. started up an active Asian department. Some in Berlin intimated that Deutsche Bank's Deutsch-Asiatische Bank and Deutsche Ueberseeische Bank might look to develop partnerships with these American institutions, as some German banks were trying – for example, Dresdner Bank with Equitable Trust – unsuccessfully to do.[18]

Even before the American–German peace treaty was signed, some old friends wanted to do business with Deutsche Bank. Schwab of Bethlehem Steel informed Schmidt that he was going to Europe and wanted to meet with Deutsche Bank representatives. He claimed to have great faith in Germany's industrial future. With profits earned thanks to the war, he and friends wanted to build a consortium of allied companies to invest a billion Marks in German stocks.[19] Although Schmidt assured Schwab of Deutsche Bank's interest and help, he warned his German colleagues about the onslaught of American money eager to buy cheap German assets.[20] Schmidt pressed Schwab for a commitment that buying assets in Germany would at least help to reduce Germany's political isolation. Though ambitious, Schwab's shopping list, which included Siemens & Halske, AEG, and Krupp, involved sizeable amounts of common stock without the intention necessarily of taking a controlling interest.[21]

Schmidt was confronted by several business problems both practical and bizarre. Right after the war he leased space from McClement, which was not a long-term solution for Deutsche Bank. Starting in May 1920, he took office space in the Equitable Building at 120 Broadway. Space was hard to come by, and rents had doubled since the beginning of the war. His departure necessitated reassuring McClement that the relationship between Deutsche Bank and McClement would not change, but there already seems to have been some conflicts brewing. The bank stopped publishing its Annual Report in English; only key financial information like revenues, profit, and total assets were provided to Americans.[22]

In July 1920, Schmidt was finally released from all his parole restrictions. The United States attorney general warned him that enemy aliens, including those who were released on parole, were still subject to internment. Although his parole allowed him to travel back to Germany for the first time since 1914, Schmidt was strictly forbidden to do anything that might be construed as hostile to the United States.[23]

Despite having only a small staff, Hugo Schmidt had his share of personnel problems.[24] In early 1920, one key member of his staff had a nervous breakdown and had to be hospitalized. His worst problem, curiously, was with another Schmidt, *Prokurist* Wilhelm, who had been sent from Germany to handle Deutsche Bank and customer claims against the Alien Property Custodian (APC). He held the position for nearly two-and-a-half years, until Hugo Schmidt and Deutsche Bank became concerned with the expenses produced by his activities, his increasing aggressiveness with the director Schmidt, and reports that he was irritating U.S. government workers in Washington.[25]

The work representing clients must have been tedious with the APC offering little immediate reward, which is probably one reason Deutsche Bank was so concerned about costs. One list of Deutsche Bank customers with claims against the APC for shares in only one company, the Baltimore & Ohio Railroad, contained fourteen accounts. Some clients held as few as three shares.[26] Each case had a separate file number.

There were the usual problems with the head office. Some departments in Berlin felt that Schmidt's staff was not responsive enough. Schmidt vigorously defended them, claiming that the division of responsibility in Berlin led to his small, overworked staff being besieged by correspondence deluging them with questions.[27] It seemed to Schmidt that too many people wanted to get involved. The legal costs of his operation, too, were mounting. The APC legal expenditures alone had come by December 16, 1925, to nearly $170,000.[28] The German government added to the workload of the U.S. office. In March 1926, someone in the United States charged that the German government had $10–12 million deposited with Deutsche Bank in New York before the United States entered the war. Deutsche Bank was asked to help refute the accusation.[29] Much of its dealings were with correspondent banks and depository accounts, such as

Alfred Blinzig circa late 1930s. Blinzig's experiences in the United States were particularly useful to the bank during the difficult 1920s. He served as one of the bank's principal point persons for negotiations about seized property, reparations, and revision of the Dawes Plan. Unfortunately, no picture of Hugo Schmidt, Deutsche Bank's representative in the United States during much of the interwar period, could be found.

those held with Bankers Trust. As always, there were many requests for market information, specific security values, and even for exchange of rumors.[30]

There were other reasons why reestablishing banking relationships was difficult for Deutsche Bank. Although bankers like Blinzig of Deutsche Bank and Thomas W. Lamont of Morgan, who had worked together before the war, could meet and discuss German economic conditions, U.S. aid to Germany, and transfers, Morgan had so committed itself to Allied financing during and after the war that the U.S. bank had little time and resources left over for Germany. Morgan's offices in London and Paris were doing some European business in New York, which probably seemed sufficient for the bank. In any case, Morgan showed little interest in making Deutsche Bank its main bank in Germany. There were too many other good choices, and Morgan began to think it did not need an intermediary. Prewar administration, among other issues, divided Deutsche Bank and some American banks. Deutsche Bank had to walk a fine line between pushing for remuneration to which it felt morally entitled and losing possible future business with powerful New York bankers.[31]

In spite of the frictions that developed in the New York banking community during the war, a sort of banking network remained intact: what Mira Wilkins describes as "cosmopolitan banking," the "intertwining of inward and outward" investing activities and institutions.[32] During the interwar period, the United States became both the source and the recipient of long-term capital and pivotal to somewhat new types of blending of direct and portfolio foreign investment, and the internal allocations of capital within firms. U.S. portfolio investment in foreign companies made direct investment into the United States possible. U.S. banks took the lead in managing portfolio investment in the United States that in turn also fed portfolio and direct investment in other countries.[33]

Not all investment flowed into New York, which had become a banking center rivaling London. The timing of some public figures' deaths, other transactions, and the strong Dollar provided encouragement for foreign investors to sell their U.S. assets. Lord Mount Stephen, for example, died in December 1921 leaving an estate full of large U.S. railroad investments. Moreover, U.S. government policies also contributed to the sale of some foreign-owned U.S. assets. Prohibition on the sale of alcoholic beverages and restrictions on foreign ownership in many sectors such as communications and banking, for example, led to foreign disinvestments in U.S. businesses.[34]

Foreign banks were anxious to be part of the action, and American banks looked more seriously to developing their international presence. Banking regulation changed considerably, but these new rules did not seem to change the form or substance of German involvement in U.S. banking. Prewar family ties, such as those provided by the houses of Warburg and Speyer, continued after the war.[35] Others chose to set up an international banking organization, which was allowed under New York state law. This structure had mixed success. The most famous example was the International Acceptance Bank (IAB), formed in New York in April 1921 by Paul M. Warburg with American capital of $276 million and foreign capital of $271 million. The M. M. Warburg & Co. of Hamburg, though not a shareholder until 1925, was actively involved. IAB specialized in banking transactions between Germany and the United States. With several successful years behind it, in 1924, IAB branched out into other services. It created the American & Continental Corporation to provide assistance to potential German borrowers. At this point, Deutsche Bank joined the group as an investor, along with several other German and non-German European banks. In December 1928, the Bank of Manhattan Company, decided to buy IAB in a stock exchange and quickly separated the acceptance business from the investment advising side of IAB.[36]

With all of these financial flows and despite the restoration of an international banking community, unfortunately Deutsche Bank had lost much of its comparative advantage. Large German firms had little reason to seek it out for their investment and borrowing in the United States. Moreover, American firms increasingly felt that they could have direct access to German markets. The steelmaker tycoon Hugo Stinnes, for example, established his own U.S. company to finance his German subsidiaries, which allowed his firm to retire much of its domestic debt. The chief underwriter for the Vereinigte Stahlwerke's (United Steel Works) was Dillon, Read & Co., not a German bank.[37] Representatives of major German companies rarely even visited the Deutsche Bank office in New York. Deutsche Bank played only a minor role in the issuing of German securities on the American market. Few of the German companies that made direct investment in the United States between 1924 and 1929 seemed to avail themselves of Deutsche Bank's services.[38] Moreover, throughout the interwar and 1940s periods, investment in the United States was of a different nature. Before World War I, companies were seeking new opportunities. After 1914, security and the avoidance of barriers to international commerce played a much greater role.[39]

Deutsche Bank and the Alien Property Custodian

One of the most important regulations affecting Germans was that involving the assets held by the APC. The APC sold off many assets and held others in trust. Its activities were marred by several scandals.[40] Although most American business historians talk about the great strategic and structural innovations of American business after World War I, few stress the competitive advantages provided by the seizure of German property. Sterling Products alone bought up 1,200 Bayer patents in December 1918. Other American chemical companies were anxious not to be excluded from the feeding frenzy. In February 1919, a nonprofit corporation, The Chemical Foundation, Inc., was established to take possession of the confiscated German patents and trademarks (4,500 in total) and license them out to U.S. companies.[41] Despite many technical problems, which led American companies to seek out assistance from the former German owners and the creation in some cases of joint ventures, the easy access to German technology gave American companies an enormous leg up in international competition during the next few decades.

Deutsche Bank's efforts to recover its assets seem to have begun in earnest in 1921. The Berlin office wanted to maintain extensive control over the process. Deutsche Bank established two departments for which the principal activity seems to have been getting back its prewar assets. Some of the letters to Schmidt with detailed instructions were more than ten pages long excluding lengthy attachments. Not only did Deutsche Bank have to reconcile what the APC thought it had had with what its New York deposit banks claimed had been with them in 1918, it also needed to gather from all its branches, domestic and foreign, what amounts they held for their own or for customers' accounts in New York. The reams of correspondence flowed in both directions and dealt with details regarding the application process. Without a detailed and verified list of all the property, the application process could not go forward. Some certificates were numbered, others not. Some were bearer bonds, others registered. All of the details had to be exact to pass the APC's muster. The list of securities held by Speyer & Co. was eleven pages long and contained approximately 300 different entries with a face value of nearly $800,000, presumably held for various Deutsche Bank clients. The Bankers Trust list was much shorter, but the nominal value was still nearly $400,000. All in all, in 1918 Deutsche Bank had left securities with fifteen New York institutions, including National City Bank, Chase, and Kuhn Loeb, with a nominal value of approximately

$4.4 million. The largest two were Blair & Co. and Guaranty Trust Co. of New York.[42]

In May 1921, Deutsche Bank estimated that its combined prewar Dollar holding in the United States – from the Berlin head office, branches, Deutsche Bank-led syndicates, and customer deposits – amounted to $1.3 million in cash and securities of $3 million. Of the total, about $3 million belonged to Deutsche Bank. One memo estimated that the application involved 1,700 cases, not including the London branch,[43] which alone submitted fifty-five different accounts in the United States for clients, some of which were trusts in Britain but presumably held in the name of Germans who thought they had hedged themselves by using London institutions for their deposits in the United States.[44] The assets in Deutsche Bank's care included hundreds of different securities from many sectors: some old friends such as Northern Pacific bonds and stock; Allis-Chalmers stock; Western Maryland common and preferred; some new investments such as California Petroleum Corporation common and preferred; and AT&T, broken up into many pools and syndicates with various securities.

Even with all efforts, there was no guarantee of success. Some estimates indicated that it would take at least two-and-a-half years to recover the assets. Other institutions and individuals were vying to represent those who had lost property.[45] At least some Americans believed that the seizure and sale of assets was in conflict with American values. Not until November 1925 did the U.S. government put into place plans to compensate Germans for the property they had lost.

The loss of these assets entailed many kinds of costs for Deutsche Bank. For some of the companies, the bank had been influential in management decisions, and the ability to control the companies was lost. Its designates resigned from the boards of companies once owned by Deutsche Bank, seemingly without consulting the bank.[46] There were valuation issues concerning which foreign exchange rates to use for transactions, for example, about which Deutsche Bank could exercise little or no influence. In addition, the bank lost some liquidity – the opportunity to get rid of investments at favorable moments.

B&O railroad securities posed a special problem for Deutsche Bank. As the managing agent of the security on the Berlin exchange (see Section I), it had to hold shares traded on the Berlin stock exchange. It was also responsible for transmitting dividends from the B&O paid into its account in New York for the German shareholders. But the shares were in the hands of the APC, and the B&O was obliged to pay the government its dividend on the shares. Mixed in with Deutsche Bank's own holding, moreover, were shares it held for the accounts of investors from neutral and even Allied nations who were customers of the bank and who ostensibly under U.S. regulations had the right to immediate return of the securities.[47] Proving ownership and complying with the APC demands for documentation was not easy. A small error in the forms – each security was numbered – had the potential of causing frustrating bureaucratic delays. Ironically, by the end of the decade B&O's own financial problems and the slowness of getting the APC shares led to the rail's delisting in Berlin.[48]

At first, Schmidt was relatively pessimistic about recovering the assets. Woodrow Wilson's Democratic cabinet, which remained in office until March 1921, believed that the differences were irreconcilable and that the Germans would never see their property again. Some thought the only hope was to offer German property as security for a credit to Germany, an idea to which some still clung in mid-1921 and which finally contributed to the settlement.[49]

From 1922 on, however, there seemed to have been a commitment by the U.S. government to return the assets. Although the new Republican administration was more sympathetic, implementation of the commitment involved new legislation and competing interest groups. It was a battle waged with money, in which salvos about the principles of American "fairness" and commitment to property rights were answered with shots about the financial guarantees of German payments to the United States, and later by mounds of paperwork designed to discourage and delay. Before the assets could be returned, the APC had to determine what assets were at issue and, sometimes, to collect them from trustees who appeared to feel it their patriotic duty to withhold information and the securities from even the U.S. government.[50]

The basic issues were articulated early on. In 1922, everyone seemed to agree that legislation releasing the seized property would be passed. By 1922, the simple confiscation and sale of German assets had stopped. The question was: Would German guarantees for the payment of American damages – and later American loans – be sufficient to insure payment? Most Americans seemed to think that losses resulting from the sinking of the *Lusitania*, for example, as well as other damages Americans ostensibly suffered should be paid out of the funds. In April 1923, the total estimated losses reached nearly $1.2 billion.[51] Although the Senate bill S. 3088, introduced on January 25, 1922, authorized former enemies to recover their property, the attorney general recommended that the bill be deferred until Germany provided the guarantees, a process that delayed its implementation.[52]

In some cases, figuring out what had been seized and when forced Deutsche Bank into uncomfortable discussions with not only the APC but also with former business partners lasting many years and involving incalculable uncertainties. One such example involved two of Deutsche Bank's oldest associations in the United States, Morgan and the Northern Pacific.[53] During the war, even though communication and transfers were difficult, Deutsche Bank continued to handle payments of Northern Pacific coupons and Morgan acknowledged its liabilities to the German bank until war broke out between the United States and Germany in April 1917.

The post-World War I dispute arose in 1921, three years after the end of hostilities, when Deutsche Bank appealed for its share of payments from the war years and during the armistice. The Berlin headquarters instructed Schmidt to try to collect the back payments, which should have been paid to Bankers Trust. Deutsche Bank in Berlin believed that the amounts might have been paid directly to the APC, but was not sure, and requested Schmidt to determine how much had been paid.[54] Schmidt urgently responded that Berlin should handle the discussions directly with Morgan because he felt that his activities during the past years in New York had made him *persona non grata* with the Morgan people.[55]

There was an odd lapse of two years before the issue came to the fore once more. In the fall of 1923, Carl Bergmann was sent to New York to try to resolve this and other matters. Bergmann met with several of the Morgan partners in November 1923, with whom he discussed the matter politely. Attesting to the long duration of banking transactions and the importance of acknowledging history, three Morgan representatives and one Deutsche Bank manager discussed contracts and transactions that had been consummated over twenty-five years before the meeting. The issue was further complicated because most of the individuals left to discuss a solution had not been around when the original contracts were signed, and therefore did not know the intentions of the original signers. The Morgan partners seemed sympathetic to Bergmann's request and promised to get back to him in a few days. After ten days, Bergmann informed the head office that he had heard nothing and that he had discovered that Morgan had done nothing to communicate with the APC about Deutsche Bank's claims.[56]

The peace treaty between Germany and the United States (the Berlin Treaty) had improved Deutsche Bank's position in the discussions, but that treaty had been signed in August 1921 and in force since October 1921. But even this agreement left many legal questions open. Was the war period from April 6, 1917, when war was declared to the Armistice (November 11, 1918), or to the signing of the treaty, or to its coming into force? This date was critical, for example, in determining which private transactions were covered by war legislation. Moreover, would the United States pass legislation allowing companies to nullify prewar contracts?[57] The overall consensus was that Deutsche Bank's legal claims were a little shaky, as it had been unable to perform services under the contract for many years, but that more importantly the overall legal climate was such that the outcome of a court battle was uncertain and the costs high. Even working through the Claims Commission that had been established entailed many risks. Nevertheless, both sides acknowledged a kind of moral obligation. In December 1923, Morgan offered $102,000 to settle the matter (an amount equal to what was owed to Deutsche Bank for the years 1919–23), on condition that the contract would be void for the future and Deutsche Bank drop any further claims. Deutsche Bank refused despite the enormous economic pressures it and Germany faced.[58] Even a related decision of the U.S. Supreme Court in December that was very favorable to German private interests did not eliminate all the uncertainty around Deutsche Bank's claims.[59] Deutsche Bank's American lawyers maintained that the German bank was entitled to all payments on transactions before April 1917, that the contract was only suspended for the duration of the war, and that the APC, having failed to seize the cash and the contracts, had now forgone the right to do so.[60]

Under these circumstances, Deutsche Bank seemed to exercise amazing restraint. It must be remembered that the early stages of the dispute were played out against the backdrop of the final stages of Germany's hyperinflation and severe capital shortages. Despite the crisis, Deutsche Bank decided to back off from the dispute, at least temporarily, perhaps in order to preserve its good relations with Morgan in hopes of winning new business.[61]

This may have been the explanation, although Deutsche Bank attributed the delay in resolving the matter to Bergmann's resignation for a position with Lazard Speyer-Ellissen in Frankfurt. Deutsche Bank pinned its new hopes on the visit of Alfred Blinzig, a member of the management board, in March 1927, and the eagerness of both sides to do new business together.[62] With Blinzig planning to visit New York in 1927 the matter was brought up again with a lengthy letter reminding Morgan of the decisive role played by Deutsche Bank in the reorganization of the Northern Pacific, including bringing the business to Morgan.[63] Morgan "pleasantly" agreed to pay Deutsche Bank $250,000 in return for the latter bank's agreement to void the 1897 contract.[64] Deutsche Bank had earned $148,000 for its patience, a virtue required in all its efforts to get back its U.S. property.

By May 1924, Deutsche Bank had a complete inventory of cash and securities with the APC, amounting to over $18 million, for which the bank applied. Accounts held in Deutsche Bank's name accounted for approximately $4 million of the total. The additional $14 million was probably made up by other Germans who turned to Deutsche Bank for assistance. Dividends and interest on the securities alone came to $3 million.[65]

Disposing of the securities held by APC was cumbersome but not impossible. On occasion, the APC sold assets without getting Deutsche Bank's formal permission, although for months the bank had indicated it would like to sell some securities. At other times, Deutsche Bank tried to execute orders for securities that were in the APC's hands. It was a long tedious process.[66] With APC initiated transactions, Deutsche Bank seemed anxious retroactively, however, to give its permission in order to get the cash that came out of the sale, which in one case finally occurred in December 1924. What provoked the sales was not always clear. Sometimes sales resulted from reorganizations of companies.[67] In some cases, Deutsche Bank proposed and APC accepted the sale of securities. Occasionally, Deutsche Bank asked the APC to exercise the bank's rights to new shares.[68] The APC was not always adverse to sales, especially if it saw a good economic justification for the transaction.[69]

For several months, Deutsche Bank negotiated with the APC for release or sale of its Banco Mexicano shares, a bank that it had helped set up with Speyer. When Speyer lost much of its interest in Mexican business in 1921, and the local bank, Banco Mexicano, went through a reorganization (liquidation), Deutsche Bank tried to sell off its own holding, which was in the hands of the APC. In order to get a better price, Deutsche Bank engineered the sale of the securities through a middleman.[70] Banco Germanico bought the shares from the APC and sold them off at a higher price, on Deutsche Bank's behalf, to a third party.[71]

Deutsche Bank wanted to unload other properties that were in the hands of the APC. Western Maryland's difficulties were so bad that Schmidt had to take phone calls at home after office hours.[72] The sale of 65,000 WMR common shares, a holding which reportedly amounted to 11 percent of the company's shares outstanding, was probably the largest sale of Deutsche Bank assets held by the APC. Deutsche Bank succeeded in arranging for the sale of the shares to B&O, but the APC held up the transaction because it had difficulty verifying that the German owners found the offer satisfactory. Although the shares were in the hands of the APC and subject to Congressional oversight, the APC had decided only to dispose of securities with the written consent of the German owners. After the eventual sales, all the funds were then deposited with the treasury subject to an ultimate decision about how they would be distributed.[73]

The process of getting a complete settlement of the APC assets meant not only a long wait but also many emotional ups and downs. Sometimes the release looked imminent, at other times as if it would never happen. In February 1924, the situation took a radical turn for the worse. The Teapot Dome scandal broke in 1923, hitting the Republican Party, which favored the restoration of German property. Politicians were totally focused on the scandal's ramifications. Although the House was still very much in favor of the return of German property, a vote during the session was unlikely and the Republicans were likely to lose a lot of seats in the 1924 election.[74] In early summer 1924, American views, moreover, about German property hardened. Secretary of State Charles Evans Hughes took the position that no German property would be released until all American claims were settled. Some thought was given to tying German claims to Dawes Plan financing (see next Chapter). Hughes, however, preferred immediate settlement of the American claims.[75]

Even after President Warren Harding ordered in March 1923 that all claims of $10,000 or less to be released[76] and while Deutsche Bank labored to maintain good relations with the APC, there were still difficulties in getting Deutsche Bank's depositors' funds paid out.[77] Foreign exchange issues and verification of Deutsche Bank's lists of securities held up disbursements of the first payments. Some of the relevant files were simply mislaid at the APC.[78] The managing director of the APC claimed that his organization was not capable of handling all the work. It could not process more than 1,000 claims a month.[79] Moreover, the APC stepped up its own propaganda to encourage the view that German assets should not be released as long as there were questions about American claims.[80] Some of the problems in finding a complete resolution lay in the division of power within the government. Although the original act called for the return of property after the war, Congress delayed voting on new legislation until the executive branch pronounced judgment about how to proceed. There was also some conflict, though not a lot, in the bills proposed by the two houses of Congress.[81]

A big step forward finally came with the passage of the Settlement of War Claims Act on March 19, 1928. But even after President Calvin Coolidge signed the Act, bringing to an end the long, drawn-out legislative battle, many administrative questions still remained. How and when, for example, would American claimants and German owners of the seized property – securities, ships, patents, and radio stations – receive the property? Distributing monies to American claimants was to receive the highest priority. Some thought that the entire process would take six months. Others hoped for a shorter period, but recognized that some sorts of property might take as long as three years to distribute.[82] American claims to be paid immediately were estimated to amount to approximately $56 million. Enemy claims in 1928 amounted to approximately $113 million, leaving $57 million (a little over 50 percent of the total), which could be awarded in the fairly near future on a pro rata basis to claimants whose awards were over $100,000.[83]

The Settlement of War Claims Act alone, however, covered only $43.2 million of the assets, but even this legislation required further regulation by the U.S. Treasury Department – a process which alone took four months – to explain how administrative details such as taxes should be handled. From July to December 1928, only 436 claims had been allowed. There were further delays in actually paying out the sums owed even for these approved claims. The APC's staff had been reduced during the year from 201 to 184, adding to the administrative challenges. Despite some early disbursements, with all the income added to the original amount seized, on December 31, 1928, the APC still held a sizeable packet of securities, real estate, and patents. There was plenty to cover its liabilities. Among the assets still held by the APC in early 1929 were 2.6 million common shares with a market value of $55 million and bonds with a market value of $75.2 million at pre-Crash prices.[84] In theory, income on the securities belonged not to the APC but to the owners. The APC, however, collected some substantial fees for the administration of the assets: 5 percent of the first $5,000 collected in income, sliding down to 1 percent for annual amounts over $25,000. In addition, though capped at $200 for each individual trust account, its custodial fee ranged from 1 percent on the first $5,000 in assets it held to one-eighth of 1 percent on amounts in excess of $25,000 per annum on amounts it had seized. Ironically, some clients were paying less than they would have with a trust bank, but it is unlikely that they got the same level of service.[85]

At the hour of victory, more problems arose. Disputes erupted among Deutsche Bank's American counselors over who did what and how the spoils should be divided. In winter 1928, A. W. Lafferty, a propagandist employed by several German institutions, was outraged by the behavior and comments of a person he himself had hired to replace him while he was sick. In any case, by this time Schmidt had lost confidence in Lafferty but feared that he could cause problems in Washington.[86] Just as Deutsche Bank received its shares, a tax bill arrived. Schmidt had to prepare a list of when and for how much each share – which had been sold by the APC – had been purchased, including the Western Maryland and Western Pacific pools. In several cases, the bank was missing the information to determine the tax basis.[87] If Deutsche Bank could come up with an estimate of its tax liability, the APC generously proposed to deduct the amount from the final award.

The payout for several banks, however, came in fall 1928. Deutsche Bank was not the first to receive its settlement. The Berliner Handels-Gesellschaft remarkably got over $7 million, which probably included customer accounts, two months before Deutsche Bank's assets were released.[88] However, Deutsche Bank and its clients fared better than did other German institutions. Those who held securities watched them increase in value; those who held patents and trademarks, for example, received back damaged goods. Fortunately for Deutsche Bank, all outstanding matters regarding share sales and ownership seem also to have been, or were about to be, resolved, and Deutsche Bank was still holding rights to most of its and its customers' prewar investments.[89]

In early 1929, it debated when to sell them.[90] As the settlement approached, prices of American securities skyrocketed. Impatient Deutsche Bank managers in Berlin were tempted to sell even securities while they were still in APC hands. Schmidt was afraid that this would cause complications with the APC, even if the bank borrowed the shares from a correspondent bank and repaid them when the shares were returned.[91] The delay was very fortunate. Heeding Schmidt's advice, Deutsche Bank waited until 1929, when it aggressively sold off shares, especially Allis-Chalmers, near their market high – some as late as early October, just before the Crash. Unfortunately, when the Crash did come, Deutsche Bank and its customers had not received all their shares from the APC.

Despite the fortunate timing, all in all the experience contributed to the motivation of many German institutions and individuals to cloak their assets, especially in the 1930s, in the hope that having some sort of stand-in would make the seizing process so much harder for the Americans that they would lose interest or run out of time to trace ownership, should another war come.[92] Even this temporary loss illustrated how political financial matters had become, and how important conserving some measure of financial independence, sometimes even from Deutsche Bank's home government, had become for businesses in the interwar period. Like many aspects of the financial scene in the 1920s, the property disputes did not end cross-border flows. They distorted them, reduced their productive value, and sometimes added to their risks.

12

Deutsche Bank and Rebuilding Cross-Border Financial Flows

> What you write me about your feelings on our co-operation in the past work is a great satisfaction to me, notwithstanding I know what large part of your compliments are undeserved and should go to Mr. Schlieper, your good self and Mr. Axhausen plus the wonderful organization of your bank. As I told you when I left Berlin, I am spoiled forever by the experience I had in these negotiations, and any future negotiations will seem to me doubly hard.
>
> Steiner of Dillon Read to H. A. Simon of Deutsche Bank after the restructuring of Deutsche Bank's $25 million loan, October 6, 1932, HADB, S4392.

> That is the finest business you have done in Germany, and I think it is the finest business that has been done in Germany.[1]
>
> Schacht to Eberstadt of Dillon Read in English, File note, September 13, 1927, HADB, S4382.

Personal Relationships and Political Solutions

Through much of the interwar period, Dollar loans in Germany became a big part of Deutsche Bank's business. Deutsche Bank developed a tenuous and often thankless role as a conduit between Dollar-rich investors and loan-hungry German clients. Its lending and borrowing practices must be seen against the background of the short-level political and economic attempt to restore financial "normality" in the wake of hostilities and an unsatisfactory peace that made Germany more dependent on international lenders.

Personal relationships were key to restoring business with the United States The war left many old friendships and habits shaken, but not destroyed. The Warburg family was one of the most interesting examples of how the ties could be maintained. The Warburg and Kuhn Loeb banks were family affairs. Paul Warburg traveled between the United States and Europe. A member of the Federal Reserve Board, he was an intimate of Benjamin Strong, head of the New York Federal Reserve, and Montagu Norman, head of the Bank of England. Throughout much of the 1920s, with a stream of letters and papers Warburg kept them informed about their counterpart in Germany, Hjalmar Schacht, president of the Reichsbank, and general conditions in Germany.

For many, the well-being of Germany and the United States was still intertwined, but they no longer shared the same worldview. In much of Europe, including Germany, the bright optimism that had shone before the war, for example, had disappeared, perhaps helping to define one of the major differences between the two regions for the next hundred years. As Paul's brother Max Warburg wrote just after his return from a two-month visit to the United States: "In America, speaking by and large, things are bright and hopeful, while all the observer sees in Europe is dark and depressing."[2] For many Germans, beset by political extremism and overall hatred of the economic and political ramifications of the Versailles Treaty, the United States offered the last vestige of hope to rebuild the world for the short and long-run. Warburg added:

> It is a matter of fairly common agreement today, that since the end of the War, governments of some of the leading European countries have done, not only obviously stupid and destructive things, but that they have committed these blunders with open eyes and often unwillingly and regretfully, simply because the pressure of home politics and war begotten passions were stronger than their conscience and reason. *If America had only been officially represented on the Reparations Commission* [underlined in the original text], her influence could have helped the forces of reason to assert themselves sooner, and some of the bitter and wasteful lessons of painful experience, that Europe is learning today, might have been avoided.[3]

In 1924, America finally attempted to help put Germany's finances on a firm footing. For optimists, the Dawes Plan – named after General Charles Dawes, the American financier who formulated the plan and later became vice president of the United States – was a phenomenal accomplishment that established a basis for working out Germany's immediate economic woes. In retrospect, though, it perhaps contributed to a whole new set of difficulties.[4] The Dawes Plan was a multifaceted ambitious financial program with limited short-term success. Although certainly no panacea, it provided hope in an otherwise bleak situation. Under the plan, nearly $15 billion in American public and private funds was organized for German public and private projects to stabilize Germany's finances by providing temporary relief and by restructuring Germany's foreign debt.[5] It had several components: one involved the APC using German property to insure repayment of a portion of the loan. The United States assigned to a trustee seized property that would guarantee reparation and other payments from Germany. The Centralverband des Deutschen Bank- und Bankiergewerbes, on whose board Blinzig sat, took a leading role in explaining the terms of the plan and organizing German institutions to maximize the return of seized German property.[6] But successful implementation of the plan required enormous financial discipline, a virtue that was in short supply during the "Roaring Twenties" and not likely to be cultivated in the Weimar political and economic culture.

Although financial gain was surely a motive, many Americans were concerned for other reasons about the political and economic climate in Germany in the 1920s. In July 1925, Benjamin Strong once again visited Germany. His reports were full of praise for Schacht and the work done by America's financial representative, Parker Gilbert. Strong believed that Schacht was completely committed to holding the Reichsmark's external value. But Schacht feared that the

$1000 $1000

GERMAN EXTERNAL LOAN 1924

Nº C 008500 Nº C 008500

DEUTSCHE ÄUSSERE ANLEIHE 1924

SEVEN PER CENT. GOLD BOND
TOTAL ISSUE IN UNITED STATES OF AMERICA, $ 110,000,000.

The German Reich (hereinafter termed the Obligor) for value received, hereby promises to pay on the 15th day of October, 1949, to the bearer of this Bond, the principal sum of ONE THOUSAND DOLLARS and to pay semi-annually on the 15th day of April and the 15th day of October in each year, until such principal sum shall have been paid, interest thereon at the rate of seven per cent per annum, in accordance with the coupons for such interest hereto attached, upon presentation and surrender of such coupons as severally they become payable.

Such principal sum and such interest will be paid in the City of New York, State of New York, United States of America, at the office of J. P. Morgan & Co. in the Borough of Manhattan in the said City of New York, in gold coin of the United States of America of the standard of weight and fineness existing on October 15, 1924, without deduction for all or any present or future German taxes, or stamp or other duties, dues or public charges of any kind whatsoever, and neither this Bond nor any other document or writing relevant to the Loan shall be subject to any German registration fees, stamp duties or other similar duties.

The Obligor further covenants that in no case or event will this Bond or the coupons for interest thereon be attached or sequestrated, and that all and any moneys in this Bond covenanted to be paid upon or in respect of this Bond will be paid in time of war as well as in time of peace and whether or not the holder of this Bond or of any of the interest coupons thereof is a subject of a State friendly or hostile to the German Reich.

This Bond is one of the Seven Per Cent Gold Bonds (hereinafter termed collectively the "Bonds of this issue") of the Obligor, for the aggregate principal amount of $110,000,000 payable in the above defined gold coin of the United States of America and issued therein, which bonds constitute part of the German External Loan 1924 (hereinafter referred to as the "Loan") for the purpose and in respect of which the Obligor has executed its General Bond dated October 10, 1924, of which General Bond a transcript in full is printed on the reverse hereof.

In accordance with said General Bond and supplementary documents and proceedings the Obligor has covenanted to pay in the above defined gold coin of the United States of America, as a sinking fund for the amortization of the Bonds of this issue, the sum of $4,620,000 a year, in equal monthly instalments of which the first instalment shall be paid on or before November 15, 1924 and succeeding instalments on or before the fifteenth day of each calendar month thereafter. Such sinking fund is to be applied from time to time to the purchase of Bonds of this issue if obtainable at or below 105% and accrued interest, or if not so obtainable to the redemption by call of Bonds of this issue selected by lot at 105% and accrued interest, the amount of the accrued interest in either case to be provided and paid by the Obligor otherwise than out of the sinking fund. The numbers of the Bonds drawn for redemption will be advertised in a newspaper of general circulation in the Borough of Manhattan, City and State of New York, United States of America not less than one month prior to the date of redemption. Drawn Bonds when presented for payment upon any such redemption must be accompanied by all coupons due subsequent to the redemption date. Payment of the above expressed sinking fund obligations of the Obligor shall be made in accordance with the relevant provisions of the aforesaid General Bond, and the administration of such sinking fund shall be in accordance with regulations prescribed by the Loan Trustees provided for in said General Bond.

This Bond is subject to redemption on October 15, 1925 and on October 15th in each year thereafter prior to October 15, 1949, by operation of the sinking fund above described, at 105% of the principal amount, the interest accrued to the redemption date being also payable upon surrender of the coupon then maturing. The sum due on this Bond, in the event of such redemption, will be paid in the above defined gold coin of the United States of America at the place of payment hereof above expressed.

This Bond shall not be negotiable until authenticated for identification in the said City of New York by the countersignature hereon of Bankers Trust Company.

The English text and the German text of this Bond are counterparts constituting a single instrument, the English text being controlling in case of any variation.

Dated October 15, 1924.

7 PROZENTIGE GOLDSCHULDVERSCHREIBUNG
GESAMTAUSGABE IN DEN VEREINIGTEN STAATEN VON AMERIKA 110,000,000 DOLLAR.

Das Deutsche Reich (im folgenden als Schuldner bezeichnet) verpflichtet sich hierdurch, am 15. Oktober 1949 dem Inhaber dieser Schuldverschreibung für empfangenen Gegenwert den Betrag von EINTAUSEND DOLLAR zu zahlen und halbjährlich am 15. April und 15. Oktober j. Js. bis zur Tilgung des Kapitals Zinsen hierauf von 7 v. H. für das Jahr laut den hierfür beigefügten Zinsscheinen gegen deren Vorzeigung und Übergabe zum Fälligkeitstage zu entrichten.

Kapital und Zinsen werden gezahlt in der Stadt New York, Staat New York U.S.A., in dem Geschäftshaus der Firma J. P. Morgan & Co. in dem Stadtteil Manhattan der Stadt New York in Goldmünze der U.S.A. zu dem am 15. Oktober 1924 geltenden Gewicht und Feingehalt ohne Abzug für irgendwelche gegenwärtigen oder zukünftigen deutschen Steuern, Stempelgebühren oder anderen Abgaben oder öffentlichen Lasten irgendwelcher Art. Diese Schuldverschreibung sowohl wie jede andere auf diese Anleihe bezügliche Urkunde soll keinen deutschen Eintragungs-, Stempel- oder ähnlichen Gebühren unterworfen werden.

Der Schuldner verpflichtet sich, fernerhin in keinem Falle diese Schuldverschreibung oder die dazu gehörigen Zinsscheine zu beschlagnahmen oder in Zwangsverwaltung zu nehmen, alle Zahlungen, zu denen er aus dieser Schuldverschreibung verpflichtet ist, zu jeder Kriegs- und Friedenszeit und an jeden Inhaber der Schuldverschreibung oder eines zugehörigen Zinsscheins, sei er Untertan eines mit dem Deutschen Reich befreundeten oder feindlichen Staates, zu leisten.

Diese Schuldverschreibung ist eine von den 7 prozentigen Goldschuldverschreibungen (späterhin insgesamt bezeichnet als "Schuldverschreibungen dieser Ausgabe") des Schuldners für den Gesamtbetrag von 110.000.000 $, zahlbar in der obenbezeichneten Goldmünze der U.S.A. und ausgestellt auf diese; diese Schuldverschreibungen stellen einen Teil der Deutschen Äußeren Anleihe 1924 dar (späterhin als "Anleihe" bezeichnet), für welche der Schuldner den Generalbond vom 10. Oktober 1924, von welchem eine Abschrift auf der Rückseite hiervon abgedruckt ist, ausgestellt hat.

In Übereinstimmung mit dem bezeichneten Generalbond, den ergänzenden Urkunden und Protokollen hat der Schuldner sich verpflichtet, als Tilgungsfonds für die Tilgung der Schuldverschreibungen dieser Ausgabe die Summe von 4.620.000 $ in der obenbezeichneten Goldmünze der U.S.A. für das Jahr in gleichen monatlichen Raten, von denen die erste Rate spätestens am 15. November 1924 und die folgenden Raten spätestens am 15. jedes Kalendermonats fällig sind, zu zahlen. Dieser Tilgungsfonds ist von Zeit zu Zeit zum Ankauf von Schuldverschreibungen dieser Ausgabe, soweit sie zu 105% oder niedriger zuzüglich aufgelaufener Zinsen erhältlich sind, zu verwenden oder falls sie nicht so erhältlich sind, zur Einlösung dieser Schuldverschreibungen zu 105% zuzüglich aufgelaufener Zinsen durch Verlosung. Der Betrag der aufgelaufenen Zinsen ist in jedem Falle von dem Schuldner bereitzuhalten und ohne Inanspruchnahme des Tilgungsfonds zu zahlen. Die Nummern der gezogenen Schuldverschreibungen werden in einer Zeitung von allgemeiner Verbreitung in dem Stadtteil Manhattan, Stadt und Staat New York U.S.A. nicht weniger als 1 Monat vor dem Tage der Einlösung bekanntgemacht. Ausgeloste Schuldverschreibungen, die behufs Einlösung zur Zahlung vorgelegt werden, müssen mit allen nach dem Einlösungstag fälligen Zinsscheinen versehen sein. Zahlungen des Schuldners auf die obenbezeichneten Tilgungsverpflichtungen sollen in Übereinstimmung mit den hier anwendbaren Bestimmungen des vorbezeichneten Generalbonds geleistet werden und die Verwaltung dieses Tilgungsfonds soll in Übereinstimmung mit den von den Anleihe-Treuhändern, die in dem Generalbond vorgesehen sind, festgestellten Regeln geführt werden.

Diese Schuldverschreibung ist einlösbar aus dem Tilgungsfonds zu 105% des Kapitalbetrags am 15. Oktober 1925 und 15. Oktober jedes späteren Jahres vor dem 15. Oktober 1949. Die bis zum Einlösungstage aufgelaufenen Zinsen sind ebenfalls zu zahlen, sofern der dann fällige Zinsschein mit übergeben wird. Die aus dieser Schuldverschreibung im Falle der Einlösung geschuldete Summe wird an dem obenbezeichneten Ort in der obenbezeichneten Goldmünze der U.S.A. gezahlt werden.

Diese Schuldverschreibung ist nicht verkehrsfähig, bis sie in der Stadt New York durch die Gegenzeichnung der Bankers Trust Company hierauf beglaubigt ist.

Der englische und der deutsche Text dieser Schuldverschreibung sind Gegenstücke eines einheitlichen Ganzen, wobei der englische Text im Falle von Abweichungen der ausschlaggebende ist.

Am 15. Oktober 1924.

This public bond certificate (Face Value Gold $1000, coupon 7 percent) for refinancing German external debt was part of the Dawes Plan. The overall amount was nearly double the U.S. government's Gold Bond Issue in 1896, which carried a coupon rate of 4 percent. The bonds, which were designed to help the German government shore up its reserves much like the U.S. issue in 1896, came due in 1947. Morgan was the paying agent. The terms, written in English and German, highlighted the German government's commitment to maintain payments even in case of war and to make regular cash payments toward retiring the debt (a sinking fund).

necessary curtailing of credit would mean a very sharp reduction of German prices and employment, which he correctly foresaw would lead to a social crisis and threaten the Dawes Plan if additional and significant new long-term loans from the United States to the German government were not forthcoming. Even if the plan was flawed from conception, many Germans and Americans desperately wanted it to work. But neither side seemed sufficiently interested in controlling *ex ante* how the new funds were applied. Much of the money was thrown into economically inefficient projects that were unsustainable even during the good days of Weimar. Schacht was not amused by the efforts of many German businesses to cover up their financial sins with foreign money, and vowed to clean up the problems in Germany,[7] a tall order considering the many problems associated with the amount and kinds of debt that Germany was building and the demands of Germany's many creditors.

In meetings throughout his visit to Germany in summer 1925, Strong emphasized that the attitudes of American investors would be highly influenced by their degree of confidence in the political conditions in central Europe. The slightest signs of social unrest would send a chill over the financial community and have an enormous impact on the ability of any German institutions to place loans in the United States. For Strong, the most significant question seemed to be whether the French, English, and Germans could come to some mutually acceptable compromise about reparations and other matters that would allow for real peace and the successful implementation of the Dawes Plan.[8] Although Strong had a lot of faith in Schacht, he also spent considerable time recounting his weaknesses and the weaknesses of the Reichsbank.[9] Nevertheless, Strong was confident that Germany would thrive once it passed through a second period of liquidation (reorganization). The country would need more loans, but only secured mortgages on high-quality assets would serve as worthwhile investments. Germany and the world had only a short window of opportunity.[10]

Deutsche Bank and U.S. Capital Markets

Although Deutsche Bank's position as a link for financial matters between the United States and Germany was weaker in 1924 than it was in 1914, it still had some competitive advantages. As a result of its persistence, it and its clients had a much better chance of receiving a substantial part of their Dollar assets, which could be used to collateralize financing from the United States. It also had preserved many of its prewar relationships. Deutsche Bank's exemplary behavior was appreciated by many in the sector at the time and allowed it to preserve many of these ties.[11]

With so much German property in the United States on the block and with the weakness of the Mark, many Americans were interested in acquiring German assets, both those held in the United States and in Germany. W. Averell Harriman, the son of the railroad tycoon, E. H. Harriman, went to Germany in 1920 to negotiate for an alliance with the Hamburg-America Line (Hapag) under the auspices of Max Warburg, the Hamburg banker. By August 1920, despite public criticism for dealing with the enemy, an agreement was announced.[12] Deutsche Bank seems to have been excluded from many of these early deliberations but, by the mid-1920s, it was once again playing a leading role in German efforts to acquire foreign money, even for Hapag.

The dynamics of American investment in Germany were highly influenced by perceived opportunities in the United States. Through much of the 1920s, the roaring U.S. stock market pulled in an enormous amount of both U.S.-sourced and foreign-sourced investments. The period witnessed a tremendous shift of interest among investors from debt to equity. In 1928, for the first time, the total value of common stock on U.S. securities markets exceeded that of bonds. In addition to the promise of extraordinary capital gains, much of the investment into the U.S. was influenced by U.S. and foreign tax considerations, as well as perceived political risk. Foreign institutions participated not only in investing, but also in underwriting and financing purchases. Some foreign institutions traded securities and served as custodians for foreign investors. Virtually all the securities bought by foreigners were denominated in U.S. Dollars. Even after the Crash in October 1929, common stocks represented 54 percent of the holdings by foreigners in U.S. assets; however, foreign ownership of U.S. investments had fallen from nearly 20 percent of U.S. GNP to less than 6 percent in 1929.[13]

One of the cruelest ironies following the war was Germany's dependence on American capital. The two countries had switched their capital market roles. Deutsche Bank's first American transaction after the war was to help float a $50 million U.S. Dollar loan for the German government to support the Mark, almost an exact mirror image of its role in Morgan's 1896 syndicate to save the U.S. currency, except that the terms were more stringent. The facility, which in large part was designed to mop up German Dollar holdings and put them at the disposal of the Reich, was a three-year loan with no coupon, just a 20 percent premium over its price to be paid at maturity, corresponding to a 6.38 percent rate. At least 50 percent of the price had to be paid in Dollars, a condition the consortium guaranteed to the government.[14] The facility had less success, for understandable reasons, than the 1896 issue. The Mark continued to tumble.

In the 1920s, U.S. market levels were so high that Deutsche Bank was tempted to list its own common shares. As early as fall 1924, Deutsche Bank sold 40 million Goldmark in common shares (20 percent of Deutsche Bank's total common) through a syndicate on the American market. In addition to National City Bank, the syndicate included Bankers Trust, Chase, Speyer, and International Acceptance Bank, but not Morgan.[15] Many of the shares were bought up by foreign banks in private sales.

In spring 1929, Deutsche Bank inquired into New York listing costs and procedures. This came as a great reversal to its attitude in the early 1920s, when the bank considered ceasing to pay for announcements about its earnings in American journals, as it had done before the war, a practice that in the early 1920s seemed expensive and perhaps frivolous.[16] It had no problem fulfilling the minimum requirements for a New York Stock Exchange listing – 50,000 shares with a market value of at least $2.5 million. The expenses of listing, printing of temporary and definitive certificates, agreements, issuing tax, cables, legal fees, depository fees, application fees, and miscellaneous expenses of between $16,000 and $35,000 depending on how many shares the bank listed, were not extraordinary. The bank also looked into listing its own bonds.[17] Coming six months before the Crash, market prices must have been tempting. With Deutsche Bank's reputation in the United States and its need for fresh capital sufficiently high, listing its shares in New York offered many advantages. But there were several technical obstacles. These included the registration of shares, which was not typical for German companies. The biggest risk, however, was the transfer of voting rights to Americans. These considerations must have been too onerous, because Deutsche Bank did not go ahead with the listing (40 million Reichsmark), but there is no record of exactly why.[18]

The bank did issue some special certificates on an early form of the Over-the-Counter (OTC) market. In December 1928, Deutsche Bank along with two other large German banks offered their shares on the so-called "New York Curb Market." The Curb brokers literally operated in the street in front of the "Big Board," limited their activities to securities that were not listed on the New York Stock Exchange, sometimes just before their listing. Many new, risky securities began trading on the Curb, which was for some a stepping stone to a formal listing. For much of its history, the Curb operated without a formal organization, but by 1911 brokers entered into an association and into some affiliation with the New York Stock Exchange. Although the Curb flourished in the vibrant 1920s, the Securities Exchange Act of 1934, which passed much control of stock exchange activities into federal hands, effectively ended its activities.[19] The agreement of Guaranty Trust Company and Kassenverein of Berlin to accept deposits of the shares of the German banks approved by the Curb Market and to issue certificates against them (a form of American Depository Receipts) represented an important step in broadening the Curb Market with foreign securities. According to *The New York Times*, these banks were the first foreign firms to issue securities on the market with a New York institution issuing the Depository Receipts, though many other foreign shares with a market value of $5 billion were already admitted through non-New York institutions.[20]

The vast changes in its interests and activities in the United States required Deutsche Bank to change how and with whom it did business. While in New York in the late 1920s, Blinzig laid out Deutsche Bank's key interests: Bring United States funds to Germany in the form of equity and place German debt in American investment syndicates. During the mid-1920s, Deutsche Bank shifted its New York banking loyalties. It developed a much stronger relationship to Dillon Read, which also encouraged Deutsche Bank to issue new share capital and list it in New York.[21] Speyer seemed incapable of taking the lead. Although James Speyer entertained Blinzig and his colleagues royally during their strenuous visit to New York, Blinzig found the bank deeply troubled and feared that it would soon go out of business. Others courted the Germans' attention, such as National City Bank. Many of the New York banks were already investing in Europe, circumventing their "old friend."[22] But by 1926, Deutsche Bank was once again underwriting American securities, although to be sure in vastly smaller relative amounts. In December 1926, for example, Dillon Read offered

Deutsche Bank a 1 percent participation in Standard Oil's $50 million bond issue, which Deutsche Bank sold in Germany.[23]

The feasibility of cross-border finance was highly dependent on the success or failure of the Dawes Plan. By 1927, some observers fretted over the use to which Dawes Plan funds were applied and to the speculative bubble it had encouraged. Many worried that Germany had no intention of honoring its reparations or other financial commitments. At the very least, undermining the apparent economic recovery in Germany and America's financial markets were insufficient foreign trade and international specialization, falling commodity prices, and high unemployment in many countries, which exacerbated overcapacity and imbalances worldwide. During their U.S. visit in 1927, at the height of Weimar enthusiasm, Alfred Blinzig, Arthur Erdmann, and Willi Schoendke had to fend off many questions about the German economy. Although at times they cautioned Americans not to expect immediate results from the Dawes Plan, in May Blinzig was far less tentative. He could not contain his enthusiasm: "Germany is fast getting back on its feet. Our money is on a sound basis and German industries are progressing so well that there is no longer any doubt about Germany being able to meet all her debt obligations."[24]

Although much of the American investment community, too, was guardedly optimistic about financial conditions in Germany – or at least anxious to make money – well into 1928, some caveats to Blinzig's rosy view were already evident. As the Institute of International Finance, for example, pointed out, Germany's "first economic miracle" contained some causes for concern. Although it praised Germany's ability to pay substantial portions of its reparations and raise new capital since 1923 as one of the most important and positive developments following the war, by 1927, many New York bankers openly conceded the necessity of revising the Dawes Plan.[25] The Institute noted that never in the history of the world had a nation succeeded in borrowing so much, so quickly, abroad. This was a mixed blessing. Servicing this debt and paying the planned $600 million reparations bill for 1928–29 was a Herculean task, especially in light of Germany's consistent trade deficit during the mid-1920s. As America's portion of the foreign loans ran around 70 percent, the question of priority of payment was acutely felt in the United States.[26]

Nevertheless, it took a lot to shake America's thirst for high-yielding German assets.[27] International lending involved a lot of risk and many layers of government. Bankers asked the U.S. Treasury Department for its opinion about loans to Germany during the 1920s. The treasury repeatedly replied with a stock answer. It had no specific reason to object, but it advised the banks to be particularly careful because there were so many loans. The treasury drew the banks' attention to the fact that even the German authorities were concerned and that there was a great deal of foreign exchange risk. Wisely, the treasury pointed out that only loans that helped Germany improve its productivity and, thereby, its ability to pay its obligations, made sense. At the very least, the banks had the "duty to advise clients" of the risks.[28]

Given the size of American loans to Germany in the 1920s, the small amount of U.S. direct investment in Germany was remarkable. America and Germany could have profited from closer equity ties, especially ones that involved long-term commitments. Germany was the gateway to central European markets. The first few years after the war presented particular opportunities for foreign direct investment. But for some, the psychological effects of the war, revolution, and disastrous economic conditions contributed to Germans' and foreigners' loss of confidence, confusion about the true economic value of things, and fear of foreign invasion or, conversely, foreign entanglements. The collapse of the German banking system aided American banks, which had an image of solidity that compared favorably to the weakened German institutions. For those willing to take risks in the early 1920s, Germany's assets seemed undervalued, because of the economic chaos and depreciating Mark but German resistance to foreign control was a substantial hindrance.[29] To German clients, however, American banks at least appeared as the lesser of two evils: foreigners, but not from hostile European countries.[30]

Although clearly everyone did not agree, foreign direct investment could have been mutually beneficial. By investing in German companies, American investors would gain German experience, a sense of system, organization, models, patterns, machinery, as well as the value of reliable and competent local talent. German workers were experienced, capable, and cheap. The most serious problem for German companies – lack of raw materials – would be eliminated by association with an American company with capital and connections.[31]

Despite the advantages of foreign direct investments, most of the funds that poured into Germany were in the form of foreign denominated debt. The problem with the German capital dependencies was not so much its amount, but its form. The vast majority was portfolio investment, which was much more liquid (easier to remove) than investments in whole companies or real estate. The whole international financial architecture and national systems were based on limiting the control foreigners could have of domestic property. Germany's net inward investment from 1924 through 1929 amounted to $3.8 billion, with annual amounts peaking in 1927 at $1 billion before starting to drop and then reversing the flow beginning in 1931.[32] Of that total inward investment, only a little over $.2 billion was direct foreign investment as measured in book value.[33] Moreover, foreigners understandably demanded to have all their debt in Goldmark or foreign currency.[34] In short, if there were a panic, the flows could quickly reverse themselves and exacerbate the economic problems.

Deutsche Bank's $25 Million Loan

The flow of money from the United States to Germany created dilemmas and opportunities for Deutsche Bank. Many Americans bypassed Deutsche Bank and other German banks, and some clients went straight to U.S. capital markets. Excluded from much of the large private Dollar-funding deals that came to Germany, in 1927 Deutsche Bank turned to helping *Mittelstand* exporters fund their businesses, medium-sized companies that could not access the New York markets directly. The idea seems to have been spawned, or at least discussed for the first time in the United States, during Blinzig's 1927 meetings in New York with Ferdinand Eberstadt of Dillon, Read & Co. The loan also had a wider political significance for the bank. In the 1920s, Deutsche Bank was heavily criticized in many quarters for its insensitivity to the *Mittelstand*.[35] For much of its existence, Deutsche Bank did not have a strong branch network and therefore its involvement with smaller companies outside Germany's main cities was limited.

Dillon Read was an up-and-coming American private bank of Jewish origins, a prototypical American success story.[36] Dillon Read evolved out of a small bond dealer, William A. Read & Co., established in 1905, just before the 1907 Panic. In the prosperity that followed, this small financial firm, relying on the conservatism that had brought it through the crisis, seemed to thrive in a banking community dominated by five or six vastly larger enterprises. It even established a London office in 1908. In 1909, Read was joined by a Harvard-trained son of a Polish Jew, who converted to Protestantism and changed his name from Lapowski to Dillon. Clarence (Lapowski) Dillon had no intention of becoming a banker after graduation and joined Read only by accident, but in short order he became one of the leaders – to some the "Baron" – of Wall Street.[37] By 1929, Dillon Read was second only to Morgan, with $192 million in new bond issues brought to market as principal issuer, including $35 million for Siemens & Halske.[38]

One of the many achievements of Dillon Read during the period was the creation of the United States & Foreign Securities Corporation, which held assets in December 1929 of nearly $54 million at historical value, an amount that was reportedly still $8.3 million below its market value over two months after the crash – a remarkable decrease on the year of only $2.7 million.[39] With securities in American and foreign banks, railroads, public utilities, industrial stocks, and other entities, such as the German Credit & Investment Corporation, it served as a kind of mutual fund. As early as December 1925, Dillon Read bought a block of shares in Disconto-Gesellschaft, which merged with Deutsche Bank a few years later.[40]

Deutsche Bank's interest in Dillon Read's activities seems to go back to July 1920, when Schmidt lauded the predecessor firm, William A. Read & Co., as being "in every dimension first-class."[41] Despite Schmidt's praise and one partner's visit to Berlin, in 1920 Dillon Read declined to handle the sale of Deutsche Bank's own shares in the United States, due to the bad market conditions in both the United States and Europe, but the U.S. bank expressed the desire to revisit the issue when market conditions improved.[42]

The *Mittelstand* loan owed much to the efforts of Ferdinand Eberstadt – a well-connected, well-educated (Princeton undergraduate and Columbia Law), and well-traveled (including a few years in Germany before and after World War I) financier. He had been a partner in an affiliated firm before joining Dillon Read officially in 1926. Through him, Dillon Read became the leading Wall Street firm in refinancing German private and public institutions. Eberstadt first established an office in the Adlon Hotel in Berlin, but by the winter of 1928 had moved his headquarters to Paris. Deutsche Bank feared that he would try to market securities directly to its customers.[43] Although the firm never quite achieved Eberstadt's dream of issuing one billion Dollars worth of German bonds, thus becoming Germany's *de jure* banker, the firm underwrote the paper of Siemens & Halske, Disconto-Gesellschaft, Gelsenkirchen Mining, Vereinigte Stahlwerke, and many other German institutions, including Deutsche Bank.[44] Despite its heavy German involvement and the legislative investigation of its investment trust charges of exorbitant fees and stock manipulation, Dillon Read survived the defaults of the early thirties relatively well.[45]

The first record of a serious intention to issue debt for the *Mittelstand* was in August 1927. Oscar Wassermann, spokesman of the management board 1923–33, and Eberstadt met in Berlin to discuss pricing, amounts, and maturity.[46] For a few days the two haggled about what role Speyer, which must have been very jealous, would play.[47] By the time Deutsche Bank wrote to Schacht, the president of the Reichsbank, whose consent seemed to be required, the banks had decided on a five-year, $25 million note, with a coupon of 6 percent that would hopefully sell for 99.5.[48] Schacht seemed smitten by the project. To him, for internal German financing long-term foreign credits were better than short-term ones, especially for companies that usually had to settle for credits that could be called at any time.[49]

The Deutsche Bank $25 million issue was the first to be listed under the New York Stock Exchange's new rules for foreign securities, which allowed participation certificates, now called American Depository Receipts. According to *The New York Times*, the listing was conditional on Deutsche Bank offering its own common shares on a similar basis. Oddly, Deutsche Bank failed to fulfill this requirement and seemed to avoid any repercussions.[50] Perhaps their sale in the Curb market was considered sufficient.

Despite Schacht's enthusiasm, from the beginning the issue was plagued with problems, sometimes for reasons unrelated to the solvency of the actual debtors. In September, rumors hit the market about the financial problems of several of Deutsche Bank's clients, for example, Daimler-Benz and Ufa, whose financial health, or lack thereof, might adversely influence the bank's.[51] Although Dillon Read claimed that the distribution was one of the widest and most thorough of all the German issues – with 152 houses making an average of ten sales each, plus those by Dillon Read itself meant that the note had nearly 2,000 holders – the market was in general weak for German bonds in fall 1927. Dealers who had at first picked up the issue were now returning them unsold. The price had fallen to 98. The only consolation for Deutsche Bank was that the bonds of other German banks were doing even worse.[52] Yet Deutsche Bank got other benefits out of the loan. Although the rest of the German stock market was declining in September, reports of its new loan kept its share price steady at 160.[53]

The registration statement was a very complete document, even by modern standards. It included not only Deutsche Bank's latest balance sheet but also comparative historical financial data. The debt itself was not listed on the exchange. The notes were deposited with Equitable Trust Company, which actually issued American Participation Certificates. The notes came in $1,000, $5,000, and $10,000, denominations, which entitled the holder to the amounts

Equitable received from Deutsche Bank for those denominations. Oddly, the section about the purpose of Deutsche Bank's note was a little misleading. It stated that "the proceeds of the Note will be used by the Bank in the general conduct of its business."[54] For its listing, Deutsche Bank agreed to publish its earnings annually, including a statement of its financial condition, an income statement, and a balance sheet; to maintain a transfer agent in New York; and not to make any changes in the transfer agent or the participation certificates without the permission of the exchange.[55] Some of the investors were in Germany.

This kind of arrangement had been used by Swiss and Swedish banks to provide financing for their medium-sized firms and clearly had advantages for both Deutsche Bank and the *Mittelstand*. The notes seemed to be the epitome of a win-win undertaking. Deutsche Bank had issued debt ($25 million, bearing 6 percent interest, due September 1, 1932) in its name in New York, thus getting a better rate by virtue of its name and the size of the issue, which the smaller commercial firms could not get. With it, Deutsche Bank kept its hand in the private capital markets. Medium-sized firms borrowed from Deutsche Bank in smaller allotments of Dollar loans with ample security at rates that they would almost never get by themselves, even though they had to pay a spread to Deutsche Bank and accept a shorter repayment schedule than had been desired. The loan allowed Deutsche Bank to combat criticism that, like other large money-centered banks, it ignored small and mid-sized firms, which for many, especially on the growing extreme right, represented the mainstay of German capitalism and culture. As Gerald Feldman pointed out, "Not only did the Deutsche Bank have the distinction of being the first German company to float an issue on the American market, but also it was praised by Schacht for raising long-term money for genuinely productive purposes."[56]

Deutsche Bank's profit margin on the transaction was rich, but perhaps not rich enough. It was not running a charity for the *Mittelstand*. For the money it was borrowing at 6 percent plus some transaction cost, it was looking to lend out at 8 percent.[57] The head office advised its branches to reserve the credit only for high-quality firms whose financial situation and prospects were such to make surprises at maturity highly unlikely.[58]

Unfortunately for almost all the participants, who were congratulating themselves in September 1927, fissures in the German, American, and international financial system began to widen over the next two years. The maturity of the loan was indeed not long enough. By the time the principal came due, a moratorium to reparations had been called, Germany had reinstituted foreign exchange controls, and called for a 25 percent reduction in all interest payments. Several German and Austrian banks had failed, and the first of many Standstill Agreements had to be negotiated.

But part of the problem was that even these *Mittelstand* companies, whose liability was in Dollars, would have to have access to Dollars.[59] Not all the companies could earn Dollars, therefore they would have to buy them from the Reichsbank out of general sources. Although these payments had a relatively high priority for Deutsche Bank and the Reichsbank, because they were a symbol of Germany's overall credit worthiness,[60] unfortunately – like so many of the German credits of the period – Deutsche Bank's Dollar notes ended up in default or in broad financial rescheduling plans, which were a cause or at least a very public part of the breakdown in financial relations among the great powers. Although some public and private institutions in Germany rigorously tried to adhere to their commitments, neither sector had the consistent understanding, support, and resolve to avoid building financial structures on what they should have known was unstable land. In a nutshell, Germany and the world rested on a financial faultline made up of debt instruments, most relatively short-term, denominated in foreign currency, and owed to foreigners, a common element of macroeconomic political risk.

13

Deutsche Bank and the Collapse of the Fragile World Order

> The brusque and unexpected disregard by Germany of such unanimous and considered opinion of her creditors cannot but have a most unfortunate effect upon German credit in general and upon the many thousands of individual investors who have bought German bonds.
>
> Dillon Read, Speyer & Co., Kuhn, Loeb & Co. et al., Banking houses that issued German debt, to Schacht, December 26, 1933.

Consolidation and International Banking

Deutsche Bank's problems of rescheduling its notes were part of a much deeper crisis in financial markets that undermined American and German relations. As the two largest creditor and debtor nations during the interwar period, it should not be surprising that the two nations suffered the most from the weakness in their own and global financial architecture. When the Crash came, blaming international bankers and other nations seemed politically expedient in both countries. From 1929 to 1945, Deutsche Bank went, in the eyes of American observers, from the best hope of German finance to a political and economic pariah. Its strategic environment in Germany and relationship to the United States was dominated from 1929 to 1945 by economic crises, production of war materials, and their eventual deployment.

In fall 1929, a few weeks before the New York stock market Crash and a year after German stocks had nosedived, Deutsche Bank announced steps to make itself more efficient. It merged with Disconto-Gesellschaft, its older Berlin rival. The merger, a reflection of already greater cooperation between the two leading banks, was a colossal event by the standards of the 1920s, which had witnessed many such fusions. The combined bank would represent 34 percent of the loans, 37 percent of the liquid assets, and 33 percent of all the accounts of German credit banks.[1] Secretly negotiated by a few directors, the merger was heralded as a trendsetting event for German banking. The announcement of the record merger advanced the shares of both banks and brought rumors of foreign participation in the new bank.[2]

Some American reactions to the merger were extraordinarily enthusiastic. According to most American accounts, the new bank would be far more competitive in Germany and around the world. It was two-and-a-half times larger than the next largest German bank and the largest French banks, and nearly as big as the largest British and American banks, as measured by deposits. As the largest nongovernment bank on the continent, the new bank would be in a strong position with foreign lenders to renegotiate debt and muster more capital, something desperately needed in Germany. A state department report described it as "[t]he most outstanding transaction in German banking history..., an essential step in responding to banking conditions in Germany."[3] Like many sectors, banking plainly had too much capacity for the amount of commercial and industrial activity in Germany. Although savings accounts and other forms of capital formation were far lower than in the pre-World War I period, the five main Berlin banks maintained 750 branches, compared with the 300 they had in 1913. In many small towns, all five banks operated branches even though there had been a steady decline in securities trading. The consolidation eliminated duplicate branches in eighty to one hundred towns, saving 20–30 million Reichsmark. Because both banks owned or had large holdings in four other banks, the merger contributed to further financial sector consolidation.[4] Moreover, because the two banks also had large holdings with and played an important role in the management of many industrial firms, their merger was expected to contribute to the consolidation of commercial companies, which the report also hoped would make German exports stronger, especially in central Europe. (Although the name of the bank for a few years officially became Deutsche Bank und Disconto-Gesellschaft, I will continue to refer to the merged entity as Deutsche Bank.)

The whole banking system itself desperately needed to reduce costs, but opinions differed about how to achieve greater efficiency. Before World War I, operating costs at Disconto-Gesellschaft were 40 percent of gross profit. In 1929, that figure was 80 percent.[5] Consolidation would help lessen overhead and thereby unit costs in all sectors. To be sure, the report acknowledged that not everyone was enthusiastic about the merger, which would eliminate approximately 3,000 jobs. Although the bank was expected to pay a bonus of one year's salary to released employees, for men past the age of thirty-five or forty finding a job in Germany was very difficult because of the willingness of younger men to work for lower salaries and without the customary social allowances for married men. Representatives of salaried employees argued that the average monthly salary of the lowest paid 75 percent of bank employees was only 275 Reichsmark ($85.47). The spokesman of the management board responded that the average bank profit, which in 1913 was 146 percent of the average monthly salary of bank employees, in 1928 had fallen to 40 percent. In one area, however, there would be little reduction in employment: The new supervisory board consisted of 109 members, 63 from Deutsche Bank and 46 from Disconto-Gesellschaft. The fusion dismayed some important economic figures. Max Fürstenberg, the head of the German bank officials' association, questioned whether it would be good for Germany's overall economic and social situation.[6]

In contrast to some employees and competitors, the American government representatives seemed relieved by the consolidation. The U.S. State Department had been concerned about Deutsche Bank's financial condition for years.

These statues decorated Deutsche Bank's meeting room at the head office in Berlin as late as 1929. Each statue represents one continent. Although they predate the national tensions of the 1920s and '30s, it is tempting to read some political commentary into the choice of images. North America is represented by a "gun-toting cowboy," consistent with Siemens' first impressions in 1883. Apart from the European figure, none of the other continents is portrayed with anything that can be described as a flattering image. For the most part, they serve to highlight differences between attitudes from the early to the late twentieth century about the world.

In 1925, the Berlin Consul reported that Deutsche Bank paid a 10 percent dividend on 1924 profits, even though he considered its revalued capital as "high." Deutsche Bank had many new foreign investors who demanded greater profitability. The 1924 dividends, however, were only paid on 110 million Reichsmark of Deutsche Bank's 150 million Reichsmark of capital. The amount held by the foreign consortium, by special agreement only began receiving dividends in 1925. The report took note of the very unfavorable increase of operating expenses to gross profit. Gross profit had increased 120 percent since 1913, but net profits, after operating expenses, only went up by 35.6 percent. Despite staff reductions (48 percent from its 1923 high of 37,000), expenditures per employee had only dropped 17 percent; the number of employees was still twice its 1913 level. Detailed comparisons between 1924 and 1913 were telling. Although gross profit had climbed by just over 21 million Reichsmark, business expenditures and taxes had doubled, going from 47.8 to 96.8 million Reichsmark.[7]

Although still Germany's largest bank, even before the Depression, Deutsche Bank's worldwide financial clout had deteriorated. In 1926, it led or participated in the restructuring of IG Farben, Daimler-Benz, and the British and German Trust, and participated in the securities flotations for approximately 100 private and governmental entities. Among its international rivals, however, its position had fallen considerably. After reaching a peak in December 1928, its stock price and assets began a decade-long decline. By the 1920s, two American banks, National City Bank and Chase National Bank, held assets that amounted to nearly four and three times, respectively, Deutsche Bank's $367 million. Even though Crédit Lyonnais no longer outranked it in the league tables, two Italian banks did. Deutsche Bank had long outgrown its original function of reducing the cost of trade financing by offering a competitive choice to London, but the war and its aftermath had seriously undermined its main strength: The ability to marshal funds entrusted in it to create, fund, and help manage companies on an international scale.[8] The financial world had changed considerably. But Deutsche Bank, because of its consolidation and its foreign business, was better able to handle the shocks than many other central European banks.

Even after the Depression hit, American banks, especially Bankers Trust, were still very interested in doing business with Deutsche Bank. As late as 1930, Deutsche Bank considered selling more of its securities on the American market. Just after its merger with Disconto-Gesellschaft, Bankers Trust, for example, indicated that it would be willing to present a $50 million issue of notes or bonds in much the same fashion as Dillon Read had done, but with an even longer maturity. Despite interest in the offer, management felt that right after the merger was too soon to create another sensation. In mid-January, Bankers Trust repeated the offer but with somewhat of a twist. It wanted to create a separate entity to handle these transactions, something like the original Treuhand idea, but for U.S. investors. The American bank was pursuing these deals with other large German companies such as IG Farben, Siemens, AEG, and Vereinigte Stahlwerke. Deutsche Bank liked the idea, but because of its relationship with Dillon Read, some managers felt that that bank would have to be included. The potential profits must have seemed enormous. Bankers Trust indicated that it would be willing to take all of the $50 million with a 7 percent coupon at 97,[9] which considering the amount of deflation during those years was a very high real interest rate. Bankers Trust seems to have been particularly aggressive in the German market at this time. From its Paris office, it even planned to create a giant corporation to acquire German utility firms with Deutsche Bank, aptly named Superpower Corporation.[10] Although other American banks felt overextended with German loans, Bankers Trust did not even seem to be intimidated when the Austrian and German banking systems began to melt down in summer 1931.[11] This attitude soon changed. Despite its German commitments, Bankers Trust seemed to weather the Depression well. Its 1933 net income was just under $11 million. Although much of this was achieved by cutting operating expenses, Bankers Trust also dropped its German holdings from $27.3 million in 1931 to $12 million in 1933.[12]

The 1931 Banking Crisis

Even before the Crash hit in October 1929, world financial and political leaders recognized that the Dawes Plan had to be restructured. They could not come to a meeting of the minds, however, about how to react, especially one that was politically acceptable to national constituencies. Though actually spreading German annual reparations over a much longer period created a more sensible plan for German debt payments, the Young Plan, negotiated by Germany's Foreign Minister Gustav Stresemann in 1929, unleashed a political whirlwind over foreign influence in Germany, which helped to radicalize German politics. Even supporters of international cooperation seemed to lose faith. On March 7, 1930, Hjalmar Schacht, for example, shocked the German political community with his resignation from a four-year term as president of the Reichsbank over the terms of the Young Plan and other matters.[13]

The Depression exacerbated the resentments of many Germans, even members of the banking community. In March 1931, even before the nadir of the economic crisis, Hans Luther, Schacht's successor as president of the Reichsbank, a year after Schacht's resignation delivered an impassioned plea for more restraint among German creditors. He criticized the foreign media for blowing up the significance of certain international financial transactions. Given the dire German and world economic circumstances in February, with a quarter of the German workforce unemployed (five million in Germany, twenty million worldwide), and extraordinary internal political conflicts, Germany's efforts to keep its financial house in order and prove its trustworthiness to its creditors should be praised, not minimized. In a less than subtly concealed barb, Luther complained that Germany unlike some countries lacked limitless "*Lebensraum*" (he did not use the word, he said *Volksraum*) for expansion, nor was it an island, cut off from its nearest neighbors. Quite correctly, Luther warned that the whole capitalist system had come under intense scrutiny. The future of that system was dependent on the wisdom of decisions about "political payments" that would be made by both creditors and debtors. He argued that most economists had come to believe that the reparations had exceeded sound limits, especially in light of the unwillingness of most nations to open their borders to trade, despite repeated calls for a tariff truce that were part and parcel of the Geneva Conference and the Young Plan. Unable to export sufficiently to pay for reparations and long-term debt, short-term indebtedness had become an "invisible army of occupation" for Germany.[14]

Although most of the developed world already was very somber in 1930, the full impact of the downturn was measured not just by its depth but also its length, disruption to capital flows, and international tension. The Depression devolved from an ordinary downturn to full-fledged crisis with the collapse of Österreichische Credit-Anstalt für Handel und Gewerbe in spring 1931. The Austrian crisis spilled over into Germany. On June 20, 1931, President Herbert Hoover proposed a one-year moratorium on German reparations and other intergovernmental war debt. German reparations, which had partially covered Allied debts to the United States, never resumed. Hoover's action temporarily, at least, buoyed stock prices in Germany and slowed capital flight from Germany[15] but much of the damage was done; $11.7 billion of U.S. government loans had evaporated. "[W]hat did not evaporate, however, was the anger of many Americans at the defaults, which would cast a dark cloud over American policies throughout the 1930s."[16]

The international banking system tried to salvage Austrian and German banks. Indeed, for much of the rest of 1931, the world banking community discussed how to redeem international finance. In late June just after the crisis began, the Federal Reserve Bank of New York, the Bank of England, the Banque de France, and the Bank for International Settlements organized a loan of $100 million for the Reichsbank.[17] Other private credit lines followed to German financial institutions supported by pledges of assets. Most of the big American banks were among the institutions participating – including the largest ones: National City Bank, Chase, and Guaranty Trust Company. Notably absent was Morgan. Interestingly, several institutions with European investors, such as IAB, were also pledging funds.[18]

But new facilities and the moratorium merely forestalled a German economic crisis. By July, the Danatbank, one of Germany's largest banks, collapsed, and the rest of the banking houses closed by government decree for a few days. The German government imposed exchange controls and took over much of the banking sector, further weakening those dependent on cross-border flows. Competitive devaluations and tariffs followed in nearly every developed country. The next decade would be punctuated by only brief periods of optimism. Ironically, the measures seemed to have added to German enthusiasm for American portfolio investment, and contributed to higher interest rates and distorted flows – just what the world did not need – in many countries, because of the perception of greater political risk.[19] Along those lines, Franklin Delano Roosevelt's election to the presidency in November 1932 reinforced fears that the Dollar would not be supported, which contributed to a pre-emptive sale by many foreigners of their American securities. As political conditions worsened, though, voluntary and involuntary foreign investment picked up, both as a hedge in perceived "safe havens" such as the United States, where some assets suddenly also seemed cheap after the Dollar devaluation in January 1934. In other countries where funds were blocked, such as Germany, profits accumulated. Though greatly reduced from their levels in the 1920s, by the mid-1930s foreign investment of both kinds – voluntary and involuntary – became a significant source of funds for cash-strapped economies engaged in a life and death struggle for resources. In their own way, each undermined stability and productive investment.

Many smaller banking houses failed on both sides of the Atlantic. Speyer & Co. tried to bail out its one-time German "parent." The effects were short-lived. When Eduard Beit von Speyer, the head of Lazard Speyer-Ellissen, died in 1933, his venerable firm had to be liquidated. Paul and Felix Warburg had to lend $9 million to their brother Max to keep the German bank afloat. Bank of Manhattan had to be reorganized, and IAB liquidated.[20] By 1931, Deutsche Bank had much less invested in the United States than many other European and Asian banks. In the 1930s many foreign banks maintained agencies or founded international trust companies, although on a reduced scale. Deutsche Bank still relied on a representative office and correspondent banks, yet even that presence became smaller.[21]

Standstill Agreements

Germany basically defaulted on its short-term foreign debt. Like nearly all defaults by a nation, a long series of renegotiation sessions began and agreements were worked out.[22] In Germany's case the sessions and agreements became nearly annual affairs during the 1930s. The creditor countries were furious, but divided and virtually powerless. For the debtor institutions, such as Deutsche Bank, the actions of the German government in 1931 created an enormous opportunity that only the Nazi regime fully exploited. Faced with a choice between reducing credit lines at a considerable cost or trusting in an eventual improvement in the German political-economic situation, many banks, especially those in London, opted for trusting their German associates until late in the 1930s, a decision that sadly helped financially nurture a regime the bankers, like many others, had badly misjudged.[23] Ironically, in the space of twenty years, Deutsche Bank's relationship with American finance shifted from managing American defaults to managing American anger over German defaults.

The first Standstill Agreement was the product of the first London Conference called in July 1931 to deal with the crisis in Austrian and German banking, and in some sense was a reaction to the Hoover Moratorium, which froze all reparation payments to countries other than the United States. The Agreement's intention was to create a temporary measure to shore up Germany's short-term borrowing problems. The idea was to ensure sufficient orderliness and payment to the main creditor country banks for those institutions to continue to extend short-term credit to German institutions, mainly bank acceptances that allowed for trade. On September 19, 1931, representatives of ten creditor nations signed the first Standstill Agreement, originally designed to run for only six months. Ostensibly, all existing credits were left at their original amounts, though this was not exactly the case. Servicing of debt was guaranteed, but the agreement only covered between one-third and one-half of all short-term debt, depending on whose estimate is to be believed. American and French institutions were particularly reluctant to accept its terms. From the beginning, the participants recognized that as long as no comprehensive governmental solution over reparations and other issues was attained, the agreement could not possibly salvage the situation before the end of the Hoover Moratorium.[24]

The negotiations were critical to Deutsche Bank's business future. Deutsche Bank had five representatives on the Banking Committee of the Deutsche Ausschuss für das Deutsche Kreditabkommen von 1932. That committee represented the interests of the German banks and manufacturing companies. Gustaf Schlieper, a member of Deutsche Bank's management board from 1929–37, was part of the German delegation that represented Germany along with the Reichsbank and Deutsche Golddiskontbank in the negotiations with the banking and industrial committees of the United States, Belgium, Czechoslovakia, Denmark, Britain, France, the Netherlands, Italy, Norway, Sweden, and Switzerland. In 1933, he and Otto Jeidels of Berliner Handels-Gesellschaft headed the German delegation.[25] In a sense, the repetition of the agreements transformed short into long-term credits. Before the ink was dry on the February 1932 agreement, plans were made for a July meeting. The parties began to focus more attention on how German exchange controls affected trade. Some non-German participants pushed the German delegation to use the Standstill funds for long-term financing and to further trade.[26]

In October 1932, as Germany's political situation deteriorated, reports hit the newspapers that Germans were buying back from French creditors facilities covered by the Standstill Agreement at a discount of 15 percent or more, a practice that infuriated many creditors. The repurchased credits were being used to finance exports by allowing Germans to undersell competitors, a kind of trade subsidy.[27] The issue was a political hot potato, which led many participants to bend the truth. According to Deutsche Bank, these reports were unfounded. "All funds subject to the Standstill Agreement are registered with the Reichsbank, to whom application must be made for any transfer or release of such funds."[28] Only transactions compatible with the spirit of the agreement received the Reichsbank's permission. Even outstanding funds not covered by the Standstill Agreement were strictly controlled. Some transactions of blocked Marks, balances that could not be withdrawn due to foreign exchange regulations, however, did occur on occasion. These usually involved sales of long-term securities, and were also ostensibly strictly regulated and restricted to a few instances.

Deutsche Bank Dollar Notes

The crisis created some opportunities for those institutions with access to convertible funds and enough savvy to exploit market turmoil. Deutsche Bank did not want to default on its Dollar notes, but the bank was well prepared in some respects for the eventuality. When the notes came due in September 1932, the Reichsbank effectively blocked their repayment. The news plunged the bank into debt rescheduling negotiations and a worldwide campaign to redeem its reputation. Ostensibly, Deutsche Bank's client *Mittelstand* firms could repay their obligations, at least in the form of the equivalent sums in Reichsmark, and Deutsche Bank itself was ready to deposit the necessary Reichsmarks with the Reichsbank for Dollars at the then-prevailing rate of 4.20 Reichsmark to one U.S. Dollar. Deutsche Bank saw the problem coming and embarked on two related courses. The first was to buy up as much of the U.S. debt instrument as it could, thereby effectively allowing it to convert the obligations into Reichsmark debt. The second was to float a new issue in New York, allowing the old-note holders to convert their old notes for ones that were redeemable in three years for Dollars, carrying the same interest rate and an immediate cash premium of 2 percent, or the same amount in blocked Reichsmarks in Germany (*Sperrmarks*).[29] According to the sales bulletin, probably put out by Dillon Read, unlike many other issuers of German securities on the New York market, Deutsche Bank had the Reichsmark funds for payment, would continue interest payments, and had acted on a timely basis to give investors several reasonable alternatives.[30]

The only hitch in the plan was that 25 percent of the bondholders could legally stop the conversion, and disgruntled creditors, even if they could not block the transaction, could cause unfavorable publicity for Deutsche Bank and Dillon Read. Both institutions were understandably concerned about their reputations. Moreover, the new issue had to be listed on the exchange, and, therefore, pass its rules. Ironically, Deutsche Bank appealed to John Foster Dulles of Sullivan & Cromwell, who would later lead the investigation against German companies that profited from trading in their own American debt, for advice.[31] Both banks had much that they wanted to keep under wraps and had worked out a public relations plan in July 1932, even before contacting Dulles.[32] Both an outright default on the debt and complete knowledge of how the parties managed to avoid it would be very embarrassing. At the least, they would lead to higher transaction costs and perhaps further seizures of German property in the United States.[33] On the other hand, rumors of default and statements by government officials about the shortage of foreign exchange and further limits on interest payments could only help reduce the price for repurchasing the notes.

At first the bank did not seem to handle the initial announcement of payment problems well. Even though Deutsche Bank was completely capable of paying the loan off in Reichsmarks – its only problem being the refusal of the Reichsbank to make Dollars available – rumors of the default affected Deutsche Bank's worldwide reputation. Its difficulties acquiring foreign exchange were regarded as a bank failure as far away as China.[34] Reuters reported the news from Dillon Read and stressed that the "default" was very serious, given the bank's size and importance to world finance. Japanese banks and the Deutsch-Asiatische Bank along with its branches were affected by the rumors of Deutsche Bank's problems without sufficient reference to a proposed alternative redemption scheme.[35] Deutsche Bank held Reuters responsible for the misleading reports in Sweden, the Netherlands, and Italy and attempted to organize a campaign against the incorrect characterization of the situation.[36] Deutsche Bank got support, which it gratefully acknowledged, from Dillon Read in its efforts to communicate correctly its redemption plan to the international financial community, an undertaking it viewed as having "the utmost importance to German credit in general."[37] The bank realized that it should have acted earlier. Once the reports had circulated, it was harder to correct them. Even the success of the reorganization was not widely reported, and particularly the special American circumstances (so many bondholders) should have been better communicated to journalists.[38]

Deutsche Bank was understandably skeptical that many foreign owners would be interested in the blocked accounts.[39] The Sperrmarks held numerous advantages, but mainly for German exporters, who could exchange their foreign currency at a more favorable Reichsmark rate.[40] American investors could only hope to negotiate the sale of blocked funds to German companies, a tricky business with only a small hope of netting a higher Dollar return. Those choosing the extension of the notes were supposedly also going to receive regular interest payments. In any case, by the end of September 1932, 96 percent of the bondholders had chosen one of the two alternatives, an outcome that Deutsche Bank had already guaranteed, as will be discussed.[41] The vast majority of the bonds still in public hands chose the Dollar option, which reinforced Deutsche Bank's Dollar exposure.[42]

The other side of the ledger was also problematic. What was to be done with the loans to the German *Mittelstand*? Should Deutsche Bank give their customers an alternative too? Allowing them to pay in Reichsmark could potentially leave the bank with a terrible mismatch of liabilities and assets.[43] The bank was between the proverbial "rock and a hard place." It had set as a condition for the extension of the loans the acceptance by the borrowers of the gold-Dollar clause. It was doubtful, however, whether many clients, even the good ones, could hold to the foreign exchange clause. If the bank were tough with all its clients, many might perceive an opportunity to renege on the Dollar clause. For all of these difficulties, the bank considered raising its rate by 1 percent over the original average of 8.25 percent to be paid by the *Mittelstand*.[44] In the end, Deutsche Bank insisted on its customers' sticking to the gold-Dollar clause and tacked on some additional charges. Despite an enormous amount of pressure to relent, only customers who could buy back in Dollars the same amount of Deutsche Bank notes as they owed were released from their foreign currency obligations. Although Deutsche Bank still had a large foreign exchange risk, the bank and some of its clients had reduced their risk substantially by buying back many of the notes with Dollar funds they held outside of Germany. For the Sperrmark deposits (blocked Reichsmark payments on the notes), there was the other option, however, which removed the foreign exchange component of the rescheduling. Deutsche Bank's head office, and the head office only, had received permission on a case-by-case basis to release these funds to settle export bills at what amounted to favorable foreign exchange rates, a way of using the note payments to encourage exports.[45] Although Deutsche Bank's efforts seem to have been reasonably successful with the rescheduling, in November 1932 the New York Stock Exchange officially delisted Deutsche Bank's first security publicly traded in the United States. The notes were still selling, however, between 80 and 88, a fairly high price considering the circumstances.[46] Moreover, well into the crisis, cash-rich investors seemed willing to throw good money after bad.[47]

Deutsche Bank's repurchase program of the Dollar obligations in the United States also contributed to the notes' relatively strong price. Deutsche Bank had seized the opportunity provided by the capital market crisis to reduce its foreign exchange liability – which arguably was in the interest of all involved – while making a substantial profit. For a long time, well before its announced "default," Deutsche Bank had been buying back the notes, at times above their face value, but for many years at a steep discount, which had been nearly 40 percent in times of dire crisis (that is, at a price of 63–64 percent of principal). The bank even encouraged the exporting *Mittelstand* companies, with permission by the Reichsbank and with the complete understanding of Dillon, Read & Co., to use their hard currency earnings to do the same. In such a manner, Deutsche Bank, Dillon Read, the Reichsbank, and the ultimate debtors all realized their ends at the expense of the former note holders, some of whom received only 63–64 cents on the Dollar. Deutsche Bank avoided complete default by employing a tactic that would ignite a public and regulatory outcry today. Dillon Read handled the new listing and many of the purchases, no doubt earning good fees, and avoiding legal problems as the transfer agent in New York along with Chase. The Reichsbank conserved foreign exchange. And, finally, the German debtors presumably relieved themselves of a liability at a discount. Deutsche Bank enlisted its branch offices and surrogates in other countries. They labored hard to keep their activities secret in order to make as many purchases as possible before the price of the notes climbed.[48] All of this required careful planning with the Reichsbank, which had to approve all elements of the plan and its implementation.[49]

By May 1932, three months before payment was due, they already had purchased $7 million of the estimated $8.5 million still in circulation.[50] In fact, by August 1932, Deutsche Bank and Dillon Read knew that the conversion could not be blocked because they had already bought back 75 percent of the notes, unbeknownst, most likely, to the other note holders, who were left with a *fait accompli*. At least, though, for the first note holders, the price in August once again floated between 79 and 93.[51] Once the operation was complete, the bank's foreign exchange position would be greatly improved. If the price of the new security moved to par, Deutsche Bank's prestige would also be secured. After the first buyback's success, the bank even considered one with the rescheduled issue. Later, Deutsche Bank also considered doing a debt/equity swap for its own common shares.[52]

Through the mid-1930s, Deutsche Bank labored to get the loan completely off its books. In 1938, it applied to the Reichsbank for currency to pay Hfl 2.5 million on what it still owed to Bary & Co. for notes it had purchased. Deutsche Bank was even willing to use the 5,510 common shares it received from the 1917 reorganization of Davis Coal & Coke Company to pay off the loan. There was one hitch. No one wanted to buy its 9.1 percent holding. Even the Rockefellers, who owned 75 percent of the Davis company already, were uninterested. Other parties did not present themselves. In principle the shares were selling at 40 percent of their nominal value, but not for a block trade of this size. The prospects of the brown coal sector in general and Davis Coal & Coke in particular looked pretty grim. Deutsche Bank hoped to convince the Rockefellers to have the Coal & Coke Company use its cash for a special dividend. If they agreed, Deutsche Bank's share would be more than enough to cover its payment to Bary & Co. and if the Reichsbank allowed the bank to use the foreign exchange for that purpose, a large portion of its remaining U.S. debt would be settled.[53] With the agreement of the Rockefellers and the Reichsbank, Deutsche Bank was able to settle its last remaining debt connected with the Dollar notes shortly before World War II began.[54] These considerable successes with difficult U.S. transactions should have given some reason for optimism. Unfortunately, Deutsche Bank's problems in the 1930s could not be disentangled from the general collapse of world financial markets and of liberal democratic politics.

Deutsche Bank and the United States in the Shadow of the Third Reich

By the time Hitler became Chancellor of Germany in January 1933, Deutsche Bank and the other German banks were in pretty bad shape. Already, in the best year of Weimar, assets and profits were far less than their 1913 amounts. During the early '30s, the bank's stock price had lingered at around one-quarter of its high of nearly 200 Reichsmark in the 1920s. A year after Hitler coming to power, Deutsche Bank's stock had lost nearly 50 percent of its December 1932 value. From 1931 to 1934, Deutsche Bank paid no dividend at all. Although the merger with Disconto-Gesellschaft had helped Deutsche Bank in relative terms, the whole banking system was plagued by weak economic circumstances and was awkwardly dependent on a hostile home government, with an antifinance and anti-international ideology, and on continuing negotiations with international competitors and foreign authorities.[55]

With the coming to power of the National Socialist regime, the creditor nations, too, were faced with a much more difficult situation. The new regime was much more willing to repudiate its country's debt and to destabilize foreign trade, a fact that encouraged some countries and institutions, especially those from the United States and France, to cheat on their agreements and desert the Standstill Agreement.[56] Even though the Foreign Bankers' Committee reported that the first six months of the agreement witnessed a mixture of good and bad results, the position of the creditor nations had deteriorated decidedly. Unfortunately, the more favorable balance-of-trade numbers were not due to higher exports, but lower imports. Foreign exchange collections coming into Germany were falling. Only 75 percent of exports were paid in foreign currency, the rest were by blocked clearing agreements with various central European countries, the Far East, South American countries, and Russia, a device that had become a considerable part of the export business for large German companies in regions where the normal payment terms were two years. Although the terms of the agreement were holding, foreign trade in general was decreasing and unemployment increasing.[57]

The new National Socialist regime moved quickly to harness the blocked funds for export subsidies and debt buybacks.[58] The third round of Standstill talks was going on as Hitler came to power. Some in Britain, the United States, and in Germany felt confident that even after the *Machtergreifung*, foreign policy and financial matters remained in the hands of the same experienced men.[59] The *Frankfurter Zeitung* observed that the National Socialists had made some effort to articulate an economic system but lacked the maturity to make it independent and understandable.[60] Hitler reappointed Schacht to head the Reichsbank. His experienced hand reassured the foreign and domestic business communities. Although he knew how to leverage Germany's financial situation for the country's benefit, Schacht set a course to limit some of the regime's most destructive plans.[61]

Despite or perhaps because of the new Nazi position in the government, the third conference extended the Standstill for another year, amounting to the rescheduling of 4 billion Reichsmark in short-term facilities into the long-term blocked funds, 2.5 billion for banks, and the rest for industrial concerns, mostly in the form of bank acceptances.[62]

Toward the end of 1933, the financial crisis deepened. In December, Schacht announced that the Reichsbank did not have enough hard currency to pay even 50 percent of its interest obligations. "Playing hard ball," the president of the Reichsbank claimed that Germany had to demand yet another delay in payments to foreigners.[63] It was a clear choice between interest for foreigners or dividends for Germans. No world power could protect countries from the destruction caused by denying peaceful work to its citizens. A week later, he announced that with few exceptions only 30 percent of some of the Reichsbank's obligations to foreigners would be transferred for the first half of 1934. No other payments in hard currency would be made for the rest of the year. Instead, Reichsmarks were to be deposited with the Reichsbank for use in Germany. The Reichsmark amounts could be used or sold. American protest was quick and sharp.[64]

Because of Schacht's and his predecessor's efforts, Germany's indebtedness had actually lessened. From July 1931 to September 1933, it fell from 23.8 to 14.8 billion Reichsmark, short-term debt from 13.1 to 7.4 billion Reichsmark, and long-term from 10.7 to 7.4 billion, with the amounts covered by the Standstill Agreement falling from 6.3 to 3 billion Reichsmark.[65] Some, including

British observers, gave the National Socialists credit for the improvement, but this improvement was threatened by increased import needs and the inability to stimulate sufficient exports. For this, many factors were to blame, not the least of which was the government's own anti-Semitic policies.[66] Nevertheless, the balance of payments improved and rumors floated about the Reichsbank having a secret stock of hard currency.[67]

The discussion took on an ugly but familiar form. As the Dutch representative summed up the situation when the Germans attempted to drop the amount of their payments in late 1933:

> The Committee of Experts gave it as their opinion that Germany could pay 50% and the Committee was right. The Germans have made the percentage very small in order to depreciate the value of their own bonds abroad and to repurchase them at a cheap price. Dr. Schacht gave no notice of his intended action, did not attempt to negotiate with the representatives of the bondholders, and behaved in a reprehensible and arbitrary fashion.[68]

One Dutch journal went even further about Germany's canceling the gold clause in its debt, which reduced its value by 20 percent.

> Germany has certainly in no small degree contributed to the trampling of the comprehension of justice. It is unnecessary to be a Shylock to recognize that the country's attitude toward its creditors is steadily becoming more audacious.[69]

Some U.S. investors demanded a government or SEC investigation.

For many reasons, America had a special role to play in all of the debt negotiations. An enormous amount of the total German debt was in Dollars. How the United States treated its own currency was of importance to the entire community of creditors. Congress's decision in June 1933, for example, to remove the gold clause from U.S. Dollar debt contracts and devalue the Dollar, in some sense, eliminated 40 percent of the value (42 billion Reichsmark) of the total 105 billion Reichsmark of German debt.[70]

The long-term debt holders voiced their dismay, which was often at odds with their own governments and other parties' interests. In December 1933, John Foster Dulles was chosen by the American banking houses with German debt to investigate the situation (Foreign Bondholders Council). He concluded that the National Socialists were consciously ignoring the rights of the bondholders. All improvements in Germany's financial situation were being used to better conditions in Germany. The Reichsbank had improved its reserves by 180 million Reichsmark, 100 million of which Dulles guessed was from non-recurrent factors such as the repatriation of German nationals' foreign assets after a new law stiffening penalties for disobeying foreign exchange regulations. The use of foreign currency export subsidies served only to help Germans retire debt. Between November 11, 1931 and September 30, 1933, an estimated 657 million Reichsmark in external German debt had been bought up by Germans and in many cases retired.[71]

Although this reduced the nominal amount of long and short-term debt, Dulles feared that Germany's actual exports were still significantly lower than the amounts reported. In the long run, the export schemes employed were not sustainable because many countries, including the United States and Great Britain, were already considering antidumping measures. To Dulles, Germany had already chosen to sacrifice its creditors to pay for a trade stimulus, which sadly would only be short-term. Payment of debt was a question of will, not means.[72]

The German government dangled the carrot of preferential trade agreements in front of some of its neighboring creditors – the Netherlands and Switzerland in particular – to get them to break ranks from other creditors such as those from Britain and the United States. Their greater trade interest coupled with smaller financial risk for those countries made them relatively easy targets. There were some elements in Germany who also wanted to use the available resources for the purpose of gaining political and economic leverage with Germany's neighbors. The United States would not for a number of years be an important enough factor, politically or financially, for Germany to worry a lot about its obligations to that country.[73]

Based on Dulles' report, the issuing houses rejected Schacht's calls for yet another rescheduling of the debt just six months after the last reduction in payments and before it had been given a fair trial in light of Germany's more favorable balance of payments and, especially, in light of the rapid rate at which German institutions were using the arrangements to repatriate German debt.[74]

Despite these complaints and continued improvement in Germany's short-term obligations,[75] those expecting interest and dividend payments were given some uncomfortable new choices. First, they could hold on to their rights and hope for the best. Second, they could convert their interest and dividends into notes guaranteed by the German state carrying 3 percent interest with repayment of principal at a rate of 3 percent a year. Any remaining balance would be paid on January 1, 1945. Lastly, they could sell their receivables for hard currency at 40 percent of their face value.[76]

The economic and political pressures were enormous. International trade wars, depression, and skeptical creditors, losing their lust to throw good money after bad, only reinforced Germany's new government's commitment to autarky and rearmament. Ironically, too, each year, with the volume of trade dropping, the trade financing arrangements that the German government had negotiated to be kept open went unused. Germany clearly lacked sufficient exports to pay its foreign obligations, and the Nazis had no intention of devoting precious hard currency to pay debts to their potential enemies. Sadly, both creditors and debtors seemed to find the circumstances and the regular renegotiations more and more normal. Investors, not only in America, but in many other countries were indignant, but powerless. With blocked funds used to subsidize exports, the financial distress of German borrowers turned into a competitive advantage for German exporters. American bondholders felt, with some justification, that whatever hard currency German firms earned should be applied to paying foreign debt first.[77] For political as well as economic reasons, Deutsche Bank was drawn into the melee.

Deutsche Bank and Other Dollar Loans

The Banking Crisis in the summer of 1931 exposed many weaknesses in the German banking system and in the Reichsbank's ability to respond to foreign pressure to tighten the German money supply. In this stressful environment, all the weak links in the German financial system were at grave risk. Deutsche Bank, in better shape than other banks, was under considerable political pressure to do more to help the weaker ones. Although critical of some government policies, as were virtually all financial institutions, it found itself more dependent on various sorts of government assistance.[78]

Its role in the credit of Hamburg-America Line (Hapag), Germany's largest passenger shipping company, is another good case in point. Unfortunately, it is only one of many. By 1931, it was clear that neither Hapag nor the Reichsbank were willing or able to pay the shipping company's $18.6 million credit. Although the company had assets, some of which were in the form of Dollars held outside the country, it and its government seemed unwilling to allow the firm to go bankrupt, disgorge its liquid funds, or to sell off its valuable shipping property at such an unfavorable time in order to satisfy its creditors. Some of the loan consortium members pushed for a day of reckoning. Deutsche Bank and Dresdner Bank, which collectively held two-thirds of the loan, tried to work out a compromise among the various actors: the foreign banks, the shipping line, and the government.

In 1928, Norddeutsche Bank in Hamburg, a subsidiary of Disconto-Gesellschaft, and Danatbank, the first major German bank to be laid low in the 1931 crisis, put together a syndicate for a temporary $10 million line of credit for Hapag. The line of credit was designed to help Hapag with temporary cash flow problems as it waited for the return of its American assets.[79] It carried an interest rate of 6.5 percent and a fee of 0.5 percent on the total amount. Deutsche Bank started with a 10 percent share of the facility. Over the next eight years, the principal grew to $21.5 million. The participants were forced to accept payment delays and finally a swap into Reichsmark. Although many of the participants in the syndicate reduced their holding, Deutsche Bank and Danatbank increased theirs.[80] In the spring of 1930, Hapag received $11.5 million from the U.S. government for its interned property, but it had obligations to fulfill with the Reich, International Acceptance Bank, and other organizations. After these payments, only $1.5 to $2 million was left to pay down the line of credit. The final settlement of the loan would have to await some future return of property, ostensibly arriving that very year. In practice, the consortium was to receive only an interest payment, nothing more. Nevertheless, at the time, the participants were reluctant to force payment or bankruptcy. Deutsche Bank, at least, believed that Hapag could get the funds to pay off the credit line from Warburg and the International Acceptance Bank. The lenders in the consortium seemed anxious to continue doing business on these terms.[81] Nearly a year later, soon after the consortium had extended the credit for another year, but before the banking crisis of 1931, Deutsche Bank's branch in Hamburg warned headquarters in Berlin that Hapag had in the space of three days drawn down $4.5 million in cash.[82]

In July, the member banks started to demand some sort of transformation of the loan into a more liquid, marketable form, such as bills of exchange.[83] In light of the extraordinarily difficult credit market situation, they also pushed Hapag to take steps to improve its cash flow, in order to increase the likelihood that any part of the loan (58.4 million Reichsmark) – transformed (swapped) into Reichsmark bills – could be paid, a step that would make the bills more marketable.[84] The participants pledged, however, not to put them on the market, but rather to deposit them with the Reichsbank where they could presumably be discounted. In theory, the issuing of the acceptances should not have changed the terms of the loan, but as the banking crisis in July deepened, the banks became more anxious to offload at least a portion of their loan to Hapag.[85] Some banks even demanded immediate repayment of the loan.[86]

The extension of the loan and acceptances brought Deutsche Bank into the discussion with foreign creditors and exposed Deutsche Bank to foreign exchange risk. The loan was rolled over into 1932 and included the London agreement, which called for a reduction in interest rates.[87] Some of the German banks had swapped their assets with foreign banks and were having difficulty making their payments.[88] It was not clear who was responsible for the swap costs and how payments could be made from blocked accounts (*Sperrkonten*). One bank demanded of Deutsche Bank, as lead bank in the consortium, moreover, to clarify whether Reichsmark amounts deposited in Reichsmark *Sperrkonten* had to be considered repayment of the loan or whether these amounts were only security for the final settlement of the loan in Dollars.[89] With the deposits in the hands of the Reichsbank, the foreign exchange risk remained, which Deutsche Bank believed Hapag must understand and accept as its responsibility. The shipping line had to find the necessary foreign exchange.

Even for the banks, however, it was not completely clear how the system would work and what their future obligations were.[90] For the Reichsbank, for example, the fact that the twelve German banks had swapped or sold off their positions in the Hapag loan to foreign banks was not Hapag's problem. By depositing payments with the Reichsbank, Hapag had satisfied its obligations under the extension agreement. What was owed by the member banks to their foreign bankers came under the 1932 London agreement. They would have to wait their turn for foreign exchange.[91] As late as February 1933, there was no clear understanding of what would happen. One aspect was clear, however: The decisions about how foreign exchange would be used was no longer a private matter. Hapag, for example, could not pay the Dollars back even if it had them and wanted to. All foreign exchange had to be turned over to the Reichsbank, which would determine the priorities for its use, in the interest of Germany, not foreign or domestic banks.[92] All of the participants had to await legal and administrative rulings. The most the German participants could hope for was Reichsmark payments; the foreign participants blocked accounts that they could trade. As the lead bank, Deutsche Bank was the primary German institution to which foreign creditors turned to recover their foreign currency. The bank was left in a very uncomfortable position between its government, clients, and foreign banks.

By July 1933, with the full knowledge of Hapag's management, the banks, government, and Hapag had been working on a reorganization of the company for over a year. The two lead banks presented a situation report and proposal, which they hoped could be used to calm foreign investors. They reiterated to the international banks the Reichsbank's March position that the foreign currency would be unavailable for the Dollar payment of the consortium loan. The Reichsbank would, however, continue to discount the 46 million Reichsmark in outstanding notes and to guarantee final payment of this sum. For the Dollar portion, $18.6 million of the Hapag credit, Deutsche Bank demanded a higher interest rate, that the company's freed U.S. assets be pledged to pay off the consortium, and that the sums be paid on a gold, not Dollar basis, as the Dollar, too, had recently been devalued. All this would be done in return for extension of the loan for another year and its increase to $20.5 million. The agreements had stipulated that the banks should take no losses for foreign exchange or for other reasons, which included any losses due to the German debt Standstill Agreements of 1932 and 1934. Deutsche Bank agreed to put up a deposit of 100 million Reichsmark supported by Hapag ships and a deposit of the shipping line's South American subsidiary shares as a guarantee of repayment.[93]

Walking a fine line between its nation's perceived interests and those of its international colleagues, Deutsche Bank grappled with thorny foreign exchange issues. In January 1934, Hapag requested another extension of the loans, assuming that the Standstill Agreement from 1933 would become the Standstill Agreement of 1934 in virtually unaltered form, and the Reichsbank's discounting policy of the loan would continue. The Consortium was informed that the government supported the extension, believing that Hapag was not in position to pay.[94] The Reich was not terribly sympathetic to the predicament of the banks, especially the foreign holders of German debt. Given the state's overriding interest, Deutsche Bank's job was to come to terms with Hapag.[95] But with the extension there was one snag. Since the U.S. government had devaluated the Dollar, if the company paid Dollars (not gold), there would be a foreign exchange gain. Who would get it? The Reichsbank had been against transforming the foreign part of the loan into Reichsmark, which was customary with other Deutsche Bank clients. Now the debtor would make an enormous foreign exchange windfall, while the German creditor institutions would be left with fewer Reichsmark and fixed obligations to their foreign banks as the reward for their patience.[96] All this spoke for a general gold value clause in all financial contracts, at the very least because the banks had been promised it in all the extension agreements, which also stipulated that they would suffer no damages.

Hapag's fate illustrated the gravity of the situation. Notwithstanding its foreign exchange gains and extensions, Hapag's business was not viable. In spite of the political pressure, in February 1935 Deutsche Bank managers made it clear to the government that they were against any further extensions for Hapag.[97] In the end, Hapag was nationalized and the government assumed its debts, an outcome with which few were probably happy.[98]

The New York Office

The worsening economic and political circumstances inside and outside of Germany contributed to administrative and other problems with the United States for Deutsche Bank. The conflicts in the early 1930s took a toll on Deutsche Bank's American business. Deutsche Bank's financial statement in 1933 tells an interesting story. Its only long-term direct investments in foreign banks were in Bulgaria, the Netherlands, Austria, and Switzerland. All but the one with de Bary & Co. in the Netherlands was small. In Germany, it still had the Deutsche Ueberseeische Bank (11.1 million Reichsmark), its investment in the Deutsche Treuhand-Gesellschaft, its audit and bankruptcy consulting firm, but virtually no consortium Dollar investments, in or outside the United States. Virtually none of its other assets were in Dollars.[99] Antiforeign, especially anti-German sentiments mounted in America during the 1930s, limiting Deutsche Bank opportunities there. Many observers blamed foreign investors, mainly British, for Wall Street's plunge.[100]

American banks also came under heavy domestic criticism for their foreign loans. The infamous Pecora Commission wanted to know the details of all loans issued by Morgan & Co. in the last ten years but seemed content with the amounts, default rates, and the bank's profit margins.[101] Like many Germans of both the right and left, many members of Congress and the public at large believed that international banks worked for their own interest to the detriment of their nation's welfare, implicating the United States more and more in Europe's economic problems. For them, "America and the American people were helpless, hopelessly in the grip of the International Bankers." The 1936 Democratic Platform vowed "to guard against Americans being dragged into war by international bankers." Some political leaders, like the one-time head of the APC, Francis Garvan, argued that Germany had an even greater financial hold on the U.S. economy in the 1930s than it had had before World War I. Americans were infuriated by the buyback of German debt. Distinctions between public and private investment flows, as well as the differences between private investors and debtors became blurred. As the German bond defaults became greater in the 1930s, Congress passed the Harrison Resolution prohibiting any further compensation to Germany for their assets lost in World War I. The U.S. tax code became more onerous for foreign investors and more attention was focused on the "dumping" of foreign goods on the U.S. market.[102]

By the early '30s, the economic regulatory and political environment had made normal business virtually impossible. Total official German long-term investment in the United States was estimated to have been $124 million in 1937, just 2 percent of the total foreign investment in the United States, down from $1.1 billion in 1914.[103] Germany had dropped from the second largest foreign contributor of capital to the United States to the seventh, behind Great Britain,

Canada, the Netherlands, Switzerland, France, and Belgium, although some German investment may have been funneled through other countries such as Switzerland. Lack of hard currency effectively ruled out most trade and financial transactions.[104] The Reichsbank cut Deutsche Bank off from access to convertible currency that the bank had not earned itself. From the mid-1930s on, apart from debt buybacks, Deutsche Bank itself participated in virtually no major transactions with the United States. By the time war was declared in Europe, its new business with the United States was confined to a few correspondent relations and trade financings, and painfully little of that.

But as late as 1936, at least some American government officials still had a favorable view of Deutsche Bank. Although the U.S. Department of State noted that it had fallen into second place among German banks after the merger of Dresdner and Danatbank, the latter bank was receiving considerable aid from the government, which in and of itself may have been understandably a negative feature in American eyes. Like all banks, however, Deutsche Bank was increasingly implicated in government-sponsored public works projects and short-term financing. Even though its commercial loan business and general profits declined, the bank resumed paying a dividend in that year, after a hiatus of four years. Among the big branch banking establishments of Germany, Deutsche Bank stood out for its reluctance to accept state assistance after the financial crash in 1931.[105] The regular U.S. Department of State report provided by the consulate's office in Berlin did note, however, that the bank's financial statements were compiled in a completely new way that made comparison with prior years impossible. The assumedly large, but still unknown precise amount of special reserves also made normal financial analysis and determination of real profit difficult, to say the least. The consulate's report made no mention of how much money Deutsche Bank was making from buying up its own debt on American markets, as discussed earlier.[106]

Given the economic and political divisions of the interwar years, it is remarkable that Deutsche Bank could do any business at all in New York. In 1930, Hugo Schmidt retired at age sixty-seven from Deutsche Bank. In addition to his Deutsche Bank duties, representing both the bank and its South American affiliate, Banco Aleman Transatlantico (Deutsche Ueberseeische Bank), he served as vice president of the U.S. & Overseas Investment Corporation, which, in September 1929, launched 600,000 shares of common stock underwritten by the Harris Forbes Corp.[107] Despite his treatment during World War I, he had taken American citizenship. He died in 1954 in New York.[108] With the return of most German property and Schmidt's retirement, the New York office seemed to become less important. For a short period, Adolf Koehn, Disconto-Gesellschaft's representative in New York since 1920, took over Schmidt's post. Herbert Waller succeeded Koehn in May 1933.[109]

By the early 1930s, too, Deutsche Bank's physical presence and business dealings were greatly reduced. When Waller, a Berlin employee, took over for Koehn, he moved the offices to 20 Exchange Place.[110] The office was downsized. In most respects, Waller's work differed greatly from his predecessors, but some aspects remained unchanged. There were still some messy APC details to handle[111] and settlements over bonds issued before World War I.[112] To be sure, there was a steady stream of reports about American politics and economics from Waller. Although the buybacks were handled strictly from Berlin, Waller was preoccupied by foreign exchange issues. With sales of blocked Reichsmarks vigorous in New York,[113] as can be easily imagined, in the mid-1930s, Waller had to have some involvement with the buying back of German debt, at least with cultivating American clients in Germany, whose blocked funds helped make them important customers. German Scrip (Blocked Funds Certificates) was even registered under the rules of the Federal Trade Commission and the Securities Acts, so as to allow it to be used to pay agents of holders of German coupons originally paid in Dollars.[114]

In April 1937, Waller visited Germany. A file note documented the discussion and what was called "biggest issues at hand." Apart from a small lawsuit that could be settled, the meetings dealt with the ongoing but tricky repurchases of foreign debt. The Reichsbank had become stricter about permitting the repurchases. The Berlin management decided to reinforce its personal contact with Reichsbank officials in the hope of helping German clients. Great care needed to be exercised in choosing which securities to buy up. In addition, they talked about selling many of the bank's remaining U.S. securities.[115]

One of the biggest surprises of the period appears to be the extent to which Deutsche Bank was doing business with American companies in Germany. By the mid-1930s, foreign exchange controls had back-handedly increased the amount of U.S. foreign direct investments in Germany. Deutsche Bank found that it held deposits amounting to Reichsmark 27.5 million from German subsidiaries of U.S. companies, most of which could not be remitted to the United States. The competition to win these deposits was heating up. Commerzbank sent a representative to the United States to try to draw some of the American companies away from Deutsche Bank.[116] These customers included household names such as Kodak, General Motors (Opel), Singer, Woolworth's, IBM, and Coca-Cola, all of whom accumulated more cash in Germany than they needed.[117]

As with these companies, Deutsche Bank's weakened position in Germany and the United States was not primarily of its own making. Although it might have handled some situations better and avoided some transactions that tarnished its reputation in the United States, the fundamental constellation of international finance had greatly reduced the scope of mutually beneficial transactions. Beggar-thy-neighbor public economic policies set the tone for private ones. Doing appreciable business with the United States would have to wait until prosperity returned and nations improved their ability to work out their conflicting national agendas.

14

The Second Phoenix

The War and the Rebuilding of Deutsche Bank

There is another difficulty to which I made reference earlier, and that is so many of this class of which I am speaking were employees of the Treasury during the Morgenthau regime and were inculcated with a hatred of everything German to an extent that at times their main objective seemed to be not that of rebuilding Germany but smashing the little there was left of German organization and the German economic system.

Walter Lichtenstein, speech, "The German Problem: A Sequel," May 26, 1948, NARA, RG 260, Box 60, File 44,7a.

World War II and Deutsche Bank in the United States

Even before shots were fired in the new European war in September 1939, Deutsche Bank's position in the United States had become virtually untenable. Between America's slow recovery and Germany's military priorities, doing profitable normal banking business was hard to imagine. Despite America's general isolationist sentiment, government and popular support for England and France was growing. Moreover, many of Deutsche Bank's best business friends – for example Speyer & Co. – had left the commercial scene or lost their political-economic clout and, thereby, their ability to help Deutsche Bank weather the political storm.[1] As one American businessman wrote to the head of Deutsche Bank's international operations, since 1933 America's foreign policy had changed radically from disinterest with continental Europe to active hostility toward Germany and Italy, and an even more interventionist sentiment than with Japan and South America.[2]

Although the bank would continue to rent some office space for a while and kept one junior employee there for some special tasks, it announced to its correspondents, effective October 1, 1938, that it was closing its representative office.[3] Between 1936 and 1945, Deutsche Bank's transactions involving the United States were complicated and often processed through non-German banks, as had been the case during World War I.

What was true for German banks was not true for banks from other European countries. Perhaps because of the foreign tensions, foreign deposits in the United States in June 1939 reached $1.5 billion, an increase of nearly $1 billion in four months.[4] With the deposits came renewed interest by foreign banks in creating U.S. branches. Credit Suisse had already established one in July 1939. Dutch and French banks were studying the move. Notably, German banks, including Deutsche Bank, were not among the candidates.[5]

The cloaking of German assets, which had been undertaken before the 1930s in many countries, took on greater importance for German companies and became more complicated. Using nominees and complex holding company structures, German firms labored to keep funds outside of Germany and reduce their worldwide tax bite. In many cases, reduction in direct investment was coupled with licensing and technical agreements that allowed "subsidiaries" to serve not only the United States but also other markets, especially those in Latin America.[6] Once war broke out in Europe, Deutsche Bank's direct transactions with the United States – already few in number by 1939 – came to a grinding halt.

The war changed the geographic scope of Deutsche Bank's business. Even though new opportunities arose on the European continent, offshore ones declined. The Deutsche Ueberseeische Bank, Deutsche Bank's subsidiary for Latin American investments, had 215 million Reichsmark in assets in 1938, with 36 million in capital. By 1941, however, its assets had declined substantially. Originally, it maintained branches in Spain, Argentina, Chile, Peru, and Brazil, but its six Brazilian and two Peruvian branches were liquidated in 1942, which helps to explain the decline in assets.[7] Deutsche Bank's involvement in Hitler's economic war against the Jews, though less than many other financial institutions, led to some transactions involving the United States. Deutsche Bank assisted some Jewish refugees from Germany and other conquered countries, whose assets had been taken over (aryanized) by the bank or by others, to transfer more funds than allowed by German law to the United States and other countries. On at least one occasion, the bank helped mask the true nature of funds bound for the United States through Switzerland.[8] Because some of the amounts were small and because they generally passed through Swiss banks, these sorts of transaction can hardly be described as major dealings with the United States. Most precious metal transactions processed by Deutsche Bank, moreover, went through other countries.[9]

The coming war once again made communication and the coordination of banking activity more difficult. Until fall 1941, the Reichsbank and the U.S. Federal Reserve had frequent, if not completely open, correspondence with one another. Those communications came under increasing U.S. government scrutiny. The Reichsbank's last letter before war was declared against the United States echoed its earlier optimism after war broke out in Europe in September 1939.[10] In November 1941, the Reichsbank instructed the Fed to deliver all correspondence through the German embassy in Washington. Even that avenue was blocked in December and all correspondence between the two central banks was terminated by order of the U.S. State Department,[11] although U.S. officials kept meticulous records of German gold transactions in Istanbul.[12] Even earlier, in June 1941, the "die seemed to have been cast." Germany told America to close all its consular offices and American Express its travel offices in Germany and in all the occupied territories, and to get their personnel out before July 15,

1941, in part as retaliation against American restrictions on German business in the United States.[13]

Long before the United States was drawn into the shooting war, America and Germany had declared economic war against each other. On June 14, 1941, America froze German assets in the United States. On June 28, Germany responded in kind. Only assets held by the U.S. embassy, the Chamber of Commerce, and U.S. diplomats were spared, but even they were limited to withdrawing no more than Reichsmark 1,000 per month from their accounts. The decree mandated that all companies with more than 25 percent American ownership apply to dispose of any of their assets. They were also obliged to file extensive reports about their directors, boards, and the nature of their American ownership.[14] American officials demanded similar filings, but Deutsche Bank was not mentioned in the extensive report filed by the attorney general about German business's cloaking activities.[15]

In quick order, $4.5 million in foreign assets was included under the authority granted to the U.S. Treasury Department. Later, a total of approximately $8 million would come under the control of the Treasury Department. Administrating the order was complicated. Knowing which assets were foreign was often not easy, and issuing licenses that permitted some transactions was cumbersome.[16] Through much of 1941, German companies were the subject of many investigations. The Truman Committee looked at them from the standpoint of national defense, whereas the justice department, which had inherited the files of the APC, the FBI, and the State Department also actively investigated the activities of German businesses and businessmen. Even the SEC pursued foreign holding company structures. Moreover, these authorities worked with the British secret service to find out more about and hinder the activities of German companies.

As late as June 1941, German companies and individuals held $172.4 million in American assets, mostly in the form of controlled enterprises (direct investment), but sizeable amounts totaling $50.1 million were held in trusts and estates by individuals.[17] Deutsche Bank held far less than it did before World War I – nine securities with relatively little value, mostly under the name of nominees or as bearer securities. Two were particularly interesting in light of the coming war, common and preferred shares in the Russian Finance and Construction Corporation.[18]

In the battle of seizing assets, Germany found itself in a better position in 1940 than in 1914. America had invested $455 million in Germany, mostly in the form of physical property. According to one source, the German total in the United States was only $103 million. The ratio in Italy was somewhat better for the Americans. Only in conquered countries such as France, the Netherlands, and Belgium was the relationship of inward to outward investment very favorable to the United States should America try "to keep assets from Hitler."[19]

Once Germany declared war against the United States, American officials moved swiftly against German and Italian assets. On the day the United States went to war against Germany, the U.S. government shut down or took over many German companies.[20] Wildly different reports about the views and actions of Deutsche Bank representatives circulated among the authorities. The FBI maintained an extensive file on Waller, Deutsche Bank's last prewar representative. Waller elected to stay in the United States as a naturalized citizen, even though his duties for Deutsche Bank seemed to have come to an end. Although one FBI agent found no evidence of illegal activity, in another report, Waller and others from the Wilmington Chemical Company were allegedly involved in a plot to poison a man who had testified for the Truman Commission investigating German and American business connections. An informant from Bankers Trust contended, however, that Waller was a nephew of Hugo Schmidt, was violently anti-Hitler, and a Jew, which accounted for his difficulty in gaining membership to an elite New York club. Waller's resignation from Deutsche Bank was attributed to his anti-Nazi feeling and substantially Jewish heritage. But as late as 1943, J. Edgar Hoover himself connected Waller with espionage, even though he had been replaced "as German financial agent."[21]

With the exception of highly stealthy payments, financial transactions with the United States stopped. Deutsche Bank had trouble conducting business even with South America through Deutsche Ueberseeische Bank, although it helped the Reichsbank transfer gold out of Germany to Spain and to other destinations in 1944.[22] During the war, some reports came into FBI hands that Waller was involved in South American financial transfers, but the reports could not be confirmed.[23] As evidence that Germany diminished financial transactions with the United States, recent studies about German gold sales during World War II hardly mention the United States.[24] Trade and Standstill discussions ceased. From 1941 through 1951, Deutsche Bank's primary American focus was avoiding the negative effects of first the war and then Allied administration.

The Americanization of German Banking After the War

Starting in May 1945, a quite new dependency on the United States developed, one that greatly exceeded that between the First and Second World Wars. For several years, American officials replaced the Reichsbank, the Ministry of Finance, and the German court system as the principle regulators of Deutsche Bank's affairs. The bank's personnel and other administrative decisions required more input from Americans than it ever had from German regulators before 1933 and rivaled, to be sure without the same moral significance, the intrusions of the National Socialist regime. From 1945 to 1948, the bank functioned in an occupied country, whose administrators, largely Americans, Russians, and British, held big banks mostly responsible for the political disasters and moral decay of the past decade. Despite its weakened status, Deutsche Bank continued to play a leading role in German banking, German financial policy, and German representation in negotiations with the Allies about the future of German finances, especially as concerned banking regulation.

Already weakened by National Socialist attacks on the bank and banking system, the Allied occupation might have seemed like a death blow. In spring 1945, the members of Deutsche Bank's management board, most of whom had never joined the party, found themselves scattered in different Allied zones. One was shot by Russian soldiers. Many of Deutsche Bank's customers were destitute and many of its physical assets destroyed or severely damaged. Important banking records had been shipped west and many business operations, because of the impending collapse of communication and centralized political control, had been decentralized. In the chaotic situation just before and after the German surrender, Deutsche Bank managers scrambled to place assets and personnel so as to minimize the adverse impact of occupational zones. The man who was to lead Deutsche Bank through most of the next two decades escaped Berlin for Hamburg in a delivery van on April 14, just before the Russian assault on the capital. The decision to keep key personnel and cash in the British zone turned out to be fortunate: of the four Allied occupiers, Britain was the most sympathetic to the German banking predicament.[25] But assets of Deutsche Bank's largest successor bank in 1948, even in near worthless Reichsmarks, were less than 75 percent of their 1938 nominal value.[26]

Some readers may be surprised that one of the first rounds of the Americanization of Europe was not in the form of rampant liberalism but rather Progressive, New Deal skepticism of unbridled capitalism and centralized power. The first impulse of most American regulators was to destroy the economic and political power of big business in Germany in order to strengthen democracy. The attitudes of those charged with "reforming" the German banking system might best be seen in a series of *New York Times* articles. According to the paper, the German banks had reached out with an octopus-like clutch to seize foreign assets. Even with Hitler deposed, there was a risk that these bankers would maintain their grip on the German and European economies.[27]

Luckily for the German banks, the Allied banking policies, however, were not uniform over time and among the zones. By summer 1945, the Allies had established that even banks headquartered in Berlin would not be controlled by the Russians alone. The Soviets had already removed 50 million Reichsmark in currency from Deutsche Bank's Berlin office and a large amount of securities, the value of which had not yet been determined.[28] For a considerable time, while the Allies researched the German banking system with a special Private Banking Section, no clear, definitive policy was established.

In September 1945, at least the aims of its banking study for the Office of Military Government of the United States (OMGUS) were laid out. The Private Banking Section was to work with the war crimes people to find "one or more pointed examples of the war criminality of probably no more than one private bank." The value of the work would be judged on how well it "fits the requirements" of the war crimes people. An internal memo stated that the desired information was: Determining what types of transactions could constitute bank criminality, determining whether a banker could be added to the list of defendants, and determining how information derived from the banks could be included in other investigations. Almost sadly, it seems, the author concluded: "It is felt that it is unrealistic to assume that large groups of bankers will be hung as a result of our investigation." Although the most likely candidate for prosecution was Deutsche Bank's managing director, the study was more focused on uncovering patterns of financial operations. The team was less interested in cases of strong-arm methods and more intent on uncovering foreign acquisitions of Dresdner and Deutsche Bank. Given the ample number of examples of aryanization and other crimes, the author felt confident that the study needed to do little more than confirm what has been known about the big banks for a long time.[29]

Although there was some difference of opinion among the administrators – between the finance and economic sections, for example – for many of the Americans, decentralized financial institutions with limited scope in their activities was a virtual requirement for democracy. Removing Nazis from positions of power was insufficient. Most of the original American administration felt that its mission was to guide and assist "[G]erman authorities in the development of effective democratic financial machinery," putting the banking structure and money "into the hands of the people, and to place local needs ahead of the country's central politics."[30]

Given the original aims, the conclusions of the study should come as no surprise. It is hard to understand why it took until June 1947 for the investigators to state in writing their economic and moral conclusions about Germany and the banks. For them, banks and Germany were not only financially but also morally bankrupt. Germany could not pay its prewar debts. Firms with large foreign holdings were likely to undergo enforced liquidation or socialization in the Soviet zone. Long-term creditors would be better served if their debts were transferred from private to public obligations.[31] Much of the factual information could have been written before 1942 from public documents. The Forward made clear the interests of the authors and how their conclusions were drawn.

> The investigation was designed to trace the functions of the Big Banks in the development of the Nazi state, to determine the extent to which they might be considered an excessive concentration of economic power, and to gauge whether and by what means these banks might be adapted to a peacetime German economy.
>
> The findings of these bank investigations have provided the foundations for the decentralization of the German banking system which has taken place in the U.S. zone, as well as for the criminal trials against officials of the Dresdner Bank by the Office of the Chief of Counsel for War Crimes at Nuremberg.[32]

Even though no executive from Deutsche Bank was tried, Deutsche Bank and Dresdner Bank were part of the same report, painted, as it were, with the same brush. Dresdner, the previously state-owned but smaller bank had much more to atone for, but big was bad. In 1943, based on their large networks, the top six banks controlled 55 percent of the total assets of commercial banks. They dominated foreign exchange and stock market transactions. Largest of these six were Deutsche Bank and Dresdner, with assets in 1943 of 8.7 billion and 6.7 billion Reichsmark respectively. The authors gave a short history of the banks, omitting the vitriolic criticisms of the banks by many parties including the Nazis before 1933 and the hostility of the National Socialist government to the banks during its reign. The great power of the banks through interlocking directorates, stock ownership, and proxy voting provided sufficient evidence of their great political and economic power during the Third Reich. Nothing was said of the limits on supervisory board and even shareholder power during the regime. Although the report mentioned the 1943 Martin Bormann banking committee efforts to take further control of banks, the writers took it as evidence of the banks' connection to the Third Reich, not their vulnerability. Apart from a few personal relations and party memberships among managers, the fairly normal relationship between the bank and the Ministry of Economics, and some loans to companies involved in war production, the report presented painfully little in the way of any Deutsche Bank involvement in Nazi planning for the war. Its worst crimes involved cases of complicity with aryanization and profiting from institutions weakened by occupation. Nevertheless the writers concluded: "From the foregoing it is apparent that the Deutsche Bank and Dresdner Bank were active partners of the Nazis in the spoliation and economic domination of Europe."[33] More recent studies of Deutsche Bank would agree with aryanization and expansion activities, but not with the "active partner" portion of the OMGUS conclusions.[34]

All this information gathering was in large part designed to defend the proposition that all those who were in positions of importance before the war should not be after and that, along the lines envisioned by the Potsdam Declaration, big German banks should be decentralized. The most important features of the edict that followed (No. 57) were the appointment of independent custodians for the banks and for the banks to be broken up.[35]

But the Americans had set in motion the future of German banking long before the banking report was even issued. Although the Russians were more thorough, American regulators saw controlling the German banking system as part of their mission. Even before entering Germany, British and American regulators developed straightforward instructions about how to administer Germany, including guidelines that governed banking matters, the *Financial and Property Control Manual*. In contrast to the Soviet zone, banks in the U.S. zone were to be kept closed only long enough to introduce satisfactory control, to remove objectionable personnel, and to block securely certain accounts. This said, the personnel of both the Reichsbank and private banks were to be used for carrying out orders. The Manual provided for settling currency issues and reporting requirements. Within a year, in the Western zones loans were being made and securities traded.[36]

Allied administrators had instructions for debt payments to insure a reasonable amount of liquidity for banks. After the war, creating and implementing banking policy was entrusted to the Allied Control Council, which had some difficulty determining a common policy. Many Americans shared the views expressed in the Morgenthau Plan, which argued for a complete deindustrialization of Germany; others, at the very least, wanted to create a banking system modeled on the American. Much of the implementation of the policy in the American zone was in the hands of the treasury department, run by Henry Morgenthau, Jr., himself. These officials worked to break up German banks, with the aim of weakening them. Although Morgenthau resigned in August 1945 in protest over not being appointed to the Potsdam Conference delegation, Bernard Bernstein, a close friend of the secretary, and other Treasury

Department members who shared Morgenthau's views, continued to administer financial affairs in Germany. Even Bernstein's more moderate successors believed in decentralizing German banking. Although not explicitly required by any agreements, the new administrative group that included American bankers proceeded to decentralize the big banks corresponding to the larger regions of the Allied zones, not along the lines of the new smaller German *Länder* as the more radical regulators wanted. The top advisor of the Finance Division of the Allied authorities in September 1945, Joseph M. Dodge (chairman of the board of the Detroit Bank & Trust and president of the American Bankers Association) favored a banking system that resembled that of the United States, combining the twelve-regional-bank layout of the Federal Reserve with state-by-state banking for commercial banks, as well as breaking off investment banking functions and banning the banks' participation in client supervisory boards.[37] Ironically, forty years earlier, German bankers were trying with much success to get America to establish a more reliable banking system modeled on the German one. Moreover, as one scholar put it:

> Even more remarkable was the similarity between the American and the National Socialist perception of the power of the banks, and the measures they took to limit the influence of the banks on the economy. In its role as the occupier of Germany, the American government – pursuing the tradition of Jeffersonian ideal of a maximum degree of local self-determination – demanded what the National Socialists had demanded earlier: namely, to limit the proxy voting power, to restrict bankers from sitting on the supervisory boards of business enterprises, and, contrary to the centralized character of the National Socialist state, to regionalize or decentralize the banking system.[38]

In December 1945, the U.S. authorities instructed the *Länder* under their control to forbid banks to maintain branches or subsidiaries outside of the *Land* in which the principal office of the financial institution was located. The number of banks was to be reduced and eventually their geographic scope should be limited to one municipality or rural district. Once-national banks were restricted to one *Land*. Although British opposition eventually forced a compromise, as early as October Dodge had begun to urge the Allied Finance Directorate to forbid banks from dealing in securities. A banking committee of the Finance Directorate was established in June 1946 with power to enforce decentralization, though Russian opposition now prevented the four powers from reaching a unified approach to exactly how this would be done.[39]

In the end, the Western Allies acted individually. As relations between the Soviets and the other powers deteriorated, Germany's plight became greater, and various German governmental authorities and private institutions established themselves as a credible collective force, decisions about the western zones were made outside of the four-power context. A plan to merge and reorganize all the big banks along regional lines, strongly opposed by Deutsche Bank, was dropped in favor of a unilateral American plan for the American zone. Pending final determination of the structure of German banking, Deutsche Bank, Dresdner Bank and Commerzbank would have state custodians who should act independently of the interests of the shareholders and bank directors. Despite new business names, the institutional structures remained the same. The British thought the American ideas a ludicrous holdover from the Morgenthau period. Harsh treatment of German banks also received criticism from the general custodian of British and American Standstill credits, groups still awaiting payment.[40]

From an early stage, some Deutsche Bank managers were involved in helping the Allies investigate and administer banks. They were obliged to accumulate and turn over information to assist the Financial Intelligence and Liaison Branch about Deutsche Bank, and about the whereabouts and activities of other managers. In spring 1946, three of the bank's leading managers were still held by the Russians, two by the Americans. Only those in the British Zone were still at liberty.[41] The senior managers were not altogether happy about the cooperation given to the investigation by some managers. In January 1946, the informal management committee learned that the Allied banking authorities were even meeting in a Deutsche Bank branch office to work out plans for decentralizing the banks. Deutsche Bank's management had not yet been formally advised of the meetings and strongly protested against the steps, adding that it hoped Deutsche Bank employees had not participated in the discussions and that Deutsche Bank middle managers would continue to take the interests of Germany's economic health as a whole and the bank's unity as their primary objectives. These issues should only be addressed by the bank's management and supervisory boards.[42] The informal board seems to have been relatively effective at enforcing the loyalty of lower-level managers in the face of pressures from both occupying forces and perhaps their own ambition.

The bank provided the occupiers with the number and names of thirty supervisory board members, all of whom had been ostensibly selected because they were either customers of the bank or representatives of different regions, or industrial sectors, and the names, addresses, and functions of the management board members – all ten members, including their spokesman, Oswald Rösler. According to the memo, both boards adopted a collegiate system with all resolutions requiring unanimity. There were three Nazis on the management board. Until 1942, party affiliation had not been taken into consideration for board membership, but in that year the bank was informed that having only one party member on the board of Germany's largest bank would no longer be tolerated.[43]

Americans pursued their investigations of German banking, if not with unanimity, with relatively strong opinions that were not always well informed or objective. In an interim report, the officials indicated that Deutsche Bank's assets had quadrupled from 1928 to 1944, without mentioning that the bank had merged with another large bank in 1929, that the war preparations and war period brought with them inflation, and that there were strict limits on how much any institution could dividend to shareholders. The authors concluded that: "This growth demonstrates that the bank fully participated in the rapid credit expansion which took place in Germany, generated by Government financing of preparations for, and ultimate conduct of, a war of aggression." With 70 percent of its assets in government securities, the authors concluded that they were war profiteers, not victims of forced investment in what became nearly worthless paper. In addition to its vast network of branches (288 in 1940), according to the report, the bank held 50 percent ownership in Deutsche Ueberseeische Bank and a minority interest in two firms doing business in Asia and Japan. Indeed, the bank, as the report pointed out, followed the flag, acquiring twenty new banks in Austria and conquered lands.[44] Subsequent progress reports, ostensibly supported by 295 exhibits in three volumes, traced operations during the Nazi regime and established Deutsche Bank's management's complicity in the commission of economic war crimes and Deutsche Bank's influence on industry. Despite the absence of some files, the investigation had firmly "disclosed evidence of the power which was concentrated in a few hands by control of those banks."[45]

A subsequent memo addressed to the director of the finance division summed up the situation in late 1947. The German banking system was "excessive" and bankrupt – especially Deutsche Bank, Dresdner Bank, and Commerzbank, whose assets ostensibly only covered 22 percent of their liabilities. It advocated breaking up the banks into small local institutions with laws passed by the Germans themselves.[46] Understandably the Americans feared the Germans would be negligent in this area. As early as June 1947, one staff member complained to the director of the finance division that the Germans in many regions had failed to appoint custodians for the banks or to change the banks' names.[47] Germans were to enforce American directives. A few days later, the policy was stated even more clearly: "It is considered to be in the common interest, not to enforce this decentralization, but to carry it through on a voluntary basis in accordance with the provisions of the German stock laws," proposed by the parent bank. The Americans wanted it both ways: to have control and to delegate responsibility to the German authorities.[48]

By the end of December 1947, however, Deutsche Bank moved its international operations to the more friendly British zone.[49] It was perhaps a coincidence that six of twenty-four Deutsche Bank branch managers accused of party membership were also living in the British zone.[50]

In their early investigations of Deutsche Bank's foreign activities, the American authorities seemed to be interested only in the bank's Swiss, Turkish, and South American transactions and cloaking. They seemed convinced that Deutsche Bank had nothing going on in North America or that they already had all the needed information.[51]

A regional banking system was taking shape in Germany. By 1947, too, the regional institutions of Deutsche Bank had been accredited by the military governments as foreign trade banks, as a first step to relinking the German banking system with the rest of the world. The French basically supported the American decentralization policy. The banks, however, offered their own proposals. These included dividing Germany into different regions with different configurations of ownership, control, and fund-raising relationships between semi-independent regional banks and the national parent. Without any official acceptance of the plan by the Allied administration or the Reichsbank,

Deutsche Bank, for example, implemented a regional structure based on occupational zones further divided by separately named banks in each *Land*, each with a separate custodian. It also had a loose national coordination with an unsanctioned committee representing the interests of the Deutsche Bank group. In January 1948, the American authorities finally sanctioned the plan. In April, Deutsche Bank was broken up for all practical purposes, but not liquidated. Nevertheless, the decoupling only became official in 1952.[52]

The progress in developing a system was slow for many reasons. Some thought that there had been a reduction in the quality of American administrators. Walter Lichtenstein, a retired businessman who worked on the economic reconstruction of Germany as chief of the Financial Institutions Group, felt that those from private industry, who understood business and had volunteered their time, had already gone home. By 1947, only two kinds of administrators were left: those like him who looked for an opportunity for interesting activity after retirement, and young, overpaid kids from the government, many from the treasury, "who like Government officials the world over regard it as their chief task to shirk responsibility and not express any opinions."[53] To Lichtenstein, Jack Bennett, despite his considerable ability, was a good case in point.[54] Moreover, according to another colleague, Bennett had learned very little about finance since arriving in Germany. His advice to General Clay was neither objective nor informed.[55] The work was further hampered by disagreements first among the Americans, then between the Americans and the other powers, and, finally, as Germans started to have some voice, with those who would be charged with administering the new regulations.[56] Although the Americans were very committed to the principle of decentralization, they also did not want to interfere in the administration of financial matters in other zones.[57]

Despite the problems, by the time Bennett left the finance division in March 1947, he seemed quite proud. They had been men on a mission, decentralizing German finances, and, thereby, creating a "sound banking system ... for that is the very foundation upon which the future of Germany will rest."[58]

Even though the Occupation Statute signed in connection with the founding of the Federal Republic in 1949 still gave the Western powers control over the structure of German banking, Cold War politics increasingly provided Germans with more opportunities for political initiative. British representatives, who only reluctantly agreed with the Americans about decentralization and who sat on the Allied Bank Commission, which still had authority over the framework of German banking, helped Germans convince the American and French representatives, whose willingness to compromise had been heightened by tensions with the Soviets and the desire to have a strong, new ally.[59]

Already in summer 1949, everyone seemed to agree that a less ambitious and more permanent solution to decentralization had to be found to replace the interim plan. The Americans and French still wanted to liquidate the old, big banks, whereas the British were afraid that this would prejudice their prewar Standstill Agreement claims, approximately three-quarters of the DM 425 million in outstanding short-term debt. One representative from each of the three big German banks met in fall 1949 to fashion a strong argument against the American proposal for decentralization, which entailed eliminating the original bank companies. Recognizing the opposition, they stopped short of demanding recentralization, just partial recentralization, which the British would support.[60]

In February 1950, even the American position toward regional banking seemed to soften, but with the provision that no national bank could control the activities of four or five regional ones. Though it was too late to institutionalize limits on universal banking, some Americans also remained concerned that German banks would retain their influence over industrial firms. But it was no longer the case that Americans could just dictate the terms. The process of creating new legislation and new structures involved not only the perceptions and interests of the Western Allies but those of German regions, regulators, small banks, and West German legislators.[61] In the end, the legislation that passed reflected those interests and left the ban with a certain degree of flexibility.

The Western Allies, who could still veto the plan, raised many objections that led to two substantial changes. The first was to define the three banking districts. The second was to require that each successor bank of the original parent guarantee repayment of the original parent's obligations. With these conditions met, the compromise was finally approved by the Allied High Commission in October 1951 and the legislation embodying the Allied complaints was passed in March 1952 (the Big Banks Act). German banks could merge many of their separate *Länder* institutions. In 1952, Deutsche Bank began operating as Norddeutsche Bank AG, in Hamburg, Rheinisch-Westfälische Bank AG, in Düsseldorf, and Süddeutsche Bank AG, in Munich, with total assets of DM 3.8 billion, spread roughly 20 percent, 40 percent, and 40 percent among the three, respectively. Beginning in November of that year, the boards of the three successor banks met jointly every two months.[62]

Hermann Josef Abs, America, and Deutsche Bank's Revival

Since the end of the war, Allied control of the bank had been pervasive, but incomplete. Deutsche Bank knew how to adapt to changing circumstances and hostile regulators. The three Deutsche Bank management board members present in Hamburg had been suspended from their posts, in accordance with Allied policy, but they managed to influence the bank's affairs through "informal" contact with those who were allowed to continue to work. Even before the end of the war, Deutsche Bank, befitting its new situation, divided the management board members' duties not by function or international regions, but by German regions resembling the future Allied occupational zones.

By 1948, too, many of the political and economic issues that daunted Germany's and Deutsche Bank's recovery – poor and conflicting administration, lack of a stable, convertible currency and sufficient capital to rebuild – were beginning to be resolved. Unbeknownst to those struggling to make ends meet and keep up their courage, Germany's economic miracle was about to start. For them, much of their country was in ruin, on the brink of starvation, and

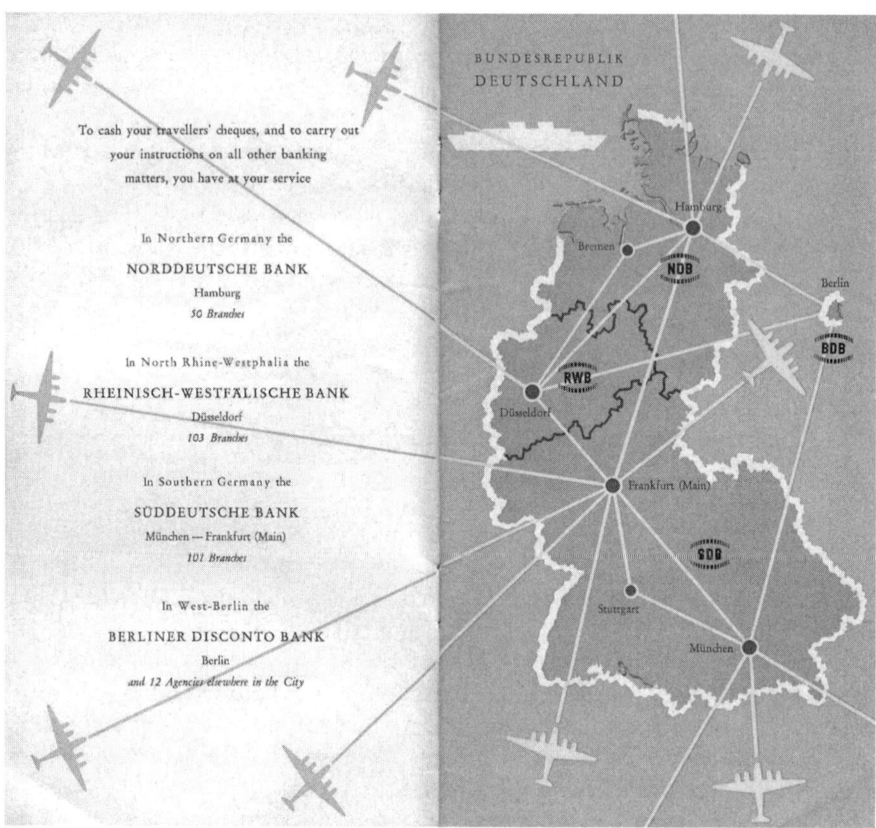

This 1953 map shows the breakdown of the areas serviced by the three banks into which Deutsche Bank had been divided after World War II. It should be remembered that not only was Deutsche Bank divided after World War II, the once-German territory that it could service was only approximately 65 percent of the economic and geographic area of Germany in 1929.

occupied by four great powers often hostile to one another. Many Germans also felt like an international pariah with few friends and seemingly no comparative advantage.

From 1952 through 1957, Deutsche Bank managers worked gradually toward freeing themselves of the vestiges of what was basically American regulation of German banking. Several experienced managers from the prewar period were in place to guide that development; one in particular stands out in the story of Deutsche Bank's reentry into world markets, the first leader of the reunited bank, Hermann Josef Abs.

One of the most controversial and powerful bankers of his time, Abs had joined the bank in 1938 at age thirty-six from Delbrück Schickler & Co. and headed up Deutsche Bank's international operations. Like many of the past leaders of Deutsche Bank, he had done an international banking circuit for his training, including a visit to New York in the 1920s at the banking house of

Schröder, before returning to Germany as an acknowledged expert in foreign exchange and trade. At the time he joined Deutsche Bank, his close connection with and handling of complicated issues in the last series of Standstill Agreements was one of the most appealing aspects of his resume to Deutsche Bank.[63] In winter 1939, Abs went to New York for the negotiations over that year's Standstill Agreement.[64]

For a few years, the Americans wanted to prosecute Abs at Nuremberg. The charges were enriching himself during the Nazi period, serving on the boards of many armament companies, helping with the transfer of foreign and domestic assets illegally obtained by the Nazis, and, lastly, having once been a partner in the private bank where Hitler and other high-ranking Nazis had their personal bank accounts. He was never formally charged, and later more sober analyses conclude that he was at worst an opportunist, at best a man of character who had to practice his profession in an inhuman system.[65]

One recent study covering his politics stated:

> Abs, although he never sympathized with the Nazi ideology and was close to some of the central leaders of the German resistance, was not a part of the resistance, and he self-consciously chose not to be a hero. He believed that in doing this, he was following the interests of his family (to whom he had a primary responsibility) and also of the bank (to which he also felt responsibility); he did not believe himself obliged to make a useless sacrifice.[66]

As early as March 1945, Abs' name appeared on a list of "Business Men and Officials Holding Leading Positions in the Organization of the German Economy." Along with 1800 others, he was accused of being an economic war criminal. In July 1945, a U.S. Senate committee reported that Abs was a banker industrialist whose rise within the Nazi economy had been phenomenal.[67] On a list drawn up by the U.S. Army in June 1946 of the leading industrialists and financiers in Germany, Abs had the honor of being the second youngest; only Alfried Krupp of the Krupp works was his junior by five years.[68] Within a few years, it was clear to most Allied administrators that Abs was a key figure to accomplishing their aims.[69]

At first the American administrators of Germany were especially suspicious of Abs. His rise in the German economy during the Nazi years was *prima facie* evidence not of competence but rather of complicity. Connected to forty banks and industrial concerns, his influence seemed pervasive. His board membership included many utilities, banking concerns in occupied territories, and companies essential to the war effort and extermination policies, such as the notorious IG Farben. Though acknowledging his strong Catholic convictions and rumors that he might have been involved in the Catholic opposition, some of the authorities concluded that resistance would have been impossible given his business activities.[70]

Under political pressure from the Americans, Abs had been arrested in 1946 and imprisoned in a camp with many other leading German industrialists. Released after three months, he met regularly with three suspended members of the management board and other managers for informal board meetings at their modest private residences. On orders from the Allies, over the next few months several of the managers were dismissed whereas others had their suspensions lifted and could go back to work. By 1948, all four of the inner circle, however – Abs, Clemens Plassmann, Erich Bechtolf, and Fritz Wintermantel, who were among the youngest members of the management board before 1945 – had been reinstated and would serve to provide Deutsche Bank with leadership and continuity during the difficult days to follow.[71]

Accusations about Abs' work during the Nazi regime followed him through much of the rest of his career and remain a matter of debate among historians to this day.[72] During the first two decades of the postwar years, Abs proved to be the most adaptive and dynamic German financial leader outside of government, spearheading most of Deutsche Bank's and Germany's most important economic initiatives.

Like the Nazis before them, the Americans came to use him, even if they never completely trusted him. In any case, the legal bar to Abs' working was removed in April 1948, although with reservations. The head of OMGUS, General Clay, wrote in a handwritten note to Bennett accompanying the formal denazification notice about his deep misgivings, admitting that disapproval "would be more harmful than this acceptance." In any case, it could be reversed later, but "having made our bed, we must lie in it. I can only suggest careful surveillance."[73]

Time was growing short for the American officials. The American administration was under considerable pressure to get the German economy up and running. Moreover, some administrators realized that they would never prosecute all the Germans about whom they had created dossiers. The Chief Counsel for War Crimes had set a December 1947 deadline to bring individuals to trial. The existing denazification organization was not equipped to handle all the investigations. The sheer lack of manpower prevented all criminals from being brought to justice.[74] In autumn 1947, Abs ended up testifying as a voluntary witness at the Nuremberg Trials.[75]

In large part because British administrators did not share their American colleagues' view of Abs – indeed the British had a great deal of respect for him – he got out of the "American doghouse."[76] By 1948, Abs resumed his post at Deutsche Bank, at least in an informal way. Although very active in the financial affairs of Germany, until 1952 he took no formal responsibility in the successor banks into which Deutsche Bank had been divided. During those years, his professional activities involved government and quasigovernment assignments. Despite the rehabilitation, Abs' first trip to the United States after the war to negotiate new terms for the short-term obligations met with a public outcry.[77]

For the next twenty years, in addition to serving as the *de facto* leader of the bank while it was decentralized and its first spokesman of the management board after the merger in 1957, he not only was a key figure in Germany's financial system, he represented Germany in much of its financial dealings with the United States. He was at the epicenter of all negotiations between the bank and the occupying powers, and at the nerve center of the different regional offices into which Deutsche Bank was divided.

The Inaugural Committee
requests the honor of the presence of
Mr. and Mrs. Herman Abs
to attend and participate in the Inauguration of
Dwight David Eisenhower
as President of the United States of America
and
Richard Milhous Nixon
as Vice President of the United States of America
on Monday the twenty-first of January
one thousand nine hundred and fifty seven
in the City of Washington

Please reply to
The Inaugural Committee
Washington, D.C.

Robert V. Fleming
Chairman, Inaugural Committee

Abs' invitation to Eisenhower's and Nixon's second inauguration.

Well into 1948, conflicts between the Allied administration and German banking experts flared up. In April 1948, Abs was elected president of the Bank deutscher Länder in Frankfurt, the organization that was designed to oversee each of the *Länder*'s central banks for the western zones. The bank had special responsibility for foreign and public credits but was still under the control of the occupying administration (the Allied Bank Commission).[78] After five weeks of difficult negotiation over voting procedures and the powers of the board, Abs and the chairman declined the honor, refusing to take up the position to which they had been elected.[79]

By 1957, although a cloud hung over him in the popular press, Abs seems to have been completely rehabilitated in most banking circles. As early as 1949, he had been feted by the big banks during a New York visit "to take the temperature of the attitudes of New York bankers."[80] Even though the trip in 1949 itself caused a lot of controversy, Chase Manhattan invited him to lunch with both its president and the chairman of the board, as well as Laurance S. Rockefeller and Leroy Wilson, president of AT&T.[81] Others also did not ostracize Abs. In that year, the Council on Foreign Relations, which publishes *Foreign Affairs*, wanted to arrange a dinner in his honor.[82] In 1953, the *Wall Street Journal* wrote that Abs was personally responsible for trimming 50 percent of Germany's huge debt and of his efforts to achieve the London Debt Accord. The journal called him Germany's number one international banker, a man whose experience made him an ideal negotiator for settlement of German prewar liabilities and for encouraging new investment in Germany.[83] Although the relationship was not without problems, by 1955 Chase and the Frankfurt office of the decentralized Deutsche Bank were doing DM 150 million in business with one another. In 1957, Abs and his wife were invited to Eisenhower and Nixon's Second Inaugural Ball.[84] He was corresponding regularly with many of America's top bankers and planned his 1957 trip to the United States with them. They were back to exchanging information, confidences, and congratulations about the great strides made in Germany's economic development. At least one New York bank placed interns for training with Abs.[85] The American Bankers Association and Columbia University invited him to their Monetary Conference at Arden House, an event that would become a regular part of U.S. trips for him.[86]

Nowhere was Abs' contribution perceived to be greater than with his involvement in the administration of Marshall funds in Germany. Germany's and Deutsche Bank's quick recovery from the effects of the war and occupation would have been unthinkable without a large infusion of foreign capital. As early as 1947, American experts recognized that something must be done to avoid a meltdown of the German economy, if only to spare the American taxpayer. Although significant assets existed in the Western Zone, German wealth, which was less than half its 1937 level, had to be increased. The country desperately needed a sound tax system, simplified corporate structures, fewer cartels, and currency reform,[87] all of which could be aided by an infusion of capital. Inspired by two speeches given the year before by America's new Secretary of State George Marshall, the Economic Cooperation Act was passed by Congress in 1948, establishing an aid program that came to bear the General's name. The European Recovery Program, or Marshall Plan, administered by the Organization for European Economic Cooperation (OEEC) and the State Department distributed $12.4 billion in aid, roughly 2 percent of the GNP of recipient countries. Its terms were much more generous and better controlled than the interwar aid packages. With European capital severely diminished and America accounting for nearly half of the world's manufacturing, even these funds were insufficient by themselves to address the economic chaos. Stabilization required a host of other programs and reforms.[88]

Although the Kreditanstalt für Wiederaufbau (Reconstruction Loan Corporation), formed to administer the Marshall funds in Germany, had many "parents," most agreed it was Abs' "child."[89] Appointed by its administrative council as the managing board's spokesman, Abs effectively headed this organization from 1948 to 1952. With no export market, little production, and capital markets, it was charged with distributing the funds where they would do the most good.[90] One of Abs' first decisions was to bring into the new bank a former director of Deutsche Bank's Leipzig branch, Walter Tron. With a capital of DM 1 million, the Reconstruction Loan Corporation opened in January 1949. By 1953, it had channeled DM 3 billion of Marshall Plan funds into Germany.[91] With Abs leading the Reconstruction Loan Corporation, it was not surprising that Deutsche Bank's banks received a disproportionate share of subsidized export credits.[92]

Americans came to appreciate Abs' role in overseeing the Marshall Plan in Germany. For nearly a decade after the end of World War II, international finance for Germany meant aid money from the World Bank and directly from the United States. Deutsche Bank played an integral role in various ways, guiding the financial credits used to rebuild Germany. After the introduction of reforms and the Marshall Plan, within a relatively short period many observers began to see remarkable improvement in German economic and political conditions. In summer 1949, *Newsweek* reported that since the currency reform a year before, Germany had witnessed an epoch-making transformation. The black market for Dollars had virtually dried up, meaning that Germans had accepted their new currency. Despite the British Pound crisis, German production was nearly up to 1936 levels. Nevertheless, the country was still struggling with a low standard of living, high unemployment, and an enormous refugee problem.[93] Moreover, as an important member of the American financial team in Germany pointed out, there was no Western consensus, let alone one that included the Soviets, about what Germany should, could, and would become. Although Germany seemed much tamer in 1949 than it did in 1939, its potential also posed threats to long-standing English, French, and perhaps even American interests.[94] Some Germans and Americans seemed to fear, too, that American ignorance of Germany and general financial matters would ultimately hurt Germany's ability to reenter world markets.[95]

By 1953, Europe was independent of Marshall funds, but they still played a role in debt settlement negotiations and financial aid for countries in other regions. As late as 1978, Abs said of the assistance in a somewhat obligatory fashion, "I hope I have made it clear that the Marshall Plan, beyond its importance for Europe as a whole, imbued the people of the Federal Republic, including twelve million refugees and expellees, with courage and the belief that they could succeed in the reconstruction of the country's economy by hard work." It was a precondition for establishing the iron and coal community in 1950 and therefore, the European Union.[96]

As business picked up in Germany, private organizations became more interested in investment. Abs had a good many dealings with the World Commerce Corporation, a group of companies from the United States, Canada, and England, which included the Atlas Corporation, Ladenburg, Thalmann & Co., Transamerican Corporation, and Hambros Bank and that numbered Edward Stettinius, former American secretary of state, and General William Donovan as members of the board. With the approval of Generals Lucius Clay, head of the occupational forces, and Marshall, the group established representation in Germany through the Deutsche Commerz GmbH. Abs served as the main shareholder in Germany. The group was involved in rebuilding Germany through the import of machinery and materials.[97]

In spite of all these initiatives, as late as 1954 there was a perceived lack of American investment in Europe. Net of reparations, private American investment into the world remained small, and only 10 percent of long-term private investment from the United States went to Europe from 1945 to 1952, compared with 19 percent during the 1920s. Britain got the largest share of U.S. outward flows. Some Europeans were already a little ambivalent about the arrival of U.S. money. Because of Europe's heavy Dollar debt load, Dollar investment had immediate benefits but some cautioned that it might produce long-term problems.[98]

Despite Marshall funds and agreements for handling prewar debt, for two decades after the cessation of hostilities the return of German property seized after America's entry into World War II remained a contentious issue between the two countries. In 1957, there seemed to be some willingness in the United States to release property claims of less than $10,000 as had been the case after World War I, but once again the issue of American damage claims blocked a final accord. The U.S. government was reportedly holding on to $259 million in German assets, $122 million in real estate and securities and the rest in cash, including the General Aniline & Film Corporation shares of IG Farben, which alone were worth $100 million. Ninety-two percent of the claims, however, were in amounts of $10,000 or less, which negotiators were somewhat more hopeful could be quickly released.[99] For many Germans and even some Americans, the U.S. government's position was just "legalized theft," to borrow an expression from a very different context.[100]

As usual in these matters, Abs played a central role. As German Chancellor Adenauer's special envoy in 1955, Abs discussed the problem with representatives of the U.S. administration, even though or perhaps because this time Deutsche Bank had no outstanding claims. For Abs, the matter was clear. Returning the property should be part of the free world's efforts in defense of private property and the reestablishment of international confidence, a view that he shared with none other than the International Chamber of Commerce, the U.S. National Foreign Trade Council, and John Foster Dulles, the American secretary of state under Eisenhower. According to Abs, Nasser's seizing of British, French, and Israeli property was just copying the U.S.'s Trading with the Enemy Act. Ironically, some German citizens who were suffering from expropriation of their property in East Germany by the Communists had to contend at the same time with similar expropriation in the United States.[101] Abs had no trouble putting the return of German property in the context of a struggle for Western Civilization:

> I am happy to be able to wholeheartedly join all those in our western community and in particular quite a number of outstanding Americans of my personal acquaintance who still think that our traditional western principals [sic] are the only means to maintain personal freedom – and who are prepared to fight for them.[102]

In July 1955, Abs was cautiously optimistic. Dulles had told German delegates that the Republicans would sponsor a bill for the return of the small claims.[103] The Republican Senate had already tried but failed to put through a full return bill in 1952 and 1954. Although the bill for partial return of small claims was sponsored by Democrat Olin Johnston and Republican Everett Dirksen, most of the opposition came from Democrats and the Justice Department. Rather than returning the assets to Germans, George Smathers, a Democrat from Florida, proposed using the funds instead for science projects in the United States. Abs was even personally chastised in Democratic Senator Smathers' speech on the subject as a German with many contacts to the lobbyists pursuing the release of the German property. During the Senate debate, the famous American columnist Drew Pearson seemed to sum up the feelings of many Americans.[104] He remarkably wove together anti-German and perhaps a little anti-Semitic rhetoric, tainting Deutsche Bank with both:

> MEANWHILE, A TERRIFIC [bold in the original] German property lobby has thrown its weight behind Johnston. The mastermind of the lobby is Hermann Abs, former managing director [sic] of Adolf Hitler's Deutsche Bank, who came to the United States in 1950 but beat a hasty retreat after Senator Guy Gillette exposed his pro-Nazi past.
>
> As his chief American lobbyist, Abs has hired Maj. Gen. Julius Klein, past commander of the Jewish War Veterans.[105]

Despite generally improving relations between Germany and the United States, sufficient political conflicts connected to the Nazi period meant that Germans had to tread softly, even about domestic German matters, for fear of alienating the vastly more powerful and still-needed Americans. As late as the 1950s, the FBI kept tabs on Abs' social life in the United States, including a cocktail party in which the agents' boss, none other than J. Edgar Hoover, was also in attendance.[106]

During the mid-1950s, there was little doubt that Deutsche Bank managers intended to reunify the bank. Even before the three-year waiting period agreed with the Allies when the terms of the Big Banks Act were negotiated, Deutsche Bank managers circulated memos about how the reunification could

Abs (left) with Congressman John Bell Williams and General Julius Klein in 1957. During the 1950s, the German government and several German firms hired Klein's public relations firm to "sell" German interests to the American public and its government. Klein had served with the American army in Germany, spoke German, knew many of Germany's leaders, had strong connections to the Republican Party – less so to the Democrats – and was one of the founders of the Jewish War Veterans. A former newspaperman, motion picture executive, and soldier, Klein had created his own PR firm in Chicago. His lobbying activities caused him and his clients a good deal of embarrassment in the 1960s.

be accomplished. Either by actually merging the three regional banks or by creating a Deutsche Bank holding company, the managers intended to fuse the activities of the separate banks. Abs proposed an interim solution, combining the three banks into a community of interest (*Interessengemeinschaft*). This included coordinating business and sharing profits, followed by standardization of all three banks' names and introduction of an interlocking directorate. Abs' second step had to wait. With the Paris Treaties in May 1955, Germany once again had full sovereignty, but the Federal Republic was still committed to the terms promised to the Allies in 1952, which led to the creation of the Big Bank Act. The interim solution was implemented; the plans for alternative reunifications of the bank were drafted, awaiting permission from the government. Led by Deutsche Bank, which actually formulated the wording of the proposed legislation and framed the relevant tax exemptions, the big banks lobbied the government long and hard to relieve them of the decentralization requirement. Three months after the Law to Remove Limitations on the Regional Credit Institutions was passed, Deutsche Bank's successor banks signed the amalgamation agreement and Deutsche Bank was reborn, effectively ending the postwar organizational impact of American regulation.[107]

With Abs as head of the new merged institution and Germany economically vibrant and reintegrated in the world, Deutsche Bank was finally in a position to turn a new international page in its history. Its traditional services, placing securities in capital markets, granting general credit, and financing trade were all in great demand. By 1957, seemingly unhampered by the decentralization regulations, Deutsche Bank's and the other big banks' share of banking assets as a percentage of the whole German system was falling, but still substantially higher than they were in the mid-1930s. Deutsche Bank's share of the big three business was nearly 43 percent. From January 1952 to December 1957, the combined assets of the bank (regional banks in 1952) had grown from DM 3.8 billion to DM 8.4 billion. Deposits, investment banking activity, and personnel grew substantially during the same period. In 1957, its share price of 220 percent and dividend of 12 percent of nominal capital were both substantially higher than the average of German companies.[108]

Even while the bank had been decentralized, Deutsche Bank had begun to rebuild its foreign business. Former Deutsche Bank employees now in the regional banks found various devices to work together. In 1950, Deutsche Ueberseeische Bank, its subsidiary for South American, Portuguese, and Spanish business, was reactivated as a foreign bank and relocated to Hamburg, where, from 1959 onward at least, it began doing a vibrant business. In that year too, reopening ties with Istanbul and de Bary of the Netherlands was discussed. Deutsche Bank's foreign trade business was revived through a separate joint venture, the Ausfuhrkredit Aktiengesellschaft, in which Deutsche Bank had a 30 percent interest. As early as 1952, there were rumors that Deutsche Bank intended to reopen a representative office in New York, untrue but not unthinkable.

Deutsche Bank's leadership entered international markets in general and America specifically with a great deal of caution. They had received their training under less than ideal circumstances for international finance. Rocked by forty years of intermittent war, inflation, exchange rate instability, blocked funds, economic collapse, expropriation, and acrimonious political attacks on both sides of the Atlantic and division of both country and firm, Deutsche Bank executives opted for an incremental approach. Although the world seemed by 1957 to have taken a turn for the better, in light of historical circumstances, conservatism probably seemed not just to be the best policy, but the only one.

Section III

Renewal and Reentry: 1957 to 2000

And there is no doubt that, ever since the 1950s, the Americans have been the "best Europeans." In their investment policy, American companies have anticipated the integration of European economies in a Common Market and contributed to this integration earlier than European companies.

Hermann J. Abs, speech to the Manufacturing Chemists Association, Greenbrier, USA, June 12, 1975, HADB, V1/3243.

Whatever their native strengths, big banks have much of their power thrust upon them by events.

The Banker, October 1977.

Introduction

> This is of course an absolute contradiction to our system – while one in America has instituted open-door policy, in German business one actually would prefer, rather than being behind closed doors, double doors. This is just a part of a different mentality in America and Germany.
>
> Ernest Frankl to Gerhard Polfers, February 12, 1957, HADB, ZA6/99.

> "Thank you, Mister Abs, you saved my life."
>
> Chancellor Adenauer to Abs, after being warned that he should praise John Kennedy's choice of wine at a state dinner, reported by Abs in Düsseldorf, October 10, 1972, HADB, V1/3244.

Whereas the previous Section of this book began with a nearly unparalleled catastrophe of world and bank-shattering proportions, this one commences with events far less abrupt, far more foreseeable, and certainly far more welcome. The year 1957 was less dramatic than 1914, but, nevertheless, for Deutsche Bank and perhaps for much of the Western World it represented a turning point. Although East–West tensions remained deep, by then, European confidence seemed to have been restored. By 1957, to a large extent, Europe had overcome the initial deprivations and political recriminations following the war.

It is probably not a complete accident that the articles to remerge Deutsche Bank were signed (March 5, 1957) in the same month as the Treaty of Rome (March 25, 1957) establishing the European Economic Community with Germany as one of the six founding members. With a mixture of trepidation and optimism, both events had been long contemplated and were part of broader efforts to repair economic and political damage, some of which had plagued Europe since 1914. They were part of a series of decisions that heralded a new era in German relations with the world. Just under two years earlier, military occupation of West Germany ended and the Federal Republic was brought into NATO, bringing an end to that country's real and symbolic isolation from the Western community.[1]

The mid-1950s may have been the high-water mark of German-American consensus. Most Germans and other Europeans looked to the United States, within limits, as a model of not only democracy but also good economic management.[2] To be sure, the so-called cultural wars had already begun, but they were fought with special intensity in France and Italy, not in Germany. Many European intellectuals balked even then at American cultural, political, and economic hegemony, but businesses and most people appreciated the stable economic growth. America invested heavily in getting its story told, and American products were still a novelty.[3] The Cold War, Berlin Airlift, and war in Korea had not only reinforced a feeling that the whole Free World was in the same boat – a sentiment felt particularly deeply in the Federal Republic of Germany – they also led to a massive buildup in military expenditures that proved to be an enormous stimulant to the West German economy. Given the alternatives, West Germans were becoming very comfortable with their Deutsche Mark (DM) and even Germany's divided status. However, along with their comfort came a new sense of confidence and a good deal of discomfort with their one-sided dependence on a giant partner whose political and economic reliability seemed to become increasingly questionable.[4] Even though Germany flirted with other attachments, for many reasons Germany's relationship with the United States remained "special." Throughout the period, but particularly during the early stages, as the above quote reported by Abs about saving face for Adenauer is meant to imply, American relations were of the utmost importance to Germany and Deutsche Bank, even concerning apparently trivial matters. With some mixed feelings, West Germans lived with thousands of American troops based on their soil: On the front line of the Cold War, at the fringe of the Iron Curtain, uncomfortably close to their own "living rooms."[5]

This period then witnessed an enormous turnabout in European and American economic relations and attitudes about themselves and each other. In 1957, after two generations of horrors, Europe was reinventing itself, stimulating extraordinary increases in trade among Common Market countries.[6] For many years after the war, the urgency about Europe's resurgence and unity was set against vivid memories of nearly thirty years of barbarity and the threat of communism.[7]

Economic growth encouraged confidence and cooperation. As this Section opens, Germany was in the middle of its "economic miracle" and just beginning to reestablish itself on the world economic stage. In 1958, the DM, a symbol of German economic strength and European importance, became convertible for the first time in nearly three decades. With economic growth starting to slow from its fever pitch in the 1950s, Germans were aware that America offered the largest potential market for German exports.[8] The economic spirit of the times was also good for the United States. Unfortunately though, the low inflation and high economic growth of the 1950s and 1960s soon seemed like an economic Camelot compared with the decade that followed.[9]

By the end of the 1960s, Europe and America started to experience a wave of internal political tension and economic issues, which exacerbated some national frictions. From 1950 to 1970, Europe had become affluent, young, and impatient, factors that contributed to frustration as economic growth slowed. Both the so-called stagflation of the 1970s and the diminished capacity to satisfy high expectations contributed to a sense of malaise. In fact, growth in both Germany and the United States still topped 3 percent per year, but new opportunities did not keep pace with demands nor quell a heightened sense of alienation in Europe from the large, rich, and powerful cousin across the Atlantic.

Even in the 1970s, with Germany still catching up at a fast pace, the distance between it and the dominant economic power was enormous.[10] Despite Germany's high savings rate – albeit from a very low starting point – the magnitude of the difference in their capital markets was even greater.[11] In 1957, too, West Germany passed a key piece of legislation that would separate the two countries' capital markets and social systems. In contrast to the United States's creation of private savings for retirement, which pulled vast sums into equity and bond markets,[12] West Germany's Social Security Reform Act confirmed the state's role as the primary provider of retirement protection and other social services, which effectively removed the immediate incentives for giant private pension and other funds.[13]

The reunification of the bank brought with it – but not at once – many obvious organizational changes and a greater capacity to reenter world markets. Its centralization process was extensive, but slow. Although nominally incorporated in Frankfurt, for many years Deutsche Bank maintained three regional head offices. Some members of the management board remained based outside of Frankfurt. Board meetings took place in the regional headquarters and in other cities. Although Deutsche Bank tried to improve its market proximity and streamline its structure both in Germany and in the rest of the world to keep pace with market developments,[14] during the post-merger decades its efforts sometimes appeared tentative and inconsistent, especially in the United States. The pace of its international "reentry" reflected more than just generally conservative banking; it was caution honed by catastrophes.

The second half of the twentieth century witnessed an extraordinary array of political, financial, and technological changes, to which Deutsche Bank had to adapt and that would form the backdrop to its efforts to rebuild its American business. The strategic issues were daunting and changing rapidly. As this Section opens, the European Union was a distant dream, most individuals did not use credit cards – few had checkbooks and none had ever seen a cash machine – pension funds, mutual funds, and Eurodeposits were all in their infancy, and international payments among companies – even within the same group – were based on trade documents. There were no commercial jet flights between Europe and the United States and certainly no internet service.[15] Two very different and competing economic systems, led by two superpowers armed with weapons of mass destruction, vied for adherents all over the world by peaceful and, at times, military means. The financial regulation and theory that now serve as the legal and intellectual context for managing transactions were just beginning to take shape. Shareholders were becoming more mobile, and new technologies allowed for cross-border management in ways that would have startled Adams and Gwinner.

By the end of the period covered by this Section, relations among nations had been transformed. On the one hand, freed from East–West conflicts, nations pursued their own interests more vigorously. On the other, businesspeople, armed with new technologies and competitive regulation – in contrast to most politicians and their constituencies – thought less in terms of national commerce than worldwide business opportunities. By the year 2000, at Deutsche Bank, talking about American or German business as separate activities of the bank – as distinct from its global businesses such as equity trading, asset management, investment banking, or foreign exchange trading – would seem odd. In some sense, and even though many nations are represented in its offices, business lost much of its ethnic quality.

Deutsche Bank's business relationship with the United States was set against several different foreign exchange regimes. In 1957, most foreign exchange dealings were still controlled by governments at "fixed rates." The Bretton Woods System, the free world's attempt after World War II to avoid the financial problems of the interwar period, promoted free trade, U.S. Dollar convertibility into gold at a rate of $35 an ounce, and a commitment of other countries to hold their currencies at fixed rates of conversion to the Dollar, eventually extending that commitment to complete convertibility. Buttressed by new institutions such as the International Monetary Fund to support the efforts of countries to maintain foreign exchange rate stability, and a consensus among nations about foreign exchange rates and about the need to fight communism with economic as well as other means, the system scored many successes.[16]

Although some of the weakness of the system appeared relatively early on, it took decades for it to collapse. The United States, as the only advanced nation whose financial and production resources remained intact after World War II, had to run a perennial balance-of-payment deficit to allow other countries to build their reserves.[17] The United States accepted its role as the market for exported goods, and many former enemies and long time friends relished special access to this veritable temple of prosperity. By the late 1960s, U.S. resolve weakened. Fluctuating American attitudes and policies toward the value of the Dollar baffled and perturbed German bankers, and had an enormous impact on the nature and profitability of Deutsche Bank's business connected with the states. As in the pre-1914 period of this story, Deutsche Bank made money and endured risk by virtue of American ambivalence about stable foreign exchange rates. But with cross-border investment increasing rapidly and without the safeguards of the pre-1914 period, already during the 1960s Abs, for one, began to be concerned about the strength of international capital markets in light of the demands being made on them.[18] By 1970, countries were poised to "privatize" foreign exchange risk. A little over two decades after it came into existence, Bretton Woods' institutions seemed to lack sufficient authority, acting alone or in concert with others, to insure free movements of inputs while providing macroeconomic stability.[19]

Currency fluctuations and other economic risks helped shape fund-raising and investment patterns, contributing to political conflicts. Capital flows were still minuscule compared to trade but mounting rapidly.[20] In the decade before the collapse of Bretton Woods' foreign exchange regime, foreign direct investment nearly doubled in the United States, for example, the amount from Germany alone quintupled.[21] The investment flows not only significantly shifted the demand for foreign currency, in the short run at least destabilizing the system, they also shifted corporate demands for banking services. Some financial players had already devised many ways to escape national controls for short-term placements, whereas other investors were turning in droves to foreign direct investment, which was stable but which could also ignite animosity. Even Abs openly wondered whether American companies operating in Europe would really integrate themselves by adapting to national and European laws and customs. In 1969, he was even talking about European financial reforms, such as reducing taxes, unifying capital markets, and creating truly "European-wide" companies, *as the best defense* against the United States. The upsurge of government borrowing, especially in the United States, was squeezing out private companies and putting pressure on interest rates. Abs feared that shortages of capital would aggravate national passions.

As this Section begins, too, there was a great deal of continuity between interwar and post-World War II banking. Deutsche Bank's business with the United States was still built on the skills and structures it had in place before the war. In 1957, Deutsche Bank's overall business was still mostly in domestic lending, which sometimes benefited from the support of U.S. government-channeled funds, and international trade financing for its German clients. However, as firms invested in foreign facilities, more and more trade in goods and services was becoming intercompany, lessening companies' dependence on international banking facilities.[22]

Many profitable services became routine transactions with low profit margins but high volumes. As the quantity of banking transactions grew into a volume business with a lot of repetitive transactions, Deutsche Bank had to improve its transactions technology. Not only were capital markets growing to astronomical sizes, the number of people able to take advantage of various sorts of bank accounts increased exponentially. The bank's future became dependent on managing large amounts of information efficiently with little cost in a way that it never had before. Once this investment in hardware and skills had been made, planning and international expansion became even more crucial.[23] Moreover, the turbulence in capital markets and even the political frictions between the United States and Germany created an appetite for sophisticated methods to manage risk that required investment in new talent and systems.

Greater importance had to be given to internal business generation and cross-selling. With fixed costs rising in a way hardly experienced before, service sectors, like nearly every other economic sector, had to generate more business quickly to maintain profits. The bank redrew responsibilities around customer groups – such as automotive and pharmaceutical – or types of business – such as corporate finance, private banking, and foreign exchange trading – rather than domestic versus international.[24] More weight had to be placed on international diversification to recoup high fixed costs. Indeed, this period witnessed the beginnings in some sectors of an evaporation of the distinction between domestic and international. In some sense, despite or because of political frictions, the story of Deutsche Bank during this period is the story of the denationalization of finance.

The organization of the material and the nature of the sources themselves illustrate some of the changes. Whereas in the preceding Sections the changes in capital markets focused on national regulation, here international regulation and institutions play a much greater role. Gone are chapters built around specific lending or borrowing transactions. A myriad of ongoing business deals that defy individual description make up a greater part of the bank's activities and must be discussed in aggregate. Even if they could be described individually, as discussed in the Preface, I do not have access to many nonpublic primary sources. Much more space must be devoted to Deutsche Bank's foreign direct investment in the United States rather than the bank's relationships with agents and correspondent institutions. Above all, many of the events and people covered by this Section are part of a living history, a work in progress, a fact that is underscored by the contributions to this text of many of those who were actively involved in the story.

15

Divisive Issues and the Making of a New Financial Landscape

Definition of an American: "A man drinking Brazilian coffee from an English cup, while sitting on Danish furniture, after coming home in a German car, from an Italian movie, who picks up his Japanese ballpoint and writes to his Congressman demanding that something be done about all the gold that's leaving the country."

Somewhat dated joke sent to Bundesbank President Blessing from Heinrich Freiherr von Berenberg-Gossler, with the comment that it came from a British newspaper and could be "professionally" interesting for Blessing, March 8, 1962, HABBk, B330/235.

The flexible exchange rates introduced in 1973 have not fulfilled the high-flying expectations of their supporters with regard to a balancing effect on the flow of international payments.

Hermann J. Abs, Speech to the Manufacturing Chemists Association, Greenbrier, USA, June 12, 1975, HADB, V1/3243.

Deutsche Bank and Shifting German-American Relations

The economic and political confrontations between Germany and the United States are not only important to this story because they form the context of Deutsche Bank's business dealings with the United States, but also because the bank's leaders, especially Abs, were at the vortex of the debates. Some of the discussions will have an all-too-familiar ring for twenty-first-century readers. Some harkened back to interwar difficulties; whereas others seem to be omnipresent conundrums of a world struggling with seemingly ever increasing degrees of national interdependencies – globalization as it is commonly called. Many of the issues – and their resolution – that will be discussed here established the fundamental contours of our current international banking system.

Apart from some radical intellectuals in the 1960s, criticizing America was not easy for many Germans. Most who were adults during either the Nazi or postwar periods labored with a sense of guilt about their country's recent history, and were deeply appreciative of American influence to restore democracy and a vibrant economy. Eager to break with their turbulent past, German businessmen carefully avoided confronting their role in the National Socialist regime and embraced many symbols of change.[1] Abs, for one, was particularly thankful for America's role after World War II in bringing prosperity back to Germany and for making European integration possible.[2] Germany had indeed prospered. From 1949 to 1955, industrial production grew from 89 percent to

198 percent of its 1936 level. Employment more than quadrupled. From 1949 to 1955, German central bank holdings grew from next to nothing to $4.3 billion. With nearly 70 percent of Germany's productive capacity destroyed, 2.3 million apartments destroyed, and 12 million refugees arriving from the East, America's demonstration of faith in German reconstruction and its $3.2 billion in aid gave Germans confidence and helped lay the foundation for the German recovery. Abs even gave America credit for the "moral and material" support necessary to establish a market economy and a common market in Europe.[3]

But there were dark clouds on the horizon, even in 1957. By then, Germans were beginning to feel cheated over the loss of their property seized in the United States after World War II was declared. Even before 1950, the debate began, and, as in the 1920s, dragged on for well over a decade. It entailed various government and private participants, involving Germans and Deutsche Bank in American politics with unpleasant consequences. For a while, expectations for a favorable settlement for the Germans ran high, only to be dashed once again on the rocks of American political intrigues, at times with such seeming callousness that it threatened even to topple fundamental pillars of German-American cooperation.[4] Germans found America's final decision to return virtually nothing of their property an abuse of power and an attack on liberal economic principles. Understanding the threat the issue posed to foreign investment, Abs called for a Magna Carta among countries for the protection of private property, which for him clearly included German assets taken by the U.S. government when America entered World War II.[5] The whole question and long-standing rancor had an extensive impact on Deutsche Bank's decisions about how and when to do business in the United States for much of the rest of the century.

With prosperity, competition for capital and other resources as well as market share heated up. Each country wanted to preserve financial and trading privileges won after the war to rebuild economies. Workers of the world felt that they had made sufficient sacrifices for the general economy during and after the war, setting the stage for wage demands and the possibility of wage-related inflation and European social democracy. No one seemed to have an answer for simultaneously assuring foreign exchange convertibility and massive cross-border capital flows, while maintaining interest rate and foreign exchange rate stability. At the very least, whether one talked about the European or global stage, greater coordination seemed to call for the loss of national sovereignty, a prospect for which peoples and politicians seemed ill-prepared. Even in the narrow confines of the six original members of the Common Market, let alone the entire world, old national priorities were hard to shed.[6]

Cracks in European confidence in American economic and political leadership, even among conservatives, began to appear. Within the space of thirty years, world concerns seemed to shift from the fear of being overwhelmed by the American economic and political juggernaut to fears of its imminent demise, and then back again to the juggernaut. European faith in America was still strong, but the fear of American cultural influences started to broaden beyond "lefty intellectuals," with whom in the 1950s it was still mostly associated.[7]

Heinrich von Berenberg-Gossler, a Hamburg banker, for example, reported after a trip to the United States in 1964 that prosperity was still great in the United States, but the country was full of excess: Puritanism; crime; racial mixing and racism; and unrestrained borrowing. "America will always remain the country of unlimited possibilities, but probably also unlimited impossibilities."[8]

In contrast to property rights and cultural matters, for example, the formation of a tighter "European Community" did not seem to be an issue between the United States and Germany, at least during the early years covered by this Section. Abs, for one, wanted a Europe that posed no threat to German-American relations. He was a whole-hearted supporter of the expansion of Europe, but not at the expense of trade and other relations with the rest of the world. For him, the Treaty of Rome provided the basis for stimulating trade, cross-border capital flows, and especially monetary stability, which he stressed was a precondition for economic growth and financial integration. The Treaty should not lay the foundation of an economic and political block, whose distrust for other regions would stand in the way of closer cooperation. As early as 1959, Abs feared that protectionist tendencies in Europe would threaten relations with the rest of the world and tighter political union.[9]

By the late 1960s, his tone had changed considerably. Abs came to believe that a lack of financial discipline, and trade and investment barriers emanating from the United States had become a terrible impediment to commercial integration. U.S. laws, such as the 1962 Trade Expansion Act with its antidumping clauses and the 1933 Buy American Act – decades old but still on the books – which stipulated that public orders should give preference to American companies, and heavy governmental-military research and development all threatened to make foreign trade more costly and posed much more of a threat to free trade than regional associations. American policies hampered greater exchange of research and development and the harmonization of industrial policies. Even German investment in the United States was threatened by the use of antitrust regulation to protect American companies against competition.[10] By 1970, Abs worried that many groups were lining up to revive protectionism. But perhaps predictably, and certainly in line with the dangers he himself foresaw, Germany's own efforts to promote foreign trade and finance, in contrast, were to Abs merely enlightened pursuit of national interest.[11]

Many Americans, too, began to resent Europe's quicker pace of economic growth as well as the perceived favorable trading and investment terms granted to Europe as part of America's concessions to rebuild the world economy after the war. On several occasions, Abs felt obliged to defend German economic policies against American attacks.[12]

During the 1960s, a series of many other intertwined macroeconomic and political difficulties weighed on German and American relations and affected Deutsche Bank's relationship to the United States. Under pressure to stimulate exports, Americans promoted several measures that Europeans found threatening.[13] Foreign exchange management, however, dominated economic relations between the two countries for several decades. Although some economic historians believe that America's financial and other difficulties have been exaggerated as causes of the problem, in the eyes of many European bankers of the period, America's "sloppy" fiscal management was becoming an ever-increasing issue.[14] The breakdown of fixed and stable rates had far-reaching effects.[15] American importers were reluctant to do business in anything but Dollars. With few opportunities for hedging and for support from industrial groups that could help manage currency risk, some Germans, understandably, were nervous about assuming Dollar risk and the headaches currency management entailed.[16]

Between 1958 and 1967, the Bundesbank became increasingly concerned about pressures on the Dollar, but there seemed to be no easy solution.[17] It was at various times actively buying Dollars, calling for other central banks to do the same, and, along with other central banks, reaffirming its commitment to a $35 price for an ounce of gold and to convertibility. There were many skeptics.[18] By the late '60s, despite government steps to control prices and movements, the value of Sterling had already cracked under the pressure. Like today, capital and foreign exchange markets began exhibiting a power and willfulness that frustrated political actors. As a leading economic historian put it:

> The array of devices to which the Kennedy and Johnson administration resorted became positively embarrassing. They acknowledged the severity of the dollar problem while displaying a willingness to address only the symptoms, not the causes. Dealing with the causes required reforming the international system in a way that diminished the dollar's reserve-currency role, something the United States was still unwilling to contemplate.[19]

Weakness of the Dollar in the 1960s may have been a classic example of "overshoot" in political and economic matters. As countries tried to build their reserves in preparation for a restoration of convertibility, all welcomed the outflow of Dollars and many of the goals were achieved or well on their way to being achieved. Most economists recognized, though, that an essential success factor in the transition was keeping the size of world financial liquidity small.[20] In other words, if capital markets were large and funds mobile, stability would be unenforceable. Both the desired growth in trade and international investment surpassed what governments could or wanted to manage. As two economic historians recently wrote, "Bretton Woods proved untenable in the end because its rules could not reconcile independent national policy goals, pegged exchange rates, and even the limited degree of capital mobility implied by an open world trading system."[21]

Convertibility not only stimulated international capital flows but also brought a host of new challenges. Almost all major currencies suffered a threat to their stability within a few years. For most of the next few decades, American officials were more prone to live with the instability rather than maintain the necessary discipline, a tradeoff that their German colleagues found irresponsible. The system depended on undisputed American leadership and reliability as the "Banker of Last Resort."[22] By the end of the 1960s, the loss of confidence coupled with an enormous increase of "uncontrolled" cross-border monetary transfers had created a system beyond the competence of central banks, even when they worked together with international institutions.[23]

Business involving the United States came in many forms. The Deutsche Bank's Lübeck branch used a Volkswagen van as a mobile office to help American sailors and marines change Dollars into Marks in May 1962.

Although European bankers – including Abs – and government leaders, even before the war in Vietnam heated up, tended to lay the blame on U.S. government deficits, which overstimulated the American economy, this was not the whole story.[24] Europe, too, faced a dilemma. It wanted U.S. investment, which contributed greatly to the outpouring of Dollars, yet it wanted its currencies cheap in comparison to the Dollar to facilitate trade. By 1965, Deutsche Bank was publicly expressing its concern about the U.S. balance-of-payments deficit.[25] In 1967, America's shaky finances occupied one full page of Deutsche Bank's annual report.[26]

By 1973, the America-centered foreign exchange system had come apart. Politics and economics combined in the early '70s to end the foreign exchange provisions of Bretton Woods, leaving the freewheeling market-dominated system we have today. Speculative investors – using short-term, highly liquid funds (hot money) – started to bet that European currencies would have to be revalued against the Dollar, increasing the returns of those who had sold Dollars and invested in Deutsche Mark or French Franc assets, further aggravating the problem.[27] Although no one knew what any new system would look like or indeed for sure whether the gold-Dollar exchange system was effectively dead, the symptoms pointed toward a terminal illness.[28] Currency turbulences would play a major role in central and commercial bank planning and discussion for much of the next 20 years, but it was hard for bankers to envision to what extent "privatization" of foreign exchange risk would affect their businesses. No one had seen anything like what was to follow. Not only did the collapse of the Bretton Woods' foreign exchange system herald a new period – lasting to the present – it witnessed a huge upsurge in transactions and demands to hedge, which in turn contributed to reforming business structures and products.

For the next half decade, one of bankers' greatest concerns was stabilizing what seemed to be a near free fall of the Dollar.[29] With much of the world suffering from stagflation in the late 1970s, German officials continued to be aghast by American monetary indiscipline.[30] As the Carter administration came to an end, the Dollar had lost nearly half of its July 1971 value.[31]

Free floating exchange rates did not help relations between the countries. Not only were nominal rates fluctuating wildly, so too were real rates as measured by Purchasing Power Parity, making foreign demand for goods hard to judge, exacerbating the business difficulties of trading nations such as Germany. With the Dollar still the currency of record for many kinds of transactions, its fluctuations were acutely felt. From 1980 to 1985, the Dollar rose 150 percent to about its 1971 level, which prompted calls for a controlled decline.[32]

Deutsche Mark per Dollar rate, 1970 to 2000

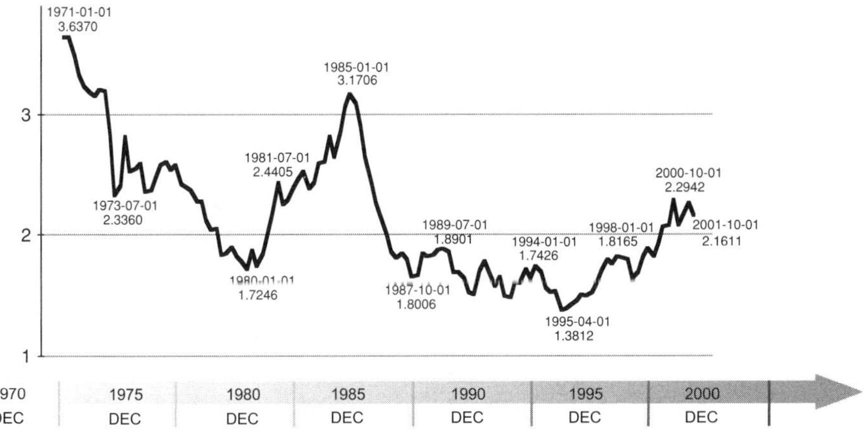

Figure source: Federal Reserve Bank of St. Louis, Economic Research, EXGEUS, Germany/U.S. Foreign Exchange Rate (discontinued series). Between 1949 and 1969, the DM moved three times against the Dollar. In 1949, it was devalued by 21 percent. In 1961, it was revalued by 5 percent, an amount considered by many to be too low, and then again in 1969, after a good deal of discussion and coordination with its trading partners, by 9 percent. For an excellent description of the foreign exchange and other economic issues within Europe and between Europe and the United States see Barry Eichengreen, *The European Economy Since 1945: Coordinated Capitalism and Beyond* (Princeton: Princeton University Press, 2007), which was published after the bulk of the research for this book was completed.

For the next ten years, the Dollar weakened and then stabilized, only to make a vigorous comeback toward the end of the millennium, bolstered by strong capital markets.

The U.S. indiscipline led many Europeans to look for an alternative to the Dollar as a reserve currency. As Europeans lost their faith in the Dollar as the bulwark of the foreign exchange system, they became increasingly drawn to the concept of composite currencies, and eventually, to the Euro. In 1969, at the Hague, representatives of the European Economic Community (EEC) agreed to pursue a monetary union beginning in January 1971. Foreseen as a long and difficult process, the creation of a common European currency was to progress in several steps and suffered many setbacks. It finally came into existence thirty years later with a much longer list of countries than originally envisioned.[33] Abs, not an early supporter of the view that a monetary union could precede complete economic and political integration, cautioned that sovereign national rights would have to be further curbed for the plan to work.[34]

Through the 1970s, as markets became more chaotic, less subject to national control, and as American hegemony seemed to be breaking down, Abs pleaded for more cooperative international economic policymaking. Like many business people of his generation, he seemed to yearn for a simpler time, when "rational control" of markets could be exercised by wise international bankers, a sort of club of enlightened, liberal economists, who knew how to balance stability and freedom. Economics had become too important for politics to be left to national policymakers. America and Europe had to work as partners, in the framework of transatlantic cooperation, which would be reinforced, not threatened by a stronger EEC.[35]

Despite political frictions and market volatility, Abs never seemed to lose his faith in the liberalization of commerce. Not greatly concerned about Third World debt, Abs focused more on the potential for greater trade by improving macroeconomic conditions coupled with allowing emerging countries to adopt limited special measures to encourage national industry and private investment. Although he praised the steps taken to encourage free trade by Western countries, Abs stressed the sloppy macroeconomic environment of trade and, by implication, America's role in that mismanagement, all the more striking because his views were expressed at a Marshall Research Foundation function. His main criticism was directed toward the lack of monetary stability in the world and its effect on trade. Although the floating system was for Abs far from a perfect monetary system, a return to fixed rates for the foreseeable future would be impossible as it required governments to pursue a monetary system and domestic stabilization policy that would reduce international inflation differentials.[36] They simply lacked the discipline.

Multinational Institutions and Instruments

The collapse of the fixed rate system was tied to a series of intertwined changes in investment and regulatory patterns that have configured our present financial system and contributed to Deutsche Bank's restructuring of its international and American business in particular. The increase in FDI, for example, was both a cause and a consequence of exchange rate volatility. The restoration of Deutsche Bank's business with America and changes in its entire portfolio of products must be seen also against the background of American assaults on the bastions of European banking. Although from many quarters there were complaints, it cannot be said that the American influence was all bad. The American banks added new techniques and new energy to the European banking sector. The wave of American banks and money helped internationalize banking in new ways. Whereas in the third quarter of the twentieth century cross-border finance was practiced in a "relatively traditional" manner with seekers of foreign capital listing on foreign markets, by the end of 1970, international finance had to a large extent freed itself from the guiding hand of any national regulatory authority. Although Deutsche Bank managers had mixed feelings about these capital market developments, from 1963 to 1977, Deutsche Bank could hardly avoid helping to lead the assault.[37]

International banking became increasingly offshore and multinational. In 1960, for example, only nine U.S. banks had offices overseas, including among them 139 branches. By 1970, the numbers had grown to eighty banks with 540 branches. Twelve years later, almost every large and medium-sized U.S. bank had foreign operations. Nine hundred U.S. branches and 758 overseas subsidiaries held $471 billion in assets. The banks of many other nations followed similar trends.[38] Driven by a resurgence of trade, the liberalization of financial markets – sometimes a mixture of new national controls coupled with blatant opportunities to escape them – as well as the general ability to profit from economies of scale and scope led banks to open up foreign operations in their home-country currency (offshore banking) and foreign operations offering services in local currency (multinational banking).[39]

Not only was the American invasion of the banking sector in the 1950s rather novel, it had an odd "David and Goliath" quality. American banks dwarfed their European adversaries. In 1953, Bank of America, the largest bank in the United States as measured by assets, was over five times the size of either of its largest continental rivals, Crédit Lyonnais and Deutsche Bank. As late as 1960, it still outvalued either of those banks by a factor of five. Only some of the British banks matched the sheer size of the American giants.[40] The Americans had a host of other strengths: the world reserve currency; a strong, large domestic economy; and a great many industrial clients investing internationally.

Curiously though, what appeared to Europeans as an American juggernaut resembled more a flock of scared geese. U.S. banking executives, eager to profit from their competitive advantages, found themselves blocked by American regulation almost everywhere they looked, except off shore. In the 1950s and '60s, American banking regulations had evolved so as to ban commercial banks from doing insurance, investment banking, stockbroking, offering interest above a legally determined limit, retail banking outside of their state of incorporation, as well as other restrictions that did not, for all practical purposes, exist in Europe. As Richard Sylla cogently put it:

> History has its ironies. US history books say that Europeans migrated to America in the seventeenth century and later to pursue economic opportunity in the New World and

to escape from oppression at home.... It appears that US banks migrated to Europe in the 1960s and 1970s for exactly the same reasons.[41]

Although one of the overriding macro factors of the last Section was the ever-growing influence of American economic, political, and regulatory hegemony over Germany and Deutsche Bank, this period was characterized in many ways by a "de-Americanization" of capital markets. In the face of new forms of banking and foreign direct investment, American political leaders and regulators – as well as those from other countries – substantially lost control not only of their own currencies but of other macroeconomic levers.

Despite the imposition of investment controls in 1968, U.S. investment abroad accelerated.[42] By the mid-1970s, some bankers recognized that the magnitude of foreign investment and foreign exchange volatility would recast financial services, but evaluating how and by how much was not easy. Though the world had known several different globalization paradigms, capital markets clearly seemed to be "sailing into uncharted waters," complicating the decisions of financial managers.

Faith in the value of foreign investment, moreover, was severely tested in business circles and in the general public on both sides of the Atlantic by increases in foreign investments involving a controlling interest of host-country assets (FDI). Although in 1963 overall European investment in the United States was higher than America's in Europe, European funds came mostly in the form of portfolio investment, without management control.[43] This would soon change. Nixon's removing the United States from the gold standard and the massive devaluation of the Dollar in 1973 helped the United States' balance-of-payments picture, but opened the floodgates for foreign investors anxious to take advantage of the lower Dollar.[44] Virtually all countries experienced waves of foreign investment and trade paranoia depending on absolute or relative national economic results. Much like Germans after World War I, many Americans felt as if treasured assets were passing in the hands of foreigners with dangerous consequences. Foreign investment in the United States appeared threatening even if it solved some problems.[45] To be sure, Germany was not the chief object of U.S. fears, but complaints about each other's trade policies persisted for decades, generally coinciding with new reports of unemployment, cross-border purchases of companies, and with the seemingly unending and still growing U.S. trade deficit.[46]

Some of the difficulties regarding foreign direct investment arose from differences in attitudes about the proper organization of capitalism and markets. A lot of attention was focused on the financial sector. In both Germany and the United States, regulators struggled with how to control the greater influx of cross-border banking. Old sore points came to the fore. America, for example, remained unconvinced that some of the German ways of managing a complex economy, such as the use of cartels and universal banking, did not retard economic growth, pose political dangers or that, conversely, they gave German firms an unfair advantage. The critics of the German banking system included Robert Roosa, then undersecretary of the U.S. Treasury, who claimed that

New York never seemed far from the minds of Deutsche Bank managers and customers, even at the bank's Hanover branch office in the early 1960s.

German banking was a tight monopoly. In an exchange of letters with Abs, Roosa maintained that a small number of German banks control German capital markets keeping interest rates artificially high, to which Abs retorted that large German banks had less of a share of the banking system in Germany than in other industrial countries.[47] Abs also felt obliged to defend universal banking in the international financial press. Citing criticism in Britain and the United States, he claimed that Germany's system of allowing financial institutions to take deposits, make loans, and issue and hold corporate securities, of which Deutsche Bank was the most notable example, could not account for Germany's high financial costs. According to Abs, the rates were a reflection of capital shortages and the risk of high inflation brought on by Germany's high growth rates.[48]

The Bundesbank evidenced concern about the increasing investment of American banks outside of the United States, especially in Germany. The number of European branches of American banks grew from 295 at the end of 1967 to 335 at the end of 1968. During the four previous years – led by First National City Bank (with 163 European operations), Bank of America (72), and Chase Manhattan Bank (49) – American banks had added 181 operations. Although Germany was not the preferred destination for American banking investment, American banking institutions there grew from three in 1960 to forty-seven at the peak in 1980.[49] Even more striking was the growth in assets, which had climbed in one year from $16 billion to $22 billion. With this network of branches, the banks expected a great profit based on obtaining local deposits and lending in foreign markets, mostly to American companies, which were anxious to finance locally instead of with funds drawn from the United States. Using London as a jumping-off point, these American branches were competing aggressively with high rates for depositors, many of whom were also eager to get better rates than were allowed in the United States.[50] For the first time, American banks were attacking Europeans *en masse* on their home turf. The American banks, for example, disrupted cozy national markets with heightened competition and innovations, such as sophisticated cash management and derivative instruments.[51] It is easy to understand why the onslaught was not welcome.

The increase in American banking investment abroad and general foreign direct investment in the United States also served as a catalyst for foreign banking investment in America. Although non-American banks lost some advantages in the United States, their position in the United States improved in the 1970s. American banks' demands for open foreign markets produced calls for reciprocity by foreign banks entering the United States and led to the relaxation of restrictions on branches of foreign banks in New York, for example. Customers' needs encouraged foreign banks to look for ways to offer a broad range of services outside of their home countries, which required changing their strategies and structures. From 1973 to 1992, the share of total U.S. business loans granted by foreign agencies and branches grew from 3 percent to 18 percent. With subsidiaries included, the figures jump from 4 percent to 25 percent of total U.S. business loans. By 1980, New York alone had 133 agencies and branches of foreign banks. Branches were integral parts of their parent's operations – not even separate legal entities. Dependent on the creditworthiness of their home institution, they could engage in virtually all banking activities except retail services and were under the primary regulatory supervision of their home country.[52]

As early as the mid-70s, bank regulators recognized the need for international cooperation, but this was not simple to devise and implement. After two bank failures in 1974 (Herstatt and Franklin National Bank), the heads of the G-10 central banks formed the Basel Committee to consider regulatory issues related to international banking in member countries. Its first decision delegated to home countries oversight for their own banks and to host countries regulation for foreign subsidiaries operating in their countries. But because offshore banking centers (banks in nonmember countries such as the Cayman Islands) were minor at the time, they were not party to the agreement, which left a huge loophole for banks to drive through. Banks based in large countries were now in competition for financial services with those from small, stable countries. By 1983, the original agreement was revised to give home and host countries joint responsibility for overseeing the solvency of foreign banks, but the emphasis was on oversight. A host of issues, such as lender of last resort questions relating to stability, were left out.[53]

The committee began issuing capital asset standards only in 1988 and to-risk-asset ratios for international banks in 1993. By then, it recognized that foreign exchange, debt, and equity trading had different kinds of risk. A complex system of valuing the risk of various forms of assets was instituted, which tended to move banks away from using their own capital for financing and away from applying personalized or relational methods of evaluation. Curiously, derivative instruments ostensibly taken on to hedge positions were excluded. By 1993, the Group of Thirty, a private association of industrialized countries, recommended self-regulation as long as bank management adhered to certain guidelines, which included the active involvement of senior management in overseeing derivatives trading. Active involvement was considered the only workable means of controlling this volatile, opaque, and sometimes illiquid portion of capital markets.[54]

The spurt in multinational banking and apparent lack of international oversight created a regulatory nightmare for domestic banking authorities. The vagueness of the term "primary regulatory supervision" troubled conservative bankers. Well into the 1970s, the Bundesbank, for example, continued to discuss the sufficiency of foreign-bank capital reserves in Germany. The central bank debated how to judge the foreign-bank branches' capital adequacy in light of their customers, sectors with which they worked, and the relationships with large and regional banks.[55]

In April 1973, the Bundesbank created a special committee to oversee the capital requirements for foreign banks in Germany.[56] Some at the central bank doubted whether a general analysis of and policy for foreign banks could be developed. Some foreign banks, even a few with long histories in Germany, required additional capital. Much depended on the parent banks' situations and the type of business attempted by the foreign operation. Currency speculation, deemed to be particularly risky, posed special problems. Widespread agreement existed for creating norms that would put the foreign banks on an "equal footing" with German banks.[57] Some felt that foreign banks, even those from the European Community, should just get rid of some of their large loans and adjust their capital requirements in accordance with the type of business the foreign operations undertook.[58]

It was not just the influx of foreign banks, but also the increase in domestic banks' opening operations outside of their jurisdiction, especially in tax havens, that worried the regulators. In August 1972, the Bundesbank warned that in the past ten years German banks had opened foreign operations to an extraordinary extent to support German exports, German firms manufacturing in foreign countries, and to be represented in Euromarket centers, which would help them react faster to the needs of investors. Unstated – but clear – was the huge increase of activity in tax havens and locations where reporting requirements could be described as more "lax." In the early 1970s, Luxembourg became a prime destination. In one twelve-month period, the assets of German banks in Luxembourg jumped from DM 2 billion to DM 6 billion. It seemed clear that this development was at least in part a reflection of bank and customer desires to escape home or host-country oversight. At least thirteen foreign subsidiaries of German banks were in operation in 1972, ten in Luxembourg alone. Deutsche Bank maintained two: one in Luxembourg, one in the United States. EAB, as a partially owned affiliate, was not listed (see next Chapter). While the foreign subsidiaries were not directly under the control of the Bundesbank, the

Bundesbank instituted a policy of regular reports from German banks about their foreign subsidiaries.[59] The banks were not happy,[60] but the Bundesbank seemed unimpressed by their pleas.[61]

American officials were confronted with similar challenges and debates. Different concepts of how the economy and the banking sector should be organized impinged on relations between the two nations and affected Deutsche Bank's business. In entering the United States, Deutsche Bank had to dance around changing federal and state multileveled regulations designed to limit a commercial bank's ability to hold shares of companies, underwrite securities, and operate in more than one state. At times, the regulations and maintaining a U.S. business threatened aspects of its operations in Germany.[62] In the mid-1970s, Abs' successor felt obliged once again to defend the whole German banking system in the U.S. press. Evidently, many in America considered Deutsche Bank's stellar performance as *prima facie* evidence of German big banks' near monopoly position in their own market and the unfair and risky breadth of their business, which included sizeable investments in and substantial control of many of Germany's largest companies. Both the complaints and the defense had a familiar ring.[63] The ability of German banks, for example, to hold shares of commercial companies particularly troubled American legislators. Moreover, regulators questioned whether American bank account insurance protection should be extended to foreign banks, whose parents the U.S. authorities could not regulate.[64]

Something New, Something Old in Financial Offerings

Nowhere was the challenge to national control more striking than in the world of financial products. Offshore banking or the Eurocurrency market emerged in London as a major force in finance in the late 1950s. Though not completely new – between the wars international banks based in London held Dollar deposits – the Euromarket (called Euro for its first location not because of Europe's new currency) owed its spectacular growth to a complicated, and somewhat contradictory, combination of political risk and economic liberation. With the shift in the denomination of foreign trade transaction from Pounds to Dollars after World War II, foreign banks, especially those in London – still an important world financial center – needed Dollar deposits to support their Dollar lending. Wary of putting money in the United States where it could be easily frozen, many investors, particularly, at first, from the Communist bloc, sought Dollar deposits held outside of the United States. National currency controls in some countries, from which the offshore Dollar accounts were exempt in several countries such as Britain, made Dollar-denominated accounts held outside of the United States very attractive. The banks in the United Kingdom holding Dollars were spared from Federal Reserve restrictions but did not come under the Bank of England's jurisdiction either. Free of U.S. reserve requirements, foreign loan and interest-rate limitations, by the late 1960s, even the subsubsidiaries of U.S. banks offered the same services in London as non-U.S. banks. They could offer depositors and borrowers more competitive rates than banks in the United States. Ironically, all the measures taken by the United States to stem the outflow of Dollars contributed to the creation of vast sums held outside of its control. Their existence and their size transformed the world of international finance.[65]

Within a decade, Eurodeposits had spread to other locations. From 1973 to 1988, fueled by higher revenues from oil producers and a surge in Asian economic activity, Eurodeposits grew from $300 billion to nearly $1.2 trillion. By the end of the 1980s, too, the market had been transformed from what was originally exclusively Dollar deposits to a mix of European and Asian currencies based in financial centers including Luxembourg, Paris, Rome, the Cayman Islands, Bahamas, Panama, Singapore, Hong Kong, and Tokyo. By 1990, Europe accounted for 50 percent of all Eurodeposits, with London alone representing one-third of the total.[66]

The startling growth of Eurodeposits led to a new kind of financing, one to a large extent independent of national regulators. It also helped account for the surprising resilience of the Dollar, despite persistent assaults and more than twenty years of huge current account deficits lasting into the twenty-first century. Although technically the financial institutions still held the Dollar deposits in the United States, as foreign banks they had more freedom to invest Dollars as they wished and could offer more competitive rates. Customers could buy and sell Dollar-based securities in a way U.S.-based ones could not. Eurodeposits funded innovations in how and where capital market transactions were conducted. By 1996, $1 trillion in new Eurobank notes and commercial paper had been issued. Even national governments borrowed on these markets. Maturities, types, and amounts of facilities grew quickly. It offered users easy terms to swap out of interest rate and foreign exchange exposures they had taken on. Transaction costs were lower, in part because companies could bypass national registration requirements. Markets reacted quickly and were very liquid. By 1996, Eurofinancing accounted for 75 percent of all international financing.[67] Finance became denationalized and banks had to be prepared to play on this ethereal plain.

National regulators appeared ambivalent about these developments. On the one hand, they were stimulated by the imposition of credit and other controls in many countries. On the other hand, regulators winked at the existence of deposits in currencies other than their national currency but in institutions based in their country. Even after the credit controls and the need to recycle OPEC funds had largely disappeared, the market offered a variety of competitive advantages to customers. By the 1980s, companies could issue short, medium, and long-term securities whose terms were regulated merely by professional groups, not national authorities. Prior to the Euromarket's rapid rise, foreign exchange transactions were limited largely to trade or foreign direct investment transactions and some travel. By the mid-1990s, the huge interbank market for trading deposits, used by banks to manage their liabilities, accounted for roughly two-thirds of all banking business transactions.[68] From 1973 to 1998, daily foreign exchange turnover jumped from $15 billion to $1.4 trillion.[69]

Ultimately, too, for Deutsche Bank taking advantage of new market opportunities meant wrestling with complex new products and regulations. The turmoil in capital markets led to the application of some old and new instruments to financial risk management. Although futures contracts for commodities can be traced back at least to seventeenth-century Japan, and forward contracts for securities and foreign exchange have been around for at least 100 years, financial derivatives virtually did not exist before 1970. A derivative is a financial instrument – such as futures, options, and swaps – which *derives* its value from another security or commodity. Traded on organized exchanges or in private (OTC) arrangements, the volume of futures and options trading grew from less than 100 million contracts in 1983 to nearly a billion by 1992. Whereas all the trading in 1983 was in the United States, by 1992 approximately half took place outside of U.S. jurisdiction.[70] An enormous body of financial theory and technique has evolved for pricing these instruments and managing their risk. Financial innovators are continually developing new and complex combinations based on the original derivatives, which can be used to reduce (hedge) or assume risk.

For some observers, all of these developments led to regulatory quandaries. Competition between national regulators for financial investors has retarded harmonization of rules and rapid innovation in financial services seems to proceed more quickly than regulatory adaptation. Deregulation in many countries allowed banks to move into new services, such as insurance and brokerage, which further complicated national and international regulatory efforts.[71]

Unlike many American counterparts, for much of the period covered by this Section, Deutsche Bank evidenced little interest in some new aspects of the financial landscape, and in the growth of equity financing and competitive bidding for financial services. With greater numbers of Germans acquiring wealth and in need of banking services, and with its large clients eager to reduce costs, this strategy might have been one of the significant obstacles to its domestic and international growth in the period under discussion. Moreover, Germany had no great pool of pension funds hungry for equity issues, and German investors well into the 1990s evidenced less interest in equity investing compared with individuals in Britain and in the United States.[72] Over the past forty years, German equity markets were and remain still a much smaller percentage of German Gross Domestic Product (GDP) than American equity markets are of U.S. GDP.[73]

As with Deutsche Bank's first venture into the American market, trade financing played a significant role, at least in the initial stages, in U.S. business after the war. With virtually no assets and no branch network abroad in 1957, Deutsche Bank pursued a business segment that had not changed substantially since the nineteenth century. It could rely on correspondent banks. Nevertheless, rebuilding its trade financing business and its network of contacts was not easy. It would, moreover, only have short-term benefits. Structural changes in international banking and customers as well as technology, which took hold in the late 1960s and '70s, eliminated much of the need for letters of credit, for example.[74]

Foreign trade was one of the principal driving forces in Germany's economic recovery after the war. With its domestic clout and international network of correspondent banks, Deutsche Bank played a leading role. By 1957, West German exports as a percentage of GNP were 16.6 percent, double what it had been in 1950. By 1990, the figure was 30 percent. Even before the bank's reunification, the separate institutions attempted to rebuild Deutsche Bank's old correspondent relationships, which seemed – at least for the time being, preferable to branches – a perfectly reasonable means of servicing clients' foreign trade requirements. By 1980, Deutsche Bank maintained 4,000 correspondent relationships in 152 countries. At its zenith, this allowed the bank to clear transactions all over the world. Deutsche Bank made short-term trade financing one of its strategic thrusts during the decades following the war. For longer term credit, it helped found and was a large participant in Ausfuhrkredit-Aktiengesellschaft.[75]

As early as 1957, Deutsche Bank took the lead in offering long-term export financing, with maturities of five to ten years. Abs used his position as head of the Kreditanstalt für Wiederaufbau to see to Deutsche Bank's involvement in the extension of new kinds and maturities of trade credit.[76] Deutsche Bank expected 20 percent to 30 percent of this new and lucrative business.[77] With the growth of foreign direct investment in the 1970s, which shifted trade from third party to intercompany, the consolidation of businesses and the process of disintermediation – which allowed many clients to access working capital funds directly from capital markets – much of this business started to disappear in the 1970s.

By the 1970s, too, new communication and cash management techniques were making corresponding banking obsolete. In 1977, SWIFT (Society for Worldwide Interbank Financial Telecommunication) allowed Deutsche Bank to hook up 200 of its domestic branches to handle international payments. Only the increase in political risk, during the oil and debt crises of the 1970s and 1980s, and the increase in trade with Communist Europe, which came with the *détente* of the 1970s, slowed down the process of converting to centralized, standardized transactions. Indeed, Deutsche Bank clients not only needed letters of credit in many countries with a high degree of country risk, such as in South America and Africa, they were also demanding confirmed letters of credit. But by the end of the 1980s, most trade and traders no longer required trade financing services provided by foreign branches or correspondent banks.[78]

Beginning in the 1960s, Deutsche Bank made some efforts to become a stronger player in the burgeoning area of foreign exchange transactions. Although Germany's foreign trade led to many foreign exchange transactions and Deutsche Bank was always a market maker for the major currencies, the bank concentrated on spot transactions. Given the low volume of more sophisticated transactions and low volatility of currency rates, Deutsche Bank branch foreign exchange trading facilities were not centralized in Frankfurt until 1967. With this reorganization, Deutsche Bank was better positioned to take advantage of the demise of the Bretton Woods system in the early 1970s as well as

Foreign exchange trading in 1971, when this shot was taken, was already an important part of Deutsche Bank's international business. During the next decade, that business would undergo an enormous transformation. The collapse of the Dollar-based foreign exchange system and spectacular increase in rate volatility added risks and opportunities for banks like Deutsche Bank. The bank and its customers needed to trade more and develop more sophisticated techniques for managing foreign exchange issues. A far cry from the activity and technology of foreign exchange trading rooms nowadays, this trading room served as one of Deutsche Bank's main links to other markets.

the growing hedging requirements of its customers. But the turmoil in markets contributed to hesitancy about establishing more branches, delayed entry into the Eurodebt market, and contributed to avoidance of aggressive expansion of its swap business. By 1973, however, market volatility and corresponding higher risks and arbitrage opportunities offered Deutsche Bank a substantial opportunity in currency trading. Revenues from trading improved in that year fivefold.[79]

For the first few years of Deutsche Bank's new existence, international lending played little role in the affairs of the bank.[80] With the gradual convertibility of the DM and increased contact with international clients, by 1960, however, Deutsche Bank once again became an active participant in international lending – but only slowly. It took several years for the bank to overcome fear of foreign exposure and the shortage of staff to manage international credit arrangements. Short of long-term funding, Deutsche Bank encouraged its clients investing abroad to seek funds in their host country. Even though the opportunities for cross-border finance were growing quickly, much of Deutsche Bank's involvement in international lending came through its joint ventures. Because U.S. companies, for example, wanted to invest more abroad and their own government was also putting them under pressure not to use funds from the United States, the lure of European financing was almost irresistible.

During the 1960s, a vast array of American companies began issuing debt on European markets. This type of financing resembled the traditional form of international financing in some respects and differed little from the flotations Deutsche Bank performed for American firms in the nineteenth century. Some were actually listed on European exchanges. In January 1968 alone, American companies issued $265 million – roughly the amount for all of 1967 – of Dollar debt in Europe, including for such household American names as Chrysler, Gulf & Western, RCA, and Standard Oil of California. Much of the debt was in the form of convertibles – bonds that could be exchanged for equity shares. Japanese, Austrian, and Scandinavian firms were also active in emitting Euro-Dollar debt.[81] According to the Bundesbank, many American companies were tapping European funds for investment back in the United States.[82] By 1969, the Bundesbank grew even more concerned that government debt, due largely to U.S. social programs coupled with the war in Vietnam, was driving up U.S. interest rates. During the summer of that year, it reported that the U.S. banking system was becoming more illiquid and that Congress had proposed to tax earned interest more heavily. Both factors contributed to increased investor and lender interest in the Eurobond market.[83]

By the mid-1960s, Deutsche Bank was once again taking the lead in issuing American securities in Europe. It was the first bank to list American securities in Germany. In 1963, it was the lead bank in listing IBM shares on the Frankfurt stock exchange.[84] As early as 1962, Ford turned to Deutsche Bank to underwrite its nonvoting Class A Common Stock throughout Europe. Deutsche Bank became Ford's transfer agent in Germany, on behalf of both the Ford Motor Company and The Ford Foundation. Although the Securities and Exchange Commission (SEC) had determined that the shares could not be offered in the United States or to U.S. citizens and companies, this limitation did not apply to holders of U.S. Dollar deposits outside of the United States (Eurodeposits). Abs had determined that distribution would be made through European banks, which could hold on to securities. Deutsche Bank had contracted for 150,000 shares, with an option for another 350,000, earning a commission of approximately 5 percent of the sales' price for its own account. The bank consortium included most of Germany's public and private banks, but no non-German ones.[85]

A good deal of this international business did not require heavy investment by the bank. As late as 1962, Deutsche Bank held very few foreign bonds in its portfolio, none were American, and only the shares of one U.S. company, Ford, were on its balance sheet.[86] Although the 1963 annual report noted an upsurge in European issues, just a year later the upsurge had turned into a tidal wave. Twenty-nine foreign stocks were issued that year on the German market.[87] In 1965, Deutsche Bank helped bring securities from six American companies to the market, pointing to another trend. Because American companies were

16.10.1963

IBM

International Business Machines Corporation

New York, N.Y.

Aktiengesellschaft nach dem Recht des Staates New York
(Vereinigte Staaten von Amerika)

PROSPEKT

für die Zulassung von

US-$ 141 152 395 auf Namen lautenden Aktien

28 230 479 Stück im Nennbetrag von je US-$ 5,—, verbrieft in Zertifikaten der Gesellschaft, und zwar:

I.

US-$ 138 817 535,— auf Namen lautende Aktien — 27 763 507 Stück —
die am 30. September 1963 bereits ausgegeben waren
mit Gewinnberechtigung vom 1. Januar 1963 an,
ausschließlich dreier bereits gezahlter Vierteljahresdividenden für 1963

II.

US-$ 2 334 860,— auf Namen lautende Aktien — 466 972 Stück —
die ausgegeben werden:

a) Aufgrund der Ausübung von Optionsrechten, die nach den „IBM 1956 and 1961 Stock Option Plans" bestehen oder noch eingeräumt werden (insgesamt 267 424 Stück)

b) Gemäß dem „IBM Employees 1961 Stock Purchase Plan" (insgesamt 199 548 Stück)

mit Gewinnberechtigung vom Zeitpunkt ihrer Ausgabe an

an der
Frankfurter Wertpapierbörse

Although Bundesbank and Deutsche Bank concerns about the Euromarkets impeded Germany's becoming a center for offshore financing, in the early 1960s Deutsche Bank was once again active in international financing. Despite many restrictions, it led the way in helping foreign companies eager to access German funds. This IBM equity listing was one of many from the period and differed little from the sort of deals arranged by Siemens and Gwinner before World War I.

turning to offshore financing and financing entities to avoid U.S. regulatory controls and taxes, many of these were not in the name of the parent but rather that of offshore financing companies or normal foreign subsidiaries.[88] The numbers continued to grow. By 1967, the list even included an old friend, the bonds of Allis-Chalmers International Finance Corporation.[89] These new issues took advantage, in large part, of American or at least Dollar funds held outside of the United States.

Although the long-term impact on the bank is not clear, Deutsche Bank's reaction to the Eurodollar market was not positive at first. Abs, like many continental bankers trained in the old school, feared that the Euromarket lacked sufficient bank and central bank administration. Deutsche Bank seemed in the 1960s to prefer cross-border lending in the old sense, with national regulatory oversight, where its know-how to list securities on the German market would give it a competitive edge. Deutsche Bank, however, became an active player on the Eurodeposit market via its Luxembourg subsidiary. Despite some Bundesbank restrictions and with a small investment in staff in Luxembourg, Deutsche Bank could generate billions in revenue and substantial profits, rivaling its banking operations in New York and London.[90] As with so many financial developments, Deutsche Bank's Eurodeposit activities required an offshore entity and ignited many regulatory concerns.

For these and other reasons, well into the 1980s its primary emphasis remained on national markets in concert with other banks, however. The bank advocated parallel issues to help harmonize European capital markets and make them more efficient. Issuing international bonds in several different national *tranches* in each country's currency or with some sort of foreign exchange clause that would effectively make the payments in each country the same would broaden capital markets.[91] Deutsche Bank's international bond business and medium-term trade financing continued to blossom through the end of the 1960s, but with little mention of the United States per se.[92] As early as 1979, fifty U.S. companies had listed their equity on the German stock exchange. Deutsche Bank managed about half of the listings.[93] Turnover of U.S. common stock on German markets in 1978 reached DM 1.1 billion. By 1986, Deutsche Bank had done over $80 billion in new launches of debt instruments, $70 billion of which was not DM denominated.[94] Investment banking included all sorts of government and quasi-government intervention as well as advisory services sometimes in conjunction with the Bundesbank.[95]

But many of the calamities of the 1980s and 1990s first reared their head in the 1960s. Central bankers understandably feared that their own efforts to liberalize short-term money movements had opened a Pandora's Box. In addition to facilitating trade and efficient capital allocation, the monetary reforms and convertibility of currencies of this period also increased the mobility of funds, which made central bank efforts to control liquidity and foreign exchange rates more difficult and aggravated balance-of-payment problems.[96] Building up unregulated Dollar deposits also contributed to several rounds of emerging market debt crises. At the very least, the capital market and exchange rate developments appeared as a mixed blessing for central as well as commercial bankers.

The New Face of Investment Banking

As the Euromarkets matured, new institutions and instruments came to dominate finance. One of the great paradoxes of the period was that much of the financial innovation came in the form of financial freedom from United States and other nations' jurisdictions, but the process was driven by American institutions. American banking regulations tended to create highly focused financial service powerhouses, freed in a sense from the low margin end of banking and other activities. For several decades, financial services were delivered in a less bundled fashion by American institutions. Consulting and due diligence, once performed or guided by U.S. banks, had to be separated by the mid-1930s, giving rise or a boost to specialized service activities like consulting and audit.[97]

Not only did American banks move abroad to offer services that they could not in the United States because of the Glass-Steagall Act and interest rate caps, American investment banks, freed from other activities, focused exclusively on investment banking. Mutual and pension funds, mostly American, moreover, grew in the over forty years covered by this Section from 6 percent of the investor pool to approximately 50 percent. As soon as in the early 1960s the Bundesbank had begun to take more seriously the emergence of American pension funds as a factor that would dramatically change capital markets and the business of German banks. From 1960 to 1965, the amount of all American pension funds increased from $75.7 billion to $133.5 billion, an annual increase of 12 percent – but that was only the beginning. From 1980 to 1989, pension funds alone grew from assets of $500 billion to $4.3 trillion.[98] Managed by experienced financial experts, these relatively flexible funds, along with other popular vehicles for gathering savings such as mutual funds, labored under strict limits on how much of any one security they could take, but with few limits on the range of possible investments, including overseas opportunities. By the 1980s, their hunger for new placements seemed insatiable.

Meanwhile, because of U.S. regulations forbidding banks to underwrite securities and to take deposits, some American banks evolved into a new type of investment bank, one that focused purely on underwriting securities and on selling services at competitive prices. With a great deal of market access and few regulatory restrictions on their placement activities, they combined aggressive pricing, innovative instruments, market knowledge, and closeness to other financial institutions – such as pension funds, mutual funds, and insurance companies – to place their new issues. German authorities tracked the progress of American investment banks. Unlike universal banks, with whom they competed for underwriting, these financial institutions neither dealt in retail banking with small customers nor developed very close ties to corporate clients, whose shares German banks often held for their own account. As the difference between the cost of cheap retail and more expensive wholesale funds diminished, their high-volume wholesale business and experience gave American investment banks greater pricing advantages with corporate clients, even in Germany where firms became less inclined to allow relationships to determine financial choices. In 1966, First Boston Corporation headed the list of the largest investment banks in the United States with nearly 20 percent of the $87.9 billion in private security launches. Several of these banks had experienced more than 50 percent growth over the previous decade. Salomon Brothers, for example, enjoyed 600 percent growth in revenues for the period.[99]

Deutsche Bank was a relatively latecomer to this type of investment banking. In 1983, it took a major step toward increasing its international investment banking and asset management activities by founding the Capital Management International GmbH (CMI) in response to changes in U.S. pension laws (Employee Retirement Income Securities Act, or ERISA). As the SEC did not allow Deutsche Bank to be used as a broker or custodian for ERISA funds, the bank established CMI as an independent asset manager. Despite some success from Germany in the U.S. pension management business, CMI opened a branch in New York in 1985. Without a track record and with different (not American) measures of performance, getting new business was not easy for CMI.[100]

Deutsche Bank tried to expand its corporate financial services for client companies in the United States and other countries in new ways. International leasing, for example, became one area that tended to replace trade financing. In 1982, the bank set up its own installment financing and leasing company, Deutsche Credit Corporation, in Deerfield, Illinois. A wholly owned subsidiary, it focused on the American market. It purchased products from German exporters and leased them to American importers. Most of the exporters were German clients of Deutsche Bank. It was a model that Deutsche Bank, in a somewhat altered form, applied elsewhere in the world. The subsidiary branched out into long-term factoring and other types of transaction. By the mid-1990s, Deutsche Credit Corporation had a large branch network in the United States.[101]

Despite these efforts, at the end of the 1980s, Deutsche Bank still realized that the greatest challenge remained investment banking. In order to help remedy this and other deficiencies in the bank's range of service offerings, in 1989 Deutsche Bank purchased Morgan Grenfell Group, one of the spinoffs of the old J. P. Morgan financial empire. Since 1984, Deutsche Bank had held a 5 percent interest in this traditional British merchant bank.[102] With Morgan Grenfell Asset Management Ltd.'s substantial, global expertise with institutional customers, the newly rechristened CMI, Deutsche Asset Management GmbH, was better positioned to deal with demanding institutional clients. Yet even with its purchase of the remaining shares of Morgan Grenfell, as will be discussed more in the next Chapter, Deutsche Bank's position in this market remained too weak for the liking of many at the bank.[103]

Compared with American and British banks, Deutsche Bank's mergers and acquisitions capacities developed relatively late. For many reasons, hostile takeovers are not part of the German business landscape. Although American and British companies went through several waves of mergers during the period covered by this Section, relatively few occurred in Germany, leaving Deutsche Bank without much chance to develop experience in its home market which it could harness to enter other markets or utilize for cross-border mergers. From 1970 to 1989, merger and acquisition activity in the United States climbed from $16.4 billion to $221 billion per year. In the decade that followed, foreign mergers by American companies and into the United States by foreign companies leaped to nearly $.5 trillion.[104] One of the most interesting areas for investment bank advisory services, hostile takeovers, was even rarer in Germany.[105] As late as 1998, Deutsche Bank had not made the top ten of merger advisors. Only two non-American banks could be found on the list of big players in this lucrative sector, and they had already combined with American institutions.[106]

As it did in many other areas, at first Deutsche Bank tried to beef up its mergers and acquisitions capacities with a joint venture. In 1971, UBS and Deutsche Bank created Atlantic Capital Corporation – which was renamed Deutsche Bank Capital Corporation in 1985 after Deutsche Bank purchased all the shares from its Swiss partners – to build up its M&A business in the United States. Although its staff acquired some experience and did a few small deals, there were no great successes. The bank hoped, however, to import some of the experience gained in New York to Germany. In 1984, it established a small company for M&A in Frankfurt, but it never really transcended its German roots. The only way to increase the number and quality of its M&A staff would be to acquire the talent by buying an experienced house, which it tried in 1989 with Morgan Grenfell. Deutsche Bank had the same problems and ultimately the same solutions for M&A business as it did with derivative instruments,[107] buying institutions that had the talent and experience. However, according to some senior management, the greatest disappointment connected with the Morgan Grenfell acquisition was its weakness in the United States.[108] During the period covered by this Section, Deutsche Bank struggled to come up with a coherent strategy for exploiting the transaction opportunities connected with the United States, which had already become the epicenter of a transnational financial world.

One of Deutsche Bank's largest M&A transactions during the period – in 1957, just two months after the reunification of the bank – and probably its only cross-border one until the 1980s – developed out of the economic problems of the interwar period and the U.S. seizure of German assets during World War II. In 1926, the Stinnes concern, soon after the death of its founder Hugo Stinnes, was reorganized as a U.S. corporation.[109] The transaction reflected the degree to which Deutsche Bank's first international investment transactions were tied to its and Germany's history. It also showed, at this stage at least, how personalized, in the form of Abs, U.S. business remained as late as the early '60s.

Heavily indebted to German banks after the German inflation, in 1926 the giant steel and coal company got a $25 million bailout from American banks. Although 99 percent of real assets were in Germany and other European countries, one of the conditions of the new financing was the transfer of the assets of the German company to an American company (50 percent owned by the Stinnes family, 50 percent by the American banks). Although the stock was divided equally, voting restrictions on the family's shares gave effective control to the banks. During the crisis of the 1930s, the German enterprises, still controlled by the Stinnes family, were unable to make payments owed to the American holding company under the terms of the loans. Nevertheless, between 1926 and 1953, a substantial amount of the loans had been retired, roughly 85 percent, though much of this was accomplished by buying up the debt in Germany, at a discount, with the permission of the Reichsbank. Given the German Stinnes company's dubious record under the Third Reich, American regulators were reluctant to return the property.[110]

But Abs intervened. By 1955, Abs had gotten the agreement of the American Justice Department that if the shares were sold, the sale would be to Germans. When the sale was announced in 1957, Abs, with the help of the German government, organized a consortium of investors, including the Kreditanstalt für Wiederaufbau, for the purchase of a large part of the shares for DM 120 million.[111] By 1961, the American shares were already in the hands of Hermann Josef Abs and the Atlantic Asset Corporation, a firm established to handle the repurchase of the U.S. shares and the reincorporation of the Stinnes holding company in Germany. It is not completely clear to what extent Abs acted on his own behalf or Deutsche Bank's.[112]

In short, as late as the mid-1960s, Deutsche Bank had not yet institutionalized its international and American businesses. Sandwiched in between the disorder of the more than four decades that preceded Deutsche Bank's reunification and the turbulence of the post-Bretton Woods era, the 1960s must have appeared to many German bankers like the "eye of a hurricane." Mindful of the "great winds" that surrounded them, they were reluctant to build structures that might easily be blown away. As is often the case in the face of great uncertainty, networks and personal relationships seemed more reliable than formal business organization for Deutsche Bank, especially in its international business. How the bank moved from a very personalized business model in the United States to one with international-management hierarchies is the subject of the next Chapter.

16

From Abs to Kopper and from Joint Ventures to Branching

The Structure of Deutsche Bank's Business in the United States

Your services to your own bank, to German banking, to the German economy, as well as to the well-being of the general public are well-known everywhere. At an age when most people think about retirement from professional life, you stand at the high point of your activities and influence.

Otmar Emminger to Abs, October 14, 1966, HABBk, N2/69.

Changing the Guard

The more than forty years covered by this part of the book were not only turbulent, they also witnessed one of the most important generational changes in German history. From 1960 to 2000, leadership passed at Deutsche Bank and most other German institutions from those who had witnessed and even participated in the events leading up to and during the Third Reich to those who were born after Hitler's *Machtergreifung* (seizure of power). For those executives trained in the interwar period, especially, preserving the bank from the consequences of another round of German isolation or worse still, lunatic autarky, was one of their principal business preoccupations. Wanting Germany to be strong, though, they stressed institutional impediments to prevent the bank operating in chaotic, uncontrolled financial markets. For some of Deutsche Bank's leaders of that generation, doing extensive business in the United States might only serve to distract it from its core competencies and values. Well into the 1980s, moreover, some members of the management board thought strengthening the bank in Europe was a necessary precondition to a stronger push in the United States. With increasing European integration and the advent of the Euro, the strategy of building a larger, stronger home market had a lot to recommend it. Some at Deutsche Bank wanted to concentrate first on Europe by expanding the bank's presence in France, Spain, and especially Italy. Whereas no one in senior management wanted to abandon the U.S. business, there were differences about priorities.[1] Some in senior management were still working with the old universal bank model, which included a heavy emphasis on retail banking and fixed income securities. There was a profound choice to be made then, and still is even now. Would Deutsche Bank be a traditional Continental European universal bank or a global financial institution focused on investment banking in the Anglo-American mold?

By 2000, Deutsche Bank's new breed of managers felt less intimidated by the interwar and Nazi periods, and much more at home with the freewheeling ways of unbridled capital markets, as well as with Deutsche Bank's ability to function unfettered by national constraints as an equal to Anglophone financial institutions based in London and New York.

From the late 1930s to the end of the 1970s, Abs was the main driving force in at least Deutsche Bank's – and perhaps Germany's – international financial strategies. Abs seemed to be everywhere, and with the right people.[2] Abs even charmed some former adversaries.[3] In spite of the controversies that surrounded him, with his many contacts and gift for languages, Abs brought a lot to the task of reviving Deutsche Bank's American relationships.[4]

He visited the United States regularly with a full schedule, which included a mix of "old" and "new" Deutsche Bank business and cultural events, as well as meetings at the International Monetary Fund and other international financial organizations.[5] In 1970, even after his retirement from the management board, during one trip his first few days included visits to the New York Fed, the president of Chase Manhattan Bank, the chairman of Mobil Oil, and to the Metropolitan Museum of Art. A great lover of classical music, the trips nearly always included concerts at Carnegie Hall and later Lincoln Center, sometimes even cultural events on the day he arrived. In a five-day period during that 1970 visit, Abs saw eight company and government officials in New York and Toronto, gave interviews, and attended a *Financial Times* symposium, where he delivered a talk, "A European Currency Counterweight to the Dollar." The guest list for the symposium included an impressive array of New York and Washington elite.[6] Thanks to Abs, Deutsche Bank's network went beyond pure banking relationships.[7]

His influence on German business was enormous. The extent of his board memberships led to a German law limiting the number of supervisory boards upon which any individual could serve at one time. Simultaneously, he chaired the boards of both Daimler-Benz and Lufthansa. Among his many contributions to German finance was playing a leading role in the creation of the DM debt market, which put Deutsche Bank at the center of a huge European-wide business. His mastery of detail and facility with numbers awed and intimidated subordinates, colleagues, and even state ministers.[8] A tireless worker, sometimes surviving for months even in his sixties with four hours of sleep a night, he demanded at least as much from subordinates, with whom he could be extremely hard but from whom he evoked much loyalty and appreciation for what they learned.[9]

No matter how his views of American economic and political policy changed, Abs never seemed to forget his debt to the United States for the Marshall funds.[10] Despite the threats to world financial stability in the latter years of his life, Abs remained guardedly optimistic that the United States would respect its commitments to the world economic order and that cooperative revisions to foreign exchange rates could ensure an orderly transition from the Bretton Woods system to convertible currencies and a new Dollar-gold parity.[11] Although cognizant of the great political efforts required and, at times highly critical of American policies, Abs still concluded, at least in front of American audiences in early 1972, that no country in the world had shown more readiness to identify with the problems of the free world than the United States.[12]

At 80, he still was very active. Even in retirement he was considered the "patriarch" of Deutsche Bank and perhaps Germany. As Honorary Chairman of the bank, Abs attended and participated in meetings of Deutsche Bank's Supervisory Board as a guest but claimed to give the current managers advice only when asked. Although forgiving of bankers' misjudgment about risk and central banks' interest rate policies, as late as 1982 Abs still feared the lack of transparency in the Euromarket. He felt more comfortable in a world of bankers and central bank oversight and control. Even though Deutsche Bank helped found the Eurodebt market, Abs regretted its growth.[13] National and even international regulations were no panacea, as the interwar period had shown, but for him, money in the '70s and '80s could be too easily recycled, making mismatches of assets and liabilities too easy.[14]

As long as Abs presided over the management board, Deutsche Bank's direct entry into the United States seemed to be blocked. Even a joint European approach to investment in the United States and other markets went against his grain at first. Abs believed that bankers should cultivate their own domestic markets and trade their knowledge and access with bankers from other countries, very much in the same way as Siemens and Gwinner had in the nineteenth century.[15] Not only should Germany learn lessons from the illiberal and undisciplined economics of the interwar years, but also from its lost property after two world wars.[16] Eventually, he came around to a scheme of shared investment in the United States. After all, alone, Deutsche Bank ran greater risks; together with British, French, Belgian, and banks from other nations it could hope to avoid expropriation in case of conflict with the United States. However, in a world of gentleman bankers, for Abs cooperation and correspondent networks were sufficient for Deutsche Bank to benefit in foreign markets from its own strengths in Germany.

For Abs banking was still divided into a German and non-German world. For the bankers who immediately followed him, the focus was less and less on what could be lost by international investment and more and more on what could be gained. The competitive world was changing. Abs ended his career, not as a "Man for all Seasons," but rather as a private banker – trained in a bygone paradigm of economic organization and institutional challenges. It was a world of "gentlemen" with personal authority and responsibility.[17] Unfortunately for this vision, as one of his successors put it, the "gentlemen" from New York were coming to Germany.[18]

Abs' successor as spokesman of the management board, Franz Heinrich Ulrich, shared much of the bank's traditional strategy, as mapped out by Georg Siemens soon after the bank was founded and applied by Abs. Combining foreign transactions, domestic deposit banking, and issuing securities for German and foreign companies on the German or European market, activities that had served Deutsche Bank so well during its first forty years, would serve the bank well in the latter part of the twentieth century.[19] All were built on a large domestic branch network, close ties to industry, good political connections, and a predominant role in the German brokerage sector, as well as an extensive correspondent network.[20]

But Ulrich's vision had to deal with several unwelcome facts. The new competitive world of global banking made maintaining home markets and penetrating foreign markets a more capital intensive exercise. Although international banking had developed briskly since the late 1950s, it had also been rocked by a series of political and economic crises. Cold War tensions, decolonialization, oil shocks, stagflation, volatile exchange rates, and debt overhang brought new opportunities and costs. Political uncertainty of many varieties, including sovereign default, were once again everyday parts of bankers' vocabulary, requiring polices for dealing with many kinds of risk and for systematically integrating guidelines from supragovernmental, governmental, and credit agencies for classifying and evaluating positions as well as the banks' ability to absorb losses.[21] Above all, many of Deutsche Bank's clients invested abroad to unprecedented degrees and demanded a multinational reach and innovative services from their house banks.

Fending off domestic and European competition while establishing a presence in the great capital markets outside of Europe must have seemed like a Herculean task.[22] With this in mind, Ulrich and his immediate successor pushed for more international investment but they hedged their bets. They were careful not to tie up a lot of Deutsche Bank's assets in the United States and not to disrupt its domestic business with non-German influence.

Ulrich was succeeded by a series of management board co-spokesmen: Wilfried Guth (1976–85) and F. Wilhelm Christians (1976–88), and then Christians with Alfred Herrhausen (1985–89). Herrhausen's life served as a dramatic illustration of how politics and banking were very much intertwined. Probably the most publicly visible German businessman after Abs, Herrhausen was murdered on November 30, 1989, two months before his sixtieth birthday, a few weeks after the fall of the Berlin Wall and a few days after the announcement of Deutsche Bank's takeover of Morgan Grenfell.

The British successor of the J. P. Morgan banking empire, though a household name and widely considered one of the leading London merchant banks, Morgan Grenfell had been wrestling with a series of problems for many years, not the least of which was its relationship to the United States. The bank's separation from Morgan Guaranty in 1981 cleared the way for building up its New York organization. In 1986, it purchased Cyrus J. Lawrence Inc., a brokerage house well known for its research, and established a presence in Tokyo, giant steps geared to support a move into the international securities business. But entry into private and government securities trading ultimately required a larger capital base. By the time of Deutsche Bank's acquisition – and despite the 1987 stock market crash, which took a toll but was not fatal – Morgan Grenfell Holding maintained respected businesses in banking, asset management, and corporate finance, but little business in the United States.[23] According to some sources at the bank, Herrhausen's untimely death as well as German

Although Alfred Herrhausen was reported by some sources to be very impatient for greater investment in the United States, during his tenure as spokesman of the management board (1985–89), he and his colleagues had to prioritize among many pressing issues confronting Deutsche Bank around the world, depicted visually by the map behind him in this 1985 photo. His untimely death probably slowed the investment process, but the consensus management at the top of Deutsche Bank insured that the basic policies which he helped shape remained intact.

reunification and all it entailed for Germany and Deutsche Bank contributed to Deutsche Bank not getting all it could from the purchase of Morgan Grenfell. Although the terms of the acquisition, negotiated with Herrhausen and others, had already called for a five-year period in which Morgan Grenfell's operations would maintain their independence – perhaps allowing the British operation to enjoy exceptional growth and profitability – one of the German bank's most articulate voices for change and for integration of Anglophone-styled underwriting had been lost.[24]

Having joined the bank in 1970, Herrhausen became co-spokesman of the management board along with Christians, and after the latter's retirement, the bank's first sole spokesman since Ulrich. Outspoken, eloquent, and charismatic, his intensity and complexity excited reaction. As the first Deutsche Bank leader who had not been an adult during World War II, he was freer from the pervasive sense of German guilt than his predecessors, and spearheaded Deutsche Bank's entry into many European markets and its diversification into many new businesses. He was the first Deutsche Bank leader since 1967 whose reputation and fame could approach Abs' business and political notoriety, which may have contributed to his murder. Like Abs, too, Herrhausen also had strong and well-thought-out views about the world order and managers' role in it.[25] Although unashamed of being German and of Deutsche Bank, Herrhausen went to his death troubled about the future of the bank and its capacity to be competitive in the ever-harsher world of international banking.[26]

Herrhausen and his colleagues set their sights on turning Deutsche Bank into a pan-European giant poised to take advantage of tumbling trade and financial barriers. In addition to Morgan Grenfell, the bank acquired Antoni, Hacker & Co., a small private Austrian bank; bought Bank of America's Italian operations; took control of MDM Sociedade de Investimento, a Lisbon investment bank; acquired majority control of Banco Comercial Transatlántico, a middle-market bank, which had been the Spanish subsidiary of Deutsche Ueberseeische Bank; and acquired H. Albert de Bary & Co., an Amsterdam bank specializing in trade financing, with which Disconto-Gesellschaft had had a strong relationship. All were a part of a drive to create, out of an inward-looking institution, a global banking titan that ranged from Moscow to Montevideo. A strong defender of German banking capitalism, Herrhausen wanted to use Deutsche Bank's dominant and highly profitable position in Europe's strongest economy as a springboard. To make up for the loss of Deutsche Bank's international businesses from 1914 to 1957, the bank would have to be an even more aggressive purchaser of foreign banks than its European and American counterparts. This would not be cheap or easy. At the very least, Herrhausen had to transform conservative German bankers into dynamic business entrepreneurs.[27]

With Herrhausen's death, leadership of the bank fell to Hilmar Kopper (1989–97), who had joined Deutsche Bank in 1954. By most accounts, he contributed a global, international banking perspective. He was a "dyed-in-the wool" banker who tried to move the bank from commercial to investment banking.[28] He both brought into the bank and encouraged a lot of investment bankers, but his greatest effort in that area, the integration of Morgan Grenfell, did not make all the hoped for contribution. Perhaps the bank was still

Hilmar Kopper with Deutsche Bank's logo around the time he became spokesman of the management board. Although committed to developing Deutsche Bank in the United States and American-styled investment banking for Germany, his tenure was filled with unprecedented opportunities and demands within the borders of Europe – the reunification of Germany, the opening of Central Europe, and the effects of the Maastricht Treaty – all of which pushed the bank to draw some attention away from the United States.

too timid. Throughout his years as spokesman of the management board, sorting out the legacy of Deutsche Bank's post-World War II investment decisions in the United States was nearly always on his mind.[29]

Deutsche Bank's European Experiment in the United States

For several years after the war, unresolved international financial disputes and other obstacles hampered the bank's involvement in the United States. During the 1950s, at least, traditional alliances with correspondent banks seemed like the best, and perhaps the only conceivable way of doing business in the United States. Its correspondent network allowed Deutsche Bank to engage in cross-border transfers and trade documentation processing for its customers, which would soon, though, become obsolete in all but the "exotic" countries. With Deutsche Bank's reunification and the growing competitive threat from American banks, the U.S. imperative became clearer. Despite domestic and foreign problems throughout the second half of the twentieth century, the American economy and its capital markets dwarfed those of the rest of the world.[30]

Deutsche Bank knew that it would have to alter its approach to financial services to enter the U.S. market. Although U.S. banking law allowed foreign banks some advantages for many years, there were still many aspects of the U.S. system with which foreign bankers were uncomfortable. The United States still discouraged universal banking and looked for ways of exercising more control in general of foreign banks. Entry into the United States might even threaten Deutsche Bank's whole business model. Since 1933, banks had been barred from the brokerage business. The New York Stock Exchange forbade foreigners to buy seats.[31] Apart from the pure regulatory differences, there were more attitudinal ones. Personal banking and responsibility, a hallmark and strength of the German system, represented for Americans too great an opportunity to extract insider information and unfair profit. The objective standards of credit worthiness extolled by rating agencies, for example, were preferred to the personal guarantees of bankers closely connected to a company.

Mastering U.S. regulations was no easy matter for foreign banks. Their decisions about how to enter the United States were still highly influenced not only by what business they wanted to do but also by the changing and overlapping state and federal regulations with which they had to live. With both American and European banks increasing their foreign establishments, competition heated up, so, too, did pressures to allow more access to one anothers' markets.[32] In the 1960s, the Federal Reserve did not impose many limits on foreign banks. According to the Fed, foreign banks could even operate in more than one state, a privilege American banks did not enjoy, but many states did prevent multistate banking by foreign financial institutions. Because of its port and vibrant capital markets, most foreign banks wanted to be in New York. In the early 1950s, New York state began to expand the forms and functions permitted to foreign controlled bank entities. Foreign agents could be converted into subsidiaries, for example. By the early 1960s, moreover, branches and agents of foreign banks, whose home countries extended the same privilege to American banks, could perform most banking functions permitted to domestic institutions. Most foreign banks elected this route for entry into the United States, later moving into other states with similar provisions and openness to multistate banking.[33] The main activities of foreign bank offices operating in New York were financing foreign trade, investment in Dollar paper in the U.S. money market, and commercial lending. Only foreign banks interested in broad banking or trust business had an incentive to open a subsidiary in New York, as opposed to a branch or an agency. Understandably, between 1960 and 1973, the vast majority of growth in new foreign bank entities and assets came from branches and agencies rather than subsidiaries.[34] Even presented with the opportunity for a branch in New York, Deutsche Bank hesitated to act alone.

In the 1970s, competitive pressure and the failures of some foreign bank entities in the United States led to calls for regulatory reform of foreign banking. As European banks became more aggressive in the United States, pressure mounted there to restrict their activities, or to at least diminish some of the competitive advantages they derived from American regulation. Both the Fed and state banking officials bolstered their oversight capacity.[35] With the federal government and twenty-five states allowing holding company structures, many foreign banks in the 1970s made effective use of the bank holding companies to organize their operations, which allowed them to do interstate banking but prohibited material investment in nonbanking activities.[36] In 1978, the International Banking Act made some basic changes to the positions of foreign banks. It permitted them to seek federal licenses, and it eliminated some restrictions on their acquisition of national banks. It also instituted reserve requirements on the U.S. branches and agencies of foreign banks having an excess of $1 billion in worldwide assets. Deposit insurance was made available to the branches of foreign banks in the United States, but it was mandatory for branches engaged in retail business. Interstate branching, once open to foreign banks, became restricted. Perhaps most importantly for Deutsche Bank's structural development in the United States, prohibitions against nonbanking affiliates under the Bank Holding Company Act were extended to branches, agencies, and commercial lending companies.[37]

Despite the complexity and changes in U.S. and New York regulations, the allure of New York was still virtually irresistible. German export companies needed trade financing and other services in the United States. Those with subsidiaries in America needed local Dollar-denominated financing to free themselves from capital shortages in Germany and to offset their long-term foreign exchange risk. German companies, some of which were unknown in the United States, had little access there to certain kinds of borrowing, such as commercial paper and private placements of securities. Many needed guidance in how to do business under American practices and norms.[38] As evidence of the foreign imperative, by 1974, one-third of Deutsche Bank's total business and balance sheet originated outside of Germany. Nevertheless its organization and manpower did not reflect the weighting of its activities.[39]

Faced with this vast array of regulatory issues and political risks coupled with economic opportunity, it is no wonder then that many banks, including Deutsche Bank, Dresdner, and Commerzbank, turned to cooperative agreements for foreign investment. During the 1960s and early '70s, creating cooperative agreements among European banks became one preferred strategy in the financial sector for dealing with a host of problems and opportunities – some of which were connected to the United States, but others not – such as American competition in Europe, European integration in the service sector, and various resource and regulatory constraints.[40] The goals of these banking groups were couched in idealistic European political terms. They wanted, in some sense, to create the same spirit in European banking that had characterized the general progressive political and economic development of the European Community.[41] Deutsche Bank's cooperative efforts began in 1963 with informal discussions with other European banks (European Advisory Committee), which eventually led to several joint ventures, two in the United States.[42]

Deutsche Bank was one of the first financial institutions to enter into an alliance with other European banks. Although lukewarm about entry into the United States with other banks, Abs came to see the whole undertaking as the beginning of a merger of banks in and outside of Europe.[43] As early as

1965, Abs stressed the importance of creating pan-European enterprises in key sectors such as banking if the European dream were to be realized.[44] On this point, in the 1960s, a consensus existed in Deutsche Bank management.[45] Reluctant to proceed with monetary integration in 1965, by 1970, Abs and other leaders began to take seriously not only monetary union – an alternative reserve currency to the Dollar – but also a single market and a unified tax system as well as even a unified banking system and the formation of large, European enterprises.[46] As with the other alliances, the consortium's project was flush with rhetoric about European integration and vague aspirations but suffered from a lack of clear strategic goals. Unfortunately, despite a great deal of enthusiasm that lasted well into the 1970s, the projects never attained their lofty goals, in part because none of the banks, even Deutsche Bank, seemed completely committed to it; perhaps too, because European integration did not produce more consolidation in the banking sector, this business model did not succeed. Like the European Community itself, sadly, the alliances suffered from asymmetrical commitment to the intermediary goals and conflicting views about ultimate aims.[47] Within ten years of the joint venture's entry into the United States, Deutsche Bank was looking for alternatives for doing business there.

In 1963, Deutsche Bank announced that Europe needed to develop a joint credit agency for foreign activities, which would extend its credit network outside of European national borders. In addition to European idealism, day-to-day practical matters also spoke for collective action. With more and more customers demanding medium and long-term credit for export and other services, Deutsche Bank's existing participations, such as that with Ausfuhrkredit-Aktiengesellschaft, appeared inadequate for future and even current needs.[48] The bank stressed that this new association would not harm its existing relationships and correspondent banking agreements. The initial alliance, the culmination of five years of talks, included four banks (Amsterdamsche Bank, Banque de la Société Générale de Belgique, Midland Bank, and Deutsche Bank), and merely entailed a European Consulting Committee for coordinating business. Abs and Ulrich represented Deutsche Bank.[49]

In 1967, the bank finally announced the group's first concrete project, a European bank for medium-term credit – up to seven years – Banque Europeénne de Crédit à Moyen Terme (the original name of BEC). With developments in the world currency system and offsetting payments with the United States, the bank prospered. By that time the "circle," as Deutsche Bank referred to the group, had expanded to seven.[50] Within ten years of its birth, BEC was doing a lively business in the Eurodebt market. It played a leading role in thirty-nine international credit consortia and participated in another fifty-one, for a total of $9.5 billion.[51]

Also in 1967, the European Advisory Council announced its intention in the following year to found a bank jointly in New York. The ownership of the bank was in the hands of Deutsche Bank, Amsterdam-Rotterdam Bank (AMRO Bank, the product of the 1964 merger of two Dutch banks), Midland, and Société Générale of Belgium. In effect, the group was taking over two

From left to right, Klaus Jacobs, Karl Klasen, and Franz Heinrich Ulrich at the opening celebration for EAB in 1968.

subsidiaries of the Belgian bank, which already existed in New York, and had their origins in the agency established in 1921 by Banque Belge pour l'Etranger, Brussels, an affiliate of Société Générale of Belgique. By 1952, the Belgian bank had turned the agency into two subsidiaries under New York law: the Belgian American Bank Corporation, a commercial bank, and a trust company to take deposits.[52]

Even under Belgian management, the banks, which had been insufficiently supported, were significant players in New York. Among the five subsidiaries of foreign banks, together they amounted to the second largest, just behind Schroder.[53] By 1964, the twenty-three branches, twenty-four agents, and five subsidiaries of foreign banks already accounted for $4.6 billion in assets or 8 percent of the New York market, making them together roughly the size of Bankers Trust Company. But the totals were deceptive. About 70 percent of their deposits, for example, came from their parent companies. A good deal of their short-term lending was to brokers and for trade financing. Like their counterparts in Europe, most of the foreign banks' business in the United States was with affiliates from their home country. Few had any success penetrating the market of American borrowers. According to Deutsche Bank analysts, the founding of the foreign bank affiliates was more a method of reinforcing the competitive position of the parent by providing financial advice to home-country clients investing in the United States, by getting involved in trade and investment decisions of clients, by doing foreign exchange trading, by reinforcing long-standing correspondent relationships, and, most curiously, by encouraging other American banks to do business in the European market.[54]

The goals of the participants were ambitious but well grounded. The joint venture aimed at not only servicing subsidiaries of European clients but also at helping to establish contacts with American companies preparing to do business in Europe. Both purely U.S. business and central bank foreign exchange transactions might be won over. The Council banks jointly contributed $20 million for the shares. The two U.S. foreign bank subsidiaries were renamed European American Bank Corporation (EABC) and European American Bank & Trust (EABTC).[55]

The two-bank structure gave the venture an incredible competitive advantage. Both were organized under New York law and each of the member banks held the same proportion of the shares. EABTC operated as a bank that could take deposits and hold securities in trust, but had strict lending limits. EABC, in contrast, was not permitted to take deposits, offer checking accounts, or serve as a trust, but had much higher lending limits. EABTC could give advances to EABC, which in turn could lend the funds out to corporate clients. The two-bank structure gave the collective entity the ability to take in cheap deposits and lend them out with few constraints at much higher rates. There were few Article 12 companies, as this New York statute was called, and the Fed, which had begun to find the structure dangerous – or at least messy – threatened regularly to take the power away from New York state, which slowly began to let in more banks with this capacity in the 1970s.[56] The employees worked for both banks, passing files from one side of their desks to the other depending on which bank should handle a particular piece of business. EABTC was also a member of the Fed, whereas EABC had been grandfathered in, allowing it to trade securities. Although other banks such as Schroder had the same structure, EAB became the leader in using it to build business.[57] In effect, it could compete with Chase and Citibank on relatively equal terms.[58] (The two subsidiaries were eventually merged in 1978 into one holding company, but I will refer to them as EAB unless the distinction is important to the narrative.)

Within two years, the two banks had assets of $439.8 million, double the amount they held when the banks were restructured in May 1968, and had opened a subsidiary in Bermuda and a branch in the Bahamas. With these successes behind it, the European Consulting Committee seemed poised to enter new ventures.[59]

In ten years of cooperation, the partner banks built an international reach. Including the member banks themselves, the joint venture operations, and their combined subsidiaries, branches, and minority investments, the consortium collectively had a presence nearly everywhere. By 1973, the European Advisory Council had added members, restructured itself into the European Banks' International Company SA (EBIC), expanded the activities of and renamed BEC (Banque Européenne de Crédit), and begun to issue financial statements.[60] The group had established a merchant bank in London in 1973 and several other ventures with varying degrees of participation by the member banks.[61] The member banks had $87.7 billion in assets, 9,350 branches, and nearly 178,000 workers. In 1973, EAB alone had $1.7 billion in assets.[62]

Much of EAB's activities consisted of giving advice to client firms from the home countries of the investing banks. The U.S. banks had a special German department principally to aid Deutsche Bank clients in the United States with financing, consulting, and other services.[63] In 1974, for example, the bank put together a book on direct investment in the United States. The book included contributions from consulting and legal firms, and dealt with issues such as the possible legal forms for entry into the United States, the choice of location, cartel regulations, and tax rates – as well as a host of facts such as labor costs, types and amounts of imports, growth rates of some sectors – and, of course, methods of financing, a chapter understandably written by the bank itself.[64]

The staffing was a mixture of Europeans on loan from their own banks and American hires. Klaus Jacobs was selected to be Deutsche Bank's first representative. With virtually no advance notice, he was signing visa applications and preparing to leave for New York.[65] The operation was run by Paul Verhagen, a Belgian who had worked for Merrill Lynch, together with four executive vice presidents, including one from Deutsche Bank, Jacobs, who worked for EAB from 1968 to 1977. Verhagen was replaced by Harry Ekblom, an American from Chase Manhattan. He remained until the early 1980s, when Ray Dempsey, an expert on turnarounds was brought in.[66] The board of directors – each of the subsidiaries had separate boards with overlapping members – also included representation from each of the member banks, usually senior managers. For example, Klasen and Ulrich served from Deutsche Bank.[67] In addition to Jacobs – who elected in 1973 to remain as a local manager and who eventually became president of EAB under chairman Ekblom, instead of returning to Germany – Deutsche Bank sent over some of its best young talent to EAB's New York office.[68] After serving for five years as Abs' personal assistant, the position Jacobs had held before him, Michael Rassmann joined Jacobs in New York. He served with EAB for fourteen years, nine of them as executive vice president, member of the board of directors, and head of the German desk.[69]

From the beginning, though, Deutsche Bank hedged its bets a little in the United States. For one thing, as mentioned, EAB did not solve Deutsche Bank's investment banking problem, for which Deutsche Bank sought out a separate joint venture. Despite the successes and rhetoric associated with EAB, as discussed Deutsche Bank created another joint venture with UBS Corporation for international listings. By 1971, the EAB banks had assets of over a billion Dollars, with loans of $833 million, largely to European subsidiaries in the United States. German companies alone accounted for DM 1.5 billion ($0.4 billion),[70] but as long as U.S. limits on mixing commercial banking and underwriting securities held, Deutsche Bank had to keep its operations very separate. It relied on joint ventures in part because they helped avoid the onerous application of New York banking and federal bank holding company laws which precluded affiliation of a commercial bank with a bank that conducted investment banking.[71] However, EAB itself had a checkered history.

Although EAB initially focused on supporting member-bank customers' local banking services in the United States – mostly financing American subsidiaries of European companies – consistent with its original objectives, it soon moved into other activities.[72] The partner banks offered customers Eurocurrency loans through offshore branches, real estate loans, straight loans, and trade services,

The German Desk at EAB circa 1972 with Michael Rassmann, standing left, and Ellen Ruth Schneider-Lenné, who later became Deutsche Bank's first female member of the management board. The other person is unidentified.

as well as deposits. EAB also set up branches in California for loan production and contact with American clients, but with no legal powers.[73] EAB had a large and diverse list of corporate clients, approximately 150 subsidiaries of German companies alone, with a variety of different facilities, including revolving credit lines, letters of credit, and short-term loans. Some individual lines were as high as $20 million.[74] Besides deposits, its financing came from its shareholders and from issuing commercial paper on the money market, which it accessed without parent company guarantees. EAB issued a $20 million ten-year fixed rate bond to an insurance company and branched out into other banking activities. From their headquarters at 52 Wall Street, the two banks had achieved a good deal of independence, but not the presence that Deutsche Bank desired.[75]

Independence and diversification created management problems. By the late 1970s, write-offs and bad loans were putting pressure on profits. Some of the write-offs were related to emerging market loans, some to EAB's acquisition (specifically EABTC) and the integration of Franklin National Bank, a New York retail bank, at a public auction brought on by Franklin's mismanagement of foreign currency transactions. With the acquisition, EAB entered U.S. retail banking.

In many respects, the purchase was a good deal for EAB. Although Franklin had a lot of bad loans, EAB's agreement with the FDIC allowed for a short period during which time EAB could reject any of Franklin's assets deemed too risky. With Franklin's branches, too – Franklin had approximately 100 branches, mostly on Long Island – EAB had much greater access to retail deposit funding instead of Eurodeposit borrowings, which then, unlike now, were much more expensive than retail funding.[76]

With this wider base, EAB was among the largest twenty-five banks in the United States, but Franklin left EAB with many problems. Managing the larger operations proved more difficult than foreseen.[77] Profits fell until 1978 when the two companies were merged via a holding company, European American Bancorp (EAB). Both EAB and Deutsche Bank got entwined separately in a suit involving a syndicate loan to a tanker group (Colocotronis). Originally brought to EAB by Deutsche Bank, the tanker company mismanaged its assets and lost a large portion of its long-term leasing deals. Difficulties with EAB's documentation of agreements made prosecuting its interests more difficult.[78] Although the suit was resolved out of court, the write-downs and payments to plaintiffs took a toll on EAB's earnings until 1978 and at least one senior manager resigned. Whereas some of the assets were recovered, only a great increase in customers and a cut in employees restored EAB's profitability.[79]

Nevertheless, EAB continued to expand in the late '70s and early '80s with a branch in Luxembourg for foreign exchange trading and Euromarket business, a venture capital company in New York and subsidiaries in Chicago and Miami. It became the first foreign company admitted to the New York Clearing House Association in 1978, and pursued new business lines, though it was forced by regulators to close the California branches. But with its expansion via Miami into South America, especially, EAB acquired many new problem loans.[80]

Deutsche Bank seemed to be getting out less than it put in. BEC and Deutsche Bank's Luxembourg operations competed for lending Eurofunds to American clients through EAB, and EAB was obliged to do business with both BEC and Deutsche Bank Luxembourg, splitting the profits it earned on prearranged agreements, even when the business was derived from German clients and Deutsche Bank. EAB and Deutsche Bank played a key role in recyling Eurodeposits and the securitization of European debt.[81] By 1973, Deutsche Bank was considered by far the strongest of the partner banks. Most of the foreign employees at the American bank came from Deutsche Bank. The great strength of the German economy required German banks to have a greater presence in the United States. With huge branch networks in Germany scooping up funds and corporate customers making new demands, Deutsche Bank had to have more capacity to channel funds and expand services.[82] Some Germans at EAB felt that Deutsche Bank's contribution to the joint venture was large enough to justify even a 50 percent ownership stake.[83]

Moreover, some other weaknesses of the joint venture were obvious. Too many decisions had to be pushed up to the board level where senior management of the parent banks sat. Although the policy had been to keep an American as CEO, the board met once a month and the Europeans made many decisions. Without a single-bank structure in Europe, competition among the member banks was rife. There was little coordination of the European side of the business by the partner banks. The hoped-for merger, at least by German managers, never happened. With the emergence of the Eurodeposit market, much of the vast sums of money produced during the oil crisis years was recycled through

European banks, especially in Luxembourg, rather than through New York. The retail and other bank functions never quite developed an American identity nor profited a lot from their European roots. Although EAB worked with large American companies such as General Motors, Ford, Chrysler, DuPont, Rockwell International, and Honeywell, until the purchase of Franklin, 70 percent of the clients were Europeans, with one-third of those coming from German (Deutsche Bank) contacts. Even after the acquisition of Franklin, 50 percent of the client base was still European and many of the American companies were with EAB because of its European connections and access to the Eurodebt markets. Although the workplace atmosphere was very international and the team seemed to work well together – animated by a sense of mission to create a truly European institution – EAB had little capacity to service the needs of new sorts of financial institutions and had not given Deutsche Bank the entrée into investment banking it needed, especially for equity issues for which Deutsche Bank still had little capacity. Some German clients, too, wanted to know where Deutsche Bank was in the United States. More and more voices in Frankfurt spoke for Deutsche Bank developing its own independent strength in the United States. For some observers and employees alike, a joint venture structure by one of the world's largest banks in the world's largest capital market seemed to be an odd strategy at best.[84]

From Dual Strategy to Integrated Entity

Announced finally in 1977, the long-rumored Deutsche Bank intention to establish a branch came, nevertheless, as a shock to many in and outside the bank. Informed during a board meeting, partner banks were reported to have been stunned. Not only were many of Deutsche Bank's representatives surprised, some felt betrayed.[85] Nevertheless, the partners and employees must have had an inkling that something was afoot. Although Deutsche Bank managers were hesitant to rush into independent foreign investments and professed their commitment to the EBIC concept, by 1977 opening a branch in the United States was publicly discussed in the press and pursued in some other countries.[86] European investment in the United States alone seemed to call for a greater presence.[87]

The branch was actually opened over a year after the announcement. Deutsche Bank did not receive the license from the New York State Banking Department to open an uninsured state branch of a foreign bank organization until July 15, 1978.[88] In 1982, branches in Los Angeles and Chicago followed. Part of the intention of opening up a direct U.S. presence was to develop stronger relationships with U.S. banks – not so much with the customers of those banks – and to better represent German commercial interests there, even if this put Deutsche Bank in competition with EAB. Deutsche Bank claimed at the time that it had no intention of selling or reducing its interest in EAB, merely that operating under its own name had acquired more importance. Deutsche Bank, moreover, saw the branch as an opportunity to attract and service foreign investors in Deutsche Bank's own equity. Foreign ownership of the bank's own

View of the Manhattan skyline, including the building in which Deutsche Bank's New York branch was located (the white framed building).

shares had already grown to a substantial 20 percent.[89] The decision seemed to have nothing to do with the Latin American debt problems, which had caught many banks off guard, or those with Franklin, but rather seemed intended to give Deutsche Bank added strength in the United States and to be part of the bank's desire to be represented in its own name in all major markets. Deutsche Bank contended that it would pursue a dual strategy with the branch and joint venture in the United States, but it was clear to many from the outset that this approach made little sense. Although one of the ostensible missions of the New York branch was to serve German clients' foreign exchange, loan, and trade-transaction needs, many of the German companies preferred the full-service EAB.[90]

The branch labored under many other hindrances. Although Abs seemed to have finally supported the decision – he was the first home-office leader to visit the New York branch office – in Frankfurt, feelings were mixed. Younger Deutsche Bank executives tended to have some reservations about the EAB concept, but the branch in the United States was not wholeheartedly supported either.[91] Detlev Staecker, who had opened both the Sydney and London offices, was tapped to move to New York and do the same there. He had experience but few employees. For over ten years, Deutsche Bank had no systematic way of moving employees back and forth from Germany to other countries.[92] Worse still, Staecker had little guidance from Frankfurt about the branch's long-term objectives. The few that were set often seemed contradictory. The head office was still looking at foreign branch operations as if they were part of the domestic business. Even though Deutsche Bank had done the first U.S. Dollar loan in Australia, Frankfurt wanted to push ahead with the bank's old product lines from Germany. No one seemed to have a coherent plan as to how to use Deutsche Bank's phenomenal brand name.[93] It even seemed to some that the leaders of the bank expected Deutsche Bank's managers on the ground, in the branch and at EAB, to figure out collectively an intelligent strategy for solving the problems.[94]

Although the branch ostensibly was to serve American companies, taking clients away from EAB was taboo. The two operations were in competition for new customers, both American and German. EAB's German customers were supposed to stay with EAB, unless they expressed a wish to do business with the branch. The potential for conflict should have been obvious. The branch did business with Hoechst and Daimler, but only by invitation. For a time, managers at the two Deutsche Bank operations hardly talked with one another. Frankfurt management had put the EAB and branch teams in New York in an impossible position. The branch was not allowed to poach staff from EAB, and few young German managers were capable or willing to join the branch in New York. EAB had virtually all the talented Deutsche Bank people with American experience,[95] whereas Staecker opened the branch with a staff of only three. Although by 1980 it had grown to fifty, he needed more people from Germany. With tight control from the head office, getting deals done, moreover, required staff with good contacts in Frankfurt, people who knew with whom to talk and how. He was obliged to take staff on loan from outside of the United States for short periods.[96]

This particular issue reflected broader problems at the bank. Herrhausen bemoaned how few people at the bank wanted to take on international positions. Hans-Otto Thierbach, who was responsible for the international operations, used to say that the difference between Barclays and Deutsche Bank was that Barclays had nearly a thousand managers with international experience. Deutsche Bank had virtually no one.

Deutsche Bank was still a very centralized organization. At first, the branch was limited to credit lines of $2 million, a tiny sum for the U.S. market. Anything above this amount had to be approved by two Frankfurt departments, credit and international, where managers passed judgment with little knowledge of the U.S. market. Frankfurt could not understand the difference between counterparty and market risk. Delays were costly.[97]

Even though the branch status allowed the bank to operate as a domestic commercial bank in the United States and to deal in foreign exchange and trade financing, there were still regulatory problems. With numerous layers of regulatory compliance in the United States, the branch had to file reports with the Federal Reserve, New York Superintendent of Banks, the U.S. Treasury, Federal Deposit Insurance Corporation (FDIC), the Bundesbank, U.S. and German tax authorities, and Deutsche Bank's own head office. No wonder Deutsche Bank sent a lawyer. Because of the Glass-Steagall Act, the branch had to keep its distance from Deutsche Bank's investment bank arm in the United States, Atlantic Capital. Although Staecker would run into Barthold von Ribbentrop, head of Atlantic Capital, by "accident," U.S. legal authorities demanded that a firewall exist between the two Deutsche Bank organizations. Not until the late 1980s, when the Fed loosened the 1933 rules and Deutsche Bank was grandfathered in, could the two Deutsche Bank representatives coordinate the businesses.[98]

Some of the regulatory problems were international in nature. Basel I forced banks to reduce their exposure to short and medium-term loans and letters of credit, both stable and profitable businesses of Deutsche Bank. As a branch, the Deutsche Bank operation was included in Deutsche Bank's consolidated statistics for Basel I reporting, but not EAB. Like most banking operations, therefore, Deutsche Bank in New York pursued guarantee business and syndications.[99]

There were other policy and procedural issues with the head office. The branch wanted to serve as the window for many small and medium-sized American financial institutions for letters of credit and back-up commercial paper lines. These banks and insurance companies were too small to have their own contacts. Until the late 1980s, however, Deutsche Bank policy forbade guaranteeing facilities of other financial institutions, which in Germany were perceived as competitors.[100] Therefore the branch could not do business with them in the United States.

In general, many of the German managers in Frankfurt had little feeling for the American problems and new facilities, which were beginning to emerge in the 1980s. Some of the issues arose because of differences in the structure of markets and the required organizational responses in both New York and Frankfurt. In Frankfurt, there was little sense of liability management, the short-term financing of an operation with commercial paper in different currencies. This was essential in New York. In 1992, Staecker even hired an expert, John Ross, to put a system in place for the American operations, but he had no counterpart in Frankfurt with whom to work. As derivative instruments became more and more important, clashes occurred over restricting traders in New York who had to make split-second decisions which the Frankfurt office could not oversee and sometimes did not understand. Eventually, in 1995, Ross was brought to Frankfurt to set up an American-style treasury operation.[101]

By 1986, the branch was doing a vibrant business in long-term debt facilities and was particularly strong in foreign exchange dealings, an area in which the Germans and other Europeans in general seemed to excel. American banks in this period seemed less interested in trade business, out of which foreign exchange trading had sprung. By this time, the branch had very good personnel for trading.[102] The branch could count many famous American companies among its clients – for example, Woolworth's, Mobil, International Harvester, John Deere, AT&T, ITT, General Motors, Ford, and Continental Can. Much of its success with these American clients – but not all, however – rested on their activities with and relationship to Deutsche Bank in Germany.[103] By this time, too, a good deal of purely German business had moved over to the branch.[104]

Deutsche Bank wanted still more of a presence in New York. Gradually the staffing problems eased. Exchanges of staff were organized between Germany and the United States and among other national operations. Eventually, around

Detlev Staecker (center) and Hans J. Buhr (left) being interviewed for the staff magazine at the Deutsche Bank's New York branch office in 1979.

120 Germans worked for a time in the American operations, many later moving into senior positions in the bank. Some Americans were sent to Germany; one even ran a branch there.[105] Despite the market crash in late 1987, in 1988 Deutsche Bank Capital Corporation expanded its securities trading business and moved into new areas, such as estate management, real estate financing, and mergers and acquisitions (M&A). In 1988, it also founded a wholly owned subsidiary, Deutsche Bank Government Securities, specializing in trading U.S. government debt. After a losing first year, management hoped that gaining status as a primary dealer in U.S. securities would allow it to turn the forty-one-person operation into a profitable undertaking.[106] But with all of these separate Deutsche Bank activities, as late as the mid-1980s if you looked up Deutsche Bank in the New York telephone directory, you got the EAB listing.[107]

By the mid-1980s, most senior managers recognized that Deutsche Bank's double strategy (dual strategies) was flawed. In 1984, Herrhausen demanded a decision from his colleagues. While he, Ulrich, Christian, and Guth shared responsibility for various aspects of business through much of the 1980s, in a 1984 exposé about the situation in the United States, it was Herrhausen – or perhaps just his staff – who implored the bank to buy the whole joint venture or get out of EAB.[108] Either Deutsche Bank should take control of EAB and fold the branch into it, or Deutsche Bank should sell its interest in EAB and focus on the branch.[109] Some of the impetus may have come from a memo written by the head of Deutsche Bank's investment banking operation in the United States. He argued that it was clear that the Glass-Steagall Act would be applied less and less and that many bank holding company restrictions would also be removed. If U.S. restrictions on interstate banks were also loosened, Deutsche Bank would no longer need to conduct its universal banking through a series of joint ventures. Instead of remaining a marginal player in the United States, it could build up a world class operation there by itself.[110] In short, as U.S. restrictions on investment and commercial banking as well as lending activity for subsidiaries and branches relaxed, the two defenses of the holding company and separate subsidiaries became less significant. The change in the regulatory and business environment did not go unnoticed among Deutsche Bank's American partners. For several years, the partners engaged a sort of "cat-and-mouse" game about relinquishing or conversely increasing their shares in EAB. No one wanted to confide his interest in leaving for fear of losing his bargaining position.[111]

In 1988, Deutsche Bank sold its 23.15 percent interest in EAB to its Dutch partners, AMRO,[112] who had approached the Germans. The deal involved not only cash but trading of some foreign subsidiaries.[113] Deutsche Bank's sale of its holding in the EAB investment, such as the earlier one to open the branch, hit its staff there hard. They had been wrestling for ten years with a tense and unsatisfying compromise. Moreover, without Deutsche Bank, the joint venture was not viable. Most of the other member banks soon made the same decision. The association disappeared, and although only two of the six member banks are still independent institutions, the dream of a European bank is still far away.

The decision solved many immediate problems. Despite its disappointment, the EAB staff behaved very professionally. The old frictions seemed to disappear as if they had never existed. Michael Rassmann and one or two other Germans moved over to the branch; some went back to Germany. Rassmann oversaw the large task of transferring EAB's German desk to the branch – credit lines and relationships (over 200 clients), a six-month undertaking that by all accounts was accomplished smoothly.[114]

Deutsche Bank still maintained a German system in New York with at least two co-managers. Staecker's 1978 arrival in New York had been quickly followed by Hans Buhr; the two split the responsibility for the branch. Staecker handled credit risk and personnel; Buhr corporate banking and international (foreign exchange trading); they jointly managed client relations, dividing the list of clients alphabetically. By 1979, the staff of forty was divided into nine departments headed by Staecker and Buhr.[115] In the mid-1980s, they were joined by Helmut von Natzmer, who handled organizational issues. His arrival made it possible to split the client list three ways instead of two. Natzmer was part of an effort to address Deutsche Bank's ongoing information systems problem. IBM had been hired to develop an integrated system for all of Deutsche Bank's operations, because each unit at the bank still had its own system. For Deutsche Bank, a very centralized operation, integrating computer systems entailed both a significant cost but also a vital control necessity. As with most companies, too few people knew the complexities of all markets. Adapting the trading system to the United States was a real nightmare,[116] but a typical growing pain for companies becoming more international while trying to absorb the eventual costs and benefits of powerful new electronic tools.

The integration of EAB's staff and activities led to several organizational changes, and coincided with still others. Buhr went back to Germany and Rassmann took over his role in the "Triumvirate."[117] The branch also began dividing clients into separate departments to focus on the specific needs of companies in different branches. By December 1986, it held $1.5 billion in deposits and issued $3.1 billion in credit lines to 550 firms, a near doubling of its business from the year before. With German customers, it stressed its ability to offer a full line of German-styled services, but new business of this sort was hard to come by. By 1987, thirteen German financial institutions were operating in New York.[118]

In 1989, Deutsche Bank moved its office uptown. Although still formally separate, Deutsche Bank's various American operations – the branch, Deutsche Bank Capital Markets Corp., and its leasing firm – were brought under one roof. The new office, rented from Shearson Lehman Hutton, provided enough space for 700 office workers. The festivities for celebrating the grand opening were decorated by a German flag that had accompanied Apollo 15 on its 1971 voyage to the moon.[119] To some observers, Deutsche Bank's hundred-year journey from the founding of Edison General Electric to establishment of the new office may have seemed more arduous.

With the combined talents of the EAB German desk and the branch staff, Deutsche Bank developed a large client base of U.S. corporations and German subsidiaries, offering money market financings, commercial paper and bonds, foreign exchange, and investment banking. Foreign exchange trading was still particularly strong, but private banking became more important. Housing 858 employees, its new space had virtually become an all "Deutsche Bank building." By 1989, the branch was already contributing 7 percent of all Deutsche Bank's business, amounting to 21 percent of all Deutsche Bank foreign branch revenue. Interest income reached $38.7 million, fee income $18.2 million, and trade and foreign exchange $9.1 million, producing a profit contribution for Deutsche Bank of $22.7 million. Its German connections laid the foundation for this success, but also created some restrictions on its activities and perhaps higher expectations for its results. With tight relations with some clients, such as Philip Morris, the branch felt compelled to exclude itself, for example, from some lucrative transactions where it perceived a conflict of interest, such as in many leveraged buyout financings.[120] Moreover, some in Frankfurt felt that the branch's profitability outlook was still pretty dismal.[121]

A New Strategy for the 1990s

It is perhaps a cliché to write that 1990 was a watershed year for Deutsche Bank, Germany, and the world, but clichés often contain much truth. In that year, Germany was reunified after forty years of separation. The Cold War came to an abrupt end, and the United States began a resurgence that baffled many Europeans. A year earlier Deutsche Bank's leading manager had been assassinated, and Deutsche Bank had purchased the successor bank of J. P. Morgan's investment bank in London, Morgan Grenfell. By many comparative benchmarks, Deutsche Bank lost in the 1990s many of its competitive strengths. However, by the end of the decade, it had taken some giant steps forward, regaining a leadership position in international banking.

As for many institutions, for Deutsche Bank globalization has been a "double-edged sword." Although globalization and deregulation opened more opportunities for banks, they also eliminated entry barriers in home markets. New competitors penetrated once-protected national markets and sectors and threatened steady sources of profit.[122] Many financial institutions witnessed an erosion of margins in their traditional, core businesses.[123] The introduction of the Euro, for example, temporarily reduced foreign exchange transactions, an activity in which Deutsche Bank excelled in the late 1990s.[124] International regulation often dampened the ability of banks to cultivate profitable domestic relationships.[125] With increased capital mobility and new vast international participants also came greater demands for international regulation of financing.[126] Under profit pressure because of the crises of the late '90s, weak trading profits, and predictions of lower growth in core banking areas, many European banks retrenched dramatically in their home markets and in some foreign activities to free up capital for more lucrative ventures.[127]

By 1990, too, American regulators had loosened up restrictions on commercial banks acting as investment bankers, making it easier for the U.S. institutions to challenge specialized American investment banks and non-American universal banks in this field. A group of worldwide players, such as Citigroup, Merrill Lynch, Morgan Stanley (later Morgan Stanley Dean Witter), and Goldman Sachs had emerged on an equal or even broader footing for underwriting than their European and Japanese competitors. These institutions offered sophisticated, worldwide corporate and individual services, took deposits, and provided research as well as made markets for initial public offerings and secondary issues.[128] Moreover, corporate clients became increasingly able themselves to access capital markets directly, sometimes even becoming bank-like in the services they offered others.[129]

Despite, or perhaps because of, America's pivotal place in financial changes, the U.S. market entailed special opportunities and obstacles. Without a serious presence there, banks could not become players in many capital market segments. By the late 1990s, the capitalization of the U.S. equity market, for example, was greater than the combined capitalizations of Japan, Germany, and Britain. Its bond market accounted for two-thirds of the outstanding global bonds.[130] As late as 1997, Deutsche Bank Securities Inc. ranked only twentieth in securities trading, capitalized at less than 3 percent of the largest, Merrill Lynch.[131] Moreover, in the United States and even in most of Europe it lagged behind many competitors, such as HSBC and Citibank, in retail banking. Although strong in private banking – a lucrative business under competitive and regulatory pressures because of its high profits and secrecy – Deutsche

Bank's $180 billion under management was less than half that of the market leader UBS, but still required 70 percent of UBS' staffing levels.[132]

By 1990, too, the world seemed poised to witness a new wave of mergers in the financial sector. With market liberalization and greater international competition, bank assets had grown faster than GNP in some countries. The larger banks were troubled by weaker profits and troubled loans. Some banks examined a variety of solutions: raising more capital; better loan evaluation and pricing; international retrenchment; new services; cost reduction; and focusing on niches. Although Germany's banks had maintained their return-on-assets ratio during the 1980s, bank valuations, including those in Germany, compared with overall market indices had fallen considerably between 1975 and 1990.[133]

As discussed, in 1989, Deutsche Bank bought the remaining 95 percent of shares in Morgan Grenfell for $1.5 billion. The decision was part of the bank's recognition that productive innovation was coming from America to Europe via England. Stopping in London may have been a result of insufficient courage at the bank to go all the way to the shores of the Hudson, but at least it provided a step toward moving closer to the heart of current financial trends – contributing senior and junior financial talent trained in Anglo-American investment banking. The bank still needed, however, young Germans who could speak the international language of banking as well as speak to the German *Mittelstand*.[134]

But the acquisition failed to deliver on much of what had been hoped. Some said that the greatest mistake was to leave Morgan Grenfell independent. According to Kopper, though, integrating Morgan Grenfell into the bank's other activities risked destroying the very entrepreneurial, investment banking spirit and high profits Deutsche Bank had sought to add with the acquisition. Much more disappointing was Morgan Grenfell's weakness in the United States and continental Europe, particularly in the equity sector, which was the German bank's weakness and an area which boomed soon after the purchase.[135] It made a great deal of money but had little impact on the culture of the rest of the bank. Deutsche Bank knew how to do relational banking and was one of the leaders in Europe, even worldwide, in fixed income issues and trading, but it was lost in the world of equity issues. Like Germany itself, it had not developed an equity culture that some at the bank began to see would become a growing source of high-margin business. The change in orientation would require vast changes not only in the structure and strategy of Deutsche Bank's business but also in German capitalism itself. Its competitors and even its customers were moving away from tight house bank relationships to competitive bidding and pay-for-service relationships. Avoiding conflicts of interest and enlarging its market required Deutsche Bank to drop substantial equity commitments in clients' stock and supervisory board insider responsibilities.[136] In short, Kopper understood and launched Deutsche Bank into an era with a very different business model, and one with a very different approach to U.S. business – a model designed to adapt to international competition and turbulence.

Competitors were branching out into many new or revived services. As fears subsided of emerging market defaults, in the early 1990s, a secondary market for developing country debt arose. By 1997, that market had grown to $6 trillion before falling off a few years later. Trading in rescheduled debt, the so-called Brady bonds for Argentina, Brazil, Bulgaria, Ecuador, Mexico, Nigeria, Panama, Peru, the Philippines, Poland, and Venezuela virtually exploded until the Asian and Russian crises dampened enthusiasm.[137] Corporate restructurings, which thrived in the United States in the form of leveraged buyouts and management buyouts as a newfound panacea to lackluster corporate earnings, moved onto the European scene. But Europe had its own special form of restructuring, which was the massive privatization of many of Europe's largest enterprises. Financial engineering and derivatives also exploded. From 1986 to 1996, financial derivatives' principal amounts outstanding increased by a factor of fifteen. In Europe alone, they increased from $13 billion to $2.83 trillion.[138] A shift in regulation and household savings patterns funneled trillions of funds away from simple savings accounts into pension and mutual funds – worth $2.4 trillion by 1995 – the management of which became either a new activity or at least a new source of investment banking funds for traditional banks.[139]

With all of these market developments, the last decade of the twentieth century was not good for Deutsche Bank. From December 1989 to December 1998, its stock price grew by only approximately 49 percent, a less than 4 percent compounded rate, despite strong world equity markets.[140] Distracted by many issues, not the least of which was German reunification, Deutsche Bank seemed during the 1990s to have lost much of its market position and cutting edge. For some, this period represented the third round of Americanization of German business. American capital markets were a magnet for all kinds of foreign investment. Not being there in force gave up this very strategic terrain. In 1990, Deutsche Bank was not among the top-twenty-five foreign banks in the United States as measured by assets. The list included sixteen Japanese banks, two British banks, two French banks, and one bank from each of four other countries. Some of the foreign banks had over ten offices in the United States.[141] Deutsche Bank recognized that its weakness in the United States was a giant soft spot in its international ambitions and strategies.

The widening and deepening of free trade zones also affected Deutsche Bank's international position. In addition to those in the United States, changes in European banking regulation during the last decade of the millennium created new opportunities and challenges for Deutsche Bank that would ultimately affect its U.S. business. Based on the principle that all barriers to trade and services should end in the European Community (European Union), in 1989 the Second Banking Directive granted any banks within the EC an automatic license to operate anywhere else within the Community. The automatic license would also be available to banks from countries that extended the same privilege to European banks. The Directive unleashed a wave of mergers in Europe. Since the new regulation went into effect, Deutsche Bank has acquired ownership and control of banks in Austria, Italy, the Netherlands, Portugal, and Spain. A decade later, the Euro also promised to promote intra-European banking by simplifying transactions among participating countries. NAFTA also promised to expand banking in North America by opening up Mexico to U.S. and

Canadian-based banks.[142] The degree of cross-border banking, multinational banking, and a series of bank failures and scandals reinforced the perception in most circles that more and better cross-border regulation of financial activity was necessary, complicating both the domestic and foreign operations of banks such as Deutsche Bank.

Despite some regulatory liberalization, foreign banking in the United States was still not easy. Many U.S. operations of foreign banks operated with losses. Because of the classic problem of managing from a distance and finding a happy medium between independence and tight control, some foreign purchases of U.S. banks, such as Midland Bank's of Crocker National, sustained such large losses that all or parts of the U.S. operations had to be sold off.[143] Although foreign banks with multistate branches had been grandfathered out of some of its provisions, the International Banking Act of 1978 required foreign-owned banks to adhere to the laws pertaining to U.S. banks and forced them to select a "home state," whose banking laws would apply. In response to the BCCI scandal, moreover, further restrictions were imposed in 1991 with the Foreign Bank Supervision Enhancement Act, which required foreign banks to obtain a license from both federal and state regulators.[144]

For some, Deutsche Bank started the 1990s with a relatively clear but rather defensive vision of its future. Under new leadership, its priority was to protect its two greatest strengths: its domestic leadership in Germany and Europe. However, that might require expansion in Europe as well as in the United States. Hilmar Kopper committed the bank to continue its push into retail in some high-margin markets, such as Italy and Spain, while maintaining a strong corporate banking presence throughout Europe, which included corporate finance, trading money, currencies, and fixed income securities, equities, and derivatives. Yet there was some schizophrenia at the bank. As Kopper revealed to an interviewer, when "I talk to a German, I stress retail, because he understands it better. Internationally, we prefer to be regarded as a corporate bank."[145] But this division of identity was workable in a world in which few Germans spoke English and few foreigners German.

Nowhere was the ambivalence more pronounced than with the Morgan Grenfell acquisition. Deutsche Bank recognized that it had paid a "full" price for the British bank and not all of the management was wholehearted about the acquisition. It was hoped that the merchant bank would complement the larger, slower continental bank the same way a destroyer complements a battleship. But both management groups had to contend with culture clashes.[146] Even though the bank had acquired a small New York brokerage firm, CJ Lawrence, which it hoped would improve its equity trading business,[147] and John Craven from Morgan Grenfell became the first non-German to join the Deutsche Bank management board, the beneficial synergies never seemed to materialize.

Even given its new international capacities and predominant position in its home market, Deutsche Bank had a long list of unfulfilled strategic objectives. Some might say that the list was so long that it itself became a weakness.[148] Despite efforts in the 1990s to cut staff, its cost structure was still high compared to some international competitors. It was weak in equity and derivative trading.

Kopper, at least, believed that growth in many of these areas would require a huge structural and cultural change in the bank. To be a market leader in Europe and in the sectors at which the bank aimed, it would have to shift its center of gravity out of Frankfurt and toward London or New York. American competition would be an obstacle, but, more importantly, Deutsche Bank could never be, in Kopper's view, a "Deutsche Sachs, or a Deutsche Lynch, in the United States."[149] It wanted to stay a universal bank. The days of having to choose between universal banking and investment banking seemed numbered even in the United States – perhaps the time had come to make an acquisition in the States. "If we saw a genuine opportunity, we would look closely at it."[150]

Deutsche Bank shared both this vision and conflicts with several of its European rivals. Some banks such as Crédit Suisse, which had purchased First Boston, despite their difficulties, were an enormous competitive threat: "They had it all, Zurich, London, New York, Tokyo." But caution had to be the watchword. Experience had taught that it was not easy to combine cultures. Kopper still preferred to grow Deutsche Bank's people talent and hoped that it would be possible to cultivate two parallel cultures and remuneration systems. But the bank's remuneration system and cultivation of talent had not yet completely caught up with the market, which hampered Germany's search for investment banking talent. With German companies unwilling to pay for advice from bankers and Deutsche Bank less willing to hold large blocks of securities on which it could earn returns, the bank sought geographic and product diversification. By 1993, most of Deutsche Bank's profits came from outside Germany, concentrated in other European countries, and in South-East Asia, not in the United States.[151] It had set its sights on becoming a major force in several aspects of investment banking for which neither the supply of ideas nor the demand for products could be found in abundance in Germany. Coming close to both seemed to require changing the bank's compensation system.

Although many at the bank wanted to maintain the traditions established by Siemens, a curious thing had happened over the past 100 years. Not only was there a separation of ownership and control, but there had become a separation between dealmakers and management within the bank. In the days of Villard and Adams, the dealmakers might have made more money than Siemens and Gwinner, but they were not employees of the bank. The division had produced an odd situation. Unlike most other companies, Deutsche Bank's most senior managers are not its highest earners.[152]

Kopper aggressively sought new blood in the United States to grow and coordinate the various business segments there. In September 1992, Deutsche Bank appointed John Rolls as president and chief executive officer of its North America Holding Corp. (DBNA), Deutsche Bank's coordination center for the bank's nearly 1,500 employees and its activities in the United States and Canada. He had a mission to make Deutsche Bank a leading player in the commercial and merchant banking business in North America, especially corporate finance and money market activities. Rolls, a Canadian by birth and raised in Mexico, had an MBA from Columbia University and years of experience as a financial officer with commercial – not banking – firms.[153]

To some observers, he was an odd choice. He spoke no German, requiring meetings of the management board in Germany, which Rolls sometimes attended, to be conducted in English. Although other foreign ventures into the United States had been frustrated by management conflicts over local autonomy and pay, Deutsche Bank seemed poised to make the same mistakes.

Because Deutsche Bank had had many false starts in North America, Rolls spent much of his first fifteen months with Deutsche Bank in meetings with its top management in Germany, formulating a strategy for success in the United States. He had inherited two distinct investment banking operations in the United States: Deutsche Bank Capital, chartered under the grandfather clause of the International Banking Act, and CJ Lawrence, the partially owned subsidiary of Morgan Grenfell, which operated under Section 20 of the Glass-Steagall Act. Although the Federal Reserve limited the revenues of Section 20 banks, none were imposed on the grandfathered institutions. The Fed feared that Deutsche Bank's ownership of the two would give it a serious advantage over its American competitors, which still could not combine their investment and commercial banking operations. Concerned about Fed retaliation, Rolls merged the two into a single Section 20 unit, CJ Lawrence/Deutsche Bank Securities, headquartered at DBNA offices at West 52th Street in Manhattan. Thanks to Deutsche Bank Securities' expensive government securities activities, the combined entity did not have much risk of exceeding the government's cap of 10 percent restriction on revenues from corporate securities. All Deutsche Bank's North American branches, its swap and option businesses (Deutsche Bank Financial Products), and asset-based lending (Deutsche Bank Credit Corp.) were brought under the same rubric of DBNA. At the heart of Rolls' strategy was helping the bank's foreign clients to sell their securities to American clients, and to cull out a large share of the foreign securities purchased by Americans, transactions that were running at $27 billion in the first quarter of 1994. Deutsche Bank intended to win the favor of its American investment banking competitors by inviting them into its own European deals, hoping then that they would return the favor. Rolls' target was to quadruple DBNA's $454 million 1993 revenues by the end of the decade.[154]

For a while U.S. management seemed confident that Frankfurt was committed to developing the U.S. operations and would allow the New York entity a great deal of autonomy, which would produce the needed cross-fertilization and sharing of talent necessary for success.[155] Rolls assembled some top-notch Wall Street talent, promising to pay them in accordance with American standards, to marshal resources, and to defend their independence.[156] He pushed for higher trading limits and to deal in new instruments at much higher levels. Unfortunately, Frankfurt managers were just not ready for many of the changes.[157] Despite many signs of progress in realizing a real meeting of minds and cultures, there were already some mumblings in Frankfurt about the loss of German and Deutsche Bank identity in the U.S. office and fears in New York of being overwhelmed by the "product and technology challenged" Germans.[158] Rolls had some success, but he lasted only three years. According to some, Rolls seemed too direct for many German managers, but this may have been an instance "of shooting the messenger." Friction grew between him and the Frankfurt office over strategy and ultimately control. He felt that the head office wanted to "micro-manage" the U.S. operations.[159] In any case, his tenure was shorter than originally planned.

For the better part of the last decade of the twentieth century, Deutsche Bank's attempts to grow in the United States internally, although enjoying some successes, had not brought it much closer to the most important strategic goal on which it had set its sights: becoming a strong player in American-styled investment banking. Some of the American influence was felt in Frankfurt. Ross went on to serve in several capacities with Deutsche Bank. He was one of the few American senior managers brought to Germany, where he served as corporate treasurer for the bank for several years and then as head of the bank's Asia/Pacific operations based in Singapore. He did a second tour as head of the Americas operations, before leading the bank's team to determine worldwide restructuring and staff reductions.[160] But the bank's culture and *modus operandi*, even in the crucial and international sector of investment banking, was still distinctively German. The series of companies that were America's operations employed around 5,000, but provided Deutsche Bank as a whole only a small part of its revenues and even less of its profits. It was still a marginal player in many lucrative banking sectors, servicing mostly German clients.[161]

Some of Deutsche Bank's leaders were convinced that a completely different approach and still greater efforts were required if Deutsche Bank was ever to become a force in U.S. banking circles and a strong participant in global investment banking and trading. But the bank's leadership moved cautiously – some would say slowly. Unlike many American institutions, there was a commitment to consensus among top management. Building a consensus around a major investment in the United States might be seen as a difficult forty-year-long process at the bank.

17

The Bankers Trust Acquisition

Deutsche Bank Fulfills Its "American Dream"

Trusting that we may have the pleasure of establishing a relation with you, we remain, yours very truly.

Benjamin Strong, then vice president of Bankers Trust, to Edward Adams, December 7, 1903, HADB, A33.

Through this acquisition, we have taken a big step towards becoming a global financial services provider. Never before has Deutsche Bank – or any other non-American bank – been in a similar situation in the United States. For the first time, the strength and network of a European universal bank are uniting with the special capabilities and experience of a big, broad-based bank in the U.S.A. This transaction has no precedent. We must set a new standard. And we fully intend to do so.

Rolf-E. Breuer, spokesman of the Deutsche Bank management board, November 30, 1998, news conference, announcing Bankers Trust acquisition.

The Urge to Merge

For the better part of the past decade, Deutsche Bank has been at the center of takeover rumors, both as an acquiring and target institution.[1] In dramatic fashion, in fall 1998 Deutsche Bank radically restructured its business in the United States and, by some accounts, all over the world, by acquiring a well-known, nearly one-hundred-year-old U.S. bank. But its acquisition of Bankers Trust was in many senses not its first piece of American foreign direct investment. Not only was Morgan Grenfell formally owned by Americans, for example, it had an American subsidiary that had already augmented Deutsche Bank's trading, sales, and research capacity, especially in high-tech sectors, in the United States.

The Bankers Trust purchase was, however, by far larger and has probably had a far greater impact on other aspects of the bank. Unlike its other acquisitions, that of Bankers Trust led to significant changes in the structure of Deutsche Bank, its investments, and its corporate governance.[2] It was part of an enormous global reshuffling of assets in the whole financial services sector.

As the world prepared for the Millennium, America remained Deutsche Bank's greatest challenge. It began the 1990s with huge real estate losses in the States. In the space of seven years, Deutsche Bank went through four top managers for the American operations. Even Deutsche Bank's handling of many

The old Bankers Trust building, which created an architectural stir when it was built in 1912, as Adams reported in his letters to Deutsche Bank, and into whose offices Strong suggested Deutsche Bank move in 1914.

financial problems in Germany met with much criticism in the United States. Its purchase of the financial subsidiary of ITT, following in the very successful footsteps of GE Capital Corporation, added many new workers but provided few synergies. The bank's attempts to buy away top talent from other investment banks ended in cost overruns and finally the resignations of 100 top technology group stars.[3]

Under competitive pressure and with a host of new, strategic opportunities, big has understandably seemed better to many bankers. In the decade preceding Deutsche Bank's acquisition of Bankers Trust, a veritable tidal wave of mergers had already run through the banking world. Business history has witnessed many merger waves during the past 130 years, some of international scope. Even a casual observer has to be struck by not only the number of banking mergers in the past twenty years but also by their vast and international reach. Banks have embarked on a wave of consolidation around the world. Mergers and acquisitions in the United States have led the way. Between 1991 and 1998, the United States recorded over 5,000 such mergers. Europe, as a whole, hosted only a quarter so many during the same period, but the number of deals was growing.[4] From 1988 to 1997, the American market alone had lost 30 percent of its banking institutions – 510 per year – through mergers and acquisitions.[5] In Europe, from 1988 to 2007, the numbers were smaller than in the United States but still impressive, including such well-known institutions as the above mentioned Morgan Grenfell, purchased by Deutsche Bank, the mergers of BNP with Paribas, Crédit Agricole with Crédit Lyonnais, and Swiss Bank Corporation with Union Bank of Switzerland. Most of these mergers have remained within the national markets of the two institutions, but cross-border deals seemed to be on the upswing.[6] The wave of consolidation, moreover, included bank mergers with nonfinancial institutions, insurance companies, and pension funds. As one observer noted about banks' ambitions at the beginning of the last decade of the twentieth century, "Everyone who was a major player in his home market, and who aspired to global prominence in the future, had his eye on making the all-world team in year 2000."[7]

By 1998, the size of mergers and acquisitions had reached unprecedented dimensions. Despite the roughly $10 billion cost of the Bankers Trust deal, it was only the tenth largest in history, equivalent to merely 15 percent of Citibank's acquisition of Travelers, and well below other megabanking deals of the late 1990s.[8] Though clearly not the first, the Deutsche Bank acquisition seemed to unleash a new chain reaction of both domestic and cross-border mergers.[9]

The reasons for this wave of acquisitions are varied and in line with other waves of consolidation in history.[10] As in earlier periods, regulation played a significant role. In the United States, passage of the Riegle-Neal Interstate Banking and Branching Efficiency Act of 1994 effectively removed the last obstacles to interstate banking. In Europe, the Second Banking Directive – passed in 1989 but implemented in 1993 – abolished geographic restrictions on member-country banks by the introduction of single bank licenses and the principle of home-country control.[11] Technological changes allowed banks to have a greater scale and to extend their services. Once any institution makes the enormous investment in information technology, adding sites usually entails few costs, at least few relative to the initial investment. More transactions can be done and internalized; therefore, the more of them you do, the lower the unit cost. Moreover, some activities, such as foreign exchange management, can be centralized with high-speed electronic connections, thereby extending customer relations and services to the farthest reaches of the globe. Many of the banks' largest customers have increased their foreign direct investment, while bringing together many financial services in money centers such as New York, London, and Paris – a positioning the large banks are virtually compelled to follow. By expanding internationally, big banks avoided one of their greatest risks, a lack of market diversity, frequently becoming so large that, in the eyes of some regulators, they were "too big to fail." With a larger size, too, banks could add more equity capital and extend their range of services, giving banks even more market flexibility and international breadth both for further additions of services and of new equity value.[12] Many of the mergers, especially the domestic ones, promised high degrees of cost reduction – sadly often in the form of staff layoffs.

For some observers, the merger was a strategic necessity for Deutsche Bank, which had recently suffered the humiliating loss on its own turf of the leadership battle for the Deutsche Telekom initial public offering to the American firm

Goldman Sachs and even the lead in Daimler's acquisition of Chrysler.[13] As one analyst put it, in short, "From this point of view, the very survival of banking institutions in national markets became fundamentally dependent on their global competitive capacity."[14]

Consolidation in the banking sector, however, was not without its critics and risks. The public and regulators feared that multinational banks would lose interest in small domestic clients and grow too powerful to be supervised adequately by their home-country regulators or even supranational agencies. There are still many legal, tax, management, and attitudinal obstacles that can prevent even the most well-reasoned mergers from becoming cost-effective, especially across national borders. According to some analysts, too, size has its limits and executive egos can be an impediment to realizing gains in merging giant institutions.[15] Banks realize that synergies, moreover, often imply many staff reductions and, at the very least, a great deal of postmerger complex coordination. Going from the slogans to the realization of having worldwide reach for a large range of financial services, as Citibank aims, or being America's banker, as NationsBank intends, requires enormous skill and perseverance in cross-selling, as well as management knowledge of many sectors.[16]

The Target

Deutsche Bank's announcement that it would buy Bankers Trust came at a time of general stock market frenzy or "irrational exuberance" as Alan Greenspan dubbed it. It unleashed a torrent of press speculation. Concerns mounted on both sides of the Atlantic. One newspaper metaphorically asked about the merger, "*Frosch oder Prinz für die Deutsche Bank*?" ("Frog or Prince for Deutsche Bank?")[17] At the time of the merger, "the frog or the prince" had a market capitalization roughly one-quarter of Deutsche Bank's 30 billion Euro and 40 percent of its 1997 assets of 500 billion Euro.[18] With the final negotiations, and approval process alone taking an additional four to five months after the first late November 1998 announcement, whether "frog or prince," the kiss was long – lasting the whole winter – and deep!

Deutsche Bank had been on the hunt for an American acquisition for some time. The original idea seems to have come from Edson Mitchell, head of Deutsche Bank's bond and currency trading. In July 1998, he reportedly made the suggestion to Rolf-E. Breuer, who had taken over from Kopper as Deutsche Bank's chief executive a little over a year earlier. Within a few days, Deutsche Bank management made up its mind that the acquisition made sense, a conviction that was only strengthened by the Russian capital market crisis, which lowered the prices of investment banks in general. With the loss of many of Deutsche Bank's investment bankers just a few months earlier in a management dispute, the acquisition was in part designed to fill a gaping hole in its staffing. Bankers Trust was not the first American bank Deutsche Bank had targeted. With one of its archrivals (Goldman Sachs) advising it, Deutsche Bank sought new talent first at the California high-tech specialists Hambrecht & Quist, and then Bankers Trust. In the fall, the principals met to iron out a deal, which Goldman Sachs had code named "Osprey" for the large hawk that picks its prey from the water with its talons.[19] For many observers, it seemed like an expensive meal.

Established in 1903 by several leading New York banks – spearheaded by the House of Morgan – Bankers Trust took deposits from individuals and corporations during its first few years of operation with a meager staff of eight in a two-room office at 143 Liberty Street. It specialized in trust services, acting as executor and trustee for wills and administrators of estates, an activity that before 1914 was forbidden to commercial banks and one that stimulated a spurt in the growth of new trust institutions, many of which were affiliated with commercial banks in order to get around the restriction. Under the leadership of several well-known bankers – including, as mentioned earlier, Benjamin Strong, its second president and later head of the New York Federal Reserve Bank – Bankers Trust became well respected in banking circles. By its fiftieth anniversary, with 4,000 employees, 17 offices, and $2.0 billion in assets, Bankers Trust was the eighth largest commercial bank in the United States as measured by assets.[20]

By the early 1970s, Bankers Trust had expanded well beyond its original functions, even establishing a large international presence and branching out into riskier activities. In the 1950s and 1960s, it grew in part through making many acquisitions, such as Title Guarantee & Trust and Lawyers Trust Co. in 1950, Commercial National Bank and Trust in 1951, Bayside National Bank in 1953, the Public National Bank & Trust Co. in 1955, and the South Shore Bank of Staten Island in 1960. Monitored regularly by the Bundesbank, it was one of the first American banks to invest internationally.[21] At a time when American banks dominated the league tables in 1962, Bankers Trust was among the twenty largest banks in the world as measured by total assets – eighth to be precise, with $3.2 billion in deposits. With nearly 25,000 shareholders and 7,000 employees, it sat six places ahead of the bank that would acquire it nearly four decades later. Tellingly, with $600 million less in assets, Deutsche Bank had twice the shareholders and three times the employees.[22] The two banks had a fair amount of contact in Germany. According to Bankers Trust representatives at the time of Deutsche Bank's reunification, the two banks – that is, Bankers Trust and the three banks that became Deutsche Bank in 1957 – had a "balanced relationship."[23]

But in the late 1970s, Bankers Trust was considered by many observers to be a "mediocre money-center bank." Despite inflation, from 1975 to 1978, return on equity did not exceed 10 percent.[24] The bank was staggering under the weight of huge losses in real estate lending, and the competitive pressures in its retail and credit card businesses. The real estate losses were particularly damaging, as Bankers Trust had positioned itself as a leader in this sector. It had to book large charges due to real estate investment trusts even before the 1973–74 national recession and New York City municipal crisis in 1975.[25] The problems facing the bank's retail and credit card business were different. Whereas it had to book losses in real estate, its credit card business lacked economies of scale. Although Bankers Trust had grown these businesses over the past twenty years, its growth had not kept pace in the highly competitive New York market. In addition, retail banking was facing a technology transformation with the introduction of automated teller machines. Improving its weak position in the market required heavy investment outlays in new technology, for which Bankers Trust was ill-prepared.[26]

By the end of the 1980s, much had changed. Both the media and peers were lavishing heavy praise on Bankers Trust for its innovation and transition into investment banking.[27] As early as 1994, Deutsche Bank's management, for example, indicated that it had much to learn from Bankers Trust.[28] By then, Bankers Trust had been transformed from a sleepy middle-sized commercial bank to one of the most aggressively innovative financial institutions in the world.

Under the leadership of Charles Sanford, who with a combination of New York savvy and Southern charm encouraged others to envision a new strategic orientation, the bank began a decade-long metamorphosis. His first public notoriety probably came in 1975, when he signaled New York City's fiscal crisis by pulling out of underwriting questionable new NYC paper and then later heading the banking community's task force looking for ways of restoring New York's access to credit markets.[29]

Sanford recognized that changes in regulation and the competitive environment for banks left financial intermediaries, like Bankers Trust, in a precarious position.[30] The liability side of the balance sheet, but not the asset side, had been deregulated. A horde of new competitors had come into the financial services sector depriving traditional commercial banks of deposits, their basic franchise and lowest cost of financing. Easy access to capital markets allowed corporations to circumvent banks with commercial paper, which could be bought up (underwritten) directly by investment banks and nonbank lenders and distributed to final investors. Without top-tier corporate relationships, Bankers Trust was particularly vulnerable with its dependence on loan business in the United States and low return on equity. Pension and other funds were switching their investment management activities away from trust departments, the crown jewel of Bankers Trust, to specialized investment managers.[31]

Sanford had the vision and courage to push the bank into uncharted waters. By 1993, it not only had become highly touted for its innovative approach to risk management but also extremely profitable, posting nearly a quarter of a billion Dollars in client-related risk management profits. Total business income rose from $125 million in 1985 to $634 million in 1992.[32] According to many accounts, the success was directly attributable to Sanford's bold new approach to banking and his efforts to change the mentality of the bank.[33] By 1990, Bankers Trust had chalked up many impressive successes, including being the first U.S. commercial bank since 1933 to underwrite commercial paper and to enter the securities business. The bank attracted clever people who were rewarded for innovative products.

As an agent of change, Sanford challenged the status quo even before becoming president of the bank. Applying an "underwrite and distribute" model of investment banking to even its lending business, Bankers Trust created loan syndications that lowered risks and reduced the percentage of assets devoted

Charles S. Sanford around the time he assumed the helm at Bankers Trust.

to loans. But Sanford's greatest contribution may have come in the analysis and control of risky instruments. Shortly after he became executive vice president for resource management, Sanford put into place a new methodology for assessing the effect of interest-rate volatility on the returns of transactions and products. This methodology – risk-adjusted return on capital (RAROC) – was eventually applied throughout the bank as a guiding principle for evaluating transactions, business units, capital allocations, and individual performance. It even influenced the control systems of many competitors.[34]

Sanford wanted to create an organization that focused on managing global risk, but that enterprise itself was fraught with uncertainty, what some might call the "risk of innovation." One foreign exchange transaction in the late 1980s led to minor regulatory issues, but according to some, it helped Sanford reinforce a greater sense of urgency in the organization about spreading the use of RAROC, making it part of the bank's internal culture. Risky transactions had to beat a high hurdle rate, usually 20 percent. Applied to individuals and whole units, the system helped management move from a pure growth strategy to a controlled one in which not all new business was treated equally. Although not infallible, the system helped convince management to move away from traditional lending into newfangled risk management and trading, whose risk-adjusted returns appeared more profitable.[35]

But by the time of the acquisition some observers wondered whether Deutsche Bank had purchased tainted merchandise.[36] All the news associated with Bankers Trust's new focus was not rosy: The process and results had its critics.

Bankers Trust took heat for its aggressive financing of leveraged buyouts. Its substantial portfolio of real estate holdings and emerging market loans led some to argue that its real credit exposure had been understated, a problem certainly not confined to Bankers Trust and one that predated Sanford's appointment as CEO. During the late 1980s, as was the case at many banks, the continued write-downs of loans made during the 1970s periodically weighed on Bankers Trust's stock price.[37]

Worse still, the very successful transformation was marred by unfortunate publicity arising from the sale of derivative instruments. In April 1994, two of its customers, Procter & Gamble and Gibson Greetings, made charges against the bank connected with it selling the clients high-risk leveraged derivatives. Although charges were different in each case, P&G alleged, for example, that Bankers Trust representatives had mispriced investments and promised quick profits, a charge Bankers Trust of course denied. Some observers suspected that the treasury staff at P&G wanted to turn that department into a profit center without fully informing or educating its own senior management of the risks. In January 1995, Bankers Trust settled with Greetings and paid a $10 million fine to several regulatory authorities. It sacked two salesmen and agreed to having its leveraged derivatives business, a business Bankers Trust later exited, reviewed by an outside examiner.[38] The bank booked another reserve against derivatives' losses and instituted other procedures to avoid further client defections.[39] Nonetheless, the publicity took a heavy toll on its stock, which declined nearly 30 percent during the second half of 1994, despite a strong market for bank stocks.[40] Even though Bankers Trust won repeated court successes against P&G and regulatory authorities took no punitive action against it, bad publicity dogged the bank. P&G continued to maintain that Bankers Trust had failed to fully inform its client of the risks of the Deutsche Mark and interest rate swaps Bankers Trust had arranged. The Cincinnati firm refused to make contractual payments. In 1996, Sanford's successor as CEO somewhat surprisingly settled the case for an undisclosed amount, even though no court had passed judgment on the allegations and some distinguished academics publicly sided with Bankers Trust.[41]

Despite heavy trading losses in the first quarter of 1995 on Latin American leveraged positions – which contributed to a steep drop on year-to-year profits and in return on equity for the year – Bankers Trust was one of the most profitable financial firms in the United States from 1985 to 1995. Its average annual return on equity was above those of J. P. Morgan, Merrill Lynch, and Citibank, for example. For six of the previous ten years, the bank enjoyed over 20 percent returns on shareholder equity. (In contrast, from 1974 to 1986, the bank averaged 12.9 percent, with a high of 16.6 percent in 1985.)[42] During the early 1990s, among Bankers Trust's peers, only Morgan Stanley and Bear Stearns outperformed Bankers Trust.[43] The bank had built strong franchises in providing financial services, especially with derivatives, syndicated loans, debt underwriting and placement, and particularly financing for leveraged buyouts.[44] With the bank's high dividend and healthy stock price growth, from 1985 to 1995, shareholders had done well. In spite of the falling out with some of its clients, Bankers Trust was named the best derivatives bank by a Greenwich Equity poll in 1994.[45] The confidence of many important clients remained unshaken.[46]

But in 1995, too, Bankers Trust's share price began a five-year-long roller-coaster ride. It bounced from its 1994 high of nearly $85 a share – almost the price Deutsche Bank paid in 1998 and above its preacquisition-rumor price – to a low of $50 in 1995. It then climbed to a new high of $133 before plummeting once again in 1998, losing nearly half of its 1997 highs shortly before the acquisition despite a buoyant stock market.[47]

Although by 1997 Bankers Trust had seemed to have overcome its derivatives troubles of the mid-1990s, a whole set of new ones popped up. At the very least, in hindsight, Sanford's early retirement at age 60 in 1996 – long planned but publicly announced in the spring of 1995 – may have been unfortunately timed. With the board somewhat spooked and unsure of a home-grown successor, it turned to Frank Newman, whose experience was with Wells Fargo, Bank of America, and the U.S. Treasury and who had been hired to head finance and administration. Despite having had little experience in the fast-moving world of capital markets, Newman was appointed in January 1996 to replace Sanford that coming spring.[48]

In 1996 and 1997, Bankers Trust's earnings and stock price growth were back on track. Despite the departure of many of Sanford's admirers at the bank, Newman continued some of Sanford's strategies – for example, focusing on financing for growth companies in the early days of the dot.com boom, which brought a great deal of praise. He pushed through Bankers Trust's acquisition of a Baltimore firm with a strong franchise in initial public offerings, with which his predecessor had already held talks. Newman hoped to bolster this business with yet another acquisition of a boutique M&A bank, an attempt regarded as less successful. He also pushed the bank back into several other unprofitable and risky areas. As early as 1997, Bankers Trust's loan portfolio – a particularly low-risk-adjusted margin and illiquid part of its business – had increased 49 percent since 1995, with international loans, especially in emerging markets, outpacing domestic exposures.[49] By 1998, Bankers Trust's commitments in emerging market loans and derivatives (both fixed income and equity), especially in Indonesia and Russia, were causing significant problems for the bank. In retrospect, it appeared that its once-vaunted and innovative derivatives business suffered from a lack of thorough central control.[50]

For the first few years, Newman's changes had little negative impact on the bank's financial results. In 1998, however, Bankers Trust took huge write-offs. Unfortunately for Deutsche Bank, the bleeding continued well into 1999.[51] With the market turmoil in Asia and Russia, Bankers Trust seemed to be in big trouble, for which finding a potential buyer seemed to be the best "fix."[52] Various aspects of its involvement with the 1998 collapse and bailout of Long-Term Capital Management had been widely criticized.[53] Bankers Trust had already been approached by Bank of New York, Mellon Bank, and State Street Corp. about buying portions of its business. By the time Deutsche Bank began talks in summer 1998, the company was already in play.[54] But for these and other reasons, some observers believed that Bankers Trust was not the ideal target company. The acquisition put Deutsche Bank into several businesses it really did not want to be in, such as the custodial business. Although Deutsche Bank expected to eventually realize $1 billion per year in pretax savings by elimination of back office personnel in Europe and the United States, the merger entailed a $1 billion charge to income for the expected pretax first-year costs. This was in addition to the understandable fears of layoffs and culture clashes in the major centers of the combined bank such as New York, London, and Frankfurt.[55]

Nevertheless, Bankers Trust's position was not weak compared with its larger German suitor, and perhaps even a bargain given its cost. Bankers Trust brought with it a great deal of experience in initial public offerings, management buyouts, and derivatives. Before the Newman era, at least, Bankers Trust had cultivated an innovative corporate culture with a great many dynamic managers. Although the shares of both companies had suffered a nosedive over the previous six months and Bankers Trust's 1998 pretax income was roughly one-sixth that of Deutsche Bank, a year earlier they were roughly equal.[56] Deutsche Bank was buying the American bank with a strong DM. Bankers Trust was selling well below its highest share price of $133 in 1997 and at a lower price-earnings ratio than many other comparable banks. Despite its troubles, too, Bankers Trust was a substantial American player with an extensive international presence. Nearly half of its 20,000 employees were outside of the United States. Even though Bankers Trust was struggling with large losses, stiff competition, and its participation in the recent bailout of Long-Term Capital Management, it was still the eighth largest U.S. bank. With assets of $850 billion, the combined bank, once all the negotiations and regulatory hurdles were cleared, would be the largest in the world, surpassing the recently merged UBS with $778 billion in total assets. With the acquisition Deutsche Bank also took a significant step toward making further inroads into U.S. investment banking.

The Announcement

Long rumored, the news of the acquisition unleashed a torrent of media coverage, speculation, and even recrimination, principally on both sides of the Atlantic, but stretching to all countries where the two banks had big offices, as far away as Australia.[57] At a share price of $93 per share, or $9.7 billion for the company, the initial purchase details implied a price 20 percent over Bankers Trust's pre-acquisition market value and 2.4 times book value, making it the largest acquisition of a U.S. banking company by a foreign firm. Much of Deutsche Bank's American staff was taken by surprise by the size and magnitude of the venture. It was very much a deal driven by Frankfurt and London management. In the face of internal and external skepticism, though, senior management appeared confident. As some on Deutsche Bank's New York staff questioned the magnitude of the price, the response from one of the initiators was: "Oh, you want to know how we got it so cheap?"[58]

U.S. markets surged on this news and that of other deals. Bankers Trust shares ended the day at $84.5, up $7, but still considerably below the offering price of $93, indicating perhaps that much still had to be done. Despite regulatory hurdles and last-minute negotiations about the new structure right after the announcement, Deutsche Bank's shares jumped 2 percent, a welcome relief for shareholders who had seen their stock lose nearly half its value over the previous six months. The market makers seemed to believe that the advantages of combining Deutsche Bank's healthy balance sheet with Bankers Trust's market position and know-how seemed to outweigh the cultural and other difficulties of combining a German commercial bank with an American investment bank.[59] Four days later both boards approved the deal.

Some of the initial international response was relatively favorable. The deal would make Deutsche Bank the second largest asset manager in Europe. It represented a major step in the bank's efforts to make its investment banking – which had been hurting, especially on the equity side – more robust. Even if it was not the perfect target and difficult to integrate, the acquisition of Bankers Trust was a step in the right direction. The two banks together had many common activities which could be serviced with roughly the same infrastructure, a tremendous opportunity to improve profits. For both, the merger represented an opportunity to diversify into new areas and strengthen others in which they had not reached critical mass. Moreover, parts of the Anglo-American press viewed the acquisition as a trendsetter, "the most visible sign of a much broader upheaval in European finance" to deal with new competition.[60]

But those competitive pressures were not only coming from outside of Europe as many critics of globalization claimed, but rather from Europe's own ambitions and constraints. As the *International Herald Tribune* put it two days after the announcement: "The introduction of the single European currency, the Euro, in 11 countries in January has increased the pressures on national banks to reinvent themselves as European players."[61] So long as many European countries blocked foreign entry into the banking sector – for example, France – and Germany's banking system remained dominated by nonprofit financial institutions, deals within Europe or in Germany itself would be difficult. The real opportunity for expansion would come from mergers involving institutions outside of continental Europe.[62]

Despite the need to consolidate and develop a broad international presence, there were also many critics of the acquisition. Skepticism was by far the most prevalent attitude. After an initial bounce in its stock price, by the middle of the day following the announcement, Deutsche Bank's share price had dropped nearly 5 percent. Quoting bankers from other institutions, several newspapers doubted whether the planned synergies could be realized and whether the purchase price could be justified. Although widely acknowledged as a courageous step, some thought that the price was a little expensive for what Deutsche Bank was getting, especially considering the problems that the merger would unleash.[63] The purchase left the combined banks at only eleventh among institutions issuing new stocks and bonds in the United States, and fourteenth worldwide. Integrating the bank would be a challenge for Deutsche Bank managers, whose problems with Morgan Grenfell in 1989 were deemed by many to have been a fiasco. Earlier difficulties there had sparked the departure of two hundred executives. Investment bankers were still furious that the bank's structure forced them to hawk the bank's low margin services such as cash management and trade financing.[64]

Rolf-E. Breuer, Deutsche Bank's spokesman of the management board who had spearheaded the deal, had his hands full. He felt that the merger would determine his legacy at Deutsche Bank. Hired as an intern in 1966 after completing his doctorate in law, in typical German fashion Breuer served in a large array of positions before joining the management board in 1985. Before his appointment as spokesman of the management board in 1997 and chairman of its supervisory board in 2002, he had headed Deutsche Bank's stock exchange department. Most insiders believed that Breuer seemed to have a flair for international banking. Worldly and experienced, he seemed endowed with a direct sincerity that could be part of his charm and perhaps his undoing. Under his leadership, the bank's stock price had increased substantially (20 percent), but it lagged behind in several bank indices. Breuer was convinced that the bank needed to make a bold move. He knew the risks. A few days before the announcement, after introducing several central bank chairmen at a podium discussion, he pronounced, what for some – perhaps prematurely – appeared to be his own epitaph: "I am a mortal next to the Gods."[65]

Despite the poor track record of foreign bank mergers and the probable elimination of jobs in many overlapping centers, management was optimistic. According to Breuer at the press conference about this almost unprecedented integration of two huge international financial service entities, "Bankers Trust is a platform on which we shall build an opening into the United States."[66] If the bank's ambitious goals of growth and increased profits were to be realized, speed was of the essence.

On Monday, November 30, Breuer and Newman made the formal announcement of the deal and of the respective boards' approval of the roughly $10 billion takeover.[67] Deutsche Bank reported that it hoped to achieve by 2001 cost savings of DM 1.7 billion ($1 billion) and improve earnings per share by 10 to 15 percent. As early as 2000, the acquisition was supposed to have a positive effect on earnings. In the short run, however, there were many disappointments. Management announced that it intended to fund the purchase with a combination of new equity (DM 4 billion), ready cash, profit-sharing certificates, and the sale of bonds, straight or convertible. With DM 20 billion in cash reserves in September, the financing plan seemed reasonable. Although he spoke no German, Newman had been tapped to join Deutsche Bank's management board in April when the deal was complete. Not only did the merger create the largest bank in the world, it also formed the fourth largest fund manager and the twelfth largest underwriter of stocks and bonds, with a special strength in growth sectors such as high-tech and health care.

The Press Reaction

It was a busy couple of weeks for Deutsche Bank's press department. During the first days after the announcement, there were on occasion multiple articles about the acquisition in the same newspaper. On the very day of its Bankers Trust announcement, rumors appeared about how Deutsche Bank would finance the acquisition. Two possibilities often mentioned were the sales of its Daimler-Chrysler or Allianz holdings, which had market values of DM 20 and 15 billion respectively, even though both of these sales under the German tax law would lead to a sizeable capital gains tax.[68] Several German papers picked up the theme of the possible sale, which would have wide-ranging consequences for other German companies and perhaps the whole German financial system.[69]

Within a few days, Deutsche Bank began denying rumors that it would dispose of securities, but as one paper pointed out there were tax effective ways of synthetically profiting from a sale without actually unloading the shares. Allianz, for example, had issued a bond backed by its shares in Deutsche Bank to finance its acquisition of Assurance Générale (Asset-Backed Security), in effect placing a bet on whether the German tax authorities would relieve firms of their capital gains burden on sales of shares in other companies. If Deutsche Bank had been listed on U.S. exchanges at the time of the Bankers Trust deal, moreover, it could have offered its shares, or shares in another company, in exchange for those of Bankers Trust, which would have made the purchase less costly than a cash deal in which the target company's shareholders had a virtually immediate tax liability.[70] Investors and rival banks expressed dismay that Deutsche Bank might be able to avoid issuing new share capital to finance its acquisition by using a loophole in German capital adequacy standards. German regulators had decided to permit Deutsche Bank to use international accounting standards, which would increase its Tier 1 capital base, and to write off the Goodwill ($5 billion) in the acquisition price over ten years instead of immediately.[71]

Before the end of the week following the announcement, Deutsche Bank was in the headlines again for its acquisition of Crédit Lyonnais's Belgian subsidiary for a price of DM 1 billion.[72] Under an agreement with the European Commission, Crédit Lyonnais was obliged to sell off many assets in exchange for approval of French government aid. For Deutsche Bank the deal represented further evidence that the German bank had not lost its appetite for further expansion in Europe. Indeed, Deutsche Bank was said to be in talks to acquire Spanish banks, including Crédit Lyonnais's subsidiary there.[73] There was some speculation that acquiring a French bank would be Deutsche Bank's next step.

Personnel issues were crucial. Preserving the loyalty of Bankers Trust executives would be a great challenge. Headhunters were likely to swoop down on the best of them.[74] On another labor front, within a few days of the announcement, German and international journals began fretting about the inevitable loss of jobs as far away as Australia, where both banks had substantial staffs.[75] What for management represented synergies and cost savings amounted to around 10 percent staff reductions, potentially nearly 9,000 job losses worldwide for the combined bank. At the time of the announcement, the two banks employed around 91,000 people, roughly 76,000 with Deutsche Bank and 15,000 at Bankers Trust. The sacrifices and rewards seemed unbalanced. Even the conservative *Wall Street Journal* mused over how the mind-numbing pace of mergers could mean only one thing: "mind-numbing fees for the deal makers."[76]

Some American journals viewed the takeover as the first step in the "Americanization" of Deutsche Bank. To get significant benefit out of acquiring an American niche player, *The Wall Street Journal* reasoned that the real question was how a bank that epitomized German banking style would mesh with an institution that had always done things the American way. The potential for a clash was huge. But if the results were positive, other European banks would be emboldened to try the same. The American business journal feared that the Germans would have to do the most changing, and that they were not well known for their capacity to adapt. Safety had been the watchword and strength of German banking. How would those bankers feel in a world dominated by equities and derivatives? The independence and above all high salaries demanded by the American staff might not go down well with the German public and even with some German executives trained in the belief that managers work for the institution, not themselves. Despite Breuer's commitment to becoming a more global (more American, for some) institution, the *Journal* cautioned that changing the German banking community would not be easy for him and for his colleagues. Although Deutsche Bank had learned to be more flexible, "the analysts trying to determine whether the merger will work might like to take a break from their number crunching and watch this clash of cultures unfold."[77]

The *Journal* also mused whether Bankers Trust was the right target at all. Neither Deutsche Bank nor Bankers Trust had been among the top ten advisors on announced M&A deals involving a European target through October 1998. Other American investment banks still dominated even the European terrain. Bankers Trust, for the *Journal*, was hardly the right candidate to fill the investment bank gap in Deutsche Bank's arsenal. After all, it ranked only twenty-sixth in the United States. The acquisition seemed to be a desperate move by a European bank, which, like so many others, had difficulty entering the rarified world of mergers and acquisitions. Neither creating investment banking capabilities from scratch nor purchasing them seemed to be feasible. Only four European banks broached the top ten in even European deals. The question remained: Could Deutsche Bank draw top talent to the new bank, and was it willing to write the checks for them?[78] Investment banking at any one institution had become a kind of temporary partnership of highly mobile, talented people who just seemed to divide the profits among themselves before moving on to a new firm.

The *Journal* acknowledged, though, that the combined companies in the United States might work out, if managed well, to form a magnet for attracting high-quality new staff. Even more money might have to be put in, at least in the near term. According to the *Journal*, the new entity's greatest gains might come in Europe by expanding Deutsche Bank's clout for underwriting stocks and bonds for smaller and medium-sized companies, a sector in which Bankers Trust was particularly strong. Bankers Trust was strong, too, in some growth sectors such as new stock issues and high-yield corporate debt (junk bonds), where the *Journal* judged that the potential for growth in Europe was higher than in the saturated U.S. market. This might become particularly important if the introduction of the Euro gave a kick-start to European issuances and trading, as many expected. In short, Bankers Trust might give Deutsche Bank's European investment banking business a boost by adding a greater window to the U.S. markets and U.S. banking innovations. Finally, Bankers Trust might have been Deutsche Bank's second choice, but, unlike its first, J. P. Morgan, it was simply available.[79]

Understandably, some of the German press, too, feared that Deutsche Bank would lose its identity.[80] In Germany, one could almost feel the sense of bewilderment as one major restructuring after another, like a tidal wave, washed over icons of the German economic scene. Within a few years Daimler, Hoechst, and now Deutsche Bank were losing some of their German character. For some, too, the supposed synergy effects were spurious or represented a too-costly attempt to realize overly zealous goals. For some, the acquisition seemed like a desperate attempt by the bank's new management board spokesman, Breuer, to save Deutsche Bank's ailing fortunes. According to *Der Tagesspiegel*, Deutsche Bank's 76,000 worldwide employees felt that the great ship was adrift, moving from one restructuring to another. Deutsche Bank had not only lost its European power, it was no longer a force in determining national policies. The bank seemed more interested in itself than its clients. It seemed to lurch from one scandal and acquisition plan across countries and sectors to another.[81] The next day the same paper called into question what *Der Tagesspiegel* obviously considered an underlying assumption of the merger: whether growth had economic value considering the price. It feared that the sudden rash of mergers involving German companies was only the tip of the iceberg.[82]

Some German papers even questioned the advisability of entering the "notoriously provincial" world of American banking. Regulations intended to protect depositors in the United States by limiting interstate and investment banking, though relics of a bygone era, still influenced the worldwide operations of even the foreign banks working in the States, let alone the American ones.[83] Some competitors rejoiced at the prospect of Deutsche Bank losing its European focus and being tangled up in a long, complicated implementation process.[84] At the very least, the move entailed enormous risks. Deutsche Bank's earlier efforts with Morgan Grenfell had proven that heavy investment did not necessarily bring exceptional rewards in the investment banking sector. It was a massive investment requiring future cash input with unproven returns and severe integration problems.[85]

Whereas American economics analysts voiced concerns about realizing synergies, the German press expressed fears above all about job losses in Germany, a particularly sensitive issue there with unemployment running around 10 percent. The conservative weekly *Rheinischer Merkur* quoted Marx and Engels about the bourgeoisie's tendency to reshape the world in its own image, an image designed to further its own pecuniary interests. An economic system must produce economic gain:

> But if under profit pressure from international investment funds the floor is knocked out from under jobs in every country, the destruction of work by self-serving rationalization, today's business leaders will produce alienation from society to our detriment.[86]

Perhaps the most insightful point was raised by Peter Martin, columnist for the *Financial Times*. In an article entitled "Alice in Mergerland," he sensibly posed the question of whether any of the huge mergers of the 1990s had sufficiently considered that the economies of scale realized by the mergers also entailed huge management costs because of the new institutional complexity, which could easily reduce or eliminate the incremental economic benefit of the merger. Like "Alice in Wonderland" who grew so large she could not tie her shoes, giant companies might find it hard keeping in touch with the parts that matter. Moreover, in some sense, every acquisition was an admission of a hidden failure; failure of the target to achieve acceptable returns or failure of the acquirer to achieve adequate internal growth. What was often overlooked was whether the acquisition really provided a solution to the hidden failures. Although size can rectify many ills, some research and experience indicates that despite modern technology, beyond a certain point, economies of scale are hard to realize. Designing the appropriate communication, control, and remuneration structures provided a daunting challenge whose solutions were not particularly evident in investment banking.[87] Although investment banking paid high returns to executives, returns to shareholders were not quite so rich. Only three major investment banking houses returned more than 20 percent on equity. Neither Bankers Trust nor Deutsche Bank was among them.[88]

Regulatory Hurdles and Integration

The initial stages of integration passed relatively smoothly. Even before the official approvals, the bank had formed committees of Deutsche Bank and Bankers Trust executives to recommend organizational and personnel changes. After years of work in London and New York, Deutsche Bank had several executives within the organization who had a good deal of relevant experience. There was no long wait to find out who would stay and who would go. Senior managers had learned from the bank's experience with Morgan Grenfell nearly a decade earlier – there were to be no "coheads of businesses." Instead of leaving the "Anglo-Saxon" investment bankers as a separate, albeit very profitable entity, Deutsche Bank took steps to create a worldwide investment banking arm. Senior executives realized that it had no one in Germany who was comfortable with the equity segment of investment banking. The challenge was first to create a broadbased, young, German talent pool, then cross-national teams, which would spearhead marketing throughout Europe and the rest of the world. Like Germany, Deutsche Bank needed more of an equity culture. In bonds and M&A, Deutsche Bank was fine, but in the growing, dynamic area of initial public offerings, it lacked talent and experience.[89]

Although most observers considered the Bankers Trust deal done, there were still several regulatory and other hurdles for Deutsche Bank to jump to acquire Bankers Trust. American law still technically separated investment and commercial banking. In addition to European and other regulation, the Federal Reserve would have to pass judgment on whether the proposed merger violated the latest American regulations. Deutsche Bank's stakes in nonbanking institutions, such as its 12 percent position in DaimlerChrysler, for example, might sound some warning bells. The acquisition might also undermine Deutsche Bank's excellent (Aa1. Moody's Investors Service) credit rating.[90]

Within a few weeks of the announcement, Germany's misdeeds during World War II threatened to derail the merger, illustrating the almost imponderable duration of home-country political risk.[91] The comptroller of the State of New York warned that he would not approve the deal until all the claims relating to Holocaust victims had been settled by German companies. Organizing American pension funds against Swiss banks had proven to be a quite successful tactic to get information and the return of Jewish funds held in Switzerland. The lawyer for the victims contended that approval of the Bankers Trust deal by federal and state authorities had no chance until his clients had been satisfied.[92] Although the approval of the U.S. authorities came in May 1999, the hurdle for regulatory clearance had been persuading survivor groups of Deutsche Bank's relatively clean record during the Third Reich and openness about its role during the Nazi period.[93]

In addition to regulatory and financing issues, Deutsche Bank had to address many internal management ones. How would the two banks' structures come together? Would executives from Bankers Trust join the Deutsche Bank management board? Would the functions of German management board's members change? When and how many job cuts would be announced?[94] How would the merger affect Deutsche Bank's strategies in Germany and countries such as Italy and Spain where it had built up retail businesses? Most importantly, what kind of adjustments was Deutsche Bank prepared to make in its traditionally cautious corporate culture and the structure of its business? Could it, and did it really want to, move from a bank built on intimate relationships with customers into a more open group that provides cutting-edge services to a whole host of customers through impersonal capital markets? At the time of the acquisition, Deutsche Bank representatives sat on more than 400 company supervisory boards. It held substantial stakes in some of Germany's best known and largest companies – for example, Allianz, 10 percent of share capital, market value DM 10.4 billion; Daimler-Benz (before merger with Chrysler) 22 percent, DM 14.2 billion; Philipp Holzmann, 25 percent, DM 0.5 billion, and Metallgesellschaft, 13 percent, DM 0.6 billion.[95] Could the bank attract, encourage, and tolerate the high salaries and big egos of those investment bankers it had and would inevitably have to pinch from other firms? The bank had already had many important recent defections. Was Deutsche Bank prepared to divest of some of its unprofitable business sectors and push into new, higher margin ones in order to reach its aggressive goal of a 25 percent return on equity by 2001? Would the bank continue to follow a Europe-first strategy or move toward a more global outlook? How could the bank, moreover, avoid the missteps, delays, and squabbles associated with its Morgan Grenfell acquisition of nearly a decade earlier with a bank like Bankers Trust?[96]

Job cuts would have to come first. Emphasizing that no positions would be lost in Germany, Breuer and Newman announced that an estimated 5,500 employees in the United States, Britain, and other locations would be let go, costing approximately DM 2.2 billion in severance pay. For those Bankers Trust executives the bank wanted to keep, Deutsche Bank set aside a $400 million retention pool to be spread over many people, but denied a report that it would pay Newman and other executives $10 million apiece to stay on for an undisclosed period. The bank also announced that it intended to list its shares on the New York Stock Exchange and would issue financial statements in conformity with U.S. Generally Accepted Accounting Principles (US GAAP).[97] Some questions, such as whether the Bankers Trust name would remain for some parts of the business and whether Deutsche Bank would still pursue European expansion through a European acquisition, were left unsettled.[98] What was clear to most American observers, however, was that Bankers Trust would cease to exist as a separate institution.[99] Deutsche Bank had no intention of repeating its Morgan Grenfell strategy. What was clear, moreover, for Breuer, as quoted at the beginning of this section, and for most Germans was that the merger was just another indication that the German business world had entered uncharted waters.[100]

The job of integrating the two banks fell to Josef Ackermann, a 50-year-old Swiss banker and lecturer in monetary theory at St. Gallen University who joined Deutsche Bank thanks to a contact with Kopper. Ackermann had left Credit Suisse after a falling out with its chairman in 1996. He came to Deutsche Bank with a broad range of experience. Able to integrate many points of view, Ackermann was known as a manager who could make decisions, even unpopular ones, such as those that entailed the loss of many jobs. His merging of Deutsche Bank's and Morgan Grenfell's investment banking operations led 200 executives to quit their jobs. Ackermann, who admired Bankers Trust expertise in derivatives – securities that derive their value from other securities (options and futures, for example) – was likely to emphasize this portion of Bankers Trust's portfolio. Ackermann chose a committee to steer the consolidation process consisting of a mixture of Bankers Trust and Deutsche Bank managers – Bankers Trust chairman Newman, Yves De Ballman, Mayo Shattuck III, and Mary Cirillo from Bankers Trust, along with Edson Mitchell and Michael Philipp, heads of Deutsche Bank's global markets and equities departments respectively.[101]

The acquisition suffered, though, from some glitches. Although Deutsche Bank knew the extent and quality of the assets it acquired, it was not quite sure what it wanted to do with them. Some businesses required more investment; others had to be dropped. Senior management was not yet sure which. There were some false starts. Even after another small acquisition, Deutsche Bank was deemed to be too small in what was once a core business of both banks, custodial services. Private equity, an area in which both banks were relatively strong, was dropped. Moreover, each time Frankfurt management changed its views about the configuration of businesses and the structure of the regional operations, it changed its man on the ground. The bank went through four regional presidents in three years. As one of them put it, "One of the major hurdles for the acquisition implementation was Frankfurt's indecision about exactly what it wanted in the United States."[102]

Perhaps the biggest glitch came in the person of Newman. By spring 1999, senior managers on both sides of the Atlantic wondered whether Newman was an asset or a liability to the merger. Several Deutsche Bank members of the management board balked at his inclusion. He had been further weakened by the fallout from a scandal involving customer transfers. With the departure of some of his allies at Bankers Trust and a perceived lack of confidence among many who stayed, it was not clear whether he could lead the U.S. group or have a clear role in Deutsche Bank's new matrix organization.[103] Within six months of announcing the deal, Frankfurt management became convinced that Newman's relationship with his own staff and American regulators was sufficiently shaky that his continued involvement with the combined banks became untenable and Newman was bought out with a hefty payout.[104]

However, by 1999, Deutsche Bank was once again a leading player in investment and other banking activities. It was the fifth largest provider of syndicated loans and the largest outside of the United States, even though its activity was only 25 percent of that of the world leader, Chase Manhattan.[105] With $844 billion in assets, it was the largest bank in Germany and Europe as measured by assets.[106] During the first third of 1999, it ran approximately 200 bond issues, totaling $48 billion and nearly 8 percent market share.[107] For the first six months of that year, it led all issuers of West European corporate bonds.[108] By 1999, too, investment banking profits amounted to 60 percent of the group's total.[109]

Nevertheless, the first few years of the merger brought few profits. It was a period of big investment, not of high payouts. Unfortunately, Deutsche Bank's investment banking business was still dominated by low margin, volatile activities. The merger had bought credibility, but little immediate business.[110] Bankers Trust added something in derivatives and in leveraged buyouts, but Deutsche Bank still needed to beef up both these areas with personnel acquisitions. Much of the development of the above-mentioned capacities had to be brought in or grown internally anyway. But without the acquisition and certain key managers, such as John Ross, who knew New York's finances and politics, and could deal with the managers in Germany, it would have been impossible. In retrospect, the acquisition brought the bank a platform, an identity, an innovative spirit, and a perception on the street that it was committed to being cutting edge.[111] Deutsche Bank had realized its "American Dream," but in the fast-moving world of financial services, no institution can count on long-term value creation with one investment or collection of offerings. Truly the slogan "innovate or die" applies here more than virtually anywhere else in the global economy.[112]

Although Deutsche Bank at the Millennium had reestablished itself as a leading investment bank, it still had many issues to address. The trickiest perhaps was the paradoxical and at times conflicting necessity of shoring up its position in its domestic market – the German or European home countries – while simultaneously bolstering its reputation in the highly competitive and unsentimental international capital markets. Frustrated in many of its attempts to consolidate its position in German financial services, but aided by changes in German tax law, Deutsche Bank divested itself of many German holdings, freeing up capital for more profitable investment banking activities, and shed some of its German identity. But cultivating entrepreneurial managers for its key businesses in the face of some its home-country stakeholders, who feared the freewheeling ways of international capital markets associated with the Wild West and, for the readers of this book, with Karl May, together with the problems of Henry Villard and the Northern Pacific, will not be easy.[113] For good or ill, through the decade of the 1990s, despite many distractions, Deutsche Bank's management team had made several courageous decisions that reestablished the bank as a world-class competitor. With an international outlook and a strong foothold in the two largest capital markets in the world as well as its home market, both its own staff and external stakeholders, in and outside of Germany, had to recognize Deutsche Bank as the leading representative of German capitalism on global markets and as a formidable, multifaceted financial player.

18

Postscript

Deutsche Bank in the United States and the Future of Multinational Banking

> We have had a lot of organic growth, but we couldn't have done it without a platform and a statement of seriousness. The Bankers Trust acquisition did this for us. But the experience of 9/11 really brought people together. In the tragedy and its aftermath, we took a giant step toward establishing our commitment to the American market and New York. It helped bind us to a vision of ourselves as a powerful American component in the identity and success of a global financial institution.
>
> Seth Waugh, president of Deutsche Bank Americas.

> For future historians, the salient fact of the twentieth-century finance will be the sharp erosion of banker power – that is, the dwindling role of the financial intermediary.
>
> Ron Chernow, *The Death of the Banker*, p. xii.

This book has tried to put Deutsche Bank's nearly 140-year-long relationship with the United States – with its key individuals, events, strategies, and outcomes – in its historical context. That experience in the world's largest capital market suggests several lessons about the past and about the nature of modern finance. Unfortunately, many of these are not the sort that historians and businessmen are generally seeking. Deutsche Bank's history imparts insights that will probably neither dramatically change our overall view of the past nor provide explicit guidelines for the future. It merely may help to give those interested in international business and general history a little more of a buffer with which to avoid faddish thinking, as well as an appreciation of what is novel or commonplace about our present situation. Given the wide range of audiences to which I hope this book will appeal, I fear some of my readers may find these points trivial; while other readers may regard the very same views as incomprehensible, or worse still, false. Never one to back off from a challenge, I trust that some of what I say will strike a chord for those among my readers who share the conviction that it is impossible to truly understand the present or imagine the future without a thorough grounding in the past. My intention in this Postscript is merely to highlight a few connections between salient features of Deutsche Bank's American story and current management and financial issues.

The Timeline

First, most important actions of businessmen have long-term consequences, many of which were unforeseen when initiated. For some transactions we can legitimately record immediate gains and losses, but strategic orientations, tactical decisions, and even apparently simple, self-contained transactions often produce far-reaching results, touching a multitude of banking activities stretched over a large geographic area, which are hard to assess even with modern accounting and financial analysis.

From finally realizing a gain with Northern Pacific securities to getting back German investments after World War I, Deutsche Bank made money – or just avoided losing it – by having a long-term commitment to its investments and its customers, and by guarding its most important asset, its reputation. Not only is time a factor in and of itself, the activities undertaken create certain path dependencies. Once Deutsche Bank had committed resources to solving the Northern Pacific problems, clever businessmen realized that the bank's interest lay in cultivating and using the capacities the bank had developed. Over decades, the incremental benefits and costs of Deutsche Bank's most important American activities worked their way through its domestic and other international businesses. In the late nineteenth century, Deutsche Bank became Germany's premier universal bank in part because it offered its customers access to a large range of services over a broad geographic area. To not have had business connections in the United States and an offering of U.S. securities would have been fatal for that undertaking.

Oddly, even though key strategic and tactical decisions are imbedded in a company's business life and entail complicated, decades-long opportunity costs, few companies bother to look even at their own histories to understand better how decisions are made, which ones benefit their shareholders and other stakeholders, and why. Investing in American railroads, relying on agents, correspondent banks, and representative offices – as Deutsche Bank did through its first eighty years – and, finally, even borrowing on U.S. markets in the 1920s in the long run, for example, seemed to be a viable strategy or tactic that contributed to Deutsche Bank's great success before World War I and even helped it survive the vagaries of the interwar period. Yet evaluating those activities individually at any one time, specifically one shortly after they were initiated, would give a distorted image of their effects – both positive and negative – and certainly insufficient information about their overall business significance for the bank.

The most frequently asked question about Deutsche Bank today – was the acquisition of Bankers Trust a good idea? – perhaps needs to be seen in this perspective. Four years into the acquisition, Deutsche Bank had little to show for its efforts.[1] However, as noted in the last Chapter, the decision to buy a large American bank should be evaluated not by its immediate returns but rather in light of Deutsche Bank's long-term view of its position in financial markets, its trajectory before the acquisition, the turbulence in capital markets since that time, and the overall malaise of the German and European economies during the first few years of the twenty-first century.

Deutsche Bank's celebration of its New York Stock Exchange Listing, October 3, 2001. At the podium is Mayor Rudy Giuliani, to his right is Richard A. Grasso, head of the New York Stock Exchange, and to his left Rolf-E. Breuer.

Perhaps most importantly, Deutsche Bank's competitive position, just a few years after the acquisition, had started to show signs of dramatically improving. By 2001, investment banking accounted for 80 percent of Deutsche Bank's pretax earnings, compared with 55 percent in 2000. In 2005, Deutsche Bank earned Euro 15.9 billion in corporate investment banking revenues, approximately 60 percent of its total turnover but 71 percent of pretax profits. This sector was returning 33 percent on equity, making a significant contribution to Deutsche Bank's overall return on active equity of 24 percent.[2]

The American operations of the bank have already had a great impact on the whole company. In terms of market share and profits, U.S. operations alone have achieved many of Deutsche Bank's goals set for them. From providing losses a few years earlier, the U.S. operations already account for roughly one-third of the bank's profits. Leading the bank in many important and lucrative businesses, Deutsche Bank's U.S. operations no longer have niche-player status in the world's largest capital market. While some of its businesses, such as asset management and private banking, have not attained their potential, they are growing. In global currencies, commodities trading, and credit derivatives trading, Deutsche Bank is the number one ranked bank. In several other categories, such as emerging markets and credit trading, the bank is among the top five. In 2005, global revenues, income before taxes and net income were all growing at double digit rates – profits by over 30 percent, to which the United States was making a substantial contribution. From 1989 to 2004, while Deutsche

Bank's revenues grew nearly fourfold, America's share of total Deutsche Bank revenue went from 2 percent to 26 percent.[3] Its American management structure to govern the region has been adopted in somewhat modified form by all the bank's regions.[4]

One thing is incontestably clear: There is no longer any question about which preposition to use for describing the bank's relationship to the United States, as discussed in the Introduction. Deutsche Bank is now, beyond any shadow of a doubt, *in* the United States.

The Borderless World of Finance

Second, much of finance is now conducted on a supranational playing field, but this is not a completely new phenomenon. In many respects, today's global financial markets resemble those that existed before World War I. But today, despite the comparative ease of information and capital flows, that "globalization" seems to require much more foreign direct investment. The huge amounts of funds that poured into the United States during the pre-1914 period, however, were funneled through "supranational institutions" based on kinship or other personal connections. Like most of the large, joint stock banks, Deutsche Bank had to work closely with private, mostly family, banks that furnished the main financial bond between countries at a time when large, multidivisional and multinational organizations were still impractical. Sometimes the relationship between Deutsche Bank and the private banks was also based on family ties. Central banks, led by the Bank of England, supplied a sort of international regulation of the whole financial system not unlike that of the G-10 and Basel Committee, but the private banks whose international affiliates were run by family members added personal trust to the system in the absence of sufficient legal recourse. And like their modern counterparts, they also exploited opportunities for "superior" returns by managing uncertainty and overcoming information asymmetries.[5]

Well before World War I, Deutsche Bank and others organized investment funds, for example, for wealthy individuals and institutions to pool their funds in risky international undertakings, managed by international financial experts, to attain returns superior to those investors derived from ordinary German securities or even foreign securities listed in Germany. The funds profited not only from the expertise of some of its members but also from avoiding the costs of registering securities on the German market (a kind of offshore investment) and concentrated power over cash recipients derived from investors pooling their funds. Like modern hedge funds, in which Deutsche Bank is heavily involved as a lender and even manager for clients, these pre-World War I pools took cash from high-net-worth individuals, including senior executives of the bank and institutions, and invested them in projects and securities with above-average expected returns, often exploiting information asymmetries.

But the investment pools managed by Deutsche Bank, Speyer, and Morgan differed in some respects from their more modern equivalents. They had longer-term horizons, and, above all, they actively managed investments on behalf of or sometimes even by the participants themselves. Instead of breaking out and hedging undesired risk, as do their modern counterparts, they attempted to manage it, or perhaps better put, to control specific risk.

Not only does the Eurodeposit market form the basis for the movement and for cross-border investment of funds that are relatively free of national regulation, but also the rapid growth of hedge funds allows wealthy individuals and institutions easy access to investments all over the world with potentially above-normal returns. Though a subject of intense academic debate about their true risk-adjusted returns, diversification benefits, and about the appropriate regulatory prescriptions, several points about hedge funds are clear. Like their earlier cousins, they are structured in such a way as to avoid national laws that apply to other investments. They are growing fast and, with promises of high payouts, they are attracting some of the best fund managers in finance, whose innovations seem to outpace the best regulatory and investor efforts to control or even value them. Using sophisticated derivative instruments and traditional securities, like their pre-1914 predecessors, hedge funds are ostensibly good at identifying market "anomalies" and structuring their investments, sometimes with a great deal of leverage, so as to only take on the specific risk-reward of the precise opportunity they have identified.[6]

As was the case before World War I, Deutsche Bank is a leader in managing these cross-border flows. Not only is Deutsche Bank actively trading with and in some cases lending to hedge funds on a secured basis, it also serves as a conduit of investment into hedge funds by advising private banking clients about how to evaluate hedge funds and in which funds to place cash. Hedge funds play a large and varied role in Deutsche Bank's U.S. and worldwide business. They are replacing the preeminence of some other institutional clients for the bank, and are sources of trading volume and funding business that the bank eagerly courts. Despite some risks and compliance burdens, increasing the breadth and depth of hedge fund business is an essential part of the bank's reaching its aggressive growth targets.[7] Apart from the active management of acquired assets, practiced by Deutsche Bank before World War I in the United States, and the sophisticated mathematics they employ now, their aim, their clients, and their effect are not so different from what Siemens, Gwinner, and others were doing in 1900. Deutsche Bank learned to its detriment through the North American Company and numerous poolings that no amount of diversification and sharing of risk can save economic value if no one is watching the store. Like several of its competitors in recent times, Deutsche Bank has already been burned by relying too much on even the most skillful model makers. Having done a lot of business with Long-Term Capital Management (LTCM), the most famous hedge fund, the collapse of which in 1998 threatened the whole financial system despite the active involvement of two Noble Prize winners and some of the best traders on Wall Street, Deutsche Bank and Bankers Trust were "obliged" to help with its rescue. To its credit, the bank took an active role in LTCM's bailout.[8]

Political Risk

Third, despite the size and independence of markets and market players, national politics and regulation still play a pivotal part of the environment in which business strategies and their economic outcomes are formed. Although Deutsche Bank's whole strategy relied on relatively stable and open international capital markets, they cannot always be counted on. Business people should not take them for granted. As international as Deutsche Bank was and as cosmopolitan as its managers were, the bank could not escape the economic consequences of the great political upheavals of the past hundred years. Its business thrived when national politics and regulation were not hostile, and nosedived when they were.

Political risks have changed, but not disappeared. As recently as 2003, frictions between the United States and much of Europe made doing business in either place harder for companies of the other regions. For most of this history, while national frictions between Germany and America were minimal, Deutsche Bank could rely on cooperative undertakings and enjoy high profits from its American undertakings with minimal foreign direct investment.

Not only do relations between the two countries matter, but also the economic trajectories of each have had a great impact on Deutsche Bank's fortunes. Germany began the second half of the twentieth century as the economic powerhouse of Europe, which helped give Deutsche Bank a competitive edge in the United States. By the end, though, it was the sick man. Much of Deutsche Bank's fortunes have fluctuated with the general economic and political conditions of the country in which it is incorporated, as well as with the divisions and sluggish growth that still exist in Europe.

Deutsche Bank has by and large thrived in a world order characterized by peaceful relations among nations and a liberal exchange of goods and services, which came to a grinding halt in 1914 and took nearly fifty years to reestablish, if at all. Those who confidently greeted the end of the twentieth century as the beginning of a new halcyon period of reduced risk, high growth, and many new investment opportunities, would do well to remember the hubris of the "last Grand Illusion."[9] By 2004, the Asia Crisis, the Russian and Argentinean defaults, the Long-Term Capital Management crisis, the Enron scandal, the collapse of the dot.com bubble, and the events of September 11, 2001, as well as some of the political reaction to the destruction of the World Trade Center had taken much of the luster off capital markets and sobered up all but the most besotted Pollyannas. Poor regulation and political conflict are once again viewed as an element of political risk on both sides of the Atlantic. As a recent book on globalization noted, "Without stable political foundations, markets collapse."[10]

As today's regulatory challenges mount, they seem to transcend any single nation's ability to control them. The financial system as a whole seems too vast, too diffused, and, above all, too interconnected for one regulatory body – or perhaps even several working in concert – to maintain adequate oversight. Not even the most sophisticated bankers feel comfortable with the role of banks

Outside of Bankers Trust's former headquarters at Liberty Street after the September 11, 2001 terrorist attacks.

and the whole financial system in cushioning financial shocks. Whereas a few bankers and politicians could have had an overview of the financial system in 1900, the intricate web of positions and counterparty risk of today's derivative instruments defies any overseer. The very financial freedom that we cherish may have spawned a financial vulnerability that we cannot assess.[11] Although banks generally do not lend to hedge funds, they are exposed to risk as derivative

Inside view of the destruction in Bankers Trust's building.

counterparties, and they do lend to brokers who provide margin accounts to hedge funds.[12] In short, governments have privatized many financial risks, but the ultimate responsibility for and origin of much international investment risk is political and national nature.

One of those risks comes from a clash of cultures, an investment fact of life that has grown considerably for Deutsche Bank and business in general during the period covered by this narrative. For the first forty years of this history, when Deutsche Bank used agents to run its U.S. business and when it took on minority shares in U.S. companies, fears of being overwhelmed by each other's culture hardly surfaced. Indeed, both countries evidenced an ability to learn from one another.[13] By the 1920s, though, conflict and distrust were more the rule than the exception. Acceptance of funding from the United States was attached to unwanted loss of German sovereignty. Despite the internationalization of capital markets and perhaps because of the degree of equity investment, both portfolio and foreign direct, fears of foreign invasion have once again become a political and, thereby, a business issue.[14]

Deutsche Bank's new strategy is part of a profound change in Germany's and other corporate governance systems. Both customers and banks are breaking away from the old house-bank model of tight relationships. If Deutsche Bank wants to be a player in competitive bidding with the very specialized sort of investment banks in large part created by the American Glass-Steagall Act, Deutsche Bank's leaders believe that it will have to shed its large holdings in its clients' equity and its active role in the management of German companies, considered by most a mainstay of the German corporate governance system since the nineteenth century. These relationships entail too many conflicts of interest – as some of the stories from Deutsche Bank's pre-World War I experience in the United States illustrate – and also many costs. These close relationships are still frowned upon by American regulators just as they were encouraged by their German counterparts. In short, Deutsche Bank finds that it has more risk and fewer incentives to take long-term responsibility for the companies it brings to market.[15]

Some of Deutsche Bank's most recent legal problems can be traced back to political frustration with high European unemployment rates and fears of being overwhelmed by American-styled capital markets. They serve as an unwelcome illustration for many executives in multinational firms of unresolved national conflicts over how economies should be organized.[16] If these "rather tame-by-comparison disputes" are insufficient, then the painful reminder of September 11 provided by the highly damaged Bankers Trust building and two-year-long battles with insurers over what should be done with the damaged shell gives an all-too-clear picture of the potential impact of political conflict.[17]

The Management Factor

Last, people and the institutions they create still count in economic value creation, but creating the proper balance of control and freedom on an international scale is a monumental task. This may be self-evident for some, but the role of certain human activity is a fact often forgotten in modern financial theory and practice. For many, capital markets are deemed to be efficient in the sense that all risk-adjusted financial gain, above what models predict as expected return, is a statistical delusion. As one financial theorist put it, people are "fooled by randomness" into thinking that they have really done something constructive.[18]

It is hard to reconcile this view of the world with financial intermediation. But despite many predictions of their imminent demise, banks continue to thrive, especially in some sectors. The history of Deutsche Bank suggests that the role of intermediaries has changed considerably over the past 130 years, but also that banks still have a role to play to supplement direct access to financial markets, overcome information asymmetries, and to evaluate and to control unique risk (uncertainty). Even if markets provide all the right information, moreover, there is no guarantee that this information will be correctly integrated into prices.[19] It is not just the information but also who is using it that counts.

It is beyond question that capital markets have evolved extraordinarily since Deutsche Bank began investing in U.S. securities. Moreover, economic theory has provided a host of tools for managing the risk-reward relationship of investing in securities, which have revolutionized financial practice. Much of modern finance is predicated on market efficiency and a related concept of the Law of One Price, which states simply that identical assets must have the same price; if not, an arbitrage (a risk-free investment) opportunity exists. The absence of costless arbitrage opportunities, for example, is fundamental to options pricing.[20] Assets are believed to be correctly priced given our best knowledge of their return and best assessment of the risk-adjusted cost of purchasing them. Paradoxically, one of the basic lessons of finance teaches that real profit only comes from ventures that provide gains which exceed market expectations for their return.[21]

The history of Deutsche Bank in the United States is inconceivable without the passions of highly motivated individuals pursuing the greatest possible gain. The bank's successes and failures point to the vital role that individuals and organizations still play in value creation. In the early part of this history, a few individuals ran Deutsche Bank's businesses, even those that spanned several continents. Though important, most of its employees were occupied with routine matters, record keeping, letter copying, and filing. Only a few key managers made and monitored deals. Thanks to modern technology and despite great numbers of transactions, routine functions are largely automated now.

What has not changed, however, since the days of Siemens and Gwinner, is that Deutsche Bank's triumphs and tragedies are still determined by its organizational capacities, its ability to attract and utilize talent. Through much of its history, several cosmopolitan managers played key roles in building its business. Without the Siemenses, Gwinners, Blinzigs, and Abses, and their knowledge of international business and languages, the early stages of Deutsche Bank businesses would have been unthinkable. Likewise, from 1960 to 1990, the bank's shortage of Rassmanns and Staeckers limited the feasibility of further investment in the United States. Today, whatever success Deutsche Bank has in the United States and other key markets is not only contingent on attracting talent, but also on ensuring that talented individuals work together to invent new products, highlight new market opportunities, understand customer needs, and, most importantly, to share that information within the bank. Despite communication improvements, for Deutsche Bank and for its competitors the nature of multinational banking in the twenty-first century has created extraordinary management demands.

The history of Deutsche Bank in and with the United States points to a great paradox in financial and other service sectors: the explosion of foreign direct investment and an enormous increase in the management demands to control it.[22] In a period in which we are thought to have unparalleled geographic and informational access and once unheard of opportunities to divide and reintegrate assets and risks – a world in which national borders for funds have become so porous and so many sales weightless – financial institutions seem to need more foreign direct investment, not less.[23] Not only technical but financial activities seem to require centers of excellence. In addition to modern technology providing separate corporate entities with a means to communicate and do business with one another – establish networks – it also gives very large enterprises a greater facility to cultivate innovation and to expand the geographic coordination and integration of new products. The trick to internalizing these functions and reaping high rewards is to develop the management skills to link efficiently the various disparate centers of innovation, users of information, and customers.

Deutsche Bank's experience in the United States before World War I was not the exception in international finance but the rule. Whether one fears or welcomes globalization, all can agree that large multinational firms have become a kind of glue for the world order and their frictionless internal financial flows its lifeblood, if I may be allowed to mix my metaphors. Deutsche Bank's history not only points to the paradoxical need for greater investment, it also suggests that the process is incomplete and still full of minefields. Today's configuration, as opposed to that in 1900, entails many opportunities but also new costs, new risks, new management difficulties, and new clashes of national cultures.[24]

Like Deutsche Bank, its competitors can roll out new products with lightning speed. But maintaining a large presence in many countries entails a substantial fixed cost that must be covered by many transactions and new financial instruments, with little or no patent and copyright protection to forestall their becoming quickly copied – transformed into commodities, as it were, that suffer intense price competition – soon after introduction.

The only response to competitive pressures and reduction of entry barriers is continual product and management innovation. Like innovators in the sciences, financial innovators need clusters – cities and other meeting points – where they can talk with people who are dealing with similar problems, with those who can provide ancillary services, and where their efforts are rewarded monetarily or with less materialist signs of status. Ideas need incubators: For finance, that means financial theorists, business schools, law firms, accountants, and a good deal of freedom to change. Not every place is conducive. Some locations historically have exercised too much control, others lack sufficient regulation or amenities. The history of science and business should teach us that real innovation is virtually impossible to achieve without a community of people raising similar questions, paired with institutions that are able to transform ideas into actionable plans.[25]

Deutsche Bank's entry into the United States has added a lot of management complexity to its business. Fifty years ago, it did not operate a single legal entity in the United States, not even a joint venture.[26] Today, although down from its peak in 1999, the bank still operates more than 600 legal entities in the United States, including special purpose corporations, branches, representative offices, holding companies, joint ventures, and operating subsidiaries. The New York office oversees more than 700 legal entities that are part of Deutsche Bank Americas. They are held together in a holding company, Taunus Corporation, into which all the Americas operations and all of the Bankers Trust legal entities, including many in Europe and Asia, were folded. The North American portion not only includes 541 operations in the United States, but also 52 in the Cayman Islands alone. Although it has multiple legal entities in many states, in the state of New York alone Deutsche Bank operates nearly 250. Imagine Siemens' and Gwinner's surprise if they learned that Deutsche Bank today had more legal entities in Bermuda than were ever contemplated in all of North America in their lifetimes.[27]

Successfully marshalling the bank's skills to respond to the numerous and sometimes conflicting regulatory and shareholder demands being made on it requires coordinating business units both locally and with their counterparts all over the world. To cope with this managerial complexity, Americas group, for example, operates three-committee systems, which meet regularly, for managing its business: a regional business board, which discusses the specific goals and problems of the business units; the control and governance committee, which focuses on administrative and regulatory issues; and finally the executive committee, which handles overlapping issues.[28]

Real multinational banking, as this book illustrates, is still a young pursuit. Banks such as Deutsche Bank are continually working on ways to improve their transnational capacity, which may lead to further international mergers in the financial sector.[29] Moreover, like most banks, Deutsche Bank must face an array of challenges in its home market and host markets, which for it includes European banking overcapacity as well as potential confrontations with various regulatory bodies.[30]

Attracting, keeping, and controlling those with a flair for modern banking pose both managerial and technical problems. Senior managers are not only under pressure to pay high bonuses to attract the right talent, but also to give traders, for example, freedom to react quickly to market movements and opportunities, a practice that seems necessary for trading but is anathema for controlling.[31] According to the *Financial Times*, Deutsche Bank managers recognized that in the rarefied, fast-growing areas of credit derivatives, for example, which are highly innovative, sometimes illiquid but important sources of new business, control by risk managers was problematic at best.[32] Although derivatives are far from new, they have enjoyed explosive growth in recent years, especially noncommodity instruments.[33]

Thanks in part to new forms of derivative trading and other innovations banks have been relatively successful at maintaining their profit margins. By adding new products and shedding many costs – savings achieved largely through consolidation of independent institutions – banks have been able to increase their profitability and allay some regulatory concerns, but they have added others. After a rocky ride in the 1980s – U.S. bank return on equity, for example, bounced from 13 percent to less than 2 percent – from 1994 to 2003, bank profits jumped to a much higher, consistent level. During those ten years, return on equity reached a comfortable plateau of between 13 percent and 15 percent. U.S. bank failures during the same period dropped enormously. At the same time, bank capital adequacy ratios, boosted by greater profitability, climbed significantly in most countries. In Germany, for example, from 1993 to 2003, the average ratio climbed from 10 percent to 13 percent; in the United States, from 9.5 percent to 13 percent, well above the 8 percent Basel minimum.[34] This success has come at a price, however.[35]

Forging a New Global Financial Institution

Like many multinational institutions, Deutsche Bank is walking a cultural tightrope, for which good management serves as the only balancing rod for finding an optimal equilibrium between three polls: the demands of regulators, investors, and other stakeholders who do not always share a common national identity. Although multinational companies contribute to international integration, some studies indicate that national norms are still very important to company management, even in multinational firms.[36] Deutsche Bank is learning how to balance bringing together seamlessly complex functions over huge geographic areas with respecting regulatory constraints as well as local norms and expectations. Deutsche Bank's strategies and actions over the past fifteen years reflect a deep desire to shed, at least in part, its purely German character, while maintaining a deep link to its strongest market and to the players in international capital markets. Despite keeping its headquarters in Frankfurt, Deutsche Bank is trying to emulate more profitable banks based in London and New York.[37] However, Deutsche Bank is still a continental European universal bank and subject to European, German, and international regulation.

The approximately $10 billion spent on Bankers Trust was just part of an ambitious strategy to remake Deutsche Bank. For many Deutsche Bank leaders the pursuit of a greater presence in the United States is a means to a larger end: to inject the virtues of Anglo-American investment banking into the German bank. For them, Deutsche Bank needed to become more entrepreneurial, in some sense returning to its roots before World War I. It is, as it were, looking for a new generation of Siemenses and Gwinners, even Adamses and Villards. In contrast to the nineteenth century, this now seems to require a greater presence in the United States. Even high immediate financial rewards are not sufficient to attract and retain highly motivated innovators who could keep the bank supplied with a steady stream of cutting-edge ideas. Deutsche Bank must convince current and future employees as well as customers and competitors that the bank is in the United States to stay.[38]

Nevertheless, there are several aspects of the German tradition of capitalism – financial institutions committing to local communities, offering a wide range of services, and maintaining a very strong position in their home markets as springboards to international development – which Deutsche Bank is likely to continue to cultivate. Despite their focus on international capital markets, Deutsche Bank managers in the United States invest a lot in the American image of its operations. The existence of this history is in itself testimony to the bank's desire to understand the cultural similarities and dissimilarities between the United States and Europe, as well as the desire to help current employees appreciate the deep historical interdependence of Deutsche Bank and U.S. capital markets. Despite cost-cutting pressures, the bank maintains many of its traditional activities to help current employees and other stakeholders understand Deutsche Bank's core values and to reinforce a sense of corporate values. Understanding the history and values of the bank is part of Deutsche Bank's DNA, which allows Deutsche Bank to be both a local and international institution, and to replicate itself over time and space. Even in our materialist world and even in a business in which compensation has reached astronomical proportions, Deutsche Bank managers recognize money is not the only motivator for key employees.

With the first years of the merger behind it, Deutsche Bank in the United States is focusing on creating an American identity that is part of a greater whole. Sadly, September 11 helped shape that identity. The tragedy bound the staff together as probably nothing else could. Deutsche Bank's decision to stay in Wall Street as well as other contributions to New York City after the attack have helped to achieve an extraordinary goal: that a German bank is often perceived by many customers and competitors as an American institution.[39] As part of its desire to be part of its community, Deutsche Bank supports numerous cultural and other projects in the United States.[40] As the newest and biggest Manhattan tenant and a powerful financial institution, Deutsche Bank has its own political clout, for which circa 1900, as described in Section I, it was obliged to depend on J. P. Morgan, Sr.

Deutsche Bank's management seems wedded to a two-pronged strategy of constantly seeking new financial innovations while continuing to service selectively some traditional market segments and clients, a strategy for which the American operations play a vital role. Although no one can foresee precisely what those innovations will be, the bank hopes that preserving a climate of innovation, where creativity is rewarded and outmoded practices can be jettisoned, will keep the bank ahead of its competition. At the same time, by maintaining the universal bank concept, along with a large client base and a long list of services, Deutsche Bank will buttress its capacity to draw on diverse sources of funding and a wide range of market mechanisms for distribution. This may entail further external investment and alliances to build up a specialized retail business in the United States and to increase its geographical and sector presence in the European Union, which Deutsche Bank now considers its *home market*.[41] Two decisions symbolize its mixed identity: holding on to the name Deutsche Bank everywhere and using American financial statements.

The current management of the bank is a reflection of its international, investment banking orientation. For many, Ackermann typifies an American style of management. In early 2002, the statutory German management board was reduced from eight to four members, and in effect replaced by an executive committee, on which the management board members also sit. By late 2006, the eleven-person executive committee contained seven non-Germans, four of whom spoke English as their first language, along with three Swiss. Although the changes were approved by German banking authorities, the double management board and the autonomy of managers for their business segments are unusual structures for Germany, where collective responsibility of the management board is preferred to the individual responsibility of business-line managers.[42] According to *The Economist*, this new structure was created in part to accommodate the fractional nature of Deutsche Bank, which was more like "a bunch of franchises that include an investment bank, an asset-management arm, a retail bank, a commercial bank, and a private bank for the well-off."[43] Many of the world's largest banks share the belief that these various bits can be forged into an effective whole, while still allowing the "frontier spirit" of individual managers enough autonomy to build their individual businesses.

As the new century begins, Deutsche Bank truly has a global reach. It has invested in people, buildings, and equipment in nearly every corner of the globe, including many of the former and still nominally communist countries. Deutsche Bank now has operations in approximately seventy countries outside of Germany, divided into five groups: Europe; the Middle East and Africa; Asia Pacific; Japan; and the Americas. New York is one of its key centers, the others being London, Frankfurt, and Singapore. Its North and South American operations are run out of New York, only one of thirteen U.S. cities in which it has offices.

Although Chernow is no doubt right in the previously quoted passage about the great transformation of banking being one of the salient features of modern financial history, he may also have been premature in pronouncing the death of the banker, at the very least we might prepare to sit longer than the traditional seven days of *shivah*. Indeed, banks and financial intermediation have changed but they are far from entering the "dustbin" of history, if I might mix my metaphors once again with a reference to Friedrich Engels.

Deutsche Bank has seemed by most accounts to have turned a financial corner. It seems poised to attain its extraordinary goal of a 25 percent return on equity. Much of the investment community, which includes competitors, has given the bank high marks for its recent results. Although some areas were disappointing, equity sales and trading as well as private capital asset management overshot estimates. In 2005, only Goldman Sachs and Morgan Stanley enjoyed better equity sales and trading results. Cost cutting and other measures have shown a financial discipline admired by Wall Street. Some analysts foresee a doubling of earnings per share from 2004 to 2007, and a significantly higher share price, an achievement for which the U.S. operations will have to make a sizeable contribution.[44]

Deutsche Bank's overall market share seems to warrant optimism. With global bonds and equity underwriting reaching $6.5 trillion in 2005 – up from $5.8 trillion the year before – Deutsche Bank's 6.4 percent market share and third position in the league tables, just behind Citigroup and Lehman Brothers, left the bank in an enviable position in this lucrative segment. Although Deutsche Bank was still strongest in debt instruments, the bank had increased its activities with equities, too.[45]

Deutsche Bank's personnel in the United States reflect the bank's American past as well as current economic realities, and the bank's need to move beyond both its own and Bankers Trust's histories. At the time of the merger, Deutsche Bank employed 3,800 and Bankers Trust 10,000, making a total of nearly 14,000. Today its total staff is under 12,000. Although there are substantial numbers of Deutsche Bank and Bankers Trust legacies, roughly equal amounts, 1,872 and 2,112 respectively, approximately two-thirds of its current Americas workforce (7,638) was hired after the merger.[46] In contrast to earlier investments in American bank operations and elsewhere, moreover, Deutsche Bank has made the effort to integrate the Americas into its overall business structure.

Some multinational institutions like Deutsche Bank have taken the lead in bridging gaps between cultures and economic systems. By integrating divergent cultures they have been instrumental in creating a new international synthesis among often antagonistic national perspectives. This story presents a great deal of evidence that Deutsche Bank has survived and at times thrived not only by providing normal banking services, but also by serving as a contact point between cultures for well over a hundred years.

Internalizing cross-border functions has forced global firms to rethink traditional ways of doing business. With new strategies comes also the need for relentless reexamination of whether the organizational strengths of each firm are up to its goals. The real challenge seems to be not what particular products and services the bank offers today but how to develop the organizational capabilities to respond continually to the demands of an ever-changing market. Global firms such as Deutsche Bank need to build cross-border cost advantages through centralization of operations, while simultaneously exploiting their closeness to markets. It is an extraordinary undertaking. In additional to geographical breadth of operations, unlike their nineteenth-century predecessors, not many managers today can hope to perform more than a few of the wide range of corporate tasks. As one recent history of British management put it, "A key characteristic of modern management is its diversity, even within organizations functionally, vertically, and laterally, which also provide dimensions of the growth of management."[47]

According to many management theorists, the essential task involves leveraging learning, cultivating organizational strengths, and establishing a diverse, committed workforce.[48] Firms need to avoid being trapped by organizational tables and a false reliance on their ability to solve core problems. Unfortunately, all of this is not simple. To achieve this ambitious end, firms need to understand how they evolved, to develop and practice a strong sense of core values, and to learn how to balance diverse opinions and cultures within the confines of organizational rigor. Legitimizing diversity requires understanding how diversity contributes to an organization and what rational limits must be set to produce a well-integrated whole. In this schema, international operations are no longer just a means of reducing costs or avoiding barriers to trade, but rather parts to building a worldwide infrastructure of resources to deal with tumultuous factor costs, market fluctuations, and technological changes. The first step is self-knowledge. Most companies ignore their administrative heritage. As two well-known management theorists put it:

> In deciding how to manage their worldwide operations, most managers we studied focused intently on where they were going. They seldom asked themselves where they were coming from, although this question often turned out to be crucial. Companies had to respond to new environmental demands in the context of their existing organizational capabilities as shaped by various historical and structural factors. This administrative heritage represented both a major asset and a powerful impediment to the change process.[49]

It is my hope that this book has made a contribution to this specific process by shedding light on the roots of Deutsche Bank's organization in the United States. Although some think that a forward looking organization should ignore its past, more enlightened business people recognize that, as with individuals, any rational organization must examine its past before setting out to reinvent itself. Yet, as one German philosopher put it, both too much of a sense of history and too little can be dangerous for individuals – and, I would add, to organizations. Looking just backward or just forward tends to rob individuals of a capacity for rational action. As in many areas, Deutsche Bank's commitment to unearthing its past while pushing into innovative services and organizational structures may indicate that it is poised as an organization to create the kind of synthesis in the business world Nietzsche had in mind for individuals.[50]

Appendix I

Returns to Deutsche Bank Investors in Three Separate Periods and Comparative Returns in the New Millennium

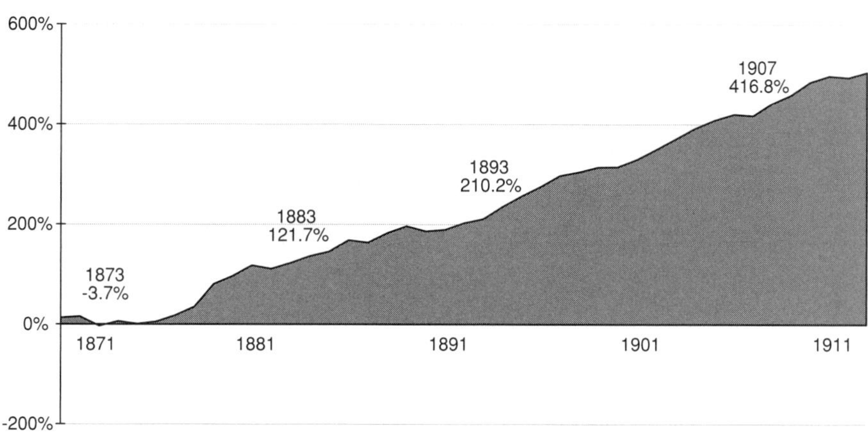

GRAPH 1. Cumulative Return to Deutsche Bank Shareholders, 1871 to 1913.
Source: Adapted from www.bankgeschichte.de. It includes dividends and capital gains (change in share price from the beginning to the end of the period) from the end of December 1870 to the end of December 1913, just before World War I began. An investor who bought a Deutsche Bank share in December 1870 at its then market price of 108% of nominal capital between dividends and capital gains quintupled his investment, a remarkable return, considering the period's extremely low inflation and the steadiness of his return (low volatility) compared with other periods. Although real equity returns are a matter of great debate in finance, there is much evidence that in purely nominal terms (unadjusted for volatility) they were lower before World War I than after, making Deutsche Bank's return to investors even more impressive during the period. Once the bank survived the Panic of 1873, returns increased fairly steadily, despite dips, especially in the early 1880s and 1890s and 1907. It is impossible to know precisely what role American business played, but after the Northern Pacific crisis, Deutsche Bank's shareholders enjoyed high and steady returns. Despite the poor regulation and traumas in the world's largest economy for most of the period, it is perhaps a truism to point out that these results owe a lot to the combination of favorable macroeconomic and political circumstances coupled with astute management. From 1871 to 1913, Deutsche Bank's total revenues grew from 3 million to nearly 130 million Mark. During that time, trading in bank acceptances and bills, two very international businesses collectively represented a steady 20% of revenues. Securities trading, in contrast, fluctuated between 5% and 20% of revenues. Hook, Tables 9 and 10.

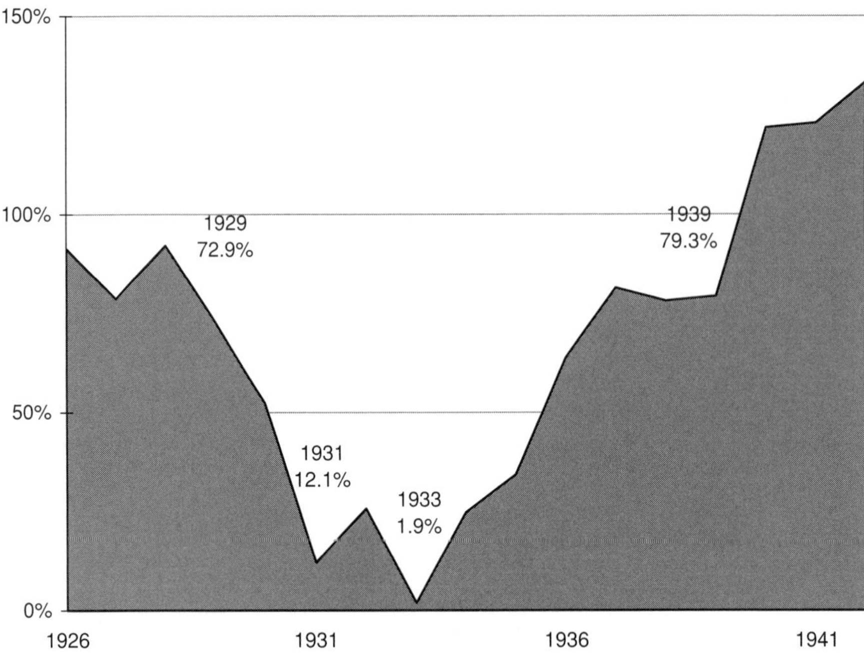

GRAPH 2. Cumulative Return to Deutsche Bank Shareholders, 1926 to 1942.
Source: Adapted from www.bankgeschichte.de. It includes dividends and capital gains (change in share price from beginning to the end of the period) from the end of December 1925 to the end of December 1942, when operations were suspended on German stock markets. The contrast to the previous period could not be more dramatic. After a couple of years of extraordinary gains, by 1933 considering dividends and capital losses, an investor had earned virtually nothing, barely holding on to his principal that had been paid out to him in the form of dividends (approximately 50% of the value of the original investment). By 1942, an investor who had bought Deutsche Bank shares in December 1925 had barely doubled his money during the period, which witnessed extraordinary volatility, at times significant inflation, and risk that funds in Germany could not be converted to other currencies.

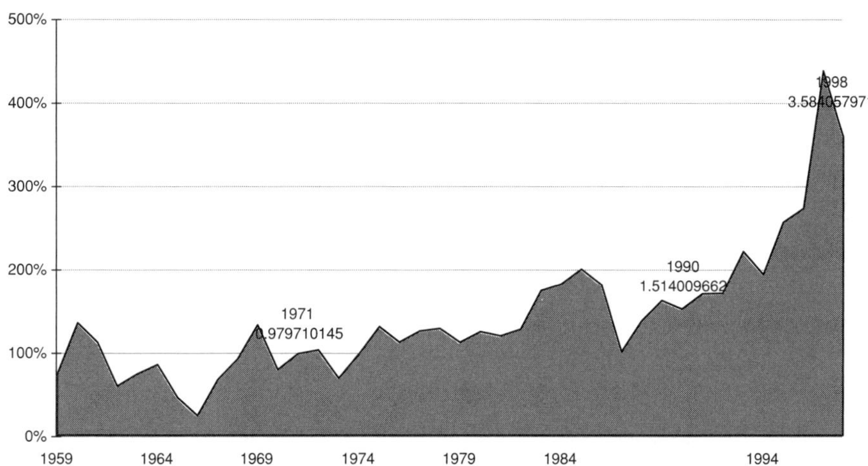

GRAPH 3. Cumulative Return to Deutsche Bank Shareholders, 1959 to 2000.
Source: Adapted from www.bankgeschichte.de. It includes dividends and capital gains (change in share price from the beginning to the end of the period) from the end of December 1958, Deutsche Bank's first full year as a reunited bank, to December 2000. Just after the three banks consolidated, Deutsche Bank's shares enjoyed a huge increase, but then they languished until the 1980s. Although much of the world's equity markets witnessed extraordinary growth in the 1990s, Deutsche Bank's stock price was highly volatile.

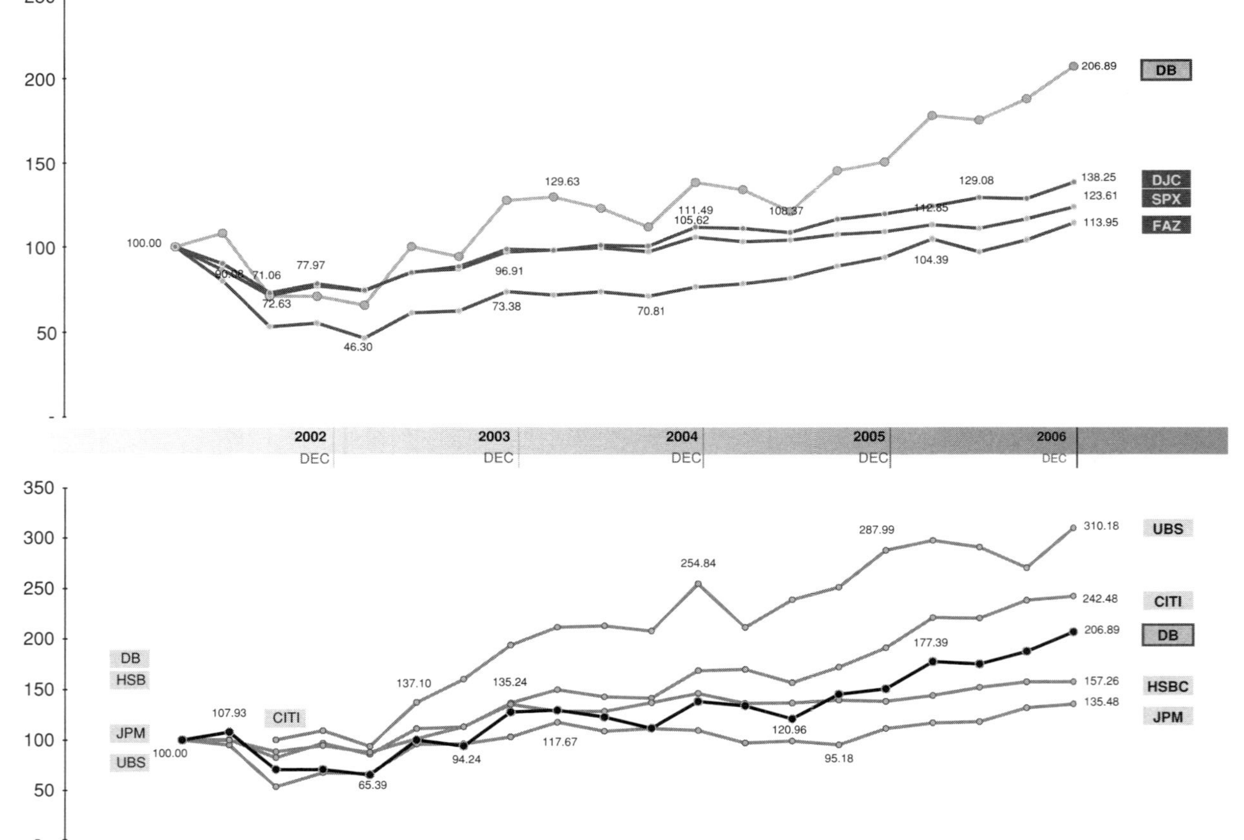

GRAPH 4. Deutsche Bank's Share Performance Against Selected Competitors and Indices, 2002 to 2006.
Source: Datamonitor. The changes in Deutsche Bank's share price are compared with several stock market indices (Dow Jones, Standard and Poor's, and Frankfurter Allgemeine Zeitung) as well as four of its main competitors from early 2002 to the end of 2006. As seen from the graphs, Deutsche Bank's stock outperformed all of the indices and two of its major competitors during the period.

Appendix II

Deutsche Bank in Comparison with Other Banks

TABLE 1. *Sources of Profits*

Germany's Three Largest Banks in 1904	In thousands of Marks or percent	
	Foreign Exchange, Bills, and Interest	Securities Emissions and Trading
Deutsche Bank with its Subsidiaries	27,252	15,375
% total bank profit	45	25
Dresdner Schaaffhausen with Subs	17,070	5,497
% total bank profit	52	17
Disconto-Gesellschaft with Subs	13,831	8,350
% total bank profit	46	28

Source: Jeidels, p. 129, adapted from *Kölnische Zeitung*, April 3, 1904. Unfortunately, no accurate breakdown of bank profits or revenues by international versus domestic sources is available. This table gives some indication of how important Deutsche Bank had become to German banking and how international its business had become by the turn of the century. Profits from its securities business – much of which was international in origin – exceeded the combined amounts of the next two largest banks. Foreign exchange, bills, and interest made up nearly half of Deutsche Bank's profits. From 1871 to 1910, Deutsche Bank had increased its assets tenfold, making the bank over 40% and 50% larger as measured by assets than Dresdner Bank and Disconto-Gesellschaft, respectively. Hook, Table 11.

TABLE 2. *European and American Banks by Assets – 1925 (in thousand Dollars)*

Country Bank	Total Assets	Amt. of Deposits	Capital	Reserve	Total Capital & Reserves
Germany					
Deutsche Bank	366,636	295,035	35,700	13,090	48,790
Disconto-Gesellschaft	222,606	135,544	23,800	8,330	32,130
Dresdner Bank	276,775	238,892	18,564	5,569	24,133
Darmstädter und Nationalbank	240,837	204,473	14,280	9,520	23,800
France					
Crédit Lyonnais	293,507	260,278	9,750	8,775	18,525
Banque de Paris et des Pay-bas	136,959	108,548	7,800	5,141	12,941
Holland					
Amsterdamsche Bank	186,031	25,426	22,000	17,200	39,200
Rotterdamsche Bankvereeniging	108,175	60,169	20,000	8,000	28,000
Italy					
Banca Commerciale Italiana	592,490	266,828	28,000	18,400	46,400
Credito Italiano	391,096	192,827	14,118	5,200	19,318
United States					
National City Bank	1,281,494	963,554	50,000	63,133	113,133
Chase National Bank	931,651	813,426	40,000	36,764	76,764

Source: HADB S4382 – This table shows some of the effects of World War I on international banking. Whereas not one American bank was among the world's ten largest banks in 1913, by the mid-1920s National City Bank alone was approximately four times larger in terms of assets, capital, and deposits than the four German banks listed. Not one Continental European bank comes close to the size of the two American banks listed.

TABLE 3. *The Largest "Free World" Banks by Assets – 1962*

Asset Rank	Bank *Head Office*	Total Assets	No. of Shareholders	No. of Employees
1	Bank of America Nat'l Trust & Svgs. Assn. *San Francisco, United States*	$13,417,140,809	. . .	26,700
2	Chase Manhattan Bank *New York, United States*	10,932,323,095	100,000	. . .
3	First National City Bank *New York, United States*	10,280,323,775	67,817	19,800
4	Manufacturers Hanover Trust Co. *New York, United States*	6,532,402,555	44,040	10,345
5	Barclays Bank Limited *London, U.K.*	5,756,285,458	84,535	26,491
6	Morgan Guaranty Trust Co. *New York, United States*	5,313,607,035	38,606	5,998
7	Midland Bank Limited *London, U.K.*	5,275,667,562	88,000	23,000
8	Chemical Bank New York Trust Co. *New York, United States*	5,246,135,618	34,273	8,000
9	Royal Bank of Canada *Montreal, Canada*	4,810,987,818	25,339	17,566
10	Lloyds Bank Limited *London, U.K.*	4,647,675,856	74,987	24,000
11	Banca Nazionale del Lavoro *Rome, Italy*	4,449,606,105	. . .	9,972
12	Canadian Imperial Bank of Commerce *Montreal, Canada*	4,425,368,296	25,233	16,090
13	Security First National Bank *Los Angeles, United States*	4,301,925,186	18,179	10,917
14	National Provincial Bank Limited *London, U.K.*	4,263,470,813	65,000	16,000
15	Fuji Bank Limited *Tokyo, Japan*	4,198,289,434	23,329	11,867
16	Mitsubishi Bank Limited *Tokyo, Japan*	4,087,582,783	20,368	10,769
17	Continental Illinois Nat'l Bk. & Tr. Co. *Chicago, United States*	4,045,325,172	16,360	5,407

(continued)

TABLE 3 *(continued)*

Asset Rank	Bank *Head Office*	Total Assets	No. of Shareholders	No. of Employees
18	Sumitomo Bank Limited *Osaka, Japan*	4,001,573,920	16,426	10,311
19	Bankers Trust Co. *New York, United States*	3,934,580,367	24,494	6,803
20	Sanwa Bank Limited *Osaka, Japan*	3,929,489,322	17,467	12,072
21	Bank of Montreal *Montreal, Canada*	3,802,327,704	22,666	15,835
22	First National Bank *Chicago, United States*	3,716,732,225	8,931	3,540
23	Crédit Lyonnais S. A. *Paris, France*	3,680,721,567	...	25,700
24	Westminster Bank Limited *London, U.K.*	3,380,591,374	63,000	18,200
25	Deutsche Bank *Frankfurt, Germany*	3,303,002,789	50,000	21,333
39	Dresdner Bank *Frankfurt, Germany*	2,493,151,000	45,000	14,921
47	Rheinische Girozentrale und Provinzialbank *Dusseldorf, Germany*	2,021,682,000	...	1,993
51	Commerzbank *Dusseldorf, Germany*	1,978,130,256	25,000	10,600
53	Hessische Landesbank-Girozentrale *Frankfurt, Germany*	1,713,054,031	...	...
60	Swiss Bank Corporation *Basle, Switzerland*	1,593,307,708	...	5,459
61	Swiss Credit Bank *Zurich, Switzerland*	1,576,760,169	...	3,539
62	Bayerische Hypotheken- und Wechsel-Bank *Munich, Germany*	1,520,451,009	...	6,750

Source: The American Banker, Aug. 7, 1963. Although the sector's focus on size was in its infancy, this early ranking shows where Deutsche Bank stood in relation to its competitors inside and outside of Germany shortly after the reunification of the bank. Six of the largest banks are American. By this time, too, there were a considerable number of Japanese and European banks whose asset base was much larger than Deutsche Bank's. It was still significantly larger than its German and Swiss rivals. Interestingly, while First National City's assets were nearly three times larger than Deutsche Bank's, the two banks had roughly the same number of employees.

TABLE 4. *Banking Rankings, 1978 and 1979*

Rank '79	Rank '78	Bank *Head Office*	Assets Less Contra Accounts	Capital and Reserves	Total Revenue	Pretax Earnings	Revenue on Assets (%)
1	2	Crédit Agricole	104,997	6,024			
		Paris	*17.4*	*20.0*			
2	1	BankAmerica Corp.	103,919	3,462	9,450	948	9.65
		San Francisco	*13.0*	*13.9*	*35.7*	*12.3*	
3	3	Citicorp	102,742	3,598	10,904	871	11.62
		New York	*21.1*	*12.9*	*44.3*	*5.3*	
4	5	Banque Nationale de Paris	98,859	1,386	7,663	145	8.52
		Paris	*22.0*	*9.4*	*37.0*	*10.6*	
5	4	Deutsche Bank	91,188	2,942	7,075	634	8.06
		Frankfurt	*8.2*	*15.9*	*23.5*	*2.5*	
6	6	Crédit Lyonnais	91,085	1,115	7,376	229	8.79
		Paris	*18.7*	*5.8*	*33.2*	*89.3*	
7	7	Societe Generale	84,914	1,402		282	
		Paris	*22.5*	*7.9*		*−15.0*	
8	9	Dresdner Bank	70,331	1,981	5,181	307	7.70
		Frankfurt	*9.4*	*6.3*	*23.0*	*10.4*	
9	19	Barclays Group	67,474	3,906		1,178	
		London	*27.0*	*29.3*		*41.8*	
10	8	Dai-Ichi Kangyo Bank	66,581	2,517			
		Tokyo	*19.4*	*4.9*			
11	21	National Westminster Bank	64,393	4,175		982	
		London	*30.4*	*16.4*		*44.4*	
12	10	Chase Manhattan Corp.	61,975	2,027	6,079	550	9.97
		New York	*3.4*	*11.3*	*36.3*	*50.3*	
13	16	Westdeutsche Landesbank-Girozentrale	60,080	1,906	3,952		6.92
		Dusseldorf	*11.0*	*7.8*	*21.3*		

(continued)

TABLE 4 *(continued)*

Rank '79	Rank '78	Bank *Head Office*	Assets Less Contra Accounts	Capital and Reserves	Total Revenue	Pretax Earnings	Revenue on Assets (%)
14	11	Fuji Bank	59,833	2,485			
		Tokyo	*19.4*	*8.7*			
15	20	Commerzbank	58,271	1,442	4,120	193	7.53
		Dusseldorf	*14.0*	*16.4*	*29.7*	*365.3*	
16	12	Sumitomo Bank	58,022	2,438			
		Tokyo	*18.1*	*6.1*			
17	13	Mitsubishi Bank	57,344	2,307			
		Tokyo	*17.8*	*4.3*			
18	14	Sanwa Bank	55,301	2,084			
		Osaka	*16.6*	*5.3*			
19	15	Norinchukin Bank	53,663	2,130	2,761	55	5.65
		Tokyo	*21.7*	*4.4*	*12.1*	*10.9*	
20	17	Banco do Brasil	49,130	3,262	4,215	485	11.51
		Brasilia	*103.8*	*63.6*			

Source: Adapted from *The Banker*, June 1980. As banks and those who followed the sector perceived the greater direct competition among international banks, relative size and other comparisons seemed to become more important. *The Banker* also adjusted assets for contra accounts, those items that appear as both assets and liabilities on banks' balance sheets, such as collateral accounts, which do not, therefore, represent funds for the bank's own use. All figures on first line in $ millions or percentages (far right column); second line shows percentage growth in local currency in past twelve months. Helped by the Dollar's loss in value, Deutsche Bank and other non-American banks climbed in the league tables. The two American banks still left among the top ten were joined by four French, two German, and one Japanese. One South American bank broke into the top twenty. Although Deutsche Bank's revenue growth was substantial, it lagged in local currency terms behind its two larger American rivals in profit growth and overall profitability.

TABLE 5. *The 20 Largest Commercial Banks, 2001 (in millions of Dollars)*

	Market Capitalization
1. Citigroup (*United States*)	250,143
2. HSBC (*United Kingdom*)	140,693
3. J. P. Morgan Chase (*United States*)	103,113
4. Wells Fargo (*United States*)	89,251
5. Bank of America (*United States*)	82,745
6. UBS (*Switzerland*)	73,673
7. Royal Bank of Scotland (*United Kingdom*)	62,865
8. Lloyds TSB (*United Kingdom*)	60,663
9. Crédit Suisse (*Switzerland*)	55,719
10. Barclays (*United Kingdom*)	53,630
11. Deutsche Bank (*Germany*)	51,047
12. BSCH (*Spain*)	48,311
13. Bank of Tokyo-Mitsubishi (*Japan*)	46,986
14. BBV Argentaria (*Spain*)	46,774
15. Bank One (*United States*)	46,395
16. Fleetboston Financial (*United States*)	46,022
17. Bank of New York (*United States*)	41,466
18. Fortis (*Belgium/Netherlands*)	39,368
19. BNP Paribas (*France*)	38,367
20. ABN AMRO (*Netherlands*)	35,370

Source: Youssef Cassis, *Capitals of Capital: A History of International Financial Centres, 1780–2005* (Cambridge: Cambridge University Press, 2006), p. 267. Adapted from the *Financial Times*. Despite its purchase of Bankers Trust, Deutsche Bank early in the new millennium seemed to lag especially behind in its American and U.K. competitors' ability to attract equity capital. Although larger than some in terms of assets, Deutsche Bank's market valuation remained well below several American, Swiss, and British banks.

TABLE 6. *The top 10 Investment Banks, ranked by value of deals done in 2001 (in billions of Dollars)*

	Worldwide mergers and acquisitions, value of deals
1. Goldman Sachs *United States*	594
2. Merrill Lynch *United States*	475
3. Morgan Stanley *United States*	445
4. Crédit Suisse First Boston *Switzerland/United States*	387
5. J. P. Morgan *United States*	383
6. Citigroup/Salomon Smith Barney *Switzerland/United States*	262
7. Deutsche Bank *Germany*	221
8. UBS Warburg *Switzerland*	211
9. Lehman Brothers *Switzerland/United States*	125
10. Dresdner Kleinwort Wasserstein *Germany*	120

Source: Youssef Cassis, *Capitals of Capital: A History of International Financial Centres, 1780–2005* (Cambridge: Cambridge University Press, 2006), p. 269. Adapted from the *Financial Times*. By 2001, however, Deutsche Bank had established itself as a major player in the lucrative area of M&A deal making.

TABLE 7. *Banks Ranked by Tier One Capital Strength*

		Bank *Head Office, Year-end*	Strength Tier One Capital $m	Strength Tier One Capital %ch	Size Assets $m	Size Assets Rank	Size Assets %ch	Profits Pretax Profit $m	Profits Pretax Profit %ch	Performance Profits on Av. Capital % latest	Performance Profits on Av. Capital % prev.	Return on Assets %	Return on Assets Rank	Cost/inc. Ratio %
1	1	Citigroup *New York, N.Y., U.S. (12/31/04)*	74,415	11.3	1,484,101	2	17.4	24,182	−8.2	34.2	41.8	1.63	303	65.38
2	5	J. P. Morgan Chase & Co. *New York, N.Y., U.S. (12/31/04)*	68,621	59.0	1,157,248	7	50.1	6,223	−38.0	11.1	24.9	0.54	745	79.68
3	3	HSBC Holdings *London, U.K. (12/31/04)*	67,259	22.6	1,276,778	4	23.5	17,608	37.4	28.8	27.3	1.38	373	54.74
4	4	Bank of America Corp. *Charlotte, N.C., U.S. (12/31/04)*	64,281	45.9	1,110,457	10	50.8	21,221	33.6	39.2	36.5	1.91	229	55.07
5	2	Crédit Agricole Groupe *Paris, France (12/31/04)*	63,422	6.1	1,243,047	5	4.3	10,437	30.5	16.9	15.1	0.84	603	64.14
6	8	Royal Bank of Scotland *Edinburgh, UK (03/31/05)*	43,828	17.0	1,119,480	9	28.3	13,358	12.3	32.9	33.7	1.19	458	56.27
8	6	Mizuho Financial Group *Tokyo, Japan (12/31/04)*	38,864	5.9	1,295,942	3	3.8	8,785	7.0	23.2	23.7	0.68	675	73.36
9	11	HBOS *Edinburgh, U.K. (12/31/04)*	36,587	15.2	759,594	19	7.9	8,868	21.9	26.0	24.1	1.17	465	42.26
10	10	BNP Paribas *Paris, France (12/31/04)*	35,685	1.9	1,233,912	6	15.7	10,338	19.9	29.2	26.0	0.84	606	60.17
11	29	Bank of China *Beijing, People's Republic of China (12/31/04)*	34,851	52.8	515,972	32	11.1	4,178	243.8	14.5	5.4	0.81	622	40.02
12	22	Santander Central Hispano *Santander, Spain (12/31/04)*	33,259	44.1	783,707	18	63.7	6,040	8.1	21.4	25.8	0.77	641	54.19

(continued)

TABLE 7 *(continued)*

		Bank	Strength Tier One		Size			Profits		Performance					
			Capital		Assets			Pretax Profit		Profits on Av. Capital		Return on Assets		Cost/inc. Ratio
		Head Office, Year-end	$m	%ch	$m	Rank	%ch	$m	%ch	% latest	% prev.	%	Rank	%
13	13	Barclays Bank *London, U.K. (12/31/04)*	32,178	11.1	992,103	11	15.9	8.890	19.7	29.1	26.3	0.90	579	59.88
14	15	Rabobank Group *Utrecht, Netherlands (12/31/04)*	30,810	15.1	647,084	25	17.8	3.826	16.9	13.3	13.1	0.59	712	66.95
15	9	Sumitomo Mitsui Financial Group *Tokyo, Japan (03/31/05)*	30,389	−8.7	896,909	14	−2.9	1,011	−126.8	−3.2	11.9	−0.11	971	91.79
16	14	Wells Fargo & Co. *San Francisco, CA, U.S. (12/31/04)*	29,060	15.9	427,849	38	10.3	10,769	12.3	39.8	41.2	2.52	126	58.21
17	17	ING Bank *Amsterdam, Netherlands (12/31/04)*	28,792	10.8	839,654	15	13.8	4,301	56.4	15.7	10.9	0.51	755	69.97
18	19	Wachovia Corporation *Winston-Salem, N.C., U.S. (12/31/04)*	28,583	19.8	492,606	33	22.8	7,633	22.7	29.1	27.5	1.55	321	64.49
19	18	UBS *Zurich, Switzerland (12/31/04)*	27,440	4.3	1,533,036	1	25.2	9,433	27.9	35.1	29.4	0.62	700	74.01
20	20	ABN AMRO Bank *Amsterdam, Netherlands (12/31/04)*	26,993	8.6	828,961	16	15.1	7,424	10.8	28.6	27.8	0.90	580	69.15
21	12	Deutsche Bank *Frankfurt, Germany (12/31/04)*	25,507	−13.4	1,144,195	8	4.5	5,488	46.2	20.0	12.4	0.48	782	79.92
22	30	Groupe Caisse d'Epargne *Paris, France (12/31/04)*	25,056	26.6	740,821	20	42.9	3,285	14.4	14.7	15.6	0.44	804	72.60
23	23	Société Générale *Paris, France (12/31/04)*	25,008	8.4	818,699	17	11.4	6,904	18.4	28.7	26.6	0.84	602	67.93

TABLE 7 *(continued)*

		Bank *Head Office, Year-end*	Strength Tier One Capital $m	%ch	Size Assets $m	Rank	%ch	Profits Pretax Profit $m	%ch	Performance Profits on Av. Capital % latest	% prev.	Return on Assets %	Rank	Cost/inc. Ratio %
24	27	Crédit Mutuel *Paris, France (12/31/04)*	24,773	18.9	527,611	31	9.1	3,578	6.2	15.7	17.8	0.68	674	66.00
25	21	China Construction Bank *Beijing, People's Republic of China (12/31/04)*	23,530	4.5	471,792	35	9.9	6,067	11059.1	26.4	0.3	1.29	417	39.17
26	26	Lloyds TSB Group *London, U.K. (12/31/04)*	22,644	4.5	540,446	29	11.0	6,746	−19.7	30.4	42.0	1.25	436	54.44
27	33	Credit Suisse Group *Zurich, Switzerland (12/31/04)*	21,736	9.8	962,783	13	13.2	7,337	43.6	35.3	27.6	0.76	646	45.59
28	24	UFJ Holdings *Osaka-shi, Japan (03/31/05)*	21,550	6.4	730,394	21	−0.2	2,185	na	−10.5	−14.0	−0.30	975	na
29	32	HypoVereinsbank *Munich, Germany (12/31/04)*	21,412	9.4	636,622	26	−2.5	3,103	na	−15.1	−12.8	−0.49	981	65.64
30	34	Banca Intesa *Milano, Italy (12/31/04)*	21,199	8.9	374,010	43	5.5	3,585	34.6	17.6	14.1	0.96	548	59.90

Source: The Banker, July 2005. While Deutsche Bank still ranked among the ten largest banks as measured by assets, by Tier One Capital (paid-in equity capital plus disclosed reserves, principally retained earnings) now used by *The Banker* for its principal bank ranking, it had dropped to number twenty-one in the world. Tier One Capital is one of the main components in evaluating bank capital adequacy agreed by most major central banks in 1988. In addition to the strong showing of American, United Kingdom, and Japanese banks, Chinese banks had entered the ranking under this measure. Deutsche Bank still remained the largest bank in Germany by this measure, but its profitability and cost ratio lagged behind many of its global competitors.

Notes

Preface and Acknowledgements

1. Marc Bloch, *The Historian's Craft* (New York: Knopf, 1971), p. 64.
2. For this period, apart from some documents that have mysteriously disappeared – for example, minutes of the management board meetings up through 1945 and a collection of documents reported to have been seized in 1917 by the American government from Deutsche Bank's New York office that both Mira Wilkins and I have attempted to find and failed to locate – I have had ample, perhaps too much, material to work with.
3. Per H. Hansen, "Writing Business History Without an Archive. Newspapers as Sources for Business History – Possibilities and Limitations," in Carl-Johan Gadd, Staffan Granér, Sverker Jonsson, eds., *Markets and Embeddedness. Essays in Honour of Ulf Olsson* (Göteborg: Göteborg University, 2004), pp. 99–120. See also Christopher Kobrak, "Varieties of Business History," ABH Meeting, London, 2006. Http://www.busman.qmul.ac.uk/abh/conference.
4. The accuracy of much of the public information provided by companies is supposedly protected by the force of law, but we all know that those who write annual reports sometimes "play" with the truth. The press's primary objective is to report the news, but some members of the fourth estate have very definite ideas of how they will make the world better and often have little sympathy for or even understanding of the workings of business. Even the memories of those who actually were there may be distorted by time or wishful thinking. As discussed, I have a preference for internal documents. Though by no means perfect, their authors, especially before 1914, probably had little idea that they would be used by an outsider, and they needed to convey information sufficiently accurate to run businesses. As always I am indebted to Fritz Stern, ed., *The Varieties of History: From Voltaire to the Present* (New York: Meridian Books, 1956) as a guide to the responsibilities of and issues in writing history.
5. Through the offices of its representative in the United States, Deutsche Bank arranged for Helfferich's book to be sent out to the 16,500 institutions and individuals that received its annual report, as well as to other institutions and individuals connected with the German Society located at Columbia University. Adams to Deutsche Bank, Nov. 10, 1913, HADB, A39. Sadly, the far smaller number of copies purchased by Deutsche Bank of this volume probably has less to do with a change in Deutsche Bank's generosity than a reduction in the number of interested readers. I hope that a change in the quality of the two books is not the explanation. As a matter of fact, not everyone was impressed with Helfferich's assessment of the strengths of the German economy. See *The Times Literary Supplement*, Dec. 11, 1913.
6. Michael Jensen, "The Modern Industrial Revolution, Exit, and the Failure of Internal Control Systems," *Journal of Finance*, Vol. 48 (1993), no. 3.

1. Overview of the Title and Terrain

1. Some recent research has helped to refine our image of the Gold Standard, how it functioned and how well it worked. It clearly was not simple, nor was it a panacea for all economic and social woes. Some of our esteem for it, moreover, may be more a reflection of the economic chaos that followed. A good argument could be made that the financial history of post–World War I is best seen as many failed attempts to restore the currency stability and convertibility

of the forty years before August 1914. See Barry Eichengreen and Marc Flandreau, *The Gold Standard in Theory and History* (London: Routledge, 1997). For the transition, see an excellent new collection of essays, *International Financial History in the Twentieth Century: System and Anarchy*, Marc Flandreau et al., eds. (Cambridge: Cambridge University Press, 2003).

2. *The MIT Dictionary of Modern Economics*, ed. David Pearce (Cambridge, MA: MIT Press, 1992). The *American Heritage Dictionary* defines a market as "a public gathering held at regular intervals for buying and selling merchandise." The *MIT Dictionary of Modern Economics* takes a broader view, defining a market as "any context in which the sale and purchase of goods and services takes place" (p. 266). It goes on to define market forces as a "free play of market supply and demand" (p. 267).
3. Ron Chernow, *The Death of the Banker* (New York: Vintage Books, 1997), p. 33.
4. The question of U.S. influence over the political–economic decisions in Europe and Japan have been one of the most interesting areas of research over the past few decades, but goes back at least to Jean Jacques Servan-Schreiber's *Le défi Américan* (Paris: Denoël, 1967). Many more recent studies have taken up the issue. See Volker R. Berghahn, *The Americanization of West German Industry, 1945–1973* (Leamington Spa: Berg, 1986), Jonathan Zeitlin and Gary Herrigel, eds. *Americanization and its Limits: Reworking U.S. Technology and Management in Post-war Europe and Japan* (Oxford: Oxford University Press, 2004), Mary Nolan, *Visions of Modernity: American Business and the Modernization of Germany* (Oxford: Oxford University Press, 1994), and Stefano Battilossi and Youssef Cassis, eds., *European Banks and American Challenge: Competition and Cooperation in International Banking under Bretton Woods* (Oxford: Oxford University Press, 2002), Richard Whitney, *Divergent Capitalism: The Social Structure and Change of Business Systems* (Oxford: Oxford University Press, 2000), Mary O'Sullivan, *Contests for Corporate Control: Corporate Governance and Economic Performance in the United States and Germany* (Oxford: Oxford University Press, 2000), Werner Abelshauser, *The Dynamics of German Industry: Germany's Path Toward the New Economy and the American Challenge* (New York: Berghahn Books, 2005), David Coates, *Varieties of Capitalism, Varieties of Approaches* (London: MacMillan, 2005) and, most recently, Volker R. Berghahn and Sigurt Vitols, eds., *Gibt es einen deutschen Kapitalismus: Tradition und globale Perspektiven der sozialen Marktwirtschaft* (Frankfurt: Campus, 2006), for example.
5. My thanks to Youssef Cassis, who was the first to raise the issue of using the preposition "in" at a conference, a 2005 ABH Meeting in Glasgow.
6. We still do not know enough about the political and other dimensions of foreign direct investment, especially in the financial sector, despite the excellent work of Mira Wilkins, Geoffrey Jones, Mark Casson, and Adrian Tschoegl, which will be noted in this text. A more precise discussion of Deutsche Bank's relationship to the United States based on internal documents can shed light on a host of interesting business questions including: What role do ownership and location advantage play in foreign investment decisions of service companies; how does that role change over time and under different economic-political circumstances; how effective is internalization of banking functions as opposed to networks; how useful are financial intermediaries in corporate governance systems; and, finally, what effect does political risk have on service companies and what options do they have for dealing with it?
7. Daniel T. Rodgers, *Atlantic Crossings: Social Politics in a Progressive Age* (Cambridge, MA: Belknap Press of Harvard University, 1998), p. 11.
8. Ranking based on Tier 1 capital as defined by the Basel Bank for International Settlements (BIS). *The Banker*, Vol. 154 (July 2004), no. 941. Deutsche Bank was ranked sixth by assets.
9. See, for example, Harold James, *The Deutsche Bank and the Nazi Economic War Against the Jews* (Cambridge: Cambridge University Press, 2001).
10. See O'Sullivan, pp. 259–288.
11. Although Siemens and other members of Deutsche Bank's leadership were raised to the German peerage, I will always drop the "von" from their names, as a changeover in the middle of the narrative would probably just confuse me and the reader.
12. Lothar Gall, "The Deutsche Bank from its Founding to the Great War," in *The Deutsche Bank, 1870–1995*, Lothar Gall et al. (London: Weidenfeld & Nicolson, 1995), p. 10. At

least one other bank was established in Germany in that year to perform a similar function. In 1870, a group of private bankers established Commerz- und Disconto-Bank to further German trade, especially that emanating from Hamburg, and financial independence. *Hundert Jahre Commerzbank, 1870–1970* (Dusseldorf: Commerzbank Aktiengesellschaft, 1970), pp. 39–40.

13. Otto Jeidels, *Das Verhältnis der deutschen Grossbanken zur Industrie, mit besonderer Berücksichtigung der Eisenindustrie*, 2nd printing (Leipzig: Duncker & Humblot, 1913).
14. Gall, "The Deutsche Bank," pp. 21–23.
15. Youssef Cassis, *Capitals of Capital: A History of International Finance, 1870–2005* (Cambridge: Cambridge University Press, 2006), pp. 43, 51–53, and 92.
16. See Niall Ferguson, *The House of Rothschild: The World's Banker, 1849–1999* (New York: Viking, 1999), pp. 65–68, who contends this was a near fatal flaw in Rothschild's international reach.
17. By 1913, manufacturing in the United States was more than double that in England. Mira Wilkins, *The History of Foreign Investment in the United States to 1914* (Cambridge, MA: Harvard University Press, 1989), p. 142.
18. Fritz Stern, *Einstein's German World* (Princeton: Princeton University Press, 1999), p. 4.
19. Ibid.
20. Wilkins, *History of Foreign Investment in the United States to 1914*, p. 170.
21. Wilkins, *History of Foreign Investment in the United States to 1914*, p. 169.
22. Wilkins, *History of Foreign Investment in the United States to 1914*, p. 176.
23. Adams to Deutsche Bank, Oct. 19, 1900, HADB, A30. Mexico and Russia were also big recipients of American money.
24. Cassis, *Capitals of Capital*, pp. 72–73.
25. Wolfgang Zorn, "Wirtschaft und Politik im deutschen Imperialismus," in *Wirtschaft, Geschichte und Wirtschaftsgeschichte: Festschrift zum 65. Geburtstag von Friedrich Lütge*, Wilhelm Abel et al., eds. (Stuttgart: G. Fischer, 1966), p. 342.
26. Gall, "The Deutsche Bank," pp. 55–61.
27. Deutsche Bank to Adams, March 12, 1901, HADB, A30.
28. Deutsche Bank to Adams, Oct. 22, 1900, HADB, A30. Gwinner informed Adams that all cable messages from Germany were going through the new Deutsch-Atlantische Telegraphen-Gesellschaft, even though there had already been complaints and some reason to believe that there had been additional delays. Cables through England, if specially requested, however, would cost 0.30 Mark more per word.
29. See Edward Hallett Carr, *Nationalism and After* (London: Macmillan, 1968), and Christopher Kobrak, *National Cultures and International Competition: The Experience of Schering AG, 1851–1950* (Cambridge: Cambridge University Press, 2002).
30. Scholars have pointed out that the "value creating assets" of service firms is in their human capital, but the backgrounds, training, and personalities of managers in this sector have played only a small role in academic business history literature. See, for example, Cyril Bouquet et al., "Foreign expansion in service industries: Separability and human capital intensity," *Journal of Business Research*, Vol. 57 (2004) for an excellent discussion of human capital in this sector. There are several popular biographies of bankers, but modern business literature had de-emphasized personal history. For some recent attempts to get at the profiles of bankers, see Youssef Cassis, "New Literature on the Social Backgrounds and Social Attitudes of Bankers," and Ganette Kurgan-van Hentenryk, "The Social Origins of Managers," both papers at EHA, Athens, 2004, and Hartmut Berghoff and Ingo Köhler, "Redesigning a Class of Its Own Social and Human Capital Formation in the German Banking Elite 1870–1990," *Financial History Review*, Vol. 14 (2007) issue 1, pp. 63–87.
31. See Karl Helfferich, *Georg von Siemens: Ein Lebensbild aus Deutschlands grosser Zeit*, 3 Vols. (Berlin: Julius Springer, 1921–23), and Arthur von Gwinner, *Lebenserinnerungen* (Frankfurt: Knapp, 1975).
32. Deutsche Bank to Adams confirming receipt of his telegrams, Sept. 10, 1901, HADB, A30. Adams reported to Berlin after McKinley's assassination that his death was already factored into equity prices and "conservative public consider Vice-President too young and restless

impulsive headstrong laking [sic] proper experience for nearly full-term presidency." Weak interest in capital markets was also likely to lead to gold outflows.

33. Adams to Deutsche Bank, Sept. 20, 1901, about management of Greene Consolidated Copper Co. ("extravagant and not conducted upon conservative lines"), HADB, A30. He mentions Allis-Chalmers Company, the first time I have seen such mention. Another example is in an Oct. 30, 1901 letter to Deutsche Bank about the management of Goldman, Sachs & Co. "wealthy, able, ambitious, bold, intimate with Kuhn, Loeb & Co., National City Bank. Moral tone not as conservative as Redmond Kerr." HADB, A30.
34. Adams to Deutsche Bank, May 9, 1902, HADB, A32. This has a lot of interesting comparative information about money center banks in 1902.
35. On one occasion he wrote directly to Arthur Gwinner as a director and large shareholder in the Central and South American Telegraph Co. (CSAT), asking Gwinner to use his influence with the German authorities to get the Deutsch-Atlantische Telegraphen-Gesellschaft to use CSAT to route messages to South America. He promised better and cheaper service, as well as a reciprocal agreement. This alliance would offer the German Empire many advantages, not the least of which is that it would avoid going through England. Adams to Gwinner, Dec. 9, 1902, HADB, A32.
36. See Paul Miranti, "The Mind's Eye of Reform: The ICC's bureau of Statistics and Accounts and a Vision of Regulation, 1887–1940," *Business History Review*, Vol. 63 (1989), no. 3, pp. 469–509.
37. See Jeff Fear and Christopher Kobrak, "Origins of German Corporate Governance and Accounting 1870–1914: Making Capitalism Respectable," Economic History Conference, Helsinki, August 2006. http://www.helsinki.fi/ichc2006/.
38. 2002 figures from Deutsche Bank's Annual Report. Unfortunately, that same region contributed a 600 million Euro loss.
39. Gertrude Himmelfarb, *The New History and the Old* (Cambridge, MA: Belknap Press of Harvard University, 1987), p. 47.

Section I. Introduction

1. David S. Landes, *The Wealth and Poverty of Nations* (New York: Norton, 1998), p. 232, and Landes, *The Unbound Prometheus: Technological Change and Industrial Development in Western Europe from 1750 to the Present* (Cambridge: Cambridge University Press, 1960). Although its economy was only slightly larger than those of the United States and Germany, it was the world leader by many other indices of development, including exports, technological sophistication, energy usage, and urbanization. In 1869, the U.K.'s coal consumption and pig iron production, for example, were roughly four times that of the region that became Germany (p. 194). See also Cassis, *Capitals of Capital*, pp. 74–94, for an excellent discussion of Britain's general economic and financial clout.
2. Niall Ferguson, *The Cash Nexus: Money and Power in the World Order 1700–2000* (New York: Basic Books, 2001), p. 131. For the size of German capital markets before World War I, see Kurt v. Reibnitz, "Der internationale Effektenkapitalismus und Deutschlands Wiederaufbau," *Der Wirtschaftsprüfer*, May 31, 1932.
3. A. G. Kenwood and A. L. Lougheed, *The Growth of the International Economy 1820–2000*, 4th edition (London: Routledge, 1999), p. 30.
4. Niall Ferguson, "The City of London and British Imperialism: New Light on an Old Question," in *London and Paris as International Financial Centres in the Twentieth Century*, Youssef Cassis and Éric Bussière, eds. (Oxford: Oxford University Press, 2005), p. 63.
5. See Geoffrey Jones, *British Multinational Banking 1830–1990* (Oxford: Oxford University Press, 1993), and Jones, *Multinationals and Global Capitalism: From the Nineteenth to the Twenty-First Century* (Oxford: Oxford University Press, 2005), pp. 113–114.
6. Youssef Cassis, "Introduction," *London and Paris as International Financial Centres*, p. 2.

7. Peter Hertner, "German Banks Abroad Before 1914," in Geoffrey Jones, ed., *Banks as Multinationals* (London: Routledge, 1990), pp. 99–120.
8. Harold James, *The End of Globalization* (Cambridge, MA: Harvard University Press, 2002).
9. Barry Eichengreen and Marc Flandreau, "Introduction," in *The Gold Standard in Theory and History*, eds., Barry Eichengreen and Marc Flandreau (London: Routledge, 1997).
10. Robert Triffin, "Myth and Realities of the Gold Standard," in *The Gold Standard in Theory and History*, eds., Barry Eichengreen and Marc Flandreau (London: Routledge, 1997), p. 151.
11. Indeed, the Mark, Pound, and Swiss Franc exchange rates from 1900 to 1914 can be graphed by a straight line. Gerold Ambrosius, "Internationale Wirtschaftsbeziehungen," in *Moderne Wirtschaftsgeschichte: Eine Einführung für Historiker und Ökonomen*, Gerold Ambrosius et al., eds. (München: Oldenbourg, 1996), p. 334.
12. Sidney Pollard, *Peaceful Conquest: The Industrialization of Europe, 1760–1970* (Oxford: Oxford University Press, 1995), p. 264.
13. Pollard, p. 259. Although tariffs for most countries were low, the United States and Germany were two countries in which protectionist voices were quite strong. U.S. tariffs on all imports were just below 20%.
14. Niall Ferguson, *Empire: The Rise and Demise of the British World Order and the Lessons for Global Power* (London: Penguin, 2002).
15. Kenwood and Lougheed, p. 129.
16. Kenwood and Lougheed, p. 20. During the same period the entire developed world enjoyed impressive growth.
17. Landes, *Wealth of Nations*, p. 232.
18. For a benchmark, at the end of 2005, the value of Deutsche Bank's equity represented only a third of 1% of Germany's GDP. The largest bank in the world by most measures, Citibank, is still around 1% of U.S. GDP, GE around 2%.
19. Deutsche Bank, annual report 1913.
20. Deutsche Bank, annual reports 1880 and 1913.
21. The risks and rewards were indeed high as indicated by interest rates. From 1870 to 1914, bond yields in the United States were higher than in Russia, Canada, and Australia. Ferguson, "The City of London," p. 66.
22. See Geoffrey Jones, *The Evolution of International Business* (London: Routledge, 1996), pp. 187–193. Although there was much cross-border finance, international transactions were serviced by correspondent banks. Domestic banks did little foreign direct investment in their own operating capacities, such as retail services or wholesale banking. Until the 1960s, most large banks did not operate a network of subsidiaries. Those that existed prior to 1960 were mostly in colonies or former colonies.
23. Claudia Langen, *Tradition, Expansion und Kooperation: Deutsch-amerikanische Bankenbeziehungen von 1900 bis 1917* (Dissertation, Cologne, 1995), pp. 1–5.
24. The precondition for effectively internalizing many activities were not there. See Oliver E. Williamson, *The Mechanisms of Governance* (Oxford: Oxford University Press, 1996) for an excellent general discussion of economics of transaction costs, trust, and family business, which was so important to international banking at the end of the nineteenth century. For a specific discussion of family banking as an alternative to multinational banking, see Christopher Kobrak, "The Rise and Fall of Family International Banking: Private Banks, Capital Markets and the Democratization of Finance," Business History Conference, Cleveland, May–June 2007, http://www.hnet.org/business/bhcweh/anmeet/general07.html.
25. Langen, pp. 5–29. Although most of this narrative covers investment banking activities, Deutsche Bank's toehold in the American market probably served to give the bank a taste of the profits from the routine transactions it directed through its correspondent bank network, but these transactions are neither sufficiently well documented nor dramatic enough to play a role in this story. It is hard to discuss servicing the banking needs of immigrants in the United States of which there were many, because of a lack of documents in the files. Tourism also played an increasing role. Americans traveling to Europe grew from 80,000 in 1892 to 375,000 in 1913.

26. Langen, pp. 5–29.
27. Langen, p. 5. German politics played little direct role in the decision to invest in the United States, but later events would show that without a direct tie to the United States, Germany was left with a severe military disadvantage *vis-à-vis* many of its European rivals.
28. *New York Times*, April 23, 1910. Americans remained, for their part, suspicious of German and other foreign intentions in the United States. As *The New York Times* reported in 1910, "Closely bound up in the Deutsche Bank are not only matters financial and economical, but political and social as well."
29. In the mid-nineteenth century, approximately nine U.S. banks were partially owned by foreign banks. Mira Wilkins, *The History of Foreign Investment in the United States to 1914* (Cambridge, MA: Harvard University Press, 1989), p. 455.
30. Bernard Desjardins et al., *Le Crédit Lyonnais, 1863–1986* (Paris: Droz, 2003), pp. 563–572. Deutsche Bank and Crédit Lyonnais cooperated on many projects including the sale of American securities in Europe. The French bank also suffered in the 1920s, not because of its national origin, like Deutsche Bank, but because its Russian office was seized by the Communists: Russian émigrés to the United States and Western Europe kept the bank in a long series of court cases and hostile press reports over their lost deposits.
31. Francis Lees, *Foreign Banking and Investment in the United States* (New York: Wiley & Sons, 1976), pp. 10–11.
32. Wilkins, *Investment in the United States to 1914*, p. 464.
33. Harold B. van Cleveland and Thomas F. Heurtas, *Citibank 1812–1970* (Cambridge, MA: Harvard University Press, 1985), pp. 1–31. Between 1838 and 1852, federal law prohibited branching and set minimum capital requirements and limits on loans. While the law from 1852 to 1865 (the free banking period) lowered capital requirements and dropped lending limits, it still set limits on deposits and prohibited branching, effectively limiting a bank to one site. The National Banking Act (1865–91), which was in effect for the first twenty years of Deutsche Bank's involvement in the United States, created for the first time federally charted banks, national banks. When National City Bank, the forerunner of Citibank, was established as a national bank under the law in 1865, it had a minimum capital requirement of $200,000, lending limits, and a prohibition against branching.
34. Wilkins, *Investment in the United States to 1914*, pp. 455–456.
35. See Kobrak, "The Rise and Fall of Family International Banking."
36. Eugene Nelson White, *The Regulation and Reform of the American Banking System, 1900–1929* (Princeton: Princeton University Press, 1983), pp. 35–38. Private bank assets peaked in 1909 at $246 million, but their number started falling around the turn of the century.
37. Niall Ferguson, *The House of Rothschild*, pp. 64–68. Despite the difficulties of controlling investments in the United States from Europe, the Rothschilds reluctantly allowed August Belmont to handle their affairs, at least on the east coast of America. Even though he brought them a lot of business, according to Ferguson, this turned out to be the single greatest mistake the family ever made. No male member of the family wanted to live in the United States and the partners, while respecting Belmont's knowledge, seemed to trust him less than Deutsche Bank's managers trusted their representatives through most of the period leading up to World War I. Evidence from Deutsche Bank's affairs in the United States as well as other sources indicate the volume and intensity of Rothschild business dealings in the United States may have been much greater than Ferguson indicates. Ferguson devotes very little space to Belmont Senior or his son. See Wilkins, *Investment in the United States to 1914*, pp. 184–186.
38. Wilkins, *Investment in the United States to 1914*, pp. 454–455. Wilkins argues that despite this lack of investment in state and local banking, Deutsche Bank was the only one of the top ten international banks that had truly important stakes in American assets. I hope this story will confirm this impression.
39. Mark Casson, "Evolution of Multinational Banks: A Theoretical Perspective," in *Banks as Multinationals* ed. Geoffrey Jones (London: Routledge, 1990) and Geoffrey Jones, *The Evolution of International Business* (London: Routledge, 1996). As Mark Casson and Geoffrey Jones have argued, finding the justification for foreign direct investment in the banking sector is somewhat more difficult than for some other sectors.

2. First Steps

1. Helfferich, Vol. 1, pp. 245–253.
2. Helfferich, Vol. 2, pp. 222–223. Helfferich was a conservative journalist and economist and Siemens' son-in-law. He served on Deutsche Bank's management board from 1908–15.
3. Helfferich, Vol. 2, p. 222. Some of the ways Helfferich expressed himself about the United States would have delighted some contemporary American politicians and upset many of his European colleagues. They may have been affected by Germany's new post–World War I financial and political dependence on the United States.
4. Helfferich, Vol. 2, p. 225.
5. Ibid.
6. Langen, pp. 71–75.
7. James Foreman-Peck, *A History of the World Economy: International Economic Relations since 1850* (New York: Simon and Schuster, 1983), p. 259.
8. Friedrich-Wilhelm Henning, *Industrialisierung in Deutschland, 1800–1914*, 7th edition (Stuttgart: Fischer, 1989), p. 172.
9. Langen, p. 86.
10. Deutsche Bank, annual report 1872.
11. Wolfgang Hinners, *Exil und Rückkehr: Friedrich Kapp in Amerika und Deutschland, 1824–1884* (Stuttgart: Heinz, 1987). Kapp's son, Wolfgang, the leader of the infamous *Kapp-Putsch* that temporarily seized power in Berlin after World War I, was a member of the Deutsche Bank's supervisory board from 1912–20. See HADB, P10130.
12. Kutter to Siemens, July 12, 1872, HADB, A1343.
13. Gebhard to Deutsche Bank, Aug. 13, 1872, HADB, A1343.
14. Undated correspondence between agent and Berlin head office, HADB, A1343.
15. Knoblauch to Siemens, Aug. 6, 1872, HADB, A1343.
16. Geschäfts-Instruction für die Commandite der Deutschen Bank in New York, Sept. 13, 1872, HADB, A1343.
17. Ibid.
18. Siemens and Wallich to K&L, Sept. 14, 1877, HADB, A1343.
19. Hertner, pp. 99–101.
20. Helfferich, Vol. 1, pp. 249–250.
21. London branch to Deutsche Bank Berlin, Nov. 27, 1880, HADB, A1359.
22. Siemens to K&L, Oct. 5, 1877, HADB, A1359.
23. Siemens to Marcuse, Aug. 12, 1885, HADB, A1343.
24. Marcuse to Siemens, Aug. 13, 1885, HADB, A1343.
25. Wilkins, *Investment in the United States to 1914*, pp. 479–480. For example, the relationships of Disconto-Gesellschaft with Kuhn Loeb and Dresdner with Morgan became closer.
26. Langen, pp. 83–87. With cable volume running at around 300,000 a year, a German-owned service was established through the Azores. In 1907, America had 1,200 miles of telephone wire, but no international service. A plan to link the United States and Germany before World War I was cut off by the onset of hostilities. With rising trade between the two countries (5 percent per year from 1896–1913), many shipping lines had regular service between Europe and the United States. Nevertheless, with a voyage to the United States still taking ten days in 1900, businessmen would have to commit around three weeks for the round trip alone.
27. Gary M. Walton and Hugh Rockoff, *History of the American Economy* (New York: Harcourt and Brace, 1998), pp. 354–355. The uneven growth in operational track topped 60 percent per decade from 1860–90, nearly 6 percent per year. Despite downward pricing and erratic returns, the sector accounted for 20 percent of U.S. gross capital formation in the 1870s and 15 percent in the 1890s.
28. Alfred D. Chandler, Jr., comp. and ed., *The Railroads: The Nation's First Big Business* (New York: Harcourt and Brace, 1965), and Chandler, *The Visible Hand* (Cambridge, MA: Harvard University Press, 1977).
29. Jonathan Barron Baskin and Paul J. Miranti, Jr., *A History of Corporate Finance* (Cambridge: Cambridge University Press, 1997), pp. 146–157.

30. Wilkins, *Investment in the United States to 1914*, pp. 197–198.
31. Chandler, *Railroads*, p. 17.
32. Wilkins, *Investment in the United States to 1914*, p. 169.
33. London branch to Deutsche Bank Berlin, HADB, A1359.
34. Helfferich, Vol. 2, p. 225.
35. Many events in Villard's early life are described in his oddly written autobiography, some of which was transcribed from his notes after his death and written in the third person. He fled his homeland and changed his name to avoid being traced by his father, but by the 1890s this wealthy and famous outcast reestablished contact with his siblings. *Memoirs of H. Villard: Journalist and Financier, 1835–1900*, Vols. I and II (Westminster: Archibald Constable & Co., 1904).
36. Dietrich Buss, *Henry Villard: A Study in Transatlantic Investment and Interests, 1870–1895* (New York: Arno Press, 1978), pp. 1–29.
37. Buss, pp. 30–55.
38. Alexandra Villard de Borchgrave and John Cullen, *Villard: The Life and Times of an American Titan* (New York: Doubleday, 2001), pp. 296–298. This is a very intimate portrait – surprisingly frank – of one of the author's great-grandfathers. Even she concedes that Villard was "overly optimistic, disinclined to focus on details, and prepared to risk all for the sake of a worthy but shaky enterprise," pp. ix–x.
39. Helfferich, Vol. 2, pp. 226–228.
40. Buss, pp. 85–111.
41. Buss, p. 98.
42. Buss, pp. 112–150.
43. Helfferich, Vol. 2, pp. 228–229.
44. Buss, p. 121.
45. The line was just south of the Little Big Horn, where General George Armstrong Custer perished with much of the Seventh Cavalry in June 1876. The rail workers still had to be protected from Indians by soldiers. Sitting Bull, Chief of the Sioux and victor over Custer, attended the ceremony of driving in the last spike at Cold Creek, Montana on Sept. 8, 1883. *The Life and Times*, pp. 322–331. There is no record of their meeting, but the idea of Sitting Bull, President Grant, and Siemens mixing among the onlookers is intriguing.
46. Buss, pp. 130–138. Shortly after moving into his new palatial house on Madison Avenue, Villard's fellow directors became nervous about the company's finances. He reportedly lost everything, including the new house, which had just been completed and took up a whole city block. His great-granddaughter estimated that he lost $5 million, but even this was not enough to silence charges of gross incompetence and even dishonesty. *The Life and Times*, pp. 337–339.
47. Buss, p. 98.
48. Helfferich, Vol. 2, pp. 230–231. For some interesting impressions see Nicolaus Mohr, *Excursion through America*, ed. Ray Allen Billington (Chicago: Lakeside Press, 1973).
49. Buss, p. 142.
50. Buss, p. 151.
51. Helfferich, Vol. 2, pp. 232–233. See also Fritz Seidenzahl, *100 Jahre Deutsche Bank, 1870–1970* (Frankfurt: Deutsche Bank, 1970), pp. 83–100.
52. Buss, pp. 151–187. *New York Times* reference in Buss, p. 155, Sept. 30, 1883.
53. *Vossische Zeitung*, October 26, 1883, HADB, A1144.
54. Buss, pp. 151–187.
55. Buss, pp. 151–187.
56. Helfferich, Vol. 2, pp. 233–235.
57. Jean Strouse, *Morgan: American Financier* (New York: Random House, 1999), pp. 240–241.
58. *Der Aktionär*, Dec. 20, 1885, HADB, A1144.
59. Helfferich, Vol. 2, pp. 236–237.
60. Georg von Bunsen, *Friedrich Kapp: Gedächtnisrede* (Berlin: Simion, 1885), p. 21.
61. Helfferich, Vol. 2, pp. 235–250.

62. Helfferich, Vol. 2, pp. 236–237. According to his son-in-law, Siemens even wrote to Villard about his conflicts with other members of Deutsche Bank's management board and his gambit to force matters to a head at the bank, which led to the consolidation of his power at the bank in the late 1880s.
63. One reason that Villard was asked to represent the bank was the failure of management to report directly to the bank after his departure. Deutsche Bank to Villard, July 8, 1885, HADB, A744. This need also included other companies and more general conditions. Deutsche Bank to Villard, Nov. 22, 1887, HADB, A744.
64. Deutsche Bank to Northern Pacific, July 8, 1885, HADB, A744, and a letter to Villard, Nov. 22, 1887, HADB, A744, asking him to write articles for German newspapers about America and the American markets to drum up interest, a role that he was doubly well suited to perform.
65. Gall, p. 15.
66. Helfferich, Vol. 2, p. 238.
67. Handwritten contract and addendum, signed by Villard and Siemens in Berlin, Sept. 29, 1886 (addendum May 2, 1888), HADB, A401. Villard was allowed an allowance for three-quarters of his out-of-pocket costs for running the office (*laufende Kosten*, personnel, rent, etc.) to a maximum of $7,500 per month. Although Deutsche Bank and allied institutions set Villard up in a New York office (the Mills Building), he had his hand in many businesses, sometimes only tangentially related to Deutsche Bank's interests. Villard was juggling many balls at one time. From 1888–92, for example, he served as president of Edison General Electric, another holding company, oversaw Deutsche Bank's interest in Northern Pacific and other investments, and played an important role in Grover Cleveland's 1892 presidential election campaign, among other interests.
68. Bank statement, January 1886, Baker Library, Villard Collection, Box 100, Folder 753.
69. Marcus, a German who had worked for Rütten & Bonn, a small private bank in New York, will play an important role in this narrative. Marcus to Villard, Nov. 2, 1876, Baker Library, Villard Collection, Box 105, Folder 811.
70. Siemens to Drexel Morgan, Nov. 21, 1885, HADB, A1142. During the 1880s, Deutsche Bank seemed very anxious to drum up more business at the Northern Pacific, as demand in Germany for rail securities was very high.
71. Helfferich, Vol. 2, p. 246.
72. Helfferich, Vol. 2, pp. 238–239. The bank was obviously very interested in doing more business with the United States. Siemens wrote directly to Drexel Morgan in 1885 about the high demand in Germany for Northern Pacific bonds and how similar new issues were eagerly awaited.
73. Helfferich, Vol. 2, p. 239–241.
74. Helfferich, Vol. 2, p. 240–241.
75. Drexel to Villard, April 14, 1891, about Deutsche Bank withdrawing its support, Baker Library, Villard Collection, V84a, 459.
76. *Wall Street Journal*, April 13, 1891, about Deutsche Bank's 1890 financial results. The amounts were 75 million Mark, deposits 208 million Mark, and loans of 59 million Mark.
77. Undated unsigned memo, later references make it clear that the proposal came from Villard, HADB, A1245.
78. Steinthal to Villard about the rejection of a Baltimore & Ohio securities purchase, May 23, 1890, HADB, A1246.
79. Siemens to Marcus, May 23, 1890, HADB, A404, and Marcus to Siemens, Dec. 5, 1890, HADB, A1246. Siemens stressed that he wanted this message repeated to Villard, a sign perhaps that Siemens no longer trusted his U.S. representative.
80. Villard to Deutsche Bank, December 20, 1889, HADB, A1245.
81. Marcus to Siemens, May 27, 1890, HADB, A1246; see also Marcus to Siemens, Dec. 5, 1890, HADB, A1246, for a discussion of controlling the market in Europe for American securities.
82. Marcus to Siemens, May 27, 1890, HADB, A1246. The words "hierfuer" and "London zum Zusammentreffen" were underlined in heavy pencil in the text, probably by Siemens. Marcus

repeated the emphatic plea to go ahead with the B&O loan, which they considered very important, and the "threat" to go elsewhere in several other letters.

83. Marcus to Siemens, June 24, 1890, HADB, A1246.
84. Marcus to Siemens, June 11, 1890, HADB, A1246.
85. *Wall Street Journal*, June 16, 1890.
86. Various internal documents and newspaper articles, HADB, A671.
87. Strouse, p. 305.
88. Villard to Deutsche Bank, Nov. 14, 1890, HADB, A671.
89. Marcus to Siemens, Dec. 5, 1890, HADB, A671.
90. *The Life and Times*, p. 368.
91. By late December NAC shares, once worth $50, were selling at $2.50. Marcus to Siemens, Dec. 24, 1890, HADB, A671.
92. Villard to Deutsche Bank, July 24, 1891, HADB, A1247.
93. Balance sheet, Dec. 8, 1891, HADB, A671.
94. Various, HADB, A674.
95. *The Life and Times*, pp. 360–363. His young son, Henry Hilgard, died after his father created the North American Company.
96. Helfferich, Vol. 2, pp. 243–245.
97. Villard to Deutsche Bank, July 24, 1891, HADB, A1247.
98. Various correspondence, HADB, A1249.
99. Drexel to Villard, April 14, 1891, Baker Library, Villard Collection, V84a, 459, and a letter seemingly to Villard but not clear from whom, saying that Villard had lost the support of Siemens and that there were disputes with the Treuhand. April 17, 1891, Baker Library, Villard Collection, V84a, 459.
100. Stern and Deutsche Bank to Villard, Nov. 11, 1892, HADB, A1247.
101. Villard to Deutsche Bank, Feb. 13, 1893, HADB, A1247.
102. Villard to Oakes, March 1, 1893, HADB, A1247. The letter to Oakes was in German. This may have been a translated version for Deutsche Bank managers, with whom Villard almost always communicated in German. He wrote to the board of Northern Pacific that he had decided to resign as chairman and member of the board. As his relationship to the company had been very personal, he regretted his decision. Oddly, there is no record of his discussing his decision with Deutsche Bank beforehand or of his confiding any other views about the decision or at this juncture about the state of the line to managers in Berlin.
103. Oakes to Villard, March 3, 1893, HADB, A1247.
104. Villard to Oakes, March 5, 1893, HADB, A1247.
105. Villard to Oakes, May 1, 1893, HADB, A1247.
106. Ibid. This letter is in German in the files, suggesting that it was translated by Villard or Deutsche Bank for Siemens.
107. Marcus to Deutsche Bank, Jan. 30, 1891, HADB, A722. Marcus wrote to Deutsche Bank in German. In the winter of 1891, a consortium of Kuhn, Loeb & Co, Speyer, and Deutsche Bank gave the expanding railroad a $7 million loan carrying 6 percent interest, with a 2.5 percent commission and an option on Northern Pacific Consols at 83 (83 percent of the face value). As collateral, the rail line pledged its own debt and equity securities. Some of the funds would not be used immediately and were held by participating American banks like Speyer, carrying a 3 percent interest rate. A year before the collapse of Northern Pacific, the railroad drew down on another $2 million of its revolving credit line. In January 1893, negotiations were completed for Deutsche Bank and the other participating banks to substitute capital stock of Northern Pacific Railroad Company as collateral for the loans.
108. To Speyer and Co., and as agents of Deutsche Bank, and Jacob S. H. Stern from the Northern Pacific Railroad, Jan. 13, 1893, HADB, A722.
109. Siemens to Villard, June 21, 1893, HADB, A1247.
110. James C. Bonbright, *Railroad Capitalization: A Study of the Principles of Railroad Securities* (New York: Columbia University, 1920).
111. Villard, *Memoirs*, pp. 313–329.

3. Deutsche Bank and American Electrification

1. Thomas P. Hughes, *Networks of Power: Electrification in Western Society, 1880–1930* (Baltimore: Johns Hopkins University Press, 1983), pp. 5–18. One great technical issue arose because of distribution. The controversy over direct (Edison) and alternating current finally hinged on distribution, which proved the downfall of direct current.
2. Hughes, *Networks of Power*, p. 4.
3. Hughes, *Networks of Power*, p. 1.
4. See William J. Hausman, Peter Hertner, and Mira Wilkins, *Global Electrification: Multinational Enterprise and International Finance in the History of Light and Power, 1878–2007* (Cambridge: Cambridge University Press, 2008).
5. Hughes, *Networks of Power*, pp. 76–77. See also Delbrück to Villard, May 3, 1887. Baker Library, Villard Papers, Box 78, Folder 550. The agreement called for Siemens & Halske and AEG to buy patent rights jointly from the Paris Edison Company. The Deutsche-Bank-led consortium provided AEG with the capital for the purchase.
6. Hughes, *Networks of Power*, p. 181.
7. See Thomas P. Hughes, "From Firm to Networked Systems." *Business History Review*, Vol. 79 (2005), no. 3, pp. 587–593, for an excellent discussion of firms working together to establish electrification.
8. The two seemed to have a warm, though tumultuous, relationship. Edison to Villard, Jan. 19, 1888, Baker Library, Villard Papers, Box 78, Folder 551, inviting Villard and his wife to dinner and to stay over with him in New Jersey.
9. Villard to Stern, Feb. 4, 1880, Baker Library, Villard Collection, Box 77, Folder 541. Villard wanted Stern to split the purchase of Edison patent rights for Germany, Austria, Russia, France, Italy, and Spain for about $450,000. According to Villard, it was an extraordinary opportunity "for a quick profit." Stern declined, arguing that it was too large a sum, but left the door open for a smaller amount covering fewer countries. Feb. 9, 1880.
10. Eaton to Villard, Sept. 13, 1880, Baker Library, Villard Collection, Box 77, Folder 541. He reported that there was no illumination when he visited Edison's lab.
11. Paul Israel, *Edison: A Life of Invention* (New York: John Wiley & Sons, Inc., 1998), pp. 197–211.
12. Hughes, *Networks of Power*, pp. 29–31.
13. Hughes, *Networks of Power*, pp. 40–46.
14. Vincent P. Carosso, *The Morgans: Private International Bankers, 1854–1913* (Cambridge, MA: Harvard University Press, 1987), pp. 270–272.
15. See Manfred Pohl, *Emil Rathenau und die AEG* (Mainz: Hase & Koehler, 1988), pp. 39–64.
16. Israel, pp. 321–323.
17. Israel, pp. 215 and 254.
18. Wilfried Feldenkirchen, *Siemens* (Munich: Piper, 1995), p. 362. Feldenkirchen has curiously little to say about Siemens in the United States during this period.
19. Villard to Drexel, Morgan, May 23, 1889, Morgan Library, Syndicate II, ARC-158, 254. The syndicate conditions included a provision that the shares be held until Jan. 1, 1890, which in Dec. 1, 1889 was extended to April 1890.
20. In April 1890, for example, Stern held common stock amounting to $815,000, $185,000 of the $2 million in loans that had been issued by the syndicate, and an option on more unspecified securities. Stern to Deutsche Bank, April 2, 1890, HADB, A402. Although Stern was still ready to purchase more shares in fall 1891, AEG already wanted to unload some of its holdings if the securities could be sold in such a way as to avoid driving down the market value. Stern to Deutsche Bank, Sept. 26, 1891, and AEG to Deutsche Bank, Oct. 25, 1891, HADB, A402.

    An undated handwritten calculation seems to show the breakdown of the original ownership interest. The so-called German syndicate received $3 million of the $6.9 million in common stock (not including 2.2 million common stock held in trust, or, in modern parlance, approved but not outstanding). Of the $3 million, Villard received $0.6 million as a bonus.

Of the preferred, the syndicate had an option on a further $2.7 million in shares. The German common share subscribers were divided among Deutsche Bank ($450,000 paid-in and bonus shares), Jacob S. H. Stern (the same terms as Deutsche Bank), and Allgemeine Elektricitäts Gesellschaft (AEG and Siemens with roughly $.3 million each). According to these notes, Villard and Marcus got $85,000 and $20,000 bonus shares each, in addition to the already-mentioned Villard bonus of $600,000. Oddly for American subscribers, Drexel Morgan were mentioned, but with no share allocation, only Thomas Alva Edison with $1.2 million in paid-in common and another $.2 million as bonus shares are listed with Dollar amounts. Undated and unsigned handwritten calculations, HADB, A401.

The last figure ties to Wilfried Feldenkirchen sources, which indicate that Siemens & Halske had invested 1.1 million Mark or roughly $3 million. Wilfried Feldenkirchen, "Die Anfänge des Siemensgeschäfts in Amerika," in *Wirtschaft, Gesellschaft, und Unternehmen, Festschrift für Hans Pohl zum 60. Geburtstag* (Stuttgart: Steiner, 1995), p. 882.

According to yet another source (what appears to be an early planning memo), Deutsche Bank wanted the new company to have equity of $12 million. $6.4 million in new shares would go to the shareholders of the old companies, $3.2 million would be kept in reserve (treasury stock), and the remaining $2.5 million reserved for the German–American investors, who would receive the new shares against cash or services rendered. Depending on how many of the existing shares were owned by German interests, these figures tie in with those provided by Buss on which Wilkins relies (which would have to include old share holdings or be from a later time) or with the above memo. Memo to participants, May 1886, HADB, A401.

Buss reported in Villard's files that $4 million of the capital came from Siemens, $3.8 from AEG, $0.5 million from Deutsche Bank for a total of $8.3 million. A history of AEG, for example, without citing its source, gives that company's original investment as $210,000, an amount that was later increased to $416,000. Peter Strunk, *Die AEG: Aufstieg und Niedergang einer Industrielegende* (Berlin: Nicolai, 1999), p. 28. Still another account reports that the initial offering was $3.6 million, with Deutsche Bank taking two-thirds of the shares. Carosso, p. 273.

21. Wilkins, *Foreign Investment in the United States to 1914*, p. 434, and Strouse, p. 312. According to Strouse, the original public offering was for $3.6 million, 62 percent for Deutsche Bank ($2.3 million, probably including the other German firms), Kuhn Loeb $0.4 million, and Morgan $0.6 million. Although this is at odds with some other sources, it confirms a high magnitude of investment.
22. Israel, pp. 321–334. Edison and Siemens & Halske agreed for a time that AC current was dangerous and uneconomical, which would give Westinghouse, eventually, a great competitive advantage.
23. First annual report of Edison General Electric, Jan. 2, 1890, HADB, A404.
24. Extract from an announcement by the vice president of the Edison General Electric Company, Undated, HADB, A405.
25. Annual report, Edison General Electric Company, January 1890, HADB, A401.
26. Strouse, p. 312.
27. Several letters, November, 1891, Baker Library, Villard Collection, Box 77, Folder 546. While traveling on Northern Pacific business, Villard used the staff of the Northern Pacific, for example, to analyze Edison General Electric results provided by Edison.
28. Villard to Marcus, Dec. 6, 1888, HADB, A401.
29. Ibid.
30. Villard to Marcus, Dec. 9, 1888, HADB, A401
31. Villard to Marcus, Dec. 28, 1888, HADB, A401.
32. Two cables, Villard to Marcus, Feb. 10, 1889, HADB, A401.
33. Several cables, Villard and Marcus, Feb. 11–12, 1889, HADB, A401. Villard seemed to have a good relationship to Rathenau, for whom he bought shares of other companies on the U.S. market.
34. Villard to Deutsche Bank, March 22, 1889, HADB, A401.
35. Villard to Siemens, May 28, 1889, HADB, A401.
36. Villard to Deutsche Bank, July 30, 1889, HADB, A401.

37. Edison–Villard correspondence, Baker Library, Villard Collection, Box 78, Folders 553 and 562, especially Feb. 8, 1890.
38. Stern to Deutsche Bank, Sept. 30, 1889, HADB, A401. Both Deutsche Bank and Stern decided that the securities should remain in New York. The letter included a list of syndicate securities held by Villard: shares of Oregon & Transcontinental, Rocky Fork Coal Road, Edison General Electric, Northern Pacific & Manitoba, and Wisconsin Central, totaling nearly $5 million.
39. Villard to Deutsche Bank, Oct. 15, 1889, HADB, A401.
40. Villard to Deutsche Bank, Nov. 22, 1889, HADB, A401.
41. Villard to Deutsche Bank, Dec. 4, 1889, HADB, A401.
42. Villard to Deutsche Bank, Dec. 18, 1889, HADB, A401.
43. Villard to Deutsche Bank, Jan. 3, 1890, HADB, A401.
44. Villard to Deutsche Bank, Jan. 7, 1890, HADB, A401.
45. Villard to Deutsche Bank, Jan. 7, 1890, HADB, A401.
46. Deutsche Bank to Villard, Feb. 20, 1890, HADB, A401.
47. Villard to Marcus, Feb. 26, 1890, HADB, A404.
48. Villard to Marcus, March 5, 1890 and March 7, 1890 HADB, A404.
49. Sales and Profit Analysis 1890, HADB, A404.
50. Several cables, early March, HADB, A404.
51. Villard to Deutsche Bank, Feb. 3, 1890, Baker Library, Box 78, Folder 562.
52. Siemens to Marcus, May 23, 1890, HADB, A404.
53. Villard to Deutsche Bank, June 6, 1890, HADB, A404
54. Villard to Deutsche Bank, March 7, 1890, HADB, A404.
55. Villard to Deutsche Bank, April 8, 1890, HADB, A404.
56. Villard to members of the syndicate, March 18, 1890, HADB, A404.
57. Villard to Deutsche Bank, April 8, 1890, HADB, A404. Finally, it paid the amount on April 17 and received 8,965 shares of Edison General Electric Company shares, oddly put in the name of E. D. Bray. Villard to Deutsche Bank, April 8, 1890, HADB, A404. Some of the Germans, understandably, wanted to get a firsthand impression of what was going on in the United States with their money. Rathenau came to the United States in March 1890 to inspect the Schenectady factory and the company's books. Villard to Deutsche Bank, April 1, 1890, HADB, A404. According to Villard, Rathenau seemed pleased with the factory. He visited Boston and toured the West with Villard. Villard to Deutsche Bank, April 8, 1890, HADB, A404.
58. Villard to Deutsche Bank, May 16, 1890, HADB, A404.
59. Marcus to Siemens, May 27, 1890, HADB, A404.
60. Drexel Morgan to Villard, June 28, 1890, and Villard to Drexel Morgan, June 28, 1890, Morgan Library Syndicate Book II, ARC 106. Drexel Morgan's $0.6 million and Villard's $2.3 million (representing Deutsche Bank and other German institutions) made up the bulk of the $3.6 million total.
61. Marcus to Deutsche Bank, July 30, 1890, HADB, A404.
62. Marcus to Deutsche Bank, Aug. 12, 1890, HADB, A404.
63. Marcus to Deutsche Bank, Aug. 19, 1890, HADB, A404.
64. Marcus to Deutsche Bank, Sept. 2, 1890, HADB, A404.
65. Marcus to Deutsche Bank, Sept. 19, 1890, HADB, A404.
66. Marcus to Deutsche Bank, Oct. 3, 1890, HADB, A405.
67. Marcus to Deutsche Bank, Oct. 10, 1890, HADB, A405.
68. Marcus to Deutsche Bank, Dec. 15, 1890, HADB, A405.
69. Marcus to Deutsche Bank, Dec. 16, 1890, HADB, A405. Copied to Stern and Rathenau.
70. Villard to Deutsche Bank, Jan. 16, 1891, HADB, A405.
71. Marcus to Deutsche Bank, Feb. 3, 1891, HADB, A405. Deutsche Bank and Stern agreed to contribute 1,000 shares jointly to the block offered to the Vanderbilt family.
72. See Fear and Kobrak, "The Origins of German Corporate Governance."
73. Siemens to Villard, May 22, 1891, HADB, A405.
74. Ibid.
75. Marcus to Deutsche Bank, July 14, 1891, HADB, A405.

76. Marcus to Deutsche Bank, Oct. 27, 1891, HADB, A405.
77. Marcus to Rathenau, Oct. 27, 1891, HADB, A405.
78. J. H. Henrich, VP Finance EGE, to Morgan, Sept. 9, 1891, Morgan Library, Syndicate II, ARC 72.
79. Announcement, Nov. 28, 1891. Morgan Library, Syndicate II, ARC 72.
80. As Villard had noted years earlier, avoiding "wasteful" competition was in both companies' interests.
81. Villard to Marcus, March 3, 1890, and other telegrams, HADB, A404.
82. W. Bernard Carlson, *Innovation as a Process: Elihu Thomson and the Rise of General Electric, 1870–1900* (Cambridge: Cambridge University Press, 1991), pp. 203–219.
83. Villard to Marcus, March 3, 1890, HADB, A404. Some authors give Morgan and Thomson credit for the idea of the merger. It is hard to know who thought of it first but ample material presented here indicates that Villard supported the consolidation earlier on.
84. Marcus to Deutsche Bank, Feb. 5, 1892, HADB, A406.
85. Edison to Deutsche Bank, Aug. 19, 1889, HADB, A401. In 1889, the bank wrote for Edison, while he was visiting Europe, a letter of introduction to Friedrich Krupp, for which Edison was extremely grateful.
86. Carosso, p. 391.
87. Marcus to Deutsche Bank, Feb. 9, 1892, HADB, A406.
88. The Kiernan News Co., Feb. 5, 1892, HADB, A406.
89. Undated unsigned memo about Thomson's financial position, HADB, A401.
90. Carlson, p. 299.
91. With roughly the same sales in 1891, Thomson-Houston profits were $2.7 million compared with EGE's $1.4 million, with respective return on capital of 26 percent to 11 percent. Carlson, pp. 294–296.
92. Marcus to Deutsche Bank, Feb. 12, 1892, HADB, A406.
93. Marcus to Deutsche Bank, Feb. 16, 1892, HADB, A406.
94. Wilkins, *Investment in the United States to 1914*, pp. 434–436. It seems hard to believe that sizeable lots of shares were sold at this time, though they may have been purchased by the North American Company. The merger was not until 1892 and the market, by all accounts, was quite illiquid.
95. Wilkins, *Investment in the United States to 1914*, pp. 436–437.
96. Strunk, p. 28. Strunk claims that Rathenau found the deal too good for the Americans, but he wanted to keep close relations with the new company, perhaps even cooperating to divide markets.

4. The Northern Pacific Bankruptcy Saga

1. See Braunfels of Stern to Villard, April 1892, Henry Villard Papers, Box 99, Folder 741, Baker Library, Harvard University. Braunfels complained that U.S. bonds had been listed in Europe under the assumption that default was virtually impossible.
2. Chandler, *Railroads*, p. 17.
3. Chandler, *Railroads*, p. 13.
4. Reorganization of the Northern Pacific Company, 1896 Announcement by the Reorganization Committee, pp. 3–6, HADB, A1149.
5. Reorganization of the Northern Pacific Company, 1896 Plan of Reorganization, pp. 7–16, HADB, A1149.
6. Deutsche Bank to Marcus, April 5, 1892, HADB, A1142.
7. Marcus to Deutsche Bank, May 10, 1893, HADB, A1142.
8. Elmus Wicker, *Banking Panics of the Gilded Age* (Cambridge: Cambridge University Press, 2000), p. 64.
9. Strouse, pp. 318–319. For discussions of the underlying causes, see Milton Friedman, *Episodes in Monetary Mischief* (New York: Harcourt and Brace, 1992), and Charles P. Kindleberger, *Manias, Panics and Crashes* (New York: Basic Books, 1978).
10. Marcus to Deutsche Bank, June 20, 1893, HADB, A671.

11. Various telegrams, HADB, A674.
12. Marcus to Deutsche Bank, June 25, 1893, HADB, A1142.
13. Exchange of telegrams between Marcus and Deutsche Bank, July 27–Aug. 16, 1893, HADB, A1142. With farm prices down, Deutsche Bank even considered buying some commodities. Defaults of related companies were also weighing on Northern Pacific.
14. Marcus confessed that he feared that the company managers would lose their heads, which would make that panic step even more necessary. Marcus to Deutsche Bank, July 19, 1893, HADB, A1142.
15. Marcus to Deutsche Bank, July 25, 1893, HADB, A674.
16. Marcus to Deutsche Bank, July 25, 1893, HADB, A1142.
17. Deutsche Bank to Marcus, Aug. 15, 1893, HADB, A1142.
18. Marcus to Deutsche Bank, Aug. 15, 1893, HADB, A1142.
19. Villard to Deutsche Bank, Aug. 3, 1893, HADB, A718.
20. Villard to Deutsche Bank, Aug. 5, 1893, HADB, A718.
21. Villard to Siemens, Aug. 15, 1893, HADB, A1142.
22. Although he did not say it, for Villard, as for many Americans, the receivership was a way to manage the debt burden until revenues improved.
23. Helfferich, Vol. 2, pp. 250–251. Many early warning signs had clearly been ignored. As early as October 1892, the shareholders demanded that a commission look into the operations of the company. The commission was highly critical of the financial management of the firm, but was optimistic about its prospects.
24. *The Life and Times*, p. 375.
25. Helfferich, Vol. 2, pp. 253–254. Helfferich's account contains a lot of useful information, but he is very anxious to emphasize the degree to which the news of the bankruptcy came as a complete surprise to his father-in-law and other Deutsche Bank managers. Although the bankruptcy news coming after the close of business on that particular day may have indeed been a surprise, the grave financial distress and risk should not have been.
26. Helfferich, Vol. 2, pp. 252–253.
27. Peter Tufano, "Business Failure, Judicial Intervention, and Financial Innovation: Restructuring U.S. Railroads in the Nineteenth Century," *Business History Review*, Vol. 71 (1997), no. 1, pp. 1–40.
28. Helfferich, Vol. 2, pp. 250–256.
29. Ibid.
30. Notes to Besprechung mit Herrn Braunfels, Aug. 10, 1893, HADB, A1147, and in the Circuit Court of the United States for the Seventh Judicial Circuit and Eastern District of Wisconsin, The Farmer's Loan and Trust Company complainants against the Northern Pacific Railroad, Aug. 15, 1893, HADB, A1147. According to a petition from the receivers – Thomas Oakes, Henry Payne, and Henry Rouse – sent to Circuit Court, the St. Paul line, for example, was essential to the Northern Pacific and should be kept under its control, even if that objective required purchasing the stock of the St. Paul line to get out of the lease payments.
31. Telegram from Marcus to Deutsche Bank, Aug. 16, 1893, HADB, A1147. The Rockefeller family had acquired a substantial portion of Northern Pacific and other securities that will be discussed throughout this Chapter. The incredible success of John D.'s refining operation provided the family with such ample cash flow that he and his brother William were hard-pressed to find sufficient securities on the market for investment. Chernow, *The Death of the Banker*, pp. 34–51.
32. Memo to Roland-Lücke with background and instructions, no date, but presumably just before his departure in August for New York, HADB, A1147.
33. Ibid.
34. Siemens file note, Aug. 22, 1894, HADB, A712.
35. Handwritten draft of what appears to be a telegram to the receivers, no date, HADB, A1147, also Marcus to Deutsche Bank management, Aug. 24, 1893, HADB, A1147.
36. Marcus to Deutsche Bank management, Aug. 24, 1893, HADB, A1147, and Marcus to Deutsche Bank management, Aug. 25, 1893, HADB, A1147.
37. Marcus to Deutsche Bank management, Aug. 18, 1893, HADB, A1147.

38. Hammacher to Siemens, Jan. 20, 1895, HADB, A713.
39. Helfferich, Vol. 3, pp. 341–345.
40. *Bradstreet's*, Nov. 4, 1893, HADB, A1144.
41. Helfferich, Vol. 2, pp. 258-259. At first, Siemens thought that he could make some use of Villard for the audit, but then thought better of it. He was so angry that he could not even sleep "under the same roof as Villard." His parting words to Villard indicate how embittered Siemens was toward his old confidant: "My greatest regret about you is that, despite the collapse of the Northern Pacific, you remain a rich man" (Helfferich, Vol. 2, p. 260). Villard escaped the experience, as Siemens indicated, virtually unscathed, even though some investors were even more angry with him than Siemens was.
42. Wallich to Siemens, Oct. 3, 1893, HADB, A713.
43. Marcus to Deutsche Bank management, Aug. 29, 1893, HADB, A1147, also Marcus to Deutsche Bank management, Sept. 5 and 10, 1893, HADB, A1147, for the discussion of strategy.
44. Roland-Lücke to Deutsche Bank, Sept. 15, 1893, HADB, A1147. Marcus wrote the receivers to urge them to put the delinquent subscribers under pressure. At the early stages, collection of these unpaid subscriptions seemed critical to the Northern Pacific's ability to cover its current obligations.
45. Siemens to Braunfels, Feb. 8, 1894, HADB, A713.
46. Several letters from Marcus to Deutsche Bank, late September and early October 1893, HADB, A1147. Belmont and Villard hated each other and Deutsche Bank wanted to avoid Belmont's assuming any representation for German interests.
47. Marcus to Deutsche Bank, Oct. 20, 1893, HADB, A1147.
48. Adams to Deutsche Bank, Oct. 20, 1893, HADB, A683. Deutsche Bank seemed to be already learning the mechanics of the agency problem, ensuring the mutual interest of investors and their agents. Having failed with Villard to assure a common financial interest, Deutsche Bank would work harder in the future with Adams to avoid financial conflicts of interest. It would be an ongoing issue even for the banks' employees. For the basics of Agency Theory, see Michael Jensen, *A Theory of the Firm: Governance, Residual Claims, and Organizational Forms* (Cambridge, MA: Harvard University Press, 2000).
49. *Who's Who in America*, 1930–31. J. G. Bartlett, *Edward Dean Adams* (privately printed, 1926).
50. Although Adams and German managers conversed in English, their correspondence dealt with many personal matters and general political issues, to a much larger extent than had been the case with Villard.
51. Deutsche Bank to Siemens, Oct. 26, 1893, HADB, A713.
52. List of shareholders holding more than 1,000 shares at Sept. 15, 1893, HADB, A1147. Interestingly, neither Villard nor Deutsche Bank is on the list. Some of those listed may have been representing others. Notice to shareholders, Sept. 15, 1893, HADB, A1147.
53. "Northern Pacific Company" *Vertraulich*, Roland-Lücke, January 1894, HADB, A1147. In November Villard wrote the *Evening Post* a long letter in which he defended his actions. It had a pathetic ring. He bemoaned the loss of esteem – something every man covets – that he had suffered through the insolvency of the Northern Pacific. Although under the by-laws of the company he could not exercise any executive functions, his fellow board members would testify that he always counseled caution. In addition, he did not personally initiate any construction, make any purchases, or disburse any funds. He was merely one of thirteen board members. He respected the limits on his authority to speak for the other members and accepted responsibility for his share in any bad decisions made by the board, but these decisions included many that helped the rail line grow enormously, especially in light of the enormous competition it faced. In contrast to those such as Siemens, who felt that he had made a fortune through his activities, he claimed that he had lost millions – more than any other single investor, but was vague about how he measured that loss. Denying charges that he had sold the company's shares short or arranged for purchases unfavorable to the Northern Pacific from companies he controlled, he pleaded guilty to only one thing: unwavering

faith in the future of the Northern Pacific. Letter to the *Evening Post*, Nov. 4, 1893, HADB, A1144.

54. Albro Martin, *James J. Hill and the Opening of the Northwest* (New York: Oxford University Press, 1976), pp. 7–57.
55. Michael Bliss, *Northern Enterprises: Five Centuries of Canadian Business* (Toronto: McClelland and Stewart), pp. 213–378. Clever tactics by Stephen, a banker, allowed the group to gain control of rail property that linked the Canadian border, St. Paul, and Manitoba.
56. Bliss, p. 298.
57. Martin, p. 436.
58. Martin, p. 441.
59. Martin, p. 440. When the line demanded a 15 Dollar per share assessment from investors, some shrewd shareholders forfeited their shares.
60. Martin, p. 135. In 1897, he got Minnesota politicians to effectively transfer some of the Northern Pacific's assets to him.
61. Hill even got involved in several of Schiff's Jewish charities. Martin, p. 438. Kuhn Loeb had very close relations to the Warburgs. Hill and Schiff seemed to have been genuinely fond of each other.
62. Martin, p. 132. As Hill's biographer described him, "tall, slender, impressive of countenance, sartorially elegant, . . . a shrewd judge of money-making opportunities and a skilled negotiator whose self-confidence, bordering on arrogance, was a telling asset."
63. Martin, p. 436.
64. Heather Gilbert, *Awakening Continent: The Life of Lord Mount Stephen*. Vol. 1, *1829–1891* (Aberdeen: Aberdeen University Press, 1977), p. 74.
65. Martin, pp. 440–441.
66. Gilbert, Vol. 1, p. 73.
67. Martin, p. 441. Martin cites as evidence of Adams' prissy cultivation Hill's indignation over Adams' choosing to go to the opera rather than take a meeting with him. Judging from Hill's rough appearance and simple frontier upbringing both the story and the indignation appear plausible.
68. Quoted in Gilbert, Vol. 1, p. 75.
69. Gilbert, Vol. 1, p. 76.
70. Gilbert, Vol. 1, p. 77.
71. Gilbert, Vol. 1, p. 78.
72. "Northern Pacific – Great Northern," *Wall Street Journal*, April 30, 1895.
73. "Northern Pacific," *Wall Street Journal*, May 10, 1895. Other investors at the time were preoccupied with getting the receivers to cooperate with their suit against Villard and others in order to recuperate $3.5 million.
74. May 10, 1895, letter to Edward D. Adams confirming discussions, HADB, A1149. See also Gilbert, Vol. 2, pp. 82–83. See also Memorandum of Agreement, signed A. Gwinner, June 5, 1895, HADB, A1149.
75. Ibid. The syndicate would be in a position to delay payments and give short-term financing to the company. By consolidating the debt, the syndicate would reduce conflicts between the various categories of debt holders. Deutsche Bank only got a majority of the creditors to sign on to the committee with great effort. The Second Mortgage Holders set up their own committee, however, which with the help of the Belmont banking house, won a relatively strong position.
76. Gilbert, Vol. 2, pp. 83–84.
77. Ives to Leon Brothers, London, July 2, 1895, HADB, A220.
78. Bank für Handel und Industrie to Gwinner, Jan. 18, 1894, HADB, A738.
79. Martin, pp. 449–450. Hill believed Adams had a part in the negative publicity in order to delay Hill's takeover of the line and to keep his lucrative post as head of the reorganization committee as long as possible. Some lawyers believed that since the charter of the Great Northern predated the relevant legislation, it would be exempt.
80. Copy of the resolution, undated, HADB, A1149.

81. Martin, pp. 449–450. Although the Sherman Anti-Trust Act of 1890 forbade combinations in restraint of trade, it had not yet been applied to railroads that were not obviously "parallel or competing." For Hill, this combination would benefit customers and was the only alternative to a Darwinian struggle for "survival of the fittest" (Gilbert, Vol. 2, p. 83). Driven as he was, Hill, unlike the bankers, had little objection to taking on public opinion, the courts, and even legislators to get his way.
82. Gilbert, Vol. 2, pp. 83–94.
83. Gilbert, Vol. 2, pp. 94–95.
84. Adams to Gwinner, Feb. 23, 1896, HADB, A24.
85. Adams to Deutsche Bank, Feb. 29, 1896, HADB, A24.
86. Deutsche Bank to Adams, March 7, 1896, HADB, A24. Under the terms of the new agreement, Adams stood to make one-third of what all the committees would receive as compensation for their participation in the plan.
87. Adams to Gwinner, March 8, 1896, HADB, A24. Adams reported that Rockefeller was buying. He also included the prices of securities and margins.
88. Deutsche Bank to Adams, March 20, 1896, HADB, A1268.
89. Adams to Gwinner, March 21, 1896, HADB, A1268.
90. Memorandum of Agreement, March 16, 1896, HADB, A1149.
91. Statistics of the Northern Pacific System, March 9, 1896, HADB, A1149. Most carried an interest rate of 6 percent, but with a much higher effective yield given the large discounts at which the bonds traded.
92. Reorganization of the Northern Pacific Company, Plan of Reorganization, pp. 7–16, HADB, A1149.
93. Reorganization of the Northern Pacific Company, Announcement by the Reorganization Committee, pp. 3–6, HADB, A1149. The new financing and organization offered many advantages to those who subscribed. The retirement of the old mortgage bonds would not affect the rights of the bondholders to have the proceeds of land sales up to an amount of $500,000 per year. The proceeds of those sales could not be used for the repurchase of the prior lien bonds. With the object of maintaining the integrity of the firm, the reorganization managers believed that increased planning could establish security and produce good results for all interested parties.
94. Reorganization of the Northern Pacific Company, Plan of Reorganization, pp. 7–16, HADB, A1149. Preferred shareholders who deposited $100 in par value old preferred shares and paid an additional $10 in cash would receive $50 in new preferred and new common shares, effectively trading half of their preferred position for common shares and adding $10 of new capital to the firm for every 100 Dollars in par value preferred ($3.6 million). The common shareholders, on the basis of their capital holding, would receive the same amount of new common for an additional cash payment of $15 ($7.5 million). Total equity would then be brought up to $150 million at par value (up from $75 million, not all of which was paid in before the collapse), $72.5 million of preferred (4 percent non-cumulative), and $77.5 million in common.
95. Reorganization of the Northern Pacific Company, Plan of Reorganization, pp. 7–16, HADB, A1149.
96. Memorandum of Agreement, Nov. 6, 1896, HADB, A1149.
97. Letter to Gwinner, Oct. 28, 1896, HADB, A1149. The general traffic manager of the railroad consulted Arthur Gwinner about some of the firm's advertising material. The plan created a governance structure that would give the bank a good deal of power, but also much responsibility. Adams' first job seems to have been to convince Hill to agree to reductions of service, equalizing the speed of trains – Great Northern trains were evidently faster between different points – and more evenly sharing postal contracts. These tasks were not made easier by the distance between New York and the Northern Pacific property, roughly the distance of Berlin to Moscow. Adams to Deutsche Bank, April 17, 1896, HADB, A1268.
98. Mankiewitz to Gwinner, Nov. 13, 1896, HADB, A1149. The London office was selling $200,000 of 4 percent bonds at 84.38, and 3 percent bonds at 52.75 percent, in hopes of offloading some of its stock by year-end. In order to keep the market orderly it was buying equities. The head of Deutsche Bank's London branch reported that there was limited interest

in the new 4 percent bonds and the initial speculative interest in preferred shares was waning, especially compared to the Berlin market's enthusiasm. Many of the transactions in London were merely arbitrage deals designed to exploit price differences between Paris and London. The price for common and preferred were hovering around 17.75 and 30 percent (as a percentage of their par values) respectively. Trades were earning an unpromising 1.75 percent margin between the buy/sell.

99. Reorganization of the Northern Pacific Company, Plan of Reorganization, pp. 7–16, HADB, A1149.
100. Ron Chernow, *The House of Morgan* (New York: Touchstone Books, 1990), p. 68.
101. Voting Trust of Northern Pacific Railway Shares, March 16, 1896, HADB, A1145.
102. Memorandum of a conference held in London on April 2, 1896, present and signing, J. P. Morgan, Lord Mount Stephen, James J. Hill, and Arthur Gwinner to C. H. Coster, Oct. 28, HADB, A1149.
103. Ibid.
104. Ibid.
105. Adams to Deutsche Bank, Aug. 27, 1896, HADB, A44.
106. Mankiewitz to Gwinner, Nov. 10, 1896, HADB, A1143.
107. Gwinner to Adams, Nov. 30, 1896 and Gwinner to Mount Stephen, Jan. 15, 1897, HADB, A1149.
108. Gwinner to Mount Stephen, Jan. 15, 1897, HADB, A1149.
109. Two letters, Adams to Deutsche Bank, Jan. 29, 1897, and attachment, HADB, A1149.
110. Mount Stephen to Arthur Gwinner. Feb. 6, 1897, HADB, A1149.
111. *The Railway Age*, May 7, 1897, "Railway Matters and Railway Men."
112. Maury Klein, *The Life and Legend of E. H. Harriman* (Chapel Hill: University of North Carolina Press, 2000), p. 151.
113. See letters, April 1897, HADB, A741. One in particular, a handwritten note from Adams to Deutsche Bank indicating that he had found evidence of Winter's insider trading, may provide the explanation.
114. Adams to Deutsche Bank, May 1, 1897, HADB, A741.
115. Adams to Gwinner, April 26, 1897, HADB, A741. This charge, his support of Winter's resignation, and finally his support of Lamont for the presidency coupled with Ives' conniving played a great role in Adams' problems with Morgan. Adams to Deutsche Bank, May 4, 1897, HADB, A741
116. Adams to Gwinner, Aug. 19, 1897, HADB, A741.
117. Resumé, HADB, A741.
118. Mellen to Adams, Aug. 30, 1897, HADB, A741.
119. Gwinner to Morgan, June 21, 1897, HADB, A1143.
120. Gwinner to Mount Stephen, May 1, 1897, HADB, A433.
121. Hill to Mount Stephen, June 15, 1897, HADB, A433.
122. Mount Stephen to Hill, June 16, 1897, HADB, A433.
123. Hill to Mount Stephen, July 5, 1897, HADB, A433.
124. Extract of a letter from Hill, July 2, 1897, HADB, A433.
125. Perhaps he felt that Adams' new association with Deutsche Bank had made him insufficiently grateful for Morgan's past favors. There were some concerns voiced about Adams succumbing to conflicts of interest. In January, Mellen asked Adams to consider forming a land grant company to purchase all Northern Pacific's land grant holdings. Adams reported that he personally was willing to purchase the land at $25 per acre, paid partially in bonds and partially in cash, which would amount to around $12 million. Mellen advocated offloading the land in hopes of reducing the company's land grant taxes, increasing miscellaneous income, and removing the management problems (expense, friction, and local prejudices). Outsourcing the selling activity would introduce an element of urgency into the sales. Mellen seems to have wanted to get rid of a headache and the transaction had many potential benefits, but the sale entailed many issues with security holders and equity investors. Adams to Deutsche Bank, Jan. 13, 1898, HADB, A865. Despite the obvious conflict of interest, Adams claimed that he could satisfy the bondholders by using the funds to retire debt, and that the transaction would

stimulate interest in the market for all Northern Pacific's securities. Adams to Deutsche Bank, Jan. 18, 1898, HADB, A865. Deutsche Bank's first reaction to Adams' offer was swift and negative. Somehow, the assumption seemed to have arisen that Deutsche Bank would finance Adams. Deutsche Bank seemed to have found Adams' offer unfairly low. Although the bank seemed to think that Adams was taking advantage of the situation, it held out the possibility that with revised terms it might consider the offer. It was also pessimistic that the idea would be approved by the other participants. Various correspondence, HADB, A865. The whole issue proved a turning point in the dynamics of the group. From right around that time and onward, Morgan and Hill, who could not agree on very much else, both soured on Adams. His leadership role representing the interests of Deutsche Bank had been severely undermined.

126. Adams to Gwinner, April 13, 1897, and Gwinner to Adams after London meeting, May 19, 1897, HADB, A44.
127. Hill to Mount Stephen, July 5, 1897, HADB, A434.
128. Hill to Mount Stephen, Aug. 2, 1897, HADB, A433.
129. Mount Stephen to Gwinner, Aug. 13, 1897, HADB, A433.
130. Gwinner to Mount Stephen, May 14, 1897, HADB, A434.
131. Adams to Deutsche Bank, Oct. 3, 1897, HADB, A434.
132. Gwinner to Morgan, June 21, 1897, HADB, A1143. Gwinner claimed that the German group that he represented still owned a large chunk of the company's shares. Impatient with American legal constraints and far from American public pressure, those shareholders who bought expressly "with the expectation that as soon as possible" the London Agreement would be put into effect were particularly agitated. Part of the friction was over personnel matters.
133. Minutes to Aug. 5, 1897 meeting of the management of the two railroads, HADB, A1143. One of the issues complicating the relationships among the participants was the disposition of the Northern Pacific's Land Grant holding. The conflict of interest posed by the issue poisoned Adams' relationship to Hill and Morgan, and even threatened his close ties to Deutsche Bank. Some of that property was disputed by settlers (squatters), who had taken possession of unused land. In June of 1898, the U.S. government determined that the settlers could keep the land and that the Northern Pacific would be compensated with new land in states into which it was expanding. *New York Herald*, June 10, 1898. The management of all three companies met in violation of the Sherman Act for the specific end of gaining greater cooperation between the Oregon Railway & Navigation Company and the other lines. With both Adams, as chairman of the board, and Winter, as president, in attendance, they tried to reach some conclusions about how to work together to avoid "aggressive action" against one another, which might impair their revenues. They agreed not to "invade" each other's territories, for each line to cease operation in some contested areas, to work with other railroads, to avoid giving free rail service, to coordinate short- and long-haul business, to share some common assets, and to consult about rate changes in territories in which all three lines operated.
134. Hill to Morgan, Sept. 27, 1898, HADB, A1143.
135. Morgan to Hill, Oct. 8, 1898, HADB, A1143.
136. Morgan to Hill, Oct. 8, 1898, HADB, A1143.
137. Adams to Gwinner, Nov. 4, 1898, HADB, A45.
138. Adams to Gwinner, Nov. 28, 1898, HADB, A45.
139. Mount Stephen to Gwinner, Nov. 15, 1898, HADB, A45.
140. Adams to Siemens, Nov. 25, 1898, HADB, A679.
141. Adams to Deutsche Bank, Nov. 25, 1898, HADB, A679.
142. Ibid. In the discussion, Hill moves back and forth between debt and equity. Coster catches him in this. Mount Stephen said that Coster was always getting the better of arguments with Hill. Hill seems in general to have been better at running railroads than making financial deals. Interestingly, Hill called both debt and equity liabilities.
143. Gwinner to Adams, Dec. 24, 1898, HADB, A45.
144. Adams to Gwinner, Feb. 14, 1899, HADB, A45.
145. Arthur Hill to C. H. Coster, Oct. 28, 1898, HADB, A1149.
146. Adams to Deutsche Bank, Feb. 14, 1899, HADB, A679. In 1898, in the state of Washington, Northern Pacific was shipping eight times more bushels than the Great Northern. OR&N led with 20 million.

147. Deutsche Bank to Adams, March 27, 1899, HADB, A680. Deutsche Bank wrote to Mount Stephen asking him to appeal to Hill.
148. Mellen to Adams, Undated, HADB, A679. He succeeded in winning back the lost business and forcing Hill to finally rescind his reductions for first-class mail.
149. Gwinner to Mount Stephen, March 14, 1899, HADB, A434. Gwinner's correspondence with Lord Mount Stephen was generally very friendly – the two families socialized, many of their letters dealt with the two gentlemen's respective health and political conflicts in the world – and revealed a lot about the difficulties and advantages of unifying the Great Northern and Northern Pacific. According to some accounts, Hill and Morgan formed an alliance against Deutsche Bank, but that does not seem to be the case at all. If anything, Deutsche Bank and Hill's group seemed closer to each other than Morgan. Gwinner and Stephen corresponded regularly, especially in 1898, sometimes three and four times a month. During the period of the Voting Trust, Siemens had less and less to do with the affairs in the United States.
150. Mount Stephen to Gwinner, May 7, 1900, HADB, A434.
151. Ibid. and Mount Stephen to Gwinner, Dec. 4, 1900, HADB, A434.

5. The Fallout

1. Gwinner to Morgan, Sept. 3, 1900, HADB, A1143.
2. Gwinner to Jacob Schiff, Kuhn Loeb, March 5, 1901, HADB, A1143.
3. Chernow, *The House of Morgan*, pp. 69–70.
4. Adams to Gwinner, March 20, 1900, HADB, A681. Adams had his office at 35 Wall Street and the House of Morgan was at 23 Wall Street.
5. Chernow, *The House of Morgan*, p. 94.
6. *The Life and Times*, pp. 379–380. Schurz and Edison attended the funeral. His wife Fanny survived him by nearly three decades.
7. There were a few odd pieces of business that passed between the bank and Villard after 1896. The last letter from/to Villard in the Deutsche Bank files is dated Jan. 10, 1900. It is from Gwinner and talks about general economic and political matters. Deutsche Bank continued for many years to have an ownership interest in a mining company in Red Lodge, Montana – a supplier to the Northern Pacific and Great Northern – along with Villard and the Northern Pacific. See several letters in Baker Library, Villard Collection, Vol. 89, Stofford to Fox, October 1897 to January 1898. Most of Villard's correspondence after he left Deutsche Bank's service was handled by his personal secretary.
8. Villard, pp. 368–369. Both Hill and Adams had been involved in its management, even though Adams was highly critical of the mine's operating methods.
9. *The Life and Times*, pp. 374–376.
10. *World Sunday*, Sept. 9, 1894, HADB, A1144.
11. *The Life and Times*, pp. 376–380. In the end, his great legacy may have been in politics and journalism. See Susie J. Lee, "The Content of Character: The Role of Social Capital in the Expansion of Economic Capital," Dissertation, Cornell University, 2004. His son, Oswald Garrison Villard, went on to own and edit *The Nation* and the *New York Evening Post*, as well as to report on German politics in the 1930s.
12. Siemens to Deutsche Bank, Oct. 26, 1893, HADB, A713.
13. Ibid.
14. Gebhard to Siemens, July 12, 1894, HADB, A713.
15. Adams to Gwinner, April 3, 1900, HADB, A681. Adams also reported that Northern Pacific management believed that Hill had already broken so many commitments that any agreements between him and the bank should be considered null and void.
16. Gwinner to Adams, April 27, 1900, HADB, A681.
17. Mellen to Adams, April 20, 1900, HADB, A681. With Coster gone, Mellen turned to Adams to vent his frustration at the possibility of Hill taking over.
18. Klein, *Harriman*, pp. 148–161.
19. Klein, *Harriman*, p. 238.
20. Martin, p. 440.

21. Gwinner to Adams, June 9, 1900, HADB, A45, and Adams to Gwinner, July 23, 1900, HADB, A45.
22. Gwinner to Adams, June 9, 1900, HADB, A45.
23. Adams to Gwinner, July 22, 1901, HADB, A45. Ironic, in that the two had used the insider information, not known to other minority shareholders, to buy shares for themselves.
24. Gwinner to Adams, July 20, HADB, A45.
25. Adams to Gwinner, Aug. 19, 1901, HADB, A45. Not only had much of Deutsche Bank's own direct interest in Northern Pacific disappeared, so too had its once profitable arbitrage business. Nevertheless, the bank followed developments with keen interest. Gwinner to Adams, Oct. 8, 1901, HADB, A45.
26. Adams to Gwinner, Aug. 19, 1901, HADB, A45.
27. Adams to Gwinner, Sept. 21, 1901, HADB, A45.
28. Gwinner to Adams, Oct. 8, 1901, HADB, A45.
29. Ibid.
30. Deutsche Bank to Adams, Nov. 6, 1901, HADB, A682.
31. Deutsche Bank to Adams, June 5, 1901, HADB, A682.
32. Adams to Gwinner, Nov. 21, 1901, HADB, A45.
33. Adams to Gwinner, April 30, 1902, HADB, A45.
34. Adams to Gwinner, Oct. 12, 1903, HADB, A46.
35. Klein, *Harriman*, pp. 308–313.
36. John W. Sterling of Shearman & Sterling to Mount Stephen, March 18, 1904, HADB, A434. Hill was angry at some of the justices, but calmly made plans to dissolve Northern Securities and divest of its shareholdings. Northern Securities shareholders would receive 180 shares of Great Northern and 115 of Northern Pacific for every 100 shares of Northern Securities Company stock.
37. Gwinner to Mount Stephen, Oct. 24, 1903, HADB, A434.
38. Colleen A. Dunlavy, *Politics and Industrialization; Early Railroads in the United States and Prussia* (Princeton: Princeton University Press, 1994).
39. Richard Franklin Bensel, *The Political Economy of American Industrialization, 1877–1900* (Cambridge: Cambridge University Press, 2000), pp. 291–456, and Ferguson, "The City of London," p. 66.
40. Wallon and Rockoff, pp. 364–365.
41. Kobrak, "Solid Gold Interlude: Deutsche Bank and America's Coming to Financial Age," ABH Glasgow, June 2005.
42. Walton and Rockoff, p. 421.
43. *Wall Street Journal*, April 13, 1891.
44. Dernburg of the Treuhand to Deutsche Bank, March 18, 1901, HADB, S1929.
45. Deutsche Treuhand-Gesellschaft to Georg Siemens, Jan. 11, 1892, HADB, S1929.
46. Dernburg to Siemens, Jan. 29, 1892, HADB, S1929. Bernhard Dernburg, an experienced banker who worked for Berliner Handels-Gesellschaft and Deutsche Bank, asked Siemens to whip up interest in the German public for the Edison securities and to remove objections posed by AEG. On occasion Siemens was asked to use his influence to solve problems or drum up enthusiasm for a security.
47. See Fear and Kobrak, "The Origins of German Corporate Governance," and Jeffrey Fear and Christopher Kobrak,"Diverging Paths: Accounting for Corporate Governance in America and Germany," *Business History Review*, Vol. 80 (2006), no. 1.
48. Undated worksheet, HADB, A1149.
49. Deutsche Bank to Charles S. Mellen, Aug. 12, 1901, HADB, A1143. Mellen announced his resignation in the fall of 1903.
50. Siemens to Morgan, Nov. 26, 1897, HADB, A739.
51. Deutsche Bank, annual report 1901.
52. Report to holders of Trust Certificates, Nov. 12, 1900, HADB, A739.
53. Trust Agreement, Dec. 1, 1896, HADB, A739.
54. Gwinner to Steinthal, April 12, 1901, HADB, A105. Steinthal replied that he thought Gwinner had ignored another $6 million in commissions.

55. Gwinner to Steinthal, April 13, 1901, HADB, A105. Gwinner said that at one time, date unspecified, Deutsche Bank held $25 million in Northern Pacific securities, and $11 million in other railroads.
56. Hill to Gwinner, May 25, 1909, HADB, A1365.
57. *New York Times*, June 5, 1910.
58. Gwinner to Mount Stephen, Sept. 9, 1905, HADB, A434.
59. Adams to Gwinner, April 25, 1904, HADB, A46.
60. Adams to Gwinner, Jan. 16, 1906, HADB, A46.
61. Office of John Moody, March 7, 1912, HADB, A1143.
62. Siemens to Morgan, Aug. 3, 1897, HADB, A739, and October cables, HADB, A739.
63. Ives to Coster, Oct. 17, 1896, HADB, A220. Ives, who seems to have been representing Belmont's interests and had served on the board representing a regional bank, lobbied to replace Adams as chairman of the board, once again associating him with the hated Villard. If he could not have the position, he recommended that no one get it, to avoid a powerful chairman dominating the company president or conflicts between the two.
64. Adams to Siemens, Oct. 20, 1893, HADB, A683.
65. Villard's statement to the court, December 1896, HADB, A220.
66. Villard, pp. 341–343.
67. James B. Hedges, *Henry Villard and the Railways of the Northwest* (New Haven: Yale University Press, 1930).
68. Adams, Aug. 19, 1901, and Adams to Gwinner, July 22, 1901, HADB, A45.
69. Julius Grodinsky, *Transcontinental Railway Strategy, 1869–1893: A Study of Business* (Philadelphia: University of Pennsylvania, 1962), pp. 130–140.
70. Thomas Bender, *A Nation Among Nations: America's Place in World History* (New York: Hill and Wang, 2006), pp. 246–288.

6. Other Transportation and Commercial Investments

1. Walton and Rockoff, pp. 12 and 354–355.
2. Fritz Stern, *Gold and Iron; Bismarck, Bleichröder, and the Building of the German Empire* (New York: Knopf, 1977), p. 217.
3. Deutsche Bank's most ambitious railroad underwriting, but not its only, in that and other parts of the world, was the famous Baghdad Railway. Gall, "The Deutsche Bank 1870–1914," pp. 67–76. As early as 1875, the length of American open rail lines was greater than those of Great Britain, Germany, France, Canada, Italy, India, and Russia combined. Foreman-Peck, p. 34.
4. Chandler, *The Visible Hand*, pp. 81–205. In 1906, there were thirty-three companies with more than 1,000 miles of track and $100 million in capitalization in the United States. During the 1890s and in the early part of the twentieth century, railroad construction, coordination, and restructuring played a crucial role in the development of countless ancillary sectors, government regulation, accounting practice, general management, and capital market formations.
5. Blinzig to Deutsche Bank Berlin from United States, December 1903 (no precise date), HADB, A211.
6. Adams to Gwinner, Dec. 12, 1907, HADB, A47. In the midst of the crisis, the second letter of the day.
7. Ibid.
8. Ibid.
9. Braunfels to Villard, July 7, 1892, Villard Papers, Baker Library, Box 99, Folder 741.
10. Various newspaper articles, dates and journals unclear, HADB, A1140. One of the oldest railroads in the United States, it received a concession from the state of Maryland to run a line from Baltimore to Virginia in 1827. That corporate charter broadened over the years to include the entire Ohio River Valley. By the turn of the century, it had received the right to buy the stock in other companies and through building lines, leasing, and acquiring other companies, controlled a system of nearly 4,400 miles.

11. Memorandum of Agreement, Baltimore & Ohio Syndicate Agreement, Dec. 15, 1898, HADB, A1140, and notice to Deutsche Bank of terms of its participation in B&O Reorganization Syndicate, Dec. 23, 1898, HADB, A1140. Presumably, the difference between the $8.9 million and $9 million was to be kept by the syndicate managers.
12. John F. Stover, *History of the Baltimore and Ohio Railroad* (West Lafeyette, Indiana: Purdue University Press,1987), pp. 185–200.
13. Credit Suisse to Deutsche Bank, Nov. 10, 1903, HADB, A1140. Credit Suisse took the lead in Europe by listing B&O common shares in Switzerland. Despite Adams' reservations, a few weeks later, Deutsche Bank followed by taking a similar step on the Berlin market.
14. Speyer to Mankiewitz, Sept. 15, 1903, HADB, A210. It received a commission for the sales, the profit derived from the difference between its purchase and sales price, as well as the fees pledged by the B&O to handle all dividend payments and other transactions in Germany.
15. Deutsche Bank to Adams, Oct. 31, 1903, HADB, A210. Alfred Blinzig, a member of the management board from 1920–34, was sent to the United States for the first time to work with Speyer, Adams, and the B&O to write the German version of the prospectus, which involved changes to the original disclosures and organization of accounting information to bring them into conformity with German regulatory requirements.
16. Mankiewitz to Speyer, Nov. 25, 1903, HADB, A210. If the B&O could sell its financial condition as a company that would at least maintain its dividend of 4 percent even if economic circumstances in the United States worsened, while offering some upside of increased dividends in the event of an upsurge in activity, Deutsche Bank was confident the launch would be an enormous success.
17. Credit Suisse to Deutsche Bank, Dec. 4, 1903, HADB, A1140.
18. File note, "Rolling Equipment in Service June 3, 1903" HADB, A210. From 1902 to 1903, net earnings had climbed by approximately 15 percent. With common shares of $124.3 million, preferred of $59.4 million, and bonds of $234 million, it was one of the largest railroads in America. It owned or controlled 1,769 locomotives, 1,158 passenger cars, and 84,742 freight cars, a fact that provides some indication of how dependent the line was on the region's coal mining sector.
19. Deutsche Bank's confidence in foreign business dealings and its deep, multifaceted relationship with the United States added confidence to German capital markets, understandably still nervous about American securities since the Northern Pacific affair.
20. Gesuch Zustimmung der Landesregierung zur Zulassung der Stamm-Aktien über je 100 Dollar der Baltimore & Ohio Railroad Company zum Handel an der Berliner Börse, from Deutsche Bank addressed to Eurer Excellenz, Dec. 9, 1903, HADB, A210. Over the previous three years, the B&O share price, for example, had fluctuated between 72 and 119 Dollars a share. Written in English in the original document.
21. Collection of articles, early 1904, *The New York News Bureau*, Jan. 22, 1904, HADB, A210.
22. Speyer & Co. to Deutsche Bank, Jan. 29, 1904, HADB, A211.
23. Mankiewitz to Speyer & Co., Feb. 15, 1904, HADB, A211.
24. Deutsche Bank to S. Mattersdorff, Jan. 10, 1908, HADB, A1138.
25. Deutsche Bank to Adams, Aug. 30, 1910, HADB, A1138.
26. Various newspaper articles, dates and journals unclear, HADB, A1140.
27. Speyer to Deutsche Bank, Jan. 7, 1913, HADB, A1138. In early 1913, Speyer contacted Deutsche Bank about yet another B&O issue, this time $64 million in 4.5 percent twentieth year convertible bonds at 110 for common shares up to March 1, 1923. Speyer indicated that the bonds might be paid in foreign currency, if desired. Preferred and common shareholders would be offered the bonds at 95.5 with payments accepted in three *tranches*. See trip report Axhausen in the U.S., May 19, 1913, HADB, A1138.
28. *Wall Street Journal*, April 4, 1932, Feb. 20, 1929, *New York Times*, and various newspaper articles, dates and journals unclear, HADB, A1140. B&O was a huge railroad. Its 1929 proposed reorganization would have given it 13,814 miles of track and $2.2 billion in capital, and it was bought by Pennsylvania Railroad, its great trunk line competitor. In 1931, its assets were nearly $1.2 billion, preferred and common shares $315 million, and mortgaged debt nearly $600 million. Even during the worst years of the Depression, with declining sales and

profits, the B&O made some money (sales down by 24 percent, profits down by 82 percent, $132 million sales, and $3.8 million profit). Daniel Willard, still president, asked for help from shareholders and regulators. Since 1930, the company had been in receivership.

29. Adams to Deutsche Bank, Feb. 27, 1907, HADB, A1088. Those terms included interest of 6 percent paid quarterly and a drop of the option price on the bonds to 80. The railroad also had to apply to list the bonds on the New York Stock Exchange, thus making them more liquid.
30. Maury Klein, *The Life and Legend of Jay Gould* (Baltimore: Johns Hopkins University Press, 1986), p. 3.
31. Klein, *Gould*, pp. 75 and 485–486.
32. Adams to Deutsche Bank, March 11, 1908, HADB, A1088.
33. Evaluation by J. H. McClement to W. S. Pierce, chairman of the board of Western Maryland Railroad Company, June 12, 1907, HADB, A1088. McClement was a financial advisor to Pierce, who did audits and made forecasts. He would later help represent Deutsche Bank's interest in the United States (see next Section).
34. Klein, *Harriman*, p. 250.
35. Letter to Stern Brothers, London, presumably from Deutsche Bank, but author unclear. March 7, year unclear, HADB, A1088.
36. Adams to Deutsche Bank, June 8, 1907, HADB, A1088.
37. Adams to Deutsche Bank, Oct. 17, 1907, HADB, A1088. The property's production had increased by 10 million tons during the previous year, but Gould took possession of it at a bargain-basement price.
38. Adams to Gwinner, Jan. 8, 1908, HADB, A47. Gould informed Adams that they intended to sell 25,000 acres of West Virginia Coal lands at cost to a new company that would issue shares and bonds to a syndicate to finance two large mines. They offered Deutsche Bank participation in the syndicate as an added perk for the debt financing of WMR. The operation should benefit the WMR by relieving the line of the debt that it had incurred to acquire the land. This would in turn increase the value of Deutsche Bank's option on WMR's debt by reducing WMR's other expenses.
39. Gwinner to Adams, Feb. 8, 1908, HADB, A47.
40. Adams to Gwinner, March 26, 1908, HADB, A47.
41. Gwinner to Adams, March 7, 1908, HADB, A1088.
42. Adams to Deutsche Bank, March 9, 1908, HADB, A1088.
43. Ibid.
44. Adams to Deutsche Bank, March 11, 1908, HADB, A1088.
45. Ibid.
46. Ibid.
47. Adams to Deutsche Bank, April 16, 1908, HADB, A36.
48. *New York Times*, Jan. 19, 1909.
49. Adams to Gwinner, Jan. 19, 1909, HADB, A47.
50. Adams to Gwinner, May 27, 1908, HADB, A47. Even the relationship between Adams and Deutsche Bank suffered. Many later internal documents indicate that the bank was dissatisfied with his handling of the Gould situation. As will be discussed later, so great was this disappointment that it played a role in the planning for his replacement.
51. Adams to Deutsche Bank, July 17, 1912, HADB, A39.
52. Exchange of telegrams, Adams and Gwinner, April 28 and 30, 1908, HADB, A47. Gwinner to Adams, Sept. 11, 1911, HADB, A38.
53. Gwinner to Mankiewitz, July 23, 1898, HADB, A1104. He recommended listing Union Pacific shares on behalf of Kuhn Loeb.
54. Adams to Deutsche Bank, July 14, 1908, HADB, A36.
55. Adams to Deutsche Bank, March 20, 1906, HADB, A42.
56. Adams to Deutsche Bank, June 17, 1902, HADB, A32. In 1902, Adams got wind of GE's desire to invest in Russia. Because of "its business and financial strength it shows in its business policy more aggressiveness than it has for a number of years." As reports indicated that Westinghouse already had a strong toehold in Russia, and the Russian government was

not terribly protective of foreign investments, Adams reasoned that GE would not enter that market. Deutsche Bank agreed that the experiences of most companies investing in Russia were disappointing. French and Belgian companies had lost millions of Francs in the iron industry.

57. Gall, *Deutsche Bank*, p. 36.
58. Gwinner to Mount Stephen, March 14, 1899, HADB, A434.
59. Wilkins, *Investment in the United States to 1914*, p. 437.
60. S&H to Deutsche Bank, July 3, 1903, HADB, S1278.
61. Adams to Deutsche Bank, Oct. 7, 1903, HADB, S1278. The terms of their payment were ironic considering the future problems posed by Allis-Chalmers to the negotiations.
62. Briefing memorandum to Adams from S&H, dated Berlin, July 4, 1903, attached to a July 3, 1903 letter to Deutsche Bank, HADB, S1278.
63. Wilkins, *Investment in the United States to 1914*, pp. 436–437.
64. Briefing memorandum to Adams from S&H, dated Berlin, July 4, 1903, attached to a July 3, 1903 letter to Deutsche Bank, HADB, S1278. S&H reminded Coffin that the agreements with its American subsidiary were for dynamos, motors, and electric light and power machinery. Other branches, such as electrolysis, electric cables, and telephone equipment, were specifically exempted.
65. Adams to S&H, and draft contract, Nov. 13, 1903, HADB, S1278.
66. Adams to S&H, Dec. 8, 1903, HADB, S1278.
67. Ibid.
68. Adams to S&H, Dec. 16, 1903, HADB, S1278.
69. Ibid.
70. Ibid.
71. Adams to Deutsche Bank, Jan. 22, 1904, HADB, S1278.
72. Deutsche Bank to Adams, Feb. 5, 1904, HADB, S1278. S&H did not even think it worthwhile to invest in determining exactly what had been done, since the patents were of little interest.
73. S&H to Deutsche Bank, Feb. 10, 1904, HADB, S1278. It was, however, not enthusiastic about Coffin's suggestion to wipe out the Siemens name from the subsidiary and to promise not to use it in the United States for ten years. The Germans' aim was to be released from their obligations to the American company; whether this was obtained by a negotiated agreement or by the liquidation of the company was a matter of indifference to S&H in Germany. If achieved rapidly, it might be willing to release the American company from any future obligation. However, striking out the Siemens name from the American company, though desirable as the subsidiary brought little honor to the concern, achieved only part of S&H's goal. At the very least, Adams should consult counsel about the desirability of any of these actions.
74. Deutsche Bank to Wilhelm von Siemens, March 10, 1904, HADB, S1278.
75. Deutsche Bank to Adams, March 12, 1904, HADB, S1278. Although he claimed that the two companies did not jointly set prices, they both tried to maintain prices as much as possible, avoiding competition. With important orders, however, especially ones that caught the public eye, the competition was sharp indeed. Westinghouse seemed particularly irate that Coffin had not run the agreement by him first.
76. Deutsche Bank to Adams, March 12, 1904, HADB, S1278. Westinghouse also mentioned that he felt that Rathenau, whom he visited after Siemens, had gotten the better of GE in their negotiations.
77. S&H to Deutsche Bank, March 17, 1904, HADB, S1278. He believed that his company and GE were too well positioned to respond to customer needs for Allis-Chalmers to become a real rival. Developing the flexibility necessary to provide the machines rapidly was beyond the means of Allis-Chalmers.
78. Westinghouse to Gwinner, April 20, 1904, HADB, S1278.
79. Gwinner to Westinghouse, April 22, 1904, date unclear, but Westinghouse refers to it in his next letter, HADB, S1278.
80. Westinghouse to Gwinner, April 29, 1904, HADB, S1278.
81. Various correspondence, the summer and fall of 1904, HADB, S1278.

82. Edward Adams, *Niagara Power: History of Niagara Falls Power Company*, 1886–1918, 2 Vols. (Niagara Falls, NY: Niagara Falls Company, 1927). Adams, who had been involved in every step of its development, was commissioned in 1918 by the directors to write a history of the venture. It is very technical and takes the story back to the early nineteenth century. It does discuss the companies' financing, but there is not one word about Deutsche Bank. Perhaps in 1927, when it was published Adams considered it "politically incorrect" to highlight a German bank's involvement. See especially, introduction and pp. 233–236, and 433–445.
83. Adams, p. 164.
84. Subscribers Agreement, Jan. 17, 1890, HADB, A1111.
85. Adams to Deutsche Bank on Cataract Construction stationery, Jan. 22, 1897, HADB, A1111.
86. Adams to Deutsche Bank, April 30, 1897, HADB, A1111.
87. Deutsche Bank to Adams, June 1898, HADB, A1111.
88. Adams to Deutsche Bank, Dec. 9, 1904, HADB, A663.
89. Adams to Gwinner, Nov. 4, 1898, HADB, A45. He wrote before the turn of the century, for example, about a different matter, that he refrained from talking about electrification in the Niagara Falls area "to prevent any applicant for power from thinking that possibly the private interests of the President of the Company in a similar business would prevent a newcomer from obtaining equal facilities."
90. Adams to Gwinner, Dec. 9, 1898, HADB, A45. In December 1898, Adams brought the Mattiesen Alkali Works to Gwinner's attention, because the Elektron Company might be considering establishing an electro-chemical works in America. It had overinvested and was deprived of low rates for transportation. The company seemed to be in play, at the very least shareholders wanted to break off and enlarge its profitable Niagara plant. The production quality seemed very high at the Niagara plant, allowing Elektron to export to South America, Mexico, Australia, China, and Japan. It also controlled the patents, with another year to run, which made Elektron the only important producer of chloride in the country.
91. Walter F. Peterson, *An Industrial Heritage: Allis-Chalmers Corporation* (Milwaukee: Milwaukee County Historical Society, 1978), pp. 1–70.
92. Peterson, pp. 109–111.
93. Wilkins, *Investment in the United States to 1914*, pp. 429–431. According to Alfred Chandler, the Allis side were immigrant Germans. Wilkins, p. 870, note 240.
94. Adams to Gwinner, Aug. 19, 1901, HADB, A45.
95. Ibid.
96. Deutsche Bank to members of the syndicate, May 2, 1901, HADB, A69.
97. Gwinner to Adams, Dec. 8, 1902, HADB, A45.
98. Adams to Gwinner, Dec. 30, 1902, HADB, A45.
99. Peterson, pp. 109–111.
100. Peterson, p. 124.
101. Peterson, pp. 124–127.
102. Adams to Gwinner, Oct. 20, 1903, HADB, A46.
103. Adams to Gwinner, Oct. 12, 1903, HADB, A46.
104. Gwinner to Adams, Oct. 31, 1903, HADB, A46.
105. Adams to Gwinner, April 25, 1904, HADB, A46.
106. Ibid.
107. Gwinner to Adams, Aug. 20, 1904, HADB, A46.
108. Adams to Gwinner, April 25, 1904, HADB, A46.
109. Adams to Gwinner, Nov. 30, 1905, HADB, A46.
110. Adams to Gwinner, May 22, 1907, HADB, A47.
111. Adams to Gwinner, June 13, 1906, HADB, A47. According to Adams, around this time Stillman was thinking about retiring from the board of National City for health or business reasons. Stillman was an intimate friend of William Rockefeller through the double marriage of their respective children. Adams reported that Stillman personally pleaded with Adams to keep his position with Allis-Chalmers.
112. Gwinner to Adams, July 1906, HADB, A47. In a July 1906 letter, Gwinner wrote to Adams that he could do nothing to help Allis-Chalmers.

113. Adams to Gwinner, May 22, 1907, HADB, A47.
114. Adams to Gwinner, Sept. 19, 1907, HADB, A47.
115. Gwinner to Adams, Dec. 13, 1907, HADB, A47.
116. Adams to Gwinner, Jan. 8, 1908, HADB, A47.
117. Gwinner to Adams, Dec. 13, 1907, HADB, A47.
118. Peterson, pp. 132–139.
119. Adams to Gwinner, Oct. 11, 1911, HADB, A48.
120. Various, HADB, A52.
121. File note, undated, but among 1913 papers, HADB, A62.
122. Peterson, pp. 237, 313, and 410. After World War I, Allis-Chalmers entered the tractor business – $10.6 of its total $45.3 million in 1929 sales – which helped cushion it through the tough times of the Depression. By 1977, its sales of farm and electrical equipment produced total revenues of $530 million and profits of $67 million.

7. A Taste for Start-Ups

1. For a good discussion of venture capital see Paul Gompers and Josh Lerner, *The Venture Capital Cycle* (Cambridge, MA: MIT Press, 1999). Today only a very small and declining portion of capital managed by venture capitalists is supplied by banks in the United States, pp. 4–9.
2. Gall, *Deutsche Bank*, pp. 64–67. Deutsche Bank's involvement in U.S. investments gave it a clearer picture than many other Europeans about the opportunities and difficulties in the petroleum sector, which suffered from a downturn in demand around the turn of the century because of increased use of electricity. The sector was witnessing an enormous consolidation in the United States. Its potential significance because of the automobile was just beginning to be appreciated. The dominant position of Rockefeller on the American market, as well as his potential role in the development of future sources of petroleum was also only beginning to be appreciated by Europeans.
3. Translation of the guarantee of Bamag and Didier to Lehigh Coke, undated, HADB, A485.
4. *New York Times*, April 28, 1910. The project had the financial backing of Deutsche Bank and the cooperation of a major customer, Bethlehem Steel, and Western Maryland Railroad, which had committed to build a spur line for deliveries of coal and finished production.
5. Deutsche Bank to Bamag, Sept. 25, 1909, HADB, A509. Although they had originally asked for half in the form of cash, Deutsche Bank wanted it decided later. They finally received only stock.
6. Deutsche Bank to Adams, Sept. 22, 1909, HADB, A509.
7. Deutsche Bank to Adams, Sept. 25, 1909, HADB, A509.
8. Ibid. The closeness of the dates evidences a high speed in business dealings. Some letters were, of course, in the form of telegrams, copied later by normal post.
9. Adams to Deutsche Bank, Nov. 12, 1909, HADB, A509.
10. Deutsche Bank to Adams, Nov. 9, 1909, HADB, A509.
11. Adams to Deutsche Bank, Feb. 25, 1910, HADB, A510.
12. Deutsche Bank to Bamag, Sept. 25, 1909, HADB, A509.
13. Rentabilitätsberechnung, unsigned, Dec. 18, 1909, HADB, A483. Assuming volumes of 4,300 tons of coal converted into 75 percent raw coke, 2.9 percent tar, and 0.82 percent sulfates, the plant would have daily revenues of 5,200 Mark from coke, 5,800 from gases, nearly 8,000 from sulfates, and nearly 3,000 from tars, or total daily revenues of around 22,000 Mark. A later letter from around the same time refers to Grumbacher's profit calculations. It warns that Deutsche Bank in the person of Adams must independently check all of the calculations and assumptions, a step which had not as yet been performed. Unsigned (probably Mankiewitz) to Eduard Arnhold, Nov. 4, 1909, HADB, A483.
14. Adams to Deutsche Bank, Sept. 23, 1909, HADB, A509.
15. Grumbacher, Report to Bamag Berlin, Oct. 22, 1909, HADB, A483.
16. Schwab to Grumbacher, Oct. 20, 1909, HADB, A483. As will be discussed in the next Chapter, the facility was finally sold to Bethlehem under duress just before America's entry into World War I.

17. Hohmann, Grumbacher, and Oskar Simmersbach to Bamag, Oct. 22, 1909, HADB, A483.
18. Hohmann to Mankiewitz, July 2, 1910, HADB, A486.
19. Ibid.
20. Christopher Kobrak, *Schering*, p. 98. Kokswerke acquired Chemische Fabrik (vormals E. Schering) in 1922. By the end of the 1920s, by dint of clever acquisitions and an aggressive financial strategy, it had become one of Germany's largest companies. By 1937, the chemical business accounted for most of its sales and growth. The company was reorganized in that year and renamed Schering AG. The research for this book has led the author to revise several views about Kokswerke's early history. When the story of Schering was written, nothing was known of its U.S. activity and financial distress before World War I.
21. Berve to Mankiewitz, Dec. 24, 1909, HADB, A483.
22. Berve to Mankiewitz, Feb. 8, 1910, HADB, A483.
23. Oberschlesische Kokswerke & Chemische Fabriken to Mankiewitz, Aug. 22, 1910, HADB, A486.
24. Abschrift, Nov. 8, 1906, HADB, A486.
25. Berve to Mankiewitz, Aug. 23, 1910, HADB, A486.
26. Deutsche Bank to Bamag, Aug. 31, 1910, HADB, A486, and several other letters in same file.
27. Mankiewitz to Arnhold, Nov. 13, 1909, HADB, A483.
28. Deutsche Bank to Hohmann, Didier, Sept. 28, 1910, HADB, A486, quoting telegrams from July and August between Deutsche Bank and Adams.
29. "Entgegnung auf das Gutachten des Herrn Dr. Caro über das Bethlehem-Project," Hohmann and Simmersbach, undated, HADB, A483. Caro's first report provoked a quick and sharp response. According to Bamag and Didier it was careless and showed little knowledge of the coking sector. They maintained that Caro had used incorrect figures and measurements. They assumed that he just did not know that American coking coal, unlike German coal, was of a consistent quality for exploitation. In any case, Bethlehem was obliged by contract to deliver suitable coal. According to the two companies' experts, Caro incorrectly asserted that American coal needed thirty-six hours distillation, instead of the twenty-two to twenty-four hours they had assumed.
30. Bamag to Mankiewitz, Dec. 20, 1909, HADB, A483, and Gewerkschaft Deutscher Kaiser to Geheimrat Klöne, Dec. 30, 1909, HADB, A484.
31. Minutes of June 9, 1910 conference (Mankiewitz, Hohmann, Grumbacher, Mayer), HADB, A487. To keep Lehigh's expenses down, some key managers were paid with stock. Others would be paid by the construction company, with amounts included in the guaranteed total price.
32. Minutes of the conference of May 21, 1910, HADB, A486. In spring 1910, it was proposed that Adams serve as chairman of the board and of the executive committee of the coke company, which also included M. Loeb, F. Grumbacher, E. F. Mayer, W. H. Mayer, W. H. Blaufelt, and E. L. Marston of Blair & Co. The final decision would be made in Berlin after discussions with Bamag-Didier.
33. Contract of Guaranty of March 26, 1910, HADB, A512. The original September 1909 plans were "bolstered" by a formal guarantee from Bamag-Didier in March 1910. Whereas Didier-March had agreed to build a complete coking plant near South Bethlehem, Pennsylvania, for Bethlehem Steel Company for the production of coke and coke by-products with a capacity of 3,360 net tons of coke per day (see amended agreement, Feb. 4, 1910), Lehigh Coke would pay Bamag-Didier thirty-five thousand shares of preferred stock and thirty-seven thousand common of the Coke company. Deutsche Bank on behalf of its associates would pay those companies $3,250,000. The two German companies jointly and separately guaranteed to construct the facility with a capacity of 4,300 tons of coke per day, including all necessary machinery, storage facilities, replacement parts, and other infrastructure necessary for the installation and construction in a first-class manner by Aug. 1, 1912. The bank and its associates pledged to make payments from time to time but not to exceed $3,250,000 and not to include the builder's profits and compensation to certain employees, which the builder would have to finance. For a fixed sum of 500,000 Mark per year, Bamag-Didier provided a covenant to cover the cost of maintaining and renewing the plant in complete working condition until its delivery to Bethlehem.

34. Bamag-Didier to Deutsche Bank, May 31, 1910, HADB, A512.
35. Adams to Deutsche Bank, Dec. 14, 1910, HADB, A513.
36. Adams to Deutsche Bank, Oct. 13, 1910, HADB, A512.
37. Employment contract of Aug. Putsch, July 30, 1910, HADB, A512. The contract says that he lived in South Bethlehem, but that he moved from Killamarsh, England. Much of his correspondence is in German, though.
38. Adams to Deutsche Bank, Oct. 3, 1910, HADB, A512, and Didier-March to Adams, Sept. 13, 1910, HADB, A512.
39. Hohmann and Grumbacher to Adams, Oct. 11, 1910, HADB, A512.
40. Adams to Deutsche Bank, Oct. 14, 1910, HADB, A512.
41. Minutes of meeting to Adams, Julius Goldman, the lawyer for Bamag-Didier, and Bruno Axhausen, Oct. 2, 1910, HADB, A512. Even Goldman confided that Adams' reading of the Berlin conference minutes was better than his client's and that some of his client's suggestions were not legal in the United States.
42. Adams to Deutsche Bank, Oct. 13, 1910, HADB, A512.
43. Mankiewitz to Axhausen, Oct. 24, 1910, HADB, A512.
44. Goldman to Grumbacher, Nov. 3, 1910, HADB, A512. In his seven-page description of his meeting with Adams, Goldman noted that Adams behaved very correctly and that Adams was right that American by-laws did not contain provisions for dividends. Somehow, the two sides had different copies of the Berlin minutes. Adams' copy contained the outline of the by-laws, Grumbacher's did not. As a matter of fact, the copy of the minutes shown to Goldman had many differences with Adams'.
45. Adams to Deutsche Bank, Nov. 3, 1910, HADB, A512.
46. Adams to Deutsche Bank, Nov. 7, 1910, HADB, A512.
47. Axhausen to Hohmann and Grumbacher Oct. 23, 1910, HADB, A487, along with various letters from lawyers; description of New York meeting of the parties (Adams, Hohmann, Axhausen, and Grumbacher, I think), Oct. 27, 1910, HADB, A487. Deutsche Bank made no secret of the fact that it wanted to sell the shares in a few years. This left two important issues, for Bamag-Didier: If Deutsche Bank sold, who would be their new partners and how could the interests of preferred shareholders in any undividended cash be protected? The new text of the by-laws might make the sale of the shares more difficult. The Bamag group wanted something in the by-laws to prevent an anti–Bamag-Didier coalition forming once the syndicate had sold its shares.
48. Mankiewitz to Kempner, Oct. 29, 1910, HADB, A487.
49. Mankiewitz to Arnhold, Nov. 11, 1910, HADB, A487. Mankiewitz had a reputation for being outspoken, but was as harsh as I have ever seen a Deutsche Bank executive communicate with the head of another company.
50. What appears to be a file note on Deutsche Bank stationery, Nov. 18, 1910, HADB, A487.
51. Adams to Mankiewitz, Dec. 8, 1910, HADB, A513.
52. Adams to Deutsche Bank, Dec. 12, 1910, HADB, A513.
53. Adams to Mankiewitz, Nov. 15, 1910, HADB, A512, several other letters, and two cables that day. See also Briessen to Adams, Nov. 12, 1910, HADB, A513.
54. Adams to Deutsche Bank, Dec. 8, 1910, HADB, A513.
55. Bamag to Deutsche Bank, Feb. 18, 1913, HADB, A497.
56. Mankiewitz and Axhausen to Adams, Jan. 5, 1911, HADB, A513.
57. Adams to Deutsche Bank, Jan. 16, 1911, HADB, A0513.
58. See several letters, HADB, A537, 7 percent preferred ($3,500,000 issued) and $4,000,000 in common shares.
59. General letter, presumably to clients, "Vertraulich," Jan. 26, 1911, HADB, A537. They covered the 7 percent cumulative preferred payments, repurchased the preferreds at 140 percent in twenty years, reserve of $150,000 per year up to a cumulative maximum of $1,000,000, a 10 percent bonus to executives, a 7 percent noncumulative dividend on common, and eventually bonus dividends on both preferred and common. The memo listed the company's location and purpose, key people, and relationships and discussed the construction guarantee.

60. Various letters, HADB, A537.
61. Hohmann to Mankiewitz, July 2, 1910, HADB, A486.
62. Axhausen to Mankiewitz, July 31, 1911, HADB, A490. Deutsche Bank to Adams, July 14, 1911, HADB, A490. Bergmann to Mankiewitz, Aug. 14, 1911, HADB, A490.
63. Deutsche Bank to Bamag, Aug. 15, 1911, HADB, A490.
64. Adams to Deutsche Bank, Jan. 19, 1912, HADB, A517.
65. Axhausen to Mankiewitz, July 19, 1911, HADB, A490.
66. Mankiewitz to Axhausen, Aug. 2, 1911, HADB, A490.
67. Lehigh Coke Company to Deutsche Bank, Aug. 7, 1911, HADB, A490.
68. Adams to Deutsche Bank, Nov. 16, 1911, HADB, A535. In a handwritten note presumably by Axhausen, he endorses Adams' comments and suggestion, with the comment that Wilbur is very much like Adams.
69. Meeting between Schwab and Mankiewitz, Sept. 23, 1911, HADB, A490.
70. Adams to Deutsche Bank, Dec. 14, 1910, HADB, A513.
71. Second letter, Adams to Deutsche Bank, Dec. 14, 1910, HADB, A513.
72. Deutsche Bank to Adams, Nov. 15, 1911, HADB, A517.
73. Adams to Deutsche Bank, Jan. 19, 1912, HADB, A517.
74. Unsigned contract, Aug. 1912, HADB, A520.
75. Adams to Mankiewitz, Feb. 12, 1912, HADB, A518.
76. Adams to Mankiewitz, Feb. 12, 1912, HADB, A518. On the positive side, his personal health was better, and the president of Western Maryland Railway Company, a firm in which Deutsche Bank held securities, had informed him that the coal contracts with Bethlehem would increase the rail line's revenues by $1 million per year.
77. Adams to Deutsche Bank, Sept. 16, 1912, HADB, A519. This letter is a twenty-six-page memo in which Adams goes into enormous detail.
78. Deutsche Bank to Adams, Oct. 11, 1912, HADB, A520.
79. Ibid.
80. Deutsche Bank, presumably to clients, Oct. 14, 1912, HADB, A538.
81. Adams to Deutsche Bank, Nov. 26, 1912, HADB, A520.
82. Ibid.
83. Mankiewitz to Kempner (copy to Arnhold, Bamag-Didier top management), Nov. 26, 1912, HADB, A577.
84. Ibid.
85. Caro trip report, date not clear, HADB, A501.
86. Didier-March to Stettiner Chamottefabrik, Dec. 26, 1913, HADB, A502.
87. Bethlehem to Didier-March, Dec. 18, 1913, HADB, A502.
88. Mankiewitz to Marston, April 29, 1914, HADB, A535.
89. Various correspondence, February through June, 1913, HADB, A523.
90. Mankiewitz to Marston of Blair, April 29, 1914, HADB, A535.
91. Lehigh Coke Company, Deutsche Bank to the Syndicate Associates, May 11, 1912, HADB, A535. The information and compromises worked out were largely based on Caro's March 12, 1912 report to Deutsche Bank, which supported the idea that some of the extra costs involved construction not envisioned in the original contract. According to Caro, Bamag-Didier had foregone extra payments that they might have won in a German court, and Lehigh Coke, by not accepting the amended plan, might lose out on some important advantages, especially those involving extra capacity and cost reduction. For the increased capacity and profits, not only the ovens but the whole installation had to be altered. About the selection of coal, he now believed that the ovens could be constructed to adapt to the coal in the area. At the very least, it was incumbent on the engineers to adapt them or develop a mix of coals that would be suitable. Interestingly, his report indicates that the batteries would be opened on a staggered basis, beginning July 1, 1912 and ending Jan. 1, 1913. English Translation, HADB, A573.
92. Deutsche Bank to Smith (code name for Hugo Schmidt), Feb. 11, 1915, HADB, A563. The seventeen-page letter is in German, signed apparently by Mankiewitz and Axhausen, and is

addressed oddly enough to Lieber Herr Smith. There were some other half-hearted attempts to code names.

93. Compensations for Adams, McIlvain, and Dettmann, file note, Axhausen, April 2, 1914, HADB, A504. Already in April 1914 there was enough optimism for a partial division of the rewards made to the Americans. Adams, for his four-and-a-half years of effort expected $40,000 to $50,000 as a cash payment instead of the original $5,000 promised. Axhausen suggested that, although the bank wanted to make sure that both Adams and McIlvain did better than originally promised because of their great service, Adams should be asked, however, to wait until the company was making money, accepting more stock in lieu of the extra cash now – perhaps $15,000 guaranteed now and the rest later. Of Deutsche Bank's original $400,000 stock commission, Adams might take his normal 12.5 percent or $50,000 (an amount equivalent to $4 million today). For McIlvain, Axhausen recommended $10,000 in stock and $5,000 in an additional cash bonus.

8. Transitions

1. See Fear and Kobrak, "Diverging Paths," pp. 3–8.
2. See Kobrak, "The Rise and Fall." August Belmont, Sr.'s arrival and career in the United States is one of the best illustrations of this phenomenon. On his way to Havana to handle some Rothschild business, he landed in New York in the middle of the May 1837 crisis which followed the collapse of the second central bank. In the midst of the panic, when the Rothschilds still knew nothing of what was happening, he started sorting out the family's affairs, earning him their gratitude and the post of representing its affairs in New York. He became one of the leading private bankers in New York, involving himself in Southern trade and Democratic politics, which may have weakened the Rothschild's business in the United States. See Irving Katz, *August Belmont: A Political Biography* (New York: Columbia University Press, 1968), pp. 6–98.
3. Langen, pp. 121–193.
4. Jones, *Multinationals*, p. 21. Although Jones points out that in 1913 nearly one-third of foreign investment was direct and that foreign direct investment as a percentage of world output only surpassed that of the pre–World War I period in the 1990s, the vast majority of the investment before World War I was concentrated in natural resources and foodstuffs in dependent regions.
5. Langen, pp. 309–321.
6. Youssef Cassis and Eric Bussières, eds. *London and Paris as International Centres in the Twentieth Century* (Oxford: Oxford University Press, 2005), and Cassis, *City Bankers: 1890–1914* (Cambridge: Cambridge University Press, 1994).
7. Dan Rottenberg, *The Man Who Made Wall Street: Anthony J. Drexel and the Rise of Modern Finance* (Philadelphia: University of Pennsylvania, 2001).
8. Theresa M. Collins, *Otto Kahn: Art, Money, & Modern Times* (Chapel Hill: University of North Carolina Press, 2002), pp. 43–49.
9. Ibid.
10. "Speyer Becomes Investment Unit," *Wall Street Journal*, June 14, 1934. In 1934, however, like many smaller banking houses, it chose to focus solely on its investment banking operations.
11. "Rise of New York's Great Investment Houses," *New York Evening Post*, Oct. 15, 1926.
12. Gwinner to Edgar Speyer, Jan. 14, 1905, HADB, A1323.
13. James Speyer to Gwinner, June 21, 1904, HADB, A1323.
14. Gwinner file note to Direktion, Dec. 12, 1906, HADB, A47.
15. *Die Disconto-Gesellschaft 1851–1901, Denkschrift zum 50jährigen Jubiläum* (Berlin, 1901).
16. Gwinner file note to Direktion, Dec. 12, 1906, HADB, A47.
17. Ibid.
18. Speyer-Ellissen to Deutsche Bank, Nov. 21, 1895, HADB, A152. For example, in 1895, Speyer proposed that Deutsche Bank buy U.S. Treasury Bonds from it, whereas Deutsche Bank wanted to underwrite them directly.

19. Speyer-Ellissen to Deutsche Bank, Dec. 13, 1895, HADB, A152, and other correspondence through the winter 1895–96.
20. Siemens advised his colleagues not to discuss some aspects of the Northern Pacific problems with Stern. Dec. 12, 1895, HADB, A148.
21. Internal Memo, March 8, 1905. "Verhältnis zu den Firmen Speyer's," Gwinner signed off. HADB, A1323. Nevertheless, Deutsche Bank and Speyer ended up cooperating with one another in setting up a Speyer subsidiary in Mexico and launching Mexican securities on the market.
22. Adams to Gwinner, Aug. 16, 1909, HADB, A47.
23. Adams to Albert Kahn, Aug. 8, 1910, HADB, A47.
24. Trip Report, HADB, A1364.
25. Adams to Gwinner, April 25, 1904, HADB, A46.
26. Gwinner to Adams, Dec. 24, 1898, HADB, A45.
27. First National City Balance Sheet compared with Deutsche Bank's 1900 annual report, July 15, 1901, HADB, A45.
28. Adams to Gwinner, Feb. 14, 1899, HADB, A45.
29. Adams to Gwinner, Feb. 14, 1899, HADB, A45.
30. Gwinner to Braunfels, Jan. 12, 1901, HADB, A337.
31. Adams to Gwinner, Aug. 4, 1899, HADB, A45.
32. Ibid.
33. Collins, pp. 43–49.
34. Gwinner to Adams, Nov. 6, 1905, HADB, A33.
35. Adams to Gwinner, June 18, 1904, HADB, A46.
36. Gwinner to Adams, Aug. 20, 1904, HADB, A46. Stillman felt that the Great Northern and Northern Pacific difficulties would finally have to be settled in the courts, a prediction that turned out to be true.
37. Langen, pp. 43–94 and 309–319.
38. Adams to Deutsche Bank, Nov. 25, 1898, HADB, A29.
39. Richard Hofstadter, *The Age of Reform* (New York: Vintage Books, 1955), pp. 20–21.
40. Strouse, pp. 573–596.
41. Chernow, *The House of Morgan*, p. 122.
42. Adams to Gwinner, June 13, 1906, HADB, A47.
43. Adams to Gwinner, Dec. 28, 1906, HADB, A33.
44. Adams to Gwinner, Jan. 9, 1907, HADB, A47.
45. Adams to Gwinner, Feb. 26, 1907, HADB, A47.
46. Adams to Gwinner, June 13, 1906, HADB, A47. See also his Sept. 21, 1907 letter to Gwinner, HADB, A47.
47. Adams to J. Edward Simmons, Nov. 10, 1907, HADB, A47. America had to give up its dislike of a central bank, even if the treasury could assume the function temporarily. America's stock of gold was large enough to increase the currency up to $250 million.
48. Adams to Gwinner, Sept. 21, 1907, HADB, A47.
49. Ibid.
50. Adams to Gwinner, Dec. 12, 1907, HADB, A47. Second letter of the day.
51. Adams to Gwinner, May 27, 1908, HADB, A47.
52. Gwinner to Adams, Feb. 8, 1908, HADB, A47.
53. Langen, pp. 130–183.
54. *New York Times*, Jan. 4, 1911.
55. Adams to Gwinner, Nov. 11, 1912, HADB, A48.
56. Adams to Deutsche Bank, Sept. 22, 1911, HADB, A38.
57. Ibid.
58. *New York Times*, Dec. 15, 1912.
59. See various letters, HADB, A41–A48.
60. Adams to Gwinner, Jan. 8, 1908, HADB, A47. Adams thanks Gwinner for the gift of a fourth-century Greek coin, for example.

61. Adams to Gwinner, Aug. 16, 1901, HADB, A45. See also Gwinner to Adams, Oct. 8, 1901, HADB, A45. Adams, for example, did not like how Siemens & Halske treated him over termination and payment of fees on a contract with them.
62. Obituary, *Electrical World and Engineer*, July 30, 1904, HADB, A46.
63. Adams to Gwinner, Feb. 26, 1905, HADB, A46.
64. Gwinner note, May 12, 1905, HADB, A423.
65. Gwinner file note to Direktion, Dec. 12, 1906, HADB, A47, and James Speyer to Gwinner, June 21, 1904, HADB, A1323. Speyer had some misgivings about Adams' technical competence.
66. A French self-made banker with strong ties to financial circles in the United States and Europe – though no relation to Otto Kahn of Kuhn Loeb – Kahn tried to form a consortium of banks to further international financing activities. Born Abraham, Albert was the son of a modest merchant and had a good working relationship with Crédit Lyonnais, Société Générale, and the Rothschilds. After completing his rabbinical studies in 1876, he went to Paris as a sales apprentice, studied, and met Henri Bergson, who became a lifelong friend. With a year of experience in a bank, Albert took off for South Africa on a cargo ship. There he met DeBeers, who hired him to sell shares in his company in Europe on commission, which earned the young man a small fortune, enough to buy an estate in Boulogne on the Seine, which is still a museum. His social circle included literary giants such as Anatole France and Paul Valéry, and politicians such as the future President of France, Raymond Poincaré. He used his wealth to finance numerous artistic and scientific ventures. In addition to his more literary endeavors, he became a force in international finance, traveling all over the world promoting his business and artistic interests. In the 1929 crisis, he lost nearly everything, was involved in numerous scandals, and finally fled France and died shortly before the Nazis arrived in 1940. *Dictionnaire de Biographie Française*, Sous la direction M. Prevost, et al. (Paris: Librairie Letouze et Ané, 1994).
67. Kahn was a close associate of James Rosselli, a member of Crédit Lyonnais's board and responsible for branches, including the U.S. representative office. He arranged that Kahn use the Crédit Lyonnais office in New York at 52 Williams Street, in the same building as Kuhn Loeb, and that the French bank's representative make introductions for Kahn, whose ideas also seem to have appealed to Rosselli. Crédit Lyonnais was painfully aware that its responsibilities as a bank that took deposits, made buying and holding securities, especially foreign ones, necessary for international underwriting, seem irresponsible, morally if not legally. Participating in a syndicate that took charge of the securities, however, might be easier. See Rosselli to Buchanon, June 3, 1905, and July 13, 1905, DAE, 7113. Kahn made his headquarters at the office of Crédit Lyonnais, which in 1913 was the fourth largest bank in the world as measured by deposits and which operated an agency in New York.
68. Adams introduced Kahn to many New York business leaders including Morgan, who had a private meeting with him in his famous library. Adams reported that Kahn had not received much encouragement for his international bank, in part because the idea of an American Central Bank was being received more favorably. Evidently, part of the idea of forming an international bank was to serve some of the supra-bank functions of a central bank. Morgan and others, however, were more interested in enlarging their international presence. Yet they seemed to see little split between the private and public functions of such a large, international bank, which might help facilitate America's growing international trade and investment. Adams to Gwinner, Nov. 29, 1907, HADB, A47.
69. Various correspondence between Gwinner and Adams, 1907, HADB, A47.
70. File note, Gwinner, March 21, 1903, HADB, A121. The International Banking Corporation was founded in 1902 to do business in Latin America, Europe, and Asia, much as the Deutsche Ueberseeische Bank had been designed.
71. Various correspondence, Gwinner and Adams, 1898–1902, HADB, A45.
72. In 1909, for example, he was given a wide range of prices at which he could sell Deutsche Bank shares. Deutsche Bank to Adams, Dec. 31, 1909, HADB, A37.
73. Adams to Gwinner, April 25, 1904, HADB, A46.

74. Siemens to Deutsche Bank, Oct. 26, 1893, HADB, A713.
75. Gwinner to Adams, July 20, 1901, HADB, A45.
76. Adams to Gwinner, Aug. 16, 1901, HADB, A45.
77. Gwinner to Adams, Dec. 8, 1902, HADB, A45.
78. Adams to Gwinner, Dec. 30, 1902, HADB, A45.
79. Adams to Gwinner, May 22, 1907, HADB, A47. Nevertheless, that year he rented a car and hired a chauffeur, traveling across Europe with his wife.
80. Gwinner file note to Direktion, Dec. 31, 1906, HADB, A47. Gwinner found the Kuhn Loeb people egotistical. He naturally preferred Speyers because of the tight personal relationship to the Frankfurt house Deutsche Bank had. In contrast, Kuhn Loeb had family ties to the Warburgs in Hamburg.
81. Gwinner file note to Direktion, Dec. 12, 1906, HADB, A47.
82. Adams to Gwinner, Jan. 19, 1909, HADB, A47.
83. Gwinner to Adams, Oct. 31, 1911, HADB, A46.
84. To W. Greif, at Adams office, author unclear, Nov. 11, 1911, HADB, A38. The letter indicated that it was critical that Greif avoid the impression he was sending unpleasant reports from Adams' office to Berlin.
85. Axhausen trip report, undated, HADB, A38. In case of his death, Adams' will made clear that Deutsche Bank had power to determine how his assets would be disposed.
86. Gwinner to Adams, June 20, 1914, HADB, A48. Gwinner quotes the earlier message.
87. Gwinner to Adams, Oct. 31, 1911, HADB, A46.
88. Gwinner to Adams, Feb. 28, 1913, HADB, A48.
89. Gwinner to Adams, Feb. 8, 1908, HADB, A47. Empire Engineering was using Deutsche Bank credits against Deutsche Bank's wishes.
90. Gwinner to Adams, Oct. 31, 1911, HADB, A46.
91. Lees, pp. 10–11.
92. Gwinner to Adams, June 20, 1914, HADB, A48.
93. Adams to Gwinner, Feb. 10, 1910, HADB, A47.
94. Blinzig to Marston, Aug. 15, 1908, HADB, A222. Blinzig reminded Marston of the differences between Germany and the United States. America had quick panics and corrections. In Germany, in contrast, the processes of readjustment were long and "orderly." Even though the German market was still suffering from a slowdown caused by the American crisis, there were many good reasons to invest. He advised Marston to get ahead of the curve. See various letters between the two, 1908–10, dealing with WMR, politics, and even family matters, HADB, A222.
95. Deutsche Bank, Bilanz-Inventur, Dec. 31, 1913, HADB, B302.
96. Adams to Deutsche Bank, Feb. 6, 1899, HADB, A29.
97. G. W. Wilson, Acting Commission of Internal Revenue, to Charles H. Treat, Collector, 2nd District, Jan. 24, 1899, HADB, A29.
98. Adams to Gwinner, Feb. 10, 1910, HADB, A47. Acting on Morgan's advice, for example, Adams had purchased United States Steel shares at less than $30. As the price skyrocketed, Adams sat on a paper profit of $2 million. He added another packet of shares, bringing his average price to $92. With the threatened antitrust investigation of United States Steel, the price of his shares tumbled. Morgan refused to make a market and Adams sold off a substantial number of shares at $75.
99. Adams to Gwinner, March 26, 1908, HADB, A47.
100. Gwinner to Mount Stephen, Oct. 24, 1903, HADB, A434.
101. Strong became Governor of the New York Federal Reserve Bank in October 1914.
102. Langen, p. 429.
103. Strong's trip to Europe May–June 1914, Federal Reserve Bank of New York, Strong Papers, 1000.1.
104. Ibid.
105. Strong to Schmidt, June 13, 1914, Federal Reserve Bank of New York, Strong Papers, Strong's correspondence with German bankers, 1914, 1925–28, 1130.

106. Strong's trip to Europe May–June 1914, June 13, 1914, Federal Reserve Bank of New York, Strong Papers, 1000.1.
107. Adams to Gwinner, July 13, 1914, HADB, A48.
108. Langen, p. 419.

Section II. Introduction

1. The title is an allusion to Gerald Feldman's *The Great Disorder*, which deals with German economics and politics from 1914 to 1924. The phrase might also have been applied to the whole period addressed in this section.
2. Mira Wilkins, *The History of Foreign Investment in the United States 1914–1945* (Cambridge, MA: Harvard University Press, 2004), preface.
3. Landes, *Unbound Prometheus*, p. 359.
4. Harold James, *Europe Reborn: A History, 1914–2000* (London: Pearson, 2003), pp. 26–48.
5. James, *Globalization*.
6. Cassis, *Capitals of Capital*, pp. 143–162.
7. Mark Mazower, *Dark Continent: Europe's Twentieth Century* (London: Penguin, 1998), p. 111. See Volker Berghahn, *The Americanization of German Business* (Leamington Spa: Berg, 1986), and Jonathan Zeitlin and Gary Herrigel, *Americanization and its Limits* (Oxford: Oxford University Press, 2000).
8. Ambrosius, "Staat und Wirtschaft," p. 374.
9. Average annual central government deficits as a percentage of national product went from surplus or small deficit during the period 1890–1913 to substantial deficit in most developed countries between 1919 and 1938. Ferguson, *The Cash Nexus*, p. 122. The government debt to gross national product ratios of the United Kingdom, the United States, and Germany were all below 60 percent in 1912. By 1928, those of the United Kingdom and Germany were well over 100 percent. Ferguson, p. 126. By the 1920s, debt servicing in both the United Kingdom and Germany was nearly 50 percent of government expenditures.
10. Walter Hook, *Die wirtschaftliche Entwicklung der ehemaligen Deutschen Bank im Spiegel ihrer Bilanzen* (Heidelberg: Winter, 1954), Tafel 5.
11. See Christopher Kobrak and Per Hansen, *European Business, Dictatorship and Political Risk: 1920–1945* (New York: Berghahn Books, 2004), and Jones, *Multinationals*, pp. 80–87.

9. Personal, Communication, and Financial Breakdowns

1. Cassis, *Capitals of Capital*, pp. 143–145.
2. Blinzig to Marston, Sept. 10, 1914, HADB, A223.
3. Blinzig to Marston, March 15, 1915, HADB, A223.
4. Schmidt to Blinzig, May 10, 1915, HADB, A464.
5. Marston to Blinzig, April 30, 1915, HADB, A223.
6. See, for example, Blinzig to Marston, Jan. 19, 1920, HADB, A223. Blinzig thanks Marston for his New Year greetings.
7. Blinzig to Marston, January 19, 1920, HADB, A223. McClement was already handling the WMR problems, which had caused so many difficulties between Deutsche Bank and Adams.
8. Langen, p. 426.
9. Gwinner to McClement, July 27, 1914, HADB, A1027.
10. Adams to Gwinner, Nov. 2, 1914, HADB, A457. Adams enclosed a list of eleven letters to which he had had no response. Most of the letters were in Deutsche Bank's files, but it is hard to know when they got there. Only his name appearing on the list of steamship arrivals alerted Adams to seek Schmidt out at the dock in November 1914.
11. Adams to Gwinner, Dec. 9, 1914, HADB, A457.
12. Adams to Gwinner, Jan. 28, 1915, HADB, A457.
13. Schmidt to Blinzig, Dec. 23, 1914, HADB, A1027.
14. Ibid.
15. Blinzig to Schmidt, Jan. 15, 1915, HADB, A1027.

16. Schmidt to Blinzig, Feb. 16, 1915, HADB, A1027. Marston asked the question at a breakfast with Adams and Schmidt. Schmidt had to wait until Adams left the table to explain the situation as he saw it.
17. Schmidt to Blinzig, Feb. 16, 1915, HADB, A1027. McClement, who had his offices at 165 Broadway, was not popular with everyone. On one occasion, James Speyer complained bitterly about how McClement had handled Deutsche Bank's request that McClement join the B&O board. In fairness to McClement, his rejection on that occasion by Willard, the president of the B&O, seemed to be a result of how Deutsche Bank itself had communicated with the parties and the bank's diminished importance to the railroad, an assessment the bank seemed to accept. Although McClement performed several tasks for Deutsche Bank, their relationship never seemed as deep or as broad as Adams' with the bank. Blinzig to Schmidt, March 15, 1915, HADB, A1027.
18. Blinzig to Schmidt, July 7, 1915, HADB, A464. The letter discusses a wide range of business issues, the resolution of which, because of the distance, seemed increasingly hard to realize.
19. Schmidt to Blinzig, June 25, 1915, HADB, A464.
20. Deutsche Bank to Schmidt, Jan. 12, 1916, HADB, A464. See also, Schmidt to Blinzig, Jan. 13, 1915 (I believe that the date of 1915 is in error; it is sandwiched between other January 1916 correspondence), HADB, A464.
21. Schmidt to Blinzig, Feb. 14, 1916, HADB, A464.
22. Schmidt to Deutsche Bank Berlin, Jan. 30, 1915, HADB, A464.
23. Ibid. See also the copy of attestation of American Management and Control for insurance purposes as well as *Abschrift*, addressed to Adams, Nov. 14, 1914 about payment for nominee (trustee) A. C. Woodman, approved by Gwinner. Discussing cloaking operations, Deutsche Bank was more careful to use codes.
24. Schmidt to Blinzig, Jan. 13, 1915 (I believe that the date of 1915 is in error; it is sandwiched between other January 1916 correspondence), HADB, A464.
25. Deutsche Bank to Schmidt, Jan. 17, 1916, HADB, A35.
26. Adams file note, Jan. 7, 1916, HADB, A35.
27. Adams to Deutsche Bank, Feb. 16, 1916, HADB, A35. This letter was written with small print and lines very close together, reflecting the wartime necessity to conserve space in shipments of letters.
28. Robert K. Massie, *Castles of Steel: Britain, Germany, and the Winning of the Great War at Sea* (New York: Random House, 2003), pp. 77 and 162.
29. Gwinner and Blinzig to Axhausen, Sept. 5, 1914, HADB, A460.
30. Deutsche Bank to National City Bank, Sept. 26, 1914, HADB, A460.
31. Deutsche Bank to Credit Suisse, Nov. 27, 1914, HADB, A460. Among other early glitches, on a few occasions – probably confused by the number of accounts Credit Suisse had with First National City Bank – transactions were booked to the wrong Credit Suisse New York account.
32. Langen, pp. 335–341.
33. Langen, pp. 341–347.
34. Langen, pp. 348–349.
35. Deutsche Bank Berlin to Munich branch, Aug. 18, 1914, HADB, A461.
36. Deutsche Bank London branch to Credit Suisse, Aug. 7, 1914, HADB, A462, and *The Times*, Aug. 8, 1914.
37. Luchsinger & Co. to Axhausen, Sept. 8, 1914, HADB, A462, and *The Times*, Aug. 13, 1914.
38. Langen, pp. 350–363.
39. Several letters, Axhausen to Deutsche Bank, Berlin, August–September 1914, HADB, A461.
40. Deutsche Bank to Axhausen, Aug. 24, 1914, HADB, A459.
41. Deutsche Bank to Schmidt, April 27, 1915, HADB, A464.
42. Edward Adams, New York Kontobestand, no date, but among letters from fall 1914, HADB, A41. When the war began, Adams was holding on to nearly $1 million (3.9 million Mark) in securities. Most of the securities were in railroad and mining and coal processing shares. The bank's Western Maryland Railroad interests alone were worth nearly 2 million Mark. Lehigh

Coke was valued at 0.6 million Mark. Notably, none of Deutsche Bank's Allis-Chalmers pool shares and electric investments were on the list.

43. Axhausen to Deutsche Bank, Aug. 15, 1914, HADB, A459.
44. *The Times*, Aug. 26, 1916. The report is not clear, whether the two were arrested in New York for the letters or the jewels they were also smuggling. The article does make a lot of the secret organization of converging letters and Hugo Schmidt's role in the affair.
45. Adams to Foreign Exchange Department, The Merchants Loan & Trust Company, Nov. 14, 1914, HADB, A41.
46. Deutsche Bank to Adams, Dec. 28, 1914, HADB, A41.
47. Deutsche Bank (Gwinner and Blinzig) to Axhausen, Sept. 5, 1914, HADB, A461. A risk involved in this arrangement was the prompting of hostile feelings between Germany and Switzerland. Deutsche Bank was eager to settle a dispute that arose between the *Berliner Tageblatt* and the *Neue Zürcher Zeitung* over "anti-German sentiments." Deutsche Bank to Axhausen, Sept. 18, 1914, HADB, A461.
48. Wilkins, *1914–1945*, pp. 1–4.
49. *New York Times*, May 21, 1916.
50. Various newspaper articles, generally unnamed journals, HADB, A2.
51. "War Loans Now Nearly Sixteen Billion Dollars," *Wall Street Journal*, July 15, 1915.
52. Heinrich Charles to Frank Vanderlip, president of National City Bank, Oct. 5, 1915, HADB, A2.
53. Heinrich Charles to the secretary of the treasury, Sept. 6, 1915, HADB, A2. On Sept. 14, 1915, Charles reminded W. G. McAdoo, the secretary of the treasury, of the administration's pledge at the beginning of the war not to allow either side to borrow extensively in the United States. He hoped that a new loan request of $1 billion would be vetoed, to no avail. HADB, A2.
54. Heinrich Charles to James Hill, Sept. 15, 1915, HADB, A2.
55. Heinrich Charles to James Hill, Sept. 16, 1915, HADB, A2.
56. Heinrich Charles to superintendent of insurance, Albany, Oct. 6, 1915, HADB, A2
57. Wilkins, *1914–1945*, pp. 10–15.
58. Ibid.
59. Wilkins, *1914–1945*, p. 17.
60. Axhausen cable to Deutsche Bank Berlin, Sept. 7, 1914, HADB, A461, reporting an American's observation about the German food situation.
61. Wilkins, *1914–1945*, pp. 44 –45.
62. Wilkins, *1914–1945*, p. 19.
63. Various Declarations, purpose unclear, Aug. 11, 1916 by Deutsche Bank, HADB, A464.
64. Hugo Schmidt to Gwinner, March 4, 1916 (received March 27), HADB, A464.
65. Hugo Schmidt to Deutsche Bank, Feb. 17, 1916, HADB, A464.
66. Adams to Gwinner, Sept. 22, 1914, HADB, A457.
67. Adams to Gwinner, Oct. 19, 1914, HADB, A457.
68. Ibid.
69. Langen, pp. 363–397.
70. *Frankfurter Zeitung*, Oct. 14, 1916.
71. The very early stages of hostilities led to a Dollar drain. Worried about the future, Americans cut back on expenditures and companies cut back on dividends. Inflation and unemployment were mounting, and likely to continue to soar. Several letters, Adams to Deutsche Bank, fall 1914, HADB, A41. Adams was not convinced that the New York Stock Exchange could be reopened without a collapse in prices. In previous wars, neutral countries were used to handle settlements among markets. Now the United States seemed to be the only market that could perform that function, but American markets were not free from financial strains. Although the war disrupted much of the economy, it may have saved the United States from a serious recession.
72. Adams to Deutsche Bank, Oct. 5, 1914, HADB, A14.
73. *Frankfurter Zeitung*, Sept. 26, 1916.
74. *Frankfurter Zeitung*, Sept. 28, 1916.

75. *Frankfurter Zeitung*, Oct. 6, 1916.
76. Colin Simpson, *Lusitania* (Boston: Little, Brown and Company, 1972). There is a good deal of evidence that *Lusitania*, a British merchant ship, was carrying munitions, in violation of American law. Nevertheless, in the absence of proof of the German charges, an extensive British anti-German campaign in the media, the loss of life – especially American lives – coupled with the loss of a lucrative American export to Britain poisoned American–German relations and contributed to America's ultimate decision to enter the war against Germany.
77. Company Report for the years 1915–16, undated, HADB, S108
78. Internal memo, Dec. 10, 1916, HADB, S108.
79. Contract, Nov. 15, 1915, HADB, S108, various other correspondence, HADB, S108.
80. Deutsche Bank to Deutsche Ozean-Reederei, April 1, 1916, HADB, S108.
81. Unadated internal memo, HADB, S108.
82. Internal memo, Dec. 10, 1916, HADB, S108.
83. Company Report for the years 1915–16, undated, HADB, S108.
84. *Frankfurter Zeitung*, July 11, 1916.
85. Deutsche Bank to Herrmann, Sept. 5, 1923, and Deutsche Ozean-Reederei to Deutsche Bank, Dec. 15, 1925, HADB, S108.

10. War Supplies, Espionage, and Expropriation

1. Mankiewitz to Adams, Dec. 11, 1914, HADB, A527.
2. Deutsche Bank to Adams, Dec. 16, 1914, HADB, A527.
3. File Memorandum in English, Dec. 8 1914, HADB, A527.
4. Deutsche Bank to McIlvain, Dec. 30, 1913, HADB, A527.
5. Wilkins, *1914–1945*, p. 31. Wilkins relies on William McAdoo, *Crowded Years* (Boston: Houghton Mifflin, 1931), and Gerald D. Feldman, "Deutsche Bank from World War to World Economic Crisis, 1914–1933," in *The Deutsche Bank 1870–1995*, Lothar Gall et al. (London: Weidenfeld & Nicolson, 1995), pp. 154–155. The origin of the "misinterpretation," however, is an Alien Property Custodian (APC) Report, n° 14. The APC reports often contained useful information, but then proceeded to use that information in ways designed to help justify the seizure of enemy property by the U.S. government.
6. Adams to Deutsche Bank, Dec. 31, 1914, HADB, A527.
7. Adams to Deutsche Bank, Dec. 31, 1914, HADB, A527. The passages in the letter were underlined by a reader, followed by two exclamation points.
8. Axhausen file memo, Feb. 2, 1915, HADB, A507.
9. McIlvain to Deutsche Bank, Nov. 6, 1914, HADB, A527.
10. Deutsche Bank to Smith (code name for Hugo Schmidt), Feb. 11, 1915, HADB, A563.
11. Ibid.
12. Ibid. Internal documents make clear that "Smith" and "Dean" refer to Schmidt and Adams. "*Jedenfalls sollte weder Edward* [presumably Adams, my note] *noch die Herrn von der Coke Company von Ihnen erfahren, daß wir aus prinzipiellen Gründen dem Benzol-Projekt unsere Zustimmung nicht* [underlined in original] *geben können, solange der Krieg dauert.*"
13. File memo, Feb. 12, 1915, HADB, A563. Though dated after the letter to Smith, the memo seems to record a meeting that actually occurred before the letter went out to Smith. Smith was instructed to start negotiations with Bethlehem while Deutsche Bank was lining up government support for its alternative plan.
14. Mankiewitz and Wassermann to Königlich Preussisches Kriegsministerium, May 14, 1915, HADB, A563.
15. Adams to Deutsche Bank, July 14, 1915, HADB, A528.
16. Ibid.
17. Schmidt to Mankiewitz, March 23, 1915 and April 1, 1915, HADB, A505.
18. Mankiewitz to Schmidt, May 12, 1915, HADB, A505.
19. Price Waterhouse Report, Feb. 16, 1915, HADB, A527.
20. Mankiewitz to Adams, Aug. 14, 1915, HADB, A528.
21. Ibid. Message repeated in several letters and telegrams around this date.

22. Deutsche Bank to McIlvain, Sept. 1, 1915, HADB, A528.
23. Deutsche Bank to McIlvain, Sept. 8, 1915, HADB, A528.
24. Mankiewitz to Adams, Nov. 20, 1915, HADB, A528. He apologized that his duty to his country required imposing so many conditions, and implored Adams to make sure that Toluol, the most vital by-product, would be stored, not sold.
25. Various correspondence, fall 1915 and winter 1916, HADB, A529.
26. Deutsche Bank to McIlvain, March 16, 1916, HADB, A529.
27. Deutsche Bank to Adams, Jan. 28, 1916, HADB, A529.
28. Adams to Mankiewitz, July 14, 1915, HADB, A565.
29. Adams to Mankiewitz, Sept. 25, 1915, HADB, A565.
30. Contract between Lehigh Coke, Deutsche Bank, and Carl Still of Recklinghausen, Germany, Sept. 10, 1915, HADB, A564.
31. File memo, Jan. 19, 1916, HADB, A564.
32. Mankiewitz to McIlvain, Jan. 19, 1916, HADB, A564. For the chemical shortages, see Gerald D. Feldman, *Army, Industry and Labor in Germany, 1914–1918* (Oxford: Berg, 1992). In 1916, the German government began to take note of the serious shortages of raw materials, but it is hard to imagine that Benzol and its by-products were among them. According to Gerald Feldman, coal shortages, not coke gases, became acute in the winter of 1916–17 and were due largely to transportation difficulties, which would not have been alleviated by shipment from the United States, pp. 253–55.
33. Deutsche Bank to the Kriegsministerium, Feb. 1, 1916, HADB, A564.
34. *Frankfurter Zeitung*, July 23, 1916.
35. File note, Jan. 7, 1915, HADB, A505. During the first six months of the war when Lehigh had more difficulty selling its products in the United States and was storing a lot of chemicals, Deutsche Bank approached the American ambassador in Berlin and American Cynamid about the American interest in exporting sulpher, for example, to Germany.
36. Axhausen to Mankiewitz, reporting on meeting with von Papen and Caro, Feb. 14, 1916, HADB, A564.
37. Ibid.
38. Deutsche Bank to Kriegsministerium, Aug. 11, 1916, HADB, A564.
39. Axhausen file memo, Jan. 16, 1916, HADB, A506.
40. McIlvain to Deutsche Bank, Oct. 12, 1915, HADB, A529.
41. Ibid. According to Schmidt, McIlvain complained at board meetings that the Germans had little trust for local management. These comments from Berlin might have been designed to assuage his hurt feelings. According to Schmidt, at one meeting McIlvain declared that "he [McIlvain] sometimes felt he was being treated like an office boy" ("kaeme sich manchmal wie ein Office-boy vor"). Schmidt to Deutsche Bank, March 22, 1915, HADB, A505.
42. Deutsche Bank to Adams, Dec. 17, 1915, HADB, A529.
43. See several letters, HADB, A540, particularly Deutsche Bank to Süddeutsche Disconto-Gesellschaft, July 25, 1916.
44. Nordegg to Mankiewitz, Nov. 27, 1916, HADB, A508. The size of the print and closeness of the lines used in the letters during this period remind the reader of war pressures, especially the difficulty of sending messages, which were transported by submarine, a vessel in which size and weight counted even more than with normal surface craft.
45. Mankiewitz to Nordegg, Jan. 8, 1917, HADB, A508. He seems to be responding to Nordegg's late November letter. If the response took five weeks to get to New York, it arrived just days before the sale was concluded. Mankiewitz regretted that their only means of communication was by submarine messages.
46. Axhausen to Deutsche Bank, Dec. 15, 1916, HADB, A508.
47. Mankiewitz to McIlvain, Dec. 11, 1916, HADB, A530.
48. Mankiewitz to Adams, Dec. 7, 1916, HADB, A530.
49. Deutsche Bank circular, Jan. 31, 1917, HADB, A540.
50. Nordegg to Deutsche Bank, Feb. 9, 1917, HADB, A508.
51. List of shareholders Jan. 12, 1917, HADB, A541. Except for the last group – those who received shares for services, such as Bamag-Didier and Adams – the shareholders held both

common and preferred shares, but not always in the same proportion. Some, such as Adams, were on several lists.

52. Various correspondence, HADB, A536, and Didier to Deutsche Bank, Feb. 14, 1917, HADB, A541.
53. Deutsche Bank to Adams, Dec. 17, 1915, HADB, A529.
54. Deutsche Bank to Syndicate, Feb. 14, 1917, HADB, A541.
55. Gebrüder S. & M. Reitzes to Deutsche Bank, Feb. 17, 1917, HADB, A541.
56. Bamag-Didier, Feb. 21, 1917, HADB, A541. Some of the investors, such as the French and British, would not be paid until after the war, in Mark with a greatly diminished value (strange as the price was in Dollars). Deutsche Bank to Gans & Cie. and Union Corp. Ltd., March 15, 1920, HADB, A541.
57. Deutsche Bank to Adams, Dec. 23, 1915, HADB, A529.
58. Mankiewitz to Adams, Dec. 23, 1915, HADB, A529.
59. *New York Times*, Nov. 23, 1915.
60. *New York Times*, July 6, 1917.
61. Deutsche Bank to Auswärtiges Amt, Minister von Haniel, April 23, 1917, HADB, A464.
62. Note from Deutsche Bank Filialbüro, June 30, 1917, HADB, A464. The bank received a letter from Schmidt in which he indicated that no direct correspondence was allowed, especially no political news and letters from third persons. Schmidt reported that he was being constantly watched and had to adhere exactly to all orders from U.S. officials.
63. Conference in Room 501, Old Post Office Building, July 24, 1917. Present: Hugo Schmidt, representing Deutsche Bank; W. B. Conway, Guaranty Trust Co.; L. P. Reed, counsel for Guaranty Trust; F. E. Carstarphen, special asst. to the attorney general; and Dale Parker, commercial agent, department of commerce. NARA, M1085, FBI Reports, 763.72112/5227.
64. *New York Times*, Oct. 6, 1917. The assets mentioned may have included funds held in the bank's name for customers, but was still far more than the APC had actually seized (see next Chapter).
65. *New York Times*, Oct. 6, 1917.
66. *New York Times*, Oct. 8, 1917.
67. Telegram page to secretary of state in Washington, Nov. 7, 1917, NARA, State Department Records, 13/60.
68. *New York Times*, Jan. 20, 1918.
69. Ibid.
70. *New York Times*, Jan. 21, 1918.
71. The author, as well as Mira Wilkins, tried together with U.S. federal and New York state archives to locate the missing documents to no avail. There are several possibilities. The documents may have been stored but not indexed, destroyed, or returned to Deutsche Bank and then mixed with files that are in Deutsche Bank's possession. In any case, many of the letters would have been on file in Berlin. In addition to these files, the reader should be aware that there are many records at the NARA, indexed and which pertain to these matters that have disappeared.
72. *New York Times*, Feb. 4, 1918.
73. *New York Times*, Nov. 3, 1918.
74. *New York Times*, Dec. 21, 1918.
75. *Wall Street Journal*, Sept. 4, 1919.
76. Wilkins, *1914–1945*, p. 79.
77. Wilkins, *1914–1945*, p. 48.
78. A.W. Lafferty, the attorney for several property holders such as Stollwerck, to APC, March 17, 1922, HADB, A1035. The Connecticut chocolate factory of Stollwerck Brothers of Cologne, for example, was seized and sold, with a million Dollars in cash kept by the APC for an extensive period.
79. Wilkins, *1914–1945*, pp. 63–65.
80. Ralph Izard of the justice department, Milwaukee, to A. B. Bielaski, Department of Justice, Washington, Jan. 29, 1918, NARA, RG65, M1085, Federal Bureau of Investigation, Old

German Files, OG 148. The President of Allis-Chalmers reported that Adams had represented Deutsche Bank on that company's board and was succeeded by McClement, although neither of the individuals nor Deutsche Bank had a controlling interest in the company. The B&O railroad reported that Deutsche Bank held $181,609 in six months of dividends on 74,126 common shares of stock.

81. Wilkins, *1914–1945*, p. 72. There are the reported structures, but German efforts to cloak ownership make the numbers hard to assess. See Christopher Kobrak and Jana Wüstenhagen, "International Investment and Nazi Politics: The Cloaking of German Assets Abroad, 1936–1945," *Business History*, Vol. 48 (2006), no. 3, pp. 399–427.
82. Wilkins, *1914–1945*, p. 80.
83. Ralph Izard of the Justice Department, Milwaukee, to A. B. Bielaski, Department of Justice, Washington, Jan. 29, 1918, NARA, RG65, M1085, Federal Bureau of Investigation, Old German Files, OG 148.
84. Special Report, agent Frank Stone, Aug. 17, 1917, NARA, RG65, M1085, Federal Bureau of Investigation, Old German Files, OG 148.
85. Report, J. F. Kropidlowski, Nov. 24, 1917, Department of Justice, Washington, Jan. 29, 1918, NARA, RG65, M1085, Federal Bureau of Investigation, Old German Files, OG 148.
86. Letter on Neutrality Matters, March 3, 1915, NARA, RG65, M1085, Federal Bureau of Investigation, Old German Files, OG 148.
87. File memo, Nov. 24, 1917, prepared by J. F. Kropidlowski, for APC, NARA, RG65, M1085, Federal Bureau of Investigation, Old German Files, OG 148.
88. File memo, Dec. 18, 1917, NARA, RG65, M1085, Federal Bureau of Investigation, Old German Files, OG 148.
89. File memo, Dec. 20, 1917, NARA, RG65, M1085, Federal Bureau of Investigation, Old German Files, OG 148.
90. File memo, Dec. 18, 1917, NARA, RG65, M1085, Federal Bureau of Investigation, Old German Files, OG 148.
91. Bergmann to Blinzig, Oct. 3, 1921, HADB, A1034. Bergmann was in New York at the time.
92. Deutsche Bank to Wilhelm Schmidt, Aug. 18, 1922, HADB, A1034.

11. Salvaging Assets and Business Prospects in the War's Immediate Aftermath

1. Christopher Kobrak, *National Cultures*, pp. 67–69. Although the precise impact of peace and the actual reparations is of great historical debate, there is little doubt that the payments as outlined in 1921 had a disruptive effect on Germany's political and economic life. See Gerald D. Feldman et al., eds., *The Treaty of Versailles: A Reassessment after 75 Years* (Cambridge: Cambridge University Press, 1998).
2. Charles H. Feinstein, Peter Temin, and Gianni Toniolo, "International Economic Organization: Banking, Finance, and Trade in Europe between the Wars," in *Banking, Currency, and Finance in Europe between the Wars*, ed. Charles Feinstein (Oxford: Clarendon Press, 1995), p. 14.
3. Gerd Hardach, "Banking in Germany, 1918–1939," in *Banking, Currency, and Finance in Europe between the Wars*, pp. 269–295.
4. Arthur von Gwinner, "Who Were the War Criminals of 1914?," *Current History*, Vol. 26, no. 2, May 1927, pp. 241–244.
5. Invitation, HADB, A35.
6. Management board to Adams, April 8, 1925, HADB, A35.
7. "The Debt of Engineering to Edward Adams," *Electrical World*, April 3, 1926, Vol. 87. The committee credited Adams with demonstrating the possibility of generating and transmitting multiphase alternating currents on a large scale. Adams' great contribution was to have put together thirty-five years earlier a group of eminent international engineers to solve a multitude of technical problems.
8. Adams to Deutsche Bank, March 29, 1929, HADB, A35.
9. Adams to Gwinner, Dec. 10, 1930, HADB, A35.

10. For the defining study of the period see Gerald D. Feldman, *The Great Disorder: Politics, Economics, and Society in the German Inflation, 1914–1924* (Oxford: Oxford University Press, 1993).
11. Harold James, *The German Slump* (Oxford: Clarendon Press, 1986).
12. C. H. Feinstein et al., "Banking, Finance, and Trade in Europe," in Charles H. Feinstein, ed., *Banking, Currency, and Finance in Europe between the Wars* (Oxford: Clarendon Press, 1995), p. 10.
13. Wilkins, *1914–1945*, pp. 183–185.
14. *New York Times*, Nov. 25, 1924. Soon after the Dawes loans became available, J. Henry Schroder & Co. of London and Speyer & Co. of New York bought 40,000 gold Mark shares of Deutsche Bank common ($10 million at par), nearly one-third of Deutsche Bank's total share capital, which they ostensibly sold into their respective markets.
15. *New York Times*, June 21, 1929.
16. Wilkins, *1914–1945*, pp. 166–176. Although a 1911 act permitted foreign banks to establish "licensed agencies," Deutsche Bank kept only a small administrative office in New York. The act forbade foreign banks from taking deposits, but they could conduct other banking business such as Dollar acceptances, which were beginning to compete seriously with Sterling acceptances, and trade foreign exchange. By the end of 1923, there were thirty-eight such agencies of foreign banks, including Italian, Japanese, Polish, Romanian, and South African banks. No German bank chose to establish an agency.
17. Wilkins, *1914–1945*, p. 294.
18. Deutsche Bank to Schmidt, June 8, 1921, HADB, A1031.
19. Schmidt to Deutsche Bank, July 27, 1921, HADB, A1031.
20. Ibid.
21. Ibid. See also Schmidt to Blinzig, July 28, 1921, HADB, A1031. Schmidt wrote two letters about Schwab's visit, seemingly because when Alwin Krech, president of Equitable Trust visited, neither Gwinner nor Mankiewitz were in Berlin to greet him.
22. Deutsche Bank to Schuchard in New York, June 11, 1920, HADB, A1027.
23. Francis Caffey to Hugo Schmidt, July 8, 1920, HADB, A1027.
24. Bergmann to Blinzig, Oct. 3, 1921, HADB, A1034. Bergmann was in New York at the time. In 1921, the office employed a staff of twelve.
25. Various correspondence, March 1922 through June 1924, HADB, A1027. See Blinzig to Bergmann, April 4, 1924, for the final decision. Wilhelm went over Hugo's head to Blinzig with complaints about how the New York office was being run and about the importance of his own work. Later, he vilified his eventual successor. Bergmann came to Hugo Schmidt's defense, and Blinzig's own independent investigations about the situation convinced him that Wilhelm was unstable, probably still suffering from the effects of his military service. The ruckus lasted several months. Despite his knowledge of the files, experience with the APC, and vigorous defense directed through Blinzig, Deutsche Bank repatriated him to Germany after Wilhelm spent some vacation time traveling in the United States.
26. Undated list, HADB, A209. The average was about fifteen shares.
27. Schmidt to Deutsche Bank, Nov. 13 and Nov. 30, 1925, HADB, A1030.
28. Internal memo, Dec. 16, 1925, HADB, A1030.
29. Deutsche Bank to Schmidt, March 18, 1926, HADB, A1030.
30. About the rumors, see Deutsche Bank to Schmidt, Feb. 3, 1927; about the founding of a new German company in the United States, HADB, A1032.
31. Blinzig to the Deutsche Bank management board, April 28, 1927, HADB, A685.
32. Wilkins, *1914–1945*, p. 189.
33. Wilkins, *1914–1945*, pp. 190–191.
34. Wilkins, *1914–1945*, pp. 81–95.
35. Wilkins, *1914–1945*, pp. 121 and 166–167.
36. Wilkins, *1914–1945*, pp. 166–167 and 180–183.
37. Wilkins, *1914–1945*, p. 195.
38. Wilkins, *1914–1945*, p. 215.
39. Wilkins, *1914–1945*, p. 447.
40. Wilkins, *1914–1945*, p. 114.

41. Wilkins, *1914–1945*, p. 123. Wilkins is a notable exception.
42. See reconciliation sheets, March 15, 1921, HADB, A1034.
43. Deutsche Bank to Schmidt, Jan. 10, 1923, HADB, A171. This particular tome was fifteen pages long.
44. Wilhelm Schmidt to Deutsche Bank, April 4, 1923, HADB, A172.
45. Deutsche Bank to Schmidt, March 16, 1921, HADB, A171. See also Schmidt to Deutsche Bank, April 19, 1921.
46. Schmidt to Deutsche Bank, Feb. 17, 1921, HADB, A171.
47. Blinzig to Eugen Meyer, Sept. 25, 1919, HADB, A1369. The plight of small investors' accounts was perhaps best illustrated by a letter from Blinzig to a Swiss friend living in Berlin who had held securities in New York with Deutsche Bank. The friend's initial application for release of the securities had been rejected even though he was Swiss, merely because he lived in Germany. Under the terms of the Peace Treaty, America had the right to sell German property and use the proceeds to, eventually, settle up with the German government. The exchange rate to be used and other details, however, had not been worked out. Blinzig was cautiously optimistic with his friend that America would not exercise this right and would eventually return the property, but no one knew when. He advised his friend to try again to prove that he was Swiss, which required signing and sending four enclosed forms and proof of his citizenship, all notarized, to the United States.
48. Numerous letters between Deutsche Bank and the B&O, 1921–30, HADB, A170. As late as April 1930 Deutsche Bank lobbied the Ministry of Finance to restore B&O shares. Reminding the officials of the importance of the 1904 listing to German interests, Deutsche Bank once again argued that it would add to German prestige and ultimately bring in foreign exchange. For German readers, this period of American financial history is best compared with that of determining ownership and property rights after German reunification in 1990, except the former owners in the American case were foreigners with whom the country had just fought a war.
49. Schmidt to Blinzig, July 28, 1921, HADB, A1031.
50. As late as Jan. 24, 1922, Speyer battled the government on behalf of Bankers Trust not to be required to turn over securities held by the Trust company for clients of Speyer. APC to Speyer, Jan. 24, 1922, HADB, A1035.
51. *New York Times*, April 9, 1923.
52. Lafferty to August Merckens, Reed Chocolate Co., March 9, 1922, HADB, A1035.
53. See several letters between Morgan and Deutsche Bank, June and July 1907, HADB, A169. In 1897, among the many agreements entered into by the two banks regarding the affairs of the Northern Pacific was one to share the responsibility of serving as transfer agent for payments on the railroad's securities. All fees were to be split, two-thirds for Morgan, one-third for Deutsche Bank. As early as 1907, Morgan disputed the agreement claiming that its share of the transaction called for a revaluation of the split. After several exchanges of letters in which Deutsche Bank clearly proved that the contract was to run until the Northern Pacific securities matured, Morgan backed off and issued an apology for bringing the whole matter up.
54. Deutsche Bank to Schmidt, March 18, 1921, HADB, A169.
55. Schmidt to Blinzig, April 21, 1921, HADB, A169. A curious comment for the bank's representative to make. It is not clear whether the activities were "espionage related" or had to do with something else.
56. Bergmann to Deutsche Bank, Nov. 23, 1923, HADB, A169.
57. Internal memo, Deutsche Bank, Abteilung Friedensvertrag, to Blinzig, Dec. 7, 1923, HADB, A169. It is interesting that Deutsche Bank had a whole department for the Peace Treaty.
58. Various correspondence between Bergmann and Deutsche Bank, mid-December 1923, HADB, A169.
59. Internal memo, Deutsche Bank, Abteilung Friedensvertrag, to Blinzig, Dec. 28, 1923, HADB, A169. The Supreme Court found that certain insurance contracts were merely suspended, not dissolved, by the war legislation.
60. Legal opinion of Franklin Nevius, Kellogg & Rose, April 30, 1924, HADB, A169. As evidence of the cost of litigation, the bill for the twelve-page opinion came to $1,500, around $17,000

in today's money, a little over $1,400 a page. Schmidt negotiated the final bill down to $1,000. See various correspondence, HADB, A169.

61. Letter from Bergmann in Germany to Schmidt, Feb. 1, 1924, HADB, A169.
62. Letter from Deutsche Bank to J. P. Morgan & Co., March 8, 1927, HADB, A1149.
63. Deutsche Bank to Morgan, March 8, 1927, HADB, A169. An understanding of history counts.
64. Blinzig to Deutsche Bank, April 27, 1927, HADB, A169.
65. Abschrift, APC beschlagnahmten Deutsche Bank Bestände, May 21, 1924, HADB, A1371.
66. APC to Guaranty Trust, Nov. 28, 1923, HADB, A1028.
67. Schmidt to Deutsche Bank, May 29, 1923, HADB, A1028, and Bergmann, who was in New York, to Deutsche Bank Berlin, Dec. 18, 1923, HADB, A1029. Even though the APC acknowledged that Guaranty Trust had indicated it wanted to sell one packet of shares on behalf of Deutsche Bank in May 1919, the first record of a direct discussion of a sale between the APC and Deutsche Bank came in May 1923, precisely four years later.
68. Schmidt to APC, March 7, 1924, HADB, A1029.
69. APC to Schmidt, Feb. 17, 1927, HADB, A1029.
70. Schmidt to Deutsche Bank, Feb. 1, 1924, HADB, A1029. This whole issue seems to have caused some conflict with Speyer.
71. Schmidt to Deutsche Bank, Feb. 20, 1924, HADB, A1029. Here Schmidt is confirming the bank's cables to him.
72. Schmidt to Deutsche Bank, March 12, 1927, HADB, A1033.
73. *New York Times*, Feb. 11, 1927.
74. Schmidt to Deutsche Bank, Feb. 19, 1924, HADB, A1029.
75. Schmidt to Deutsche Bank, June 28, 1924, HADB, A1029.
76. Schmidt to Deutsche Bank, March 5, 1923, HADB, A1028.
77. Schmidt to Deutsche Bank, March 21, 1924, HADB, A1029.
78. Thos. Bradley to Deutsche Bank, June 30, 1923, HADB, A1028.
79. Schmidt to Deutsche Bank, March 23, 1923, HADB, A1028.
80. Schmidt to Deutsche Bank, March 5, 1923, HADB, A1028. Excerpts from the first APC report, provided by Schmidt to Deutsche Bank.
81. Lafferty to APC, March 17, 1922, HADB, A1035.
82. Whaley-Eaton Service to clients, March 12, 1928, HADB, A5.
83. "Analysis of the Settlement of War Claims Act of 1928," Carl G. Grossman, Compliments of International Germanic Trust Company, HADB, A5.
84. Annual Report of the Alien Property Custodian 1928, Feb. 14, 1929, U.S. Government Printing Office, Washington, D.C., HADB, A177.
85. Schmidt to Deutsche Bank, June 6, 1923, HADB, A172.
86. Schmidt to Deutsche Bank, Jan. 13 and Jan. 19, 1928, and Lafferty to Schnitzler, April 21, 1928, HADB, A4.
87. Schmidt to Deutsche Bank, Oct. 9, 1928, HADB, A6.
88. Deutsche Bank to Schmidt, Oct. 31, 1928, HADB, A1033.
89. Schmidt to Deutsche Bank, Dec. 21, 1928, HADB, A 1033.
90. Deutsche Bank to Schmidt, Feb. 6, 1929, HADB, A1033.
91. Schmidt to Deutsche Bank, April 11, 1928, HADB, A1030. See also Deutsche Bank to Schmidt, Jan. 22, 1927, HADB, A1032.
92. Kobrak and Wüstenhagen, "International Investment and Nazi Politics."

12. Deutsche Bank and Rebuilding Cross-Border Financial Flows

1. File note, Sept. 13, 1927, HADB, S4382. Schacht was not always so accommodating with Deutsche Bank. In December 1929, he put the kibosh on a $75 million credit for the Reichsbahn and Reichspost, upon which the bank had been working for nearly nine months with Dillon Read, Bankers Trust, and Harris Forbes. Perhaps the times or customers made a significant difference for the president of the Reichsbank. Several letters among the participants, 1929, HADB, S2719.

2. "The German Problem" by Max Warburg, Confidential – Not to be published. Undated, but probably sometime in late 1920. Federal Reserve Bank of New York, Correspondence Files, Strong Papers, Warburg to Strong, 1918–28, No. 120.
3. Ibid. Warburg was quick to add wisely that the United States could not help Europe unless Europe was willing to help itself. Much of the paper deals with Germany's desperate situation and the unwillingness of other European countries to recognize or react to the gravity of the situation. Unlike Germany after the French defeat in 1871, the French were demanding reparations while doing little to preserve Germany's ability to pay. Moreover, even the greatly reduced reparations bill of $32 billion represented 40 percent of the country's asset value.
4. Schacht to Paul Warburg, May 31, 1924, Federal Reserve Bank of New York, Correspondence Files, Strong Papers, Warburg to Strong, 1918–28, No. 120.
5. William McNeil, *American Money and the Weimar Republic* (New York: Columbia University Press, 1986).
6. Centralverband des Deutschen Bank- und Bankiergewerbes, Circular No. 103, Dec. 11, 1925, HADB, A177.
7. Conversations with Schacht, July 22, 1925, Federal Reserve Bank of New York, Correspondence Files, Strong Papers, Strong's Trip, July 7–30, 1925, No. 1000.6.
8. Strong's Discussions at the Reichsbank, Drs. Schacht and Luther, and Mr. Stresemann, July 11, 1925, Federal Reserve Bank of New York, Correspondence Files, Strong Papers, Strong's Trip, July 7–30, 1925, No. 1000.6.
9. Strong to Jay, July 20, 1925, Federal Reserve Bank of New York, Correspondence Files, Strong Papers, Strong's Trip, July 7–30, 1925, No. 1000.6. Although the Reichsbank reserve covered a great deal of its outstanding currency, the foreign exchange drain on those reserves through mid-1925 was considerable. Capital flight would surely speed up if Germany and France could not come to some reasonable conclusion and long-term loans could not be arranged.
10. Strong to Jay, July 20, 1925, Federal Reserve Bank of New York, Correspondence Files, Strong Papers, Strong's Trip, July 7–30, 1925, No. 1000.6.
11. Gerald D. Feldman, "Deutsche Bank from World War to World Economic Crisis, 1914–1933," p. 225.
12. Wilkins, *1914–1945*, pp. 120–121.
13. Wilkins, *1914–1945*, pp. 186–189.
14. File note, May 3, 1923, HADB, S2718. See the *Frankfurter Zeitung* for a discussion of the value and purpose of the borrowing. March 30, 1923.
15. National City Bank of New York to Schmidt, Nov. 24, 1924, HADB, A1029.
16. Schmidt to Deutsche Bank, Dec. 29, 1924, HADB, A1030.
17. Frederick H. Brandi to Schmidt, April 12, 1929, HADB, A1030.
18. Brunswig memo to Millington-Herrmann, no date, HADB, S4371.
19. George Garvy, "Rivals and Interlopers in the History of the New York Security Market," *Journal of Political Economy*, Vol. 52 (1944), no. 2, pp. 139–141.
20. *New York Times*, Dec. 13, 1928.
21. Blinzig to Deutsche Bank in Berlin, April 15, 1927, HADB, A1352.
22. Blinzig to Deutsche Bank in Berlin, April 23, 1927, HADB, A1352.
23. Deutsche Bank to Dillon Read, Dec. 4, 1926, HADB, A1036.
24. *Evening Herald*, May 13, 1927.
25. Blinzig to Deutsche Bank Berlin, April 11, 1927, HADB, A1352.
26. Institute of International Finance, conducted by the Investment Bankers Association of American in Cooperation with New York University, Nov. 7, 1928, No. 19, HADB, A1033.
27. Schmidt to Deutsche Bank, Oct. 9, 1930, HADB, A1033. Nevertheless, even after the Crash two years later, according to Schmidt, American investors were not panicked about conditions in Germany. A year after Black Friday Schmidt wrote Berlin that, despite the weakness of German capital markets and the decline of German bonds in the United States, he expected no credit restrictions or further withdrawals of American deposits.
28. Various letters, U.S. Treasury, NARA, RG111, Box 157.
29. Gerald D. Feldman, "Foreign Penetration of German Enterprises after World War I: The Problem of Ueberfremdung," in Alice Teichova et al., *Historical Studies in International Corporate Business* (Cambridge: Cambridge University Press, 2002), pp. 87–110.

30. "Investment of American Capital in Germany," two memos, "Banks and Trust Companies" and "Industrial Enterprises," no exact date, but they appear to have been sent to the State Department in January 1920 by Frederick J. Schussel, former vice consul in Munich after his return from Germany. Schussel was born in Germany and appears to be one of those American citizens who attempted to make money representing Germans in America or Americans in Germany after World War I. NARA, RG 59, 862516/419.
31. Ibid.
32. United Nations, *International Capital Movements During the Inter-war Period* (Lake Success: Arno Press, 1949), p. 11.
33. United Nations, p. 31.
34. Christopher Kobrak, "Foreign-Currency Transactions and the Recovery of German Industry in the Aftermath of World War I," *Accounting, Business & Financial History*, Vol. 12 (2002), no. 1, pp. 25–42.
35. Harold James, *The Nazi Dictatorship and the Deutsche Bank* (Cambridge: Cambridge University Press, 2004), p. 3.
36. In 1929 and 1930, Dillon Read was third behind Morgan and Kuhn Loeb in syndicate lead management. News release, HADB, A1033.
37. Robert Sobel, *The Life and Times of Dillon Read* (New York: Truman Talley Books, 1991), pp. 28–43.
38. Eberstadt to Schlieper, Deutsche Bank, April 24, 1930, HADB, A411. By this time, Eberstadt was ensconced in his new offices at 39 Rue Cambon in Paris.
39. 1929 annual report and *New York Times*, Jan. 11, 1930, HADB, A411. The fund later became a target of legislative investigation.
40. *New York Times*, Dec. 13, 1925, HADB, A411.
41. Schmidt to Deutsche Bank, July 6, 1920, HADB, A411.
42. Ralph Bollard to Mankiewitz, Oct. 21, 1920, HADB, A411.
43. Axhausen to Wassermann, Feb. 21, 1928, HADB, A411.
44. Sobel, pp. 98–118.
45. See *Wall Street Journal*, Oct. 4, 1933, for discussion of the Pecora investigation of the trust. The charges seemed to have come to nothing.
46. Eberstadt to Wassermann, Aug. 1, 1927, HADB, S4382. For a three-year facility of $20 million, Eberstadt reckoned on a price of 98 and a coupon of 6 percent, for five years a price of 96.75 with the same coupon.
47. Schmidt to Deutsche Bank, Sept. 9, 1927, HADB, A1029. During the first week of September, Berlin managers communicated about its planning to Schmidt in New York and to the Reichsbank.
48. Deutsche Bank to Schacht, Sept. 9, 1927, HADB, S4382.
49. Schacht to Wassermann, Sept. 13, 1927, HADB, S4382. For a facsimile see Seidenzahl, between pp. 260 and 261.
50. *New York Times*, Nov. 11, 1927.
51. Deutsche Bank to Dillon Read, Sept. 13, 1927, HADB, S4382.
52. Schmidt to Deutsche Bank, Nov. 4, 1927, HADB, S4382.
53. *Wall Street Journal*, Sept. 9, 1927, HADB, S4383.
54. Deutsche Bank filing for American Participation Certificates, $25 million loan, adopted by the Governing Committee, Nov. 10, 1927, HADB, S4383.
55. Agreement for listing, Oct. 25, 1927, HADB, S4383.
56. Feldman, "Deutsche Bank from World War to World Economic Crisis," p. 229.
57. Deutsche Bank circular, Sept. 28, 1927, HADB, S4382.
58. Deutsche Bank circular, Sept. 30, 1927, HADB, S4382.
59. Deutsche Bank circular, Oct. 11, 1927, HADB, S4382.
60. Deutsche Bank to Dillon Read, Aug. 4, 1931, HADB, S4410.

13. Deutsche Bank and the Collapse of the Fragile World Order

1. Feldman, "The Deutsche Bank from World War to World Economic Crisis," pp. 230–236.
2. *New York Times*, Sept. 27, 1929.

3. "Fusion of Two Largest German Banks," Consulate Reports, Nov. 5, 1929, NARA, RG 59, 862516/419.
4. Ibid.
5. Ibid.
6. *New York Times*, Oct. 30, 1929.
7. Consul Report, April 2, 1925, NARA, RG 59, 862516/419.
8. Deutsche Bank filing for American Participation Certificates, $25 million loan, adopted by the Governing Committee, Nov. 10, 1927, HADB, S4383.
9. File note, Waller, Jan. 31, 1930, HADB, A 1355.
10. John Stahl (Bankers Trust) to Schlieper, July 14, 1930, HADB, A1355.
11. File note, Schlieper, June 2, 1931, HADB, A1355.
12. *Wall Street Journal*, Jan. 12, 1934, HADB, A1355.
13. *New York Times*, March 8, 1930. Just before the Reichstag debates over the plan, he announced that it was not workable as conceived and that he could not guarantee fulfillment of the Reichsbank's commitments under its terms. Coming at a time during which there were already acrimonious debates, his decision was highly criticized in many quarters. Nevertheless, some German newspapers, such as the *Vossische Zeitung*, the *Deutsche Allgemeine Zeitung*, and the *Berliner Tageblatt* had mixed feelings about Schacht's resignation. They pointed out that Wall Street had reacted with equanimity to the announcement, that Schacht's views over the past few months seemed less and less sound, and that the crisis and fears that were created even among the left-wing parties might lead to fruitful discussion about how to handle the reparations issues. Colletion of news reports, Federal Reserve Bank of New York, Policy and Procedures, 1926–30, C261.
14. Address by Hans Luther, delivered at the press reception of the Leipzig Fair, March 1, 1931, Druckerei der Reichsbank, Berlin (English translation).
15. Telegram from Federal Reserve Bank New York to Luther, June 24, 1931, Federal Reserve Bank of New York, Policy and Procedures, C261.
16. Wilkins, *1914–1945*, p. 307.
17. Telegram from Harrison to Luther, June 25, 1931, Federal Reserve Bank of New York, Policy and Procedures, C261.
18. Telegram from Reichsbank to Federal Reserve Bank New York, July 4, 1931, Federal Reserve Bank of New York, Policy and Procedures, C261. July 4 was a Saturday. The telegram was received on Sunday, July 5, a measure of the seriousness of the situation. The revolving credit line was to last until July 1, 1932. The participants received a commitment fee of 1.25 percent for two years paid in advance with the fund managers. The interest share was 100 basis points above the Federal Reserve Board's ninety-day commercial bill rate.
19. Wilkins, *1914–1945*, p. 307.
20. Wilkins, *1914–1945*, pp. 316–317.
21. Wilkins, *1914–1945*, p. 429.
22. For an excellent discussion of the evolution of Standstill negotiations and their political significance, see Neil Forbes, "London Banks, the German Standstill Agreements, and 'Economic Appeasement' in the 1930s," *Economic History Review*, Vol. 40 (1987), no. 4, pp. 571–587.
23. Neil Forbes, "London Banks."
24. Neil Forbes, *Doing Business with the Nazis: Britain's Economic and Financial Relations with Germany 1931–1939* (London: Frank Cass, 2000), pp. 33–46.
25. Deutscher Reichsanzeiger, Feb. 18, 1932.
26. Forbes, *Doing Business with the Nazis*, pp. 33–46.
27. H. G. P. Deans of Continental Illinois Bank and Trust Company to Schlieper, Oct. 11, 1932, HADB, P10396.
28. Schlieper to Deans, Oct. 25, 1932, HADB, P10396.
29. See statement prepared by W. Beutner and F. Kempner about what could be done with blocked funds, (no date), HADB, S4393.
30. Sales Bulletin received Aug. 20, 1932 in Berlin, probably put out by Dillon Read, HADB, S4391.
31. Deutsche Bank to Sullivan & Cromwell, Aug. 5, 1932, HADB, S4391.

32. Memo from New York office to Steiner in Berlin, July 20, 1932, HADB, S4391.
33. File note, March 5, 1932, HADB, S4390.
34. Deutsche Bank Hamburg Branch to Berlin Head Office, Sept. 6, 1932, HADB, S4392.
35. Ibid.
36. Internal letter, Sept. 9, 1932, HADB, S4392.
37. Wassermann and Schlieper to Dillon Read, Sept. 16, 1932, HADB, S4392.
38. Internal memo, Sept. 21, 1932, HADB, S4392.
39. Deutsche Bank to Richard Rosendorff, Sept. 8, 1932, HADB, S4392.
40. See Christopher Kobrak, "The Foreign-Exchange Dimension of Corporate Control in the Third Reich: The Case of Schering AG," *Contemporary European History*, Vol. 12 (2003), no. 1, pp. 33–47, and file note, Blinzig and Axhausen, Sept. 24, 1932, HADB, S4392, in which the authors suggest discussing using the notes in the next "Export-Schema."
41. Deutsche Bank to C. Hepner, Amsterdam, Sept. 27, 1932, HADB, S4392.
42. Deutsche Bank to Dillon Read, Jan. 13, 1933, HADB, S4392.
43. Deutsche Bank Filialbüro to Rösler, Sept. 28, 1932, HADB, S4392.
44. Ibid.
45. Deutsche Bank circular (signed by Wassermann and Blinzig) to the branches, Nov. 14, 1932, HADB, S4392. See also Kobrak, "The Foreign-Exchange Dimension."
46. Koehn to Deutsche Bank, Nov. 1, 1932, HADB, S4392. The high price may have been due to Deutsche Bank repurchases.
47. File note about conversation with Dillon Read representatives in Berlin, April 2, 1930, HADB, A411. Even as things were turning further south with world financial conditions and the first loan in 1930, Dillon Read suggested a new facility worth at least $100 million, because less would be uninteresting for Deutsche Bank, which could be used to cover the $25 million coming due and for other purposes. The Dillon Read representatives thought the market could bear this and that ten-year notes would be cheaper than the rate on the $25 million facility.
48. Exposé betreffend Sperrmarkaufrechnung gegen ausländische Valutaschulden, HADB, S4390.
49. File note on meeting with Reichsbank representatives Hechler and Hartenstein, and Wassermann, Blinzig, and Schlieper from Deutsche Bank, March 13, 1932, HADB, S4390.
50. Gesamtbesitz Deutsche Bank notes, May 15, 1932, HADB, S4390.
51. Price information, August 1932, Worksheet, Feb. 4, 1936, HADB, S4393.
52. File note, June 13, 1935, HADB, S4393.
53. Deutsche Bank to Reichswirtschaftsministerium, Nov. 28, 1938, HADB, A1382.
54. Deutsche Bank Rechtsabteilung to Generalsekretariat, Jan. 3, 1939, HADB, P136.
55. James, *Nazi Dictatorship*, pp. 1–37.
56. Forbes, *Doing Business with the Nazis*, pp. 74–92.
57. Report of the secretary, Foreign Bankers' Committees, Berlin, Oct. 1932, HADB, P10396. The office of the secretary of the foreign creditors had received few complaints. Ten percent of the amounts due had been paid off (preferred rights), and the Golddiskontbank had already started meeting the first installment payments it had guaranteed. 25.3 million Reichsmark had been made in payments on acceptance credit lines, 6.6 million Reichsmark in short-term cash advances had been converted to long-term lines, and another 0.5 million Reichsmark in other payments were made.
58. Kobrak, "The Foreign-Exchange Dimension of Corporate Control in the Third Reich."
59. *Berliner Börsen-Zeitung*, Jan. 31, 1933.
60. *Frankfurter Zeitung*, Feb. 5, 1933.
61. Christopher Kopper, *Hjalmar Schacht: Aufstieg und Fall von Hitlers mächtigstem Bankier* (Munich: Hanser, 2006), pp. 1–5. Schacht was later fired by Hitler, thrown in 1944 into a concentration camp, and later acquitted at Nuremberg.
62. *Vossische Zeitung*, Feb. 10, 1933.
63. *Berliner Börsen-Courier*, Dec. 12, 1933.
64. *Berliner Tageblatt*, Dec. 27, 1933.
65. *Frankfurter Zeitung*, March 17, 1934.

66. Gilbert C. Layton (Director of *The Economist* in London), "Vor der neuen deutschen Schuldenkonferenz," *Berliner Börsen-Zeitung*, April 12, 1934.
67. *Berliner Tageblatt*, April 14, 1934.
68. Laurits S. Swenson to the U.S. Secretary of State, Jan. 9, 1934, NARA, State Department, RG LM 193, 862.51 Bondholders/26.
69. *Handelsblad*, Dec. 19, 1933, Summarized translation to American Legation, The Hague, NARA, State Department, RG LM 193, 862.51 Bondholders/26.
70. *Berliner Börsen-Zeitung*, May 1, 1934.
71. "Report of John Foster Dulles on Berlin Debt Discussions of December, 1933," Dec. 23, 1933, State Department, RG LM, 193, NARA, 862.51, Bondholders/23.
72. Ibid. There were sufficient foreign reserves to continue some of the export subsidies and to maintain the current breakdown of cash and differed payments in scrip at 50 percent, not 25–75 percent, as the Germans were demanding. Whatever the figures, though, Dulles cautioned that they must be taken with a grain of salt, as they could be easily manipulated by Reichsbank to tell the story that it wanted to tell.
73. Ibid.
74. Cable to Schacht from U.S. banks, Dec. 26, 1933, State Department, RG LM, 193, NARA, 862.51, Bondholders/23.
75. *New York Herald Tribune*, Feb. 17, 1934.
76. *Frankfurter Zeitung*, May 31, 1934.
77. "Dr. Schacht Pleads Poverty," American Council of Foreign Bondholders, Jan. 4, 1934, NARA, State Department, RG LM 193, 862.51, Bondholders/26.
78. James, *Nazi Dictatorship*, pp. 6–11.
79. Norddeutsche Bank in Hamburg and Danatbank to Deutsche Bank, March 8, 1928, HADB, S388.
80. Ibid.
81. Deutsche Bank to Hamburg branch, July 16, 1930, HADB, S388.
82. Hamburg branch to Deutsche Bank Head Office, April 2, 1931, HADB, S388.
83. Deutsche Bank to consortium members, July 15, 1931, HADB, S388.
84. Cuno, July 16, 1931, HADB, S388.
85. Ibid.
86. Dresdner Bank to Deutsche Bank, July 16, 1931, HADB, S338.
87. Reichsbank to L. Behrens & Söhne, Sept. 8, 1932, HADB, S346.
88. Kleinwort, Sons & Co. to J. H. Stein, Sept. 22, 1932, HADB, S346.
89. L. Behrens & Söhne to Deutsche Bank, Sept. 30, 1932, HADB, S346.
90. Deutsche Bank to Hamburg branch, Oct. 4, 1932, HADB, S346.
91. Reichsbank to Deutsche Bank, Oct. 5, 1932, HADB, S346.
92. File note, Fürstenberg, Feb. 27, 1933, HADB, S347.
93. Various correspondence, HADB, S348.
94. Deutsche Bank and Dresdner Bank to Hapag, Jan. 9, 1934, HADB, S349.
95. Deutsche Bank to Reichsbank, Jan. 23, 1934, HADB, S349.
96. Deutsche Bank and Dresdner Bank to Reichsbank, May 11, 1934, HADB, S349.
97. Deutsche Bank to Reichsbank, Sept. 5, 1935, HADB, S349.
98. Deutsche Bank to Münchmeyer & Co., Sept. 5, 1935, HADB, S349.
99. 1933 Detailed financial statements, HADB, B305.
100. Wilkins, *1914–1945*, pp. 298–299.
101. Harrison, confidental memo to files, March 28, 1933, Harrison's conversations, 1927–1940, Federal Reserve Bank of New York, no. 2610.1.
102. Wilkins, *1914–1945*, pp. 360–362.
103. Wilkins, *1914–1945*, pp. 365 and 9.
104. Deutsche Bank to Landesfinanzamt Berlin, Stelle für Devisenbewirtschaftung, Jan. 29, 1932, HADB, S4411.
105. "The Deutsche Bank und Disconto-Gesellschaft's Report for the Year 1935," June 5, 1936, Analysis by General consulate, Berlin, Germany, NARA, State Department, RG LM 193, 862.516/675.

106. "The Deutsche Bank und Disconto-Gesellschaft's Report for the Year 1935," June 5, 1936, Analysis by general consulate, Berlin, Germany, NARA, State Department, RG LM 193, 862.516/675.
107. *Wall Street Journal*, Sept. 13, 1929.
108. *New York Times*, Sept. 30, 1954, Obituary.
109. Deutsche Bank circular M.68/33, March 23, 1933, HADB, A1072.
110. Telegram, date unclear, HADB, A1072.
111. Herbert Waller to Deutsche Bank, Aug. 11, 1937, HADB, A1072.
112. Deutsche Bank to Waller, July 23, 1934, HADB, A1072.
113. Waller to Schlieper, Sept. 20, 1932, HADB, A1072.
114. Deutsche Bank to Waller, Jan. 17, 1934, HADB, A1072.
115. File note, April 26, 1937, HADB, A1072.
116. Waller to Deutsche Bank, April 1, 1936, HADB, A1072.
117. Deutsche Bank Berlin to branches, undated, but all the correspondence with the branches is in winter 1936, HADB, A1072. In 1936, Deutsche Bank asked all its branches to determine which American companies were doing business with them, what the volumes were, and what were the types of transactions.

14. The Second Phoenix

1. Several letters from Waller and Schmidt, January–July 1938, HADB, P24156. The letters were ostensibly written to help inform potential German visitors to the United States.
2. President of Argo Corp. to Abs, Dec. 20, 1938, HADB, P24156.
3. Deutsche Bank (Abs) to Waller, Sept. 28, 1938, HADB, P24156.
4. *New York Times*, July 7, 1939.
5. *New York Journal and American*, July 19, 1939.
6. Kobrak and Wüstenhagen, "International Investment and Nazi Politics."
7. "Germany: Money & Bankers," prepared by the Department of Justice, February 1942, NARA, RG 60, Box 83. Oddly, there is nothing in the report about Deutsche Bank's activities in the United States, pp. 128–157.
8. Harold James, *The Deutsche Bank and the Nazi Economic War Against the Jews* (Cambridge: Cambridge University Press, 2001), pp. 75 and 94.
9. Jonathan Steinberg, *The Deutsche Bank and its Gold Transactions during the Second World War* (Munich: Beck, 1999).
10. Telegram from Reichsbank to the Federal, Dec. 3, 1941, Federal Reserve Bank of New York, Policy and Procedures, C261. See August and September telegrams from Reichsbank. The Reichsbank reported that German markets were "cheerful."
11. Letter from D. J. Liddy, Manager Foreign Department to the Department of State, October 1945, Federal Reserve Bank of New York, Policy and Procedures, C261.
12. Steinberg, *Gold Transactions*.
13. Deutsche Bank, Presse Berichte, June 20, 1941, HADB, S2181.
14. "Trade News Letter," Board of Trade German–American Commerce, July 31, 1941, Vol. XVI, No. 1, NARA, RG 131, General File, Box 171.
15. NARA, RG 131, Box 171.
16. Wilkins, *1914–1945*, pp. 452–470.
17. Wilkins, *1914–1945*, p. 445.
18. "Eigene Effekten in den Vereinigten Staaten," Nov. 23, 1939, HADB, A1382.
19. From "Babson's Washington Reports: Confidential Forecasts of Coming Developments," W-376, July 29, 1940, HADB, A198. The Netherlands investment into the United States was by far the largest at $1 billion, followed by France at $0.6 billion and Belgium $0.3 billion. American investment into Germany, $455 million, was the largest of the countries listed.
20. Wilkins, *1914–1945*, pp. 452–470; see also Kobrak, *National Cultures*, pp. 296–341.
21. Various FBI Rec. 230-97-1157, Box 1, 2/2.
22. File note, Schneider and Wodtke, Aug. 8, 1944, and letter to Albrecht Seeger, Aug. 2, 1946, unsigned, HADB, K8/18. For the complexity of South American transfers even in late 1941,

see series of telexes between head office and South American offices, October–November 1941, HADB, K8/18.

23. Various FBI Rec.230, Box 1, 97–1154.
24. Jonathan Steinberg, *Gold Transactions*, and Peter Hayes, *From Cooperation to Complicity: Degussa in the Third Reich* (Cambridge: Cambridge University Press, 2004).
25. Carl-Ludwig Holtfrerich, "The Deutsche Bank 1945–1957: War, Military Rule and Reconstruction," in Lothar Gall et al., *The Deutsche Bank 1870–1995* (London: Weidenfeld & Nicolson, 1995), pp. 357–382. See also Theo Horstmann, *Die Alliierten und die deutschen Grossbanken: Bankenpolitik nach dem Zweiten Weltkrieg in Westdeutschland* (Bonn: Bouvier, 1991), and Joachim Scholtyseck, "Die USA vs. 'The Big Six.' Der gescheiterte Bankenprozeß nach dem Zweiten Weltkrieg," *Bankhistorisches Archiv*, Vol. 26 (2000), no. 1, p. 27–53.
26. Holtfrerich, p. 505.
27. *New York Times*, May 16, 1943.
28. Finance Division Report, July 29, 1945, NARA, RG 260, Box 115, Folder 11.
29. Helga Wolski to Captain Henry Collins, Headquarters U.S. Group Control Council, Investigation of Cartels and External Assets, Sept. 24, 1945, NARA, RG 260, Box 180, Folder 7. Interestingly this is the first memo by a woman that I have found.
30. Jack Bennett, head of Finance Division, to William Hagard, acting director, Office of Public Relations, Dec. 27, 1946, NARA, RG 260, Box 64, Folder 9.
31. Cable from Jack Bennett, July 7, 1947, NARA, RG 260, Box 60, File 44.7.
32. Special report, Dresdner and Deutsche Banks, June 1947, NARA, RG 260, Box 60, File 44.7.
33. Special report, Dresdner and Deutsche Banks, June 1947, NARA, RG 260, Box 60, File 44.7.
34. See James, *Nazi Dictatorship*, for example. James argues that, by the time the Nazis embarked on the war, the banks had lost input on policy and even how implementation would be carried out.
35. Special report, Dresdner and Deutsche Banks, June 1947, NARA, RG 260, Box 60, File 44.7.
36. Holtfrerich, pp. 396–402.
37. Holtfrerich, pp. 402–408.
38. Holtfrerich, p. 408.
39. Holtfrerich, pp. 414–430.
40. Ibid.
41. Bancroft to Kagan, Aug. 22, 1946, U.S. Army, June 3, 1946, NARA, RG 260, Box 174, Folder 1.
42. Apparently a translation of letter written by the Deutsche Bank directing office in Hamburg, not clear to whom, Jan. 11, 1946, NARA, RG 260, Box 70, Folder 7.
43. Translation of Organization of Deutsche Bank, provided by Häussler, June 6, 1946, NARA, RG 260, Box 190, Files 21.30.
44. Progress Report, Paul Brand, chief of Deutsche Bank Team, Dec. 3, 1945, NARA, RG 260, Box 179, Folder 5.
45. Progress reports, Paul Brand, chief of Deutsche Bank Team, for the month of December 1945 and July 1, 1946 to June 30, 1947, NARA, RG 260, Box 179, Folder 4.
46. David Schwartz to Theodore Ball, Director of the Finance Division, December 10, 1947, NARA, RG 260, Box 136, Folder 7.
47. R. P. Aikin, chief, Financial Institutions Division, to Theodore Ball, Director of the Finance Division, June 3, 1947, NARA, RG 260, Box 143, Folder 2.
48. Saul Kagan to R. P. Aikin, chief, Financial Institutions Division, June 9, 1947, NARA, RG 260, Box 152, Folder 12.
49. Kessler and Feske of Deutsche Bank to OMGUS, NARA, RG 260, Box 135, Folder 10.
50. List of branch managers in NSDAP, no date, NARA, RG 260, Box 70, Folder 7.
51. Various reports and letters, April 1944 to July 1947, NARA, RG 260, Box 534.
52. Holtfrerich, pp. 414–430.
53. Lichtenstein to Leonard Crum, March 26, 1947, Harvard University Archives, Walter Lichtenstein Papers, HUG(FP) 43.12. These seems to have been a Harvard clique there.
54. Lichtenstein to Donald McLean, March 24, 1947, Harvard University Archives, Walter Lichtenstein Papers, HUG(FP) 43.12.

55. Adolphe Warner to Lichtenstein, April 15, 1948, Harvard University Archives, Walter Lichtenstein Papers, HUG(FP) 11.29
56. Ibid.
57. Lichtenstein, memorandum for the files, March 15, 1946, NARA, RG 260, Box 137, Folder 1.
58. Notes to the staff meeting of finance division, March 17, 1947, NARA, RG 260, Box 103, Folder 17.
59. Holtfrerich, pp. 439–468.
60. Ibid.
61. Ibid. Banks could operate in no more than six *Länder*, except North Rhine–Westphalia, whose banks could not operate elsewhere because of the size of that *Land*. But for this, the regional banks had to be decoupled from the original parent company.
62. Holtfrerich, pp. 439–468.
63. Lothar Gall, *Der Bankier Hermann Josef Abs: Eine Biographie* (Munich: Beck, 2004), pp. 1–37.
64. Gall, *Der Bankier*, p. 72.
65. See Gall, *Der Bankier*, and several works by James, *Nazi Dictatorship*.
66. James, *Nazi Dictatorship*, p. 218
67. Gall, *Der Bankier*, p. 100.
68. "Twenty-Six Leading German Industrialists and Financiers," U.S. Army, June 3, 1946, NARA, RG 260, Box 176, Folder 5.
69. Gall, *Der Bankier*, p. 130.
70. Finance division, portrait of Abs, undated, NARA, RG 260, Box 152, Folder 13.
71. Holtfrerich, pp. 357–382. See also Horstmann, *Die Alliierten und die deutschen Grossbanken*.
72. James, *Nazi Dictatorship*, pp. 214–218.
73. William McCurdy to General Clay, April 17, 1948, NARA, RG 260, Box 90, Folder 6.
74. Ferencz to General Taylor, March 22, 1947, NARA, RG 260, Box 172, Folder 12.
75. Gall, *Der Bankier*, p. 130.
76. Holtfrerich, p. 433.
77. Holtfrerich, p. 444.
78. Abs to Gero von Schultze-Gaevernitz, June 5, 1948, HADB, V1/2350.
79. Gall, *Der Bankier*, pp. 138–140.
80. File note Abs, Dec. 17, 1949, HADB, V1/2350. Abs' visit was sufficiently controversial that Senator Guy Gillette demanded that the state department answer five questions about the visit. The questions involved his meetings with banks over the Standstill Agreements, his sponsorship by the Board of German Reconstruction, his freedom of travel, by whose authority he was traveling, and where and with whom he was staying. Excerpts of the Bulletin of the Department of State, Dec. 26, 1949, HADB, V1/2350. In December 1949, *U.S. News and World Report* was not alone in maintaining that pro-Nazi parties were growing in strength and that bankers who had helped Hitler to power were themselves coming back into power. Abs is mentioned by name. HADB, V1/2150.
81. Executive committee lunch with Abs, Nov. 30, 1949, HADB, V1/2350.
82. George Franklin to Abs, Nov. 17, 1949, HADB, V1/2350.
83. *Wall Street Journal*, Nov. 13, 1953, HADB, V1/2077.
84. Invitation, HADB, V1/2085.
85. Various correspondence, HADB, V1/2134.
86. Invitation letter, Oct. 9, 1956, HADB, V1/2132.
87. Richard H. Whitehead's Report to General Lucius Clay, Sept. 25, 1947, HADB, V1/2351. Whitehead went on to work for East West Commerce Corporation, which dealt with sales to Germany.
88. James, *Europe Reborn*, pp. 230–231.
89. See Heinrich Harries, *Wiederaufbau, Welt und Wende: Die KfW – eine Bank mit öffentlichem Auftrag, 1948–1998* (Frankfurt: Knapp, 1998), and Manfred Pohl, *Wiederaufbau: Kunst und Technik der Finanzierung 1947–1953. Die ersten Jahre der Kreditanstalt für Wiederaufbau* (Frankfurt: Knapp, 1973).
90. Gall, *Der Bankier*, pp. 142–149.

91. Holtfrerich, p. 458. Unable to come to an agreement with the Russians, in June 1948 the Western powers put through a currency reform of the Reichsmark, which was converted at a rate – apart from a few exceptions, mostly small amounts held by individuals – of 100 Reichsmark to 6.50 new Deutsche Mark (DM).
92. Plassmann to Abs, July 14, 1949, HADB, V1/2020, and Plassmann to Abs, July 13, 1949, HADB, V1/2020. German banks received 1.5 percent of the interest charged, but had to assume the credit risk, even though they did not supply the funds.
93. *Newsweek*, Aug. 15, 1949, HADB, V1/2351.
94. Walter Lichtenstein, speech, "The Future of Germany," March 1949, HADB, V1/2351.
95. "Zur Wiederherstellung des deutschen Auslandskredits," what appears to be the text of a speech, Adolphe Warner, no date, HADB, V1/2351.
96. Address by Hermann J. Abs before the George C. Marshall Research Foundation and the Foreign Policy Association, Oct. 31, 1978, HADB, V1/3247.
97. Abschrift, undated, HADB, V1/2351. K. W. Banta, who worked for World Commerce Corporation at 25 Broad Street, New York, was one of the few correspondents in the files on a first name basis with Abs.
98. *Financial Times*, Feb. 22, 1954, HADB, V1/2309.
99. *Börsen-Zeitung*, Nov. 30, 1957.
100. *Frankfurter Rundschau*, Aug. 2, 1957.
101. "Stellungnahme von Herrn Abs zu dem Bericht von Senator Smather [sic]," April 6, 1957, V1/5088.
102. Ibid.
103. Hermann J. Abs, "Das deutsche Vermögen in den USA – Volle oder Teilrückgabe?" *Recht der internationalen Wirtschaft*, Vol. 1 (1954/55), pp. 145–147.
104. Drew Pearson, "Next: Another 'Giveaway' Hassle," *Washington Post*, March 31, 1957.
105. Ibid.
106. NARA, RG 230 – FBI – Box 1, Abs – 56532 – Sec. 1. The report repeats the usual accusations about Abs and a criticism about Klein.
107. Holtfrerich, pp. 468–486.
108. Holtfrerich, pp. 486–521.

Section III. Introduction

1. Gerold Ambrosius and William H. Hubbard, *A Social Economic History of the Twentieth Century* (Cambridge, MA: Harvard University Press, 1989), p. 295, and Holtfrerich, p. 484. Just a few weeks after the reunification of the bank, Abs published an article in *The New York Times* about the decision. He felt compelled to defend Deutsche Bank and other German banks against charges of monopolizing the financial sector in Germany. "Reintegration of the Big German Banks," *New York Times*, March 24, 1957.
2. Berghahn, *The Americanisation of West German Industry*, and Jonathan Zeitlin and Gary Herrigel, eds. *Americanization and its Limits: Reworking US Technology in Post-war Europe and Japan* (Oxford: Oxford University Press, 2000).
3. See Volker R. Berghahn, *America and the Intellectual Cold Wars in Europe* (Princeton: Princeton University Press, 2001), Victoria de Grazia, *Irresistible Empire: America's Advance through Twentieth-Century Europe* (Cambridge, MA: Harvard University Press, 2005), and Jean-Jacques Servan-Schreiber, *Le Défi Américain* (Paris: Denoël, 1967), the *célèbre* "call to arms" to awaken European governments and business to the American economic challenge is no longer in print in France. Optimists might conclude that the problems have been resolved.
4. Tony Judt, *Postwar: A History of Europe Since 1945* (New York: Penguin, 2005), pp. 129–226.
5. Judt, pp. 273–274.
6. From 1958 to 1970, for example, French trade with EEC countries went from 30 percent to 57 percent, German from 37 percent to 57 percent. Harold James, *Europe Reborn: A History, 1914–2000* (London: Pearson, 2003), p. 272.
7. See Mark Mazower, *Dark Continent* (New York: Penguin Books, 1998).

8. Ambrosius and Hubbard, p. 144. Real national product grew in West Germany from 1950 to 1960 by 7.8 percent annually, but fell to 4.4 percent in the next decade, a steep drop but still impressive by most standards.
9. Gary M. Walton and Hugh Rockoff, *History of the American Economy*, 8th edition (New York: Dryden Press, 1998). In the 1960s, real per capita gross national product grew at nearly 3 percent per year, one of the highest growth decades in American history.
10. Herman van der Wee, *Prosperity and Upheaval: The World Economy 1945–1980* (New York: Penguin, 1991), p. 51. German GNP (total and per capita) as a percentage of U.S. total and per capita GNP had nearly doubled since 1950, but as late as 1970 it represented only 21 percent of America's total and 74 percent per capita.
11. Whereas German stock market valuations were approximately the same percentage of GDP in each country in 1913, in 1960, U.S. capitalization was nearly twice that of Germany's as a percentage of GDP. By 1999, it was two-and-a-half times that of Germany. Raghuram G. Rajan and Luigi Zingales, "The Great Reversals: The Politics of Financial Development in the Twentieth Century," *Journal of Financial Economics*, Vol. 69 (2003), pp. 5–50.
12. See Mark Roe, *Strong Managers, Weak Owners: The Political Roots of American Corporate Finance* (Princeton: Princeton University Press, 1994), pp. 102–145, for an excellent discussion of legislation that created mutual and pension funds, and their impact on capital markets and corporate governance in the United States.
13. Judt, p. 372.
14. Hans E. Büschgen, "Deutsche Bank from 1957 to the Present: The Emergence of an International Financial Conglomerate," in *The Deutsche Bank 1870–1995*, Lothar Gall et al. (London: Weidenfeld & Nicolson, 1995), pp. 523–525. For example, in the 1970s, Deutsche Bank adopted an OM Model (organization and management) designed to deliver customers one-stop-shopping at branches.
15. Some things would not change. Just a month before Deutsche Bank's reunification, Abs complained about the behavior of some British passengers on a PanAm flight from New York. PanAm responded that alcoholic beverages were expected by passengers on its Clipper flights but that the airline would try to avoid serving those who were already intoxicated. The trip by propeller plane took approximately two-and-a-half times as long as a flight today and required one stop. PanAm to Abs, March 7, 1957, HADB, V1/2081. British Airways instituted the first jet flights from Europe to New York a year later.
16. Cheol S. Eun et al., *International Financial Management: Canadian Perspectives* (Toronto: McGraw-Hill, 2005), pp. 26–37.
17. Ibid.
18. Series of letter exchanges between Abs and Henry Fowler, U.S. secretary of the treasury, 1965 and 1966, HADB, V1/3224.
19. Hermann J. Abs, "The United States and Europe, Competitors or Partners? American Direct Investment in Europe," Institute International d'Études Bancaires, 1969.
20. "Die Entwicklung des Auslandsgeschäftes der Deutsche Bank AG im Jahre 1959," Internal report, March 15, 1960, HADB, V1/2859. In 1957, German exports and imports grew at a 16 percent and 13 percent rate, respectively. Although the United States was a large importer of German products and a large exporter to Germany, in 1958 it was not the largest. Business relationships remained very regional but still led to a great deal of economic growth. Germany's Western European neighbors accounted for well over half of its exports. From 1957 through 1959, Deutsche Bank handled approximately 32 percent of all Germany's foreign trade financing and transactions. Although imports and exports were running at roughly DM 40 billion (DM 35.8 and DM 41.2 billion to be exact), purchases and sales of foreign securities by Germans in 1959 amounted to a paltry DM 1.9 and DM .6 billion respectively.

    Foreigners did a little better, buying up DM 2.5 billion in German securities while selling DM 2.1 billion. What foreign investment that did occur went mostly to the Americas, with Western Europe and South Africa also getting substantial shares.
21. Lees, p. 78.
22. *The New York Times* reported that a long list of German firms intended to invest in the United States. By 1961, DuPont, for example, had already invested heavily in Europe – $85 million in assets at book value, just since 1956 – reflecting a 10 percent increase since 1961, with

planned 1962 investments jumping by 25 percent over the previous year. *New York Times*, April 13, 1962.

23. "Bericht über die Studienreise für Bankfachleute nach den USA," Oct. 20 to Nov. 7, 1960, Walter Hook, Georg Behrendt, and Günther Mecklenburg, HADB, V1/2859. In 1960, the bank sent three young managers to the United States to study how American banks organized their work, attracted depositors, processed transactions, and automated their activities. They concluded that many American methods and investment in machinery had to be adopted, albeit in an adapted form and at a slower pace, in Germany. Ironically, there was some urgency, but lower German labor costs allowed for greater time to reflect and implement.
24. Büschgen, pp. 530–533.

15. Divisive Issues and the Making of a New Financial Landscape

1. See S. Jonathan Wiesen, *West German Industry & the Challenge of the Nazi Past* (Chapel Hill: University of North Carolina Press, 2001) for an excellent study of the attitudes of German business about the past and Americanization of Germany after World War II.
2. Address delivered by Hermann J. Abs at the dinner of the United States Council of the International Chamber of Commerce, Inc., in New York, Jan. 16, 1957, HADB, V1/2294.
3. Ibid.
4. See Hans-Dieter Kreikamp, *Deutsches Vermögen in den Vereinigten Staaten: Die Auseinandersetzung als Aspekt der deutschen-amerikanischen Beziehungen 1952–1962* (Stuttgart: Deutsche Verlags-Anstalt, 1979), and Gall, *Der Bankier*, pp. 235–236.
5. See Christopher Kobrak and Jana Wüstenhagen, "American Seizure of German Property, Political Risk, and Globalization," EBH, Geneva, September 2007.
6. Address delivered by Hermann J. Abs at the dinner of the United States Council of the International Chamber of Commerce, Inc., in New York, Jan. 16, 1957, HADB, V1/2294.
7. Berghahn, *America and the Intellectual Cold War*.
8. Heinrich Freiherr von Berenberg-Gossler, report on his trip to the United States, in Blessing's files, June 22, 1964, HABBk, B330/235.
9. See Hermann J. Abs, "European Integration," *European Atlantic Review*, April 1960, and "A Banker Looks at International Money Movements," *Manchester Guardian*, Nov. 17, 1959.
10. "Abs Supports Concept of Regional Groups," *International Banker* (International Edition of *American Banker*), Feb. 28, 1967.
11. Abs to Charles Taguey, Oct. 20, 1970, HADB, V1/1970.
12. "German Banker Cites Similarities Between American and German Economic Growth Environment," news release, Sept. 26, 1962, HADB, V1/2621. At the September 1962 meeting of the American Bankers Association in Atlantic City, for example, Abs defended German fiscal policy against charges that deficit spending there contributed to its faster economic growth. He offered an alternative explanation, which included the willingness of German workers to work for lower wages, and Germany's monetary discipline.
13. "Report to the President of the United States From the Task Force on Promoting Increased Foreign Investment and Increased Foreign Financing," (Washington, D.C.: U.S. Government Printing Office, 1964). In October 1963, a task force appointed by President John F. Kennedy to find ways to defend the U.S. gold reserves recommended broad and intensive efforts to market U.S. securities of private companies to foreign investors, and to increase the availability of foreign financing for U.S. businesses operating abroad. In effect, these measures were designed to break down foreign restrictions on American institutions financing on foreign markets.
14. Barry Eichengreen, *Globalizing Capital: A History of the International Monetary System* (Princeton: Princeton University Press, 1996), pp. 113–117. Eichengreen contends that the very success of the Bretton Woods system in redistributing wealth and reserves called for a revaluation in rates. Both the U.S. fiscal and balance of payments deficits were reasonable throughout the period 1950–70.
15. Protokoll, der 155. Sitzung des Zentralbankrats der Deutschen Bundesbank, Dec. 5, 1963, HABBk, B330/426/1. The Bundesbank, for example, worried about continued American capital investment in Germany, which seemed to have outlived its "economic usefulness" and

put a strain on its own ability to hold down the value of the DM. Reminiscent of the 1920s, officials at the central bank fretted over drops in German capital market price levels, which would make that foreign investment easier.

16. Robert Ellscheid to Ludwig Erhard, Minister of Economics, May 27, 1961, HABBk, B330/258.
17. Memo, Aug. 5, 1958, HABBk, B330/292.
18. Press release of the Deutsche Bundesbank, Nov. 26, 1967, HABBk, B330/257.
19. Eichengreen, p. 129. For an excellent discussion of the rise and fall of Bretton Woods, see Eichengreen, pp. 93–135.
20. van der Wee, p. 456.
21. Maurice Obstfeld and Alan M. Taylor, *Global Capital Markets: Integration, Crisis, and Growth* (Cambridge: Cambridge University Press, 2004), p. 160.
22. van der Wee, p. 456.
23. Eichengreen, *Globalizing Capital*, pp. 125–135, and J. Orlin Grabbe, *International Financial Markets* (New York: Elsevier, 1991), pp. 12–25.
24. "European Bankers View of the Dollar Now," *Bankers Monthly Magazine*, Jan. 15, 1963, HADB, V1/3937. Abs is quoted making the point in the article that the U.S. federal deficit had to be restrained. Again, see Eichengreen, pp. 129–133.
25. Deutsche Bank, annual report 1964.
26. Deutsche Bank, annual report 1966.
27. "How Far Has the U.S. Changed: Hot Money Patterns?" *Financial Times*, Aug. 15, 1963.
28. Protokolle der 345. und 346. Sitzung des Zentralbankrats der Deutschen Bundesbank, Aug. 25 and Sept. 1, 1971, HABBk, B330/6163/1 and 2.
29. Protokoll der 430. Sitzung des Zentralbankrats der Deutschen Bundesbank, Feb. 6, 1975, HABBk, B330/7885.
30. "Money Supply: The Dilemma Facing the Fed," *Financial Times*, July 19, 1978.
31. van der Wee, p. 492.
32. Robert Solomon, *Money on the Move: The Revolution in International Finance since 1980* (Princeton: Princeton University Press, 1999), p. 3.
33. Joseph Daniels and David Van Hoose, *International Monetary and Financial Economics* (New York: Thomson, 1999), pp. 50–52. The original goals – merely full convertibility and immutable rates among the European Economic Community currencies – were more limited than in the final version. Once this was established, creating a common currency, it was thought, would only be a formality.
34. Hermann J. Abs, "A Counterweight to the Dollar," *Financial Times*, Dec. 3, 1970.
35. Hermann J. Abs, Speech to the Manufacturing Chemists Association, Greenbrier, U.S.A., June 12, 1975, HADB, V1/3243.
36. Address by Hermann J. Abs to George C. Marshall Research Foundation and Foreign Policy Association, New York City, Oct. 31, 1978, HADB, V1/3247.
37. Stefano Battilossi, "Introduction: International Banking and the American Challenge in Historical Perspective," in *European Banks and the American Challenge: Competition and Cooperation in International Banking Under Bretton Woods*, eds. Stefano Battilossi and Youssef Cassis (Oxford: Oxford University Press, 2002), pp. 14–20. From 1964 to 1975, the Eurocurrency market grew from $20 billion to $480 billion.
38. Meir Kohn, *Financial Institutions and Markets* (New York: McGraw-Hill, 1994), p. 270.
39. Kohn, pp. 271–272.
40. Youssef Cassis, "Before the Storm: European Banks in the 1950s," in *European Banks and the American Challenge: Competition and Cooperation in International Banking Under Bretton Woods*, p. 41.
41. Richard Sylla, "United States Banks and Europe: Strategy and Attitudes," in *European Banks and the American Challenge: Competition and Cooperation in International Banking Under Bretton Woods*, eds. Stefano Battilossi and Youssef Cassis (Oxford: Oxford University Press, 2002), p. 55.
42. Susan B. Foster, "Impact of Direct Investment Abroad by United States Multinational Companies on the Balance of Payments," *Federal Reserve Bank of New York, Monthly Review*, Vol. 54, July 1972. As measured by book value, it had already grown from a little over

$30 billion in 1960 to $80 billion in 1970. But American companies also repatriated funds, from profits and by other means, which might ultimately improve the balance of payments picture. Some believed, too, that American investment helped U.S. overall competitiveness and, therefore, in the long run the balance of payments. Manufacturing and petroleum accounted for over $50 billion. Although approximately $40 billion of the total went to the Americas, Europe received around $25 billion.

43. Private Kapitalanlagen der USA in Westeuropa, insbesondere in den EWG-Ländern, Deutsche Bundesbank, March 15, 1963, HABBk, B330/3436. Payments on private and public investment in Germany grew from DM 602 million in 1959 to DM 791 million, a significant increase in the Bundesbank's foreign transfers, even though during the same period its London debt payments, included in the totals, dropped from DM 138 million to DM 86 million. Most U.S. investment in the world and into Europe was private, but total U.S. investment into Europe (private and public) amounted to only $19.2 billion, less than 30 percent of America's total. Total private western European investment in the United States was 40 percent higher than the United States in Europe. But direct investment made up 67 percent of the U.S. total into Western Europe, whereas European direct investment in the United States was only 33 percent of the total. In 1961, of the common market countries, West Germany was the leading recipient of U.S. direct investment, accounting for nearly 40 percent but still way behind the $3.5 billion which the United Kingdom had received. From 1956 to 1961, Germany averaged $100 million per year in new flows of U.S. direct investment. From 1949 to 1961, the stock had grown from $173 million to $1.2 billion, but on a per capita basis Germany still lagged behind the Netherlands and the Benelux countries in the stock of U.S. origin FDI. By 1960, the automotive, machine, and chemical sectors led the way.
44. "U.S. Payments Upturn Confounds Experts," *International Herald Tribune*, Dec. 26, 1973. Despite price elasticity and other factors, the United States even realized a trade surplus in 1973, with exports, led by raw materials and agricultural products, rising by an unheard-of 47 percent.
45. James E. McCarthy, *Across the Board – The Conference Board Magazine*, December 1976, pp. 21–29. By 1975, seven foreign companies had subsidiaries of more than a billion Dollars in the United States, though six of the seven were Canadian and British firms. The largest, Shell, was actually a British/Dutch firm. Hoechst, the largest German, only had $617 million in sales but nearly 9,000 workers.
46. See, for example, Bruce Stokes, "Facing up to Germany," *National Journal*, Nov. 29, 1986.
47. Abs to Roosa, Oct. 19, 1962, HABBk, B330/226. Abs wrote that only 20 percent of total short-term deposits and 1,200 of 31,000 banks were in the hands of big banks and copied the letter to Blessing.
48. Hermann J. Abs, "'Universal Banking System' Absolved of Blame for German Capital Woes," *American Banker*, Oct. 26, 1966. The German banks at times even tried to bring down rates. The universal banks served to restore the balance between savings and investment, a role which they served brilliantly during the early years of German "rehabilitation" and for which they were still needed as a brake to overheated investment.
49. Carsten Hartkopf, *Die Geschäftspolitik amerikanischer Banken in Deutschland, 1960–1990* (Frankfurt: Peter Lang, 2000), p. 2.
50. Memo, Deutsche Bundesbank, Hauptabteilung Ausland, June 12, 1969, HABBk, B330/15705.
51. Hartkopf, *Geschäftspolitik amerikanischer Banken*.
52. Adrian E. Tschoegl, "Foreign Banks in the United States since World War II," in *Foreign Multinationals in the United States: Management and Performance*, eds. Geoffrey Jones and Lina Gálvez-Muñoz, (London: Routledge, 2002), pp. 149–168.
53. Shelagh Hefferman, *Modern Banking in Theory and Practice* (New York: Wiley and Sons, 1996), pp. 251–262.
54. Hefferman, pp. 251–262.
55. Emminger to Mitglieder des Zentralbankrats, March 21, 1973, HABBk, B330/6705/1. In March 1973, there were thirty-five foreign banks with branches in the Federal Republic, among them many American and European, but also Brazilian and Iranian banks with a great variety of capital levels ranging from 3.2 percent of business activity to 46 percent.

56. Ibid.
57. Ernst Fessler to Rolf Gocht, April 3, 1973, HABBk, B330/6705/1. The banks were too differentiated and the Bundesbank was not anxious to bring foreign capital into Germany. It decided to give permission for reduced capital infusions, planned for two Japanese banks that it deemed to have sufficient reserves.
58. Gocht to Fessler, April 11, 1973, HABBk, B330/6705/1.
59. Schlesinger, Vorlage für den Zentralbankrat, Aug. 18, 1972, HABBk, B330/29554.
60. Bundesverband deutscher Banken to Bundesbank, Nov. 24, 1972, HABBk, B330/29554. They felt that the reporting system would hurt their business, because it discriminated against German firms, making them disclose more than banks from other European Community countries and the United States.
61. Bundesbank to Bundesverband deutscher Banken, Dec. 5, 1972, HABBk, B330/29554.
62. Paul Verhagen, president of EAB, to Abs, June 2, 1969, V1/3236. In 1969, the United States contemplated changing the 1956 Bank Holding Company Act, the original purpose of which was to restrict the rampant growth of bank holding companies. Many U.S. banks used holding companies to circumvent interstate branching restrictions and limits on banking activity (Glass-Steagall). Deutsche Bank feared that these changes would have a negative impact on its business. Although perhaps more theoretical than actual and more cumbersome than really threatening, proposed legislation in the United States would have meant that Deutsche Bank would be considered a bank holding company, would have to submit reports to the Federal Reserve and other U.S. government agencies, and that U.S. officials would have the right to examine Deutsche Bank subsidiaries in other countries. There was even a risk that bank holding companies might have to divest themselves of nonbanking activities, a stipulation that would obviously have a huge impact on Deutsche Bank. Some of those advising Deutsche Bank hoped that the bank would be exempted by virtue of a grandfathering clause, but Democratic opposition in Congress to any exceptions was very strong. Hefferman, p. 240. The final Act, passed in 1970, emphasized restrictions on nonbanking activities but did little to stem the tide of bank holding companies' creation.
63. "The German Example: Three Rich Powerful Banks Dominate Germany," *Business Week*, April 19, 1976. Deutsche Bank's profits were climbing quickly, rising 30 percent from 1974 to 1975. From 1970 to 1975, the bank's assets had doubled.
64. *Börsen-Zeitung*, June 22 and 23, 1978.
65. van der Wee, pp. 469–470, and Grabbe, pp. 245–259, also Ekkehard Storck, *Euromarkt: Finanz-Drehscheibe der Welt* (Stuttgart: Schäffer-Poeschel, 1995)
66. Kohn, pp. 273–278.
67. Daniels and Van Hoose, *International Monetary and Financial Economics*, pp. 173–189, and Alan C. Shapiro, *Multinational Financial Management*, 7th edition (Hoboken: Wiley & Sons, 2003), pp. 441–468.
68. Hefferman, pp. 79–81.
69. Daniels and Van Hoose, *International Monetary and Financial Economics*, pp. 173–189, and Shapiro, *Multinational Financial Management*, pp. 441–468.
70. Kohn, pp. 635–666. A futures contract is a standardized agreement to buy something at some future date at a price fixed today. An option is a right by the purchaser to buy or sell something for a fee and at a price agreed upon today. A financial swap is an agreed exchange of something (usually flows like interest) in the future in amounts agreed upon today.
71. Hefferman, pp. 259–261.
72. Circa 1993, pension funds and households owned 25.8 percent and 50.2 percent of American equities. The corresponding figures in Germany were 7.7 percent and 16.6 percent. Equity shares ended up on the balance sheets of German banks, insurance companies, and commercial companies, 14.3 percent, 7.1 percent, and 38.8 percent, respectively. Clark and Bostock, p. 238.
73. Rajan and Zingales.
74. Büschgen, pp. 656–658.
75. Büschgen, pp. 656–663.
76. Abs to Helmuth Pollems of Deutsche Bank, July 5, 1957, HADB, V1/3740.

77. Oswald Rösler to Abs, July 11, 1957, HADB, V1/3740.
78. Büschgen, pp. 656–663.
79. Deutsche Bank, annual report 1973.
80. The term international lending refers to borrowing transactions when the suppliers of funds and borrowers are in different countries. In 1955, Klaus Jacobs, who later was Deutsche Bank's first representative at EAB in New York, worked in the Auslandssekretariat, where export financing, project financing, and international securities issues were just beginning. Süddeutsche Bank operated a Foreign Department *(Auslandsabteilung)* for routine matters, such as transfers and letters of credit, which were used for all trading nations and which were handled through correspondent banks. Interview with Klaus Jacobs, July 11, 2006.
81. Memo, Deutsche Bundesbank, Hauptabteilung Ausland, Feb. 12, 1968, HABBk, B330/15705.
82. Memo, Deutsche Bundesbank, Hauptabteilung Ausland, Feb. 29, 1968, HABBk, B330/20697.
83. Memo, Deutsche Bundesbank, Hauptabteilung Ausland, July 21, 1969, HABBk, B330/20697.
84. Tombstone for International Business Machines Stock Listing, and other correspondence 1963, HADB, V1/3218.
85. Minutes of meeting Jan. 23, 1962, and letter of intent, Jan. 3, 1962, HADB, V1/3211. As lead bank, Deutsche Bank took a third of the shares, Dresdner and Commerzbank a total of 30 percent with the rest divided into small increments of between 6 and 1.5 percent.
86. Deutsche Bank, annual report 1962.
87. Deutsche Bank, annual report 1964.
88. Deutsche Bank, annual report 1965.
89. Deutsche Bank, annual report 1967.
90. Ekkehard Storck, "Die Bundesbank und Auslandsbeteiligung deutscher Banken," *Börsen-Zeitung*, Dec. 8, 1973.
91. Deutsche Bank, annual report 1963.
92. Deutsche Bank, annual report 1968.
93. Internal document, Oct. 31, 1979, HADB, V1/3246.
94. Deutsche Bank, annual report 1986.
95. Roloff to Blessing, Oct. 20 and 25, 1960, HABBk, B330/292. W. T. Roloff of RCA Victor's Canadian company kept Blessing informed about his negotiations with Abs and Deutsche Bank informed about projects. See also Blessing to Roloff, Feb. 6, 1963, HABBk, B330/292, and Krebs to Roloff, April 19, 1966, HABBk, B330/292.
96. *Financial Times*, July 13, 1962.
97. Christopher D. McKenna, *The World's Newest Profession: Management Consulting in the Twentieth Century* (Cambridge: Cambridge University Press, 2006), pp. 20–47.
98. Kohn, p. 419.
99. Memo, Deutsche Bundesbank, Hauptabteilung Ausland, April 20, 1966, HABBk, B330/5170
100. Büschgen, pp. 690–691.
101. Büschgen, p. 664.
102. Kathleen Burk, *Morgan Grenfell 1838–1988: The Biography of a Merchant Bank* (Oxford: Oxford University Press, 1989), preface and p. 257.
103. Interview with Hilmar Kopper, Jan. 23, 2006.
104. Patrick A. Gaughan, *Mergers, Acquisitions, and Corporate Restructurings* (New York: Wiley, 1999), p. 43 and 58.
105. Jeremy Edwards and Klaus Fischer, *Banks, Finance and Investment in Germany* (Cambridge: Cambridge University Press, 1994), pp. 190–194. The close relationship to customers put German banks in a delicate position concerning mergers.
106. Gaughan, p. 9.
107. Büschgen, pp. 694–695.
108. Telephone interview with Hilmar Kopper, Oct. 18, 2006.
109. See Gerald D. Feldman, *Hugo Stinnes* (Munich: Beck, 1998) for an excellent study of the family and business.
110. Statement of Cläre Hugo Stinnes-Wagenknecht, to the subcommittee of the judiciary, United States House of Representatives, to amend the Trading with the Enemy Act. Undated. HADB, V1/1735, Prospectus Hugo Stinnes Corporation, May 15, 1957, HADB, V1/1733, and Wilkins,

1914–1945, p. 195, for details of the 1920s' transaction. Wilkins points out that the Stinnes holding in Germany was actually in the hands of two Maryland corporations. Effectively, inward direct investment into the United States was used to direct American funds to Germany. Interestingly, too, there is no record of Deutsche Bank's involvement in the 1926 deal, except perhaps as recipient of funds owed to it by the Stinnes estate.

111. Gall, *Der Bankier*, pp. 160–161.
112. Several documents, file notes, HADB, V1/1735. Although Abs, who ostensibly directly owned shares, was willing to give up future claims against the former shareholders of the company, for example, he maintained his right to process claims against the United States and German governments. This interpretation of the transaction as a very personal Abs' transaction has been confirmed by his assistant during these years, Klaus Jacobs, interview, July 11, 2006.

16. From Abs to Kopper and from Joint Ventures to Branching

1. Telephone interview with Hilmar Kopper, Oct. 18, 2006.
2. Program and speech for October 3, 1962 dinner, HADB, V1/3213. Abs also held a talk defending the view that "structural" foreign trade imbalances could still be worked out over time. In 1962, the Investment Bankers Association of America placed him at the "special guest" table along with David Rockefeller, and several other dignitaries at its October gala dinner at the Waldorf Astoria (its 42nd such occasion).
3. Correspondence, 1969–70, Clay and Abs, HADB, V1/3234, and interview with Klaus Jacobs, July 11, 2006. Klaus Jacobs served as his personal assistant between 1957 and 1964.
4. In the decades following the war, Abs was one of the few German bankers known and respected among bankers and businessmen in New York and London. In 1962, Abs was chosen as one of the five international bankers to advise the International Finance Corporation of the World Bank. The others included the heads of Morgan Grenfell and the House of Rothschild, *New York Times*, Feb. 27, 1962.
5. The September 1962 trip lasted a month from the departure on the SS *France* to his departure from Chicago. It included seven U.S. cities in three weeks. HADB, V1/2490.
6. Programm fuer den Besuch von Herrn Hermann J. Abs, U.S.A./Canada, Nov. 28 to Dec. 3, 1970, V1/2505. He made time for prewar business associates forced into exile. On the day after his arrival, Sunday Nov. 29, he was driven from the Drake Hotel to the Scarsdale home of the Petschek family, which had fled Czechoslovakia when the Nazis arrived.
7. Several letters, see, Jan. 7, 1966, Peter Gil to Klaus Jacobs, HADB, V1/2621. Starting in 1966, he hosted MIT's Sloan Fellows, a kind of touring Executive MBA program with middle to senior managers from mostly American companies. The programs generally included plant tours and talks by distinguished German businessmen such as Abs.
8. Interview with Klaus Jacobs, July 11, 2006.
9. Interviews with Michael Rassmann, Jan. 9, 12, and March 7, 2006. Born in Breslau in 1936 and trained in management in Germany and the United States (Harvard), Michael Rassmann worked for Deutsche Bank for nearly forty years. He played a significant part in Deutsche Bank's history during this period and is one of our most important sources of information. Rassmann recounted that his years as Abs' assistant were his most interesting professionally but they were hard on his marriage, with Abs sometimes calling in the middle of the night. On occasion, however, after a long day, Abs would invite him for a drink, fall into the familiar "du," and even discuss his feeling about the Nazi period. Rassmann, like Detlev Staecker and Klaus Jacobs, was a part of a relatively rare breed of German-born Deutsche Bank manager who combined traditional bankers' virtues with a spirit of adventure that brought all three to the United States and even to settling in the United States for all or most of their life after retirement.
10. See Henry C. Wallich of Yale and U.S. Fed, HADB, V1/12498 and V1/3232.
11. Speech at Harvard Business School Club in New York, April 12, 1972, HADB, V1/3238.
12. Ibid.
13. Gall, *Der Bankier*, p. 289.
14. "Hermann Abs at 80," *Institutional Investor*, February 1982, p. 108.

15. Interview with Klaus Jacobs, July 11, 2006. Jacobs worked as Abs' personal assistant for six years and became Deutsche Bank's first representative to EAB. Jacobs recalled Abs' successor telling him years later that one reason he was selected to go to New York was that selecting his "favorite" might make Abs, who by then was chairman of the supervisory board, more comfortable with the project. After leaving Abs, Jacobs became a German branch manager. For many other reasons, he was an excellent candidate. Having traveled with Abs to the United States many times, he knew most of Abs' contacts.
16. Gall, *Der Bankier*, p. 259.
17. Gall, *Der Bankier*, p. 254.
18. Interview with Hilmar Kopper, Jan. 23, 2006.
19. Norris Willatt, "The Deutsche Bank Bonanza: The Goldmine for the Great German Bank Is Europe's Most Successful Economy and Deutsche Bank Has Mined Deep and Well," *Management Today*, September 1973.
20. "Germany's Powerful Banks," *Dun's Review*, January 1979.
21. Joint Memorandum, "Program for Improved Supervision and Regulation of International Lending," April 7, 1983, V1/635.
22. According to some international economists, most international business is still, even in the twenty-first century, more regional than global, a point of view for which this book contributes a good deal of evidence. Through most of its history, Deutsche Bank's competitive advantage on global markets rested on its strength in its home market and in Europe. As late as 1997, 73 percent of German exports were still within Europe, only 8.6 percent to the United States. See Alan Rugman, *End of Globalization* (New York: Pearson, 2002) for an excellent study of how bound regionally trade still is. However, Rugman is virtually silent about financial services, p. 133.
23. Burk, pp. 256–258.
24. For the terms of the acquisition, E-mail from Mark Yallop, Jan. 4, 2007.
25. Alfred Herrhausen, *Denken – Ordnen – Gestalten: Reden und Aufsätze*, ed. Kurt Weidemann (Berlin: Siedler, 1990). Herrhausen believed that managers needed to understand the social and political environment of business to guide investments properly.
26. "The Battle Plans of Hilmar Kopper," *Euromoney*, January 1994.
27. "Deutsche Bank's Bigger Reach," *New York Times*, June 30, 1989.
28. Interviews with Michael Rassmann, Jan. 9, 12, and March 7, 2006.
29. Interview with Hilmar Kopper, Jan. 26, 2006.
30. van der Wee, p. 196.
31. *Wall Street Journal*, Jan. 8, 1972.
32. Lees, p. 12.
33. Lees, pp. 14–42. In 1975, of the total foreign banking entities in the United States, roughly two-thirds were in New York, as were three-quarters of representative offices, agencies, or branches, p. 15. See first Section for the discussion of the difference between a branch and agent. See also Mira Wilkins, *The History of Foreign Investment in the United States since 1945*, forthcoming.
34. Lees, pp. 24–25. Some foreign banks – such as Credit Suisse with Swiss American Corp. – had established joint stock companies. Some foreign banks still chose to work with a representative office and correspondent banks. Others, like the National Bank of Greece, had taken over American banks, and still others were allowed to open investment companies, such as Belgian-American Banking Corp. Lastly, some twenty foreign banks, for example, Swiss Bank Corp., kept the right to have a "licensed agency." New York law also required foreign owned banks, for example, to pay a special fee to operate in the state. Rudolf M. Littauer, "Die rechtliche Stellung ausländischer Banken in New York," *Zeitschrift für das gesamte Kreditwesen*, Vol. 7 (1954), pp. 253–255 and 289–291.
35. *Wall Street Journal*, March 28, 1979.
36. Lees, 47.
37. Paul Gardner, Jr., "Foreign Investment in U.S. Banking," in J. Eugene Marans, Peter C. Williams, and Joseph P. Griffin, eds., *Foreign Investment in the United States 1980* (Washington, D.C.: District of Columbia Bar, 1980), pp. 333–335.

38. Michael Rassmann, "Bankkredite in USA sind in der Regel günstiger," *Handelsblatt*, May 7, 1974.
39. *Financial Times*, Oct. 3, 1974.
40. Duncan M. Ross, "Clubs and Consortia: European Banking Groups as Strategic Alliances," in *European Banks and the American Challenge: Competition and Cooperation in International Banking Under Bretton Woods*, eds. Stefano Battilossi and Youssef Cassis (Oxford: Oxford University Press, 2002), pp. 135–160.
41. Deutsche Bank, annual report 1977.
42. Ursel Steuber, "Foreign Engagement by German Banks," *Intereconomics*, Vol. 8 (1973), no. 7.
43. "Challenge to European Industry: To Accelerate Common Ties," report on a symposium organized by *The Financial Times*, in *The New York Times*, Dec. 3, 1970.
44. Hermann J. Abs, "Financial Aspects of Industrial Investments in the European Community," a speech to executives in the Sloan Management School (MIT) MBA, Oct. 11, 1965, HADB, V1/2582.
45. Interviews with Michael Rassmann, Jan. 9, 12, and March 7, 2006.
46. "Challenge to European Industry: To Accelerate Common Ties." Report on a symposium organized by *The Financial Times*, in *The New York Times*, Dec. 3, 1970.
47. Ross, "Clubs and Consortia," pp.148–153.
48. Deutsche Bank, annual report 1962.
49. Deutsche Bank, annual report 1963.
50. Deutsche Bank, annual report 1966.
51. Deutsche Bank, annual report 1977.
52. Mira Wilkins, "Dutch Multinational Enterprises in the United States: A Historical Summary," *Business History Review*, Vol. 79 (2005), p. 230. Not all foreign banks chose to convert to subsidiaries. Algemene Bank Nederland, for instance, turned its agency into a branch in 1963 when New York law began to allow foreign branches to do so.
53. Memo Thierbach and Lederer, Nov. 16, 1967, HADB, ZA47/557.
54. Ibid.
55. Büschgen, p. 755.
56. Mira Wilkins, *Foreign Investment in the United States Since 1945*.
57. Interview with Klaus Jacobs, July 11, 2006.
58. Ibid.
59. Deutsche Bank, annual report 1969.
60. Büschgen, pp. 753–755.
61. EBIC, 1977 European bank reports.
62. Deutsche Bank, annual report 1973.
63. Deutsche Bank, annual report 1967
64. Leonard C. Yassen, ed., *Direktinvestitionen in den USA* (Würzburg: Universitätsdruckerei H. Stürtz, 1974)
65. Interview with Klaus Jacobs, July 11, 2006.
66. Interviews with Rassmann and Jacobs.
67. Undated brochure, with other documents, spring of 1971, HADB, V1/2747. Interviews with Detlev Staecker, Feb. 13 and 14, 2006.
68. Interview with Klaus Jacobs, July 11, 2006.
69. Michael Rassmann's resume provided by Michael Rassmann.
70. Deutsche Bank, annual report 1971. As already discussed, in 1978, Deutsche Bank even purchased UBS's 50 percent interest and renamed the bank Atlantic Capital Corporation. By 1978, Deutsche Bank was a participating underwriter in 210 American and international listings, giving it an important position among Wall Street investment banks. Deutsche Bank, annual report 1978. As discussed in the last Chapter, despite EBIC's leasing operation, in 1982, Deutsche Bank established its own export leasing U.S. company.
71. Jacobs to Ulrich, Feb. 3, 1970, HADB, V1/606.
72. EAB, whose ownership shifted amounts among EBIC member banks, started with a $20 million investment by Deutsche Bank. With its holding varying between 14 percent and

22 percent as partners came in and out of the alliance, Deutsche Bank maintained roughly a 20 percent holding in EAB until 1988.

73. Interview with Klaus Jacobs, July 11, 2006.
74. Kreditengagements deutscher Kreditnehmer und deren auslaendischer Tochterunternehmen per 30. November 1971, HADB, V1/2747.
75. Undated brochure, with other documents, spring of 1971, HADB, V1/2747, and press release, March 18, 1971, HADB, V1/2747. Also, interviews with Rassmann.
76. Interview with Klaus Jacobs, July 11, 2006.
77. For management problems, interview with Klaus Jacobs, July 11, 2006.
78. Ibid.
79. Büschgen incorrectly ascribes the problem to business derived from Franklin, p. 755.
80. Büschgen, pp. 755–756. The partners became reluctant to invest more, but American regulators were not ready to release them from their responsibilities.
81. Interview with Michael Rassmann, May 31, 2006.
82. Werner Blessing, "Structural Changes in German Banks Permit Wider International Focus," *American Banker*, July 31, 1973.
83. Interview with Klaus Jacobs, July 11, 2006. Jacobs suggested to Guth that Deutsche Bank negotiate with its partners that they give up 30 percent of their joint holding to Deutsche Bank. Guth rejected the idea.
84. Interviews with Michael Rassmann, Jan. 9, 12, and March 7, 2006. Although rumors abounded long before, the decision to establish a branch coincided roughly with Abs' retirement from the supervisory board. Though Abs resisted direct U.S. investment, his caution had nothing to do with anti-American feelings over treatment by the United States after the war. He encouraged young German managers, in and out of Deutsche Bank, to do much of their training in the United States as he himself had done. Among some of his coworkers, he recounted anecdotes about his stay in New Orleans where he was based for several months in the 1920s. Abs recognized that the United States was just too important to ignore. Under his leadership, Deutsche Bank still maintained particularly close business ties with Chase Manhattan, Chemical Bank, and Manufacturers Hanover.
85. Ibid.
86. Deutsche Bank opened agencies in Sydney and London in 1973, followed by a branch in London in 1976. By 1977, the other EAB partner banks also founded their own presence in London. In *Euromoney*, March 1976, Wilfried Guth indicated that Deutsche Bank would be conservative with foreign investment but that the bank would add branches beyond the one already opened in London.
87. H. E. Ekblom, "European Direct Investments in the United States," *Harvard Business Review*, July–August, 1973.
88. E-mail from Victoria Pagano to Rosemary Lazenby, New York Fed, re. Deutsche Bank, April 28, 2004.
89. "Deutsche Bank zeigt in New York Flagge," *Börsen-Zeitung*, May 3, 1979. The article does not cite the amount of shares owned by Americans. As mentioned in Section II, as early as the 1920s a substantial portion of Deutsche Bank's equity was owned by non-Germans. Through the rest of the century and into the new millennium, Deutsche Bank's interest in and dependence on foreign equity capital grew.
90. Interviews with Michael Rassmann, Jan. 9, 12, and March 7, 2006.
91. Interviews with Detlev Staecker, Feb. 13 and 14, 2006. The Germans had contributed, for example, the Deutsch-Asiatische Bank to EBIC but not the Deutsche Ueberseeische Bank. Christians led those on the management board who thought the time had come for Deutsche Bank to have a presence in its own name in New York, but his views were not accepted by all his colleagues. Wilfried Guth, who had once been a strong supporter of EAB, together with Herrhausen, also wanted to do more in the United States than the joint venture promised.
92. Interview with Otto Steinmetz, July 6, 2006. Steinmetz reported that he had to make most of the arrangements for his own moves from Germany to America and then back again. Deutsche Bank had no procedures well into the '90s for handling housing, foreign exchange rate changes, and cost differentials.

93. Interviews with Detlev Staecker, Feb. 13 and 14, 2006.
94. Interview with Otto Steinmetz, July 6, 2006. A former employee of Deutsche Bank who worked at both EAB and the branch in New York, Otto Steinmetz is a member of Dresdner Bank's management board.
95. Interviews with Detlev Staecker, Feb. 13 and 14, 2006.
96. Ibid.
97. Ibid.
98. Interviews with Detlev Staecker, Feb. 13 and 14, 2006. In the late 1980s, the investment banking group even moved into the same office building as the branch at 52nd Street.
99. Interviews with Detlev Staecker, Feb. 13 and 14, 2006.
100. Ibid.
101. Ibid.
102. Ibid.
103. Ibid.
104. Interview with Otto Steinmetz, July 6, 2006.
105. Interviews with Detlev Staecker, Feb. 13 and 14, 2006.
106. Deutsche Bank, annual report 1989. Other German banks had similar difficulties entering the United States. Commerzbank came to the United States through a sort of back door. In 1967, it took a 20 percent interest in the International Commercial Bank Ltd. (£ 3.5 million). The British bank financed itself on the European capital markets and focused on middle- to long-term credits, working very closely with First National Bank of Chicago and Irving Trust in New York. *Hundert Jahre Commerzbank, 1870–1970*, p. 150.
107. Interview with Otto Steinmetz, July 6, 2006.
108. Interviews with Michael Rassmann Jan. 9, 12, and March 7, 2006, and Detlev Staecker, Feb. 13 and 14, 2006.
109. Interviews with Detlev Staecker, Feb. 13 and 14, 2006.
110. Barthold von Ribbentrop to Christians, Guth, and Herrhausen, Jan. 12, 1984, HADB, V1/604.
111. Telephone interview with Hilmar Kopper, Oct. 18, 2006.
112. Mira Wilkins, "Dutch Multinational Enterprises in the United States: A Historical Summary," *Business History Review*, Vol. 79 (Summer 2005), pp. 252–253. By 1991, the two largest Dutch banks merged to form ABN AMRO and took full control of EAB.
113. Telephone interview with Hilmar Kopper, Oct. 18, 2006.
114. Interviews with Detlev Staecker, Feb. 13 and 14, 2006.
115. Foreign Office, HADB, V1/604.
116. Interviews with Detlev Staecker, Feb. 13 and 14, 2006.
117. Ibid.
118. Steinmetz presentation, March 15, 1987, HADB, ZA43/1077. Its credit business was divided into several categories: U.S. prime rate loans (10 percent share), Europe loans (65 percent), standby letters of credit (15 percent), and other forms of borrowings (10 percent).
119. *Börsen-Zeitung*, July 13, 1989.
120. Staecker presentation, March 29, 1989, HADB, ZA43/1077.
121. Interview with Klaus Jacobs, July 11, 2006, reporting conversations with senior Deutsche Bank management in Frankfurt. Jacobs was contracted to headhunt new leadership for the New York branch.
122. Hefferman, p. 29.
123. "Biggest Banks Face Hurdles," *National Mortgage News*, Vol. 29 (June 6, 2005), Issue 37, p. 11.
124. Jane E. Hughes and Scott B. MacDonald, *International Banking* (Boston: Addison Wesley, 2002), p. 202. Deutsche Bank was not as hard hit as some of its competitors, and the bank quickly restored growth in this area. The introduction of the Euro also gave a boost to its bond trading, derivative, and other businesses. E-mail, Mark Yallop, Jan. 4, 2007.
125. Hefferman, pp. 252–259.
126. Building on Basel I and responding to criticism, in 1999, Basel II, among other proposals, called for minimum capital requirements, more internal assessment, greater market discipline, geographic dispersion, and greater disclosure.

127. Alan Kline, "Why so Shy about International Trade Financing?" *American Banker*, Jan. 13, 2004. See also the rescue of Long-Term Capital Management, in Hughes and MacDonald, pp. 244–248.
128. Hughes and MacDonald, p. 157.
129. General Electric Capital (GE Capital) is the financial services subsidiary of GE. In the mid-90s, it issued more commercial paper than any other institution in the United States, supplied consumer credit for department stores, and insured private homes. Hefferman, p. 29.
130. Hughes and MacDonald, p. 158.
131. Hughes and MacDonald, p. 159.
132. Hughes and MacDonald, pp. 176–178.
133. "Bank of England Analyses the Performance of Major International Banks in the Period 1980–91," *Bank of England Quarterly Bulletin*, August 1992.
134. Interview with Hilmar Kopper, Jan. 23, 2006.
135. Telephone interview with Hilmar Kopper, Oct. 18, 2006.
136. Interviews with Rolf-E. Breuer and Hilmar Kopper, Jan. 23, 2006.
137. Hughes and MacDonald, p. 150.
138. Hughes and MacDonald, p. 153.
139. Hughes and MacDonald, p. 155.
140. Deutsche Bank's Financial Website.
141. Kohn, pp. 279–281.
142. Kohn, pp. 282–286.
143. Geoffrey Jones, *British Multinational Banking: 1830–1990* (Oxford: Clarendon Press, 1993), pp. 386–387.
144. Kohn, pp. 282–284. Permission was based not only on the bank's U.S. operations, but also on the bank's worldwide reputation and control system, indeed, even on the bank's home-country system of supervision. Special permission was required from the Federal Reserve Board for any foreign bank to acquire more than 5 percent of a U.S. bank. In addition, to obtain federally funded deposit insurance, foreign banks had to create separately capitalized subsidiaries. To administer its new regulations, the Fed hired 250 examiners just for foreign banks.
145. "The Battle Plans of Hilmar Kopper," *Euromoney*, January 1994. His models were J. P. Morgan and the Swiss banks.
146. Ibid.
147. Ibid.
148. "The Battle Plans of Hilmar Kopper," *Euromoney*, January 1994. In 1993, Deutsche Bank's profits were greater than the combined total of the next five largest German banks, far surpassing even Dresdner Bank – its nearest rival in Germany – despite that bank's close links to Allianz, Germany's largest insurance company. According to *Euromoney* it ranked second to Goldman Sachs in international bond underwriting and first in bond trading. In 1998, too, it was the biggest bank measured by stock market valuation outside of Japan.
149. Ibid.
150. Ibid.
151. Ibid.
152. Interview with Hilmar Kopper, Jan. 23, 2006.
153. Presse-Information, Deutsche Bank, Sept. 29, 1992.
154. "John Rolls' Grand Plan," *Investment Dealer's Digest*, Aug. 29, 1994.
155. Ibid.
156. Ibid.
157. Interviews with Detlev Staecker, Feb. 13 and 14, 2006. Klaus Jacobs, one of the first senior managers of EAB and who was president of the executive search firm Tosa, found Ross and Rolls, who was then chief financial officer of United Technologies, for the U.S. operations.
158. "John Rolls' Grand Plan," *Investment Dealer's Digest*, Aug. 29, 1994.
159. Interviews with Detlev Staecker, Feb. 13 and 14, 2006.
160. Interviews with John Ross, Jan. 16, 2006.
161. Interviews with Detlev Staecker, Feb. 13 and 14, 2006.

17. The Bankers Trust Acquisition

1. See "Deutsche Bank wagt Kauf in den USA," *Finanz und Wirtschaft*, Nov. 25, 1998, for an interesting analysis of Deutsche Bank's share movements annotated by announcements of other finance sector mergers and rumors of its own interests.
2. Axel Wieandt and Rafael Moral y Santiago, "Growing in the U.S. – Review of Deutsche Bank's M&A Strategy in North America," in: Kai Lucks (ed.), *Transatlantic Mergers & Acquisitions: Opportunities and Pitfalls in German-American Partnerships* (Erlangen: Publicis, 2005), pp. 85–97.
3. "Für die Deutsche Bank war Amerika bislang voller Stolpersteine," *Frankfurter Allgemeine Zeitung*, Nov. 30, 1998.
4. Hughes and MacDonald, pp. 427–428. While the number of acquisitions in the United States peaked in 1995–96, the Dollar volume soared to a record $350 billion in the two years ending in December 1998.
5. Eduardo Strachman et al., "Worldwide Concentration in the Banking Sector," IPEA, 2002.
6. R. V. Vennet, "Cross-Border Mergers in European Banking and Bank Efficiency," Gent University, 2002. From 1995 through the first half of 2000, there were 2,153 mergers and acquisitions of credit institutions in the European Union; 1,807 were domestic deals, but of the remaining 346, most were between Europe and other regions.
7. Roy C. Smith, *The Global Bankers* (New York: Plume, 1990), p. 351.
8. "Deutsche Bank – Aufbruch nach Amerika," *Frankfurter Allgemeine Zeitung*, Nov. 25, 1998. Nations of Bank America (1998) $60 billion; Natwest of Wells Fargo (1998) $34 billion; Mitsubishi Bank of Bank of Tokio (1995) $34 billion; Banc One of First Chicago (1998) $30 billion; Schweizer Bankverein of UBS (1997) $25 billion. Few of the deals were cross-border.
9. See Stephen A. Rhoades, "Bank Mergers and Industrywide Structure, 1980–1994," Washington: Board of Governors of the Federal Reserve System, January 1996, and Steven J. Pilloff, "Bank Merger Activity in the United States, 1994–2003," Washington: Board of Governors of the Federal Reserve System, May 2004, for a list of the important bank mergers in the United States 1950 to 2004. From 1950 to 1989, there were twenty-six considered important. During the fourteen years that followed, there were sixty-two mergers. See also *The Times*, Nov. 24, 1998.
10. The great merger waves are usually considered in the United States between 1897 and 1904, 1916 to 1929, 1965 to 1969, 1981 to 1989. Although the European experience is different, this periodization roughly holds for that area, too. In these other periods, technological and regulatory changes have also played an important role in stimulating the consolidations. Many analysts speculate about whether we have begun a new round of consolidation. Patrick A. Gaughan, *Mergers, Acquisitions and Corporate Restructurings* (New York: John Wiley & Sons, Inc., 1999), pp. 21–59.
11. Vennet et al.
12. Karina Robison, "The Driving Forces in Bank Mergers," *The Banker*, 2002.
13. Hughes and MacDonald, pp. 429–430.
14. Strachman.
15. Ken Elkins, "Merger of Egos," *Bank Director Magazine*, 2nd quarter, 1998, about the 1998 giant merger of National Bank and BankAmerica, which created an institution with a 8.1 percent United States market share, close to the top allowed by regulation, a coast to coast U.S. presence, the highest market share in some of the fastest growing regions in the United States, and the largest pure banking operation in the United States.
16. Lisa Reilly Cullen, "Citicorp vs. Nationsbank," *Money*, Oct. 19, 1998.
17. *Die Tageszeitung*, Nov. 25, 1998.
18. "Hoffnung auf Einsparungen durch Übernahme," *Die Welt*, Nov. 25, 1998.
19. Bloomberg-Ticker, Nov. 30, 1998.
20. *New York Times*, March 30, 1953.
21. See Memos, Deutsche Bundesbank, Hauptabteilung Ausland, Feb. 7, 1966, and June 13, 1966, HABBk, B330/5170.

22. "98 Free World Banks with Assets of $1 Billion," *American Banker*, Aug. 7, 1963. With the world still suffering the effects of World War II, Bank of America topped the league tables with $13.4 billion in assets. Nine of the top twenty were American banks. British and Canadian banks were the only others to make it into the top ten. Japanese banks were beginning to develop a very powerful position in world banking with four of the top twenty. Deutsche Bank was by far the largest in Germany, well ahead of Dresdner Bank, but not the largest in continental Europe, an honor that Banca Nazionale del Lavoro held.
23. M. E. Gevers, Sept. 30, 1957 file not distributed to Bankers Trust officers. HADB, K50/9/36. Bankers Trust managers seemed a little concerned about the "hot money" coming into Germany from speculators (about $1 billion). Managers from the two banks met regularly. The contact seemed particularly strong with Krebs and Jacobs. See also correspondence HADB, K50/9/34 and K50/9/35.
24. Bankers Trust, annual reports 1975–78.
25. Real estate investment trusts are groups of lenders organized as mutual funds to support construction and real estate development. In 1973, real estate loans amounted to $884 million or 10 percent of Bankers Trust's total loan portfolio.
26. Interview with Charles S. Sanford, Jr., and Gene Guill, March 9, 2006.
27. Shelagh Hefferman, *Modern Banking in Theory and Practice* (New York: Wiley and Sons, 1996), pp. 417–419.
28. "The Battle Plans of Hilmar Kopper," *Euromoney*, January 1994. Vol. 29, no. 4, pp. 28–44. Kopper singled out Charles Sanford as one of the bankers he admired most for his courage and determination in successfully turning Bankers Trust around.
29. "New York City Is Still on the Brink," *Fortune*, July 1977.
30. Interviews with Charles S. Sanford, Jr., March 9, 2006 (during first interview, with Gene Guill, a former Bankers Trust employee, who left to join Deutsche Bank in 1994) and March 14, 2006. A graduate of the University of Georgia (1958) and the Wharton School (1960, MBA), Sanford joined Bankers Trust in 1961 in commercial banking and then moved into money and securities trading. He joined the management committee in 1979, became president in 1983, deputy chairman in 1986, and chairman and chief executive officer in 1987. See also Chernow, *The Death of the Banker*, for a good discussion of the evolution of banking activities.
31. An address by Charles S. Sanford, Jr., "Managing the Transformation of a Corporate Culture: Risks and Rewards," Nov. 14, 1996, delivered as part of the 1996–97 Musser-Schoemaker Leadership Lecture Series at the Wharton School, University of Pennsylvania.
32. Bankers Trust, annual report 1995.
33. "New Tricks to Learn," A Survey of International Banking, *The Economist*, April 10, 1995.
34. See Robert A. Bennett, "Sanford's New Banking Vision," *The New York Times*, March 17, 1985, and interviews with Charles S. Sanford, Jr., and Gene Guill, Sept. 12, 2006, and Bankers Trust, annual report 1995.
35. "New Tricks to Learn," A Survey of International Banking, *The Economist*, April 10, 1995, pp. 17–19. It involved a system by which allocations of capital were made to transactions by allocating 99 percent of the expected loss to the capital based on the historical loss experience of different markets. Even though the positions may be of a shorter duration, RAROC assumed that they would take a year to unwind. On this basis, expected returns were recalculated.
36. See, for example, "Die amerikanische Herausforderung," *Frankfurter Allgemeine Zeitung*, Nov. 25, 1998.
37. Hefferman, pp. 417–418.
38. Hefferman, p. 427.
39. Ibid.
40. "Bears Clawed Bank-Investor Bulls in 1994," *American Banker*, Dec. 27, 1994.
41. See "Judge Denies Award in Derivatives Suit against Bankers Trust," *American Banker*, April 22, 1996. At least some academics sided completely with Bankers Trust on the appropriateness of the hedge, but the case points to a management difficulty of selling highly complex products to corporate clients who may not understand or want to understand the different payouts and risks.

42. This may not sufficiently show the contrast between the two periods. If the losses of Less Developed Country Loans had been booked to the earlier years when the business was done, as opposed to 1987 and 1989, the 1974–86 average return would have been less than 1 percent.
43. Bankers Trust, annual report 1995.
44. Ibid.
45. *Derivatives Week*, May 23, 1994.
46. "Bankers Trust Wins Votes of Confidence," *Pension & Investments*, Oct. 16, 1995, p. 39.
47. Bankers Trust, annual report 1997, for the stock price up to year-end 1997. Some analysts believed that Bankers Trust stock price stayed as high as it did during the mid-90s only because of its high dividend.
48. E-mail from Gene Guill, July 26, 2006. Newman, who had been appointed as president on Oct. 19, 1995, assumed the position of CEO on Jan. 1, 1996. Sanford, who remained as chairman until April 16, 1996, effectively relinquished operating control in January.
49. Bankers Trust, annual report 1998 (10-K).
50. Mark Yallop interview, Dec. 11, 2006, chief operating officer, ICAP, formerly of Deutsche Bank, member of Due Diligence Team.
51. Bankers Trust, annual report 1998 and 1999, first and second quarter 10-Qs.
52. "Mr Fix-it Aims to Get Bankers on the Mend," *Financial Times*, Nov. 30, 1998.
53. Roger Lowenstein, *When Genius Failed: The Rise and Fall of Long-term Capital Management* (New York: Random House, 2001). In addition to Bankers Trust being a major lender to LTCM, Newman was singled out as someone who threatened the success of the bailout. P. 224.
54. *New York Times*, Nov. 24, 1998.
55. Ibid.
56. *Berliner Zeitung*, Nov. 24, 1998.
57. See "Breuer's Mating Dance," *Institutional Investor*, November 1998. By the time this issue came out, Bankers Trust seemed to be the leading candidate to fulfill Deutsche Bank's ambition to buy an American financial institution, even though Lehman Brothers and J. P. Morgan were also mentioned and despite Rolf-E. Breuer's nondenial denials. Breuer contended that he was always talking to executives at Bankers Trust as part of normal business and that he had nothing to tell shareholders.
58. Interviews with Michael Rassmann, Jan. 9, 12, and March 7, 2006, reporting the announcement meeting and Michael Philipp's response to a question.
59. Reuters-Ticker, Nov. 24, 1998, *Berliner Morgenpost*, Nov. 24, 1998, and *The Times*, Nov. 24, 1998.
60. "Deutsche Deal Seen as a Trend-Setter," *International Herald Tribune*, Nov. 26, 1998.
61. Ibid.
62. Ibid.
63. "Experten sehen Banken-Deal skeptisch," *Die Welt*, Nov. 25, 1998.
64. "Deutsche Bank – Aufbruch nach Amerika," *Frankfurter Allgemeine Zeitung*, Nov. 25, 1998.
65. "*Ich bin nur ein Sterblicher neben diesen Göttern.*" "Aufstieg in den Olymp," *Die Woche*, Nov. 27, 1998.
66. Bloomberg-Ticker, after conference, Nov. 30, 1998.
67. Press reports of the price varied. Some used the pure purchase price, others included some additional charges.
68. Bloomberg-Ticker, Nov. 24, 1998.
69. "Gemischtes Finanzierungspaket der Deutschen Bank erwartet," *Börsen-Zeitung*, Nov. 25, 1998, for example.
70. "Deutsche Bank Plans to Keep DaimlerChrysler," *Wall Street Journal*, Nov. 26, 1998.
71. "DaimlerChrysler Shares 'Not for Sale'," *Financial Times*, Nov. 26, 1998.
72. DPA-Ticker, Dec. 2, 1998.
73. "Deutsche Bank in Belgian Buy," *Financial Times*, Dec. 3, 1998.
74. Bloomberg-Ticker, Second, Nov. 24, 1998.
75. See, for example, "Bank-Fusionen kosten Arbeitsplätze," *Frankfurter Neue Presse*, Nov. 25, 1998, *The Age* (Australia), Nov. 25, 1998, and the *Herald Tribune*, Nov. 25, 1998.

76. "Bankers Reap Gains as Merger Frenzy Persists," *Wall Street Journal*, Nov. 25, 1998.
77. "Americanizing Deutsche Bank," *Wall Street Journal*, Nov. 25, 1998.
78. "Is Deutsche Bank Hunting Big Game with the Wrong Gun?," *Wall Street Journal*, Nov. 23, 1998.
79. Ibid.
80. See, for example, "Die amerikanische Herausforderung," *Frankfurter Allgemeine Zeitung*, Nov. 25, 1998.
81. "Die Deutsche Bank – Ein Gigant im Nebel," *Tagesspiegel*, Nov. 24, 1998.
82. "Wachstum um jeden Preis?" *Tagesspiegel*, Nov. 25, 1998.
83. "Die Deutsche Bank bringt das globale Fusions-Karussell auf Touren," *Süddeutsche Zeitung*, Nov. 25, 1998.
84. "Deutsche Bank Threatens Focus with U.S. Deal," *Wall Street Journal*, Nov. 27, 1998.
85. "Die Deutsche Bank riskiert alles," *Handelsblatt*, Nov. 27, 1998, and "Deutsche Bank Push into U.S. Market Seems to Be a Bumpy Ride," *Wall Street Journal*, Nov. 27, 1998.
86. "*Aber wenn unter dem Renditedruck internationaler Investmentfonds jede nationale Bodenhaftung und jedes Verantwortungsgefühl für die Erhaltung von Arbeitsplätzen im Lande verlorengeht, ja der Abbau von Arbeitsplätzen als zulagenwürdiger Rationalisierungserfolg gilt, provozieren die Wirtschaftsführer von heute die Entfremdung der Menschen von unserem bewährten Wirtschafts- und Gesellschaftssystem und tragen mittelfristig zur Beschädigung dieser zwar sozialgebundenen, aber prinzipiell freien Wirtschaft bei.*" Michael Rutz, "Hat Marx doch recht?," *Rheinischer Mekur*, Dec. 3, 1998.
87. Peter Martin, "Alice in Mergerland," *Financial Times*, Dec. 1, 1998.
88. "Deutsche's Foray into America Will Offer Little to Its Shareholders," *The European*, Nov. 30, 1998.
89. Interview with Rolf-E. Breuer, Jan. 23, 2006.
90. *Neue Zürcher Zeitung*, Nov. 25, 1998.
91. See Christopher Kobrak, "Home-Country Political Risk: The Case of German Business," European International Business Academy, Jerusalem, December 1998.
92. *Financial Times*, Dec. 8, 1999.
93. *The Economist*, Nov. 27, 1999.
94. "Die Deutsche Bank läßt noch viele Fragen offen," *Die Welt*, Nov. 26, 1998.
95. "Breuer Aims for the Top," *Financial Times*, Nov. 26, 1998. See also "Ein ziemlich schwerer Brocken," *Die Zeit*, Nov. 26, 1998.
96. "The Battle of the Bulge Bracket," *The Economist*, Nov. 28, 1998.
97. Reuters-Tickers, Nov. 30, 1998 and Dec. 1, 1998. The British press was quick to bemoan the likely loss of 3,000 jobs in London. See "Deutsche's $10bn Deal to Cost 3,000 City Jobs," *The Times*, Dec. 1, 1998. The American press was also concerned about the job losses in New York and the bonuses for the elite bankers. See *International Herald Tribune*, Dec. 1, 1998, two articles.
98. The French journal *Les Echos* seemed particularly interested in the latter question, Dec. 1, 1998.
99. "Deutsche Bank Gets Bankers Trust in Line," *Wall Street Journal*, Dec. 1, 1998.
100. "Die neue Welt AG," *Der Spiegel*, Nov. 30, 1998.
101. Bloomberg-Ticker, Nov. 29, 1988.
102. Interview with John Ross, Jan. 16, 2006.
103. *Financial Times*, June 21, 1999.
104. Interview with Rolf-E. Breuer, Jan. 23, 2006.
105. Hughes and MacDonald, p. 27.
106. Hughes and MacDonald, p. 53.
107. Hughes and MacDonald, p. 145.
108. Hughes and MacDonald, p. 149.
109. *The Economist*, May 27, 2000.
110. Ibid.
111. Separate interviews with Seth Waugh and Gary Hattem, Jan. 6, 2006.
112. See *The Economist*, Sept. 25, 1999.
113. See *The Economist* Feb. 2, 2000 and May 27, 2000.

18. Postscript

1. "The great Swiss hope," *The Economist*, May 18, 2002. By 2002, Deutsche Bank was not even in the top twenty banks as measured by stock market value. With a lamentable share price, Deutsche Bank was the subject of frequent takeover rumors. At the very least, during the first few years of the new century, Deutsche Bank did not seem to be well positioned to participate in the likely continuation of bank-sector consolidations. Lloyds TSB, with which Deutsche Bank discussed a merger in 2001, had a market value, in 2002, 40 percent greater than the German bank, despite having less than half its assets.
2. "Deutsche's American dream," *The Economist*, Feb. 2, 2002, and Deutsche Bank's 2005 annual report.
3. Internal documents provided and interview with Donna Milrod and Frank Fehrenbach, Jan. 13, 2006. As this book was being written, in the United States, the bank's priorities included turning around asset management, growing private wealth management profitably, and profiting more from the combination of sales and trading.
4. Interview with Seth Waugh, president of Deutsche Bank Americas, Jan. 6, 2006, and interview with Donna Milrod and Frank Fehrenbach, Jan. 13, 2006.
5. See, Christopher Kobrak, "The Rise and Fall of Family International Banking: Markets, Regulation, and the Democratization of Finance," Business History Conference, Cleveland, May–June 2002, http://www.h-net.org/~business/bhcweb/annmeet/generalo.7.html.
6. See Franklin R. Edwards and Stav Gaon, "Hedge Funds: What Do We Know?," *Journal of Applied Corporate Finance*, Vol. 15 (2003), no. 4, pp. 8–21 for an excellent overview of hedge fund activities. For an insightful discussion of the difficulty of assessing the true risk-adjusted rewards of hedge funds, see Hélytette Geman and Cécile Kharoubi, "Hedge Funds Revisited: Distributional Characteristics, Dependence Structure and Diversification," *Journal of Risk*, Vol. 5 (2003), no. 4. Although hedge funds are said to have sprouted up in the 1940s, an argument might be made that they had their origins in the pre-World War I era and were merely curtailed by the instability during the interwar period.

   Over half of these funds are offshore, or unregistered, and organized outside the United States in places such as the Cayman Islands with favorable tax and other regulation. In 2001, by some estimates, there were 7,000 hedge funds and $600 billion in assets, a small but growing fraction of total funds under management by mainstream investment vehicles such as mutual funds.
7. Interview with Frank Fehrenbach, Sept. 12, 2006.
8. Lowenstein, pp. 136–224. The consensus among Deutsche Bank's management was that Long-Term Capital Management was an isolated problem. Management of the bank was impressed by how the Fed had intervened to contain the crisis. Indeed, the spillover effects were relatively mild and losses surprisingly limited. Telephone interview with Rolf-E. Breuer, Nov. 16, 2006.
9. See Thomas Friedman's "Gold Arches Theory," which postulates that war is virtually impossible between two nations with McDonalds restaurants – *A Brief History of the Twenty-first Century* (New York: Farrar, Strauss, and Giroux, 2005) for a wonderful example of careless optimism, and compare it with Norman Angell's *The Great Illusion*, which argued that the "economic cost of war was so great no one could possibly hope to gain by starting a war the consequences of which would be disastrous," published a few years before World War I.
10. Paul W. Doremus et al., *The Myth of the Global Corporation* (Princeton: Princeton University Press, 1999).
11. Massimo Sbracia and Andrea Zaghini, "The Role of the Banking System in the International Transmission of Shocks," *World Economy*, Vol. 26 (2003), no. 5, pp. 727–754.
12. Neil O'Hara, "Banks' Counterparty Risk," *U.S. Banker*, Vol. 115 (June 2005), Issue 6, pp. 1–12.
13. See first Section on the United States wanting to learn from Germany about maintaining the Gold Standard and creating a central bank, and German enthusiasm for American entrepreneurial values.
14. "The Great Swiss Hope," *The Economist*, May 18, 2002. Breuer, for example, has been sued over his remarks about the creditworthiness of Leo Kirch, a Deutsche Bank customer. Breuer, who recently resigned over the issue, in part, because he sat on the supervisory board of the

company, was doing something for which in the United States he has a fiduciary responsibility.

15. Deutsche Bank will in all likelihood exercise less "voice and more exit," to use the terms of the Harvard economist Albert Hirschman. This shift represents an enormous departure from the German banking tradition of more active management of corporate clients. See interviews, Breuer and Kopper, Jan. 23, 2006, and Albert O. Hirschman, *Exit, Voice, and Loyalty* (Cambridge, MA: Harvard University Press, 1970).
16. "Ackermann to Face Retrial," *Financial Times*, Dec. 22, 2005. The charges arose from the Vodafone acquisition of the German firm Mannesmann in 2000. Ackermann, along with other members of the Mannesmann board voted management large bonuses – huge by German standards – for their efforts to wring out a higher price from Vodafone. Much of the German public was incensed by the payout. Under German law, the supervisory board is not allowed to vote management bonuses for which the company is not contractually obliged. Acquitted on the first go-round, in December 2005, the appeals court threw out the original acquittal, contending that the payments were excessive and served no purpose for the company. The case is very difficult for Americans to understand. The case was not initiated by irate shareholders, whose money ostensibly had been given away. In addition to the government bringing the case to court when shareholders had complained, in Germany both defendants and the prosecution can appeal decisions.
17. Bankers Trust's building near the World Trade Center was rendered effectively unusable after the attacks. For nearly two years, the issue of what would be done and how much the insurance companies would pay was left unsettled. In April 2004, the parties came to agreement, removing one of the hindrances to the Lower Manhattan Development Project. *The New York Times*, Feb. 10, 2005.
18. See Nassim Nicholas Taleb, *Fooled by Randomness: The Hidden Role of Chance in Life and in the Markets* (New York: Thomson, 2004). Bad and good outcomes, as well as extraordinary events, "black swans," are part of a stochastic process, best understood by rigorous mathematics. Large numbers of standardized events inducing statistical patterns allow us to predict reasonably the likelihood of future events and make decisions accordingly. Along these lines, financial actors overestimate their own knowledge and competencies in determining causality, when outcomes are merely a matter of luck.
19. This implies that "market efficiency" is a kind of "ideal type," a moving target, which leaves some opportunity for "abnormal gain" in its wake. Recognition of this institutional role has contributed to one of the most interesting new directions in financial theory. Behavioral finance takes as its starting point that human beings are not always rational. Nicholas Barberis and Richard Thaler, "A Survey of Behavioral Finance," in *Handbook of the Economics of Finance*, eds. George M. Constantinides, et al. (Amsterdam: Elsevier, 2003), pp. 1054–1119.
20. Robert Whaley, "Derivatives," in *Handbook of the Economics of Finance*, eds. George M. Constantinides et al. (Amsterdam: Elsevier, 2003), pp. 1131–1159. The United States, most other developed, and even many emerging markets during the second half of the twentieth century increased their transparency, standardization, and oversight and, thereby, contributed to reducing specific (diversifiable or unique) risk and a myriad of transaction costs.
21. Frank Knight articulated the notion that risk (in the narrow sense) was that part of future contingencies (risk in the broad sense) that was quantifiable and therefore insurable. Although his idea that real profit is only derived from managing unique risk rather than just diversifying it away is consistent with modern finance, managing uncertainty gets short shrift in most finance textbooks. *Risk, Uncertainty and Profit* (Chicago: University of Chicago Press, 1921).
22. Management theorists do not have a great sense of the reasons for financial service FDI; they keep reasoning from manufacturing, ownership, and location advantages. Even when management theorists talk about services, they hark back to theories developed out of manufacturing. See for example, Peter J. Buckley and Pervez N. Ghauri, *The Internationalization of the Firm: A Reader* (London: Thompson, 1999), which has only about eight pages dealing with service firms, most of them not financial. Even those sections, such as the essay by Buckley et al., "The Internationalization of Service Firms: A Comparison with the Manufacturing Sector," does so by way of exception to theories developed from manufacturing.

23. See Jeremy Rifkin, *The Age of Access* (New York: Penguin Books, 2000), and Robert J. Shiller, *The New Financial Order: Risk in the 21st Century* (Princeton: Princeton University Press, 2003).
24. For a discussion of the importance of clusters, and the growth and challenges of multinationals, especially in the service sector, see Michael Porter, *The Competitive Advantages of Nations* (London: Macmillan, 1990), and Geoffrey Jones, *Multinationals and Global Capitalism: From the Nineteenth to the Twenty-first Century* (Oxford: Oxford University Press, 2005).
25. See Richard R. Nelson, ed. *National Innovative Systems: A Comparative Analysis* (Oxford: Oxford University Press, 1993), an excellent work which says nothing about financial innovation. Strangely, although there is much discussion about national systems and clusters of innovation, that literature has not integrated financial services. As with many academic pursuits, there is a curious disconnect between banking history and those who write about innovation theories and strategies.
26. Amazingly, running a series of subsidiaries in money market centers is no more bizarre for banks today than it was for Siemens and Gwinner operating branches in Hamburg, Frankfurt, and Bremen in 1900. Improvements in technology and the breakdown of national constraints to funds flows make internalization of banking activities over a wide patch of the world feasible.
27. DB Americas Legal Vehicle Network Analysis, Taunus Structure, as of March 31, 2005. Internal Deutsche Bank document.
28. Interview with Donna Milrod and Frank Fehrenbach, Jan. 13, 2006. Interview with Frank Fehrenbach, March 8, 2006, and internal documents.
29. Several studies have found that domestic banks are much better able to control their costs than multinational ones. Banks from different countries are not equal. American banks tend to operate more efficient foreign operations than financial institutions from other countries, but the data is inconclusive. See Allen N. Berger et al., "Globalization of Financial Institutions: Evidence from Cross-Border Banking Performance," *Brookings-Wharton Papers on Financial Services: 2000*.
30. "Trust Me, I'm a Banker: A Survey of International Banking," *The Economist*, April 17, 2004. Bank net interest margins are substantially lower in Germany than in France, Britain, and the United States. Nonbanking institutions, such as the powerful insurance company Allianz, have entered the banking business in an effort to offer one-stop financial shopping for customers and to appeal to older savers worried about their retirement. Deutsche Bank's own efforts to consolidate its business in Germany have led to many frustrations and changes in direction. In 2002 the bank reintegrated its retail arm, Deutsche Bank 24, instead of spinning it off as had been contemplated. In spite of greater electronic access to banking information and a remarkable ability to transact business from nearly anywhere, for some products and activities, many customers still prefer to see their bankers.
31. Many senior managers have little grasp of the techniques used by many who commit millions in corporate resources. The Nick Leeson–Barings catastrophe, the story of how one rogue trader brought down one of the oldest merchant banks, is probably the most glaring example, but even the best run banks share the dilemma.
32. In January 2006, Deutsche Bank dismissed a senior trader for allegedly overstating his trading position by £30 million. *Financial Times*, Jan. 17, 2006.
33. Robert Whaley, "Derivatives," in *Handbook of the Economics of Finance*, eds. George M. Constantinides et al. (Amsterdam: Elsevier, 2003), p. 1132. Virtually no financial derivative contracts were traded in the 1970s. By some estimates, trading in financial derivatives has surpassed $100 trillion, roughly ten times the U.S. Gross Domestic Product.
34. "Trust Me, I'm a Banker: A Survey of International Banking," *The Economist*, April 17, 2004.
35. In the 1990s, failure to control the activities of one of its traders bankrupted one of the oldest banks in the world, Barings, and the "hedging" of Long-Term Capital Management required intervention by not only the Federal Reserve but a large group of money-center banks.
36. Doremus, pp. 1–10.
37. "The Great Swiss Hope," *The Economist*, May 18, 2002.
38. Interviews with Seth Waugh, Jan. 6, 2006, and Rolf-E. Breuer, Jan. 23, 2006.

39. Separate interviews with Seth Waugh, president of Deutsche Bank Americas, Jan. 6, 2006, and Gary Hattem, director of corporate social responsibility, Jan. 6, 2006.
40. Interview with Seth Waugh, Jan. 6, 2006.
41. Interview with Seth Waugh, Jan. 6, 2006, and Rolf-E. Breuer, Jan. 23, 2006.
42. "Deutsche's American Dream," *The Economist*, February 2, 2002.
43. Ibid.
44. See, for example, Merrill Lynch, "Comment on Deutsche Bank," Nov. 1, 2005. In contrast to German comments, many Americans have cheered Deutsche Bank's "flexibility in staff costs." Staff costs to revenues have dropped from 46.3 percent in the first quarter of 2004 to 43.7 percent in the third quarter of 2005. Despite staff reductions, severance costs have even dropped substantially.
45. "Debt Capital Markets Review," Thomson Financial, Fourth Quarter 2005, http://banker.thomsonib.com. Deutsche Bank held very strong positions, particularly in all international debt, Euro debt, global high yield debt, and especially non-Dollar, emerging market bonds.
46. E-mail from Bernadette H. Whitaker, managing director of human resources to Frank Fehrenbach, March 9, 2006.
47. John F. Wilson and Andrew Thomson, *The Making of Modern Management: British Management in Historical Perspective* (Oxford: Oxford University Press, 2006), p. 9.
48. See Christopher A. Bartlett and Sumantra Ghoshal, *Managing Across Borders: The Transnational Solution* (Boston, MA: Harvard Business School Press, 1991).
49. Bartlett and Ghoshal, p. 35.
50. See, Friedrich Nietzsche, *The Use and Abuse of History*, 2nd edition (New York: Liberal Arts Press, 1957).

Bibliography of Secondary Sources

Abelshauser, Werner. *The Dynamics of German Industry: Germany's Path Toward the New Economy and the American Challenge*. New York: Berghahn Books, 2005.

Abrahams, Paul Philip. *The Foreign Expansion of American Finance 1907–1921*. New York: Arno Press, 1976.

Abs, Hermann J. *Entscheidungen 1949–1953. Die Entstehung des Londoner Schuldenabkommens*. Mainz: Hase & Koehler, 1991.

———. *Zeitfragen der Geld- und Wirtschaftspolitik. Aus Vorträgen und Aufsätzen*. Frankfurt: Knapp, 1959.

Achterberg, Erich. "Hermann Wallich." *Zeitschrift für das gesamte Kreditwesen*, Vol. 16 (1963), pp. 228–231.

Adams, Edward D. *Niagara Power: History of Niagara Falls Power Company, 1886–1918*. 2 vols. Niagara Falls, NY: Niagara Falls Company, 1927.

Adler, Hans A. "The Post-War Reorganization of the German Banking System." *Quarterly Journal of Economics*, Vol. 63 (1949), pp. 322–341.

Adler, John H., ed. *Capital Movements and Economic Development*. London: Macmillan, 1967.

Albert, Michel. *Capitalisme contre Capitalisme*. Paris: Editions de Seuil, 1990.

Aldcroft, Derek H. *From Versailles to Wall Street*. Berkeley: University of California Press, 1977.

Alerassool, Mahvash. *Freezing Assets*. New York: St. Martin's Press, 1993.

Ambrosius, Gerold, and William H. Hubbard. *A Social Economic History of the Twentieth Century*. Cambridge: Cambridge University Press, 1989.

Ambrosius, Gerold et al., eds., *Moderne Wirtschaftsgeschichte: Eine Einführung für Historiker und Ökonomen*. Munich: Oldenbourg, 1996.

Aubert, M. Georges. *La finance Américaine*. Paris: Flammarion, 1910.

Backer, John H. *Priming the German Economy. American Occupational Policies 1945–1948*. Durham: University of North Carolina, 1971.

Barberis, Nicholas, and Richard Thaler. "A Survey of Behavioral Finance." In: *Handbook of the Economics of Finance*. George M. Constantinides et al., eds. Amsterdam: Elsevier, 2003.

Barth, Boris. *Die deutsche Hochfinanz und die Imperialismen*. Stuttgart: Steiner, 1995.

Bartlett, Christopher A. and Sumantra Ghoshal. *Managing Across Borders: The Transnational Solution*. Cambridge, MA: Harvard University Press, 1991.

Bartlett, Edward Everett. *Edward Dean Adams*. New York: privately printed, 1926.

Baskin, Jonathan Barron, and Paul J. Miranti Jr. *A History of Corporate Finance*. Cambridge: Cambridge University Press, 1997.

Baster, A. S. J. *The International Banks*. 1935. Rpt. New York: Arno Press, 1977.

Battilossi, Stefano, and Youssef Cassis, eds. *European Banks and the American Challenge: Competition and Cooperation in International Banking Under Bretton Woods*. Oxford: Oxford University Press, 2002.

Bender, Thomas. *A Nation Among Nations: America's Place in World History*. New York: Hill and Wang, 2006.

Bennett, Edward W. *Germany and the Diplomacy of the Financial Crisis 1931*. Cambridge, MA: Harvard University Press, 1962.

Bensel, Richard Franklin. *The Political Economy of American Industrialization, 1877–1900*. Cambridge: Cambridge University Press, 2000.

Berghahn, Volker R. *America and the Intellectual Cold Wars in Europe*. Princeton, NJ: Princeton University Press, 2001.

______. *The Americanisation of West German Industry 1945–1973*. Leamington Spa: Berg, 1986.

Berghahn, Volker R., and Sigurt Vitols, eds. *Gibt es einen deutschen Kapitalismus: Tradition und globale Perspektiven der sozialen Marktwirtschaft*. Frankfurt: Campus, 2006.

Berghoff, Hartmut, and Ingo Köhler. "Redesigning a Class of its Own: Social and Human Capital Formation in the German Banking Elite, 1870–1990." *Financial History Review*, Vol. 14 (2007), pp. 63–87.

Berle, Adolf A., and Gardiner C. Means. *The Modern Corporation and Private Property*. Rev. ed. New York: Harcourt, Brace & World, 1968.

Bhagwati, Jagdish N. "The Capital Myth." *Foreign Affairs*, Vol. 77 (May/June 1998), pp. 7–16.

Black, David. *The King of Fifth Avenue: The Fortunes of August Belmont*. New York: Dial Press, 1981.

Bliss, Michael. *Northern Enterprises*. Toronto: McClelland & Stewart, 1987.

Bloomfield, Arthur I. "Postwar Control of International Capital Movements." *American Economic Review*, Papers and Proceedings Issue, Vol. 36 (May 1946), pp. 687–709.

______. *International Capital Movements and American Balance of Payments, 1929–1940*. Ph.D. diss. University of Chicago, 1942.

Boelcke, Willi A. *Die deutsche Wirtschaft 1930–1945. Interna des Reichswirtschaftsministeriums*. Düsseldorf: Droste, 1983.

Böhme, Helmut. *Deutschlands Weg zur Grossmacht*. Berlin. Kiepenheuer & Witsch, 1966.

Boissevain, G. M. *Money and Banking in the United States*. Amsterdam: J. H. de Bussy, 1909.

Bonbright, James C. *Railroad Capitalization: A Study of the Principles of Regulation of Railroad Securities*. New York: Columbia University, 1920.

Bonin, Hubert. "The Development of Accounting Machines in French Banks from the 1920s to the 1960s." *Accounting, Business & Financial History*, Vol. 14 (2004), pp. 257–276.

Booker, John. *Temples of Mammon. The Architecture of Banking*. Edinburgh: Edinburgh University Press, 1990.

Borchard, Edwin, and W. H. Wynne. *State Insolvency and Foreign Bondholders*. 2 vols. 1951. Rpt. New York: Garland, 1983.

Borchardt, Knut. *Perspectives on Modern German Economic History and Policy*. Cambridge: Cambridge University Press, 1991.

Borchgrave, Alexandra Villard de, and John Cullen. *Villard: The Life and Times of an American Titan*. New York: Doubleday, 2001.

Born, Karl Erich. "Vom Beginn des Ersten Weltkrieges bis zum Ende der Weimarer Republik (1918–1933)." In: *Deutsche Bankengeschichte*. Ed. Wissenschaftlicher Beirat des Instituts für bankhistorische Forschung. Vol. 3. Frankfurt: Knapp, 1983, pp. 11–146.

______. *International Banking in the 19th and 20th Centuries*. New York: St. Martin's Press, 1983.

______. "Deutsche Bank during Germany's Great Inflation after the First World War." *Studies on Economic and Monetary Problems and on Banking History*, no. 17 (1979), pp. 11–27. Rpt. Mainz: Hase & Koehler 1988, pp. 495–514.

______. "Die Hauptentwicklungslinien des mitteleuropäischen Universalbankensystems." In: *Universalbankensystem als historisches und politisches Problem*. (Bankhistorisches Archiv; Beiheft 2). Frankfurt: Knapp, 1977, pp. 13–18.

______. *Die deutsche Bankenkrise 1931. Finanzen und Politik*. Munich: Piper, 1967.

Bouquet, Cyril, et al. "Foreign Expansion in Service Industries: Separability and Human Capital Intensity." *Journal of Business Research*, Vol. 57 (2004), pp. 35–46.

Bovykin, V. I., ed. *Transformation of Bank Structures in the Industrial Period*. Budapest: Akadémiai Kiado, 1982.

Bower, Tom. *The Pledge Betrayed. America and Britain and the Denazification of Postwar Germany*. Garden City, NY: Doubleday, 1982.

Brackmann, Michael. *Vom totalen Krieg zum Wirtschaftswunder. Die Vorgeschichte der westdeutschen Währungsreform 1948*. Essen: Klartext, 1993.

Brown, John Crosby. *A Hundred Years of Merchant Banking*. New York: privately printed, 1909.

Buchheim, Christoph. "Marshall Plan and Currency Reform." In: *American Policy and the Reconstruction of West Germany 1945–1955*. Jeffery Diefendorf et al., eds. Cambridge: Cambridge University Press, 1993, pp. 69–83.

______. "Die Währungsreform in Westdeutschland im Jahre 1948. Einige ökonomische Aspekte." In: Wolfram Fischer, ed. *Währungsreform und Soziale Marktwirtschaft. Erfahrungen und Perspektiven nach 40 Jahren*. Berlin: Duncker & Humblot, 1989, pp. 391–402.

______. "Die Währungsreform 1948 in Westdeutschland." *Vierteljahrshefte für Zeitgeschichte*, Vol. 36 (1988), pp. 189–231.

Buckley, Peter J., and Mark Casson. *The Economic Theory of the Multinational Enterprise*. New York: St. Martin's Press, 1985.

Buckley, Peter J., and Pervez N. Ghauri. *The Internationalization of the Firm: A Reader*. London: Thompson, 1999.

Buckley, Peter J., and Brian R. Roberts. *European Direct Investment in the U.S.A. before World War I*. London: Macmillan, 1982.

Bunsen, Georg von. *Friedrich Kapp: Gedächtnisrede*. Berlin: Simion, 1885.

Burchardt, Lothar. *Wissenschaftspolitik im Wilhelminischen Deutschland. Vorgeschichte, Gründung und Aufbau der Kaiser-Wilhelm-Gesellschaft zur Förderung der Wissenschaften* (Studien zu Naturwissenschaft, Technik und Wirtschaft im neunzehnten Jahrhundert; 1). Göttingen: Vandenhoeck & Ruprecht, 1975.

Burk, Kathleen. "Money and Power." In: *Finance and Financiers in European History, 1880–1960*. Youssef Cassis, ed. Cambridge: Cambridge University Press, 1992, pp. 359–369.

______. *Morgan Grenfell 1838–1988: The Biography of a Merchant Bank*. Oxford: Oxford University Press, 1989.

Burr, Anna R. *The Portrait of a Banker: James Stillman*. New York: Duffield, 1927.

Büschgen, Hans E. "Deutsche Bank from 1957 to the Present: The Emergence of an International Financial Conglomerate." In: Lothar Gall et al. *The Deutsche Bank 1870–1995*. London: Weidenfeld & Nicolson, 1995, pp. 523–796.

______. "Geld und Banken nach dem Zweiten Weltkrieg. Internationale Kapitalbewegungen, Bankensysteme, grenzüberschreitende Kooperation." In: Hans Pohl, ed. *Europäische Bankengeschichte*. Frankfurt: Knapp, 1993, pp. 455–485.

______. *Die Grossbanken*. Frankfurt: Knapp, 1983.

Buss, Dietrich. *Henry Villard: A Study of Transatlantic Investment and Interests, 1870–1895*. New York: Arno Press, 1978.

Cairncross, Alec. "Did Foreign Investment Pay?" *Review of Economic Studies*, Vol. 3 (1953), pp. 67–78.

______. *Home and Foreign Investment, 1870–1913: Studies in Capital Accumulation*. Cambridge: Cambridge University Press, 1953.

Carey, John L. *The Rise of the Accounting Profession: From Technician to Professional, 1896–1936*. New York: American Institute of Certified Accountants, 1969.

Carlson, W. Bernard. *Innovation as a Social Process: Elihu Thomson and the Rise of General Electric, 1870–1900*. Cambridge: Cambridge University Press, 1991.

Carosso, Vincent P. *The Morgans: Private International Bankers, 1854–1913*. Cambridge, MA: Harvard University Press, 1987.

______. *Investment Banking in America*. Cambridge, MA: Harvard University Press, 1979.

______. *More Than a Century of Investment Banking: The Kidder, Peabody & Co. Story*. New York: McGraw-Hill, 1979.

______. "A Financial Elite: New York's German-Jewish Investment Bankers." *American Jewish Historical Quarterly*, Vol. 56 (1976), pp. 67–88.

______. "The Wall Street Money Trust from Pujo through Medina." *Business History Review*, Vol. 47 (1973), pp. 421–437.

Carr, Edward Hallett. *Nationalism and After*. London: Macmillan, 1968.

Cassis, Youssef. *Capitals of Capital: A History of International Financial Centres, 1780–2005*. Cambridge: Cambridge University Press, 2006.

______. "New Literature on the Social Backgrounds and Social Attitudes of Bankers." Proceedings of the European Association for Banking History, May 2004, Athens.

———. *City Bankers, 1890–1914*. Cambridge: Cambridge University Press, 1994.
———, ed. *Finance and Financiers in European History, 1880–1960*. Cambridge: Cambridge University Press, 1992.
———. "Swiss International Banking." In: Geoffrey Jones, ed. *Banks as Multinationals*. London: Routledge, 1990, pp. 160–172.
———. "The Emergence of a New Financial Institution: Investment Trusts in Britain, 1870–1939." In: Jean Jacques van Helten and Youssef Cassis, eds. *Capitalism in a Mature Economy*. Aldershot: Edward Elgar, 1990, pp. 139–158.
Cassis, Youssef, and Éric Bussière, eds. *London and Paris as International Financial Centers in the Twentieth Century*. Oxford: Oxford University Press, 2005.
Casson, Mark. *The Organization of International Business*. Vol. II. London: Edward Elgar, 1995.
———. "Evolution of Multinational Banks: A Theoretical Perspective." In: Geoffrey Jones, ed. *Banks as Multinationals*. London: Routledge, 1990.
———, ed. *Multinationals and World Trade*. London: Allen & Unwin, 1986.
———, ed. *The Growth of International Business*. London: Allen & Unwin, 1983.
———. *Alternatives to the Multinational Enterprise*. New York: Holmes & Meier, 1979.
Chamber of Commerce of the United States. *Laws and Practices Affecting the Establishment of Foreign Branches of Banks*. Washington, DC: Chamber of Commerce of the United States, 1923.
Chandler, Alfred D., Jr. *Scale and Scope*. Cambridge, MA: Harvard University Press, 1990.
———. *The Visible Hand*. Cambridge, MA: Harvard University Press, 1977.
———. *The Railroads: The Nation's First Big Business*. New York: Harcourt Brace, 1965.
———, ed. *Giant Enterprise*. New York: Harcourt Brace, 1964.
———. *Strategy and Structure*. Cambridge, MA: MIT Press, 1962.
Chernow, Ron. *The Death of the Banker: The Decline and Fall of the Great Financial Dynasties and the Triumph of the Small Investor*. New York: Simon and Schuster, 1999.
———. *The Warburgs*. New York: Random House, 1993.
———. *The House of Morgan*. New York: Atlantic Monthly Press, 1990.
Cleveland, Harold B. van, and Thomas F. Huertas. *Citibank 1812–1970*. Cambridge, MA: Harvard University Press, 1985.
Clough, Shepard B., and Charles Woolsey Cole. *Economic History of Europe*. Boston: D. C. Heath, 1941.
Clough, Shepard B., and Richard T. Rapp. *European Economic History*. 3rd ed. New York: McGraw-Hill, 1978.
Coates, David, ed. *Varieties of Capitalism, Varieties of Approaches*. London: Macmillan, 2005.
Collins, Theresa M. *Otto Kahn: Art, Money, & Modern Times*. Chapel Hill: University of North Carolina, 2002.
Cottrell, P. L. *Industrial Finance, 1830–1914*. London: Methuen, 1980.
Crick, W. F., and J. E. Wadsworth. *A Hundred Years of Joint-Stock Banking*. London: Hodder & Stoughton, 1936.
Daems, Herman, and Herman van der Wee. *The Rise of Managerial Capitalism*. Louvain: Louvain University, 1974.
Daniels, Joseph, and David Van Hoose. *International Monetary and Financial Economics*. New York: Thomson, 1999.
Davis, Lance E., and Robert E. Gallman. *Evolving Financial Markets and International Capital Flows: Britain, the Americas, and Australia 1865–1914*. Cambridge: Cambridge University Press, 2001.
Davis, Lance E., and Robert J. Cull. *International Capital Markets and American Economic Growth, 1820–1914*. Cambridge: Cambridge University Press, 1994.
De Long, J. Bradford. "Did J. P. Morgan's Men Add Value? An Economist's Perspective on Financial Capitalism." In: Peter Temin, ed. *Inside the Business Enterprise: Historical Perspectives on the Use of Information*. Chicago: University of Chicago Press, 1991.
Desjardins, Bernard et al. *Le Crédit Lyonnais, 1863–1986*. Paris: Droz, 2003.
Deutsche Bundesbank, ed. *Deutsches Geld- und Bankwesen in Zahlen 1876–1975*. Frankfurt: Knapp, 1976.
Dewey, Davis R. *Financial History of the United States*. 12th ed. 1934. Rpt. New York: Kelley, 1968.

Dickens, Paul D. *The Transition Period in American International Financing: 1897 to 1914*. Ph.D. diss., George Washington University, 1933.
Diefendorf, Jeffery, et al., eds. *American Policy and the Reconstruction of West Germany 1945–1955*. Cambridge: Cambridge University Press, 1993.
Donaldson, John. *International Economic Relations*. New York: Longmans Green, 1928.
Doremus, Paul et al. *The Myth of the Global Corporation*. Princeton, NJ: Princeton University Press, 1998.
Dormanns, Albert. "Die amerikanischen Banken – das System und die derzeitigen Reformbestrebungen." *Bank-Betrieb*, Vol. 16 (1976), pp. 191–196, 241–245.
Dunlavy, Colleen A. *Politics and Industrialization: Early Railroads in the United States and Prussia*. Princeton, NJ: Princeton University Press, 1994.
Dunning, John, and Jean-Louis Mucchielli. *Multinational Firms: The Global-Local Dilemma*. London: Routledge, 2002.
Dunning, John. *Governments, Globalization, and International Business*. Oxford: Oxford University Press, 1997.
______. *The Globalization of Business*. London: Routledge, 1993.
Edwards, Franklin R., and Stav Gaon, "Hedge Funds: What Do We Know?" *Journal of Applied Corporate Finance*, Vol. 15 (2003), no. 4, pp. 8–21.
Edwards, George W. *The Evolution of Finance Capitalism*. New York: Longmans, Green, 1938.
Edwards, James Don. *History of Public Accounting in the United States*. Huntsville: University of Alabama Press, 1978.
Edwards, Jeremy, and Klaus Fischer. *Banks, Finance and Investment in Germany*. Cambridge: Cambridge University Press, 1994.
Eichengreen, Barry. *The European Economy since 1945: Coordinated Capitalism and Beyond*. Princeton, NJ: Princeton University Press, 2007.
______. "U.S. Foreign Financial Relations in the Twentieth Century." In: Stanley Engerman and Robert Gallman, eds. *Cambridge Economic History*. Cambridge: Cambridge University Press, 2000, pp. 463–504.
______. *Globalizing Capital: A History of the International Monetary System*. Princeton, NJ: Princeton University Press, 1996.
______. "Historical Research on International Lending and Debt." *Journal of Economic Perspectives*, Vol. 5 (1991), pp. 149–169.
______. *Golden Fetters. The Gold Standard and the Great Depression 1919–1939*. Oxford: Oxford University Press, 1991.
Eichengreen, Barry, and Marc Flandreau, eds. *The Gold Standard in Theory and History*. London: Routledge, 1997.
Einzig, Paul. *World Finance 1914–1935*. New York: Macmillan, 1935.
Ekblom, H. E. "European Direct Investment in the United States." *Harvard Business Review*, July–August 1973.
Emden, Paul H. *Money Powers of Europe in the Nineteenth and Twentieth Centuries*. New York: D. Appleton-Century, 1938.
______. *Money Powers of Europe*. 1937. Rpt. New York: Garland, 1983.
Emminger, Otmar. *D-Mark, Dollar, Währungskrisen. Erinnerungen eines ehemaligen Bundesbankpräsidenten*. Stuttgart: Deutsche Verlags-Anstalt, 1986.
Epstein, Gerald, and Thomas Ferguson. "Monetary Policy, Loan Liquidation, and Industrial Conflict. The Federal Reserve and the Open Market Operations of 1932." *Journal of Economic History*, Vol. 44 (1984), pp. 957–983.
Eun, Cheol S. et al. *International Financial Management: Canadian Perspectives*. Toronto: McGraw-Hill, 2004.
Fallon, Padraic. "The Battle Plans of Hilmar Kopper" (interview). *Euromoney* (January 1994), pp. 28–44.
Fear, Jeff, and Christopher Kobrak. "Diverging Paths: Accounting for Corporate Governance in America and Germany." *Business History Review*, Vol. 80 (2006), pp. 1–48.
Federal Reserve System, Board of Governors. *Banking and Monetary Statistics, 1941–1970*. Washington, DC, 1976.

Feiler, Arthur. "International Movements of Capital." *American Economic Review*, supplement, Vol. 25 (March 1935), pp. 63–74.

Feinstein, Charles H., and Katherine Watson. "Private International Capital Flows in Europe in the Inter-War Period." In: Charles H. Feinstein, ed. *Banking, Currency, and Finance in Europe between the Wars*. Oxford: Clarendon Press, 1995, pp. 94–130.

Feinstein, Charles H., ed. *Banking, Currency, and Finance in Europe between the Wars*. Oxford: Clarendon Press, 1995.

Feinstein, Martin, ed. *International Capital Flows*. Chicago: University of Chicago Press, 1999.

Feis, Herbert. *Europe: The World's Banker 1870–1914*, New York: Norton, 1965.

______. *The Diplomacy of the Dollar 1919–1932*. New York: Norton, 1950.

Feldenkirchen, Wilfried. "Siemens in the US." In: Geoffrey Jones and Lina Gálvez-Muñoz, eds. *Foreign Multinationals in the United States: Management and Performance*. London: Routledge, 2002, pp. 89–105.

______. *Siemens*. Munich: Piper, 2000.

______. "Die Anfänge des Siemensgeschäfts in Amerika." In: Wilfried Feldenkirchen et al., eds. *Wirtschaft Gesellschaft Unternehmen. Festschrift für Hans Pohl zum 60. Geburtstag* (Vierteljahrschrift für Sozial- und Wirtschaftsgeschichte; Beiheft 120). Stuttgart: Steiner, 1995, pp. 876–900.

______. "Die Rolle der Banken bei der Sanierung von Industrieunternehmen (1850–1914)." In: *Die Rolle der Banken bei der Unternehmenssanierung* (Bankhistorisches Archiv; Beiheft 22). Frankfurt: Knapp, 1993, pp. 14–39.

Feldman, Gerald D. "Foreign Penetration of German Enterprises after World War I: The Problem of Ueberfremdung." In: Alice Teichova et al., eds. *Historical Studies in International Corporate Business*. Cambridge: Cambridge University Press, 2002, pp. 87–110.

______, et al., eds. *The Treaty of Versailles: A Reassessment after 75 Years*. Cambridge: Cambridge University Press, 1998.

______. *Hugo Stinnes*. Munich: Beck, 1998.

______. "The Deutsche Bank from World War to World Economic Crisis, 1914–1933." In: Lothar Gall et al. *The Deutsche Bank, 1870–1945*. London: Weidenfeld & Nicolson, 1995, pp. 129–276.

______. "Jakob Goldschmidt, the History of the Banking Crisis of 1931, and the Problem of Freedom of Manoeuvre in the Weimar Economy." In: Christoph Buchheim et al., eds. *Zerrissene Zwischenkriegszeit. Wirtschaftshistorische Beiträge. Knut Borchardt zum 65. Geburtstag.* Baden-Baden: Nomos 1994, pp. 307–327.

______. *The Great Disorder: Politics, Economics, and Society in the German Inflation 1914–1924*. Oxford: Oxford University Press, 1993.

______. *Army, Industry and Labor in Germany, 1914–1918*. Oxford: Berg, 1992.

Feldstein, Martin, ed. *The United States in the World Economy*. Chicago: University of Chicago Press, 1997.

Ferguson, Niall. "The City of London and British Imperialism: New Light on an Old Question." In: Youssef Cassis and Éric Bussière, eds. *London and Paris as International Financial Centres in the Twentieth Century*. Oxford: Oxford University Press, 2005.

______. *The Cash Nexus*. New York: Basic Books, 2001.

______. *The House of Rothschild*. 2 vols. New York: Penguin, 1998.

Fisher, Irving. *The Stock Market Crash – and After*. New York: Macmillan, 1930.

Flandreau, Marc et al., eds. *International Financial History in the Twentieth Century: System and Anarchy*. Cambridge: Cambridge University Press, 2003.

Fleisig, Heywood W. *Long Term Capital Flows and the Great Depression: The Role of the United States 1927–1933*. New York: Arno Press, 1975.

Fogel, Robert W., and Stanley L. Engerman, eds. *The Reinterpretation of American Economic History*. New York: Harper & Row, 1971.

Fohlin, Caroline. "Universal Banking in Pre-World War I Germany: Model or Myth?" *Explorations in Economic History*, Vol. 36 (1999), pp. 305–343.

Forbes, Neil. *Doing Business with the Nazis: Britain's Economic and Financial Relations with Germany 1931–1939*. London: Frank Cass, 2000.

______. "London Banks, the German Standstill Agreements, and 'Economic Appeasement' in the 1930s." *Economic History Review*, Vol. 40 (1987), pp. 571–587.

Foreman-Peck, James. *A History of the World Economy*. 2nd ed. New York: Harvester/Wheatsheaf, 1995.

Freyer, Tony. *Regulating Big Business: Antitrust in Great Britain and America 1880–1990*. Cambridge: Cambridge University Press, 1992.

Fridenson, Patrick. "Business Failure and the Agenda of Business History." *Enterprise & Society*, Vol. 5 (2004), pp. 562–582.

Friedman, Milton, and Anna Jacobson Schwartz. *A Monetary History of the United States*. Princeton, NJ: Princeton University Press, 1963.

Friedman, Milton. *Episodes in Monetary Mischief*. New York: Harcourt and Brace, 1992.

Friedman, Thomas. *A Brief History of the Twenty-first Century*. New York: Farrar, Straus & Giroux, 2005.

Friedrich, Carl J. *American Experiences in Military Government in World War II*. New York: Rinehart, 1948.

Frye, Alton. *Nazi Germany and the American Hemisphere 1933–1941*. New Haven: Yale University Press, 1967.

Fürstenberg, Carl. *Die Lebensgeschichte eines deutschen Bankiers, 1870–1914*. Hans Fürstenberg, ed. Berlin: Ullstein, 1931.

Gaddis, John Lewis. *The United States and the Origins of the Cold War 1941–1947*. New York: Columbia University Press, 1972.

Galbraith, John Kenneth. *The Great Crash 1929*. Boston: Houghton Mifflin, 1961.

Gall, Lothar. *Der Bankier Hermann Josef Abs: Eine Biographie*. Munich: Beck, 2004.

______. "The Deutsche Bank from its Founding to the Great War, 1870–1914." In: Lothar Gall et al. *The Deutsche Bank, 1870–1945*. London: Weidenfeld & Nicolson, 1995, pp. 1–127.

Gardner, Paul, Jr. "Foreign Investment in U.S. Banking." In: J. Eugene Marans and Peter C. Williams, eds. *Foreign Investment in the United States*. Washington, D.C.: District of Columbia Bar, 1990.

Gardner, Richard N. *Sterling-Dollar Diplomacy in Current Perspective: Origins and Prospects of Our International Economic Order*. Rev. ed. New York: Columbia University Press, 1980.

Garvan, Francis P. *"Hot Money" vs. Frozen Funds*. New York: The Chemical Foundation, 1937.

Garvy, George. "Rivals and Interlopers in the History of the New York Security Market." *Journal of Political Economy*, Vol. 52 (1944), pp. 139–141.

Gaughan, Patrick A. *Mergers, Acquisitions, and Corporate Restructurings*. New York: Wiley, 1999.

Geisst, Charles R. *Wall Street: A History*. New York: Oxford University Press, 1997.

______. *Entrepôt Capitalism: Foreign Investment and the American Dream in the Twentieth Century*. New York: Praeger, 1992.

Geist, Walter. *Allis-Chalmers: A Brief History*. New York: Newcomen Society, 1950.

Gelber, Harry G. "Der Morgenthau-Plan." *Vierteljahrshefte für Zeitgeschichte*, Vol. 13 (1965), pp. 372–402.

Geman, Hélytette, and Cécile Kharoubi. "Hedge Funds Revisited: Distributional Characteristics, Dependence Structure and Diversification." *Journal of Risk*, Vol. 5 (2003), pp. 55–74.

Gibbs (Antony) & Sons, Ltd. *Merchants and Bankers, 1808–1958*. London: Antony Gibbs, 1958.

Giersch, Herbert, with Karl-Heinz Paqué and Holger Schmieding. *The Fading Miracle. Four Decades of Market Economy in Germany*. Cambridge: Cambridge University Press, 1992.

Gilbert, Heather. *Awakening Continent: The Life of Lord Mount Stephen*. Vol. 1, *1829–1891*. Aberdeen: Aberdeen University Press, 1977.

______. *End of the Road: The Life of Lord Mount Stephen*. Vol. 2, *1891–1921*. Aberdeen: Aberdeen University Press, 1977.

Gille, Bertrand. "Banking and Industrialisation in Europe 1730–1914." In: Carlo M. Cipolla, ed. *The Fontana Economic History of Europe*. Vol. 3, *The Industrial Revolution*. Glasgow: Fontana/Collins 1973, pp. 255–300.

Gimbel, John. *The Origins of the Marshall Plan*. Stanford: Stanford University Press, 1976.

______. *Amerikanische Besatzungspolitik in Deutschland 1945–1949*. Frankfurt: S. Fischer, 1971.

Glum, Friedrich. *Zwischen Wissenschaft und Politik. Erlebtes und Erdachtes in vier Reichen.* Bonn: Bouvier 1964.

Gompers, Paul, and Josh Lerner. *The Venture Capital Cycle.* Cambridge, MA: MIT Press, 1999.

Gottlieb, Manuel. "Failure of Quadripartite Monetary Reform 1945–1947." *Finanzarchiv*, Vol. 17 (1956–57), pp. 398–417.

Grazia, Victoria de. *Irresistible Empire: America's Advance through Twentieth Century Europe.* Cambridge, MA: Harvard University Press, 2005.

Grodinsky, Julius. *Transcontinental Railway Strategy, 1869–1893: A Study of Business.* Philadelphia: University of Pennsylvania, 1962.

Gwinner, Arthur von. *Lebenserinnerungen.* Manfred Pohl, ed. Frankfurt: Knapp, 1975.

Haberler, Gottfried. *The World Economy, Money, and the Great Depression 1919–1938.* Washington, DC: American Enterprise Institute, 1979.

Hansen, Per H. "Writing Business History Without an Archive. Newspapers as Sources for Business History." In: Carl-Johan Gadd et al., eds. *Markets and Embeddedness. Essays in Honour of Ulf Olsson.* Göteborg: Göteborg University, 2004, pp. 99–120.

Hall, Peter, and Soskice, David. *Varieties of Capitalism.* Oxford: Oxford University Press, 2001.

Harries, Heinrich. *Wiederaufbau, Welt und Wende: Die KfW – eine Bank mit öffentlichem Auftrag, 1948–1998.* Frankfurt: Knapp, 1998.

Harris, Charles Wesley. "International Relations and the Disposition of Alien Enemy Property Seized by the United States during World War II: A Case Study on German Properties." *Journal of Politics*, Vol. 23 (1961), pp. 641–666.

Harris, G. R. S. *Germany's Foreign Indebtedness.* London: Oxford University Press, 1935.

Hartkopf, Carsten. *Die Geschäftspolitik amerikanischer Banken in Deutschland, 1960–1990.* Frankfurt: Peter Lang, 2000.

Hausman, William J., and John Neufeld. "U.S. Foreign Direct Investment in Electrical Utilities." In: Mira Wilkins and Harm Schröter, eds. *The Free-Standing Company in the World Economy, 1830–1996.* Oxford: Oxford University Press, 1998, pp. 361–390.

Hausman, William J., with Peter Hertner and Mira Wilkins. *Global Electrification: Multinational Enterprise and International Finance in the History of Light and Power, 1878–2007.* Cambridge: Cambridge University Press, 2008.

Hayes, Peter. *From Cooperation to Complicity: Degussa and the Third Reich.* Cambridge: Cambridge University Press, 2004.

Hedges, James Blaine. *Henry Villard and the Railways of the Northwest.* New Haven: Yale University Press, 1930.

Hefferman, Shelagh. *Modern Banking in Theory and Practice.* New York: Wiley and Sons, 1996.

Helfferich, Karl. *Georg von Siemens: Ein Lebensbild aus Deutschlands grosser Zeit.* 3 vols. Berlin: Julius Springer, 1921–1923.

———. *Germany's Economic Progress and National Wealth, 1888–1913.* New York: Germanistic Society of America, 1914.

Hennart, Jean-François. "Transaction Costs Theory and the Multinational Enterprise." In: Christos N. Pitelis and Roger Sugden, eds. *The Nature of the Transnational Firm.* London: Routledge, 1991, pp. 72–118.

Henning, Friedrich-Wilhelm. *Industrialisierung in Deutschland, 1800–1914*, 7th ed. Stuttgart: Fischer, 1989.

Herold, Hermann. "Die Neuordnung der Grossbanken im Bundesgebiet." *Neue Juristische Wochenschrift, Vol.* 5 (1952), pp. 481–484, 566–568.

Hertner, Peter, and Geoffrey Jones, eds. *Multinationals: Theory and History.* Aldershot: Gower, 1986.

Hertner, Peter. "German Banks abroad before 1914." In: Geoffrey Jones, ed. *Banks as Multinationals.* London/New York, 1990, pp. 99–119.

Hidy, Ralph W. *The House of Baring in American Trade and Finance: English Merchant Bankers at Work, 1763–1861.* Cambridge, MA: Harvard University Press, 1949.

Higham, Charles. *Trading with the Enemy: An Exposé of the Nazi American Money Plot, 1933–1949.* New York: Delacorte Press, 1983.

Hilferding, Rudolf. *Finance Capital.* London: Routledge & Kegan Paul, 1981.

Hilpert, Werner, and Max Stahlberg. "Wirtschaftsfreiheit und Bankpolitik." *Frankfurter Hefte*, Vol. 4 (1951), pp. 101–112.

Hinners, Wolfgang. *Exil und Rückkehr: Friedrich Kapp in Amerika und Deutschland, 1824–1884*. Stuttgart: Heinz, 1987.

Hobsbawm, Eric J. *The Age of Capital*. London: Abacus, 1977.

______. *The Age of Empire*. London: Abacus, 1977.

Hobson, J. A. *Imperialism: A Study*. London: James Nisbet, 1902.

Hoffman, Paul. *The Dealmakers*. Garden City, NY: Doubleday, 1984.

Hofstadter, Richard. *The Age of Reform*. New York: Vintage Books, 1955.

Holborn, Hajo. *American Military Government. Its Organization and Policies*. Washington, DC: Infantry Journal Press, 1947.

Holtfrerich, Carl-Ludwig. "The Deutsche Bank 1945–1957: War, Military Rule and Reconstruction." In: Lothar Gall et al. *The Deutsche Bank, 1870–1945*. London: Weidenfeld & Nicolson, 1995, pp. 357–521.

Homer, Sidney, and Richard Sylla. *A History of Interest Rates*. New Brunswick: Rutgers University Press, 1996.

Hook, Walter. *Die wirtschaftliche Entwicklung der ehemaligen Deutschen Bank im Spiegel ihrer Bilanzen*. Heidelberg: Carl Winter, 1954.

Horstmann, Theo. *Die Alliierten und die deutschen Grossbanken. Bankenpolitik nach dem Zweiten Weltkrieg in Westdeutschland*. Bonn: Bouvier, 1991.

______. "Die Entstehung der Bank deutscher Länder als geldpolitische Lenkungsinstanz in der Bundesrepublik Deutschland." In: Hajo Riese and Heinz-Peter Spahn, eds. *Geldpolitik und ökonomische Entwicklung. Ein Symposion*. Regensburg: Transfer-Verlag, 1990, pp. 202–218.

Hughes, Jane E., and Scott B. MacDonald. *International Banking*. Boston: Addison Wesley, 2002.

Hughes, Thomas P. *Networks of Power: Electrification in Western Society, 1880–1930*. Baltimore: Johns Hopkins University Press, 1983.

Hungerford, Edward. *The Story of the Baltimore and Ohio Railroad, 1827–1927*. 2 vols. New York: G. P. Putnam, 1928.

Hymer, Stephen Herbert. *The International Operations of National Firms: A Study of Direct Foreign Investment*. Cambridge, MA: MIT Press, 1976.

Israel, Paul. *Edison: A Life of Invention*. New York: John Wiley & Sons, 1998.

Iversen, Carl. *Aspects of the Theory of International Capital Movements*. 1935. Rpt. New York: Kelley, 1967.

James, Harold. *The Nazi Dictatorship and the Deutsche Bank*. Cambridge: Cambridge University Press, 2003.

______. *Europe Reborn: A History, 1914–2000*. London: Pearson, 2003.

______, ed. *The Role of the Banks in the Interwar Economy*. Cambridge: Cambridge University Press, 2002.

______. *The End of Globalization: Lessons from the Great Depression*. Cambridge, MA: Harvard University Press, 2001.

______. *The Deutsche Bank and the Nazi Economic War Against the Jews*. Cambridge: Cambridge University Press, 2001.

______. *International Monetary Cooperation since Bretton Woods*. New York: Oxford University Press, 1996.

______. "Banks and Bankers in the German Interwar Depression." In: Youssef Cassis, ed. *Finance and Financiers in European History*. Cambridge: Cambridge University Press, 1992, pp. 263–281.

______. *The German Slump*. Oxford: Clarendon Press, 1986.

Jeidels, Otto. *Das Verhältnis der deutschen Grossbanken zur Industrie mit besonderer Berücksichtigung der Eisenindustrie*. 2nd ed. Leipzig: Duncker & Humblot, 1913.

Jensen, Michael C. *A Theory of the Firm: Governance, Residual Claims, and Organizational Forms*. Cambridge, MA: Harvard University Press, 2000.

______. "The Modern Industrial Revolution, Exit, and the Failure of Internal Control Systems." *Journal of Finance*, Vol. 48 (1993), pp. 831–880.

Jones, Geoffrey, and Gálvez-Muñoz, Lina. *Foreign Multinationals in the United States: Management and Performance*. London: Routledge, 2002.

Jones, Geoffrey, and Harm G. Schröter, eds. *The Rise of Multinationals in Continental Europe*. Aldershot: Edward Elgar, 1993.

Jones, Geoffrey, ed. *Multinational and International Banking*. Aldershot: Edward Elgar, 1992.

______. *British Multinational Banking: 1830–1990*. Oxford: Clarendon Press, 1993.

______. *Multinationals and Global Capitalism from the Nineteenth to the Twenty-first Century*. Oxford: Oxford University Press, 2005.

Judt, Tony. *Postwar: A History of Europe Since 1945*. New York: Penguin, 2005.

Kabisch, Thomas R. "Deutsche Investitionen in den USA, 1871–1914." In: Jürgen Schneider, ed. *Wirtschaftskräfte und Wirtschaftswege, Bd. 5. Festschrift für Hermann Kellenbenz* (Beiträge zur Wirtschaftsgeschichte; 8). Stuttgart: Klett-Cotta, 1981.

Katz, Irving. *August Belmont: A Political Biography*. New York: Columbia University Press, 1968.

Keim, Jeannette. *Forty Years of German-American Political Relations*. Philadelphia: William J. Dornan, 1919.

Kenwood, A. G., and A. L. Lougheed. *The Growth of the International Economy 1820–2000: An Introductory Text*. 4th ed. London: Routledge, 1999.

Keynes, John Maynard. "Foreign Investment and National Advantage." *The Nation and the Athenaeum*, Vol. 35 (1924), pp. 584–587.

______. *The Economic Consequences of the Peace*. New York: Harcourt, Brace & Howe, 1920.

Kindleberger, Charles P. *World Economic Primacy, 1500–1990*. Oxford: Oxford University Press, 1996.

______. *A Financial History of Western Europe*. 2nd ed. Oxford: Oxford University Press, 1993.

______. *Manias, Panics, and Crashes*. New York: Basic Books, 1978.

______. *The World in Depression*. Berkeley: University of California Press, 1973.

______. *Multinational Excursions*. Cambridge, MA: MIT Press, 1970.

______. *American Business Abroad*. New Haven: Yale University Press, 1969.

Kindleberger, Charles P., and David B. Audretsch, eds. *The Multinational Corporation in the 1980s*. Cambridge, MA: MIT Press, 1983.

Klein, Maury. *The Life and Legend of Jay Gould*. Baltimore: Johns Hopkins University Press, 1986.

______. *The Life and Legend of E. H. Harriman*. Chapel Hill: University of North Carolina Press, 2000.

______. *Union Pacific: Rebirth, 1894–1969*. New York: Doubleday, 1989.

Klopstock, Fred H. "Monetary Reform in Western Germany." *Journal of Political Economy*, Vol. 57 (1949), pp. 277–292.

Klug, Adam. *The German Buybacks, 1932–1939: A Cure for Overhang* (Princeton Studies in International Finance; 75). Princeton, NJ: Princeton University, International Finance Section, 1993.

Klump, Rainer, ed. *40 Jahre Deutsche Mark: Die politische und ökonomische Bedeutung der westdeutschen Währungsreform von 1948* (Beiträge zur Wirtschafts- und Sozialgeschichte; 39). Wiesbaden: Steiner, 1989.

Knox, John Jay. *A History of the Louisville and Nashville Railroad*. New York: Kelley, 1969.

Kobrak, Christopher. *National Cultures and International Competition: The Experience of Schering AG, 1851–1950*. Cambridge: Cambridge University Press, 2002.

______. "Foreign-Currency Transactions and the Recovery of German Industry in the Aftermath of World War I." *Accounting, Business & Financial History*, Vol. 12 (2002), pp. 25–42.

______. "The Foreign-Exchange Dimension of Corporate Control in the Third Reich: The Case of Schering AG." *Contemporary European History*, Vol. 12 (2003), pp. 33–47.

Kobrak, Christopher, and Per Hansen, eds. *European Business, Dictatorship and Political Risk: 1920–1945*. New York: Berghahn Books, 2004.

Kobrak, Christopher, and Jana Wüstenhagen. "International Investment and Nazi Politics: The Cloaking of German Assets Abroad, 1936–1945." *Business History*, Vol. 48 (2006), pp. 399–427.

Kocka, Jürgen. *Die Angestellten in der deutschen Geschichte 1850–1980: Vom Privatbeamten zum angestellten Arbeitnehmer*. Göttingen: Vandenhoeck & Ruprecht, 1981.

———. *Unternehmensverwaltung und Angestelltenschaft am Beispiel Siemens 1847–1914: Zum Verhältnis zwischen Kapitalismus und Bürokratie in der deutschen Industrialisierung*. Stuttgart: Klett, 1969.

Kohn, Meir. *Financial Institutions and Markets*. New York: McGraw-Hill, 1994.

Kopper, Christopher. *Zwischen Marktwirtschaft und Dirigismus: Staat, Banken und Bankenpolitik im "Dritten Reich."* Bonn: Bouvier, 1995.

———. *Hjalmar Schacht: Aufstieg und Fall von Hitlers mächtigstem Bankier*. Munich: Hanser, 2006.

Kopper, Hilmar. "Die Zeit ist reif. Neue Leitlinien und Ziele für die Deutsche Bank." *Forum / Mitarbeiter-Zeitschrift der Deutschen Bank* (1993), no. 1, pp. 2–3.

———. "Neue Aufgaben und Ziele im Marketing einer internationalen Bank." In: Rosemarie Kolbeck, ed. *Bankmarketing vor neuen Aufgaben*. Frankfurt: Knapp, 1992, pp. 107–117.

Kreikamp, Hans-Dieter. *Deutsches Vermögen in den Vereinigten Staaten: Die Auseinandersetzung um seine Rückführung als Aspekt der deutsch-amerikanischen Beziehungen 1952–1962*. Stuttgart: Deutsche Verlags-Anstalt, 1979.

Krieger, Wolfgang. *General Lucius D. Clay und die amerikanische Deutschlandpolitik 1945–1949*. Stuttgart: Klett-Cotta, 1987.

Krooss, Herman E., and Martin R. Blyn. *A History of Financial Intermediaries*. New York: Random House, 1971.

Krüger, Peter. *Deutschland und die Reparationen 1918/19. Die Genesis des Reparationsproblems in Deutschland zwischen Waffenstillstand und Versailler Friedensschluss*. Stuttgart: Deutsche Verlags-Anstalt, 1973.

Kuhn, Loeb & Co. *Investment Banking through Four Generations*. New York: Kuhn, Loeb, 1955.

Kurgan-van-Hentenryk, Ganette. "The Social Origins of Managers." Proceedings of the European Association for Banking History, May 2004, Athens.

Kuznets, Simon. *Capital in the American Economy*. Princeton, NJ: Princeton University Press, 1961.

———. "International Differences in Capital Formation and Financing." In: National Bureau of Economic Research, *Capital Formation and Economic Growth*, Princeton, NJ: Princeton University Press, 1955, pp. 19–106.

Lamont, Edward M. *The Ambassador from Wall Street: The Story of Thomas W. Lamont*. Lanham: Madison Books, 1994.

Lamont, Thomas W. *Across World Frontiers*. New York: Harcourt Brace, 1951.

———. *Henry P. Davison*. New York: Harper & Bros., 1933.

Lamoureaux, Naomi. *Insider Lending: Banks, Personal Connections, and Economic Development in Industrial New England*. Cambridge: Cambridge University Press, 1994.

Landes, David S. *The Wealth and Poverty of Nations*. New York: Norton, 1998.

———. *The Unbound Prometheus: Technological Change and Industrial Development in Western Europe from 1750 to the Present*. Cambridge: Cambridge University Press, 1969.

Laney, Leroy D. "The Impact of U.S. Laws on Foreign Direct Investment." *Annals*, 516 (July 1991), pp. 144–153.

Lanier, H. W. *A Century of Banking in New York*. New York: George H. Doran, 1922.

Langen, Claudia. *Tradition, Expansion und Kooperation: Deutsch-amerikanische Bankenbeziehungen von 1900 bis 1917*. Ph.D., Cologne, 1995.

Laves, Walter Herman Carl. *German Governmental Influence on Foreign Investments, 1871–1914*. New York: Arno Press, 1977.

Lee, Susie J. *The Content of Character: The Role of Social Capital in the Expansion of Economic Capital*. Ph.D., Cornell University, 2004.

Lees, Francis A. *Foreign Banking and Investment in the United States*. London: Wiley & Sons, 1976.

Lenin, Vladimir I. *Imperialism*. 1916. Rpt. New York: International Publishers, 1939.

Lewis, Cleona. *America's Stake in International Investments*. Washington, DC: Brookings Institution, 1938.

———. *Debtor and Creditor Countries: 1938, 1944*. Washington, DC: Brookings Institution, 1945.

Liefmann, Robert. *Cartels, Concerns, and Trusts*. London: Methuen, 1932.

Littauer, Rudolf M. "Die rechtliche Stellung ausländischer Banken in New York." *Zeitschrift für das gesamte Kreditwesen*, Vol. 7 (1954), pp. 253–255, 289–291.

Loehr, Rodney C. *The West German Banking System*. Ed. by the Office of the US High Commissioner for Germany, Office of the Executive Secretary, Historical Division, 1952.

Lowenstein, Roger. *When Genius Failed: The Rise and Fall of Long-Term Capital Management*. New York: Random House, 2001.

Madden, John T., Marcus Nadler, and Harry C. Sauvain. *America's Experience as a Creditor Nation*. New York: Prentice-Hall, 1937.

Mandeville, A. Moreton. *The House of Speyer. A Candid Criticism of Speyer Flotations*. London, [1915].

Marans, J. Eugene, Peter C. Williams, and Joseph P. Griffin, eds. *Foreign Investment in the United States 1980: Legal Issues and Techniques*. Washington, DC: District of Columbia Bar, 1980.

Martin, Albro. *James J. Hill and the Opening of the Northwest*. New York: Oxford University Press, 1976.

Massie, Robert K. *Castles of Steel: Britain, Germany, and the Winning of the Great War at Sea*. New York: Random House, 2003.

Mazower, Mark. *Dark Continent: Europe's Twentieth Century*. London: Penguin, 1998.

McKenna, Christopher. *The World's Newest Profession: Management Consulting in the Twentieth Century*. Cambridge: Cambridge University Press, 2006.

McNeil, William C. *American Money and the Weimar Republic. Economics and Politics on the Eve of the Great Depression*. New York: Columbia University Press, 1986.

Meyer, Ulrich. "Die Verwalter der Grossbanken." *Deutsche Rechts-Zeitschrift*, Vol. 4 (1949), no. 2, pp. 25–39.

Michie, Ranald C. *The London and New York Stock Exchange 1850–1914*. London: Allen & Unwin, 1987.

Miranti, Paul J. *Accountancy Comes of Age: The Development of an American Profession, 1886–1946*. Chapel Hill: University of North Carolina Press, 1990.

———. "The Mind's Eye of Reform: The ICC's Bureau of Statistics and Accounts and a Vision of Regulation, 1887–1940." *Business History Review*, Vol. 63 (1989), pp. 469–509.

Möller, Hans. "Die westdeutsche Währungsreform von 1948." In: Deutsche Bundesbank, ed. *Währung und Wirtschaft in Deutschland 1876–1975*. Frankfurt: Knapp, 1976, pp. 433–483.

Mohr, Nicolaus. *Excursion through America*. Ray Allen Billington, ed. Chicago: Lakeside Press, 1973.

Moltmann, Günther. "Zur Formulierung der amerikanischen Besatzungspolitik in Deutschland am Ende des Zweiten Weltkrieges." *Vierteljahrshefte für Zeitgeschichte*, Vol. 15 (1967), pp. 299–322.

Montgomery, Robert. *Fifty Years of Accountancy*. 1938. Rpt. New York: Arno Press, 1978.

Morgenthau, Henry, Jr. *Germany Is Our Problem*. New York: Harper, 1945.

Moulton, Harold G., and Constantine E. McGuire. *Germany's Capacity to Pay: A Study of the Reparation Problem*. New York: McGraw-Hill, 1923.

Mundell, Robert. "A Reconsideration of the Twentieth Century." *American Economic Review*, Vol. 90 (2000), pp. 327–340.

Myers, Margaret. *The New York Money Market*. New York: Columbia University Press, 1931.

Nelson, Richard R., ed. *National Innovative Systems: A Comparative Analysis*. Oxford: Oxford University Press, 1993.

Neuburger, Hugh. "The Industrial Politics of the Kreditbanken, 1880–1914." *Business History Review*, Vol. 51 (1977), pp. 190–207.

———. *German Banks and German Economic Growth from Unification to World War I*. New York: Arno Press, 1977.

Neuburger, Hugh, and Houston H. Stokes. "German Banks and German Growth, 1883–1913. An Empirical View." *Journal of Economic History*, Vol. 34 (1974), pp. 710–731.

Nipperdey, Thomas. *Deutsche Geschichte 1866–1918. Vol. 1. Arbeitswelt und Bürgergeist*. Munich: Beck, 1990.

———. *Deutsche Geschichte 1866–1918. Vol. 2. Machtstaat vor der Demokratie*. Munich: Beck 1992.

Nolan, Mary. *Visions of Modernity: American Business and the Modernization of Germany.* Oxford: Oxford University Press, 1994.
Nordyke, James W. *International Finance and New York.* New York: Arno Press, 1976.
Noyes, Alexander Dana. *The War Period of American Finance.* New York: Putnam, 1926.
______. *Thirty Years of American Finance.* 1900. Rpt. New York: Greenwood Press, 1969.
Obst, Georg. *Der Bankberuf. Stellungen im Bankwesen, Aussichten im Bankberuf, Fortbildung der Bankbeamten.* Stuttgart: Poeschel, 1921.
Obstfeld, Maurice, and Alan M. Taylor. *Global Capital Markets: Integration, Crisis, and Growth.* Cambridge: Cambridge University Press, 2004.
OMGUS. *Ermittlungen gegen die Deutsche Bank 1946/47.* Nördlingen: Greno, 1985.
______. *Ermittlungen gegen die Dresdner Bank 1946.* Nördlingen: Greno, 1986.
Osthoff, Michael. "Das Bankwesen in den USA." *Die Bank*, no. 8 (1980), pp. 371–375.
O'Sullivan, Mary A. *Contests for Corporate Control: Corporate Governance and Economic Performance in the United States and Germany.* Oxford: Oxford University Press, 2000.
Panten, Hans-Joachim. "The Come-back of the German Big Three Banks." *The Bankers' Magazine*, Vol. 184 (1957), pp. 280–283.
______. "The Growth and Activity of the West German Successor Banks." *The Bankers' Magazine*, Vol. 177 (1954), pp. 113–122.
Parrini, Carl. *Heir to Empire: United States Economic Diplomacy 1916–1923.* Pittsburgh: University of Pittsburgh Press, 1969.
Pauluhn, Burkhardt. "Everything from one Source – a Strategy for the Future." *Bank und Markt und Technik*, Vol. 20 (1991), no. 6, pp. 21–23.
Pearce, David, ed. *The MIT Dictionary of Modern Economics.* Cambridge, MA: MIT Press, 1992.
Penrose, Edith. *The Theory of the Growth of the Firm.* New York: John Wiley, 1959.
Peterson, Walter F. *An Industrial Heritage: Allis-Chalmers Corporation.* Milwaukee: Milwaukee County Historical Society, 1978.
Phelps, C. W. *Foreign Expansion of American Banks.* 1927. Rpt. New York: Arno Press, 1976.
Pinner, Felix. *Emil Rathenau und das elektrische Zeitalter.* Leipzig: Akademische Verlags-Gesellschaft, 1918.
Pitelis, Christos N. *The Growth of the Firm: The Legacy of Edith Penrose.* Oxford: Oxford University Press, 2002.
Pohl, Manfred. "Deutsche Bank in the United States 1870–1999." In: Manfred Pohl, ed. *On German and American Identity: Deutsche Bank in the USA, 1870–1999.* Munich: Piper, 1999, pp. 53–71.
______. *Emil Rathenau und die AEG.* Mainz: Hase & Koehler, 1988.
______. "Die Entwicklung des privaten Bankwesens nach 1945. Die Kreditgenossenschaften nach 1945." In: *Deutsche Bankengeschichte.* Ed. by the Wissenschaftlicher Beirat des Instituts für bankhistorische Forschung. Vol. 3. Frankfurt: Knapp, 1985, pp. 207–276.
______. *Konzentration im deutschen Bankwesen 1848–1980* (Schriftenreihe des Instituts für bankhistorische Forschung; 4). Frankfurt: Knapp, 1982.
______. "The Amalgamation of Deutsche Bank and Disconto-Gesellschaft in October 1929." *Studies on Economic and Monetary Problems and on Banking History*, no. 18 (1980), pp. 27–52. Rpt. Mainz: Hase & Koehler, 1988, pp. 543–570.
______. "Vom Bankier zum Manager." In: Hans Hubert Hofmann, ed. *Bankherren und Bankiers* (Büdinger Vorträge; 10). Limburg: Starke, 1978, pp. 145–159.
______. *Einführung in die Deutsche Bankengeschichte.* Frankfurt: Knapp, 1976.
______. "Dismemberment and Reconstruction of Germany's Big Banks, 1945–1957." *Studies on Economic and Monetary Problems and on Banking History*, no. 13 (1974), pp. 18–27. Rpt. Mainz: Hase & Koehler, 1988, pp. 343–353.
______. *Wiederaufbau: Kunst und Technik der Finanzierung 1947–1953. Die ersten Jahre der Kreditanstalt für Wiederaufbau.* Frankfurt: Knapp, 1973.
______. "Deutsche Bank during 'Company Promotion' Crisis (1873–1876)." *Studies on Economic and Monetary Problems and on Banking History*, no. 11 (1973), pp. 19–33. Rpt. Mainz: Hase & Koehler, 1988, pp. 277–293.

______. "Deutsche Bank London Agency founded 100 years ago." *Studies on Economic and Monetary Problems and on Banking History*, no. 10 (1973), pp. 17–35. Rpt. Mainz: Hase & Koehler, 1988, pp. 233–253.
Pollard, Sidney. "Capital Exports, 1870–1914: Harmful or Beneficial?" *Economic History Review*, Vol. 38 (1985), pp. 489–514.
______. *Peaceful Conquest: The Industrialization of Europe, 1760–1970*. Oxford: Oxford University Press, 1995.
Porter, Michael. *The Competitive Advantages of Nations*. London: Macmillan, 1990.
Puth, Robert C. *American Economic History*. 3rd ed. Chicago: Dyrden Press, 1993.
Rajan, Raghuram G., and Luigi Zingales. "The Great Reversals: The Politics of Financial Development in the Twentieth Century." *Journal of Financial Economics*, Vol. 69 (2003), pp. 5–50.
Redlich, Fritz. *The Molding of American Banking*. New York: Johnson Reprint, 1968.
Riegel, Robert Edgar. *The Story of Western Railroads*. Lincoln: University of Nebraska Press, 1926.
Riesser, Jacob. *Die deutschen Grossbanken und ihre Konzentration im Zusammenhang mit der Gesamtwirtschaft in Deutschland*. 4th ed. Jena: Fischer, 1912.
Rifkin, Jeremy. *The Age of Access*. New York: Penguin, 2000.
Ripley, William Z. *Railroads: Finance and Organization*. New York: Longmans Green, 1915.
Rodgers, Daniel T. *Atlantic Crossings: Social Politics in a Progressive Age*. Cambridge: MA: Belknap Press of Harvard University, 1998.
Roe, Mark. *Strong Managers, Weak Owners: The Political Roots of American Corporate Finance*. Princeton, NJ: Princeton University Press, 1994.
Ross, Duncan M. "Clubs and Consortia: European Banking Groups as Strategic Alliances." In: Stefano Battilossi and Youssef Cassis, eds. *European Banks and the American Challenge: Competition and Cooperation in International Banking Under Bretton Woods*. Oxford: Oxford University Press, 2002, pp. 135–160.
Rottenberg, Dan. *The Man Who Made Wall Street: Anthony J. Drexel and the Rise of Modern Finance*. Philadelphia: University of Pennsylvania, 2001.
Rugman, Alan. *The End of Globalization*. New York: Random House, 2000.
Salsbury, Stephen. *The State, the Investor and the Railroad*. Cambridge, MA: Harvard University Press, 1967.
Sbracia, Massimo, and Andrea Zaghini. "The Role of the Banking System in the International Transmission of Shocks." *World Economy*, Vol. 26 (2003), pp. 727–754.
Schmidt, Ernst Wilhelm. *Männer der Deutschen Bank und der Disconto-Gesellschaft*. Düsseldorf: Scherpe, 1957.
Scholtyseck, Joachim. "Die USA vs. 'The Big Six'. Der gescheiterte Bankenprozeß nach dem Zweiten Weltkrieg." *Bankhistorisches Archiv*, Vol. 26 (2000), no. 1, pp. 27–53.
Schröder, Hans-Jürgen, ed. *Marshallplan und westdeutscher Wiederaufstieg*. Stuttgart: Steiner 1990.
Schubert, Aurel. *The Credit-Anstalt Crisis of 1931*. Cambridge: Cambridge University Press, 1991.
Schwartz, Thomas Alan. *America's Germany: John J. McCloy and the Federal Republic of Germany*. Cambridge, MA: Harvard University Press, 1991.
Seidenzahl, Fritz. *100 Jahre Deutsche Bank*. Frankfurt: Deutsche Bank, 1970.
______. "A Forgotten Pamphlet by Georg Siemens." *Studies on Economic and Monetary Problems and on Banking History*, no. 8 (1969), pp. 17–21. Rpt. Mainz: Hase & Koehler, 1988, pp. 187–192.
Servan-Schreiber, Jean-Jacques. *Le Défi Américain*. Paris: Denoël, 1967.
Seifert, Werner G., et al. *European Capital Markets*, London: Macmillan, 2000.
Shapiro, Alan C. *Multinational Financial Management*, 7th ed. Hoboken, NJ: Wiley & Sons, 2003.
Sharlin, Harold. "The First Niagara Falls Power Project." *Business History Review*, Vol. 35 (1961), pp. 59–74.
Shonfield, Andrew. *Modern Capitalism. The Changing Balance of Public and Private Power*. London 1967.
Simpson, Colin. *Lusitania*. Boston: Little, Brown and Company, 1972.
Smalley, Eugene V. *History of the Northern Pacific Railroad*. 1883. Rpt. New York: Arno Press, 1975.

Smith, George David, and Richard Sylla. "The Transformation of Financial Capitalism: An Essay on the History of American Capital Markets." *Financial Markets, Institutions and Instruments*, Vol. 2 (May 1993), pp. 1–62.
Smith, Roy. *The Global Bankers*. New York: Plume, 1990.
Sobel, Robert. *The Life and Times of Dillon Read*. New York: Dutton, 1991.
______. *The Great Bull Market: Wall Street in the 1920s*. New York: Norton, 1968.
Solomon, Robert. *Money on the Move: The Revolution in International Finance since 1980*. Princeton, NJ: Princeton University Press, 1999.
Sombart, Werner. *Die deutsche Volkswirtschaft im neunzehnten Jahrhundert*. Berlin: Bondi, 1903.
Steil, Benn, et al. *The European Equity Markets: The State of the Union and an Agenda for the Millennium*. Washington: Brookings Institute, 1996.
Steinberg, Jonathan. *The Deutsche Bank and its Gold Transactions during the Second World War*. Munich: Beck, 1999.
Stern, Fritz. *Einstein's German World*. Princeton, NJ: Princeton University Press, 1999.
______. *Gold and Iron. Bismarck, Bleichröder and the Building of the German Empire*. New York: Knopf, 1977.
Steuber, Ursel. "Foreign Engagement by German Banks." *Intereconomics*, Vol. 8 (1973), no. 7.
Stevens, Mark. *The Big Eight*. New York: Macmillan, 1981.
Stevenson, William. *A Man Called Intrepid*. New York: Harcourt Brace Jovanovich, 1976.
Storck, Ekkehard. *Euromarkt: Finanz-Drehscheibe der Welt*. Stuttgart: Schäffer-Poeschel, 1995.
Strasser, Karl. *Die deutschen Banken im Ausland*. Munich: Reinhardt, 1924.
Strouse, Jean. *Morgan: American Financier*. New York: Random House, 1999.
Strunk, Peter. *Die AEG: Aufstieg und Niedergang einer Industrielegende*. Berlin: Nicolai, 1999.
Sylla, Richard. "United States Banks and Europe: Strategy and Attitudes." In: Stefano Battilossi and Youssef Cassis, eds. *European Banks and the American Challenge: Competition and Cooperation in International Banking Under Bretton Woods*. Oxford: Oxford University Press, 2002, pp. 53–73.
Taleb, Nassim Nicholas. *Fooled by Randomness: The Hidden Role of Chance in Life and in the Markets*. New York: Thomson, 2004.
Taussig, F. W. *The Tariff History of the United States*. 8th rev. ed. New York: Capricorn Books, 1964.
Teichova, Alice, et al. *Historical Studies in International Corporate Business*. Cambridge: Cambridge University Press, 1989.
______ et al. *Multinational Enterprise in Historical Perspective*. Cambridge: Cambridge University Press, 1986.
Tilly, Richard H. *Vom Zollverein zum Industriestaat. Die wirtschaftlich-soziale Entwicklung Deutschlands 1834 bis 1914*. Munich: Deutscher Taschenbuch-Verlag, 1990.
______. "Los von England. Probleme des Nationalismus in der deutschen Wirtschaftsgeschichte." *Zeitschrift für die gesamte Staatswissenschaft*, Vol. 124 (1968), pp. 179–196.
Triffin, Robert. "Myth and Realities of the Gold Standard." In: Barry Eichengreen and Marc Flandreau, eds. *The Gold Standard in Theory and History*. London: Routledge, 1997, pp. 140–160.
Tschoegl, Adrian E. "Foreign Banks in the United States since World War II: A Useful Fringe." In: Geoffrey Jones and Lina Gálvez-Muñoz, eds. *Foreign Multinationals in the United States: Management and Performance*. London: Routledge, 2002, pp. 149–168.
Tufano, Peter. "Business Failure, Judicial Intervention, and Financial Innovation: Restructuring U.S. Railroads in the Nineteenth Century."*Business History Review*, Vol. 71 (1997), pp. 1–40.
van der Wee, Herman. *Prosperity and Upheaval: The World Economy 1945–1980*. New York: Penguin, 1991.
Vatter, Harold G. *The U.S. Economy in the World War II*. New York: Columbia University Press, 1985.
Vernon, Raymond. *In the Hurricane's Eye: The Troubled Prospects of Multinational Enterprises*. Cambridge, MA: Harvard University Press, 1998.
______. "Where Are the Multinationals Headed?" In: Kenneth A. Froot, ed. *Foreign Direct Investment*. Chicago: University of Chicago Press, 1992, pp. 57–83.

———. "The Location of Economic Activity." In: John Dunning, ed. *Economic Analysis and the Multinational Enterprise*. London: George Allen & Unwin, 1974, pp. 89–114.

———. *Big Business and the State*. Cambridge, MA: Harvard University Press, 1974.

Villard, Henry. *Memoirs of Henry Villard*. 2 vols. Boston: Houghton Mifflin, 1904.

Wallich, Henry C. *Mainsprings of the German Revival*. New Haven: Yale University Press, 1955.

Wallich, Hermann, and Paul Wallich. *Zwei Generationen im deutschen Bankwesen, 1833–1914* (Schriftenreihe des Instituts für bankhistorische Forschung; 2). Frankfurt: Knapp, 1978.

Walton, Gary, and Hugh Rockoff. *History of the American Economy*. New Brunswick: Rutgers University Press, 1998.

Wandel, Eckhard. *Die Entstehung der Bank deutscher Länder und die deutsche Währungsreform 1948* (Schriftenreihe des Instituts für bankhistorische Forschung; 3). Frankfurt: Knapp, 1980.

Warren, Charles. *Bankruptcy and American History*. Cambridge, MA: Harvard University Press, 1935.

Wehler, Hans-Ulrich. *The German Empire, 1871–1918*. Leamington Spa: Berg, 1985.

Weiss, Ulrich: "Menschen in der Bank." *Zeitschrift für das gesamte Kreditwesen*, Vol. 43 (1990), pp. 872–876.

Wellhöner, Volker. *Grossbanken und Grossindustrie im Kaiserreich* (Kritische Studien zur Geschichtswissenschaft; 85). Göttingen: Vandenhoeck & Ruprecht, 1989.

Wells, Wyatt. *Antitrust and the Formation of the Postwar World*. New York: Columbia University Press, 2002.

Whale, P. Barrett. *Joint Stock Banking in Germany: A Study of the German Creditbanks Before and After the War*. London: Macmillan 1930.

Whaley, Robert. "Derivatives." In: George M. Constantinides et al., eds. *Handbook of the Economics of Finance*. Amsterdam: Elsevier, 2003.

Whaples, Robert, and Dianne C. Betts. *Historical Perspectives on the American Economy*. Cambridge: Cambridge University Press, 1995.

White, Eugene Nelson. "Banking and Finance in the Twentieth Century." In: Stanley L. Engerman and Robert E. Gallman, eds. *Cambridge Economic History of the United States. Vol. 3. The Twentieth Century*. Cambridge: Cambridge University Press, 2000, pp. 743–802.

———. *The Regulation and Reform of the American Banking System, 1900–1929*. Princeton, NJ: Princeton University Press, 1983.

White, Horace G. "Foreign Trading in American Stock Exchange Securities." *Journal of Political Economy*, Vol. 48 (1940), pp. 655–702.

Whitney, Richard. *Divergent Capitalism: The Social Structure and Change of Business Systems*. Oxford: Oxford University Press, 2000.

Wicker, Elmus. *Banking Panics of the Gilded Age*. Cambridge: Cambridge University Press, 2000.

Wieandt, Axel, and Rafael Moral y Santiago. "Growing in the U.S. – Review of Deutsche Bank's M&A Strategy in North America." In: Kai Lucks, ed. *Transatlantic Mergers and Acquisitions: Opportunities and Pitfalls in German-American Partnerships*. Erlangen: Publicis, 2005, pp. 85–97.

Wiesen, S. Jonathan. *West German Industry & the Challenge of the Nazi Past*. Chapel Hill: University of North Carolina Press, 2001.

Wilkins, Mira. "Dutch Multinational Enterprises in the United States: A Historical Summary." *Business History Review*, Vol. 79 (2005), pp. 193–273.

———. *The History of Foreign Investment in the United States: 1914–1945*. Cambridge, MA: Harvard University Press, 2004.

———. "Cosmopolitan Finance in the 1920s: New York's Emergence as an International Financial Centre." In: Richard Sylla, ed. *The State, the Financial System, and Economic Modernization: Comparative Historical Perspectives*. Cambridge: Cambridge University Press, 1999, pp. 271–291.

———. "Hosts to Transnational Investments – A Comparative Analysis." In: *Transnational Investment from the 19th Century to the Present* (Zeitschrift für Unternehmensgeschichte; Beiheft 81). Stuttgart: Steiner, 1994, pp. 25–69.

———. "Foreign Banks and Foreign Investment in the United States." In: Rondo Cameron, ed. *International Banking, 1870–1914*. New York: Oxford University Press, 1991.

______. "Banks over Borders: Some Evidence from their Pre-1914 History." In: Geoffrey Jones, ed. *Banks as Multinationals*. London: Routledge, 1990.

______. "European Multinationals in the United States: 1875–1914." In: Alice Teichova et al., eds. *Multinational Enterprise in Historical Perspective*. Cambridge: Cambridge University Press, 1989.

______. *The History of Foreign Investment in the United States to 1914*. Cambridge, MA: Harvard University Press, 1989.

Williamson, Oliver E. *Corporate Control and Business Behavior: An Inquiry into the Effects of Organization Form on Enterprise Behavior*. Englewood Cliffs, NJ: Prentice-Hall, 1970.

______. *Markets and Hierarchies: Analysis and Antitrust Implications: A Study in the Economics of Internal Organization*. New York: Free Press, 1975.

______. *The Economic Institutions of Capitalism*. New York: Free Press, 1985.

______. *The Mechanisms of Governance*. Oxford: Oxford University Press, 1996.

Wilson, Joan Hoff. *American Business and Foreign Policy, 1921–1933*. Lexington: University of Kentucky Press, 1971.

Wilson, John, and Andrew Thomson. *The Making of Modern Management: British Management in Historical Perspective*. Oxford: Oxford University Press, 2006.

Winkler, Dörte. "Die amerikanische Sozialisierungspolitik in Deutschland 1945–1948." In: Heinrich August Winkler, ed. *Politische Weichenstellungen im Nachkriegsdeutschland 1945–1953*. Göttingen: Vandenhoeck & Ruprecht, 1979, pp. 88–110.

Wolf, Herbert. "Geld und Banken nach dem Zweiten Weltkrieg. Internationale Kapitalbewegungen, Bankensysteme, grenzüberschreitende Kooperation. Länderkapitel Deutschland." In: Hans Pohl, ed. *Europäische Bankengeschichte*. Frankfurt: Knapp, 1993, pp. 517–550.

Yassen, Leonard C., ed. *Direktinvestitionen in den USA*. Würzburg: Universitätsdruckerei H. Stürtz, 1974.

Zeitlin, Jonathan, and Gary Herrigel, eds. *Americanization and its Limits: Reworking US Technology and Management in Post-war Europe and Japan*. Oxford: Oxford University Press, 2000.

Zorn, Wolfgang. "Wirtschaft und Politik im deutschen Imperialismus." In: Wilhelm Abel et al., eds. *Wirtschaft, Geschichte und Wirtschaftsgeschichte: Festschrift zum 65. Geburtstag von Friedrich Lütge*. Stuttgart: G. Fischer, 1966.

Index

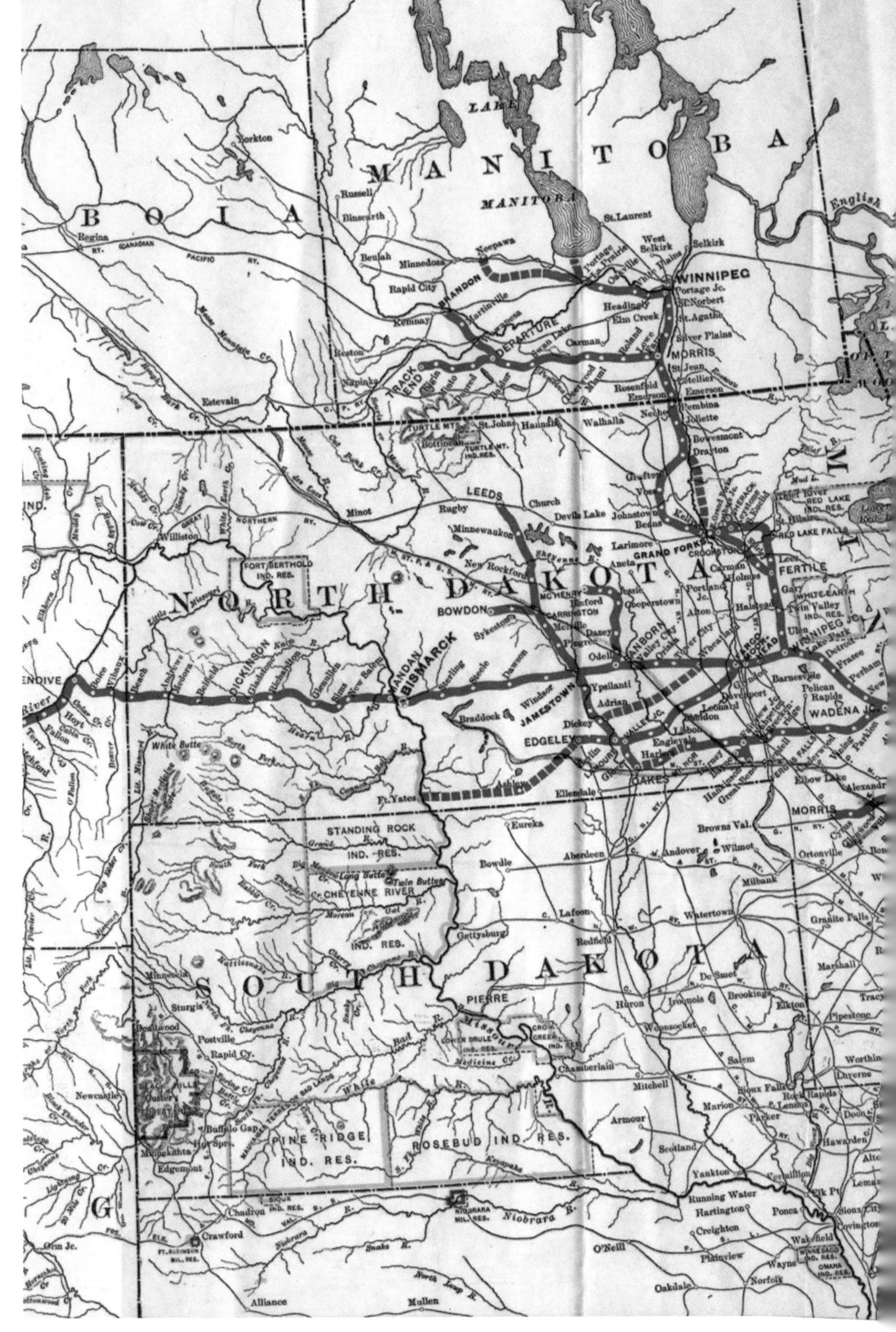
MANITOBA
NORTH DAKOTA
SOUTH DAKOTA
WINNIPEG
BRANDON
GRAND FORKS
BISMARCK
JAMESTOWN
DICKINSON
MINOT
PIERRE
ABERDEEN
STANDING ROCK IND. RES.
CHEYENNE RIVER IND. RES.
PINE RIDGE IND. RES.
ROSEBUD IND. RES.
FORT BERTHOLD IND. RES.